The Open Method
of Co-ordination in Action

The European Employment
and Social Inclusion Strategies

P.I.E.-Peter Lang

Bruxelles · Bern · Berlin · Frankfurt am Main · New York · Oxford · Wien

SALTSA

A Joint Programme for Working Life Research in Europe

SALTSA is a programme of partnership in European working life research run by the Swedish National Institute for Working Life (NIWL/ALI) and the Swedish Confederations of Trade Unions (LO), Professional Employees (TCO) and Professional Associations (SACO).

The aim of SALTSA is to generate applicable research results of a high academic standard and relevance. Research is largely project-based.

Research is carried out in three areas:
* the labour market
* work organisation
* the work environment

The Labour Market Programme

Labour market research is predominantly based on projects in collaboration with European researchers and research institutes. The focus is on ongoing and/or social partner related processes in Europe.

Aims include providing a foundation for ongoing debate, current political issues and processes involving social partners in the European labour market.

Chairman of the SALTSA Programme is Lars Magnusson and Programme Secretary is Torbjörn Strandberg.

website: www.niwl.se/saltsa

Jonathan ZEITLIN & Philippe POCHET (eds.),
with Lars MAGNUSSON

The Open Method
of Co-ordination in Action

The European Employment
and Social Inclusion Strategies

Arbetslivsinstitutet

SACO

SALTSA — JOINT PROGRAMME
FOR WORKING LIFE RESEARCH IN EUROPE
The National Institute for Working Life and The Swedish Trade Unions in Co-operation

observatoire

social

européen

•

osservatorio

sociale

europeo

"Work & Society"
No.49

© P.I.E.-PETER LANG S.A.
Presses Interuniversitaires Européennes
Brussels, 2005; 2nd printing 2005
1 avenue Maurice, 1050 Brussels, Belgium
info@peterlang.com; www.peterlang.net

ISSN 1376-0955
ISBN 90-5201-280-6
US ISBN 0-8204-6645-X
D/2005/5678/12
Printed in Germany

Bibliographic information published by "Die Deutsche Bibliothek"

"Die Deutsche Bibliothek" lists this publication in the "Deutsche Nationalbibliografie";
detailed bibliographic data is available in the Internet at <http://dnb.ddb.de>.

*CIP available from the British Library, GB
and the Library of Congress, USA.*

Table of Contents

List of Abbreviations

ACA	Allocation de chômeur âgé
AIAS	Amsterdam Institute for Advanced Labour
ALMPs	Active Labour Market Policies
ANPE	Agence nationale pour l'emploi
APNC	Anti-poverty Network Cymru
ASMK	Arbeits- und Sozialministerkonferenz (Conference of the Labour and Social Affairs Ministries)
BDA	Bundesvereinigung der Deutschen Arbeitgeberverbände
BDI	Bundesverband der Deutschen Industrie
BEPG	Broad Economic Policy Guideline(s)
BMWA	Bundesministerium für Wirtschaft und Arbeit
CASE	Centre for Analysis of Social Exclusion
CBS	Central Bureau of Statistics
CDSEI	Comité du dialogue social sur les questions européennes et internationales
CE	Community Employment
CEC	Commission of the European Communities
CEEP	European Centre of Enterprises with Public Participation and of Enterprises of General Economic Interest
CEMR	Council of European Municipalities and Regions
CEVIPOF	Centre d'études de la vie politique française
CNEL	Comitato nazionale per l'Economia e il lavoro
CPA	Combat Poverty Agency
CRE	Contrat de retour à l'emploi
CSF	Community Support Framework
CSR	Comprehensive Spending Review
DAEI	Délégation aux affaires européennes et internationales
DG	Directorate General
DGB	Deutscher Gewerkschaftsbund
DGEFP	Délégation générale à l'emploi et à la formation professionnelle

9

DIHK	Deutschen Industrie- und Handelskammertages
DIW	Deutsches Institut für Wirtschaftsforschung
DSCFA	Department of Social, Community and Family Affairs
DWP	Department of Work and Pensions
EAPN	European Anti-poverty Network
EAPP	England Anti-poverty Platform
ECB	European Central Bank
ECHP	European Community Household Panel
ECPR	European Consortium for Political Research
EEGs	European Employment Guidelines
EES	European Employment Strategy
EFCW	European Forum for Child Welfare
EGGE	Expert Group on Gender and Employment
EIS	Employment Incentive Scheme
EITC	Earned Income Tax Credit
EMCO	Employment Committee
EMU	Economic and Monetary Union
EP	European Parliament
EPC	Economic Policy Committee
ESF	European Social Fund
ESRI	Economic and Social Research Institute
ETUC	European Trade Union Confederation
EU	European Union
EUI	European University Institute
FÁS	Ireland's National Training and Employment Authority
FCC	Federation of Swedish County Councils
FEA	Federal Employment Agency
FEANTSA	European Federation of National Organisations Working with the Homeless
FEMPL	Federation of Municipalities and Provinces
FNV	Federatie Nederlandse Vakbeweging
GAIE	Gross Average Industrial Earnings
GDP	Gross Domestic Product
GNP	Gross National Product
GSSS	Graduate School of Social Science

IAB	Institut für Arbeitsmarkt- und Berufsforschung
IFO	Institut für Wirtschaftsforschung
IGC	Intergovernmental Conference
ILO	International Labour Organisation
IMA	Interministerieller Ausschuss (inter-ministerial committee)
INEM	National Institute for Employment
INPS	National Institute of Social Insurance
IPA	Institute of Public Administration
ippr	Institute for Public Policy Research
ISFOL	Institute for Labour and Training
ISTAT	National Institute of Statistics
JER	Joint Employment Report
JMC	Joint Ministerial Committees
JMC(P)	Joint Ministerial Committees on Poverty
JSA	Job Seeker's Allowance
JUMP	Immediate Programme for the Reduction of Youth Unemployment
KMK	Kulturministerkonferenz
KOLS	Konferenz der Obersten Landessozialbehörden
LAPs	Local Action Plans
LES	Local Employment Service
MEDEF	Mouvement des entreprises de France
NAPs	National Action Plans
NAPS	National Anti-poverty Strategy
NAPs/empl	National Action Plans for Employment
NAPs/incl	National Action Plans for Inclusion
NARB	National Report on Poverty and Wealth Nationaler Armuts- und Reichtumsbericht
NDA	National Disability Authority
NDP	National Development Plans
NEAP	National Employment Action Plan (NAP/empl)
NESC	National Economic and Social Council
NESDO	National Economic and Social Development Office
NESF	National Economic and Social Forum
NGOs	Non Governmental Organisations

NIAPN	Northern Ireland Anti-poverty Network
NTSN	New Targeting Social Need
OECD	Organisation for Economic Co-operation and Development
OMC	Open Method of Co-ordination
OMC/incl	Social Inclusion process
PAP-ND	Projet d'action personnalisé pour un nouveau départ
PARE	Plan d'aide au retour à l'emploi
PERP	Plan d'épargne retraite populaire
PES	Public Employment Service
PPE	Prime pour l'emploi
PRP	Programme de retraite progressive
PSAs	Public Service Agreements
QMV	Qualified Majority Voting
RAPs	Regional Action Plans
RARs	Regional Labour Market Councils
RETIS	Réseau européen transrégional pour l'inclusion sociale
RMA	Revenu minimum d'activité
RMI	Revenu minimum d'insertion
RWT	Reduction of working time
SALA	Swedish Association of Local Authorities
SCP	Social and Cultural Planning Office
SEU	Social Exclusion Unit
SGCI	Secrétariat général du comité interministériel
SIEPS	Swedish Institute for European Policy Studies
SMIC	Salaire minimum interprofessionnel de croissance
SPC	Social Protection Committee
SPTF	Social Policy Task Force
TANF	Temporary Assistance for Needy Families
UKCAP	UK Coalition Against Poverty
UKLG	United Kingdom Liaison Group
UNECE	United Nations Economic Commission for Europe
UNICE	Union of Industrial and Employer's Confederations of Europe
URGE	Research Unit on European Governance
VAT	Value Added Tax

VNG	Dutch Association of Local Government
WAGE	Center for World Affairs and the Global Economy
WAO	Wet op Arbeidsongeschiktheidsverzekering
WFTC	Working Families Tax Credit
ZDH	Zentralverband des Deutschen Handwerks

Acknowledgements

The editors would like to thank the SALTSA research program for its collaboration and generous financial support of the research for this book. We are also grateful to Martin Rhodes, Helen Wallace and the Robert Schuman Centre for Advanced Studies at the European University Institute in Florence for kindly hosting the authors' meeting in July 2003.

Jonathan Zeitlin would like to thank the University of Wisconsin-Madison's European Union Center and Center for World Affairs and the Global Economy (WAGE) for their help and support, especially David Trubek, Darya Vassina and Natalie Oldani. Philippe Pochet wishes to express his gratitude to Caroline de la Porte, David Natali and Françoise Verri.

The editors especially want to thank Valérie Cotulelli (OSE) who was, once again, indispensable for the lay-out of the manuscript.

Jonathan ZEITLIN and Philippe POCHET
January 2005

Foreword

It is obvious that the European Union today faces great challenges. The most apparent is certainly the recent enlargement and transition from EU 15 to EU 25 – which might become EU 28 in a not too distant future. To integrate the new countries into the Union is a task of great historical significance, which will have far-reaching effects not only upon the European polity and economy but also on world history. Most certainly, enlargement will have economic, social, political and cultural consequences, whose significance and content we can hardly grasp at present. Among the most important issues that we presently need to face is how an enlarged European Union shall be governed in the future. Both from experience and from new theoretical insights from the social sciences we know that good governance and robust institutions are crucial in order to achieve not only political stability but also economic development, growth and welfare. Therefore, it is necessary that a new Constitution for the European Union should be inaugurated as soon as possible which can find legitimacy among European citizens and thus contribute both to political stability and sustainable growth. For these purposes the present compromise launched in Nice 2000 is certainly inadequate in a longer time perspective.

Europe is also since Lisbon 2000 committed to a strategy of economic modernisation whose aim is to create stable growth and full employment. The kernel of this strategy is to develop the European economy into a knowledge-based economy by the year 2010. So far there are unfortunately few positive signs which suggest that this goal can be reached in such an undoubtedly short period of time. No doubt, the fulfilment of the Lisbon goals demands political stability and good governance. Only such a framework can provide for the combined policies of structural reform and increased demand that these goals necessitate.

However, Europe needs more than a new Constitution. In the present age of globalisation it also needs to develop common policies in different fields in order to enhance growth and welfare. To do this is not an easy matter. Over the last decade there have been rising concerns as to what extent the European Union has enough legitimacy to develop common policies, especially in the social field for example to avoid the danger of social or wage dumping. The so-called democratic deficit within the EU structure is a stumbling bloc for over ambitious attempts to develop common social benefits, a common tax policy or other regulations linked both to the social and economic field. For this reason, new forms of governance must be tried out and tested. Since 1997 the Open Method of Co-ordination (OMC) has been utilised as a "soft" strategy to achieve greater integration in policy fields where otherwise no progress could have been made due to the principle of subsidiarity. The first OMC process was launched at the Luxembourg summit in 1996 and eventuated in the so-called European Employment Strategy (EES). Since then other OMC processes have been launched.

In this volume of essays this Open Method of Co-ordination is discussed from different angles; its achievements so far as well as its problems and pitfalls. It goes without saying that is currently of acute importance to discuss the strengths and weaknesses of the OMC. Undoubtedly, as already observed, Europe faces great challenges in order to preserve and develop not least the various welfare regimes to which we have been accustomed for so long and have almost taken for granted. However in a world of economic globalisation even such fundamental institutions are threatened. In order to fulfil the Lisbon Strategy and achieve a stable framework of governance we must develop our political tools and institutions as well as seek legitimacy for them. The history of European integration since the 1950s suggests that there is a danger that periods of enlargement may exclude further deepening of integration. However, it seems that Europe can not afford such a standstill for more than a very short time.

Lars MAGNUSSON

INTRODUCTION

The Open Method
of Co-ordination in Question[*]

Jonathan ZEITLIN

I. The Open Method of Co-ordination
as an Unidentified Political Object

No development in European integration has aroused greater interest
or greater controversy in recent years than the Open Method of Co-
ordination (OMC). Since its annunciation as a new and broadly applicable instrument of EU governance at the extraordinary Lisbon European
socio-economic summit in March 2000, drawing on experience with the
co-ordination of national economic and especially employment policies
over the preceding decade, the OMC has been extended to cover an
enormous range of policy fields. Beyond the Broad Economic Policy
Guidelines (BEPG) introduced by the Treaty of Maastricht (1992), and
the European Employment Strategy (EES) inaugurated by the Treaty of
Amsterdam (1997), the OMC has become the central tool of EU social
policy-making in the new millennium, with formal co-ordination processes launched for social inclusion and pensions in 2001-2003, and
further proposals pending from the Commission and the Parliament for
the application of this method to health and long-term care. As part of
the "Lisbon Strategy" aimed at turning the EU into "the most competitive and dynamic knowledge-based economy in the world capable of
sustainable economy growth with more and better jobs and greater
social cohesion" by 2010, the March 2000 European Council authorised
the extension of the OMC to a host of other policy areas, such as re-
search/innovation, information society/eEurope, enterprise promotion,

[*] For helpful comments on the introduction and concluding chapter to this book,
I would like to thank Philippe Pochet, David Trubek, Gráinne de Búrca, Anton
Hemerijck, Jelle Visser, Gerben Kourthouwer, Birgitte Bentzen, Rob de Boer, Maurizio Ferrera, Mary Daly, and especially Chuck Sabel, with whom I developed many
of these ideas. I am also grateful to Natalie Oldani for invaluable assistance in preparing the references and bibliography.

structural economic reform, and education and training. Since then, OMC-type processes and approaches have also been proposed by the Commission and other European bodies as mechanisms for monitoring and supplementing existing EU legislative instruments and authority in fields such as immigration and asylum, environmental protection, disability, occupational health and safety, and even fundamental rights, as well as in areas like youth policy where the Union has few if any legal powers[1]. In addition, following recommendations from the Commission's High Level Group on Industrial Relations (CEC, 2002a), the European social partner organisations have drawn inspiration from the OMC for the monitoring and follow-up of non-binding framework agreements and guidelines at both cross-industry and sectoral levels[2].

The OMC was defined by the Portuguese Presidency at Lisbon and afterwards in terms closely modelled on the EES as involving a specific ensemble of elements:

- fixing guidelines for the Union combined with specific timetables for achieving the goals which they set in the short, medium and long term;
- establishing, where appropriate, quantitative and qualitative indicators and benchmarks against the best in the world and tailored to the needs of different Member States and sectors as a means of comparing best practices;
- translating these European guidelines into national and regional policies by setting specific targets and adopting measures, taking into account national and regional differences;
- periodic monitoring, evaluation and peer review organised as mutual learning processes (European Council, 2000: point 37).

But actual OMC processes as they have evolved since Lisbon vary considerably in their modalities and procedures, depending on the

---

[1] For overviews of the scope and applications of the OMC across different policy areas, see Borrás and Jacobsson (2004); Radaelli (2003a); de Búrca (2003); European Convention (2002); Romano (2002). On the OMC in research/innovation, immigration/asylum, and occupational health and safety respectively, see Kaiser and Prange (2004); Caviedes (2004) and Smismans (2003). For proposals that the OMC be used as a vehicle for the implementation of fundamental rights, see EU Network of Independent Experts in Fundamental Rights (2002); de Búrca (2003); Bernard (2003); de Schutter (forthcoming). A number of pre-existing European policy co-ordination processes have also been retrospectively interpreted as full or partial examples of the OMC *avant la lettre*, including the Cardiff Process for structural economic reforms, the Bologna Process for co-operation in European higher education, and the code of conduct against harmful tax competition: on these, in addition to the surveys cited above, see Foden and Magnusson (2002); Hingel (2001) and Radaelli (2003b), respectively.

[2] Agreements concluded so far have focused on the issues of teleworking and lifelong learning. For an overview of current developments, see CEC (2004a).

specific characteristics of the policy field in question, the Treaty basis of EU competence, and the willingness of the Member States to take joint action. Thus, for example, the Commission and the Council are empowered to issue joint recommendations to Member States on the implementation of the EES and the BEPG, but not on that of other OMC processes, while consultation of the European Parliament is formally required only in the case of the EES. Although most OMC processes are based on common European objectives, only the EES and BEPG involve detailed guidelines for their realisation by Member States. Common European statistical indicators or benchmarks have been established for economic policy, structural reforms, employment, social inclusion, and education, but not yet for pensions or health care. The BEPG, backed by the Stability and Growth Pact, notoriously impose national ceilings on government deficits and public debt as a proportion of GDP; the EES has fixed European employment rate targets, disaggregated by age and gender, which some countries have translated into nationally specific objectives; and the Social Inclusion OMC calls upon Member States to set national targets for the reduction of relative income poverty[3]. Member States prepare National Action Plans (NAPs) for employment and social inclusion, and National Progress Reports on structural economic reforms, but so far only more limited "National Strategy Reports" on pensions[4]. These national plans and reports are subjected to mutual surveillance and peer review by Member State representatives in the Employment Committee (EMCO), Social Protection Committee (SPC), and Economic Policy Committee (EPC) respectively, while active programs for mutual learning through exchange of good practices (also confusingly termed "peer review") have been organised within the framework of the EES and the Social Inclusion

---

[3] The Barcelona European Council of 15-16 March 2002 also fixed national childcare and R&D investment/GDP targets for Member States as part of the EES and innovation policy OMC respectively, see European Council (2002). The new employment guidelines, adopted in July 2003, include additional quantitative targets at national level for combating early school leaving and promoting participation in lifelong learning, see Council of the European Union (2003).

[4] Initially, these OMC processes also followed different timetables, with an annual cycle for the BEPG and EES, a biennial cycle for social inclusion, and a triennial cycle for pensions. But the EES and the BEPG have now been "streamlined" and synchronised with one another on a triennial cycle, with guidelines fixed in the first year, followed by annual updates and implementation reports in years two and three. OMC processes in social inclusion and social protection (likely to include health and long-term care as well as pensions) are to be synchronised with this cycle of economic and employment policy co-ordination in 2006 (CEC, 2002b, 2003 and 2004b; SPC, 2003). For a fuller discussion of the emergent architecture of social, economic, and employment policy co-ordination in the EU, see the chapter by Pochet in this volume.

process. Other so-called OMC processes are more loosely structured, involving only selective elements of the broader method, such as scoreboards, peer evaluation, and exchange of good practices[5]. Hence as Belgian Minister Frank Vandenbroucke, who played a key part in launching the social inclusion and pensions processes during his country's 2001 EU Presidency, has rightly observed: "Open co-ordination is not some kind of fixed recipe that can applied to whichever issue" but instead "a kind of cookbook that contains various recipes, lighter and heavier ones" (Vandenbroucke, 2001: 4 and 2002: xxi).

The growing political salience, proliferation, and variety of OMC processes has elicited a bewildering array of contradictory assessments from both academic researchers and EU policy actors alike. On the positive side, the OMC has been touted as a "third way" for EU social policy between regulatory competition and harmonisation, an alternative to both intergovernmentalism and supranationalism, which may open up a sustainable path between a fragmented Europe and a European super state (Larsson, 2002; British and Swedish governments quoted in Jacobsson, 2002). Some academic and political commentators have hailed the OMC as a new mode of EU governance, suitable for addressing common European concerns while respecting legitimate national diversity, because it commits Member States to work together in reaching shared goals and performance targets, without seeking to homogenise their inherited policy regimes and institutional arrangements (Hemerijck and Berghman, 2004; Hemerijck, 2002; Rodrigues, 2001)[6]. Others have emphasised the OMC's promise as a cognitive and normative tool for defining and building consensus around a distinctive European social model and policy paradigm based on common objectives and values (Vandenbroucke, 2002; Ferrera, 2001). Still others have pointed to the OMC's potential as a mechanism for promoting experimental learning and deliberative problem-solving insofar as it pushes Member States to exchange information, compare themselves to one another, and reassess current practices in light of their relative performance. Certain of its proponents, finally, have seen the OMC as a

---

[5] These techniques are also used in policy co-ordination processes not formally designated as OMCs such as the code of conduct against harmful tax competition (see Radaelli, 2003b), or the peer evaluation mechanism for national arrangements in the fight against terrorism (Council of the European Union, 2002).

[6] While acknowledging the OMC's merits in combining pursuit of common European objectives with respect for national diversity, some commentators nonetheless insist that without the capacity to impose binding sanctions this method is only likely to prove effective where Member States' interests already latently converge, whether because of institutional similarities in regime type or the underlying characteristics of the issue at stake (e.g. absence of distributive conflicts or collective action problems); see Scharpf (2002 and 2003) and Héritier (2003).

possible vehicle for enhancing democratic participation and accountability within the EU by opening up the policy-making process to inputs from "civil society" and subnational actors (such as NGOs, social partners, and local/regional authorities), while obliging Member State governments to justify their performance in meeting common European objectives to a broader public (for both this and the preceding view, see Sabel and Zeitlin, 2003; Zeitlin, 2003; Cohen and Sabel, 2003; Telò, 2002; Rodrigues, 2001)[7].

On the negative side, the OMC has been criticised as a Trojan horse allowing the EU to encroach illegitimately into policy domains reserved by the Treaties entirely or primarily to the Member States through the adoption of common European objectives and performance indicators, backed up by peer pressure (Syrpis, 2002; Szyszczak, 2001)[8]. Conversely, the OMC has also been presented as a potential threat to the "Community Method" of European integration through binding legislation and social dialogue agreements, a "soft law" option whose availability may displace the use of "hard law" instruments even in domains where the EU already possesses legislative powers (CEC, 2001; Goetschy, 2003)[9]. Against those who have pointed to the deliberative-democratic potential of open policy co-ordination, another group of critics decry existing instances of the OMC as closed, opaque, and unaccountable processes dominated by transgovernmental exchanges between national civil servants and EU officials (Berghman and Okma, 2003; Smismans, 2004; de la Porte and Nanz, 2004). Where proponents highlight the OMC's contribution to rebalancing the EU's social and economic objectives, its detractors discern instead a defensive adjustment to the constraints imposed on European social policy by the single market, EMU, and globalisation – or worse still, a mechanism for "unlearning" the positive lessons of the postwar European model of "socially embedded" capitalism (Scharpf, 2003; Offe, 2003). But the most widespread

---

[7] The original definition of the OMC by the Portuguese Presidency insisted that "the development of this method in its different stages should be open to the participation of the various actors of civil society" and that it "can also be an important tool to improve transparency and democratic participation", see Council of the European Union (2000). Cf. also the conclusions of the Lisbon Summit: "A fully decentralised approach will be applied in line with the principle of subsidiarity in which the Union, the Member States, the regional and local levels, as well as the social partners and civil society, will be actively involved, using various forms of partnership" (European Council, 2000: point 38).

[8] This has been a particular concern of the German *Länder*, which fear that OMC processes may thereby erode their reserved competences under the Federal Constitution in fields such as education and social assistance (see the chapter by Büchs & Friedrich in this volume).

[9] For a more extensive discussion, see the chapter by Trubek & Trubek in this volume.

criticism of the OMC concerns not its purportedly pernicious effects, but rather its alleged lack of substantive impact on the Member States. According to this view, the OMC in its present form amounts to little more than the European emperor's newest clothes, an exercise in symbolic politics where national governments repackage existing policies to demonstrate their apparent compliance with EU objectives (Chalmers and Lodge, 2003; Radaelli, 2003a; Scharpf, 2002 and 2003). Given such radically different interpretations, the OMC can thus be considered an "unidentified political object" *par excellence*, like the European Union itself in Jacques Delors's famous phrase (quoted in Schmitter, 1996: 1)[10].

II. Constitutionalising the OMC: The Convention Debate

This clash of interpretations has already proved politically consequential in the debate at the Convention on the Future of Europe over the incorporation of the OMC into the draft Constitutional Treaty. The Convention's Social Europe Working Group endorsed the inclusion of the OMC in the draft Constitutional Treaty (as did three other Working Groups that considered the question) provided that, as one summary of its conclusions put it, "the provision would not replace existing normative procedures or make the Open Method of Co-ordination rigid in cases where there is no specific legislative method of procedure"[11]. These provisos reflected contrasting fears among some members of the Social Europe Working Group that constitutionalisation of the OMC could undermine its flexibility and among others that it could subvert the use of the EU's existing Treaty powers to legislate in the social field. Hence a vocal minority within the Working Group and the wider Convention remained skeptical about the incorporation of the OMC into the draft constitutional treaty. The majority of the Social Europe Group insisted instead on specifying the scope and limits of the method, as well as the roles of different actors in the procedure, in ways that might have threatened its practical viability if enacted (Social Europe Working Group, 2002: §§ 37-45; see also the discussion of the Working Group debate in the Trubeks' chapter in this volume).

These differences, as academic commentators and political actors proposed at the time, could have been reconciled by a generic provision of the Constitutional Treaty defining only the fundamental aims and basic elements of the OMC; declaring that OMC processes be deter-

---

[10] For broad and balanced reviews of the debate so far, see de la Porte and Pochet (2003) and Borrás and Jacobsson (2004).

[11] Aoife Halligan, "Convention Debates Social Europe", European Policy Center (http://www.theepc.net/home.asp) 21 February 2003. For a comparison of the various Working Group recommendations, see de Búrca and Zeitlin (2003).

mined flexibly, subject to review by Parliament and other actors, unless specified otherwise by the Treaty; and disclaiming any intention to replace existing normative procedures by OMCs. To ensure the "transparency and democratic character of the OMC", which the Social Europe Working Group likewise rightly deemed essential, this generic constitutional provision could also have included specific requirements for openness and broad participation of all relevant bodies and stakeholders (such as social partners, civil society organisations/NGOs, national parliaments, local and regional authorities) in accordance with national laws and practices (de Búrca and Zeitlin, 2003)[12].

In the event, however, the Convention Presidium itself deadlocked along similar lines to the Social Europe Working Group, reflecting a *de facto* alliance of opposites between defenders of the Member States' prerogatives against further intrusions by the EU on the one hand and those who feared dilution of the "hard" *acquis communautaire* by soft law processes on the other. Hence the Presidium decided not to bring forward a proposal to incorporate the OMC into the Constitutional Treaty. Instead, Article I-15 of the draft Constitutional Treaty (Intergovernmental Conference, 2004) gives the Union general powers to co-ordinate the economic, employment, and social policies of the Member States (with explicit reference to guidelines in the first two cases). In addition, Article I-17 allows the EU to take "supporting, co-ordinating, or complementary action" in a series of other areas (industry; protection and improvement of human health; education, vocational training, youth, and sport; culture; civil protection) without harmonising Member States' laws or regulations. Part III of the Constitutional Treaty then sets out specific procedures for the co-ordination of national policies in different areas, incorporating the existing Treaty provisions for the Broad Economic Policy Guidelines and the European Employment Strategy. But this part of the Constitutional Treaty also provides for the application of key features of the OMC in social policy, research and technological development, public health, and industry, without referring to it by name. In these areas, the Commission ("in close contact with the Member States") is charged with taking "initiatives aimed at the establishment of guidelines and indicators, the organisation and exchange of best practice, and the preparation of the necessary elements for periodic monitoring and evaluation", about which the European Parliament "shall be kept fully informed" (Articles III-213, 250, 278, 279)[13].

---

[12] For related proposals, see Vandenbroucke (2003) and European Parliament (2003a).

[13] These provisions were added to the draft Constitutional Treaty at the last minute as a result of an intensive lobbying campaign orchestrated by Maria João Rodrigues, co-ordinator of the Lisbon Summit for the Portuguese presidency and the "mother of the

III. Assessing the OMC: An Empirical Deficit

Despite the high political stakes involved, the debate surrounding the OMC is widely agreed to suffer from an empirical deficit. Many assessments of the OMC, including some that claim to conduct an *in vivo* rather than *in vitro* analysis of the method (e.g. Radaelli, 2003a; Chalmers and Lodge, 2003), rely in practice on a very limited range of often outdated evidence, onto which they project their own theoretical and normative assumptions. Empirical analysis of the OMC is extremely challenging, for a series of interrelated reasons:

- the variety of distinct processes subsumed under the OMC rubric;
- the relative newness of most OMC processes;
- the horisontal and vertical complexity of OMC processes, which typically integrate multiple policy domains, and involve multiple levels of governance (EU, national, subnational) across 15 (and now 25) Member States;
- the methodological difficulties of assessing the causal impact of an iterative policy-making process based on collaboration between EU institutions and Member State governments without legally binding sanctions. Since Member State representatives continuously participate in the definition of objectives, guidelines, and indicators for OMC processes, which do not necessarily result in new legislation or justiciable obligations, standard approaches to assessing the domestic effects of "Europeanisation" based on "goodness of fit", adaptational pressures, and compliance with EU law (e.g. Cowles *et al.*, 2001; Featherstone and Radaelli, 2003) cannot be directly applied. Member State governments may also have political reasons for playing up or down the domestic influence of OMC processes in National Action Plans and evaluation reports, connected with strategies of blame avoidance and credit claiming on the one hand and efforts to present themselves either as "good Europeans" or defenders of the national interest against Brussels on the other. Hence statements

---

OMC": see Barbier (2003a). The European Parliament passed two resolutions calling for the OMC to be incorporated into the Constitutional Treaty and for an inter-institutional agreement with the Council and the Commission, "laying down rules for governing the selection of policies for open co-ordination", together with "a procedure for developing the Open Method of Co-ordination into the Community Method", which could be formalised by the Intergovernmental Conference (see European Parliament, 2003a and 2003b; Barbier, 2003b). But the IGC did not reopen the compromise reached by the Convention on this subject. For a detailed and insightful analysis of the Convention debate on the constitutional status of the OMC and its outcome, see also de Búrca (2003).

about the sources of policy change in such official documents cannot be taken at face value but must be carefully contextualised and triangulated with other evidence[14].

Despite these practical and methodological problems, there is now a very large body of material available on the empirical operation of OMC processes, particularly in the fields of employment and social policy. Such material includes numerous official reviews and reports, such as the National Action Plans, Strategy Reports, and Joint Reviews for employment (1997-2003), social inclusion (2001, 2003), and pensions (2003); the national reports (often supported by independent research papers) and Commission transversal studies produced for the five-year impact assessment of the EES (2002); and the ongoing reports of the Commission's expert groups on Gender and Employment (EGGE) and Social Inclusion (all available on the DG Employment website, http:// europa.eu.int/comm/employment_social/index_en.html). But it also includes a wide range of studies and assessments produced by European social partner organisations (e.g. the European Trade Union Institute), NGOs (e.g. the European Anti-poverty Network), local and regional authority networks (e.g. EUROCITIES), EU agencies (e.g. the Dublin Foundation for the Improvement of Working and Living Conditions in Europe), think tanks (e.g. the Observatoire social européen and the European Institute for Public Administration), academic research groups (e.g. the Govecor project on "Economic Governance through Self-Co-ordination"), and of course individual scholars[15].

This book, which grows out of an international research network organised by the University of Wisconsin-Madison, the Observatoire social européen, and the Saltsa Joint Programme for Working Life in Europe, focuses on the two most developed examples of the OMC, the EES and the Social Inclusion process, about which empirical evidence is most abundant, though some chapters also refer to the Pensions process. It concentrates on one of the OMC's most controversial but least studied dimensions, its operation and influence at national and subnational levels, though some chapters also address the OMC's broader role in EU-level governance and policy-making (for more comprehensive reviews, see Jenson and Pochet, 2002; de la Porte and Pochet, 2003). The volume comprises a combination of national and comparative

---

[14] For discussions of these methodological problems, see in addition to the other chapters in this volume, Büchs (2003); Barbier (2004); López-Santana (2004); Borrás and Greve (2004).

[15] A select bibliography of more than 140 books, papers, and reports, including links to relevant websites, is available at the University of Wisconsin-Madison's Online Research Forum on the Open Method of Co-ordination (http://eucenter.wisc.edu/OMC/index.htm).

studies, covering eight countries (Denmark, France, Germany, Ireland, Italy, the Netherlands, Sweden, and the United Kingdom) and four transversal themes (hard and soft law, participation, gender equality, activation). These studies are framed by a historical overview of the OMC's place in the development of European social and employment policy, and by a synthetic conclusion, which assesses the findings of the preceding chapters (and other available evidence on the OMC action) against the empirical and normative questions raised in this introduction.

References

Barbier, J.-C. (2003a), "Final Amendments to the Constitution", *Tomorrow Europe*, No.17, Observatoire social européen, Brussels, July 2003.

Barbier, J.-C. (2003b), "From the Convention to the Next IGC", Observatoire social européen, Brussels, July 2003.

Barbier, J.-C. (2004), "La stratégie européenne pour l'emploi: genèse, coordination communautaire et diversité nationale", Rapport de recherche pour la DARES (ministère du Travail), Paris, January 2004.

Berghman, J. and Okma, K. (2003), "The Method of Open Co-ordination: Open Procedures or Closed Circuit? Social Policy Making between Science and Politics", *European Journal of Social Security*, Vol.4, No.4, pp.331-341.

Bernard, N. (2003), "A New Governance Approach to Economic, Social and Cultural Rights in the EU", in Hervey, T. K. and Kenner, J. (eds.), *Economic and Social Rights under the Charter of Fundamental Rights of the European Union*, Hart Publishing, Oxford, pp.247-268.

Borrás, S. and Greve, B. (2004), "Concluding Remarks: New Method or Just Cheap Talk?" *Journal of European Public Policy*, Vol.11, No.2, April 2004, pp.329-336.

Borrás, S. and Jacobsson, K. (2004), "The Open Method of Co-ordination and New Governance Patterns in the EU", *Journal of European Public Policy*, Vol.11, No.2, April 2004, pp.185-208.

Büchs, M. (2003), "Methodological and Conceptual Issues in Researching the Open Method of Coordination", in Hantrais, L. (ed.), *Researching the European Social Model from a Comparative Perspective*, Cross-National Research Papers, 7th Series: European Cross-National Research and Policy, Vol.7, No.1, UK Economic and Social Research Council, Loughborough, pp.31-41.

Caviedes, A. (2004), "The Open Method of Co-ordination in Immigration Policy: A Tool for Prying Open Fortress Europe?" *Journal of European Public Policy*, Vol.11, No.2, April 2004, pp.289-310.

CEC (2001), "European Governance: A White Paper", COM (2001) 428 final, of 25 July 2001 (http://europa.eu.int/eurlex/en/com/cnc/2001/com2001_0428 en01.pdf).

CEC (2002a), Report of the High Level Group on Industrial Relations and Change in the European Union, Office for Official Publications of the European Communities, Luxembourg, January 2002 (http://europa.eu.int/comm/ employment_social/soc-dial/rapport_en.pdf).

CEC (2002b), Communication from the Commission on Streamlining the Annual Economic and Employment Policy Co-ordination Cycles, COM (2002) 487 final, 3 September 2002 (http://europa.eu.int/eur-lex/en/com/rpt/ 2002/com2002_0487en01.pdf).

CEC (2003), Communication from the Commission "Strengthening the Social Dimension of the Lisbon Strategy: Streamlining Open Coordination in the Field of Social Protection", COM (2003) final (http://europa.eu.int/comm/ employment_social/news/2003/may/lisbonstratIP280503_en.pdf).

CEC (2004a), *Industrial Relations in Europe 2004*, Office for Official Publications of the European Communities, Luxembourg.

CEC (2004b), Communication from the Commission "Modernising Social Protection for the Development of High-Quality, Accessible and Sustainable Health Care and Long-Term Care: Support for the National Strategies Using the 'Open Method of Coordination'", COM (2004) 304 final, 20 April 2004 (http://europa.eu.int/comm/employment_social/soc-prot/healthcare/com_04_ 304_en.pdf).

Chalmers, D. and Lodge, M. (2003), "The Open Method of Co-ordination and the European Welfare State", *ESRC Centre for Analysis of Risk and Regulation Discussion Papers*, No.11, London School of Economics, London, June 2003.

Cohen, J. and Sabel, C. F. (2003), "Sovereignty and Solidarity: EU and US", in Zeitlin, J. and Trubek, D. M. (eds.), *Governing Work and Welfare in a New Economy: European and American Experiments*, Oxford University Press, Oxford, pp.345-375.

Council of the European Union (2000), "The On-going Experience of the Open Method of Coordination", *Presidency Note*, No.90088/00, Lisbon, 13 June 2000.

Council of the European Union (2002), Council Decision 2002/996/JHA of 28 November Establishing a Mechanism for Evaluating the Legal Systems and their Implementation at National Level in the Fight against Terrorism, OJ L 349, 24 December 2002, pp.0001-0003.

Council of the European Union (2003), Council Decision 2003/578/EC of 22 July 2003 on Guidelines for the Employment Policies of the Member States, OJ L 197, 5 August 2003, pp.0013-0021.

Cowles, M. G., Caporaso, J. and Risse, T. (eds.) (2001), *Transforming Europe: Europeanization and Domestic Change*, Cornell University Press, Ithaca.

de Búrca, G. (2003), "The Constitutional Challenge of New Governance in the European Union", *European Law Review*, Vol.28, No.6, December 2003, pp.814-839.

de Búrca, G. and Zeitlin, J. (2003), "Constitutionalizing the Open Method of Coordination: What Should the Convention Propose?", *CEPS Policy Brief*, No.31, Centre for European Policy Studies, Brussels, March 2003.

de la Porte, C. and Nanz, P. (2004), "The OMC – A Deliberative-Democratic Mode of Governance? The Case of Employment and Pensions", *Journal of European Public Policy*, Vol.11, No.2, April 2004, pp.267-288.

de la Porte, C. and Pochet, P. (2003), "The OMC Intertwined with the Debates on Governance, Democracy and Social Europe: Research on the Open Method Of Co-ordination and European Integration", Report prepared for Frank Vandenbroucke, Belgian Minister for Social Affairs and Pensions, Observatoire social européen, Brussels, June 2003.

de Schutter, O. (forthcoming), "The Implementation of Fundamental Rights through the Open Method of Coordination", in de Schutter, O. and Deakin, S. (eds.), *Social Rights and Market Forces: Is the Open Coordination of Employment and Social Policies the Future of Social Europe?*, Bruylant, Brussels.

EU Network of Independent Experts in Fundamental Rights (2002), *Report on the Situation of Fundamental Rights in the European Union and its Members States in 2002*, European Commision, DG Justice and Home Affairs, Brussels (http://europa.eu.int/comm/justice_home/cfr_cdf/doc/rapport_2002_en.pdf).

European Convention (2002), "The Coordination of National Policies: The Open Method of Coordination. Note to the Members of Working Group on Economic Governance", CONV WG VI WD 015, Brussels, 26 September 2002.

European Council (2000), Lisbon European Council, *Presidency Conclusions*, 23-24 March 2000.

European Council (2002), Barcelona European Council, *Presidency Conclusions*, 15-16 March 2002.

European Parliament (2003a), Resolution A5-0143/2003 on Analysis of the Open Coordination Procedure in the Field of Employment and Social Affairs and Future Prospects, Rapporteur: Miet Smet, Committee on Employment and Social Affairs, 5 June 2003.

European Parliament (2003b), Resolution B5-0282/2003 on the Application of the Open Method of Coordination, 5 June 2003.

Featherstone, K. and Radaelli, C. (2003), *The Politics of Europeanization*, Oxford University Press, Oxford.

Ferrera, M. (2001), "The European Social Model between 'Hard' Constraints and 'Soft' Co-ordination", unpublished paper presented to the "Social Models and EMU: Convergence? Co-existence? The Role of Economic and Social Actors", Economic and Social Committee, Brussels, 19 November 2001.

Foden, D. and Magnusson, L. (2002), *Trade Unions and the Cardiff Process: Economic Reform in Europe*, European Trade Union Institute, Brussels.

Goetschy, J. (2003), "The European Employment Strategy, Multi-level Governance, and Policy Coordination: Past, Present and Future", in Zeitlin, J. and Trubek, D. M. (eds.), *Governing Work and Welfare in a New Economy: European and American Experiments*, Oxford University Press, Oxford, pp.59-87.

Hemerijck, A. (2002), "The Self-Transformation of the European Social Model(s)", in Esping-Andersen, G., Gallie, D., Hemerijck, A. and Myles, J., *Why We Need a New Welfare State*, Oxford University Press, Oxford, pp.173-214.

Hemerijck, A. and Berghman, J. (2004), "The European Social Patrimony: Deepening Social Europe through Legitimate Diversity", in Sakellaropoulos, T., Berghman, J., Hemerijck, A., Stergiou, A. and Stevens, Y. (eds.), *Connecting Welfare Diversity within the European Social Model*, Intersentia, Antwerp, pp.9-54.

Héritier, A. (2003), "New Modes of Governance in Europe: Increasing Political Capacity and Policy Effectiveness?" in Börzel, T. and Chichowski, R. (eds.), *The State of the European Union, Vol.6: Law, Politics, and Society*, Oxford University Press, Oxford, pp.105-126.

Hingel, A. (2001), *Education Policies and European Governance: Contribution to the Interservice Groups on European Governance*, European Commission, Directorate-General for Education and Culture, Brussels, March 2001.

Intergovernmental Conference (2004), "Treaty Establishing a Constitution for Europe", CIG 87/04, Brussels, 6 August 2004.

Jacobsson, K. (2002), "Soft Regulation and the Subtle Transformation of States: The Case of EU Employment Policy", *SCORE Working Paper*, No.2002/4, Stockholm Center for Organizational Research, Stockholm.

Jenson, J. and Pochet, P. (2002), "Employment and Social Policy Since Maastricht: Standing up to the European Monetary Union", paper presented to the Year of the Euro Nanovic Institute for European Studies, University of Notre Dame, South Bend, IN, 5-8 December 2002.

Kaiser, R. and Prange, H. (2004), "Managing Diversity in a System of Multilevel Governance: The Open Method of Co-ordination in Innovation Policy", *Journal of European Public Policy*, Vol.11, No.2, April 2004, pp.249-266.

Larsson, A. (2002), "The New Open Method of Co-ordination: A Sustainable Way between a Fragmented Europe and a European Supra State?", lecture presented to the Uppsala University, 4 March 2002.

López-Santana, M. (2004), "'Unpacking' the Policy-making Process: The European Employment Strategy and Europeanization", unpublished paper presented to the 14th International Conference of Europeanists, Chicago, IL, 11-13 March 2004.

Offe, C. (2003), "The European Model of 'Social' Capitalism: Can It Survive European Integration?", *Journal of Political Philosophy*, Vol.11, No.4, December 2003, pp.437-469.

Radaelli, C. (2003a), "The Open Method of Coordination: A New Governance Architecture for the European Union?", *SIEPS Report*, No.1, Swedish Institute for European Policy Studies, Stockholm, March 2003.

Radaelli, C. (2003b), "The Code of Conduct against Harmful Tax Competition: Open Method of Coordination In Disguise?", *Public Administration*, Vol.81, No.3, September 2003, pp.513-531.

Rodrigues, M. J. (2001), "The Open Method of Coordination as a New Governance Tool", *Journal Europa Europe*, Special Issue, No.2-3, Fondazione Istituto Gramsci, Rome, pp.96-107.

Romano, C. (2002), "La Méthode Ouverte de Coordination: Un nouveau mode de gouvernance?", Report prepared for the Task Force on the Future of Europe, European Commission, Brussels, April 2002.

Sabel, C. F. and Zeitlin, J. (2003), "Active Welfare, Experimental Governance, Pragmatic Constitutionalism: The New Transformation of Europe", unpublished paper presented to the International Conference of the Hellenic Presidency of the European Union "The Modernisation of the European Social Model & EU Policies and Instruments", Ioannina, Greece, 21-22 May 2003.

Scharpf, F. (2002), "The European Social Model: Coping with the Challenges of Diversity", *Journal of Common Market Studies*, Vol.40, No.4, November 2002, pp.645-670.

Scharpf, F. (2003), "Legitimate Diversity: The New Challenge of European Integration", in Börzel, T. and Chichowski, R. (eds.), *The State of the European Union, Vol.6: Law, Politics, and Society*, Oxford University Press, Oxford, pp.79-104.

Schmitter, P. C. (1996), "Examining the Present Euro-Polity with the Help of Past Theories", in Marks, G., Scharpf, F. W., Schmitter, P. C. and Streeck, W., *Governance in the European Union*, Sage Publications, London, pp.1-14.

Smismans, S. (2003), "Towards a New Community Strategy on Health and Safety at Work? Caught in the Institutional Web of Soft Procedures", *International Journal of Comparative Labour Law and Industrial Relations*, Vol.19, No.1, pp.55-83.

Smismans, S. (2004), "EU Employment Policy: Decentralisation or Centralisation through the Open Method of Coordination?", *Law Department Working Papers*, No.2004/01, European University Institute, Florence.

SPC (2003), Opinion of the Social Protection Committee on the Commission's Communication "Strengthening the Social Dimension of the Lisbon Strategy: Streamlining Open Coordination in the Field of Social Protection", Brussels, 29 September 2003 (http://europa.eu.int/comm/employment_social/social_protection_commitee/streamlining_en.pdf).

Syrpis, P. (2002), "Legitimising European Governance: Taking Subsidiarity Seriously within the Open Method of Coordination", *Department of Law Working Papers*, No.2002/10, European University Institute, Florence.

Szyszczak, E. (2001), "The New Paradigm for Social Policy in the EU: A Virtuous Circle?" *Common Market Law Review*, Vol.38, No.5, October 2001, pp.1125-1170.

Telò, M. (2002), "Governance and Government in the European Union: The Open Method of Co-ordination", in Rodrigues, M. J. (ed.), *The New Knowledge Economy in Europe: A Strategy for International Competitiveness and Social Cohesion*, Edward Elgar Publishing, Cheltenham, pp.242-272.

Vandenbroucke, F. (2001), "Open Co-ordination on Pensions and the Future of Europe's Social Model", Closing address to the conference "Towards a New Architecture for Social Protection in Europe?", Leuven, 19-20 October 2001.

Vandenbroucke, F. (2002), "Foreward: Sustainable Social Justice and 'Open Co-ordination' in Europe", in Esping-Andersen, G., Gallie, D., Hemerijck, A. and Myles, J., *Why We Need a New Welfare State*, Oxford University Press, Oxford, pp.viii-xxiv.

Vandenbroucke, F. (2003), Intervention presented to the Expert Hearing of Working Group 11 "Social Europe", European Convention, 21 January 2003.

Zeitlin, J. (2003), "Introduction: Governing Work and Welfare in a New Economy: European and American Experiments", in Zeitlin, J. and Trubek, D. M. (eds.), *Governing Work and Welfare in a New Economy: European and American Experiments*, Oxford University Press, Oxford, pp.1-32.

PART I

THEORETICAL AND HISTORICAL OVERVIEWS

CHAPTER 1

The Open Method of Co-ordination and the Construction of Social Europe

A Historical Perspective

Philippe POCHET

Introduction[1]

The number of papers, articles and books on the Open Method of Co-ordination (OMC) and on new form(s) of governance in the EU is growing each day. If the OMC covers different fields (economic policy, research, education, migration, for a review see Rodrigues, 2004), it is its application to social policies (employment, pensions, exclusion, health care) that has attracted most interest. These developments were not expected. Until very recently, achievements in European social policy were generally considered as – at best – weak. Most commentators underlined the imbalance between economic and monetary integration on the one hand and the social integration on the other. The difficulties of adopting a positive integration agenda (common regulation) were underlined in a context of increasing diversity in terms of welfare state arrangements and developments. The internal market had led to an "embedded liberalism". Many predicted that fiscal competition, "social dumping" and "social tourism" created by European economic integration (the single market and the single currency) would imply a race to the bottom in social policy, social protection systems being obliged to adapt through retrenchment and structural adjustment policies. It was also argued that this detrimental impact could be reinforced by the European Court of Justice. Some of its decisions have removed obstacles to a free market. In this perspective, the impact of European integration on national welfare programmes was analysed in terms of "negative integration" (Leibfried and Pierson, 1995; Scharpf, 2000). It was gener-

---

[1] Special thanks to Caroline de la Porte with whom I have traced the different aspects of the OMC. Jonathan Zeitlin gave me very stimulating comments.

ally considered that the different steps in European integration had increased its liberal and supply-side bias and had downgraded national social models without enabling the creation of a European one. Very few observers (see Cram, 1993) had predicted that the declarations and resolutions (soft law) of the mid-1990s would lead to expanding competences in social field or innovation in European social policy orientation and practices.

We can discuss whether these analyses are still relevant today but in any case there has been a radical change at least in the agenda and the method. The arrival of employment and social policies on the European agenda can be understood as an unintended consequence of European economic and monetary integration. Instead of a spillover effect, I prefer to use Dyson's term of pollination (1994: 295). There is "pollination, whether the seeds of integration germinate successfully in proximate sectors, like labour markets and budgetary policy, depends on the fertility of the soil there, in integration, fertility requires a critical mass of actors with the will and the capacity to act [...]". In the field of employment policy as well as of social protection, the dynamic can be seen as a fight between two groups of actors. The "socially-oriented" actors (Ministers of Labour, trade unions, (centre-)left governments, members of the European Parliament, high civil servants in the Commission, etc.) mobilise to control the reform agenda at European level against the economically oriented actors (Ecofin Council, Economic and Financial Committee, Economic Policy Committee, (centre-)right governments, etc.). Both groups are trying to impose their policy orientation at European level (de la Porte and Pochet, 2002; Jenson and Pochet, 2005). Despite, the aforementioned growing interest in the social dimension, as Daly (2004) rightly underlines we have still to address the questions of why and why now. The political dynamic both in term of tensions between different visions and the historically situated decision process is often lacking in accounts of the EES and OMC (Radaelli, 2003, de la Porte and Pochet, 2003 and 2004). This chapter seeks to provide the reader with an overall picture of developments in employment and social policy, by presenting the EES and OMC in a historical and contextual perspective.

This chapter is structured in three parts. The first presents the EES and the OMC in a historical perspective. Indeed, the (short) history of European social policy is the result of many trial and error processes. There is an ongoing learning process at European level about what is working and not working in a politically and economically changing environment. Each period has a dominant vision of the key themes to be addressed and a dominant form of governance. But the logics of previous periods do not completely disappear and remain alive in a limited section of social policies (Goetschy, 2005). There is a cumulative effect. The interaction between European and national level developments a will not be analysed here (for more details see Hall, 2001; Visser, 2000; Hemerijck, 2005). The second part presents the development of the EES. We highlight three main phases which partially overlap with one another. At the outset the EES was conceived as a reaction to EMU. Then it became an autonomous process and a model for the new form of governance at the EU level. Finally, it is presented as a tool to force through (difficult and unpopular) reforms at national level and is linked again with economic co-ordination in a streamlining process.

The third part presents the evolution of the OMC Social Inclusion process (OMC/incl). Here the process remains experimental and loosely linked to the EES and the BEPGs. The future streamlining process for the social protection OMCs raises fears about the autonomy of the social exclusion and poverty OMC. Finally, we draw some lessons for the future.

I.   The EES and the OMC as a New Step in the History of European Social Policy

The history of European social policy is more a story of failure than great success (measured by the number of directives adopted). Nevertheless since the beginning of the European Community at least five different attempts each with their own priorities, underlying logics and particular fields of interest (free movement of workers, social legislation or employment co-ordination for example) have followed one another. Taking this perspective, we could indicate that the OMC is only one of the possible approaches to EU social policy and certainly not the end of the story. Thus, we will present the main events of four decades of European social policy. Without entering into the details of the different phases, we underline their respective internal coherence in term of topics covered and method of governance.

Many subsequent developments are the result of initial choices. Bea Cantillon (2004: 6) reminds us that

Contrary to the US, the EEC chose in 1957 to leave the social policy to the national welfare states. This decision was taken on the basis of the Olhin report, which had been commissioned by the ILO, and which concluded that social policy differences between countries were sustainable, so the harmonisation of welfare state was deemed unnecessary.

Indeed, the ILO committee concluded:

International competition in a common market would not prevent particular countries from raising workers' living standards and there is no sound reason to think that freer international markets would hamper in any way the further improvement of workers' living standards as productivity rises, through higher wages or improved social benefits and working conditions [...]

After this initial decision, different attempts were nevertheless made to develop the social dimension of economic integration.

1) The first step, in the early 1960s, was limited to the free movement of workers. The logic was not to harmonise different national policies but to give the same rights to Community and national workers in each Member State. This included providing the possibility of cumulating benefits (e.g. pensions) acquired in different places (Pakaslahti and Pochet, 2003). In addition the European Social Fund (ESF) was created in order to retrain workers affected by economic change, partly due to economic integration.

2) In the 1970s the Community tried, in the words of the Treaty of Rome, to define a way "to promote improved working conditions and an improved standard of living for workers, so as to make possible their harmonisation while the improvement is being maintained". Several directives were adopted in a context of economic downturn and militant mobilisation at national level. Equality between men and women, health and safety in the workplace as well as certain aspects of labour law (collective redundancy, transfer of undertakings, insolvency of the employer) were involved. The first European Social Program (1974) was adopted, which can be considered as the social side of the Werner Plan for a monetary union in 1980 and the creation of a political union at the same date (Magnusson and Stråth, 2001). Finally, some directives related to collective rights were adopted (collective redundancy, transfer of undertakings, insolvency, etc.). What is generally considered the "golden age" of EU social policy corresponds (at national level) to the crisis of Keynesian economic management and the end of welfare state expansion.

3) The end of the 1970s was, then, a turning point. The Thatcher and Reagan governments indicated a neo-liberal turn which led to a pause in social regulation at European level and a process of deregulation at national level. Different proposals (the Vredeling directive on information/participation in multinational companies, reduction of working time, regulation of atypical contracts) failed to be adopted at EU level.

The Single European Act (1985) expanded the Community's social competencies, allowing the adoption health and safety measures by qualified majority (this would permit considerable development in this domain). It also contained a rather vague provision on social dialogue which launched a dynamic of non-binding agreements (joint opinions) between the European social partners (European Trade Union Confederation ETUC, UNICE and CEEP for the private and public employers respectively) (see Didry and Mias, 2005). In a unfavourable political environment, it proved impossible to continue a process aiming at harmonising national social regulation. Instead an initial debate over global competition (from US and Japan on the one hand and from the developing countries like Brazil, Taiwan, Korea on the other) fuelled controversies about social deregulation, social dumping and races to the bottom.

4) Thus, the end of the 1980s and the beginning of the 1990s were characterised by a strategy of defining minimum norms below which one should not descend in a period of triumphant neo-liberalism and globalisation. This is the true meaning of the Community Charter of the Fundamental Social Rights of Workers adopted in 1989 and the action programme which accompanied it (Jonckheer and Pochet, 1990) The basic idea was to develop a set of minimum legal regulations at European level. Nevertheless, the level of ambition was sometimes so low that the draft directives were even below the level of the ILO's international conventions. In the same period, the development of social dialogue led to the signature of the Social Agreement between the European social partners This agreement was introduced as a protocol to the Maastricht Treaty, due to the opposition of the Conservative British government. It empowers the social partners and gives them the right to sign agreements which can be extended *erga omnes* by a Council directive or voluntary collective agreement implemented by their national affiliates. The strategic idea was to mirror the national situation where in most Member States the social partners can autonomously regulate aspects of labour relations.

5) After the victory of New Labour in UK and the Socialist Party in France, an Employment Title was included in the Amsterdam Treaty (tentatively modelled on the EMU procedures) and qualified majority voting was introduced in few social areas by the incorporation of the social protocol into the Treaty. The resort to the Open Method of Coordination (OMC) is thus the fifth attempt to define the European social dimension. In a nutshell, the OMC is a flexible means of working towards shared European objectives via national plans, which are assessed in accordance with common criteria (indicators), following (in some but not all cases) guidelines and/or targets decided jointly by national ministers at European level. Without legal compulsion, peer pressure (and the force of public opinion) represents the means to ensure that national governments adhere to their European commitments. Exchange of good practices are supposed to improve knowledge and to lead to a learning process in order to improve public policies. This is an attempt to make official declarations made by Ministers at European

level morally "binding" at national level, by the implementation of a set of complex procedures. Within this framework the European Parliament and the Court of Justice play a minor role. The OMC has already been applied to economic co-ordination (the Broad Economic Policy Guidelines), to employment (the Luxembourg Process or European Employment Strategy), poverty and social exclusion, and pensions (for a general overview, see de la Porte and Pochet, 2002; Dehousse, 2004). The main objective is no longer to create a set of European rules distinct from national regulations but to favour an interaction between different levels of governance. The OMC mobilised the idea of diversity as an opportunity for improving national standards and converging on the best results (outcomes). The process through which this should be achieved is learning, a change-inducing process based on ideas (due in particular to the absence of legally binding powers). With this new multi-level arrangement, the European bodies have created a new form of intervention which is less aimed at harmonising institutions or legislation than at harmonising ideas, visions, conceptions, knowledge and norms of action, in order to have policy goals converging towards "a common political vision".

If the OMC has been at the center of academic and political attention, it should be noted that in the same time other important developments occurred which attracted less notice. The Charter of Fundamental Rights has been adopted at the Nice European Council (2000) and is now integrated in the Constitutional Treaty. It codified social rights at European level. Furthermore, the social partners adopted in 2003 their own three-year autonomous work program and have signed two autonomous agreements (teleworking and stress at work). There are also interesting developments at sectoral level (Pochet *et al.*, 2004). In the first part of the Constitutional Treaty the role of the social partners has been defined in a specific provision. Finally, the recent revision of Regulation 1408/71 (see special issue of the *Revue belge de sécurité sociale*, 2004) and its previous extension to non-EU migrant workers (Ghailani, 2003) show that the questions dealt in the 1960s and 1970s remain on the agenda (Ferrera, 2005).

Since the beginning, European social policy was institutionally very inventive (upwards harmonisation, equal treatment between national and EU workers, minimal standards, negotiated legislation, charter of fundamental rights, collective bargaining, policy co-ordination, soft law etc.). Clearly the past record shows more failures than successes in adopting European measures but European social policy has to be understood in its historical dimension as a perpetual trial and error process. The advocacy coalition (comprising trade unionists, left parties and governments, some key players in the Commission, but also academics or journalists) in favour of a more socially oriented Europe has been very active, using the windows of opportunity offered by each revision of the treaty to insert new social provisions (van Riel and van der Meer, 2002; Jenson and Pochet, 2004).

In its turn, the successive Treaty revisions had a leverage effect on the actors' resources. Nevertheless the Social Democratic governments never had a strategic vision towards creating a more social Europe. From 1995 to 2003 Social Democrats held power at national level in a majority of Member States. Their preferences have changed. On the one hand, there has been a convergence process between the left and the right parties on the role of the market (Manow *et al.*, 2004). On the other, the left parties were less pro-federal Europe and were unwilling to transfer many more competencies to the European level. On the contrary, it seems that more and more governments are trying to downgrade the traditional Community Method in favour of a more intergovernmental approach (the employment strategy and the OMC).

The departure from the traditional method is complemented by a three-pronged development of fundamental rights, social dialogue and the OMC. As noted by Szyszczak (2001: 1129)

> The distinctive features of the substance of the new social policy paradigm reveal a shift away from earlier attempts at harmonisation of social law towards creating a core of social rights in the employment field through a process of regulation, coordination and convergence. [...] Alongside these policies nestles a policy of coordinating Member States' economic, social protection and employment policies emphasizing the need to modernize, create flexibility and reduce public expenditure especially on passive labour market policies.

Table 1 below summarises the different developments according to four categories: socio-economic and political development at national level, main themes of EU social policy, governance method and national diversity.

Table 1: Development of European Social Policy

Period	National Level	Main Themes of European Social Policy	Governance Method	National Diversity
1958-1973	Economic modernisation; expansion of the welfare state; proactive Keynesianism. Christian Democrats and right govern-ments in power in all Member-States	Free movement of workers Social security of EU migrant workers European Social Fund	(Automatic) social policy convergence Equality between EU migrants and nationals in each Member State Additionality of working periods abroad	Six Bismarck-ian welfare states
1973-1981	Stagflation; social conflict. More balanced period, left in power for almost half the period and in five of the nine members states	Health and safety at work Equal treatment of men and women Protection of workers' rights Golden Age of European social policy	Harmonisa-tion in progress	Denmark, UK and Ireland (1973): Scandinavian and Anglo-Saxon models added
1981-1989	Neo-liberal moment; deregulation; privatisation, economic internationalisa-tion; end of Keynesianism Majority of right, liberal and Christian Democratic governments.	Health and safety at work Gender equality at work Structural funds doubled	Minimum standards decided by a qualified majority (QMV) in heath and safety; beginning of the European social dialogue Social Charter	Greece (1981), Spain and Portugal (1986). Presence of Southern European model.

Period	National Level	Main Themes of European Social Policy	Governance Method	National Diversity
1989-1997	Budgetary and debt constraints imposed by EMU, social pacts; welfare state retrench-ment. Change from a huge majority of right wing governments to a majority of left wing ones (1995)	Fundamental rights and minimum rights; Heath and safety; Collective interest represen-tation; Cohesion fund	British *opt-out*; minimum standard; binding Social dialogue (maternity leave, atypical contract)	Sweden, Finland and Austria (1995): reinforcing presence of high-standard welfare model
1997-2003	Structural unemployment, ageing popula-tion, less constraints by EMU (revision of Growth and Stability Pact) end of social pacts pension reforms (long term sustainability) Large majority of left wing governments at the beginning and relative 8 on 15 at the end.	European Employment strategy Autonomous Social Dialogue (teleworking, stress) Sectoral social dialogue Anti-discrimination directives, Social protection OMC	Social dialogue Open Method of Co-ordination; diversity a an asset for learning Social protection as a productive factor Minimum directives Fundamental rights (political, economic and social)	Preparation for enlarge-ment and an increased diversity of labour and welfare institutions

Source: inspired by Hemerijck (2005). The data on the right/left balance come from Manow *et al.* (2004).

Now Europe has been enlarged to take in ten new members and many others are on the waiting list. The main question is: is this a "real" enlargement (extension to new members of the previous rules) or a "new Europe" (new rules to be invented to cope with an increased diversity and growing number of players)? It is too early to say but many signs indicate that it is not simply an extension of rules and practices to more members. The co-ordination rules, whether for the Stability Pact, the BEPGs, the EES or more generally for the results of the Lisbon strategy are increasingly contested. At the time of writing, there are different views on how to improve the governance method (Kok Report, 2004, Notre Europe report on Lisbon, Commission proposal for a new Stability and Growth Pact, streamlining process for social protection etc.). Following enlargement, the right/left political balance leans once again toward the centre right in the Council and the new European Parliament. The Barroso Commission is also rather liberal. Finally the Constitutional Treaty has adopted a very restricted version of the OMC and only after a fierce battle by its supporters (de Búrca and Zeitlin, 2003; Zeitlin, 2005). The result of these different approaches and ideas about the future should find a new synthesis in the 2005 EU Spring Council.

II. The EES in Movement

Having presented the EES and OMC in a historical perspective, we will analyse the developments of the Employment Strategy as a European question. We consider that the EES has developed in three successive phases. During the first, the EES developed under the shadow of the Economic and Monetary Union integration model (section 1). The rationale behind the EES was to rebalance monetary and economic integration. Legitimised through the Employment Title in the Amsterdam Treaty, the EES progressively became a policy process in its own right (section 2). This was a phase of consolidation of the EES (by using the tool of recommendations for example) and of incremental change at European level. The underlying principles of the EES were generalised through the OMC at the Lisbon Summit (2000). The EES and then the OMC have most often been analysed under the governance rubric as a quasi-independent policy process, without any particular link with EMU. At the same time the original model, the BEPGs, proved to be not so efficient and were also analysed as a soft co-ordination process (Hodson and Maher, 2001) (section 3). The third phase began with the five-year evaluation (2003). Once again the EES was repoliticised in an environment dominated at this time by right wing governments. It was also decided to streamline the economic and employment processes (section 4). The focus shifted to the implementation of reforms at national level.

A.   A European Response to the Challenges of EMU

This section recalls how employment policy co-ordination developed and was introduced in the Amsterdam Treaty, drawing its inspiration from economic co-ordination procedures.

Two broad approaches linked EMU and employment, one centred on the national level and the other on the European.

The first approach started from the impact of EMU at national level. Indeed, monetary union was achieved with a low level of mobility of workers between the Member States and without a European budget that could play a stabilising role in case of asymmetric shock. Many authors have underlined the need to increase the flexibility of the labour market in order to create the means with which to confront an asymmetrical shock (Pochet *et al.*, 1998). This has led to a fear that industrial relations would slowly but surely become "Americanised" (Martin, 1999; Martin and Ross, 2004). This vision underpins the Swedish approach to complement EMU with an employment side (see below).

The second approach was developed more by (semi-autonomous) European actors. The main idea of these European actors (among them the trade union leadership of ETUC) was that the social side should go hand in hand with the economic one. The reflection was less in terms of content than of procedure. In this case, the EES's principal source of inspiration was the "hard co-ordination" process that led to monetary union. Mid-term objectives, indicators and pressure for convergence had to be replicated in the Employment Title of the Amsterdam Treaty. In a way, it consisted mainly of mimicking the monetary success story.

If the idea of complementing EMU with an employment side was in the air, the window of opportunity and the catalyst for action came with the economic recession following the Maastricht treaty and the rapid rise of unemployment.

In 1993 the Delors Commission published a White Paper on Growth, Competitiveness and Employment which presented an analysis of European weaknesses and a series of proposals to respond to the economic downturn. It was a reflection of the need to revitalise the European project and to counter scepticism towards Europe's monetary integration project (Arnold and Cameron, 2001; Ross, 1995). After this impulse, the Essen European Council (1994) adopted five objectives which were: to invest in vocational training, to increase employment-intensive growth, to reduce non-wage labour costs, to increase active labour market policies, and to fight youth and long-term employment, underpinned by a monitoring system which can be considered a precursor of the EES. Although there was pressure from the Delors Commission and some Member States to respond to the employment crisis in this manner, there was also a considerable amount of counter-pressure to limit any further delegation of power to the EU based on the argument that employment is created by individual entrepreneurial decisions and cannot be decided at EU level. The proposal to add an employment dimension to the European project lacked a legal base, a systematised methodology, a strong permanent structure, a long-term vision, and a control process. Member States were to proceed by simple co-operation,

47

which proved a failure (Telò, 2004). However, the White Paper was an important catalyst for raising the issue of employment on the European agenda. The subsequent European Council meetings, notably those of Madrid in December 1995 and Dublin in December 1996, contributed to the development of the process. The former identified job creation as a central objective of the EU and its Member States, in economic, political and social terms. The latter boosted employment further on the EU agenda, through the "Dublin Declaration on Employment", underlining the need to pursue a macroeconomic policy favourable to growth and employment. In addition foreshadowed in the Amsterdam Treaty, inviting the Member States to create "additional instruments for the effective monitoring and evaluation of employment and labour market policy, including the identification of 'good practice' and the development of common indicators that might allow benchmarking and explicit comparisons of policy and performance among Member States" (Arnold and Cameron, 2001: 7-8).

Based on the Commission's proposal, the Irish Presidency at the end of 1996 drafted most of what was to become the Employment Title of the Amsterdam Treaty (Arnold, 2002).

In preparation for the IGC, Allan Larsson (former Swedish Minister of Economics and future Head of DG Employment), and the Swedish representative in the IGC, Gunnar Lund, played an important role (Barbier, 2004). As a newcomer to the European Union in 1995, Sweden wished to advance its policy priorities, notably that of employment, in the European framework. Larsson's principal argument was that active labour market policies should be conceived together with the EU's project of monetary and economic convergence. The strong connection between the two is reflected in the title of his paper "A European Employment Union – to make EMU possible" written in 1995. His argument was that a strong employment policy would contribute positively to EMU through the development of a well-performing labour market (de la Porte and Pochet, 2003). In other words, economic, monetary and employment policies were to be intricately linked with each other to meet mutually supportive goals (Larsson, 1995). At Larsson's initiative, Sweden tried to convince the other Member States of the need to concretely develop an employment strategy for Europe (van Riel and van der Meer, 2002). At the time, however, France, the United Kingdom, Germany and (after the general elections) Spain were opposed (Arnold, 2002).

The EES was part of a global deal including the adoption of the Stability and Growth Pact. The new French Socialist Government led by Lionel Jospin, agreed to the Pact in exchange for adding a new Employment Title to the proposed Treaty. For most of the Member States and in particular Germany, the Pact was intended to be a key instrument for fiscal management after the selection of the members of the Eurozone. The Council agreed to the French proposal. At that time, little attention was paid to the softer side of economic policy co-ordination, which was set out as a complement to fiscal policy co-ordination. The "soft" co-ordination of economic policies was conceived to monitor the consistency of national economic policies with the economic objectives of the Union and, for Eurozone members, with Eurozone monetary policy. In the event of a deviation from the economic policies set out in the Broad Economic Policy Guidelines (BEPGs), the Council could adopt a non-binding recommendation directed to the Member State concerned. No formal sanction system is associated with the BEPGs, where the sanctions for non-compliance take the form of peer pressure, the financial markets, and public opinion. The hard fiscal and soft economic co-ordination procedures reflect the Member States' commitment to co-ordinate their economic policies with the Council to achieve common aims, including sustainable and non-inflationary growth (Hodson and Maher, 2001).

During the Amsterdam Summit (1997), agreement was eventually reached on the form that the employment strategy should take: the multilateral process associated with EMU would be adapted to employment policy. An Employment Title was integrated into the Treaty and became fully operational in 1997, although it was only ratified by all Member States in 1999. The European Employment Strategy (EES) had to be consistent with the Broad Economic Policy Guidelines through an integrative approach (Pochet, 1999; Kenner, 1999).

To operationalise the Employment Chapter, an extraordinary session of the European Council was organised in Luxembourg in November 1997. According to Juncker (2002), who had a transversal approach because he was Prime Minister, Finance Minister and Labour Minister of Luxembourg, there was a lack of consensus between the Ministers of Finance and Employment and Social Affairs. Against this background, he organised and participated in over 200 preparatory meetings, in order to reach a political consensus. Mr. Juncker himself underlined that the preparation of the Summit was a much tougher and more "tumultuous" nut to break than the Summit itself (*Bulletin Quotidien Europe*, No.7106, 24 and 25 November 1997). In terms of content, the European Commission had initially proposed that the entrepreneurship theme should act as a driving force in the strategy. The Member States, on the other hand, were overwhelmingly in favour of an approach that would principally be based on employability. It is also of interest to recall that the fourth pillar on equality of men and women was included in the guidelines upon the initiative of Commissioner Flynn, who had to prove his commitment to this theme, after he had been accused by the EP of neglecting it.

Spain, followed by Portugal, were opposed to the setting of quantitative employment rate targets, as these would, according to Spain's Prime Minister, Aznar, have require a 200% increase in spending to meet the agreed objectives to combat youth and long-term unemployment. Since the beginning of the discussions around employment, Germany was very critical about the need to address this question at European level, but eventually agreed to the EES.

Employability represented the heart of the first pillar of the European Employment Guidelines (EEGs) agreed and adopted. In addition to employability, the three other pillars that guided the Strategy were the development of entrepreneurship, adaptability and equal opportunities.

The Commission had proposed rather detailed guidelines, accompanied by quantitative benchmarks, which most Member States were unwilling to accept. The subsequent Council amendments watered down these benchmarks, including one on the reduction of the unemployment rate and another on the increase of the overall labour market participation (Trubek and Mosher, 2001). The analysis at the time was that, with an annual growth rate of 3%, it would be possible to create between 10 and 12 million new jobs in Europe in the five years that followed (*Bulletin Quotidien Europe*, No.7106, 24 and 25 November 1997).

The possibility of constructing a more demand-oriented policy was a non-issue because of the 3% deficit limit for entering the Economic and Monetary Union in the first wave. The strategy coincided with the signature of social pacts in many Member States (Fajertag and Pochet, 1997 and 2000), which acted as a counter-force to the tendency towards greater decentralisation of collective bargaining. But social pacts at national level and the EES at European level, both an answer to the liberal agenda, did not merge (Pochet, 2004). There has been a divorce between a national negotiation agenda between social partners and government (focused principally on changes in wage negotiations and to a lesser extent the welfare state in order to qualify for EMU) and a European agenda around other themes (focussed on employability, adaptability, entrepreneurship and equality between men and women). Concerning the actors, the social pact process has been driven by negotiations between social partners and the governments at national level and essentially orchestrated by the Commission and the Member States in the case of the European Employment Strategy.

B. The European Employment Strategy as an Autonomous Strategy

The EES rapidly became a policy process in its own right. The focus was on its operationalisation. Incremental changes were adopted each year at European level (Trubek and Mosher, 2001). On the one hand the tools (Joint Report, indicators, good practices, peer review etc.) were new and had to be tested. On the other hand different actors wanted to change or adapt the content at European level. In consequence the guidelines were slightly modified in content and number. In the year 2000, fundamental quantified objectives with target dates were agreed for the Union as a whole – to increase the European employment rate to 70% by 2010, and the female employment rate to 60% (European Council, 2000). Increasing the employment rate became the centre of the EES. New intermediate targets for employment rates across the Union were agreed in 2001: a 67% overall employment rate and a 57% employment rate for women by January 2005 (European Council, 2001). Moreover, in the wake of the pension debate around the ageing population, the European Council adopted a target of 50% by 2010 for the average EU employment rate among older workers (55-64). In addition to the EES's intensification in quantitative terms, it became more complex. Indeed, six horizontal objectives were integrated into the EEGs (following the conclusions of the Lisbon and Stockholm European Councils), which were linked to broader policy objectives agreed for the European Union. The first was to increase the employment rate. The second was to improve the quality of employment, which was one of the principal policy priorities of the Swedish and Belgian Presidencies (more and better jobs). In line with the employability pillar the third overall objective was to define a coherent and global strategy for lifelong learning. Another overall objective was to involve the social partners in all stages of the process (see chapter by de la Porte and Pochet in this volume). The fifth objective was to have a balanced approach to the four pillars. Finally, there was a political commitment to develop relevant social indicators.

In the process of defining the EES, some academics played a key role. Janine Goetschy was the first to characterise the EES as representing a "qualitative break" with the previous mode of governance for the social dimension of Europe (Goetschy, 1999: 130). Following this analysis, many political actors and academics have identified EES (and OMC) as a "new" governance tool, a novel approach to regulation in the European Union. The governance turn led many policy actors and academics to "the tendency to favour an approach based on form rather than on the content" (Tholoniat, 2001: 6). The debate concentrated on the differences between "hard law" (the Community Method) and "soft law" (see the chapter by Trubek and Trubek in this volume). This led many analyses to concentrate on the path through which the EES was most likely to have an effect at national level and to present a sociological view insisting on the cognitive route. "Effects may include... more subtle impact on national debates and discourses, changes in ways of thinking policy (policy principles), and collective understandings and identities" (Jacobsson, 2001: 3). In relation to European-level objectives, it seeks to encourage Member States to exchange best practices, to learn from them and to transfer and adapt them to their national contexts, in order to improve their national policies and practices (de la Porte *et al.*, 2001: 293).

The essence of this new governance approach is more than just an additional regulatory tool for the European Union (Mosher, 2000). The new governance approach is part of a new policy paradigm, to respond to the increasing complexities of the EU, as well as a period of new uncertainties (Eberlein and Kerwer, 2002). Moreover, in the current EU of 15 and especially in the view of enlargement, diversity is here to stay, and it needs to be responded to adequately (Scott and Trubek, 2002: 6-7). Benchmarking, respect for subsidiarity and adequate participation of diverse actors at different levels are central pillars of the OMC as a governance tool. These elements are in line with the "new governance" approach identified by Scott and Trubek, based on participation and power sharing, multi-level integration, diversity and decentralisation, deliberation, flexibility and revisability, experimentation and knowledge creation (Scott and Trubek, 2002: 5-6). In this manner, by seeping into domestic discourses and arrangements, the OMC is supposed to alter the beliefs and expectations of domestic actors (Knill and Lehmkuhl, 1999), thus leading to convergence in the long run. However, as Héritier (2002) states "[...] it may still be premature to advocate that the future of the European policy-making system ought to become 'a confederation of learning networks' (Beresford Taylor, 2000: 21), centered around sharing knowledge and experience, and characterised by benchmarking, peer review, and public pressure". In the same way, in employment there is not just one network for employment matters, but at least two, the first around the Employment Committee and the second around the Economic Policy Committee (EPC) and Ecofin Council.

It should be noted that internally the Commission had also developed a discourse about new practices. For example Commissioner Flynn's Green (1993) and White Paper (1994) of were in themselves a new mode of consultation and comprised some of the key ingredients of the new governance discourses. The Green Paper states for example that EU social programmes like employment, health, equal opportunity, local development etc. are based on the same approach:

they encourage innovation, good practice and policies, the exchange of ideas and experience, the transfer of know how and the development of exchange of practitioners. In a way, participants have been mobilised; partnerships at various levels have been established and developed; and the search for more coherent and comprehensive approaches on social issues has been stimulated (CEC, 1993: 11).

This discourse was further elaborated by high civil servants in DG EMPL (such as Odile Quintin, Allan Larsson or Karl-Johan Lönnroth). In 2001 the Commission adopted after many internal debates a communication on better governance which attracted many critics.

Some political and academic actors also approach OMC as a way to reinforce social Europe "If we use it judiciously, open co-ordination constitutes an offensive strategy which allows us to define concretely a "Social Europe" and anchor it firmly in the European process of co-operation as a common good" (Vandenbroucke, 2001; see also Ferrera, 2001; Pochet, 2001). Telò (2004) considers that there is an intrinsic tension between those who have a "pragmatic" vision of Lisbon (and the OMC) as a tool for domestic reform and those who have a balanced view including a new development of the European social model.

While the EES is touted as a new governance tool (under certain conditions), the efficiency of the model on which it was based, the co-ordination of economic policies and the Stability Pact, is being questioned.

C. EMU as a Soft Co-ordination Process

The 1999-2002 transition to the single currency was a frank success. Nevertheless, the central question of the beginning of the 1990s, which economic and social model in the context of a centralised monetary regime, remained unanswered. Until recently, the central bankers and the Ministers of Economics and Finance were perceived as belonging to the same epistemic community, sharing the same values and beliefs, thus facilitating the economic co-ordination procedure (Haas, 1992). In such an approach, the objectives of the Stability and Growth Pact, not only the ceiling of 3% for the budget deficit, but also maintaining a balance or a slight surplus in public finances in the medium term, were considered to be consensual and internalised by all key actors; this was supposed to indicate a (new) culture of stability. In order to achieve such stability, structural reforms had to be implemented at national level (that is the aim of the Cardiff process). After the debate about whether or not to send an early warning to Germany and Portugal, whose public deficits were approaching the 3% deficit ceiling of the Stability and Growth Pact, the fact that the recipe proposed by the Pact was by no means optimal progressively became apparent, leading the President of the

Commission Romano Prodi to label it "stupid". What was presented as a strong consensus and new conventional wisdom (not to exceed the 3% limit except in case of very strong economic recession) has now become a much more disputed theme. This first flaw was followed by the French announcement that they would not return to a balanced budget by 2004 (ultimate deadline), but would instead delay the process by three years (Hodson, 2004). Now there is a new proposal under discussion at the Ecofin Council from the Commission to modify and flexibilise the Stability and Growth Pact.

If the Stability and Growth Pact is under revision, the softer side of the new regime represented by the BEPGs has proved inefficient in its principal goal of co-ordinating economic (and social) reforms. Different analysts have come to question the real effectiveness of the economic policy co-ordination tools. The principal conclusion of a study by TEPSA (2002) for the European Parliament on the national implementation of the recommendations of the BEPGs is lack of awareness of the BEPGs nationally and therefore lack of integration into national policy processes:

> [...] the attention paid by national parliaments to the BEPGs as well as to parliamentary procedures to deal with the BEPGs and/or their implementation at the national level is uneven. In several Member States, the BEPGs do not play any significant role in parliamentary debates. Only in a few cases have the BEPGs been subject to party political debate, either on specific recommendations or on the coordination procedure as a whole.

The (non) compliance by the Member States with the BEPG's recommendations was similar to their response to the EEGs's recommendations. This recognition that economic co-ordination was not as strong as anticipated has led various authors to draw parallels between the two processes (see for example the Govecor project www.govecor.org). What is interesting to underline is that the BEPG "borrowed" some of the institutional innovations of the EES (clearer recommendations, joint report, evaluation of implementation, etc.).

Moreover the macroeconomic dialogue, set up after the Cologne European summit (1999) and involving various players – the European Central Bank (ECB), the Ministers of Economics and Finance, the Social Affairs Ministers and the European social partners – has not functioned properly. Although the Finance Ministers and the European Central Bank have various fora for conducting a more or less formalised dialogue, the originality of the macroeconomic dialogue is that it provides an opportunity for direct contact between representatives of the ECB and the social partners. Basically this dialogue remains a formal one, which means that it cannot be turned into "an effective way to approach implementing the [...] macro-economic policy forming part of the broad economic policy guidelines as pursued by the Member States" (European Council, 1999: 4), as was foreseen in the conclusions of the Cologne European Council.

It is in this context that the question of economic governance of the single currency that was wrongly assumed to be solved re-emerged. One of the six subgroups created within the Convention for the Future of Europe was to deal with the economic governance question. The European Commission (CEC, 2002a) proposed to reinforce its role and to render the recommendations more binding. Others have underlined the need to render the process more democratic, both at European and national levels (Lamy and Pisani-Ferry, 2002).

D. EES as Potential Tool for National Reforms

The return of right-wing governments to power parallels the re-emergence of a very liberal Ecofin discourse on the labour market. Kenneth Dyson, one of the best specialists of the EMU process underlined that (2002: 101):

> The ECB-centric Eurozone policy community had to absorb and accommodate the so-called Luxembourg "process" – with its annual employment guidelines and national action plans – and the Cologne "process" – the Employment Pact and the macroeconomic dialogue. These developments opened up the dialogue about EMU by transforming the definition of who was in the policy domain.

If in the first stage, the economic actors were surprised by the EES and OMC, the economic networks around Ecofin were able to regain some control of the global agenda and succeeded in "merging" the two processes. At the Barcelona Spring European Council, it was decided that the BEPGs and the EEGs, which were up to now dissociated, should be synchronised in terms of yearly scheduling, rather than having the EES take place in the autumn and the BEPGs in the spring. The BEPGs and EES should also become pluri-annual (three years) with greater emphasis on implementation.

Ten years after the Maastricht Treaty and five years after the beginning of the Employment Strategy, the processes needed to be re-thought and more interrelated systems should be created in order to cope with the requirements of the new monetary regime. The evaluation after five years of the Employment Strategy should be situated in the context of the discussion of an adequate budgetary and employment policy mix for the Eurozone. The economic context was also changing. The EES + 5 evaluation was taking place, the post-11 September 2001 economic downturn.

The EU evaluation of the EES looked at ten different issues. Efficiency was at the centre of the evaluation, while decision-making mechanisms were a peripheral issue. The ten topics subjected to evaluation were: prevention and activation policies; tax and benefit reforms; lifelong learning; social inclusion; administrative simplification and self-employment; creation of jobs in services, at local level and in the social economy; modernising work organisation; equal opportunities; and finally changes in policy-making. As it is difficult to distinguish between the European strategy and national policies, the exercise could therefore be characterised more as an evaluation of the efficiency of national policies than of the true impact of the EES. Initially, the evaluation process was rather secretive. The national research about the advantages and the limits of the method, its success and failure, followed no common methodology. More positively, it should be noted that this was the first time that the Member States evaluated their employment policies at the same time. What was initially a quasi-clandestine evaluation eventually became public under the pressure of the Commission's discourse on openness. All Member States decided to post the results of the national evaluations on the web. The transversal thematic analyses by the Commission were also made public. Most of the evaluations presented "some" evidence of change due to the EES. Indeed, most of the national + 5 EES evaluations highlighted the importance of economic growth for a healthy employment situation. The national evaluations, in spite of gaps in the methodology, allowed a widening of the number of specialists with in-depth knowledge of the European stakes and the interrelationship between national and European debates. The Commission's strategy was to reinforce its legitimacy on the basis of "scientific" analyses. It should be noted that active labour market policies received a mixed evaluation indicating some successes but also many limitations (CEC, 2002b; de la Porte and Pochet, 2003). This was in line with most of the OECD analysis (Martin and Grubb, 2001 among others) but did not influence the public political debate, which has continued to support employability as the main strategy to boost employment. But the real decisions were made through negotiations between the Member States and the Commission[2] and between the more liberal approach defended by the Ecofin Council and a more social approach supported by the Social Affairs Council (Pochet, 2003a; Jobelius, 2003).

At the same time as the "scientific evaluation took place at the political level the Informal Social Affairs Council of 19 January 2002 reached a consensus on the need for "a simplification of the process [...], par-

---

[2] Clear evidence of the influence of the Member States was the introduction of the theme of regional disparities which was an Italian priority.

ticularly by reducing the number of employment guidelines". Further, "there needs to be closer co-ordination of all the strategies launched in the social sphere, making the process more agile, enhancing its simplification and preventing duplication". This position was supported by most Member States, as the NAPs that they have to submit on a yearly basis represent an increasingly heavy workload. There was also a consensus on the need to render the Employment Strategy less technical and more politically strategic. The Member States were also calling for a longer-term perspective in order to be able to detect effects of national policy changes taken in the framework of the EES. Jobelius (2003) described in detail the making of the new EES and the political battles around the new objectives.

The Commission tried to render the EES more precise in terms of quantitative targets and at the same time more open by improving participation and the governance of the process. On the opposite side, most of the Member States wanted to be able to reinterpret the EES and feared broader participation. Rubery in this volume indicates that the European Commission presented new targets to eliminate the gender gap in unemployment rates and to halve the gender pay gap at the Member State level by 2010. This was rejected by the Council. Nevertheless, the new guidelines included a commitment to substantial reductions by 2010 in the gender gaps in employment rates, unemployment rates and pay. These tensions between centralisation and openness on the one hand and decentralisation and controlled participation on the other existed from the beginning of the process and so far have mainly been won by the Member States (see also Zeitlin in the conclusion).

In one sense, we are returning to the mid-1990s situation, where the principal question concerned the economic and social architecture that was to accompany the Monetary Union. In the economic field, the forms of co-ordination adopted (Stability Pact and Broad Economic Policy Guidelines) proved insufficient. Moreover, the economically-oriented networks are re-launching the idea that the problem is a structural question requiring an agenda of liberalisation and flexibilisation. Not surprisingly, the revival of right-wing governments has reinforced this position that appeared strongly during the Spanish Presidency (2002).

Marsh and Olsen have described the difference between expert and political processes which applies rather well to the EES.

> On the surface, one process attempts to reduce subjectivity through standardised procedures to assure verifiable knowledge; the other attempts to organise subjectivity through a set of bargains designed to assure social stability. [...] The classic outcome of confrontation of contending ideas among experts is the confirmation of one and the rejection of the others; the classic outcome of confrontation of political ideas is the building of coalitions that

makes compromises among some in order to exclude others (Marsh and Olsen, 1989: 30; see also Visser's interpretation of the difference between EES and OECD employment evaluation in this volume).

Clearly, the EES is a political compromise aiming to exclude pure neo-liberal or social democratic approaches. But as de la Porte and Pochet show in this volume it is not a pure bargaining game as the "openness" allows diverse interests, including expert evaluations, to play a part in the process.

At the end of the review, the four-pillar structure (employability, adaptability, entrepreneurship and gender equality) which had underpinned the guidelines since 1997 was replaced by three overarching objectives:

1) full employment;

2) quality and productivity at work;

3) social cohesion and an inclusive labour market.

Nevertheless, these overarching objectives do not fully dovetail with the ten guidelines that shape the new EES. These are:

1. active and preventative measures for the unemployed and inactive;

2. job creation and entrepreneurship;

3. address change and promote adaptability and mobility in the labour market;

4. promote development of human capital and lifelong learning;

5. increase labour supply and promote active ageing;

6. gender equality;

7. promote the integration of and combat the discrimination against people at a disadvantage in the labour market;

8. make work pay through incentives to enhance work attractiveness;

9. transform undeclared work into regular employment;

10. address regional employment disparities.

Each guideline comprises various sub-measures (five or six in some cases). Thus, simplification is more a matter of form than substance. On the whole, these new guidelines tend to prolong the priorities contained in the previous ones, rather than radically altering or reorienting them (for a more detailed comparison see Watt, 2004: 126-127).

From a procedural point of view, the changes are important. On the one hand, the BEPG and EES are temporally co-ordinated, on the other, both focus on implementation in a longer cycle of three years.

There is now a clear distinction between two phases: the "implementtation" phase (January-March) and the "guidelines" phase (April-July). During the implementation phase, from January onwards, the Commission presents the conclusions from its scrutiny of implementation of the previous year's European guidelines. Various documents are adopted – the report on implementation of the Broad Economic Policy Guidelines, the draft Joint Employment Report and the report on implementation of the internal market strategy – providing a detailed assessment of progress made in each of these areas. At the same time, the Commission presents its summary report for the spring European Council, which constitutes its main contribution to the European Council. We should also mention the structural indicators measuring the progress achieved.

Flow Chart of the Streamlined Policy Co-ordination Cycle

THE POLICY FORMATION PHASE	THE POLICY IMPLEMENTATION REVIEW PHASE
▷ winter ▷ spring	▷ summer ▷ autumn ▷ winter

Note : While remaining annual, guidelines would, in principle, only be fully reviewed once every 3 years (i.e. year 't', 't+3', etc.). In intermediate years, guidelines would only take account of major changes.

Mid-January
Commission presents its Spring Report and the Implementation Package covering the IR on the BEPGs and the draft Joint Employment Report. In addition, it presents its progress report on the Internal Market Strategy.

Mid March
Spring European Council (SEC) providing general political orientations.

Early April
Commission, taking account of general orientations of SEC, adopts Guidelines Package covering:
- BEPGs
- EGs & Empl. Recs.
In addition, it reviews/updates the Internal Market Strategy.

Early June
Ecofin Council formulates draft for BEPGs.

Early June
ESPHCA Council considers EGs & Empl. Recs.

June (2nd half)
Ecofin Council
European Council endorses "Guidelines Package".

Ecofin Council adopts BEPGs.

ESPHCA Council adopts EGs & Empl. Recs.

Member States to report on implementation and envisaged policy actions.

January to early March
Various Council contributions, including the Joint Employment Report.

Social Partners Tripartite Social Summit for Growth and Employment

May
European Parliament opinion on EGs.

Competitiveness Council endorses IM Strategy.

Q4
Commission reviews Implementation on the basis of information received and collected.

Other Councils follow up

Source: CEC (2002c: 9).

The spring European Council issues strategic guidelines which open up the so-called guidelines phase. On this basis, the Commission defines and presents its proposals for future action in these different areas in a "guidelines" package. The package comprises the BEPGs, the employment guidelines and the employment recommendations. Once these have been scrutinised by the European Parliament and by the relevant configurations of the Council, the June European Council draws up its conclusions. The relevant configurations of the Council adopt the BEPGs, the employment guidelines and the employment recommendations; on this basis the Member States prepare their National Action Plans and national reports during the second half of the year. And so it goes on.

This attempt at simplification and co-ordination has also affected the BEPGs. Thus the presentation of the BEPGs was changed in 2003, with a list of "general objectives" sometimes also referring back to the employment guidelines where the same subjects are covered. There are eight chapter headings and, in all, 23 general objectives. Below we indicate the general objectives (with their original number) which cover the same area than the EES or other social OMCs.

---

3. Ensure that nominal wage increases are consistent with price stability and productivity.
4. Reduce high marginal effective tax rates, reduce tax on low-paid labour, improve the application of the eligibility criteria to benefits.
5. Ensure that wage bargaining systems allow wages to reflect productivity, taking into account productivity differences across skills and local labour market conditions.
6. Promote more adaptable and innovative work organisation.
7. Facilitate labour mobility.
8. Ensure efficient active labour market policies with special attention to people facing the greatest difficulties.
11. Generate a supportive environment for entrepreneurship.
14. Enhance the contribution of the public sector to growth by redirecting [...] public expenditure towards investment in physical and human capital and knowledge.
16. Design, introduce and effectively implement reforms of pension systems. Encourage longer working lives and increase the effective retirement age. Introduce elements of funding and improve, where necessary, access to supplementary pension schemes [...]. Adapt pension systems to more flexible employment.
17. Take steps to modernise social protection systems and to fight poverty and exclusion.
18. Improve private investment in regions lagging behind, particularly by taking steps to allow actual wages to reflect productivity taking into account differences in skills and local labour market conditions.
19. Ensure that public support is focused on investment in human and knowledge capital, as well as adequate infrastructure.

The Ecofin Council drew on these guidelines to issue recommendations to the Member States. As immediately becomes apparent, the BEPGs overlap with the EES. Thus the power-related question arises: which of the two will have the last word in respect of employment policy? The Employment Committee has set out its view of the division of labour between the BEPGs and the EES:

> [...] it should be noted that the Broad Economic Policy Guidelines provide the overarching framework for economic policy coordination within the EU and should address employment issues primarily from the broad economic perspective. The Employment Guidelines – providing a comprehensive and

integrated approach – are the main tool to give direction to and ensure coordination of Member States' employment policies, dealing with employment issues in greater detail. Accordingly, the employment recommendations are the main instrument to deal with employment and labour market challenges in each Member State. References to the employment recommendations should be provided, as appropriate, in the Broad Economic Policy Guidelines (Employment Committee, 2003: 2).

The streamlining between the BEPG and EES, the limitation in numbers of the guidelines and the focus on implementation were not the only change. The clarity of the message (about necessary reforms) and the leadership of the process were also on the table. Many governments whether on the right or on the left side wanted to boost the domestic agenda for reform. The Schroeder government is a good example of such priority for change (see Agenda 2010). Following a request from seven Member States (Germany, United Kingdom, Portugal, Spain, France etc.), a European Employment Task Force was established at the Brussels European Council (March 2003). Its remit was to identify specific measures geared to helping the Member States implement the revised Employment Strategy. The Task Force was chaired by the former Social Democratic Prime Minister of the Netherlands, Wim Kok, and comprised seven other members from academic circles or representing the social partners[3]. Its report, submitted in November 2003 (Kok *et al.*, 2003), in essence paints a picture little different from appraisals of the EES and issues recommendations to Member States. It is worth noting that, for the first time in a "social" document, the subject of wages appears among the recommendations. There is nothing, however, about monetary or macroeconomic policy. The report proposes four key priority areas:

- increasing adaptability of workers and enterprises;
- attracting more people to enter and remain on the labour market;
- investing more and more effectively in human capital and life-long learning;
- ensuring effective implementation of reforms through better governance.

The Commission welcomed this report and used it to shed additional light in its evaluation report (CEC, 2004a). The Commission, which now has the necessary expertise in respect of employment policy, masterminded this group and channelled its message. Having been

---

[3]   The Task Force consisted of chairman Wim Kok and members Anna Ekström, Anette Roux, Federico Duran Lopez, Carlo Dell'Aringa, Christopher Pissarides, Maria João Rodrigues and Günther Schmid.

largely in control of the report's message, the Commission had no difficulty in incorporating it into the renewed process (CEC, 2004b). The considerations of the Kok Report are not radically different from the EES but do reinforce the liberal interpretation of it. For example, little is said about job security, and less still about quality[4]. The findings of the Task Force justified a rightward shift in the EES and a rethinking of its procedures in the sense of approved messages and a naming and shaming approach. The Commission decided to reorganise its procedures around the four key areas proposed by the Kok Report.

The fact the employment policy even in the form of co-ordination has to be tackled at EU level is still not a consensual question within the community of economists. For example, the report produced at the request of Commission President Romano Prodi, by André Sapir with six other economists and one political scientist which looks at economic policy (Sapir *et al.*, 2003), declined to take account of employment since that was not part of its remit.

At a time when political attempts are being made to align the EES and the BEPGs, each of these two key reports – Kok and Sapir – adopted a segmented view of economic and social affairs. They are indicative of the fact that, politically and intellectually, employment policy is subject to and dependent on economic policy.

Following the Kok Report, the Commission issued clearer recommendations (CEC, 2004c) and for the first time five of them were related to wage moderation (Casey, 2005). The Member States presented their first triennial NAPs and the streamlining process was tested. The enlargement to 25 also forced the participants to be more imaginative. For example the Cambridge Process (peer examination of the NAPs) was conducted in small groups of six/seven countries (see Employment Committee, EMCO/30/221104/EN). It is too early to evaluate these changes but for the first time at national level the discussions were mainly focused on implementation as the content of the guidelines is fixed – at least for three years – and cannot be changed at EU level.

After this first report, Kok was asked to present a second report on the Lisbon strategy. The European Council recognised that Lisbon has several flaws and that the targets will not be reached by 2010. Concerning policy priorities, the report highlights improved economic growth, increased employment, and productivity. Social cohesion and environ-

---

[4]   The Commission issued a communication on quality in work (CEC, 2003c). This communication revisits the ten aspects of quality defined under the Belgian presidency and conducts a country-by-country analysis. Nevertheless, once again the number one item on the agenda is not job quality but quantity, as indicated by the title of the Kok Report "Jobs, Jobs, Jobs".

mental sustainability are classified as second-order priorities. Five key policy areas are identified, one of which is the labour market. For this area, it recommended to follow the recommendations of the European Employment Task Force report (November 2003) (see supra). Other priorities highlighted include development of strategies for lifelong learning and active ageing, as well as developing reform partnerships for growth and employment. In line with the initial spirit of the Lisbon Summit, the report emphasises (Kok *et al.*, 2003: 31) increasing the employment rate and removing disincentives for female labour force participation. Other initiatives in the social protection area are also included under the labour market policy title, whether legal or soft law initiatives. These includes the temporary agency work directive, adopted in 2003, ensuring sustainability of pension schemes (an allusion to the OMC pensions process), and the OMC social inclusion process. However, there are no in-depth discussions of progress on these social issues.

In order to enhance delivery, the report calls for greater political commitment by governments, and also wider involvement by the European Parliament, called on to play a "proactive role in monitoring performance". Furthermore, the discourse on wider involvement of other actors is emphasised, notably the European social partners, but also, important for genuine national level commitment, national parliaments. The Kok Reports consider that national parliaments and social partners should be more closely involved. The second report also recommends that efforts should be made to "engage [...] citizens in its implementation". However, precisely how citizens should be involved is not spelled out. This approach giving the leading role to the Commission and based on naming and shaming was not well received by the EU Council which would like to continue to control the agenda and avoid uncontrolled pressure.

III. Social Inclusion OMC

The emergence of the OMC on Social Inclusion has followed another route than the EES. It was not directly linked to the EMU debate. On contrary, it was for years a controversial topic and in the name of subsidiarity, many thought that it should not be addressed at EU level. Though without a specific legal base, peripheral action on the fight against poverty had nonetheless been taken at European level. A sparsely funded Poverty Action Plan was introduced at the end of the 1970s and after that a European network comprised of independent experts (the Observatory on Policies to Combat Social Marginalisation). The Commission also supported the creation of a network of NGOs dealing with poverty and social exclusion (European Anti-poverty Network/EAPN; for more details see Chassard, 2001). The Commission also set up an Observatory on National Policies to Combat Social Exclusion (1990-1994). The "Poverty 3" programme was held up in the Council in 1993 because of Germany's opposition of (on grounds of subsidiarity). The Court of Justice then questioned the legality of a series of Community programmes whose legal basis was in dispute.

To understand why the poverty/exclusion OMC has come onto the European agenda and the reasons for this about-turn, the events of these last ten years need re-examination (section 1). We will then present the specificity of this OMC (section 2). Section 3 will highlight the main change in the second NAPs/incl exercise and the future streamlining process in the social protection field. Even if national governments want a stronger message about reforms at European level, they also fear losing their control over the agenda (see for more details Zeitlin's concluding chapter).

A. A Slow Process of Agenda Setting

The Social Charter for EU workers, adopted in 1989 in the form of a non-binding declaration without the UK, was in fact an important turning point. It contained an article on social protection which dealt in particular with people excluded from the labour market. The Commission's action plan for the Charter's implementation included two "community initiatives" (which would take the form of recommendations in 1992), one on general social protection (convergence of targets) and the other on common criteria on resources and sufficient benefits (Council of the European Union, 1992a and 1992b).

At that time the scope of these recommendations was generally felt to be very limited, if not completely inadequate. The non-binding character of the text was compared with the compulsory criteria for monetary union under the Maastricht Treaty. However from this moment onwards the goal was to concentrate convergence efforts on objectives rather than institutional arrangements. In other words common goals can be achieved via different means. In the case of the recommendations this was not difficult because the objectives had already been met by most Member States. As the recommendations did not go into the details of the internal organisation of national systems, the obstacle of diversity was once again partially removed, as well of that of respecting subsidiarity. Implicitly the way was opened to exchange of good practices, intended to improve national performance and make the goals more easily attainable.

Another significant aspect was the outlining of a method which today can be seen as a sort of unfinished OMC (just as it could be claimed that Essen was a pre-OMC on jobs, see above). The first recommendation stipulated that the Commission was to "submit a report assessing the progress made towards the defined objectives [...] and to establish and develop the use of appropriate indicators [...]". The second recommendation stated that the criteria should "stimulate and organise together with the Member States a systematic exchange of information and experience and an ongoing evaluation of the national provisions adopted", and to "submit a report describing [...] progress made and obstacles encountered within three years and subsequently on a regular basis".

However, these elements only emerged very slowly in the 1990s. In retrospect different discussion documents (Green Papers, White Papers, Reports, Declaration etc.) nonetheless facilitated a more common approach to the challenges.

The implementation of the two recommendations was generally a non-event. Moreover there was a debate on the European Union's legal capacity to act in the area of poverty and exclusion. All this did not prevent the Commission from regularly publishing communications and presenting every two years a report on social protection in Europe. The reasoning set to emerge from the different documents and speeches was that social protection should be considered as a productive factor and social and economic objectives reinforced rather than worked against each other.

In 1995 the Commission published a communication on "The Future of Social Protection – A Framework for a European Debate" (CEC, 1995) which highlighted the common challenges that required national systems to make certain adjustments. It also recognised that social protection is a central part of the European social model. This communication referred to problems such as a decreasing working population compared with the inactive population, the need to make social protection more favourable to employment, to review its funding, and to reform health care systems. The 1997 communication "Modernising and Improving Social Protection" (CEC, 1997) was another step which took further the idea of *"mainstreaming"*, consisting of a holistic approach to issues linked to social protection in other European policies. So the communications of the 1990s together with academic research constituted a common basis for policy innovation. This meant that an increasing awareness of the challenges facing European social protection could be based on the results of prior discussions. Moreover, choosing the "Euro" Member States and the return of economic growth opened the door to new issues. The Santer Commission fell in March 1999 and a transitional Commission sat while waiting for the new Prodi Commission to take up office. In July 1999 the Commission adopted a communication for a concerted strategy on social protection (CEC, 1999).

Four areas were identified as the pillars of a concerted strategy at European level:

- making work pay and provide a secure income (CEC, 2003a; Peña Casas, 2004);
- guaranteeing secure pensions and sustainable pension systems (Pochet, 2003b);
- promoting social inclusion;
- guaranteeing a high, sustainable level of health protection (Baeten, 2003).

The social agenda 2000-2005 adopted in Nice (December 2000) set a timetable for the priorities. First of all was the fight against poverty and exclusion, then pensions. The debate on the job trap (i.e. the minimum wage or part-time work paying less or only just above total benefit payments) and that on health were postponed to 2002-2003[5].

The communication proposed a High-Level Group on Social Protection on the model of the Employment Committee, which was soon endorsed. This went on to become a Committee on Social Protection (later made official in the Nice Treaty, article 144). The Social Protection Committee is a key element in the whole process. Its job is to develop expertise which will lead to a consensus between Member States (including the creation of indicators by a sub-group). It must also contribute to ensuring social protection occupies its rightful place between employment (and the Employment Committee) and economic policy (and the Economic Policy Committee). This committee plays an essential role in structuring the European debate in these areas, a necessary pre-condition for the creation of a policy community. Its task is also to defend a certain set of values (solidarity), which has engendered a struggle for influence between the Economic Policy Committee and the Social Protection Committee.

The Lisbon European Council (2000: point 33) invited the Commission and the Council to:

- promote a better understanding of social exclusion through continued dialogue and exchanges of information and best practice, on the basis of commonly agreed indicators; [...]
- include the promotion of solidarity in the Member States' policies on jobs, education and training, health and housing; the intervention of the structural funds while respecting the current budgetary framework supports this strategy;

---

[5] We will not present these OMCs here, see the University of Wisconsin-Madison website for useful references.

- define priority actions for specific target groups (for example minorities, children, the elderly and the disabled), the choice of the best action being left up to the Member States.

The action of two Member States (Belgium, UK) was decisive, though based on different strategies. The Belgian social affairs minister Frank Vandenbroucke supported the strategy on poverty and exclusion because he believes that diminishing poverty implies an efficient social security system. The target was less poverty itself than social protection in general (Vandenbroucke, 1999). The idea was to get things moving on a matter of general agreement – the need to fight against poverty in order to address a much more sensitive theme: social security. The UK has set itself ambitious goals for poverty reduction and child poverty in particular. The European agenda is thus a natural extension of the national agenda. Similarities between a national and European agenda strengthen national measures and gives the impressive of a pro-active role in Europe.

However, these areas of interest have become increasingly part of new national thinking over the last five years. An example in France is the setting up of an observatory on poverty and social exclusion (1998) following the "exclusion" law, and the first report on the subject in Germany (2001). Other countries like Belgium, which drew up a general report on poverty (1994), the Netherlands with the organisation of annual social conferences on these questions, Ireland which adopted a national strategy on the fight against poverty in 1997 (later confirmed in its last social pact), or Portugal which adopted a minimum wage in 1996 are all examples of how this question has been brought onto the political agenda in various countries during the second half of the 1990s (UNIOPSS, 2001). Finally, as with jobs, the Scandinavian countries do best in the poverty ratings and are better able to support such action since they do not run the risk of unwelcome interference from Europe.

This common concern does not mean that the strategies, priorities or institutions have to converge. For example, France's approach is essentially based on entitlements and participation whereas the UK is concentrating on target groups (youth, migrants, the elderly). The attempt by Portugal and the UK to make child poverty a strategic focus of Community action has failed to gain the support of most of the other Member States who feel child poverty is not a relevant category. But here too the academic community has played an important role. In an influential report for the Portuguese Presidency of the EU, Ferrera and his colleagues argued that

> As poverty and social exclusion are increasingly dynamic phenomena, as material needs and social risks change over time, so there is a clear need for commonly understood data and analysis. This is an area where monitoring

and benchmarking at the level of the European Union should take the initiative to make possible this type of problem diagnosis and policy evaluation (Ferrera *et al.*, 2000: 65).

In 2000, all ingredients were in place to implement quickly the OMC in the social inclusion domain.

B The First NAPs/incl

After their adoption at the last Social Affairs Council, the Nice European Council (December 2000) formally endorsed four major objectives including various sub-targets in this area: 1) promote employment and access to all resources, rights, goods and services, 2) risk prevention, 3) action for the most vulnerable, 4) mobilising all those concerned.

In June 2001 each of the Member States submitted their National Action Plans for Inclusion (NAPs/incl) according to the model of the National Action Plans for Employment (NAPs/empl) set to last two years. These plans were analysed by the Commission with the help of external experts. They were also submitted by each Member State to a peer review in July 2001. The NAPs/incl are based on very broad general objectives, unlike the employment NAPs which concentrate on about twenty guidelines. Moreover, in the Luxembourg process from the outset there were quantified figures on employability whereas the NAPs/incl are used to develop common indicators. It is therefore not surprising to see NAPs/incl with wide diversity both in form and in their degree of compliance with European priorities.

The Commission evaluated the national plans in its draft joint report. It distinguished between four groups of countries according to their compliance with the spirit of the exercise. The Member States strongly reacted to this judgment and obtained significant changes to the joint report adopted on December 3 by the Social Affairs Council (for more details see Ferrera *et al.*, 2002).

The Social Protection Committee was entrusted with submitting proposals on common indicators to the Laeken European Council. Its task was made easier by the publication of a report on the topic commissioned by the Belgian presidency by Atkinson *et al.* (2002). The different indicators were analysed in some detail. It is interesting to note that contrary to other OMCs the academic impulse focused less on the general content (there is a broad consensus on the relevance of this topic) that on developing common indicators to measure the different dimensions of social exclusion.

Developing common European indicators immediately runs up against the weakness of available European statistics (Peña Casas and Pochet, 2001). After lengthy debates eighteen indicators were adopted, ten primary and eight secondary. The question of (monetary) poverty, for which it was relatively easy to agree on certain indicators, must be distinguished from social exclusion, which is much more complex. There is no general definition of "exclusion" accepted by all, nor are there European indicators measuring for example social participation or access to certain services.

If you take a relative indicator for the main indicator of monetary poverty, that of 60% of the median income, it is difficult to measure the positive effects of policies. The Irish case is a good example. Because it is relative, this indicator shows that poverty got worse in Ireland. But that is only true if you compare the number of poor with the general wealth of the population, which has greatly increased over the last decade. In absolute terms, the situation of the poor has improved compared to a fixed poverty line. As it seems unlikely that the income of the poorest is increasing faster than the national average, the adoption of this indicator could have counterproductive effects for national governments, since the effects of their policy would not lead to a reduction in the relative percentage of poor measured in such a way.

The Social Protection Committee decided that the 60% threshold of average income was not poverty but low income. Every threshold is clearly a convention but the notion of low income is particularly vague. The Member States very probably were afraid that the poverty figures in table 2 were too high and preferred to choose the ambiguous term of low income, thus indicating that there were fewer "poor" people.

Table 2: At-risk-of-poverty rates* (1995-2001)

	BE	DK	D	EL	ES	F	IR	IT	L	NL	AU	P	FI	SU	UK	UE 15
1995	16	10	15	22	19	15	19	20	12	11	13	23			20	17
1996	15	9	14	21	18	15	19	20	11	12	14	21	8		18	16
1997	14	9	12	21	20	15	19	19	11	10	13	22	8	9	18	16
1998	14	12	11	21	18	15	19	18	12	10	13	21	9	10	19	15
1999	13	11	11	21	19	15	19	18	13	11	12	21	11	9	19	15
2000	13	11	10	20	18	16	20	18	12	10	12	21	11	11	19	15
2001	13	11	11	20	19	15	21	19	12	11	12	20	11	10	17	15
chge 95-2001	-3	1	-4	-2	0	0	2	-1	0	0	-1	-3	3**	1**	-3	-2

* proportion (in %) of population living in households with an income below the threshold of 60% of standardised median income.

** Finland: 1996-2001 and Sweden: 1997-2001.

Source: European Household Panel.

In combination with the OMC in this area, an action programme drawn up for a four-year period (2002-2005) was proposed by the Commission. Unlike the objectives of the former 'poverty' programmes, it was no longer a question of financing a few pilot experiments with uncertain results. This was the outline of a new strategy mainly intended to fill two gaps – knowledge ("improving understanding of social exclusion") and the abilities of the relevant participants ("developing their capacity to tackle social exclusion efficiently, in particular through European support for networks of NGOs active in the fight against poverty and social exclusion"). The Commission has funded five networks for three years: the European Anti-poverty Network, EAPN; the European Forum for Child Welfare, EFCW; the European Public Social Platform EPSE (which collapsed); the European Federation of National Organisations working with the homeless FEANTSA, and the Réseau européen transrégional pour l'inclusion sociale, RETIS.

Finally there was also the question of 'organising co-operation and exchange of experience in the context of the national action programmes, i.e. making the OMC function practically', (Community Action Programme for the fight against poverty and social exclusion, 2001). In this area the NGOs and particularly the EAPN (2001) succeeded in developing expertise and spreading among its members a good knowledge of what is at stake in Europe and the possibilities of taking action at this level. On this basis they propose a set of poverty indicators based on the experience of people living in poverty (EAPN, 2003).

C. Towards a Streamlining of All the Social Protection Processes

Most commentators agreed that the first round of NAPs/incl had to be judged as a first step and were rather indulgent about their weaknesses. The second round 2003-2005 took place at the same time that a process of streamlining all the social protection OMCs was on the table. We will first present the evaluation of the new NAPs/incl and then the debate about and timetable of the streamlining.

The evaluation by the Commission of the second NAPs/incl was rather balanced. The Joint Report identifies key trends and challenges across the Union and good practices and innovative approaches of common interest. Four main aspects were underlined (CEC, 2003d: 5):

1) The new NAPs are generally broad in scope, reflecting the multi-dimensional nature of poverty and exclusion and covering a wider range of policy fields but a truly multidimensional approach will require further attention to issues such as housing, lifelong learning, culture, e-inclusion, and transport.

2) There is a clear effort on the part of a majority of Member States to set quantitative targets for the reduction of poverty and social exclusion but the setting of targets needs to be more specific, quantified and ambitious.

3) Many Member States have significantly strengthened their institutional arrangements for mainstreaming poverty and social inclusion into national policy-making, including extending this process to regional and local levels. But more emphasis should be put on achieving and monitoring the efficiency and quality of measures designed to tackle poverty and social exclusion.

4) The participation of key stakeholders of civil society (NGOs, social partners and business community) in the preparation of the NAPs has improved. But the progress made in mainstreaming social inclusion through strengthening institutional arrangements needs to be further deepened, particularly to ensure that social inclusion goals are borne in mind in setting overall expenditure priorities.

Concerning future challenges, the Joint Report highlights six:

1) promoting investment in and tailoring of active labour market measures to meet the needs of those who have the greatest difficulties in accessing employment;

2) ensuring that social protection schemes are adequate and accessible for all and that they provide effective work incentives for those who can work;

3) increasing the access of the most vulnerable and those most at risk of social exclusion to decent housing, quality health and life-long learning opportunities;

4) implementing a concerted effort to prevent early school leaving and to promote smooth transition from school to work;

5) developing a focus on eliminating poverty and social exclusion among children;

6) making a drive to reduce poverty and social exclusion of immigrants and ethnic minorities (CEC, 2003d: 6).

This process now confronts two main challenges. The first one as all other policies is enlargement. The second is the future streamlining process.

From 2004, the process will, have to take account of the accession of ten new Member States where the nature and extent of poverty and social exclusion are often sharply different. It should be noted that ten of the fifteen Member states have updated their 2003-2005 plan in 2004 (de la Rosa, 2004).

By 2005, the social inclusion process will have reached its mid-point and an evaluation of the work carried out up to that date will be undertaken as part of the preparation for the streamlining of EU-level social protection/social inclusion processes. From 2006 onwards, it will form part of the new streamlined approach as proposed by the Commission in May 2003 and endorsed by the Council in October. The national reports on social protection and social inclusion will outline the strategy for pensions, poverty and social exclusion and health care. It should start in 2006 and will cover a period of three years. In the intermediate years 2007 and 2008 Member States will present the progress in the implementation. The same will occur at European level with the adoption of a Joint Social Protection and Social Inclusion Report which should be ready in the same time that the other reports for the Spring European Council. Many have express their fears that social exclusion would become a marginal topic compared with pension and health care which are the two main social spending items (see Marlier and Berghman, 2004). The SPC has been rather influential in guaranteeing the specific identity of social exclusion within the streamlining process. It expressed "it wish that he clear visibility of the different element of social protection process have to be preserved" and that the title of social protection and social inclusion should be used (SPC, 2003).

Although the Open Method of Co-ordination is developing relatively quickly in its different dimensions (national plans, common objectives, indicators, peer reviews etc.), there are still many pitfalls. The weakness of available indicators is one. The ability of governments to reduce monetary poverty in a more global world where social and spatial inequalities are tending more to increase than to decrease is another, especially as the question of the cost of reducing poverty has still not been tackled head on. Finally there is no question of issuing recommendations to the Member States if the agreed objectives are not respected. The financial dimension of the fight against poverty is being completely sidelined (Atkinson, 2000).

In terms of non-governmental participants, the NGOs seem to be able to use the new opportunities of the European strategy to reinforce their legitimacy at European and national levels (see chapter by de la Porte and Pochet in this volume). This involvement is also one of the four major goals approved in Nice and is supported by the Community Action Programme.

Perspectives

It is difficult to reach definitive conclusions on an ongoing process. In the first part of this chapter, we emphasised that EES and OMC are part of a dynamic of redefining the social dimension of the EU integration according to the successes and limits of the previous phases and the changing environment. This was done in a context of dominance (for the first time since the Treaty of Rome) of left-oriented governments. The new 25-member Europe has increased the diversity of welfare arrangements and levels of development. This structural fact will impact the way an EU social policy can develop in the future (de la Rosa, 2004). At the same time the limits of the EES and the OMC and even more generally the Lisbon Strategy were acknowledged in the Kok Reports (Kok *et al.*, 2003 and 2004).

An important question concerns the link between substance and procedure. There are here two broad directions for change. The first one focuses on improving the procedures, the second one on improving the prescriptions. Jonathan Zeitlin in this volume supports the first approach. He proposes to soften the prescriptions. In exchange it is necessary to harden the procedures by strengthening requirements for transparency, participation, monitoring, review of weaknesses, and self-corrective action; make OMC standards (guidelines, indicators, targets) more precise and explicit, but also more revisable; and make recommendations more transparent.

Many are supporting a different approach, mainly from the economic co-ordination actors. The aim would be to strengthen the normative recommendations to the Member States and to give more power to the Commission to force the implementation of the recommendations. The Kok Report on the reform of Lisbon strategy supports a naming and shaming approach.

Both approaches agree on the necessity of better involvement of national, regional and local actors. But the first one underlines the importance of experimentation and innovative decentralised practices. On the contrary, the second approach is much more functionally oriented and aims to improve the effectiveness of reforms. It does not seek to question the proposed reforms but rather to ensure their implementation.

When we compare the EES and the OMC/incl, the first seems to go more in a direction of centralisation, naming and shaming (through recommendations), without any broad discussion about content at European level, and the second towards a more experimental dynamic with the involvement of local and regional actors. One would be more top down and the other bottom up. It should be noted that one of the few studies about the OMC and enlargement confirms this difference between the two processes (de la Rosa, 2004).

In reality this presentation is too simplistic and tensions are occurring in both processes between centralisation and decentralisation. The same happens with the BEPGs with some arguing for reinforcing central control and the other for taking into account national circumstances.

Having analysed the various OMC from the beginning, a lesson I have learnt is to avoid excessive generalisation and drawing over too strict lessons for the future from evolving processes.

Clearly, soft governance processes are at a crossroad both from a legitimacy and efficiency point of view.

References

Arnold, C. U. (2002), "How Two-level Entrepreneurship Works: The Influence of the Commission on the European-wide Employment Strategy", paper presented at the American Political Science Association, Boston (Massachussets), 29 August-1 September 2002.

Arnold, C. U. and Cameron, D. R. (2001), "Why the EU Developed the European Employment Strategy: Unemployment, Public Opinion, and Member State Preferences", Paper prepared for delivery at the 2001 Annual Meeting of the American Political Science Association, San Francisco, 30 August-2 September 2001.

Atkinson, T. (2000), "Agenda social européen: comparaison des pauvretés et transferts sociaux", in Jacquet, P., Pisani-Ferry, J., Le Cacheux, J., Atkinson, T., Boyer, R., Herzog, P., Hel-Thelier, S., Maurice, J., Ould Aoudia, J. et Tubiana, L. (eds.), *Questions européennes*, Rapport du Conseil d'Analyse économique, No.27, La Documentation française, Paris, pp.57-70.

Atkinson, T., Cantillon, B., Marlier, E. and Nolan, B. (2002), *Social Indicators – The EU and Social Inclusion*, Oxford University Press, Oxford.

Baeten, R. (2003), "Health Care on the European Political Agenda", in Degryse, C. and Pochet, P. (eds.), *Social Developments in the European Union 2002*, European Trade Union Institute, Observatoire social européen and Saltsa, Brussels, pp.145-176.

Barbier, J.-C. (2004), "La stratégie européenne pour l'emploi: genèse, coordination communautaire et diversité nationale", Rapport de recherche pour la DARES (ministère du Travail), Paris, January 2004.

Beresford Taylor, A. (2000), "EU Moves Towards the Creation of a Network Europe", *European Voice*, Vol.6, No.24, 15-21 June 2000.

Cantillon, B. (2004), "European Subsidiarity Versus American Social Federalism: Is Europe in Need of a Common Social Policy?", unpublished manuscript.

Casey, B. H. (2005), "Building Social Partnership? Strengths and Shortcomings of the European Employment Strategy", *Transfer*, Vol.11, No.1, Spring 2005 (forthcoming).

CEC (1993), "Green Paper on European Social Policy. Options for the Union", COM (1993) 551 of 17 November 1993.

CEC (1995), Communication from the Commission "The Future of Social Protection. A Framework for a European Debate", COM (1995) 466 of 31 October 1995.

CEC (1997), Communication from the Commission "Modernising and Improving Social Protection in the European Union", COM (1997) 102 of 12 March 1997.

CEC (1999), Communication from the Commission "A Concerted Strategy for Modernising Social Protection", COM (1999) 347 of 14 July 1999.

CEC (2002a), Communication from the Commission "A Project for the European Union", COM (2002) 247 final, 22 May 2002 (http://europa.eu.int/eur-lex/en/com/cnc/2002/com2002_0247en01.pdf).

CEC (2002b), "Review of Evaluations of the Effectiveness of ALMPs – A Background to the Ongoing EES Evaluation of the European Employment Strategy", Note presented on 11 April 2002 to the Economic Policy Committee.

CEC (2002c), Communication from the Commission on Streamlining the Annual Economic and Employment Policy Co-ordination Cycles, COM (2002) 487 of 3 September 2002 (http://europa.eu.int/eur-lex/en/com/rpt/2002/com2002_0487en01.pdf).

CEC (2003a), Communication from the Commission "Modernising Social Protection for More and Better Jobs. A Comprehensive Approach Contributing to Making Work Pay", COM (2003) 842 final of 30 December 2003 (http://europa.eu.int/comm/employment_social/news/2004/jan/com_2003_842_en.pdf).

CEC (2003b), Communication from the Commission "Improving Quality in Work: A Review of Recent Progress", COM (2003) 728 final of 26 November 2003 (http://europa.eu.int/comm/employment_social/news/2003/dec/com2003_728_en.pdf).

CEC (2003c), Communication from the Commission "Progress on the Implementation of the Joint Assessment Papers on Employment Policies in Candidate Countries", COM (2003) 37 final of 30 January 2003 (http://europa.eu.int/eur-lex/en/com/cnc/2003/com2003_0037en01.pdf).

CEC (2003d), Communication from the Commission "Joint Report on Social Inclusion Summarising the Results of the Examination of the National Action Plans for Social Inclusion (2003-2005)", COM (2003) 773 final of 12 December 2003 (http://europa.eu.int/eur-lex/en/com/cnc/2003/com2003_0773en01.pdf).

CEC (2004a), Communication from the Commission on the Implementation of the 2003-2005 Broad Economic Policy Guidelines, COM (2004) 20 final of 21 January 2004 (http://europa.eu.int/eur-lex/en/com/rpt/2004/com2004_0020en01.pdf).

CEC (2004b), Report from the Commission to the Spring European Council "Delivering Lisbon – Reforms for the Enlarged Union", COM (2004) 29 final of 20 February 2004 (http://europa.eu.int/comm/lisbon_strategy/pdf/ COM2004_029_en.pdf).

CEC (2004c), Communication from the Commission "Strengthening the Implementation of the European Employment Strategy", Proposal for a Council Decision on Guidelines for the Employment Policies of the Member States,

Recommendation for a Council Recommendation on the Implementation of Member States' Employment Policies, COM (2004) 239 final, 7 April 2004 (http://europa.eu.int/eur-lex/en/com/pdf/2004/com2004_0239en01.pdf).

Chassard, Y. (2001), "European Integration and Social Protection: From the Spaak Report to the Open Method of Co-ordination", in Mayes, D. G., Berghman, J. and Salais, R. (eds.), *Social Exclusion and European Policy*, Edward Elgar Publishing, Cheltenham, pp.291-321.

Council of the European Union (1992a), Council Recommendation of 27 July 1992 on the Convergence of Social Protection Objectives and Policies (92/442/CEE), OJ L245 of 26 August 1992.

Council of the European Union (1992b), Council Recommendation of 24 June 1992 on Common Criteria Concerning Sufficient Resources and Social Assistance in Social Protection Systems (92/441/CEE), OJ L245 of 26 August 1992.

Cram, L. (1993), "Calling the Tune without Playing the Piper? Social Policy Regulation: The Role of the Commission in the European Social Policy", *Policy and Politics*, Vol.21, No.2, April 1993, pp.135-146.

Daly, M. (2004), "The Possibility of an EU Social Policy – Lisbon and After", paper presented to Lecture Series "Europeanization and Reform of National Welfare States", European Union Center, University of Madison-Wisconsin, 14 October 2004.

de Búrca, G. and Zeitlin, J. (2003), "Constitutionalising the Open Method of Co-ordination – What Should the Convention Propose", *CEPS Policy Brief*, No.31, Centre for European Policy Studies, Brussels, March 2003.

de la Porte, C. and Pochet, P. (2002), *Building Social Europe through the Open Method of Co-ordination*, P.I.E.-Peter Lang, Brussels.

de la Porte, C. and Pochet, P. (2003), "The OMC Intertwined with the Debates on Governance, Democracy and Social Europe", Research on the Open Method of Co-ordination and Social Integration prepared for Frank Vandenbroucke, Belgian Federal Minister of Social Affairs and Pensions, April 2003.

de la Porte, C. and Pochet, P. (2004), "The European Employment Strategy: Existing Research and Remaining Questions", *Journal of European Social Policy*, Vol.14, No.1, February 2004, pp.71-79.

de la Porte, C., Pochet, P. and Room, G. (2001), "Social Benchmarking, Policy-Making and the Instruments of New Governance", *Journal of European Social Policy*, Vol.11, No.4, November 2001, pp.291-308.

de la Rosa, S. (2004), "La méthode ouverte de co-ordination dans les nouveaux États membres – Les perspectives d'utilisation d'un outil de soft *law*", Paper presented at the 3rd meeting of young scholars, Aix en Provence, September 2004.

Dehousse, R. (2004) (ed.), *L'Europe sans Bruxelles? Une analyse de la méthode ouverte de co-ordination*, L'Harmattan, Paris.

Didry, C. and Mias, A. (2005), *Le dialogue social européen, le moment européen*, P.I.E.-Peter Lang, Brussels (forthcoming).

Dyson, K. (1994), *Elusive Union, The Process of Economic and Monetary Union in Europe*, Longman, London and New York.

Dyson, K. (2002), "EMU as Europeanisation: Convergence, Diversity, and Contingency", in Verdun, A. (ed.), *The Euro, European Integration Theory and Economic and Monetary Union*, Rowman & Littlefield Publishers, Lanham, pp.91-108.

EAPN (2001), "EAPN Synthesis Report on the 2001-2003 National Action Plans on Social Inclusion", European Anti-poverty Network, Brussels, November 2001 (http://www.eapn.org/docs/reports/synthesis_en.doc).

EAPN (2003), "European Project on Poverty Indicators Starting from the Experience of People Living in Poverty", *Final Report*, Vlaams Forum Armoedebestrijding, Vlaams Netwerk van Verenigingen Waar Armen het Woord Nemen, September 2003.

EAPN (2004), "National Networks' Stock-take on the Implementation of the NAPs Inclusion 2003-2005 (in the 15 'Old' Member States of the EU)", *EAPN Position Paper*, presented on the occasion of the Third European Round Table on Poverty and Social Exclusion, Rotterdam, 18-19 October 2004.

Eberlein, B. and Kerwer, D. (2002), "Theorising the New Modes of European Union Governance", *European Integration online Papers (EioP)*, Vol.6, No.5 (http://eiop.or.at/eiop/texte/2002-005a.htm).

Employment Committee (2003), Opinion of the Employment Committee on the Commission Recommendation on the Broad Guidelines of the Economic Policies of the Member States and the Community (for the 2003-2005 period) (http://europa.eu.int/comm/employment_social/employment_strategy/bepg_final_en.pdf).

European Council (1999), Cologne European Council, *Presidency Conclusions*, 3-4 June 1999.

European Council (2000), Lisbon European Council, *Presidency Conclusions*, 23-24 March 2000.

European Council (2001), Stockholm European Council, *Presidency Conclusions*, 23 and 24 March 2001.

Fajertag, G. and Pochet, P. (1997), *Social Pacts in Europe*, European Trade Union Institute and Observatoire social européen, Brussels.

Fajertag, G. and Pochet, P. (2000), *Social Pacts in Europe – New Dynamics*, European Trade Union Institute and Observatoire social européen, Brussels.

Ferrera, M. (2001), "The European Social Model between 'Hard' Constraints and 'Soft' Co-ordination", unpublished paper presented to the "Social Models and EMU: Convergence? Co-existence? The Role of Economic and Social Actors", Economic and Social Committee, Brussels, 19 November 2001.

Ferrera, M. (2005), "New Boundaries, New Structuring? On the Future of Social Protection in the EU", in Ferrera, M. (ed.), *The Boundaries of Welfare. European Integration and the New Spatial Politics of Solidarity*, Oxford University Press, Oxford (forthcoming).

Ferrera, M., Hemerijck, A. and Rhodes, M. (2000), *The Future of Social Europe. Recasting Work and Welfare in the New Economy*, Celta Editora, Oeiras.

Ferrera, M., Matsaganis, M. and Sacchi, S. (2002), "Open Co-ordination against Poverty: The New EU 'Social Inclusion Process'", *Journal of European Social Policy*, Vol.12, No.3, pp.226-239.

Ghailani, D. (2003), "L'extension de la co-ordination des régimes de sécurité sociale aux ressortissants des Etats tiers: la fin d'un périple", *Revue belge de sécurité sociale*, No.1, mars 2003, pp.213-239.

Goetschy, J. (1999), "The European Employment Strategy: Genesis and Development", *European Journal of Industrial Relations*, Vol.5, No.2, July 1999, pp.117-137.

Goetschy, J. (2005), "Bilan de l'Europe sociale: peut-on parler d'un modèle social communautaire?", to be published in Serrano Pascual, A. and Jepsen, M. (eds.), *Deconstructing the European Social Model*, European Trade Union Institute, Brussels (forthcoming).

Haas, P. (1992), "Special Issue on Epistemic Communities", *International Organization*, No.46, winter 1992.

Hall, P. A. (2001), "The Evolution of Economic Policy-making in the European Union", in Menon, A. and Wright, V. (eds.), *From the Nation State to Europe? Essays in Honour of Jack Hayward*, Oxford University Press, Oxford, pp.214-245.

Hemerijck, A. (2004), "Beyond the Double Bind of Social Europe", in Magnusson, L. and Stråth, B. (eds.), *European Social Citizenship. Preconditions for Future Policies from a Historical Perspective*, P.I.E.-Peter Lang, Brussels.

Héritier, A. (2002), "New Modes of Governance in Europe: Policy-making without Legislating?", in Héritier, A. (ed.), *Common Goods: Reinventing European and International Governance*, Rowman & Littlefield Publishers, Lanham, Md., pp.185-206.

Hodson, D. and Maher, I. (2001), "The Open Method as a New Mode of Governance: The Case of Soft Economic Policy Co-ordination", *Journal of Common Market Studies*, Vol.39, No.4, pp.719-745.

Hodson, D. (2004), "Macroeconomic Co-ordination in the Euro Area: The Scope and Limits of the Open Method", *Journal of European Public Policy*, Vol.11, No.2, April 2004, pp.231-248.

Jacobsson, K. (2001), "Employment and Social Policy Co-ordination. A New System of EU Governance", Paper for the Scancor Workshop on Transnational Regulation and the Transformation of States, Stanford, 22-23 June 2001.

Jenson, J. and Pochet, P. (2005), "Employment and Social Policy since Maastricht: Standing up to the European Monetary Union", in Fishman, R. and Messina, A. (eds.), *The Year of the Euro*, The University of Notre Dame Press, Notre Dame (forthcoming).

Jobelius, S. (2003), "Who Formulates the European Employment Guidelines? The OMC between Deliberation and Power Games", paper presented at the Annual ESPAnet conference "Changing European Societies – The Role for Social Policy, Copenhagen, 13-15 November 2003.

Jonckheer, P. and Pochet, P. (1990), "De la Charte sociale au programme d'action de la Communauté européenne", *Courrier hebdomadaire du Crisp*, No.1273-74, Centre de recherche et d'information socio-politiques, Brussels.

Juncker, J.-C. (2002), "Introduction" in Best, E. and Bossaert, D. (eds.), *From Luxembourg to Lisbon and Beyond: Making the Employment Strategy Work*, European Institute of Public Administration, Maastricht.

Kenner, J. (1999), "The EC Employment Title and the 'Third Way': Making Soft Law Work?", *The International Journal of Comparative Labour Law and Industrial Relations*, Vol.15, No.1, pp.33-60.

Knill, C. and Lehmkuhl, D. (1999), "How Europe Matters. Different Mechanisms of Europeanisation", *European Integration online Papers (EioP)*, Vol.3, No.7 (http://eiop.or.at/eiop/texte/1999-007a.htm).

Kok, W. *et al.* (2003), "Jobs, Jobs, Jobs – Creating More Employment in Europe", Report of the Employment Task Force chaired by Wim Kok, Brussels, November 2003 (http://europa.eu.int/comm/employment_social/employment_strategy/pdf/etf_en.pdf).

Kok, W. *et al.* (2004), "Facing the Challenge. The Lisbon Strategy for Growth and Employment", Report from the High Level Group chaired by Wim Kok, Office for Official Publications of the European Communities, Luxembourg, November 2004 (http://europa.eu.int/comm/lisbon_strategy/pdf/2004-1866-EN-complet.pdf).

Lamy, P. and Pisani-Ferry, J. (2002), "L'Europe de nos volontés", *Les Notes de la Fondation Jean-Jaurès*, No.27, January 2002.

Larsson, A. (1995), "A Vision for IGC 1996: A European Employment Union – to Make EMU Possible", paper written at the request of the Swedish Prime Minister Ingvar Carlsson, for the IGC 1996, mimeo.

Leibfried, S. and Pierson, P. (1995), *European Social Policy – Between Fragmentation and Integration*, The Brookings Institution, Washington DC.

Magnusson, L. and Stråth, B. (2001) (eds.), *From the Werner Plan to the EMU. In Search of a Political Economy for Europe*, P.I.E.-Peter Lang, Brussels.

Manow, P., Schäfer, A. and Zorn, H. (2004), "European Social Policy and Europe's Party-Political Center of Gravity 1957-2003", *MPIfG Discussion Paper*, No.04/6, Max-Planck Institute for the Study of Societies, Cologne, September 2004.

Marlier, E. and Berghman, J. (2004), "Open Co-ordination at EU Level in the Field of Social Protection and Social Inclusion: *Streamlining* without *Diluting*", in Girard, D. (ed.), *Solidarités collectives*, Famille et Solidarités (Tome I), L'Harmattan, Paris, pp.43-59.

Marsh, J. and Olsen, J. (1989), *Rediscovering Institutions, The Organisational Basis of Politics*, The Free Press, New York.

Martin, A. (1999), *EMU and Wage Bargaining: The Americanization of the European Labour Market?*, European Trade Union Institute and Observatoire social européen, Brussels.

Martin, A. and Ross, G. (2004), *Euros and Europeans. Monetary Integration and the European Model of Society*, Cambridge University Press, Cambridge.

Martin, J. P. and Grubb, D. (2001), "What Works and for Whom: A Review of OECD Countries' Experiences with Active Labour Market Policies", *Working Paper*, No.14, Institute for Labour Market Policy Evaluation, Uppsala.

Mosher, J. (2000), "Open Method of Co-ordination: Functional and Political Origins", *European Community Studies Association Review*, Vol.13, No.3, pp.2-7.

Pakaslahti, J. and Pochet, P. (2003), "The Social Dimension of the Changing European Union", *Sitra's publication series*, publication 256, SITRA and Observatoire social européen, Helsinki and Brussels.

Peña Casas, R. (2004), "Second Phase of the Open Method of Co-ordination on Social Inclusion", in Degryse, C. and Pochet, P. (eds.), *Social Developments in the European Union 2003*, European Trade Union Institute, Observatoire social européen and Saltsa, Brussels, pp.95-117.

Peña Casas, R. and Pochet, P. (2001), "Les indicateurs monétaires et non monétaires de pauvreté et d'exclusion sociale dans une perspective européenne", Rapport réalisé pour le ministère des Affaires sociales, de la Santé publique et de l'Environnement, Observatoire social européen, Brussels, January 2001.

Pochet, P. (1999), "European Briefing: The New Employment Chapter of the Amsterdam Treaty", *Journal of European Social Policy*, Vol.9, No.3, pp.271-278.

Pochet, P. (2001), "Méthode ouverte de co-ordination et modèle social européen", *Working Paper*, No.03/01, Institut d'études européennes, Université de Montréal-McGill University (http://www.iee.umontreal.ca/liens/WORKING PAPERS/Texte-Pochet.pdf).

Pochet, P. (2003a), "The European Employment Strategy at a Crossroads", in Degryse, C. and Pochet, P. (eds.), *Social Developments in the European Union – 2002*, European Trade Union Institute, Observatoire social européen and Saltsa, Brussels, pp.61-95.

Pochet, P. (2003b), "Pensions: the European Debate", in Clark, G. L. and Whiteside, N. (eds.), *Pension Security in the 21st Century – Redrawing the Public-Private Debate*, Oxford University Press, Oxford, pp. 44-63.

Pochet, P. (2004), "La OMC et la protection sociale: des développements ambigus", in Dehousse, R. (ed.), *L'Europe sans Bruxelles? Une analyse de la méthode ouverte de co-ordination*, L'Harmattan, Paris, pp.99-127.

Pochet, P., Beine, M., De Decker, C., Kabatusuila, F., Vanhercke, B. and Lamby, P. (1998), *Economic and Monetary Union, Employment, Social Conditions and Social Benefits, A Literature Survey*, European Foundation for the Improvement of Living and Working Conditions, Dublin, July 1998.

Pochet, P., Degryse, C. and Dufresne, A. (2004), "Dialogue social sectoriel", Research report realised for the European Commission, DG Employment and Social Affairs, Brussels, April 2004.

Radaelli, C. (2003), "The Open Method of Co-ordination: A New Governance Architecture for the European Union?", *SIEPS Report*, No.1, Swedish Institute for European Policy Studies, Stockholm, March 2003.

Rodrigues, M. J. (2004), *European Policies for a Knowledge Economy*, Edward Elgar Publishing, Cheltenham.

Ross, G. (1995), *Jacques Delors and European Integration*, Polity Press, Cambridge.

Sapir, A. *et al.* (2003), "An Agenda for a Growing Europe. Making the EU Economic System Deliver", Report of an Independent High-Level Study Group established on the initiative of the President of the European Commission, Brussels, July 2003 (http://europa.eu.int/comm/dgs/policy_advisers/ experts_groups/ps2/docs/agenda_en.pdf).

Scharpf, F. W. (2000), "Notes Toward a Theory of Multilevel Governing in Europe", *MPIfg Discussion Paper*, No.00/5, Max Planck Institute for the Study of Societies, Cologne.

Scharpf, F. W. (2002), "The European Social Model: Coping with the Challenges of Diversity", *MPIfG Working Paper*, No.02/8, July 2002 (http://www. mpi-fg-koeln.mpg.de/pu/workpap/wp02-8/wp02-8.html).

Scott, J. and Trubek, D. M. (2002), "Mind the Gap: Law and New Approaches to Governance in the European Union", *European Law Journal*, Vol.8, No.1, March 2002, pp.1-18.

SPC (2003), Opinion of the Social Protection Committee on the Commission's Communication "Strengthening the Social Dimension of the Lisbon Strategy: Streamlining Open Coordination in the Field of Social Protection", Brussels, 29 September 2003 (http://europa.eu.int/comm/employment_social/social_ protection_commitee/streamlining_en.pdf).

Szyszczak, E. (2001), "The New Paradigm for Social Policy: A Virtuous Circle?", *Common Market Law Review*, Vol.38, pp.1125-1170.

Telò, M. (2004), "Il Metodo aperto di coordinamento", *Quaderni di rassegna sindacale*, No.1, January-March 2004, pp.71-84.

TEPSA (2002), "The Broad Economic Policy Guidelines", *Final Report*, Project No.IV/2001/05/01 for the European Parliament Directorate General for Research, 24 January 2002.

Tholoniat, L. (2001), "L'Administration française et la Stratégie européenne pour l'Emploi: Jeux de légitimité et enjeux de gouvernance", unpublished manuscript, mimeo.

Trubek, D. and Mosher, J. (2001), "EU Governance, Employment Policy and the European Social Model", part of contributions to the *Jean Monnet Working Paper*, No.6/01, Symposium: Responses to the European Commission's White Paper on Governance, New York University School of Law (http:// www.jeanmonnetprogram.org/papers/01/011501.html).

UNIOPSS (2001), *Exclusion sociale et pauvreté en Europe*, La Documentation française, Paris.

van Riel, B. and van der Meer, M. (2002), "The Advocacy Coalition for European Employment Policy – The European Integration Process after EMU", in Hegmann, H. and Neumaerker, B. (eds.), *Die Europaische Union aus politökonomischer Perspective*, Metropolis Verlag, Marburg, pp.309-328.

Vandenbroucke, F. (1999), "The Active Welfare State: A European Ambition", Den Uyl Lecture, Amsterdam, 13 December 1999 (http://socialsecurity.fgov.be/active_welfare_state.htm)

Vandenbroucke, F. (2001), "Open Co-ordination on Pensions and the Future of Europe's Social Model", Closing speech at the Conference "Towards a New Architecture for Social Protection in Europe? A Broader Perspective of Pension Policies", Leuven, 19-20 October 2001.

Verdun, A. (1996), "An 'Asymmetrical' Economic and Monetary Union in the EU: Perceptions of Monetary Authorities and Social Partners", *Journal of European Integration/Revue d'Intégration Européenne*, Vol.20, No.1, pp.59-81.

Visser, J. (2000), "From Keynesianism to the Third Way. Labour Relations and Social Policy in Postwar Europe", *Economic and Industrial Democracy*, No.21, pp.421-456.

Watt, A. (2004), "Reform of the European Employment Strategy after Five Years: A Change of Course or Merely of Presentation?", *European Journal of Industrial Relations*, Vol.10, No.2, pp.117-137.

Zeitlin, J. (2003), "Introduction: Governing Work and Welfare in a New Economy: European and American Experiments", in Zeitlin, J. and Trubek, D. M. (eds.), *Governing Work and Welfare in a New Economy: European and American Experiments*, Oxford University Press, Oxford, pp.1-32.

Zeitlin, J. (2005), "Social Europe and Experimental Governance: Towards a New Constitutional Compromise?", in de Búrca, G. (ed.), *EU Law and the Welfare State: In Search of Solidarity*, collected courses of the Academy of European Law XIV/4, Oxford University Press, Oxford (forthcoming).

CHAPTER 2

The Open Method of Co-ordination
and the Debate over "Hard"
and "Soft" Law

David M. TRUBEK & Louise G. TRUBEK

The issue of the contribution of "soft law" to the construction of Europe has remerged in new form. Writing a decade ago, Francis Snyder noted that rules of conduct that may have no legally binding force may nevertheless have practical effect for European integration (Snyder, 1994: 198). In recent years, a new form of non-binding but potentially important normative system has emerged through the Open Method of Co-ordination (OMC). The OMC employs non-binding objectives and guidelines to bring about change in social policy and other areas.

The OMC originated with the European Employment Strategy (EES) and has since been applied to other areas such as social inclusion and pensions. In the short period since its formal inception at the Lisbon Summit, the OMC has generated a great deal of discussion and debate. Much of the controversy concerns the respective merits of "hard" and "soft" law in the construction of Social Europe[1].

Both those who favour the OMC as a mode of governance and those who question its desirability compare the OMC, implicitly or explicitly, with the Community Method. The Community Method is thought of as "hard law" because it creates uniform rules that Member States must adopt, provides sanctions if they fail to do so, and allows challenges for non-compliance to be brought in court. In contrast, the OMC, which has general and open-ended guidelines rather than rules, provides no formal sanctions for Member States that do not follow the guidelines, and is not justiciable, is thought of as "soft law". Proponents of the OMC argue that it can be effective despite – or even because of – its open-ended,

---

[1] Some prefer to refer to the OMC as "soft governance" rather than soft law to distinguish the OMC from situations in which non-binding forms of guidance are rendered binding by being used to interpret legal obligations and to indicate that the process has many elements beyond the objectives and guidelines (Jacobsson, 2003).

non-binding, non-justiciable qualities. Opponents question that conclusion. They not only argue that the OMC cannot do what is needed to construct Social Europe and that "hard law" is essential; they also contend that use of the OMC could undermine efforts to build the hard law they think will be needed.

On close analysis, this debate turns on a number of highly contested issues. These include the relative effectiveness of the Community Method and the OMC, the goals for Social Europe, and the nature of the obstacles to reaching those goals. When proponents of the OMC contend that it is better suited than the Community Method for certain tasks, they are not only making assumptions about the nature of the tasks and the capabilities of the open method; they are also implicitly or explicitly making assumptions about the capabilities of the Community Method. Similarly, when opponents of the OMC argue that its use should be limited in order to prevent erosion of the *acquis* or block future efforts to use hard law, they do so because of beliefs both about the OMC and the Community Method as well as assumptions concerning the proper role of the Union in social policy.

To a large degree, the people in this debate seem to be talking past each other. The policy discussion should be about the goals for Social Europe and the tasks needed to reach those goals. The institutional debate should be about the *relative* capacities of different modes to handle specific certain governance tasks, and discussion should focus on evidence relating to those capacities. Yet one often sees people on both sides making *a priori* assumptions about goals and unsupported assertions about the superior capacity of the mode they favour with little reference to data or alternative views. As a result, issues sometimes get framed in an either/or fashion: either one should only use soft law, or one should only employ hard law. Such framing not only cuts off much-needed empirical inquiry into relative capacity; it also deters exploration of hybrid (hard and soft) governance modes and possible synergies between binding and non-binding mechanisms.

The debate over hard and soft law has recently come to a head. The issue took on special importance because it was injected into the discussion of the future Constitution of the European Union where there was substantial discussion concerning the Open Method of Co-ordination. The debates in the European Constitutional Convention confirmed what was already apparent in the literature: the debate is not just about governance modes; it is also about policy options with many who favour hard law also holding a very different policy position than the proponents of softer methods.

The goal of this paper is not to resolve these debates, but to help clarify the issues and identify questions for further work. We want to unpack the arguments on both sides, identify contestable assumptions, and expose false dichotomies. While we favour continued use of "soft law" as well as hard/soft hybrids, we recognise that further work on relative capacities and their relationship to policy goals must be done before any final conclusions are reached.

I. The Battle over Hard and Soft Law – Competing Visions of the Pursuit of the Social in the EU and over the Place of the OMC in the EU Constitution

The spread of the OMC has generated real concern in certain circles in Europe. Included among the critics are some groups on the left. For a long time, many people on the left in Europe have tried to give the EU a "social dimension". They felt that the Union was too focused on economic matters and that EU economic policy could, if not counteracted by an active social policy, undermine the welfare state in the Member States. To be sure, proponents of Social Europe have very different ideas about what this concept means and how best to accomplish it. They all believe that the Union has a role to play in the maintenance and development of the "welfare state" and the preservation of Europe's commitment to solidarity. But there are very different ideas about how best to do that. While there are many approaches, they tend to stand between the poles set by two ideal-typical alternatives that we call "euro-corporatism" and "decentralised co-operation"[2].

A. Two Ideal-typical Visions of Social Europe and How to Get There

The *euro-corporatist* imagines Social Europe in terms drawn from the structure of *national* welfare states. In this vision, the European Union would have plenary power to act in all fields of industrial relations and social policy, using all appropriate modes but with a heavy emphasis on legislation. The Union's role would be to set social welfare and industrial relations standards that would have to be met in all Member States. This would be done through a corpus of uniform and binding social law passed at the EU level that creates justiciable rights. Moreover, not only would the Union develop a major corpus of uniform social standards; to the extent possible, social laws would be created not

---

[2] We have constructed these concepts as heuristics, or Weberian ideal-types. They are meant to draw out the implications of actual views on these matters, not to represent the views or position of any specific author or political faction. For a discussion of ideal types, see Weber (1968: 20-21).

through the Community Method, but by agreement between peak organisations representing labor and capital in the Social Dialogue[3].

To this vision, let us contrast an ideal-typical alternative. In the *decentralised co-operation* approach, the EU would still have an important
role to play in social policy, but it would be limited primarily to supporting and co-ordinating national-level activity while supplementing it in a
few limited cases. The approach would include efforts to develop co-
operative relations among the various stakeholders, but would reach out
to a broader range of interests and groups and concertation would be
focused at the national level. In this approach, there would be very little
legislation at the EU level: to the extent that binding rules were thought
to be desirable they would primarily be promulgated by the Member
States. The Union's role would be to establish broad objectives and then
facilitate policy reform and experimentation at the local level. By setting
some objectives, and monitoring progress towards them, the Union
would ensure that Member State social policy was sensitive to concerns
of the whole and Member state policy-makers learned from each other[4].

B. The Roots of These Visions

These two ideal-typical positions are based on very different ideas
about what is needed to preserve the European Social Model, and very
different ideas about the various instruments and modalities available to
tackle the challenges that goal involves. Thus, pure euro-corporatist
proponents of a European role in social policy would assume that without central legislation, there would be a race to the bottom in social
standards. They would believe that uniform rules in these policy domains are both feasible and desirable. They would not see a need for
much experimentation; assuming that the rules and policies needed to
preserve the social model are pretty well understood and the only problem is creating the political will to impose them. They would assume
that formal rules and justiciable rights are the only way to deal with the
asymmetric relations of power that exist between labour and capital.
They could also argue that such rules, approved in co-decision by the

---

[3]   The euro-corporatist vision is constructed by amalgamating views on separate issues
by many experts, particularity labour law experts. We do not claim that any one holds
to all, but many hold to many of them. For support on this vision, see Simitis and
Lyon-Caen (1996), Kenner (1995) and Streeck (1995) who stress the necessity for
hard law in social policy; Chalmers and Lodge (2003) emphasising the necessity for
centralised hard law at the European level; and Bercusson (2002) who sees the Social
Partners and the Social Dialogue as the route to a Social Europe.

[4]   For views that include some aspects of this model, see Sabel and Zeitlin (2003) and
Trubek and Mosher (2003).

European Council and European Parliament, alone have democratic legitimacy at the EU level.

Contrast those views with ideas that would animate a hypothetical proponent of decentralised concertation in European social policy. Such a person could argue that there is a vast amount of diversity among Member States in social policy and industrial relations. They would see the stakeholders as more varied than the traditional social partners. They would see this diversity not as a problem to be overcome by centralisation, but a lucky situation to be taken advantage of in the search for *new* solutions to seemingly intractable problems. They would stress the need for experimentation and believe this is best accomplished by fostering divergent models at national or sub-national levels. They would believe that the widest possible public participation in policy development is likely to lead to the most salutary results. They would argue that policy has to be flexible and revisable to cope with an increasingly complex and volatile world and that traditional forms of regulation may lack the necessary flexibility. They would believe that, with encouragement from the Union and advice from their peers, Member States have the capacity and will to restructure their welfare states. They would assert that Member States can fend off any "race to the bottom" pressures without the need for a centralised straightjacket and have already done so successfully in some areas. They would argue that some degree of co-ordination and monitoring at the EU level, combined with peer review and exchange of best practices, will strengthen Member State capacities and thus enhance their ability to resist pressures for a race to the bottom[5].

C. For Each Vision, the Other is a Dystopia

From each of these hypothetical viewpoints, the other would be a dystopia. If you think that centralised legislation is the only way to avoid a race to the bottom, you are not likely to be enchanted by approaches that downplay EU-level law-making. If you think that solutions are well known and all that is missing is the will to impose them on the Member States, you are likely to be suspicious of those who call for local experiments. If you feel that social policy is basically a deal between organised labor and capital to be struck in the shadow of the state, you will see widespread participation of NGOs in policy processes as at

---

[5] To these two extreme visions, one might want to add a third model which might be called "networked technocratic governance". In this model, the primary work of social and employment policy would be done by networks of technocrats at both the national and EU levels. The technocrats might employ guidelines not rules, and allow diversity, but they would rely more on expert knowledge than on broad participation and would look towards convergence. For an important study of expert governance in the EU, see Joerges and Vos (1999).

best a distraction. If, on the other hand, you think that only through experiments and mutual learning, Member States will discover new solutions that will avoid races to the bottom, if you feel that there is an irreducible degree of diversity in social policy, and if you think that experimental governance to be effective must involve all stakeholders, then you will be attracted to open processes and local autonomy and distrustful of uniform solutions coming out of deals which may affect all citizens yet are set behind closed doors by unions and management

D. Social Policy, the OMC and the EU Constitution

The European Convention debated whether to include social policy as a major objective in the proposed Constitution for the Union, and whether to give constitutional status to the OMC. The resulting debates revealed aspects of these competing visions of Social Europe and the role of hard and soft law in its construction[6].

Referring back to our ideal typical distinction between euro-corporatists and those who favour decentralised co-ordination, what might people with these competing hypothetical viewpoints have hoped for in such "constitutionalisation"? A hypothetical euro-corporatist would have hoped that the Convention would significantly expand the EU's competence so that it could legislate in all areas of social policy and industrial relations if needed, and expand the role of Qualified Majority Voting (QMV) to remove excessive veto possibilities that could block needed laws. On the other hand, a proponent of "decentralised concertation" would have hoped for a ringing endorsement of the processes and policies needed to make decentralised experimentation work. In the current context, this would mean embracing and strengthening the Open Method of Co-ordination.

The debates in the Convention over social policy and about the OMC were complex and the outcome, as reflected in the draft Treaty, suggests that no clear-cut view prevailed. The results are murky, and texts ambiguous. Although the draft does contain sections legitimating EU action in social policy, they are carefully constrained and fall far short of any move towards centralising the welfare state. And while the OMC is mentioned, albeit indirectly, it is hardly given the robust endorsement

---

[6] The Working Group on Social Europe (European Convention, 2003) illustrates the wide range of opinions between Member States in its final report. For additional discourse, see Shaw (2003) who describes the Social Working Group's deliberations, revealing the myriad of debates encompassing the inclusion of the OMC in the Constitution; de Búrca and Zeitlin (2003) who support the constitutionalisation of the OMC and Bronzini (2003) who criticises the Draft as a threat to the shrinking or stagnant European Social Model.

and full-blown constitutional status some hoped for (European Convention, 2003).

The reasons for this outcome are complex. While the lines of disagreement in the Convention do not fit neatly into our two ideal-typical categories, it can be argued that competing views on the merits of hard and soft law of the type we have sketched did play a role. In the discussions, questions were raised about the OMC that were based on assumptions the relative merits of the Community Method and Social Dialogue on the one hand ("hard"), and the OMC ("soft") on the other. Specifically, there was opposition to the OMC by people who thought that unless the "soft" option is severely restricted, it would crowd out opportunities for "hard" legislation[7]. In such a view, the OMC is sort of like a virus that needs to be quarantined before it infects the whole community. If it were let loose in areas of existing legislative competence, it would sap the Union's will and capacity to do what really needs to be done which is to pass uniform, binding, and justiciable laws.

From such a perspective, if that competence exists now, it must be saved from OMC infection. If it is not there now but might be authorised in the future, the Constitution should stop any use of the OMC in the future competence expansion areas. It seems those opposing the OMC wanted to set up rigid border controls, ensuring that no infection can occur in any area with current or future legislative competence. That way, existing areas of competence are rendered safe, and future ones will not come with a built-in tendency to "go soft".

This extremely negative view of the OMC did not prevail. The Treaty does mention the OMC process and does so without any of the clear limits on its use desired by the "hard law" camp. But at the same time the section on the OMC does not provide a strong endorsement of the method. The clause does not enshrine the OMC as a clear alternative to the Community Method nor contain many of the procedural safeguards OMC proponents had hoped for[8].

II. Transcending the "Hard/Soft" Law Debate

While the hard/soft law debate has raised important issues concerning the future of the Union, both sides of this debate over governance modes seem stuck in untenable positions. However, there is evidence

---

[7] For a critique of this point of view, see de Búrca and Zeitlin (2003).

[8] See Article I-14 (European Convention, 2003). While this article supports the overall goals of the OMC in the field of economic and employment policies, it neither uses the words "Open Method of Co-ordination" nor provides a detailed description of the process. See also EPC Draft Assessment which critiques the Draft Article as "ambiguous" and "rather restrictive" (EPC, 2003).

that some people have sensed that it is possible to transcend the debate. This section explores such efforts and their significance.

A. Seeking Theories of OMC Operation and of Hard Law Effectiveness Underlying the Move to Quarantine OMC

The first step is to get a better understanding of the some of the assumptions underlying efforts to "quarantine" the OMC. What are the views about the OMC on the one hand, and traditional EU legislative routes, on the other, that might lead one to reach such a conclusion? That is what the debate about hard and soft law is all about. Those who want to curb the use of soft law do so because they think the OMC can never "deliver the goods" the way "hard law" can. On the one hand, it is argued, the OMC cannot bring about real change or create real rights. On the other, legislation does. So to choose one over the other is to chose the simulacra of action (OMC) over the reality (hard law).

It is our view that this position is wrong on both counts. We suggest that the OMC may not be a paper tiger, but rather could emerge as a powerful tool. And the idea that all EU legislation creates hard and fast uniform rules that are easily enforced and will bring about change is a chimera that flies in the face of the record of implementation of EU directives, recent developments in the Community Method, and much of the learning in the sociology of law ever since the famed gap between the law on the books and the law and action was first identified.

B. Soft Law May Be Harder Than You Think

If you look at the OMC you may say: how can this change anything? Some of the OMCs do not even have guidelines, and those that do have few that are highly specific or yield benchmarks that are easily measured[9]. So how can one say if a Member State is "complying"? And the Member States are not subject to any formal sanctions if they do not conform to the guidelines so why do we think they would comply (assuming they knew what it would mean to "comply" with some of the guidelines, vaguely worded as they sometimes are) if they do not want to do so? Isn't the whole thing, asks the skeptic, just a charade in which the Member States pretend to make changes and the Commission pretends the EU has had an impact?

Not for those who are developing theories of how and why the OMC may bring about change, and do it in ways that might even be better than traditional legislation. While the OMC is too new for us fully to under-

---

[9] It is, however, worth noting that the Commision favours increased use of quantitative targets (CEC, 2003a).

stand its dynamics, scholars have pointed to several features that could explain why, despite a lack of clear and uniform rules or formal sanctions, it might work to bring about change. The literature identifies at least six different ways change may occur as a result of the OMC: shaming, diffusion through mimesis or discourse, deliberation, learning, and networks[10].

These mechanisms are not mutually exclusive and scholars may deploy several at the same time[11]. But it is worth noting that these accounts fall into two broad categories. Some theorists emphasise the top-down effects of the OMC, stressing how ideas developed at the EU level gradually influence developments at national or sub-national level. Others assume that the transmission of ideas and the vectors of influence for policy change may be as much bottom-up as top-down. Thus in the top-down approach, we find more stress on shaming, diffusion through mimesis and discourse, and one version of network theory. In the bottom-up category we find more attention to deliberation, experimentation, learning and another version of network theory.

One explanation for how the OMC might bring about change is through "*shaming*". This account is closest to the "hard law" model because it treats the clarification of guidelines through preparation of specific recommendations as somewhat similar to a judicial interpretation of general statutory language and the informal sanction of "shaming" as more or less equivalent to formal sanctions. In this account, Member States will seek to comply with the guidelines in order to avoid negative criticism in peer reviews and Council recommendations. The "recommendations" issued by the Council are often in fact rather pointed observations about poor performance: the assumption is that nations will seek to avoid such negative publicity and thus will either make policy changes in advance to avoid future recommendations or quickly adopt the recommendations once issued in order to limit the negative publicity they generate.

---

[10] An additional mechanism that could influence national policy along lines indicated by the OMC is the use of the European Social Fund to support projects that further OMC goals. For example, in employment, the objectives of the EES and those of the ESF are similar, and these two processes are supposed to be co-ordinated. Were the co-ordination tight, and especially if allocation of some of the funds were conditional on national performance under the EES guidelines, the ESF would be a powerful tool. However, there is evidence that the two processes are not well co-ordinated at the national level in many Member States. And, at least formally, conditionality is limited (Hartwig, 2002).

[11] For an excellent study that integrates most of these elements in a comprehensive theory of how the OMC operates as a change-inducing process, see Jacobsson (2005).

A second approach relies on *diffusion* to explain the relationship between the EES and national policy change. In this approach, change is said to come about through the diffusion of models developed in other polities and/or promoted by international organisations. The diffusion approach can, in turn, be divided into two sub-theories. One stresses diffusion through mimesis. The other emphasises diffusion through discursive transformation.

In the mimesis approach, the guidelines and information provided by the Commission and peer Member States put before national policymakers a coherent policy model they are encouraged to copy. The EES processes for benchmarking and peer review further facilitate mimesis since they require Member States to study the experiences of others and enter into a dialogue with them about "good practices". Member States adopt these models from a variety of motives.

Another way diffusion may come about is through discursive transformations. Jacobsson describes discourse-driven change as the construction of a new "[…] perspective from which reality can be described, phenomena classified, positions taken, and actions justified" (Jacobsson, 2005). She points out that the EES has introduced a series of concepts such as employability, adaptability, flexibility, active welfare etc. Some of these concepts are reinforced by being reflected in statistical indicators and annual "league tables". As policy-makers begin to take these concepts and indicators on board, adopting them as their own way of organising reality, they tend to shift policy orientation.

Discursive diffusion theory suggests that various processes, including the requirement for annual reports, committee meetings of various types, peer review and various monitoring efforts, subtly transform national discourse and thus national policy. Thus when reports must be written in terms set by the guidelines, new concepts, with definitions of reality embedded in them, come to be accepted at national level. When national administrations come to see their performance measured qualitatively through peer review and Council recommendations and quantitatively through indicators and league tables they must confront new policy paradigms and take on board new concepts and vocabularies. This process requires them to adopt new cognitive frameworks, a transformation facilitated and reinforced by the need to prepare annual National Action Plans and defend performance to various audiences that themselves employ the discourse of the EES. Such changes in the way issues are conceptualised, it is suggested, may lead to policy change.

A third, overlapping account of how the OMC might bring about change is through the creation of *new policy networks.* The networking generated by OMC occurs at several levels. In the EES, because the NAPs require co-operation from many ministries, EES can create new networks of government officials at the Member State level. Second, since the EES procedure requires input from social partners and civil society, it can expand the national level networks to reach beyond government. Finally, through the Employment Committee and otherwise, processes operate to link civil servants and others from all Member States with the Commission and Council staff in a multi-level, public/private transnational network through which new ideas diffuse and from which a common set of policy positions emerge (Jacobsson, 2003). If the process works as it should, people from Labor, Welfare and Finance Ministries will co-operate at national level, and then meet with counterparts from other EU Member States to deliberate about the best way to deal with common problems. At the same time, employers, unions, and NGOs would have an opportunity to engage with the process at both levels. Finally, as these contacts go on, a common European way of thinking about employment should emerge and eventually affect actions at the national level.

The network idea is really a part of other approaches and thus there are different ways to conceptualise the function of networks in the OMC. Networks can be seen as part of a top-down model, with the networks serving as transmission belts for ideas coming from the top. But in alternative accounts, they are the settings for deliberation and mutual learning, and thus can be channels to move ideas "up" as well as "down".

That takes us to a very different set of theories about how the OMC may bring about change. Where shaming, mimesis, and discursive transformation theories focus on how ideas originating at the top and embedded in the guidelines "diffuse" throughout the EU, alternative accounts stress ways in which the new processes foster *experimentation, deliberation and learning.* These accounts see the policy-change process not as a strictly top-down enterprise, but rather as one in which forces for change operate in both directions. In this approach, the diversity of the EU is a great asset, for it means that there will be many different policies being tried out at any time. In such a context, the process of annual planning and review, the exchange of best practices, and the system of multilateral surveillance all help Member States find new solutions to problems often thought to be unsolvable. Trubek and Mosher (2003: 46-47) note that policy learning is facilitated by:

> [...] mechanisms that destabilize existing understandings; bring together people with diverse viewpoints in settings that require sustained deliberation about problem-solving; facilitate erosion of boundaries between both policy domains and stakeholders; reconfigure policy networks; encourage decentralized experimentation; produce information on innovation; require sharing of good practice and experimental results; encourage actors to compare

results with those of the best performers in any area; and oblige actors collectively to redefine objectives and policies.

The EES contains all these elements to one degree or another. The guidelines challenge national policies in many countries. The process engages diverse groups and crosses intra-public and public-private boundaries thus creating opportunities for policy dialogues. Indicators, benchmarking, peer review and exchange of good practices bring new ideas to the surface and encourage poor performers to rethink their strategies. Moreover, the EES process is iterative and iteration fosters deliberation concerning the best way to solve problems. For a visual illustration of these varying accounts and their interrelation, see figure 1:

Competing Models of How the OMC
May Bring about Policy Change

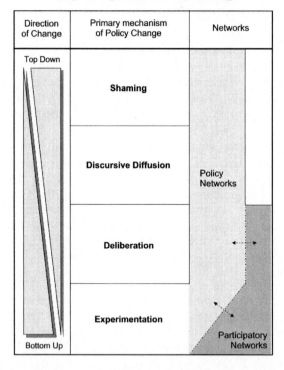

Of course, regardless of which of these theories or combination of theories, you accept, the question remains whether the hypothesised mechanisms actually operate in the ways the theories predict. To be sure, there is new empirical evidence that supports the claim that the EES has made a difference in some countries in some areas (e.g.

Jacobsson and Vifell, 2004). Yet there remains disagreement about how much change in employment policy has actually occurred since EES was created; to what degree any change that has come about can be attributed to the EES rather than purely domestic factors; and just how the EES influenced change when it can be shown to have been a factor.

There is evidence that suggests that it does not always work as it is ideally pictured, and that in some areas it has little, if any, impact. Governments may treat the NAPs as a routine administrative burden, not an opportunity for real debate and deliberation; peer reviews and benchmarking may be paper exercises; social partners may be unwilling to participate actively; some countries may resist change because they think the EES model does not fit their labor markets; others may feel they need not change because they have largely met the EES goals (Trubek and Mosher, 2003).

Nonetheless, we think the theoretical discussion is robust, and the limited empirical data positive enough, to erect a presumption that in the current situation of EU governance in social policy, "soft law" in the form of the OMC can make a difference and that the EES can be a useful instrument to deal with the employment problem. This view is strengthened by recent developments, which indicate that the Commission and the Council, rather than walking away from the EES, decided to recalibrate the process in order to make the process more focused and effective (European Council, 2003).

C. How Hard is Hard Law Anyway?

In any overall assessment of the hard-soft law debate, one also has to take into account how "hard law" really works. Since by definition the case against "soft law" in general is also a case for some kind of "hard law", and thus the case against the OMC is largely a case for the Community Method, we have to ask what assumptions are being made about that method and its capabilities. Here we must examine two very different issues.

The first are the changes in the Community Method in recent years. Note that like the OMC, the Community Method is, in part, a process designed to bring about changes in *national* law. To become law, directives must be transposed into national law. Under what Scott and Trubek (2002) call the "Classic Community Method", this process led to the creation of more or less uniform rules throughout the Union. But in part under the influence of the *Protocol on the Application of the Principles of Subsidiarity and Proportionality*, the Community Method has changed and, as a result, many newer directives are quite open-ended, leaving Member States with much more flexibility and discretion in shaping national legislation than under the "classic" approach (Scott and Trubek,

2002). At the same time, these new directives may mandate broad participation in the processes by which general principles are incorporated into national law. By allowing Member States more flexibility and diversity and relying heavily on participation to provide legitimacy, the new approach to Community legislation has somewhat blurred the distinction between "hard law" and the OMC (Scott and Trubek, 2002; Sabel and Zeitlin, 2003).

A second issue that must be taken account of in making the relative assessment of the capacity of hard and soft law is the famed gap between law on the books and law in action. Proponents of "hard law" tend to assume that if uniform rules could be passed through the Community Method, they would be automatically transposed into binding national law that would then be effectively enforced. This seems to be an heroic set of assumptions, especially in view of what is known about the problems of transposition of EU law as well as those of implementation in all legal systems. There is substantial room for delay and slippage in the transposition process. And even if EU-level hard law is successfully transposed, enforcement may prove difficult. Anyone familiar with the sociology of law knows that behind the façade of formal law operate many informal processes. That may modify or even negate the impact of formal rules. To say there is a rule or a right on the law books is not to say it is enjoyed in reality. For example, Claire Kilpatrick (2003) has noted that, even with clear and uniform norms in an area like employment discrimination, a purely rights- and litigation-based enforcement system may not be fully effective in achieving the equality goals.

In any comparison of governance modes, it is important to be sure we are contrasting a realistic picture of hard law, not an idealised model. When opponents of the OMC suggest it is weak in comparison with the hard law of the Community method, they may be comparing an idealised version of the capacities of the mode they prefer, not a realistic picture.

D. Hybrid Constellations: Can the EU Combine Hard and Soft Mechanisms for Optimal Results?

Finally, we have to get beyond the idea that there must be a choice between hard and soft law. These are not mutually incompatible and perhaps the most promising ideas are those that would yoke the two together. This possibility has been recognised by policy-makers: thus, in a report to the European Convention on the OMC, the Convention Secretariat noted that:

> The Open Method of Co-ordination therefore proves to be an instrument of integration among others. For the same subject-matter and within the limits

of the Treaties, it can therefore be combined with and linked to other instruments of Community action, including traditional Community legislative action (European Convention, 2002: 16).

Scholars have also suggested the utility of hybrid combinations. For example, Fritz Scharpf (2002) has proposed the use of framework directives combined with on OMC to monitor and co-ordinate national responses under the framework which could, in turn, provide information for revision of the framework itself. And Claire Kilpatrick (2003) has shown that such coupling has already started to occur in the area of employment law and employment policy. Kilpatrick notes that hard and soft law can play different but mutually reinforcing roles in dealing with issues such as part-time work and gender discrimination. She demonstrates that such hybrid combinations have existed at Member State levels for some time and suggests that the EU's adoption of hard/soft hybrids may be a continuation of a general trend.

Similar ideas are set forth by Edward Best of the European Institute of Public Administration. In an article entitled "Alternative Regulations or Complementary Methods? Evolving Options in European Governance", Best (2003: 2) reminds us that "in many areas, European policy is formulated and implemented through a mixture of methods both legal and non-legal, European and national, public and private [...]". In a review of how these several modes operate and interact, he stresses the importance of exploring possible complementarity between these methods.

One area where soft law is being used with hard law, and hybridity seems to be well developed, is EU environmental law. This area is especially important because unlike employment where the EU's legislative competence is quite limited, this is an area where the EU has substantial legislative powers. In that context, the fact that nonetheless the EU has chosen to proceed in part through OMC-like mechanisms suggests that it is fully aware of relative functional capabilities and prepared both to use different modes for different issues and to combine them when they are complementary (Scott and Trubek, 2002; de Búrca, 2003; Best, 2003).

E. The OMC and the EU Charter of Fundamental Rights

Another area that has recently attracted attention is the possible use of the OMC to strengthen fundamental rights. Gráinne de Búrca (2004) has suggested that the OMC might be used in conjunction with the EU Charter of Fundamental Rights if, as expected, the Charter becomes part of the EU Constitution. The proposal seems to envision two different roles for the OMC. In one area it would complement judicial action; in another it would, in essence, substitute for judicial enforcement.

This bifurcated proposal comes about because of ambivalent language inserted in the draft Treaty that limited the justiciability of the Charter of Fundamental Rights. While it is clear that the political and civil rights provisions of the Charter would be justiciable, those that deal with economic and social rights may not be. Thus, in an apparent effort to avoid judicial enforcement of social and economic rights, a clause was inserted in the draft that limits the judicial cognisability of those provisions of the Charter which "contain principles". If this awkwardly worded clause is interpreted to refer to economic and social rights, then direct judicial action in this sphere will be precluded.

In this context, de Búrca argues, the OMC could be used both to buttress judicial enforcement of political and civil rights, thus mixing "hard" and "soft" elements, and to strengthen economic and social rights. In former case, OMC mechanisms might be used to supplement judicial decision-making, spreading best practices and encouraging proactive reforms. In the latter case, the OMC might substitute for direct judicial action by creating the kind of proactive and dense processes of measurement, monitoring, and shared problem-solving in the economic and social rights field that exists under the EES and other OMC mechanisms. In this area, the rights themselves could function like guidelines, and efforts might be made to translate them into specific benchmarks, measure progress through common indicators, and encourage experimentation and deliberation on ways to ensure fidelity to the norms.

Conclusion: Legal Theory, Hybrid Solutions, and Integration through Law

If we examine the views of people like Scharpf, Best, de Búrca and Kilpatrick, we can see that unlike a hypothetical euro-corporatist, they do not see a fundamental cleavage between hard and soft approaches. And once we see that there may not be a need to choose between these approaches, we have to ask: what is really going on in debate over hard vs. soft law in the EU? Is it possible that those who object to soft law are seeing these phenomena through a theoretical vision that precludes any possibility of casting it in positive terms? At the same time, is it possible that some proponents of soft law are so wedded to their approach that they fail to see the importance of hard law?

To the extent that this is true, it would represent a failure both of theoretical vision and empirical inquiry. Proponents of hard law have a theory of the nature of law that makes them incapable of grasping the value of soft law processes. When this theory of law is linked to a theory of European integration that stresses the importance of law in promoting and sustaining European integration, we can see how the OMC could unsettle conceptual frameworks for it purports to be a tool of integration while lacking key features of prior legal mechanisms. We suspect that it is the combination of these two theoretical commitments leads to the observed hostility to the OMC and similar soft law processes.

It is not hard to see why soft law processes challenge both aspects of this body of thought. First, if one thinks that law by its nature must establish uniform rules, the rules must bind the behavior of all to whom they are addressed, the rules, to be legitimate, must have the sanction of elected representatives of the people, that the rules cannot be changed without the consent of those representatives, and that to the extent that the rules create rights, they must be enforceable by courts or quasi-courts, then whatever else a "soft" mechanism is, it cannot and should not be called "law". Second, if one believes that law, so defined, has been important to the integration of Europe, and that the progress of integration can in part be measured by the number of areas that are brought under uniform rules originating at the EU level, then any shift from hard to soft "law" means a decline in the possibility of integration itself.

At the same time, it is possible to understand why proponents of soft law may ignore the continuing importance of binding, uniform, and justiciable norms. Because of the dominance of the hard law model in our imaginations, proponents of the newer, soft measures have had to carry a heavy burden of proof. That has included efforts to demonstrate the weaknesses of traditional regulatory measures, perhaps clouding their ability to pay attention to the positive features of such regimes and the situations in which they will be most needed and effective. What we need is more careful attention to the relative capacities of the different modes in operation and to their combination in hybrids. Until we have a more realistic assessment of relative capabilities, as well as complementarities between modes, people will keep talking past one another.

Especial attention needs to be given to developing a theory of hybrids. The discussion of hard/soft hybrids is just beginning. We are seeing more and more instances of such hybrids, suggesting this constellation represents an adaptation of legal culture to new circumstances and challenges. Scholars have yet to develop explanations for this trend, or to craft the robust theories concerning the relative capacities of hard and soft law that is necessary to create a functional theory of hybrids.

We know that such combinations exist. And we know their interrelationship depends on the objectives sought and is context-specific Thus, for example, Kilpatrick (2003) notes that the EU went from a hard law to a hybrid hard-soft approach to part-time work when it shifted from a largely negative approach to one that promotes part-time work as a means towards employment stimulation and increased competitiveness. And she shows that effective hybridity in this area may operate differently than in employment discrimination, another context in which hard/soft hybridity has emerged. These observations should help us as we seek to move past dichotomous thinking and fully engage hybrid constellations.

Once we understand the limits of approaches that stress one mode at the expense of the other, recognise that every judgment must be comparative and look at relative capacity for specific objectives in varied contexts, see that there are ways these approaches can be combined, and recognise that such combinations may be essential to accomplish specific goals, we should be able to transcend the terms of the hard/soft debate. And in doing that we will find ourselves with a new and richer understanding of what we mean both by "law" and "European integration".

References

Bercusson, B. (2002), "The Institutional Architecture of the European Social Model", Interdisciplinary Seminar "Economy and Politics in Europe after the Erosion of the Nation-State: Historical, Socio-Political and Legal Perspectives", European University Institute, Florence, November 2002.

Best, E. (2003), "Alternative Regulations or Complementary Methods? Evolving Options in European Governance", *Eipascope*, No.2003/1, European Institute of Public Administration, Maastricht, pp.2-11.

Bronzini, G. (2003), "The European Social Model and the Constitutional Process of the Union", speech available at http://europa.eu.int/futurum/forum_convention/documents/contrib/acad/0053_c4_en.pdf.

CEC (1997), "An Employment Agenda for the Year 2000, Issues and Policies" (http://europa.eu.int/comm/employment_social/elm/summit/en/papers/emploi2.htm).

CEC (2001a), "European Governance – A White Paper", COM (2001) 428 final, 25 July 2001.

CEC (2001b), Communication from the Commission "The Future of Health Care for the Elderly: Guaranteeing Accessibility, Quality and Financial Viability", COM (2001) 723 final, 5 December 2001 (http://europa.eu.int/eur-lex/en/com/cnc/2001/com2001_0723en01.pdf).

CEC (2002a), Communication from the Commission on Streamlining of the Annual Economic and Employment Policy Cycles, COM (2002) 487 final, 3 September 2002 (http://europa.eu.int/eur-lex/en/com/rpt/2002/com2002_0487en01.pdf).

CEC (2002b), Communication from the Commission "Taking Stock of Five Years of the European Employment Strategy", COM (2002) 416 final, 17 July 2002 (http://europa.eu.int/comm/employment_social/news/2002/jul/com_eval_en.pdf).

CEC (2003a), Communication from the Commission "The Future of the European Employment Strategy (EES). 'A Strategy for Full Employment and

Better Jobs for All'", COM (2003) 6 final of 14 January 2003 (http://europa. eu.int/eur-lex/en/com/pdf/2003/com2003_0006en01.pdf).

CEC (2003b), Proposal for a Council Decision on Guidelines for the Employment Policies of the Member States (http://europa.eu.int/comm/employment _social/employment_strategy/prop_2003/gl_en.pdf).

Chalmers, D. and Lodge, M. (2003), "The Open Method of Co-ordination and the European Welfare State", *ESRC Centre for Analysis of Risk and Regulation Discussion Papers*, No.11, London School of Economics, London, June 2003.

Council of the European Union (2000), "The On-going Experience of the Open Method of Coordination", *Presidency Note*, No.90088/00, Lisbon, 13 June 2000.

de Búrca, G. (2003), "The Constitutional Challenge of New Governance in the European Union", paper presented at workshop on "New Governance and Law in EU", Minda de Gunzburg Center for European Studies, Harvard University, 28 February 2003.

de Búrca, G. (2004), "Beyond the Charter: How Enlargement Has Enlarged the Human Rights Policy of the EU", *Fordham Journal of International Law*, Vol.27, pp.679-714.

de Búrca, G. and Zeitlin, J. (2003), "Constitutionalising the Open Method of Coordination: What Should the Convention Propose?", *CEPS Policy Brief*, No.31, Centre for European Policy Studies, Brussels, March 2003.

Dehousse, R. (2002), "The Open Method of Coordination: A New Policy Paradigm?", Paper presented at the first Pan-European Conference on European Union Politic "The Politics of European Integration: Academic Aquis and Future Challenges", Bordeaux, 26-28 September 2002.

Employment Committee website, http://europa.eu.int/comm/employment_ social/employment_strategy/index_en.htm

EPC (2003), "The Draft Constitutional Treaty – An Assessment" by EPC Convention Team, *EPC Issue Paper*, No.5, The European Policy Center, Brussels, July 2003.

Esping-Andersen, G. (1990), *The Three Worlds of Welfare Capitalism*, Princeton University Press, Princeton.

European Convention (2002), "Coordination of National Policies: The Open Method of Co-ordination", WG VI, WD 015, 26 September 2002.

European Convention (2003), Draft Treaty Establishing a Constitution for Europe, CONV 850/03, 18 July 2003.

European Convention (2003), Final Report of Working Group XI on Social Europe, CONV 516/1/03 REV1, 4 February 2003.

European Council (1997a), Amsterdam European Council, *Stability and Growth Pact*, 16-17 June 1997.

European Council (1997b), Luxembourg Summit, *Extraordinary European Council Meeting on Employment*, 20 November 1997.

European Council (2000a), Lisbon European Council, *Presidency Conclusions*, 23-24 March 2000.

European Council (2000b), Nice European Council, *Presidency Conclusions*, 7-9 December 2000.

European Council (2001), Stockholm European Council, *Presidency Conclusions*, 23-24 March 2001.

European Council (2003), Council Decision 2003/578/EC of 22 July on Guidelines for the Employment Policies of the Member States, OJ L 197, 5 August 2003, pp.0013-0021.

Ferrera, M., Hemerijck, A. and Rhodes, M. (2001), *The Future of Social Europe: Recasting Work and Welfare in the New Economy*, Oxford University Press, Oxford.

Goetschy, J. (2003), "The European Employment Strategy, Multi-level Governance and Policy Coordination: Past, Present and Future", in Zeitlin, J. and Trubek, D. M. (eds.), *Governing Work and Welfare in a New Economy: European and American Experiments*, Oxford University Press, Oxford, pp.59-87.

Hartwig, I. (2002), "La mise en œuvre à double voie de la stratégie européenne pour l'emploi: un monstre de papier après l'élargissement? – Instituting a Double Path in the European Strategy for Employment: A Paper Monster after Enlargement?", *Eipascope*, No.2002/2, European Institute of Public Administration, Maastricht.

Hemerijck, A. (2002), "New Modes of Governance in Europe: Policy Making Without Legislating?", in Héritier, A. (ed.), *Common Goods: Reinventing European and International Governance*, Rowman & Littlefield Publishers, Boulder.

Jacobsson, K. (2003), "Soft Regulation and the Subtle Transformation of States: The Case of EU Employment Policy", Paper presented at the Seminar on the OMC, Minda de Gunzberg Center for European Studies, Harvard University, 28 April 2003.

Jacobsson, K. (2005), "Between Deliberation and Discipline: Soft Governance in EU Employment Policy" in Morth, U. (ed.), *Soft Law in Governance and Regulation: An Interdisciplinary Analysis*, Edward Elgar Publishing, Cheltenham (forthcoming).

Jacobsson, K. and Vifell, Á. (2005), "New Governance Structures in Employment Policy Making? Taking Stock of the European Employment Strategy", in Linsenmann, I., Meyer, C. and Wessels, W. (eds.), *Economic Governance in the EU*, Macmillan, Palgrave (forthcoming).

Jenson, J. and Pochet, P. (2002), "Employment and Social Policy Since Maastricht: Standing up to the European Monetary Unit", Paper presented for "The Year of the Euro", Nanovic Institute for European Studies, University of Notre Dame, 5-8 December 2002.

Joerges, C. and Vos, E. (1999) (eds.), *EU Committees: Social Regulation, Law and Politics*, Hart Publishing, Oxford.

Kenner, J. (1995), "EC Labour Law: The Softly, Softly Approach", *The International Journal of Comparative Labour Law and Industrial Relations*, Vol.11, No.4, pp.307-326.

Kenner, J. (1999), "The EC Employment Title and the 'Third Way': Making Soft Law Work?", *The International Journal of Comparative Labour Law and Industrial Relations*, Vol.51, No.1, pp.33-60.

Kilpatrick, C. (2003), "Hard and Soft Law in EU Employment Regulation", Paper presented at the 8th Biennial International Conference of the EU Studies Association, Nashville TN, March 2003.

Sabel, C. F. and Zeitlin, J. (2003), "Active Welfare, Experimental Governance, Pragmatic Constitutionalism: The New Transformation of Europe", unpublished paper presented to the International Conference of the Hellenic Presidency of the European Union "The Modernisation of the European Social Model & EU Policies and Instruments", Ioannina, Greece, 21-22 May 2003.

Scharpf, F. (2002), "The European Social Model: Coping with the Challenges of Diversity", *Journal of Common Market Studies*, Vol.40, No.4, November 2002, pp.645-670.

Scott, J. and Trubek, D. M. (2002), "Mind the Gap: Law and New Approaches to Governance in the European Union", *European Law Journal*, Vol.8, No.1, March 2002, pp.1-18.

Shaw, J. (2003), "A Strong Europe is a Social Europe", Paper delivered at the first workshop of the UACES study group on the debate of the Future of Europe, Federal Trust (available at www.fedtrust.co.uk/eu_constitution).

Simitis, S. and Lyon-Caen, A. (1996), "Community Labour Law, A Critical Introduction to its History", in Davies, P., Lyon-Caen, A., Sciarra, S. and Simitis, S. (eds.), *European Community Labour Law: Principles and Perspectives, Liber Americorum Lord Wedderburn of Charlton*, Clarendon Press, Oxford, pp.1-22.

Snyder, F. (1994), "Soft Law and Institutional Practice in the European Community", in Martin, S. (ed.), *The Construction of Europe*, Kluwer Academic Publishers, Deventer, pp.197-225.

Streeck, W. (1995), "From Market-making to State-building: Reflections on the Political Economy of European Social Policy", in Liebfried, S. and Pierson, P. (eds.), *European Social Policy: Between Fragmentation and Integration*, The Brookings Institution, Washington D.C., pp.389-431.

Trubek, D. M. and Mosher, J. (2003), "New Governance, Employment Policy, and the European Social Model", in Zeitlin, J. and Trubek, D. M. (eds.), *Governing Work and Welfare in a New Economy: European and American Experiments*, Oxford University Press, Oxford, pp.33-58.

Vandenbroucke, F. (2001), "La Coordination ouverte et le vieillissement: quelle valeur ajoutée pour l'Europe sociale?", *Europa-Novas Fronteiras*, No.9/10, December 2001, pp.59-66.

Weber, M. (1968), *Economy and Society; An Outline of Interpretive Sociology*, Bedminster Press, New York.

PART II

NATIONAL STUDIES

CHAPTER 3

Trying to Reform the
"Best Pupils in the Class"?

The Open Method of Co-ordination
in Sweden and Denmark

Kerstin JACOBSSON

Introduction

Both Sweden and Denmark were eager to place employment at the top of the EU agenda and the two countries played an instrumental role in the initiation of the European Employment Strategy (EES) (Johansson, 1999). The two governments consider the Open Method of Co-ordination (OMC) an apt and appropriate co-operation method in the nationally sensitive areas of welfare policy. Both regard employment and social policy as national competences. Thus, they have somehow to handle the tension between employment and social policy as a matter of national responsibility *and* the perceived need to develop a joint and co-ordinated European strategy.

This chapter investigates and compares the functioning of the OMC employment and social inclusion respectively in Sweden and Denmark. It looks at which national players are involved and how the OMC interacts with national policy-making. It also investigates the types of impact that the OMC has had in these countries as well as barriers to further impact.

The chapter shows that the EES is not well integrated into the national policy-making and implementation systems in Sweden and Denmark, but concerns a rather limited group of officials at national ministries. In contrast, the OMC in social inclusion has developed in a more participatory direction in the two countries. The chapter argues that the two governments have tried to maintain a gate-keeping function in the EES, but that this has been more difficult in the OMC social inclusion, which is a more explicit participatory process and, arguably, where social actors at national and European level have more interest in creating allies in the Member States. By way of conclusion, the chapter points to a number of tensions inherent in the OMC, and which partly explain the ambivalent handling of the processes on behalf of the two governments[1].

I. The OMC and Domestic Opportunity Structures

Knill and Lehmkuhl (1999) and Knill and Lenschow (2003) have identified three mechanisms by which European policy-making impacts on domestic policy: coercion, incentive structures, and learning. The use of coercion is best exemplified by the traditional Community method, which relies on supranational legislation. In the OMC, the hierarchical element is only present in the monitoring requirements, most evidently so in employment policy with its treaty-based monitoring procedure. In the absence of legal norms and mechanisms of enforcement, domestic change in the OMC is likely to follow from the two other mechanisms: by changes of domestic incentive structures, or rather opportunity structures, or by changes of beliefs among domestic actors, i.e. by learning effects.

While Knill and Lenschow (2003) emphasise peer pressure as the main incentive mechanism in the OMC, this chapter argues that there are also other ways of manipulating incentive structures at work: the consultation requirements, strategic use of the European Social Fund (ESF), Commission funding of transnational networks of local authorities or civil society actors are all examples of measures which may empower and give incentives to actors domestically. Likewise, there are other aspects of learning at work than the use of best practice models, which Knill and Lenschow (2003) mention. There is so far limited evidence of policy transfer following from the exchange of best practices in the OMC. However, this does not mean that there is no collective learning going on. Examples include joint problem identification and analysis in labour market policy as well as a self-reflective type of learning, where policy-makers are forced to review their own policy choices in the light of others as well as in the light of the common framework. Arguably, both peer pressure and learning from best practices are overemphasised in the literature on the OMC. Rather, actor-centred analyses of the use of openings provided by new opportunity

---

[1] The chapter is based on research conducted during 1999-2003, supported by the Swedish Research Council and the European Commission, through the support of the Govecor project under the 5th framework programme (www.govecor.org). I am grateful for the collaboration of Kenny Larsen, Herman Schmid and Åsa Vifell in data collection and analysis.

structures are highly relevant in order to understand the functioning of the OMC (see also Jacobsson and Vifell, 2005).

In this perspective, the OMC is likely to exert an impact mainly by changing domestic opportunity structures in various ways and by putting in motion various types of dynamics at national and sub-national level:

- it may function to shift power relations and resources;
- it may imply changed rules of the game and changes in institutional balance between different players;
- it may empower actors and provide them with an opportunity for voice and participation in public policy-making;
- it may foster new alliances between actors and strengthen them as pressure groups;
- it may foster new practices of co-operation, co-ordination and networking;
- it may provide fuel in national debate and provide "ammunition" to certain interests in their arguments for policy change and thus provide support for and justification of domestic reform (Radaelli, 2000);
- it may "infuse" the national policy debate with new knowledge and ideas, such as policy concepts, causal beliefs, links between policy areas and thus change the ways actors conceive of problems and solutions, a discursive type of impact (Jacobsson, 2004a and 2004b), that, again, may empower certain interests on expense of others;
- it may provide actors with a new arsenal of policy instruments.

In all these cases, the impact of the OMC will depend on the domestic conditions – present situations and needs as well as institutional and actor structure and resource distribution – which, by the way, is to a large extent true also of the domestic impact of the Community Method itself (Risse *et al.*, 2001). In particular, the impact will be dependent on the way domestic actors take on board EU guidelines and objectives. Since the EU norms are not formally binding, they must be accepted and effectively integrated into existing practices in order to have any impact (Jacobsson and Schmid, 2002). The fact that the OMC is so dependent on actor reception and action in the Member States means that the OMC may possibly strengthen the two-level game (cf. Moravcsik, 1998; Putnam, 1988), providing government with a gate-keeping function. However, this is not the whole story since there are, as we will see, examples of the Commission allying with sub-national actors and non-state actors in order to, if not bypass, at least put pressure on governments. Thus, even if national governments do play an instrumental role in the OMC, they are not able to act totally as gatekeepers in relation to EU and domestic levels (see Jacobsson and Vifell, 2005). Hence, we find a multi-level framework the most appropriate.

Reform pressure of course correlates with the degree of "fit" between the EU policy norms and the domestic policy (Risse *et al.*, 2001). Sweden and Denmark have the highest employment rates and among the lowest unemployment rates in the Union. They also have low poverty rates. How can the OMC improve the "best pupils in the class"? In fact, as will be shown, there are actors in the two countries that feel empowered by the OMCs, and others that question the marginal role granted to them in the production of the National Action Plans (NAPs). It is important not to conceptualise domestic action merely as adaptation to pressures from the EU level. EU-level processes may imply both opportunities and constraints for domestic actors, who may also work pro-actively to change EU-level opportunity structures. In order to do so, they must divert part of their attention and strategies towards the EU. Indeed, this has been the case both for the social partners, the networks of social NGOs, and local authorities in relation to the OMC.

II. Distinctive Features of the Swedish and Danish Systems

Sweden and Denmark have similar political systems but with some differences of possible relevance for understanding the operation of the OMC. Sweden has a system of collective decision-making, which means that the government is collectively responsible for all decisions that are made and the civil service is responsible to the government as a whole. Co-ordination between the ministries is therefore considered necessary, is well developed and also formalised. The executive agencies are organisationally separated from the ministries, and constitutionally, the agencies retain a certain level of independence from the political ministries. They are supposed to implement policies without ministerial interference, and ministries can only steer agencies by formal government approval documents. In contrast, Denmark has a system of ministerial rule. The minister is responsible for all actions within his department (Jørgensen, 2002), and agencies do not have the same independence as in Sweden. Co-ordination between ministries is well developed also in Denmark but is more informal. Municipalities and county authorities perform similar functions in the two countries. The municipalities have a dual role as units of local self-government *and* units of local state administration. In both countries municipalities have assumed increasing responsibilities for the welfare policies the last decades, such as primary education, child care, care for elderly, social assistance but also for supporting and activating those unemployed who are not insured in an unemployment fund. As it will be elaborated later, labour market policy is decentralised in Denmark, more so than in Sweden.

Social dialogue is institutionalised in both countries, but has remained stronger in Denmark. In Sweden, corporatism has become considerably weaker with the decision of the Swedish employers in the early 1990s to withdraw from all tripartite bodies and with the end of central collective bargaining. Wage formation has been decentralised in both countries in the 1980s and 1990s. Professional autonomy has been preferred to legislation in both countries but more so in Denmark, where collective agreements are strong and where many issues are handled by the social partner organisations independently. In Sweden, legislation has increased as a complement or replacement of collective bargaining since the 1970s, which was one of the reasons why the employers increasingly lost interest in tripartite collaboration, experiencing that the government took the trade unions' side. Today, again, the trade unions tend to emphasise that social partner agreements are preferable to state interference.

In relation to EU policy, Parliament has a stronger position in Denmark than in any other Member State. Before negotiating in the Council of Ministers, the Danish government is obliged to seek a mandate from the parliamentary EU Committee. Its Swedish counterpart, the parliamentary EU Advisory Committee, is, as the name indicates, merely advisory. However, since the OMC is not a legal process, both committees have an advisory role in the areas studied in this chapter.

III. The European Employment Strategy in Sweden and Denmark

A. *Production of the NAP*

In Sweden, responsibility for the National Action Plan for Employment (NAP/empl) is shared between the Ministry of Industry, Employment and Communications and the Ministry of Finance. Other ministries participate in the drafting, mainly by providing information. Co-ordination between ministries is well developed. However, notable in the case of the EES is that there is limited interaction between officials working with *domestic* labour market policy and those working on the NAP and participating in EU policy networks. Officials working on domestic labour market policy at the Ministry of Industry are not directly involved in the production of the NAP. Those civil servants who are actively involved in the EES-related work tend to think that it works very well, while most other civil servants consider the EES relatively unknown outside the core group of people (Statskontoret, 2002;

111

Jacobsson and Schmid, 2002). The production of the NAP has been a concern for a small number of officials at the two ministries, a highly centralised procedure. Knowledge about the NAP and the EES was not well disseminated in the labour market administration, neither at national, regional nor local levels. Realising this, the government in 2002 launched an information campaign on the EES addressed to the labour market administration at all levels, municipalities, and social partners. Information pamphlets were distributed and seminars held in various places across the country. There turned out to be a huge interest (Jacobsson and Vifell, 2003). A seminar on the EES organised by the Ministry of Industry, Employment and Communication in Spring 2004 gathered more than 100 participants and had two government ministers on the list of speakers. Dissemination of knowledge about the EES has accordingly improved over the years.

The links between ministry and state agencies in relation to the NAP work are not well developed, in contrast to the position in labour market policy generally. Two state agencies, the National Labour Market Board and the ESF Council, do provide background information for the NAP. However, interviewed officials there do not feel much involved or concerned with the NAP or the EES generally, and they are critical of the passive role assigned to them. A study for the five-year evaluation of the EES confirmed that the EES is not well known or perceived to have any particular impact on the state agencies, which do not feel bound to follow the strategy as long as the government does not explicitly instruct them to do so (Statskontoret, 2002). The government sees the NAP as its report to Brussels, and it has no function as a steering document or a plan of action in Sweden. In order to be operational, proposals would have to be taken the "ordinary way", first by budgetary bills and then by government approval documents directed to the state agencies. There are a few such examples where concerns of EES are reflected in the directions to the National Labour Market Board, such as the request that all unemployed should have an individual action plan worked out within three months, and that the Board must report what measures have been taken to reduce gender segregation in the labour market. The Board was also in 2003 given a special assignment to address integration of immigrants in the labour market by establishing methods for assisting their entrance into the labour force. Sweden has been repeatedly recommended by the Council to take measures to break the gender segregation and was in 2002 and 2003 also recommended to improve the labour market integration of immigrants.

Because the NAP is not mainstreamed into the domestic procedure for making and implementing labour market policy, it has turned out a rather "insular" process. The Parliament has no decision-making capacity in relation to the NAP, but is merely informed in the relevant committees. There is usually some, but not much, parliamentary debate about the NAP and about the recommendations directed to Sweden. The non-socialist opposition typically criticises the government for taking the employment policy guidelines as an *à la carte* menu, and not implementing sufficiently the recommended tax reductions.

In Denmark, responsibility for co-ordinating the NAP work rests with the Ministry of Employment's International Office. Other ministries concerned participate in the drafting process[2]. The Labour Market Authority is consulted, but does not play a central role. In Denmark, the NAP is also considered a government document. The Parliament is merely informed about the NAP in the parliamentary committees concerned and mostly after it is already produced. Since the NAP is not a legal act and the OMC not a legislative process, the government does not ask for a formal mandate from the EU committee but only for its opinion.

As in Sweden, the NAPs are not operational documents but reports on domestic policies for the EU level. A major reason is the perception that Danish policies are already ahead of the EU agenda, and thus that there is little pressure on Denmark to improve its policies. Also, the standardised template that NAPs have to follow makes it difficult to orient them towards the future and writing the NAPs easily takes on the character of "filling in" a European form. NAPs thus are mainly backward-looking documents (Jacobsson and Schmid, 2002; Rydbjerg Müller and Sand Kirk, 2003). It is also a problem that the NAPs are produced by officials in the international office with limited contact with those officials who are in touch with the daily Danish labour market policy and system (interview, Danish Association of Local Authorities, 2003).

B. Involvement of Local Actors

In Sweden, labour market policy is the responsibility of the state and its regional and local bodies. Municipalities, however, have a strong incentive to engage in employment policy since they are responsible for the well-being of their citizens, are dependent on tax revenues, and also carry the costs of social assistance for those who are not qualified for unemployment benefit. Municipalities are also engaged in education, social inclusion policy, regional development, i.e. in many of the areas

---

[2]   The new bourgeois government after taking office in 2001 set up the Ministry of Employment. Earlier the Ministry of Labour was in charge of the NAP. In Sweden a similar reform took place in 1999 when the Ministry of Industry, Employment, Communication replaced the earlier Labour Market Ministry.

addressed by the EES. In addition, municipalities employ a large number of people. However, the government has regarded it as difficult to involve the sub-national levels in the production of the NAP since it sees the latter as a presentation of governmental policies. During the first years there was virtually no input from the local and regional authorities into the NAP process, even though the Swedish Association of Local Authorities (SALA) and the Federation of Swedish County Councils (FCC) were represented at the national social partner consultation. However, as a response to a Commission communication (CEC, 2000) and a Council guideline on local development, the Swedish NAP for 2001 included a section where the Swedish Association of Local Authorities and the Federation of Swedish County Councils declared their interest in acting regionally and locally for employment. In 2001, the Swedish Association of Local Authorities together with six municipalities started a project to prepare Local Action Plans (LAPs) for employment, co-funded by the European Commission. This initiative was directly related to the Commission initiative on "acting locally for employment", even if, in Sweden, there were already municipalities working on developing local employment strategies, notably Malmö, independently of this particular initiative. In 2002, the Swedish Association of Local Authorities, the Federation of Swedish County Councils together with eight municipalities and local employment services started a new project, also with the aim of developing LAPs (using the same methodology as in the environmental Agenda 21 work), and also including awareness raising of the EES locally. This work was done within the transnational project Capacity, co-funded by the Commission. The Swedish Association of Local Authorities also offers other municipalities education about the EES and about local networking and partnerships as well as exchanges of experiences with other municipalities. Moreover, one Swedish county (*Östergötland*) in 2003 started a EU-funded project aiming at developing local employment strategies in all its thirteen municipalities. In contrast to the NAPs, the LAPs are intended to be tangible action plans, i.e. operational documents which should be followed up and results evaluated (SALA, 2001). The EES message on the need for improved co-ordination and collaboration between policies and agents corresponds well to the perceived need locally. The ESF projects fill the same function: to foster co-operation and co-ordination between local state agencies (like public employment services), municipalities, social partners and other non-state actors, like training institutions and enterprises, that is to break down traditional boundaries between organisational domains.

There are accordingly local initiatives developing in relation to the EES in Sweden, mostly initiated by the Swedish Association of Local Authorities and individual municipalities. However, these initiatives have not been strategically related to the NAP, and the actors involved feel little support for and openness to dialogue from the national political level. The government officials working on the NAP have not considered involving local actors more strategically or making use of their experiences (interview, Ministry of Industry, 2002). Labour market policy is seen first and foremost as a national responsibility and local actors as implementers of national policy. The Swedish Association of Local Authorities (SALA, 2001) has pleaded for more of a bottom-up perspective. The EES has so far mainly developed as a superficial and centralised process *in parallel* to the existing structures, instead of linking up systematically with the latter locally and regionally, such as the structures developed in relation to the European Social Fund projects. Here partnerships and broader co-operation frameworks, including civil society actors, are already developed.

In Denmark, local and regional actors play an important role in labour market policy, and this has been further strengthened in the 1990s by the introduction of a new steering system in labour market policy. Fourteen corporatist bodies, the Regional Labour Market Councils (RARs), were set up, each consisting of the social partners and representatives of the county and municipalities. The public employment service (PES) services the board, which has decision-making authority, and it also functions as the executor of the policy (Jørgensen, 2002: 181). The idea is that implementation of labour market policy requires co-ordination with regional enterprises, counties, municipalities, unemployment offices, and education institutions. Regional strategies based on regional needs are thus worked out, and the RARs have certain autonomy in forming their strategies. The RARs are obliged by a contract with the national Labour Market Authority to provide a regional planning document specifying objectives, action guidelines, output requirements and bi-annual progress reports, which reflect regional needs and priorities. The Labour Market Authority provides economic resources according to agreed activity specifications and is responsible for co-ordinating the fourteen regions in a national perspective (Jacobsson and Schmid, 2002). In turn, 150 local co-ordination committees, also corporatist, are tied to the RARs. To our knowledge, there is no co-ordination between the NAP and the work of the RARs. Local employment co-operation and strategies are developed in a large number of Danish municipalities (www.kl.dk), mostly independently from the EES. However, the Danish Association of Local Authorities together with six municipalities, supported by the Commission, in 2001 developed LAPs as part of the implementation of the EES (LGDK, 2001). As in Sweden, collaboration across organisational and administrative boundaries is considered necessary locally.

The Danish Association of Local Authorities and the Association of County Authorities participate in the social partner consultation in relation to the NAP. According to a representative of the Danish Association of Local Authorities, the important employment and labour market policy work conducted by municipalities has not been reflected in the Danish NAPs so far. However, she believes that this may be improved with the new Ministry of Employment which has replaced the former Ministry of Labour, which was too much focussed on the state system at expense of other actors. The employment related work of the municipalities was previously the responsibility of the Social Ministry but has now moved to the new Ministry of Employment. This official feels that the staffs with a background at the Social Ministry are more open to the role of other actors and a more integrated view of employment policy than the staffs at the previous Ministry of Labour (interview, 2003).

C. Social Partner Involvement

Sweden has traditionally had a strong social partner involvement in labour market policy-making but this was considerably weakened in the 1990s. In 1991, the employers unilaterally decided to withdraw from all tripartite bodies and the bourgeois government in 1992 consequently decided to dissolve interest representation in the boards of the state agencies. Employers still participate in advisory but no longer in decision-making bodies.

A formal social partner consultation on EU-related issues takes place about once a month at the Ministry of Industry, Employment and Communications[3]. Sometimes a working group on the NAP meets between these meetings, and the social partners can also submit their opinions unilaterally. The government is concerned to integrate the social partners in the NAP work, and they have been invited to produce the text for the NAP on the guidelines directed to them. This they have done on those issues on which they can agree since the NAP 2000. In those parts both the government and the social partners stand behind the NAP.

The social partners are well aware of the EES and active at the level of their peak organisations. The sectoral organisations are much less active and interested. A study has shown that also within the peak organisations knowledge about the strategy is limited to the persons

---

[3]   The social partners participating are the three main trade union confederations; the Confederation of Swedish Enterprise representing private sector employers; and the Swedish Agency for Government Employers, the Swedish Association of Local Authorities, and the Federation of County Councils representing public sector employers.

directly involved and that the EES-related work is not integrated with the work on "national" issues (Statskontoret, 2002). Still, the three trade union confederations are highly supportive of the EES and are concerned to be involved. The employers also participate actively. The employers' association refers to the EU policy guidelines to support its plea for lower taxes, and criticises the government for failing to respond enough to this recommendation. The trade unions also make references to the EES to support their claims, but for them, the main value of the NAP procedure is that it has brought the employers back to a joint dialogue, after having left the tripartite decision-making bodies. The NAP work has meant new dynamics in social partner participation in Sweden. However, there has been a certain fatigue experienced by of the social partners over the last few years, compared to first NAP cycles. Both trade union and employer representatives have expressed that their willingness to continue to participate is a function of what they gain from it. Especially on the employers' side there is doubt about the real importance and impact of the EES. They experience the consultation as being more about sharing information than as a real solicitation of their views or negotiation. Nor does the Swedish Association of Local Authorities find the social partner consultation very rewarding and sometimes does not bother to take part. As long as the NAP is not an action plan, the representatives have to consider whether to spend resources on it or not. They also experience reluctance on the part of the government to let others into the EES process, manifested among other things in the lack of interest in the LAP projects (interview, 2003).

No NGOs have been invited to the NAP consultation but only the social partners, in contrast to the ESF partnerships where NGO representatives also participate. (The reason this type of wider partnership developed there was because the ESF regulation required it). In 2002, the Ministry of Industry did receive comments during the production of the NAP from a disability organisation. A network of NGOs established in December 2000 also expressed interest in participating. Both the ministry and the social partners refused to open up the proceedings to broader participation, even if they were supportive of receiving input from the NGOs. They already have an institutionalised co-operation in labour market policy, and moreover the social partners are considered – and consider themselves – precisely *partners* and not just any participant. The trade unions also tend to question the representativeness of the NGOs, arguing that they only represent themselves, while the trade union, besides having a very high degree of membership (about 85%), also have internal democratic structures for representation. The trade union tend to see themselves as representatives of all the relevant interests in labour market policy, while the NGOs argue that the trade unions fail to represent people outside of, and sometimes far from, the labour market, like the chronically ill, immigrants or disabled people, who have difficulties in entering the labour market, or homeless people. While the social partner consultation has not yet been opened up to the NGOs, in 2003, the Ministry of Industry, Employment and Communications invited twelve representatives from civil society to a dialogue on employment policy (see also below). That dialogue has since continued.

In Denmark, there is a well-developed tripartite system, which satisfies the social partner participation in regular labour market policy-making, and is developed as well as at central, regional and local levels. In relation to the NAP, social partners are consulted through the institutionalised social dialogue and there is also a more informal work group on the NAP. The contributions of the social partners are since 2001 attached to the NAP at full length[4]. The social partners are generally satisfied with their input to the NAP (EIRO, 2002), even though some consider the NAP a backward looking document and prefer to be involved in formation of the national employment strategy and the implementation of the NAP (Rydbjerg Müller and Sand Kirk, 2003). A representative of the Danish Association of Local Authorities expresses that her organisation has come in too late when the NAP has already been more or less finalised (interview, 2003). Like its Swedish counterpart, the Danish Association of Local Authorities thinks that it is only worth devoting resources to the NAP work if it is possible to have an impact, which has not really been the case so far.

As in Sweden, there is limited interest in the EES within the social partner organisations except for the peak level experts. As in Sweden, the Danish employers refer to the guidelines to support their demands, for instance for reduced indirect labour costs. The Danish Confederation of Trade Unions does not make many references to the EU guidelines to support their demands since Denmark already largely fulfils them. However, they consider the guidelines important for other Member States, and improving their policies is considered a Danish interest due to the risk of spillovers (Rydbjerg Müller and Sand Kirk, 2003). NGOs do not participate in the production of the NAP on employment, with the exception of occasional inputs by the Danish Council of Organisations of Disabled People. As in Sweden, the social partners argue that not everyone should be consulted but only those actors who have a role to play in employment policy (interviews, Danish Association of Local

---

4 The social partners consulted are the Danish Employers' Confederation and the Danish Confederation of Employers' Association in Agriculture representing private sector employers; the National Association of Local Authorities in Denmark, the Association of County Authorities and the State Employers' Authority representing public sector employers, and the main trade union confederations, the largest of which is the Trade Union Congress.

Authorities and the Association of County Authorities, 2003). The social partnership is even more "cemented" in Denmark, and during the revision of the EES, the Danish government outspokenly resisted a greater involvement of civil society actors in the EES, as proposed by the Commission. NGOs are perceived as an unpredictable factor in a stable and well-functioning social partnership.

D. Policy Impact of the EES in Sweden and Denmark

The employment guidelines are very much in line with the Swedish Social Democratic government's policy. That is particularly true of the guidelines related to employability, adaptability, and equal opportunities, but also of most of the guidelines related to entrepreneurship. The guidelines on decreased taxation, review of tax and benefit systems, and revised labour market regulation are potentially controversial, but the government accepts the direction of the guidelines in principle. The non-socialist opposition also supports the general orientation of the guidelines, but wishes to see better implementation of the recommendations on reduced taxation and generally improved conditions for enterprising. To the extent the government only pays lip service to the common guidelines, the opposition considers the EU employment co-operation as less relevant. It has also criticised the government for trying to avoid having to reconsider its policy choices, since the government has argued that the total tax burden is not a relevant measure and that the marginal effects rather ought to be in focus. The trade unions' view is also that indirect taxation is not the problem but rather the marginal effects of direct (income) taxation. The government, thus, questions how the EU measures fiscal pressure.

The impact of the guidelines and recommendations in terms of policy decisions is difficult to assess with certainty since it is difficult to establish the causal connections. Policy decisions may have different origins and rationales. Swedish labour market policy is largely in line with, yet preceded, the EES. In some cases, Sweden has more ambitious goals than the EU. Sweden has a more ambitious definition of long-term unemployed (six months for adults and 100 days for young people), and the goal that 80% of the population aged 20-64 shall be in regular employment by 2004. The target with respect for social justice is to halve welfare dependency between 1999 and 2004[5]. It would still be possible for the government to include in the NAP more ambitious

---

[5] Sweden has used quantitative targets for some time already and considers them useful tools. In 1996, the government set itself the objective to halve the open unemployment to 4% during 2000 which was reached. The government decided in 1997 on a medium-target for public finances: the budget surplus should amount to an average of 2% of GDP seen over the business cycle. This has been reached and followed.

targets for reduced unemployment in particular areas, such as sparsely populated areas in the North of Sweden or suburbs with high levels of unemployment, or for particular groups, such as immigrants or disabled persons, who are less well-off at present. This has not been done.

Sweden has been recurrently recommended by the EU to decrease taxation on labour, particularly for low and middle-income earners, and to review tax and benefit systems to improve job incentives. The position of the government is that taxation is an issue of national competence. It is not considered to be in line with the subsidiarity principle to have European goals for the level of taxation. So far, the recommendations on tax reductions on labour have been acceptable, but not a specific target for them, a recommendation issued in 2001 to which the government did not respond. Indeed, there is an increased willingness on behalf of the government to consider tax reductions, even if the employers and the non-socialist opposition think it is not sufficient. In 2001, what the government sees as a major tax reform was initiated. Tax reductions have been implemented with special emphasis on low and medium wage earners (mainly achieved by compensating for individual contributions used to finance earnings-related and supplementary pensions and by raising the limit for national tax). Further tax cuts were launched in 2002, including lowered taxation on income, on property, on capital, and reduced VAT on books. The government's view is that public finances then allowed for tax reductions, and that these would have come about also without the EU guidelines (Junestav, 2002). Still, the EU recommendations put pressure on Sweden to move in the direction of lower labour taxation. EU policy-making, in combination with an internationalised economy generally, probably has some impact on taxation in Sweden. Sweden is moving in the same direction as others, but slowly and only to the extent that state finances allow for it, and, thus, domestic factors are favourable.

In response to the recommendation to review the tax and benefit systems, the government refers to a reform of the unemployment insurance in 2001 (participation in active labour market measures no longer qualifies for a new benefit period and there will be stronger pressure on unemployed to commute, move, or change profession in order to get a job). Incentives to take up work have also been strengthened by the tax reform, the pension reform (according to which pensions are based on a person's total life earnings) and a maximum fee for child care, and most recently, by lowering the levels of benefit in the sick insurance. While these measures are well in line with the EU recommendations, it is difficult to sustain that they are there *because of* these recommendations rather than the domestic situation. In 2003, Sweden was recommended not only to proceed with the tax reform, but also to take measures to try to reduce the high number of persons on sick leave, both by improving work situations and by strengthening job incentives. This is currently one of the most burning and difficult questions facing the government.

Sweden has repeatedly been recommended to try to break the gender segregation in the labour market. The National Labour Market Board has been instructed by the government to do so, which has resulted in special funding for projects aiming to break gender segregation, and also in attempts to reduce part-time unemployment through collaboration with the employers. In 2002, Sweden was recommended to improve measures to break long-term unemployment, particularly in the case of ethnic minorities, and the National Labour Market Board in 2003 received a special assignment on this topic. These are examples of government action in direct response to Council recommendations, even if there had also been work to reduce gender and ethnic segregation before. On the other hand, these are not very demanding or substantive actions. By giving instructions to the Labor Market Board to take action, the government can show the EU that it is responding to the recommendations. However, gender and ethnic segregation remains a problem, and is not easily solved by a number of targeted projects. In 2003, the Council recommendation on increased participation of immigrants was maintained while the one on gender segregation was lifted.

Due to the economic downturn, the government announced in autumn 2003 that it would have to give up the goal of having 80% of the population in regular employment by 2004 (Regeringskansliet, 2003). The level of open unemployment was also forecasted to be higher than the target of 4%. The government also feared that it would have to give up the objective to halve the number of people on welfare dependence. The budget bill also announced that the amount of money to be spent on active labour market policy measures would *decrease*, except for the money spent on guidance at Public Employment Services. The Trade Union Confederation (LO) has criticised the decision to, as it saw it, spend more money on passive support and reduce the amount spent on active support (news report, *Rapport*, 29 September 2003). The Labour Market Board has been criticised for inefficient programmes, which may be one explanation. Still, this decision was not altogether in line with the EES. Yet the strengthening of work incentives is, and shows that the EES is somewhat janus-faced in terms of its ideological content. However, later in autumn 2003, the government announced that it will give the Labour Market Board more money for training measures, as an attempt to reduce the number of people in open unemployment.

Most policy actors involved – civil servants at ministry and agency levels as well as the social partners – have the impression that the EES has not had any substantial impact on Swedish policy. What has happened would have happened also without the EES. This does not mean that they consider the EES useless. It has contributed to new dynamics in social partner dialogue, improvement of policy integration and a more comprehensive perspective on employment policy, and better co-ordination between policy areas within their own organisations. It is also considered important to have Swedish policy evaluated annually and shortcomings identified (Statskontoret, 2002). There is an interest in what others have to offer, such as information of other policy choices and the exchanges of best practice, even if, in practice, policy actors have limited time to review other countries' NAPs in a systematic way. Interviewed policy actors tend to believe that the exchange of best practice and the peer review is valuable and may have an impact in a longer perspective.

Denmark implemented a number of important labour market reforms in the 1990s in response to high long-term unemployment and the recognition of unemployment as structural in character. Activation was strengthened by tightened eligibility criteria and by connecting the right to benefits to a duty to participate in active labour market measures. Workfare principles were introduced, even if in the Danish type of acti-vation policy, education and training are at least as important as the dis-ciplinary elements. Interventions were also tailored to individual needs and personal action plans for the unemployed introduced (Jørgensen, 2002). While very much in line with the EES, Danish labour market policy change preceded the EES and the implementation of the strategy has accordingly not led to any significant shift in Danish policies (SFI, 2002). Rather, Danish policy actors feel that Danish policy has been exported to the EU and that Denmark is ahead of other countries.

One exception where Danish policy is not completely in line with the EU guidelines is the high level of unemployment benefits and the high income tax, which is not seen to comply with the objective to increase incentives to work. (While eligibility criteria were tightened in the 1990s, Denmark chose to retain a high level of benefit.) Like Sweden, Denmark has repeatedly been recommended to increase work incen-tives, reduce taxation on labour, and reduce gender segregation. All these recommendations have been responded to but not always along the lines suggested by the Commission, i.e. "work incentives" recommenda-tions were responded to by the tightening of eligibility criteria for unemployment benefit but not by any general changes in the level of benefit. Special target groups for increased work incentives have been families with children, especially lone parents, and older workers, to avoid early retirement. There has been an increased focus on the need to increase the participation rates of specific groups, including gender, age and immigrants in the NAPs from 2001 onwards. The five-year evaluation concluded that changes in the Danish tax system had not been generally directed towards increasing work incentives, as required by the EES (SFI, 2002). The bourgeois government replacing the former Social Democratic one in autumn 2001 expressed a greater willingness to make tax reductions, and also to strengthen financial incentives in terms of benefits/allowances (NAP, 2003). The government's medium-term economic strategy includes a tax freeze and reduction of taxes on earned income. The political programme of the new government also includes creating more flexible jobs.

The Danish government, like its Swedish counterparts, is concerned to make a good showing in international comparisons. It tries actively to avoid recommendations since they are perceived as political sanctions and can be used against the government by the domestic opposition (Rydbjerg Müller and Sand Kirk, 2003). The recommendation on gender segregation was lifted in 2001, after government action. Equal opportunities acts have been changed several times since 1997, in compliance with EU directives or recommendations (e.g. the legislation of gender mainstreaming in 2000 and the Equal Wages Act in 2001). This is one example where the EES has clearly had an impact (official quoted in Rydbjerg Müller and Sand Kirk, 2003: 105). The recommendation was sensitive since it went against Denmark's self-perception of as a society with a high level of gender equality. Yet, the five-year evaluation concluded that the gender perspective is still to a great extent missing in general labour market policy in Denmark (SFI, 2002). In 2002 and 2003, Denmark was also given a recommendation to strengthen the labour market integration of immigrants, a group with considerably lower participation rates than the average. The bourgeois government, being dependent on the populist and xenophobic Danish People's Party, is notorious for its restrictive attitude to immigrants, and the EU recommendation in that perspective has a symbolic as well as substantive dimension. The NAP for 2003 committed the government to the objective that "persons with a different ethnic background than Danish should be integrated so that they will participate in working and social life on an equal footing with the rest of the population", and devised a new integration strategy to this end. In 2002, a four-party agreement between the government, the social partners, and the municipal parties laid down a new integration policy, and in 2003, the government also set up a ministerial group on better integration.

It is hard to see any major practical implications of the EU guidelines for the development of Danish employment policy, but at least the EES has supported the work to avoid early retirement and improve labour market integration of special groups. As in Sweden, the actors involved, both government actors and social partners support the EES. They believe that the EES has been instrumental in fostering a common European approach to employment and social policy, and that the method brings a potential in learning from others. Yet, there are also sceptical voices, claiming that the experiences from the Peer Review Programme have only been used to a limited extent, and that there is more window-dressing and -shopping than learning from best practices (quoted in Rydbjerg Müller and Sand Kirk, 2003). The five-year evaluation nonetheless concluded that the EES serves as a source of inspiration for policy developments in Denmark and that a number of precise targets and deadlines have entered Danish policy through the NAPs (SFI, 2002).

IV. The Social Inclusion OMC in Sweden and Denmark

In Sweden, the Ministry for Social Affairs is responsible for the production of the NAP for social inclusion (NAP/incl). Other ministries are consulted as well as state agencies concerned, such as the National Board of Health and Welfare. The social partners are involved through their regular consultation, which meets at the Ministry for Social Affairs about every second month. But the social partners give priority to the NAP/empl. However, interestingly, a network of NGOs was mobilised in 2000 in response to the new OMC process. It is a loose network, an arena for dialogue rather than a formal organisation, consisting of more than forty groups, including representatives of churches, the social economy and disability organisations, and mobilised for the purpose of influencing the NAP/incl. It meets about every other month and also organises seminars on related topics.

The network was consulted in the NAP work in 2001. This first year, consultation was mainly a question of being informed before and after the NAP, and could not influence the plan, which was merely a report of measures already taken and not what the network considers as an action plan. Instead, it produced its own alternative action plan (interview, NGO representative, 2002). At the ministry, the civil servants stress that the NAP is the government's plan and that NGOs cannot expect to influence its content. In the ministry's view, action plans in response to the EU processes, i.e. the NAPs, by necessity acquire a different status than action plans in Sweden usually, since the latter are preceded by much more throughout preparation and are passed the "ordinary way", i.e. by public investigations and then government bills which provide funding. In the NAP/incl 2003, it is explicitly stated and explained that the plan is not guiding welfare policy development in Sweden.

Anticipating the second NAP process in 2003, the NGO network already sent in autumn 2002 proposals to the Ministry of Social Affairs in order to try to influence the Council decision on EU objectives. The dialogue between the ministry and the network has improved, and they also have regular meetings outside the formal social partner consultation. The network has been invited to submit its own positions in an appendix to the NAP. In its comment to the NAP 2003, the network stated its support for the OMC but argued that a clearer framework for consultation is needed actively to engage public authorities and voluntary organisations both in the shaping and the implementation of the action plan at both local and national levels. It also pleaded for a user and bottom-up perspective and for cross-sectoral co-ordination and a holistic policy perspective. The network, but also the Social Affairs ministry, stresses the importance of a local dimension for the OMC. The municipalities of Stockholm, Gothenburgh and Malmö are all preparing local action plans and strategies for employment and social inclusion, in the context of the European network EUROCITIES. The three municipalities provided an appendix to the NAP 2003, where they pleaded for cross-sectoral co-operation and partnership and for a bottom-up perspective. They committed themselves to diffusing knowledge about the OMC and to identifying models for analysis of needs, for identification of best practice, and for documentation of good working method and tools.

The good working relations between the local actors and civil society actors and the social ministry can partly be explained by the fact that the ministry needs allies in relation to other ministries and policy actors. Acting through the NGOs is also an indirect way for the ministry to try to influence and encourage the municipalities, which the state cannot steer directly, in their work on social inclusion. As mentioned above, the network has also requested to participate in the consultation at the Ministry of Industry about the NAP/empl, since it views the two NAPs as interrelated – participation in the labour market is the best way to achieve social inclusion. It has been determined to "break the monopoly" of the social partners (e-mail communication, 2002). Both the ministry and the social partners have refused to accept broader participation in their institutionalised consultation. However, in autumn 2003 the Ministry of Industry had a first meeting with a delegation of NGOs precisely on labour market policy, and the dialogue has continued. Since 2003, the chairperson of the Employment Committee is a Swede. This has put additional pressure on the Swedish government to live up to the "good governance" requirement of the reformed EES. In any case, the social NGOs saw this meeting as something of a "break-through".

Compared to the 2001 NAP/incl, the 2003 Plan speaks much more about the need for partnership. Yet, the government still sees the NAP as the government's responsibility. Parliament is informed through the committees concerned, but plays no active role. The network of NGOs has proposed that Parliament address the issue of guidelines for the NAP. The network has also tried to influence the content of the NAP, stressing the importance of empowerment, the role of the social economy, and the importance of integrating the NAPs on social inclusion and employment. The network thus wants to mainstream the NAP into the regular policy procedure. It has also contacted the relevant parliamentary committees as well as individual members of Parliament, and it also has direct contact with the minister responsible for social inclusion.

It is still too early to see any direct policy impact of the OMC social inclusion in Sweden. Sweden is addressing problems in its traditional way, through a welfare policy based on the principles of universalism, individualism, and income support in times of labour market interruptions, tied to eligibility criteria. High participation rates and low unemployment rates remain corner stones of welfare policy (Halleröd, 2003). As mentioned, the Swedish government has set itself the target to halve the number of welfare-dependent people and to increase the employment rate to 80% by 2004. The 2003 NAP also listed a number of other targets, such as to halve the number of sick-leave days by 2008; to reduce the proportion of people with below-median incomes; to lower the number of children leaving school without completing their secondary education; and to increase the number of drug addicts who undergo treatment. According to the European Commission, Sweden could do more, for instance to achieve better integration of immigrants, and other groups at risk of social exclusion. The network of NGOs certainly believes that much remains to be done to achieve social inclusion.

Arguably, the EU policy on social inclusion is formulated in a selective manner, with special policies for special groups, which is not evidently compatible with the universalist principles of the Swedish welfare state (Halleröd, 2003). Social exclusion has not been a policy concept used in Sweden, and I think it is fair to say that the policy discourse on social exclusion/inclusion has been introduced in there through the EU. The problems of social segregation and marginalisation have in any case been put high on the agenda since the late 1990s, and there are some indications of new strategies. One example is the development of special urban policies for the metropolitan areas, aiming at breaking down social and ethnic segregation in these areas. This is implemented by local development agreements between the government and local authorities. The discourse on social inclusion in combination with the OMC's focus on the most vulnerable groups and the mobilisation of all relevant actors has empowered the social NGOs, and given them a role in policy-making. So far this is the clearest example of impact of the social inclusion OMC. There is more actor dynamism in the social inclusion process than in the EES, and also more interest from the ministry in what local actors may contribute.

The Swedish government is somewhat hesitant about the social protection co-ordination processes. When the procedure started in 1999, civil servants at the Ministry of Social Affairs were happy to be included in an EU-level process. They felt that they had not been effectively integrated in the EES, and that social issues had not been placed on an equal footing with economic and employment policy. With the new co-operation procedure, the Social Ministry would gain a better position vis-à-vis the other ministries, as well as a new platform for "its issues" (interviews, 2000). Social issues would be put on the EU agenda and treated in their own right – not being reduced to financial concerns. At the same time, the Swedish government has had certain reservations about a co-operation procedure in social policy, emphasising the subsidiarity principle. The government supports exchange of information and experiences but stresses that the OMCs must take different shapes in different areas. It does not want to see common guidelines and recommendations in the fields of social protection or health care and care for the elderly (interviews, Ministry of Social Affairs, 2002). The government's view is that there is not a Treaty base for as far-reaching co-ordination in the field of social protection as in the field of employment, and that the co-operation must not lead to a process that would give the Community level influence over, for instance, national pension policy. Also sources in the Commission confirm that Sweden is one of the most reluctant Member States when it comes to an OMC process in social protection since it fears harmonisation (colleague's interview, 2002). The tension in the OMC between exchange of good practices and compliance with a common strategy became clear in 2001 when the Commission in its Draft Joint Report on social inclusion had made a ranking between countries according to how well the NAPs corresponded to the common objectives. The Member States protested and in the final Joint report there was no such ranking. The Commission position remains that the NAPs have to be put in relation to one another and to a common approach if the process is to be meaningful (Syrén, 2002). Sweden was among the countries objecting strongly to such comparative ranking of Member State policy[6]. Still, Sweden considers the exchange of best practices an important element and thinks that the social co-ordination

---

[6] Sweden was not among the highest ranked in the Commission proposal. The Commission wanted the NAPs to be something more than the sum of what is being done in any case. The Swedish NAP did not contain such a strategic and long-term perspective. The Swedish view was that a ranking of countries would be to compare "pears and apples", countries with very different starting positions (colleague's interviews, 2002).

process contributes to a better balance between economic, employment, and social policy. However, the process is moving too fast (interview, Ministry of Social Affairs, 2002). Also the Swedish Parliament is hesitant about the social co-ordination processes and where they may lead.

In Denmark, the NAP/incl is produced by the Social Ministry, with all ministries being invited to submit contributions. Social partners and NGOs are consulted. Compared with the first NAP in 2001, which was produced with little involvement and public awareness, the ministry has in the second round been concerned to involve actors and thus to respond to this EU objective. In the NAP process 2003, a large number of actors, including social NGOs, the Copenhagen municipality, and the social partners, were invited to a large seminar to initiate the NAP work. The aim was to invite contributions, such as examples of "good practices", but also to make the NAP better known. Two more meetings were later held, with an opportunity for the parties to submit comments on a first and second draft of the NAP (interviews, Social Ministry, 2003). Moreover, NGOs are consulted on the draft NAP through a formal contact committee for social voluntary work at the Social Affairs ministry, which has existed since the early 1980s. An interviewed member of this contact committee has the impression that the NAP/incl is so far a fairly unknown document among NGOs but that the ministry is truly concerned to involve them in the process. Interviewed representatives of the Danish Association of Local Authorities and a disability organisation clearly regard the NAP/incl process as more open and participatory than the NAP/empl (interviews, 2003). As mentioned, the Danish government actively resisted a stronger role for civil society actors other than the social partners in the revised EES. It is, thus, much more open to the role of social NGOs in social policy than in labour market policy, where actor relations have long been highly institutionalised.

In Denmark, too, the NAP is regarded as the government's document and it is a report on current policies rather than a plan of action. There is typically no debate in Parliament on the NAP but Parliament is informed about it through the specialised committees and the EU committee.

As in the case of employment policy, the Danish government sees itself as a leading country in social inclusion policy, and has actively tried to influence the EU objectives. There are so far no obvious examples of the OMC process having introduced new policy elements in Denmark. Danish policy is considered by policy actors to be well in line with the EU objectives. Still, with the NAP an overall picture of measures directed to weak and exposed groups is produced for the first time. The NAP thus systematises the existing policy, which is considered important by several interviewees.

The Danish government, the new one as well as the former one, is supportive of the OMC. However, like the Swedish government, it considers social policy a matter of national competence and does not want to see as detailed a process as the EES, and it does not accept recommendations or European targets. However, the government supports setting of national targets, an innovation which was introduced for the second NAP round, and several interviewees believe that the NAP process is likely to contribute to the development of Danish anti-poverty targets. Targets set in the 2003 NAP/incl include increasing the number of treatment places and shelters for drug users; substantially reducing the number of heavy alcohol abusers; taking special initiatives aimed at the mentally ill; and making sure that people of non-Danish ethnic background are integrated and able to participate in the labour market and social life on par with the rest of the population.

In Denmark as in Sweden, participation in the labour market is seen as the best way to avoid social exclusion. However, activation in relation to social policy is much more emphasised in Denmark than in Sweden. In the Danish NAP/incl in 2001 as well as 2003, the notion of an "inclusive labour market" is a key concept, and another important notion is that of "active social policy". In the 2001 NAP/incl the overall objective of active social policy was defined as: to enable individuals to support themselves by taking responsibility for and being in charge of their own lives. Thus, the active and personalised approach is shared both by the former and the present Danish governments. Yet, the social policy agenda of the bourgeois government which took office in autumn 2001 implied some novelties in relation to the previous government. For instance, an explicit objective was to help the weakest and the most marginalised members of society, such as homeless, mentally ill, and drug abusers, through the reform programme "Our Collective Responsibility", and to increase the involvement of voluntary organisations. A Council for Socially Disadvantaged People was established in 2002 to monitor policy development.

Like in Sweden, one of the challenges identified by the Commission, but also by the government, is the integration of immigrants. The unemployment rate for immigrants and their descendents is double as high as for the general population (11.5% compared to 5.2% in 2001). A stronger focus on the labour market participation of ethnic minorities can be seen in recent years (Non-Government Expert Report on Social Inclusion in Denmark, 2003). The new Danish government has also, in various ways, employed stricter regulations in asylum policy.

V. Domestic Uses of the OMC

As pointed out at the beginning of this chapter, the OMC may operate to change domestic opportunity structures in various ways. This
section will summarise the findings on the domestic uses of the OMC in
Sweden and Denmark.

Both countries' governments have an ambiguous attitude to the
OMC. In principle, they are highly supportive of the processes, as are
most other domestic policy actors. At the same time, the governments
are concerned to stay in control of the processes. In the Employment
Strategy, they have taken a defensive attitude in relation to other actors,
except for the social partners. In both countries, there is a weak institutional and political "anchorage" of the EES. It is not well integrated into
the national structures for making and implementing policies – and less
so than other EU-related work. The EES is seen as a transgovernmental
process and a governmental responsibility. NAPs are not used as strategic tools for domestic policy-making but are reports to the EU. Except
for the social partners, other actors are not strategically integrated, but
involved on an *ad hoc* basis for the purpose of contributing information
for the NAP. Parliamentary bodies are not integrated for the purpose of
decision-making. However, there are indications of change, especially in
Sweden where there are actors demanding participation and wanting to
see the EES moving in a more participatory and bottom-up direction,
and where the government launched an information campaign on the
EES after the five-year evaluation had revealed that it was not well-
known even within the labour market administration.

Both countries have well-developed systems for policy-making in
the employment and labour market field, and the OMC is not easily
integrated here. For instance, to fit the system, the NAP has to be considered as a government report rather than a policy-guiding document.
In Sweden, the EES has stimulated social dialogue by bringing employers back into dialogue, while in Denmark the EES has added little to the
existing social partnership. In both countries, governments and social
partners alike have tried to resist a wider involvement of civil society
actors in the EES, which would break with the traditional dominance of
unions and employers in this field.

However, the fact that knowledge about the EES is not well spread in
the labour market policy administration does not mean that it has had no
influence. In Sweden, the introduction of individual activation action
plans can be traced back to the EES. In both countries, the EES has
contributed to increased attention to gender segregation, the labour
market situation of immigrants, and the increased work incentives. The
terminology of the EES, such as the use of the concept of employability,

has also spilled over into domestic policy discourses. Still, the EES has not led to any major policy shifts in the two countries.

The EES adds no extra resources apart from the ESF. However small in the context of total labour market policy investment in Sweden and Denmark, the ESF is an important source of funding for local actors, especially municipalities, and allows for some experimental projects. However, in neither country there is much sign of the good experiences of the ESF projects having a major impact on the labour market policy at large. Yet the ESF projects have fostered co-operation and partnerships at local level between various types of actors. Apart from the ESF, there is little financial incentive to co-operation in the case of the EES. However, national associations of local authorities and a number of municipalities in both countries have responded positively to the Commission campaign launched in 2000 on "acting locally for employment", with the accompanying possibility to apply for funding for developing LAPs. The Commission has also supported transnational networking among local actors and civil society actors in relation to the EES and OMC social inclusion. For the Commission, allying with local actors in the Member States has been a way both to improve the implementation of the EES and increase its legitimacy. Engaging other actors, including civil society actors, has also been a way of putting pressure on the governments to live up to the commitments in the common guidelines and objectives. The OMC processes have spurred some local and regional dynamics, despite the lack of interest on behalf of the government.

In contrast to the EES, in social inclusion there is an interest in both countries from the ministries' side in developing the local dimension and encouraging participation and contribution of other actors. The social ministries have greater need of such external support for their policy priorities in relation to other ministries and interests. Officials at the Ministry of Social Affairs in Sweden feel empowered in relation to the other ministries by the EU social co-ordination processes. The OMC social inclusion has also provided NGOs with a legitimate claim to "voice" in social policy-making. This mobilisation of actors in relation to the social co-ordination process seems the most important achievement of the OMC in both countries so far. In Sweden, the social NGOs have also used the opportunity to try to influence labour market policy. The NGO engagement in labour market policy in Sweden is one example of the OMC's contributing to destabilising equilibria and reconfiguring policy networks (see chapter by Trubek and Trubek in this volume). Possibly, this may also open the way for new policy thinking.

At ministerial level, the OMC has implied improved co-ordination. Officials in both countries believe that the OMC has contributed to improved integration of policies, a view shared by other policy actors. For instance, according to the Swedish trade union confederations, the EES has contributed to improve national employment policy in three respects: 1) by covering a broader field of political issues than mere labour market policy; 2) by strengthening the involvement of social partners; 3) by the benchmarking procedure forcing Swedish actors to rethink and improve some of their own measures (joint answer to the ETUC questionnaire, 2001). Officials in both countries support the OMC. They consider the exchange of best practice and the peer review valuable and believe it may have an impact in a longer perspective, even if they cannot point to any particular examples of this kind of learning so far and despite not having time to read other countries' NAPs. Those involved believe in the potential for learning, e.g. about what policies work under what conditions. A positive side-effect of the OMC processes is that Member State administrations must collect and bring together information about what is done in various policy fields, which gives a good overview of present policies. Peer reviews and Commission evaluations point out shortcomings in national policies, which are considered valuable.

EU benchmarking is potentially a means for holding the government accountable regularly for its performance or lack of it. The OMC processes may empower actors in the national debate and provide justification and legitimacy for domestic policy change. The common strategies provide governments with a strong argument in relation to other domestic interests and may facilitate domestic reforms. Internally within the government, the EES has on several occasions been referred to as an argument for a certain policy line (interview, State Secretary, Ministry of Industry, Sweden, 2001; personal communication, minister, 1999). This is not to say that EU recommendations are decisive for policy change. Rather, they provide one argument among others. In both Sweden and Denmark, employers' organisations have supported their plea for lower taxes by references to the EU recommendations. The opposition parties have also used EU recommendations.

Due to the goodness of fit with existing policy, there has been weak adaptational pressure from the OMC in employment and social policy on Sweden and Denmark. In the areas where the "fit" is less good, i.e. the area of taxation and levels of benefit, both countries have tended to defend their present policies, while moving slightly in the direction of the EU norms. The EU policy priorities in the two OMC areas are not perceived to be a major challenge or contribution to Sweden and Denmark but rather to be important for other countries. In both countries, the perception is that they already ahead of the others and have a good policy. Yet, there are areas where the OMCs *could* provide challenges for the two countries to improve their policies, such as social inclusion policies and equal opportunities. Here the OMC has, at least, put pressure on governments to take action. In terms of new knowledge and ideas, the two OMC processes have not had much visible impact in Sweden and Denmark, again mainly because of the goodness of fit with existing policy ideas. Yet, the OMC processes have reinforced the idea of policy integration and of partnership, even if neither is new to the two countries. It has also placed social inclusion high on the agenda.

The OMC does exert a certain pressure on the Member States. As a minimum, governments have to actively defend their positions if they are not willing to conform to the common norms and they have to "think twice" before introducing measures that go against the common norms. (It is quite unlikely that the governments would *increase* the taxation on labour for instance). Indeed, the OMC is perceived to exert some pressure. As put by a State Secretary in Sweden: "Peer pressure is felt" (interview, 2001). Both the Swedish and Danish governments actively attempt to influence the employment guidelines in order to ensure that they are nationally acceptable, which indicates that recommendations are experienced as entailing a certain pressure. Both governments also tried actively to influence the reform of the EES in the wake of the five-year evaluation, and supported the revision of the strategy.

VI. Unresolved Tensions in the OMC

These case studies of Sweden and Denmark illustrate a number of tensions inherent in the OMC: 1) A tension between the OMC as a transgovernmental co-operation process, with governments as the relevant actors and gate-keepers in relation to other interests, *and* the OMC as a wider mobilisation process, and the related tension between openness and closeness in the process. The Swedish and Danish governments have been reluctant, especially in the case of the EES, to open up the process to a wider set of actors. 2) A tension between employment and social policy as a matter of national concern *and* the perceived need to develop a joint and co-ordinated strategy. The Swedish and Danish governments have so far resisted country-specific recommendations in the social policy field, while at the same time supporting EU-level co-operation on these issues. 3) A tension between a top-down type of learning *and* a voluntary lesson-drawing type of learning, and the related tension between the striving for convergence *and* the acknowledgement of diversity and thus an acceptance of national differences and priorities. 4) A tension between the OMC as a technocratic top-down strategy, where policy is made at European level and supposed to be implemented by actors in the Member States *and* the OMC as a process of political opinion-formation, where support must be built up within in the Member States. Related to this is the role of other actors: constructive contributors to, or mere implementers of, EU policy?

Do Member States compare and compete with each other or with themselves? If mainly the latter, the OMC could provide a challenge also for countries like Sweden and Denmark which today feel "relaxed" in the sense that most objectives are already met, and which prefer to see the OMC as useful for other countries. But then diversity must be accepted as legitimate and the openness for national characteristics and institutions maintained while avoiding a one-size-fits-all approach. Openness to a wider circle of participants is anyway less likely to support top-down European convergence ambitions but more likely to put pressure on national governments to improve their policy performance according to national priorities and traditions (Jacobsson and Schmid, 2003). The fear of "illegitimate", "external" pressure for policy reform, or even *de facto* harmonisation, is probably one reason why these two governments have an ambiguous relation to the OMC, another being the fact that the OMC poses challenges to the traditional institutional structures of policy-making, e.g. by engaging social NGOs in social and labour market policy.

How, then, can the OMC improve the "best pupils in the class"? Precisely by helping to identify shortcomings in current policy, encouraging the setting of more ambitious national and sub-national targets, empowering actors with a weaker position in the structure of policy-making, and fostering cross-sectoral networking. This would not be a small achievement.

References

CEC (2000), Communication from the Commission "Acting Locally for Employment – A Local Dimension for the European Employment Strategy", COM (2000) 196 final of 7 April 2000.

CEC (2001), Communication from the Commission "Strengthening the Local Dimension of the European Employment Strategy", COM (2001) 629 final of 6 November 2001 (http://europa.eu.int/eur-lex/en/com/cnc/2001/com2001_0629en01.pdf).

CEC (2002), "The Swedish National Evaluation of the European Employment Strategy", *Summary Report*, March 2002.

de la Porte, C. and Pochet, P. (2002) (eds.), *Building Social Europe through the Open Method of Co-ordination*, P.I.E.-Peter Lang, Brussels.

EIRO (2002), "Social Partner Involvement in the 2002 NAP", European Industrial Relations Observatory On-line (www.eiro.eurofound.ie), 24 June 2002.

Halleröd, B. (2003), "The Fight against Poverty and Social Exclusion", *Nongovernmental Expert Report*, No.1c/2003 (Sweden) (http://europa.eu.int/comm/employment_social/soc-prot/studies/Sweden_1st_report_final_en.pdf).

Jacobsson, K. (2001), "Arbetsmarknadens parter i EU:s sysselsättningsstrategi", in Jacobsson, K., Johansson, K. M. and Ekengren, M. (eds.), *Mot en europeisk välfärdspolitik? Ny politik och nya samarbetsformer i EU*, SNS Förlag, Stockholm, pp.132-182.

Jacobsson, K. (2004a), "A European Politics for Employability. The Political Discourse on Employability of the EU and the OECD", in Garsten, C. and Jacobsson, K. (eds.), *Learning to Be Employable: New Agendas on Work, Responsibility and Learning in a Globalizing World*, Palgrave Macmillan, Houndmills, Basingstoke, pp.42-62.

Jacobsson, K. (2004b), "Soft Regulation and the Subtle Transformation of States: The Case of EU Employment Policy", *Journal of European Social Policy*, Vol.14, No.4, pp.355-370.

Jacobsson, K. (2005), "Between Deliberation and Discipline: Soft Governance in EU Employment Policy" in Mörth, U. (ed.), *Soft Law in Governance and Regulation: An Interdisciplinary Analysis*, Edward Elgar Publishing, Cheltenham (forthcoming).

Jacobsson, K. and Schmid, H. (2002), "Real Integration or Just Formal Adaptation? On the Implementation of the National Action Plans for Employment", in de la Porte, C. and Pochet, P. (eds.), *Building Social Europe through the Open Method of Co-ordination*, P.I.E.-Peter Lang, Brussels, pp.69-95.

Jacobsson, K. and Schmid, H. (2003), "The European Employment Strategy at the Crossroads: Contribution to the Evaluation", in Foden, D. and Magnusson, L. (eds.), *Five Years Experience of the Luxembourg Employment Strategy*, European Trade Union Institute, Brussels, pp.111-139.

Jacobsson, K. and Vifell, Å. (2003), "National Report for Sweden", 4th Round, produced for the Govecor project (www.govecor.org).

Jacobsson, K. and Vifell, Å. (2005), "New Governance Structures in Employment Policy Making. Taking Stock of the European Employment Strategy", in Linsenmann, I., Meyer, C. and Wessels, W. (eds.), *Economic Governance in the EU*, Palgrave Macmillan, Houndmills, Basingstoke (forthcoming).

Johansson, K. M. (1999), "Tracing the Employment Title in the Amsterdam Treaty: Uncovering Transnational Coalitions", *Journal of European Public Policy*, Vol.6, No.1, pp.85-101.

Junestav, M. (2002), "Labour Cost Reduction, Taxes and Employment. The Swedish Case", in de la Porte, C. and Pochet, P. (eds.), *Building Social Europe through the Open Method of Co-ordination*, P.I.E.-Peter Lang, Brussels, pp.137-176.

Jørgensen, H. (2002), *Consensus, Cooperation and Conflict. The Policy Making Process in Denmark*, Edward Elgar Publishing, Cheltenham.

Knill, C. and Lehmkuhl, D. (1999), "How Europe Matters. Different Mechanisms of Europeanization", *European Integration online Papers (EioP)*, Vol.3, No.7, 15 June 1999 (http://eiop.or.at/eiop/texte/1999-007a.htm).

Knill, C. and Lenschow, A. (2003), "Modes of Regulation in the Governance of the European Union: Towards a Comprehensive Framework", *European Integration online Papers (EioP)*, Vol.7, No.1, 12 February 2003 (http://eiop. or.at/eiop/pdf/2003-001.pdf).

LGDK (2001), "Local Action Plans in Six Danish Municipalities", *Final Report*, Local Government Denmark, Copenhagen.

Moravcsik, A. (1998), *The Choice for Europe: Social Purpose and State Power from Rome to Maastricht*, Cornell University Press, Ithaca.

PLS Ramboll Management (2003), "Non-Government Expert Report on Social Inclusion in Denmark", *Report*, No.1, June 2003 (http://europa.eu.int/comm/ employment_social/soc-prot/studies/denmark_1st_report_final_en.pdf).

Putnam, R. (1988), "Diplomacy and Domestic Politics: The Logic of Two-Level Games", *International Organization*, Vol.43, No.2, pp.427-460.

Rydbjerg Müller, M. and Sand Kirk, J. (2003), "The European Employment Strategy: An Assessment of How Member States's Participation in the EES Influence the Development of National Employment Policy-Making", Masters Thesis, Roskilde University.

Radaelli, C. M. (2000), "Whither Europeanization? Concept Stretching and Substantive Change", *European Integration online Papers (EioP)*, Vol.2, No.8, 17 July 2000 (http://eiop.or.at/eiop/texte/2000-008a.htm).

Regeringskansliet (2001), "Att stödja nationella strategier för trygga och stabila pensioner genom ett integrerat förhållningssätt", *Faktapromemoria*, No.2001/ 02:FPM03, Stockholm.

Regeringskansliet (2003), "Budgetpropositionen för 2004" [The Budget Bill for 2004], *Prop.*, No.2003/04: 1, Stockholm, 22 September 2003.

Risse, T., Green Cowles, M. and Caporaso, J. (2001), "Europeanization and Domestic Change: Introduction", in Green Cowles, M., Caporaso, J. and Risse, T. (eds.), *Transforming Europe*, Cornell University Press, Ithaca and London, pp.1-20.

SFI (2002), "Impact Evaluation of the European Employment Strategy – Denmark", *Synthesis Report*, The Danish National Institute of Social Research, Copenhagen, February 2002.

Statskontoret (2002), "EU:s sysselsättningsstrategi och utformningen av den nationella politiken", *Statskontoret Report*, No.2002:2, Stockholm (http:// www.statskontoret.se/upload/Publikationer/2002/200202.pdf).

SALA (2001), "With Lap within NAP", *Final Report*, Swedish Association of Local Authorities, Stockholm.

Syrén, R. (2002), "To Lisbon and Beyond. Actors and Interests in the EU Social Protection Policy", Masters Thesis, Södertörn University College.

Troedsson, H. (2003), *ESS Europeiska sysselsättningsstrategin / EES – European Employment Strategy*, Svenska kommunförbundet/Landstingsförbundet, Stockholm.

CHAPTER 4

The Open Method of Co-ordination and National Institutional Capabilities

The Italian Experience

Maurizio FERRERA & Stefano SACCHI

Introduction: Can the OMC Enhance Domestic Institutional Capability?*

Although the Open Method of Co-ordination (OMC) is primarily intended to orient Member States' policies towards common strategic priorities and the adoption of shared action frameworks for bringing about desired outcomes, it also has a subsidiary goal[1]. This is the ambition to influence policy-making arrangements as such – at the national level, quite obviously, but also at the sub-national level. In this vein, it is revealing that the instances of the OMC analysed here have come to be commonly known as the "Luxembourg process" and the "Social Inclusion process". This evokes a set of procedural rules (a "process") by means of which the actors involved – at various institutional levels – are supposed jointly to achieve the overall objectives specific to the instance of the OMC in question. From a politico-institutional perspective, therefore, the OMC (or perhaps better, the various applications of the

* This paper is part of a larger research project on "The Open Method of Co-ordination and National Institutional Capabilities", based at the Research Unit on European Governance (URGE) of Consorzio Collegio Carlo Alberto of Moncalieri, Turin (www.urge.it). We are grateful to URGE and the Consortium for their support. The paper has been jointly discussed and planned by the authors. M. Ferrera wrote the introduction and the section on the EES, while S. Sacchi wrote the section on the Social Inclusion process and the conclusions. We would also like to thank the editors of this book for extremely valuable comments and all the participants in the workshop on "Opening the Open Method of Co-ordination" held at the European University Institute (EUI) in Florence on 4 and 5 July 2003. The usual disclaimer applies.

[1] On the Open Method of Co-ordination see Mosher (2000), de la Porte et al. (2001), Hodson and Maher (2001), de la Porte and Pochet (2002), Scott and Trubek (2001), Trubek and Mosher (2003), Sabel and Zeitlin (2003) and Radaelli (2003).

OMC) can be seen as an important and original experiment in the pro-motion of policy change on a continental basis, geared towards modify-ing not only objectives and policy measures, but also the interaction dynamics among the many actors operating in the relevant issue-areas.

As is well known, both the European Employment Strategy (EES) or Luxembourg process and the Social Inclusion process involve a periodi-cal sequence of issuing guidelines or objectives, presenting national action plans, drawing up joint reports and so forth. Our question is: beyond this "liturgy", what directions of "processual" change have been promoted by the OMC? There exist codified lists of substantive objec-tives for each OMC process: the original four pillars of the EES[2], which have now been replaced by three overarching objectives and ten "result-oriented priorities"[3], and the four common objectives of the fight against poverty and social exclusion[4]. The processual objectives, by contrast, have not been codified, although what can be called "guidelines for good governance" attached to the new employment guidelines, the "arrange-ments for implementation" of the Nice objectives and the fourth Nice objective itself all explicitly promote procedural patterns[5]. However, such processual objectives can be inferred from official documents with sufficient clarity as to allow us to categorise them as follows:

1. vertical integration;
2. horizontal integration;
3. cross-sectoral integration;
4. strengthening Member States' institutional capabilities.

The objective of *vertical integration* requires that policy action at the various levels of government be "virtuously" co-ordinated. The underly-ing assumption is that employment and social inclusion policies need to be territorially calibrated, and thus demand wide involvement of re-gional and local governments. However, in order to bring about virtuous co-ordination this involvement must take place within a framework of

---

[2] The three overarching objectives of the new EES are: full employment, quality and productivity at work, and social cohesion and inclusion. In pursuing them, the Mem-ber States must take account of ten specific guidelines "which are priorities for ac-tion" (Council of the European Union, 2003).

[3] *Ibid.*

[4] The four common objectives in the fight against poverty and social inclusion were endorsed by the Nice European Council in 2000 and then revised in 2002. They are: to facilitate participation in employment and access by all to the resources, rights, goods and services; to prevent the risks of exclusion; to help the most vulnerable; to mobilise all relevant bodies (the fourth objective, "mobilise all relevant bodies", clearly involves procedural issues) (see Council of the European Union, 2002).

[5] See Council of the European Union (2003) and (2002), respectively.

institutional arrangements and (positive and negative) incentives established at higher levels of government.

Tightly coupled with the objective of vertical integration is that of *horizontal integration*, requiring adequate representation of functional interests and a high level of participation by such interests in the decision-making process – a policy-making mode which might be called *governance through social partnership*. The reference to social partnership is highly explicit and visible in the OMC instances analysed here, so among the four processual objectives listed here horizontal integration is probably the most straightforward.

Our third process objective, *cross-sectoral integration*, involves the need to disrupt the watertight compartmentalisation – all too often cognitive as well as organisational – between different domains of public intervention. Significant gains in the ability to manage externalities and interdependence are to be expected from pursuing this objective. Exhortations to promote explicit and more effective ways of co-ordinating employment, inclusion, social protection, education and tax policies have multiplied and proceed hand in hand with the improved focus on inherently cross-sectoral substantive objectives, such as "to make work pay". "Contamination" (or cross-fertilisation) at the level of substantive objectives can be seen in the third overarching objective of the new EES (strengthening social cohesion and inclusion) and the first Nice objective (to facilitate participation in employment).

The fourth process objective has to do with *strengthening the institutional capability* of the collective action system pertaining to a policy area (see box 1). The inherent focus of the OMC on "learning and mimicking" (Hemerijck and Visser, 2001), policy updating and review in the light of a country's own policy experience on the one hand and mutual learning and lesson drawing on the other obviously highlights the learning component[6]. However, all the elements comprising institutional capability are highly relevant here. The identification of relevant challenges for setting policy priorities and specifying targets (the planning component) has always been demanded of the Member States, and the objectives discussed above of vertical and horizontal integration are clearly connected with the decision-making component of institutional capability. Lastly, a focus on implementation seems to be high on the

---

[6] Although the emphasis is generally put on mutual learning, in drawing up national action plans national policy-makers are also led to identify weaknesses in the effectiveness or fairness of policies or bottlenecks and strains in institutional co-ordination (e.g. between national and local levels). This is what we have elsewhere called the *maieutic potential* of the OMC (Ferrera *et al.*, 2002).

agenda as regards the policy areas covered here, following the Conclusions of the Barcelona European Council[7].

Box 1: Institutional Capability

Institutional capability of a system of collective action is the extent to which the latter is able – by means of interactive dynamics – to: 1) elaborate responses to environmental challenges; 2) transform such responses into decisions of a political nature; 3) implement such decisions; 4) learn from experience. The connotation of the concept of institutional capability comprises therefore a planning component, a decision-making component, an implementation component and a learning component.

The *planning component* relates to the ability to diagnose functional challenges in an informed way, to identify the range of possible and then feasible options, to evaluate these options in the light of socially and politically relevant interests and publicly defensible normative criteria.

The *decision-making component* relates to the ability to build social coalitions and political majorities able to make decisions given the extant formal and informal rules (or to change these rules in legitimate ways).

The *implementation component* relates to the ability to implement decisions in adherence to their basic goals, but taking also into account local variations and the existence of policy legacies and thus of inevitable interaction effects.

The *learning component* relates to the ability to monitor and evaluate the three preceding components of institutional capability and to revise them intentionally in the light of experience.

Member States have reacted in different ways to the stimuli stemming from the EES or the fight against poverty and social exclusion to pursue these processual objectives. This difference is due not only to the varying degrees of congruence between existing policy-making modes (the initial conditions, so to speak) and those envisaged under the OMC, but also to the existence and time path of endogenous dynamics of change not ascribable to the OMC, dynamics that – when occurring – may facilitate or hinder adjustment towards the suggested objectives. This *ex ante* indeterminacy of the effects of such endogenous dynamics on the pursuit of processual objectives must be resolved through empirical research.

In addition to endogenous dynamics of change, it should not be overlooked that the strength of the stimuli varies across OMC processes, as a consequence of their different structural features (unlike the Social Inclusion process, the Employment process is Treaty-based, involves

---

[7]   "[...] the focus must be on action for implementation, rather than on the annual elaboration of guidelines" (European Council, 2002: point 49).

guidelines and recommendations, has a yearly cycle) and different dates of birth.

In each of the policy areas covered here (employment and social inclusion), Italy has suffered from a twofold handicap. On the one hand, initial congruence of Italy's policy-making process with the process objectives was low as regards both the EES and the fight against poverty and social exclusion. On the other, in both policy fields endogenous dynamics of change have significantly interacted with the exogenous push related to the EES and the fight against poverty at EU level. Thus in the field of employment services and active labour market policies, there has been an ongoing process of devolution of administrative powers to regional and local governments. In the field of social inclusion, the key developments have been the approval in 2000 of a Framework Law reforming the institutional setting of social assistance, followed by a number of other changes, above all the constitutional reform of 2001 which has devolved further powers to the Regions and upset the implementation of the Framework Law. More often than not these endogenous dynamics, rooted in quarter-century old political debates, have hindered the pursuit of the four process objectives envisaged by the OMC.

The next two sections of this chapter are devoted to assessing the extent to which Italy has pursued the fourth processual objective, that of strengthening its institutional capabilities, in the context of the EES and the fight against poverty and social exclusion, taking into account the initial conditions and the interaction effects induced by endogenous dynamics of change unrelated to the OMC. The concluding section sums up, comparing the two cases and suggesting clusters of plausible factors that may help to explain variance across them, to be further refined through future research.

I. The Impact of the EES on Italian Policy-making

Since 1998, the Italian government has simultaneously had to cope with the new European Employment Strategy on the one hand, and the ongoing process of administrative decentralisation in various policy areas – including that of employment – which culminated in the constitutional reform of 2001, on the other[8]. Given the dismal initial condi-

---

[8] The constitutional reform affecting Heading V of the Constitution was enacted in March 2001 and then approved by the electoral body in a popular referendum held in October 2001. Heading V (*Titolo V*) of the Constitution establishes the prerogatives of the regions, the provinces and the municipalities. Among other things, the new Heading V of the Constitution provides for three types of legislative competence over policy areas: exclusive competence of the state over enumerated policy areas, shared

tions obtaining at the time the EES was launched, the result of this interaction – if assessed in terms of institutional capability – can be deemed moderately positive[9].

For Italy, responding to the demands of the EES raised multiple problems. The strategy took shape within Anglo-Saxon and northern European policy paradigms and values, resting on the primacy of prevention, active labour market policies and efficient public employment services. Moreover, in the early stage of the EES, the employment guidelines tended to emphasise adjustment in terms of suggested policy measures rather than achievement of targets on the part of the Member States. By so doing, the EES tended to place a heavy burden on those Member States whose employment policy system was less attuned to the northern European paradigm[10]. By contrast, the Italian model of labour policy was marked by the dominance of passive policies, by a hyperbureaucratic system of placement and by the lack of evaluation and monitoring capabilities. The organisational structure of the Labour Ministry, characterised by high internal fragmentation and by the juridical culture of its staff, did not favour any development of problem solving and ex-post evaluation skills. Its peripheral offices, vested with employment service functions, were likewise ill-equipped to perform the counselling and orientation tasks connected with active labour market policies and a preventive approach to unemployment. When the EES took off, the Italian government had virtually no institutional equipment for collecting and analysing data and thus for formulating articulated empirical diagnoses of the existing challenges and elaborating policy solutions along the general lines set by the European strategy. In 1987 a General Direction for the Labour Market Observatory had been created and the need to set up a Labour Market Information System providing on-line information to employment offices had slowly emerged. An *ad hoc* commission had been established, but the political and material support for such initiatives remained weak and thus little progress had been made. Representation of the Labour Ministry in international bodies and decision-making arenas was also scarcely formalised. The relationships with institutions like the OECD, ILO and the European Union were conducted on the basis of personal ties and contingent events.

(concurrent) competence over other enumerated policy areas, and then residual exclusive competence of the regions over all policy areas which are not listed.

[9] On employment policies in Italy, see Fargion (2001 and 2002), Ferrera and Gualmini (2004) and Graziano (forthcoming).

[10] Moreover, the Anglo-Saxon and northern European mould reflected fears of negative labour supply incentives of generous unemployment benefits, fears which are of relatively little importance for Italy (see Sestito, 2002).

To sum up, at the time the EES was launched initial conditions in the field of employment policies were very unfavourable: the dissonance between the Italian model and that underpinning the employment guidelines could hardly have been more pronounced.

In addition, the pressures coming from the EU combined with domestic reforms and in particular with the launching of administrative decentralisation in 1997, whose consequence for the Labour Ministry was the gradual loss of important competencies and responsibilities: the reforms foresaw for the Ministry only a role of general orientation, control, supervision and international representation. Endogenous decentralisation dynamics inaugurated a phase of institutional transition, which made the response to the new EU soft laws more difficult and complicated. All this may have had a disturbing effect on adjustment towards the objective of strengthening national-level institutional capability in the field of employment policy.

The process of administrative decentralisation was initiated by Law No.59 of 1997 – known as the "Bassanini Law" after the minister who acted as a policy entrepreneur to push through administrative reforms. Under this Law Parliament delegated powers to the government to issue devolution decrees in many policy fields. In employment policy, this delegated power was exercised by the government though Legislative Decree No.469 of December 1997. This devolved to the regions and local authorities all the functions related to employment services and active labour market policies, but still within an overall framework set by the national level of government, which retained a "general role of orientation, promotion and co-ordination". In particular, while leaving the administrative organisation of employment services to subsequent regulation to be issued by each region, the Legislative Decree still imposed a framework on their institutional architecture, providing for the establishment of regional co-ordination agencies and of regional and inter-institutional bodies for concerted action. However, the reform did not establish an agency at the national level, aimed at co-ordinating the various regional systems from the centre, like Germany's *Bundesanstalt für Arbeit*. The latter is no longer an option, after the constitutional reform of 2001 which established shared legislative competence between the state and the regions over employment policies. This means that the regions are vested with legislative and regulatory capacity, to be exercised however in accordance with legislation on the fundamental principles regarding employment policies, which remains in the hands of the state.

In addition to devolving governance of active labour market policies to the regions and management of employment services to the provinces, reform bills aimed to promote a preventive approach to placement instead of the old bureaucratic one, and allowed the entry of private organisations into the provision of employment services, after fifty years of state's monopoly.

The reform of employment services still constitutes one of the main challenges for Italy, and in particular for the country's regional and local governments.

Between 1998 and 1999, Italian regional governments were involved in passing regional laws implementing national prescriptions. Job centres were set up throughout the country at the provincial level (one for each 100,000 inhabitants). As mentioned earlier, a new body was created at the regional level, under a variety of different names (Labour Agency, Employment Authority etc.), aimed at governing and co-ordinating employment measures. Besides their control and supervisory functions, the new Labour Agencies have the duty to provide technical support to the provinces implementing the reform, through the co-ordination of the Computerised Employment Information System (*Sistema Informativo Lavoro*, an electronic data base covering labour demand and supply that is still in its early stages), through the development of research into the local dynamics of the labour market, and through the monitoring and evaluation of labour policy impacts. Furthermore, two important bodies were created for integration and concerted action: the Tripartite Regional Commissions (*Commissioni regionnali tripartite*) and the Inter-institutional Co-ordination Committees (*Comitati interistituzionali di coordinamento*). While the former include representatives of regional public institutions, trade unions and employers' organisations, the latter include representatives of the various levels of local government (regional, provincial and municipal). Compared to the old Regional Employment Commissions (*Commissioni regionali per l'impiego*), these new bodies should be more involved in the planning and implementation of labour policies, thus avoiding possible conflict. Similar tripartite commissions were also established at the provincial level.

The reform of employment services, so important for a strategy such as the EES to succeed (resting as the latter does on preventative and active measures) still does not appear to have been achieved in full. In the northern regions, the implementation process has been more rapid and efficient, while – as recognised by the 2003 National Action Plan for Employment (NAP/empl) – in some southern regions delays and inefficiencies continue to jeopardise the reform. The shift from a bureaucratic culture to a preventive, result-oriented approach appears to be slow. In particular, some critical factors can be identified that have obstructed the path of reform implementation. To begin with, both the newly established job centres and regional employment agencies (Labour Agencies) were mainly staffed with personnel from the former placement offices, basically trained to perform routinely administrative, "certificatory" functions. The adjustment to selection, counselling and orientation tasks has proved to be lengthy and difficult. Alongside staff coming from former placement offices, other personnel came from different offices, with more technical backgrounds. Heterogeneity of skills and expectations among staff has caused problems as regards training needs, and different previous staff affiliation has bequeathed wage differentials for personnel performing the same tasks. Moreover, successive and overlapping regulations for job placement have overburdened the new job centres in their start up stages, despite being informed by a welfare-to-work approach fully consistent with, and indeed suggested by, the employment guidelines. As remarked by Italy's 2003 NAP/empl, the biggest problems seem to lie in services to firms, placing the whole new edifice on shaky foundations since these determine the extent to which employment services facilitate the match between labour demand and supply.

To sum up, the process of devolution in the field of employment policies has (obviously) reduced prospective capacity for action at the national level, without – at least for the time being – achieving homogeneous results at the regional and local levels in relation to core aspects of the EES such as employment services and the ability to implement active labour market policies.

Hence the introduction of the EES found Italy struggling with initial conditions very different from those presupposed by the strategy itself, and undergoing a process of endogenous reform that, although aiming at the same substantive goals, tended to cripple the institutional capability of central government, reducing national authorities' scope for governing an increasingly complex employment policy network.

Nevertheless, the EES has prompted in Italy a slow process of structural adjustment (concerning the organisational network responsible for employment policies) and cognitive learning (concerning the norms, beliefs and preferences of the various actors of this network) – a process characterised at first by extemporaneity and improvisation, but which subsequently led to some degree of institutionalised innovation and change.

In order to draw up the first NAPs, those for 1998 and 1999, two *ad hoc* commissions were set up inside the Labour Ministry, composed of a small group of external experts (about ten people each), without any direct involvement of the Ministry's staff, which indeed opposed various bureaucratic obstacles to these new initiatives. The 1999 NAP was marked however by a broadening of the circle of actors involved: the Presidency of the Council (held by D'Alema) got involved in the preparation of the plan through its economic department, which precisely in those months had undertaken an internal re-organisation with a view to equipping the Prime Minister office with greater capabilities in the most crucial sectors. The 1999 experience taught an important lesson: the NAPs have not only to be prepared and packaged in order to submit them to Brussels, but they also need to be defended within the peer review processes and bilateral meetings with the European Commission that occur after the formal submission. They must be accompanied all the way through the Luxemburg process, all year round (and especially when the Joint Employment Reports are drafted). In 1999, despite the institutional investment made in its preparation, the Italian NAP was not adequately supported in the follow-up to its official presentation: the expert Committee responsible for the document disbanded after the formal deadline and the ministerial bureaucracy felt neither involved nor capable of performing this delicate task. The change of Labour Ministers during the summer of 1999 (Bassolino left his post to Salvi, both from the party of the Democrats of the Left, DS) did not improve the situation: the "expert committee" system revealed itself as an inadequate organisational response to the increasingly articulated demands of an increasingly institutionalised process of multi-level governance of European labour markets and domestic employment policy regimes. Another lesson that had to be learnt in the critical juncture of 1999 was the urgent need to develop monitoring and evaluation skills in order to respond not only to the "declarative" demands of the EES (what are your plans?), but also to its "accounting" demands (have you reached your targets?). The obligation to produce an Implementation Report to be attached to the NAP/empl could not be immediately met, given the lack of comparable and updated data on existing policies.

The turning point in Italy's participation in the EES came in 2000. In the winter of that year a new unit called the "Monitoring Group" was established within the Ministry's cabinet with the task of compiling an updated database on labour market trends and policies. The Group operated as an inter-service committee of administrators belonging to various directorates and ministries (Presidency of the Council, ISTAT/ National Institute of Statistics, INPS/National Institute of Social Insurance, ISFOL/Institute for Labour and Training etc.). This was indeed a relevant step in the overall reorganisation of the policy-making process: a new actor capable of providing empirical data and technical knowledge on the real dynamics of the labour market appeared on the scene, with firm roots in the central administrative apparatus. It began to play a pivotal role in the existing, loose and inconclusive employment policy network, acting as a link between different administrations and an orchestrator of their joint efforts. Soon after its creation, the Monitoring Group started to produce a series of Monitoring Reports on labour market trends and policies, which have rapidly established themselves as the standard reference source for knowledge and analysis and thus as a reliable basis for policy planning and evaluation. If compared to the 1997 status quo, the progress made by Italy in terms of institutional capacity building (and its learning component in particular) appears as remarkable, as explicitly recognised also by recent Joint Employment Reports.

The creation and activism of the Monitoring Group seem to have had a multiplier effect, inspiring organisational changes and new initiatives within the Labour Ministry itself, adding to institutional capacity building. Two, in particular, can be mentioned: on the one hand, the organisational strengthening of the Directorate General vested with research and statistical tasks, which now works in close association with the Monitoring Group. On the other hand, there have been remarkable efforts on the part of the Directorate General of Employment and Training to upgrade its own skills and know-how. This powerful DG – one of the most important ministerial branches in Italy – seems to have reacted to the establishment of the Monitoring Group with an attitude of (virtuous) organisational competition. This Directorate General can now make an autonomous contribution to monitoring and evaluation tasks, both by mobilising internal resources and by relying on external expertise.

In the wake of such progress, starting from the third round of the EES (2000), the Italian government began to play a more active role not only in the "descending" phase (application of guidelines, new NAP formulation, old NAP evaluation), but also in the "ascending" phase (definition of guidelines, NAP defence and peer review, contents of the Joint Employment Reports). From a technical point of view, a small but dynamic epistemic community (including not only the Monitoring Group but also the Italian delegates to the Employment and Social Protection Committees and some economic advisors of the Labour Ministry and the Presidency of the Council) gradually formed and started to perform brokerage functions between the national arena and the supranational one. From the political point of view, both Salvi (as Labour Minister) and D'Alema (as Prime Minister) mobilised to shape the agenda of the Lisbon European Council (spring 2000), seeking alliances with other countries on issues considered relevant for Italy. One of the achievements of this strategy was the recognition of the importance of the regional dimension of the labour market (and thus of employment policies) in the conclusions of the Lisbon summit and in the 2001 guidelines.

The elaboration of the 2001 NAP (the fourth round) was also assigned to an *ad hoc* committee co-ordinated by a technician, but this time the expert committee worked in close contact with the Monitoring

Group. The May elections and the change in government (from Amato to Berlusconi) disturbed Italy's participation in the 2001 round of the EES. At the end of the summer, the new government submitted to Brussels an addendum to the May NAP, putting greater emphasis on flexibility. But that same addendum also included, for the first time, some quantitative targets, based on the scenarios elaborated by the Monitoring Group. Starting from 2002, the whole NAP/empl process at the national level has been internalised within the executive machine. External experts have lost their prominence, and the process is now managed by the Labour Ministry itself, under the close supervision of one of the deputy ministers.

In sum, between 1997 and 2002 the EES has been incorporated into Italy's policy-making system and there can be little doubt that this has prompted a marked upgrading of crucial dimensions of institutional capability in the field of employment policy.

Again, this can be seen in relation to the monitoring activities, which remain very high on the policy agenda and are being constantly improved. The labour market reforms enacted in 2003 (Law No.30 of February 2003, known as the Biagi Law after the labour lawyer who drafted it and was killed by the new Red Brigades in 2002, and the Legislative Decree No.276 of September 2003) provide new tools for exploiting administrative databases and establishing common indicators for monitoring employment policies at the territorial level, to be developed by the central and regional authorities. More generally, the EES's impact the on Italy's institutional capability can be assessed by taking into account firstly the White Paper on the Labour Market, and then the country's contribution to the impact evaluation of the EES itself.

The White Paper on the Labour Market, issued in October 2001, outlined a comprehensive reform of Italy's labour market that was then partly implemented in 2003. The White Paper draws extensively, but at the same time highly selectively, on the EES as a justification for the government's reform agenda[11]. The document itself is presented as a tool for fostering policy debate in order to meet the requirements of the EES and the recommendations issued to Italy[12]. However, only certain

---

[11] To the extent that in some academic quarters the White Paper on the Labour Market was considered as a merely instrumental exploitation of the Community debate. See for instance Giubboni, who describes the White Paper as the epitome of an "instrumental and improperly opportunistic usage of Community (social and/or labour) law and/or policy" (Giubboni, 2003: 593).

[12] "To all these requests (those embodied in the employment recommendations) Italy will have to respond promptly and effectively, given that they are duties stemming from Italy's membership in the European Union" (Ministry of Labour and Social Affairs, 2001: 2).

aspects of the EES are highlighted, partly an adaptation to Italy's peculiar labour market context and partly because they fit well with the government's agenda, while other aspects would not. This can clearly be seen with reference to the issue of better jobs and "quality in work". In June 2001 the Commission issued a communication proposing various dimensions of the concept of quality in work and indicators to assess such dimensions (CEC, 2001a). The Laeken European Council of December 2001 then approved a list of indicators based on the ten dimensions proposed by the Commission[13]. The White Paper on the Labour Market of October 2001 re-framed the quality issue almost exclusively in terms of flexibilisation and desegmentation of the labour market and the fight against undeclared work, the two priorities of government's employment policy at the time. More generally, quality in work is defined in the White Paper in terms of the future labour market chances of individuals ("quality of work must be measured not only and not much in terms of specific wage and non-wage features of single, actual work relationships, but rather in terms of the chances of further progress within the labour market associated with such relationships, and mostly in terms of future chances" [Ministry of Labour and Social Affairs, 2001: 59]), thus disregarding all the other dimensions in order to emphasise the flexibility side of flexicurity[14].

Now, what is relevant here is that the EES is used intentionally, strategically and selectively to justify reforms, both functionally and normatively. This requires a degree of sophistication that shows some kind of improvement on what we called the planning component of Italy's institutional capability in the employment field[15].

---

[13] The ten dimensions are: intrinsic job quality; skills, lifelong learning and career development; gender equality; health and safety at work; flexibility and security; inclusion and access to the labour market; work organisation and work-life balance; social dialogue and worker involvement; diversity and non-discrimination; and overall work performance.

[14] It is noteworthy that, after the issue of "quality in work" was given a broad connotation in the Community debate, to encompass the ten dimensions listed in footnote 13, and included as the second of the three overarching objectives of the new EES, Italy has been trying to reduce its salience, as it has done with the objective of social cohesion and inclusion. The Joint Employment Report 2003/2004 notes that issues of quality and social inclusion are not explicitly discussed in Italy's 2003 National Action Plan for Employment.

[15] To be clear, we are *not* arguing that the impact of the EES on Italy's institutional capability lies in the government's ability to use it to justify reforms. Rather, its strategic use by the government can be taken as a mark of the institutionalisation of a network of actors with sufficient skills to elaborate sophisticated policy plans that can be justified both functionally and normatively. What we ascribe to the EES is an impact on the institutionalisation of this network, antecedent to the episode of the White Paper.

Another illustration of the effect of the EES on Italy's institutional capability lies in the national contribution to the EES impact evaluation[16]. In the final impact evaluation report, issued in March 2002, the Italian authorities highlighted some features of the old EES that they perceived as limits and shortcomings of the Luxembourg process, at least when looked at through the lenses of Italy's specific labour market problems and disparities, and put forward proposals for improving both the process and its contents. This clearly indicates an enhanced – if not outright novel – capacity for deliberate examination and evaluation of the structures and processes in which Italy participates at the European level, in addition to better consideration of domestic phenomena. It actually translated into action at the European level, insofar as specific guidelines No.9 and 10 of the new EES – that is, two out of ten – concern issues Italy had vocally pushed for and which were identified as important limits of the EES vis-à-vis the domestic situation: those of undeclared work and regional employment disparities. In particular, "a broad approach towards reducing regional employment and unemployment disparities", as guideline No.10 now reads, has been a very important issue for Italy's policymakers in their struggle to cope with socio-economic problems of the South after the demise (in 1992) of the so-called "extra-ordinary intervention", which had failed to achieve the expected results. The new local development strategy was launched in 1996, following the Employment Pact signed by Prime Minister Prodi, the unions and the business associations. Under the heading "negotiated planning" (*programmazione negoziata*) one can find a wide range of policy measures designed to foster local entrepreneurship, valorise local resources and institutional capabilities, and create new jobs. The numerous programmes are primarily based on a mixture of training and job creation, qualification and work. The most widespread and significant measures are territorial pacts and area contracts, which also have wider goals of territorial development and revitalisation[17]. Both are designed

---

[16] As foreseen by the Social Agenda approved in Nice in December 2000, an exercise of impact assessment of the EES was jointly carried out in 2002 by the Commission and the Member States in order to take stock of the experience of five years of the EES. The results are available on the website http://www.europa.eu.int/comm/ employment_social/employment_strategy/impact_en.htm.

[17] Territorial pacts consist of operative procedures and bargaining tools designed to promote the development of businesses, co-operatives and employment measures in a given area, through the utilisation of productive and natural resources that characterise that area. Bargaining does not rely upon the traditional triangle of unions, employers and the government, but on a wider network of private and public actors (such as banks, chambers of commerce, non-profit-making associations etc.), who are to share common policy problems and jointly fund the various measures. In 2000, more than one hundred territorial pacts had been submitted to the National Committee for the Economy and Employment (*CNEL/Comitato Nazionale per l'Economia e*

to encourage job creation and skill upgrading in depressed areas. Harsh words were reserved in Italy's impact evaluation of the EES for the alleged incapacity of the old employment strategy to understand the importance for the development of Italy's *Mezzogiorno* of negotiated planning policies. Alongside the labour market reform and the envisaged pension reform, local development strategy is one of the cornerstones of Italy's 2003 National Action Plan for Employment.

In conclusion, the European Employment Strategy has clearly had a positive impact on Italy's institutional capability, if only one considers the mileage travelled since 1997. This has percolated, then, to actual policies: the (novel for Italy) focus on active labour market policies is mainly, if not exclusively, a consequence of the EES. But two dark spots remain in the picture. The first concerns the relatively restricted network involved in the process at the domestic level, and its still incomplete institutionalisation. We have seen that the NAP/empl is now drawn up within the Labour Ministry – indeed, it tends to be a document internal to the ministry, with little involvement on the part of the regions (many of which are more interested in the aspects related to the structural funds than in the EES *per se*) and little if any involvement of the social partners. Moreover, if institutionalisation is defined as "the process by which organisations and procedures acquire value and stability" (Huntington, 1968: 12), then it could be argued that both the network of actors and the procedures that guide Italy's participation in the EES are still at an early stage of institutionalisation, to the extent that if left without some key policy middlemen the whole edifice might well collapse[18]. The second dark spot is related to the ongoing trend of devolution of powers to lower levels of government, culminating in the constitutional reform of 2001, which delegated most competences in the field of employment to regional and local governments. The institutional capability of these actors is still relatively weak and extremely varied across the national territory. While regions such as Piedmont, Lombardy, Emilia-Romagna or Tuscany have made significant efforts to equip themselves with the skills to perform the new tasks (and some have even started to experiment with Regional Action Plans for employment, in full syntony with the EES), most southern regions lag far behind, while

---

il Lavoro – the body competent for recommending public funding), 71 for the South and 38 for the Centre-North. Ten of these pacts are "European pacts", that is, ones financed by special European funds. Area contracts have the same goal as territorial pacts: i.e. to preserve and/or create jobs in under-developed areas. They differ from the pacts in that they cover areas where industry already exists (albeit in crisis). They are signed in order to avoid mass redundancies. Unions are prepared to waive the national contractual standard and to agree to wage and administrative flexibility.

[18] The importance of "policy middlemen" in the policy process, and for learning in particular, is highlighted by Heclo (1974).

at the same time facing the highest problem loads in terms of unemployment and labour market modernisation. The new framework of centre-periphery relations rests on co-ordination and support mechanisms which are still in a fluid state and poorly effective. Thus what has been gained in terms of institutional capability at the national level since 1997 in the wake of the EES has been partly offset by the centrifugal dynamics of administrative devolution.

II. The Impact of the Social Inclusion Process on Italy's Policy-making

At the time the EU strategy on social inclusion was launched in spring 2000, the issue of poverty and social exclusion was gaining increasing salience in Italian policy-making[19]. Plans were underway to build an integrated system of social services and interventions which was to link and co-ordinate the various levels of social assistance governance and provide citizens with homogeneous benefits across the whole national territory. These efforts were aimed at breaking away from a long-standing situation of marked territorial differentiation and paucity of resources affecting Italy's social assistance sector[20].

Largely marginal in the national debate and policy agenda for decades, the issue of poverty and social exclusion came to the political fore in the mid-1990s when the wider question of an overarching welfare state reform started to be discussed as a consequence of the intersection between changing labour markets, family structures and demographic trends on the one hand and the now binding post-Maastricht budgetary constraints on the other. The situation of Italy's "assistenza" (the aggregate of all non-contributory transfers and all non-health services) was apparent to both social and political actors: high institutional fragmentation, overlapping of measures, a bias towards cash transfers and against services, the lack of a safety net of last resort, and marked territorial differentiation. In particular, citizens enjoyed rights that varied considerably from place to place, depending not so much on their needs *per se* but, rather, on their place of residence. At the same time, the task of combating poverty at a national level was (and to a large extent still is) mainly left to categorical transfers such as the social pension and pension supplements and to disability pensions used as a functional equiva-

---

[19] This section draws on in-depth interviews with key informants conducted in Rome and Brussels in 2003 and 2004. Sometimes in what follows excerpts from some of these interviews are cited. In such cases, the interview is identified by a coded letter, to provide to the anonymity of those interviewed.

[20] On social assistance policies in Italy see Baldini *et al.* (2000), Boeri and Perotti (2001) and Sacchi and Bastagli (2005).

lent for the missing safety net. In pursuit of EMU membership, the government led by Romano Prodi in 1997 charged a commission of experts with the task of advancing proposals for comprehensive reform of the Italian welfare state. The Commission for the Analysis of Macroeconomic Compatibilities of Social Expenditure (*Commissione per l'Analisi delle Compatibilità Macroeconomiche della Spesa Sociale*), chaired by the economist Paolo Onofri and hence known as the "Onofri Commission", came up with a project of gradual re-calibration both *within* social assistance and *between* social assistance and social insurance (especially pensions), resting on the following broad orientations:

- universalisation of potential access to benefits, linked to the implementation of effective selectivity criteria and mechanisms for ascertaining beneficiaries' needs and determining deserving households;
- establishment of a safety net;
- promotion of a wider array of decentralised services, with a reduction of territorial disparities;
- rationalisation of existing cash transfers, separating more clearly the anti-poverty function from that of supporting family responsibilities.

The new approach to social assistance put forward by the Onofri Commission found its legal embodiment in the Framework Law No.328 of 2000, awaited since the late 1970s. In 1977 responsibilities for social assistance had been devolved to the regions and local authorities while the state maintained authority over contributory or insurance measures. In transferring responsibilities, the 1977 reform had not established guiding principles or general standards to be respected by the regional and local levels of governments: it simply stated that these principles and standards would be set by a national law which would regulate social assistance (reforming the social assistance law in force, dating back to 1890) and by regional laws. As mentioned earlier, the national law was promulgated only in 2000.

The Framework Law No.328 of 8 November 2000, which reformed the institutional setting of Italian social assistance, was drawn up in accordance with the ongoing decentralisation and with principles of subsidiarity, while at the same time establishing the national government's competence for fixing general guidelines. In 1997 a sweeping reform (discussed in section 1 above) had deeply modified the relationships between state, regions and local authorities, devolving administrative functions to the lower levels of government. The directive functions were reserved to the state, while regional planning functions were assigned to the regions and local service implementation to the local institutions. The Framework Law on social assistance of 2000 was consistent with the administrative reform of 1997 as regards the attribution of responsibilities across levels of government. At the same time, it promoted policies of a more universal nature (addressed to all individuals and families in a situation of need and not only to certain categories) and provision of services and in-kind benefits to complement monetary transfers, particularly in favour of children, the elderly and the poor. The Framework Law also addressed another weakness of the social assistance sector: the low level of financial resources allocated to it, and established that social assistance measures should be financed with resources from the National Fund for Social Policies[21].

The Italian system of policy planning following the Framework Law can be described as multi-level, multi-actor and multi-sector planning. The multi-level character of the planning process consisted of a rather detailed division of labour between the responsibilities of the central government, the regions and the municipalities (or sets of municipalities grouped in "zones"). Its multi-actor character rested on the involvement of social partners and NGOs in the identification of priorities as well as in the actual implementation of measures. Finally, the multi-sector character of Italy's social planning lay in the parallel presence of several action plans at various levels – the main plans being the Social Plan (intended to be issued every three years), the National Action Plan on Employment, the Education Plan (2000-2006), the Health Care Plan (every three years), plus a series of other, more circumscribed plans (for the disabled, children and teenagers, drug addicts, the elderly). All these plans contain measures that address social exclusion. Particularly relevant however is the Social Plan for 2001-2003[22]. It identified five policy priorities: supporting family responsibilities, enhancing children rights,

---

[21] The National Fund for Social Policies (*Fondo Nazionale per le Politiche Sociali*), henceforth Social Fund, was first introduced in 1998 in order to finance at a central and local level social policies aimed at children, the elderly, the disabled, the prevention of drug abuse and the rehabilitation of addicts, family support and the integration of foreign citizens. Law 328/2000 established that starting from the year 2002, the total appropriation of the Fund is determined by the annual Budget Law and no longer by the sum of appropriations made by single laws. This should facilitate a more co-ordinated programming of social policies at all institutional levels. The national government is in charge of the allocation of the financial resources, which takes place after an agreement is reached between the national and the regional governments.

[22] Law 328/2000 established that the government must prepare a National Plan of Social Interventions and Services (henceforth: Social Plan) every three years. The Social Plan should have determined – amongst other things – the priorities for action in the social assistance field. For reasons that will soon become clear, after the Constitutional reform of 2001 the central government is barred from issuing a new Social Plan to replace the one that expired in 2003.

combating poverty, supporting dependent persons (especially the severely disabled) through home help services, and promoting the inclusion of specific problem groups (immigrants, addicts, teenagers).

The Framework Law No.328 of 2000 also had two further aims, both related to institutional capability building in the field of social assistance: on the one hand, it intended to remedy the lack of data on social policies; on the other, it provided for increased staffing of the office dealing with social assistance within the Italian administration.

As for the informational deficit, since Italian social assistance is scattered and mostly delivered at the local level, data on social policies are all too often simply not available. The Framework Law intended to overcome this problem by instituting a system of comprehensive data gathering on social policy outlays, measures and social needs, involving all levels of government (state, regions, provinces and municipalities) in its operations[23].

As for the organisational aspects, the functions of policy planning, monitoring and evaluation in the social assistance field were vested in an office formally subsumed under the Prime Minister's branch within the government (albeit headed by a minister), the Department of Social Affairs. Far from being a liability, the lightness of the organisational structure of this office – a department of the Presidency of the Council of Ministers rather than a department within a Ministry – appears to have been an asset for the scope and depth of its action. Comprised of about 100 young, committed officers, it had strategic vision and planning capabilities. In order to enable the Department of Social Affairs to cope with the new tasks of co-ordination, monitoring and evaluation envisaged by the reform, the Framework Law provided for doubling the Department's staff by hiring 100 new personnel.

To sum up, at the time the EU strategy against poverty and social exclusion was launched in Lisbon, the initial conditions were fairly unfavourable: Italy's policy-making in the social assistance field was *de facto* rather incongruous with the four processual objectives of the OMC, with the partial exception of good planning capability on the part of the Department of Social Affairs. At the same time, however, endogenous dynamics of change were under way that worked in the same direction as the OMC, at least as regards the four processual objectives. The integrated system of social services and interventions envisaged under Framework Law No.328 of 2000 was intended precisely to promote vertical, horizontal and cross-sectoral integration, while at the same time setting the stage for an improvement of Italy's institutional

---

[23] *Sistema informativo dei servizi sociali*, Information System of Social Services, which was never built (see *infra*).

capability in the social assistance sector, especially as regards its planning and learning components. Our hunch is that if these dynamics had had the time to run their course, the Social Inclusion process would have made a greater impact on Italian policy-making in the social assistance field than it has done so far.

The first product of the Social Inclusion process on the Italian side, the National Action Plan on Social Inclusion (NAP/incl) 2001-2003, was built around the provisions of the Framework Law, and highlighted all the features of the new system of policy planning. In the words of the European Commission, Italy's NAP/incl 2001-2003 contained "elements of a national strategy that is being improved in order to reflect new realities or made more coherent"[24]. However, the NAP/incl did not go much farther than that. It provided an inventory of the main challenges in terms of poverty and social exclusion and of the existing policies to combat them, but did not build on the identification of such challenges – nor on examples of virtuous policies – to innovate, set targets or make new commitments. Three path-breaking measures introduced in 1998 which epitomised the new phase of Italian social assistance (a benefit for large families, a maternity benefit for women without insurance-based entitlements and the experimental introduction of a minimum income scheme) were given scant consideration in country's first NAP/incl, and the Nice objectives were not systematically used to reformulate problem diagnoses and strategic approaches. In particular, the fourth Nice objective (mobilising all stakeholders), so important for the new Italian strategy to succeed, did not receive focussed attention. No targets were set concerning stakeholders' mobilisation, and the section on the preparation of the NAP/incl was confined to a list of actors and meetings which did not specify the mode of interaction involved (likely to have been predominately "consultative")[25].

The first Italian NAP/incl was disappointing insofar as it neither set targets nor made new commitments, while tending to assume that policy planning *per se* would go a long way towards combating poverty and social exclusion, But some of these faults and weaknesses appear to have been widely shared by other Member States' NAPs in the first round of the Social Inclusion process (Ferrera *et al.*, 2002). Moreover, the drafting of 2001 NAP/incl overlapped with Italy's general elections, held in May 2001. The task of drafting the NAP/incl had been assigned to an internal team within the Department of Social Affairs and, despite

---

[24] First Draft Joint Report on Social Inclusion (CEC, 2001b: 22).

[25] The actors listed include central administration agencies, organisations of regional and local administration, trade unions, third sector associations, the national statistical office and policy evaluation agencies. It is noteworthy that the employers' associations were not listed.

its policy salience, it is a reasonable guess that the electoral campaign involving the Minister might have somewhat diverted the attention of her staff from the action plan.

As we have already observed, it appears likely that had the endogenous dynamics occurring during the early stages of the Social Inclusion process been allowed to progress, they would have actually reinforced the clout of the OMC in relation to national policy-making in the social assistance sector. As already seen, Law No.328 of 2000 was pursuing the same "processual" objectives as those of the OMC. Like all framework laws, however, Law No.328 was an "open" law: it established principles and defined priorities, but required for their realisation the enactment of a rather long list of implementation provisions, involving various institutions at different levels of government. Now, in the two-year span between the first and the second Italian NAP/incl, some new dynamics developed that upset the implementation of Law No.328 of 2000 and indeed hindered Italy's adjustment towards the four processual objectives in the social assistance sector. These are related to the change of government, to organisational changes in the offices responsible for social policy at the state level and – most importantly – to the constitutional reform affecting Title V of the Constitution, enacted in March 2001 and applied in October 2001, after a popular referendum held in the same month[26].

The greatest impediment to the implementation of Law No.328/2000 has been the reform of Title V of the Constitution, which establishes the prerogatives of the regions, the provinces and the municipalities. Not being enumerated among the exclusive competences of the state, nor among the shared competences of the state and the regions, social assistance is now an area subject to exclusive regional legislation[27]. However, the fixing of essential levels of provision concerning social rights to be guaranteed across the whole national territory remains in the hands of the state, which furthermore retains the power to substitute for lower levels of government in order to assure that citizens enjoy such essential levels of provision, once established[28]. In fact, and also considering how difficult it is to fix essential levels of provision of non-

---

[26] Constitutional Law No.3 of 18 October 2001.

[27] Unless social assistance provisions can also perform functions pertaining to areas subject to shared competences. This principle was upheld by the Constitutional Court in late 2003, when it declared that regulation of crèches, albeit traditionally considered part of the assistance sector, is subject to shared competence given that crèches also serve educational purposes, education being a matter for concurrent legislation. See ruling of the Constitutional Court No.370 of 17-23 December 2003.

[28] Essential levels of provisions must be set by law or according to a procedure set by law. See ruling of the Constitutional Court No.88 of 13-27 March 2003.

monetary benefits (and those regarding the prevention of exclusion and promotion of inclusion in particular; see Gori, 2003), it seems fair to argue that the constitutional reform has at least partially disembowelled the reform of social assistance embodied in the Framework Law. The constitutional reform has deprived the national government of those tools for co-ordination and planning that it had acquired shortly before, after a quarter-century wait[29]. As a consequence of the new constitutional provisions, the state cannot issue a new Social Plan to replace the one that expired in 2003, and co-ordination of lower-level policy action into a coherent whole has become considerably more difficult than before. Implementation of the Framework Law is haphazardly occurring at the only territorial level now vested with legislative and regulatory capacity in the social assistance sector (except for the setting of essential levels of provision): the subnational level. The drawback is that, with no guidance from the national level, implementation is left to voluntary compliance by regional and local governments, thus perpetuating precisely what Framework Law No.328 of 2000 was intended to counteract: territorial disparities in the enjoyment of social rights, particularly between the north and the south. To put it bluntly, Italian citizens living in northern regions tend to have access to a relatively wide range of social services and cash benefits, while their regional and local governments have approved regional and "zonal" social plans and developed monitoring systems. At the same time, many citizens living in southern regions have little if any access to social services and can claim no cash benefits, while their regional and local governments have not implemented Law No.328[30].

Such a centrifugal drift has found no countervailing forces from within the centre-right government led by Silvio Berlusconi, voted into office in spring 2001. The government has taken a markedly low-key approach towards the possibility of launching initiatives aimed at creating a reference framework for local social assistance. Even under the new constitutional provisions, there might be more scope for action on the part of the central government than what the Berlusconi government seems keen to undertake. Juridical relations between Law No.328 of 2000 and the constitutional reform do not seem to have been investigated thoroughly, and the task of monitoring the implementation of the Framework Law was no longer assigned to any office within the Wel-

---

[29] It is to be noted that it was the same centre-left parliamentary majority that endorsed both the framework law and the constitutional reform.

[30] "There are entire areas in the south where there is no social assistance whatsoever, and the only channel of help to citizens is through the NHS general practitioner, or the priest" (interview V).

fare Ministry starting from 2003[31]. Apparently, the government seems eager to consider Law No.328 of 2000 obsolete and in February 2003 it issued a rather vague "White Paper on Welfare" which is of little practical use as a guidance document. The White Paper identifies two "new priorities": "to manage demographic change" and "to put the family at the core of policy action"[32]. However, the way it deals with the role of the family within the welfare system seems completely at odds with the normative conclusions of mainstream contemporary social science research (see, for instance, Esping-Andersen, 1999), insofar as it assumes that the family is, and must remain in the future, the main welfare provider and the cornerstone of Italy's welfare system, disregarding the poor efficiency and distributional consequences of such an approach[33]. But the most relevant feature of the White Paper on Welfare is that only general priorities are set, while the issue of financial resources necessary to implement such (vague) priorities is evaded completely[34]. A proposal put forward by the White Paper which, if followed, could have helped to overcome the governance problems of social assistance sector stemming from the constitutional reform is that of establishing an OMC-type mechanism at the national level. This mechanism would have consisted of procedures "founded on the establishment of common macro-objectives, the identification of [...] indicators, the definition of operational goals and implementation times" (Ministry of Labour and Social Affairs, 2003: 37), involving all levels of government by means of regional and local action plans on social inclusion, with decision-making open "should it be deemed necessary, to all the other actors involved in the system" (*ibid.*). The objectives were never specified, while the OMC-type mechanism was never implemented[35].

---

[31] The Ministry or Labour and Social Policies (also known as the Welfare Ministry) incorporated the Department of Social Affairs as of June 2001 (see *infra*).

[32] It is worth noting that the family model implied by the White Paper is the traditional one, based on wedlock.

[33] Giubboni (2003: 590) calls the approach of the White Paper one of "'conservative modernization' of the familism which is typical of Italy's welfare regime".

[34] In the words of the non-governmental expert report on the Italian NAP inclusion 2001, issued within the context of the Community Action Programme to combat social exclusion, "a wide debate followed considering the White Paper as a generic proposal without timed objectives for social and labour insertion" (Strati, 2003: 29). See, for instance, the contributions by Del Boca (6 February 2003), Saraceno, Boeri and Perotti, and Ranci (20 February 2003) posted on the web journal *La Voce* (www.lavoce.info, accessed 14 June 2004).

[35] Evidence we collected from independent sources points in the same direction. "Open co-ordination is a method, but you have to give yourself objectives first. But objectives are totally lacking. There are declared objectives that are completely general, mainly relating to employment, but also that of enhancing fertility. But the objective of building a network of services to families where such services are lacking that

Prima facie, therefore, the state has backed away from the social assistance sector – and consequently from political action to combat poverty and social exclusion – even more than would be congruent with the constitutional reform. More accurately, however, it could be said that the Berlusconi government reoriented priorities within the social assistance field away from an overall, comprehensive strategy and towards haphazard categorical interventions aimed at the elderly and families[36]. A clear manifestation of this is the decision not to proceed with a generalisation of the minimum income scheme which was introduced experimentally in selected municipalities between 1999 and 2002 and highlighted as a best practice in the first NAP/incl[37]. Such a measure could well be one of those essential levels of provision concerning social rights that the state is entitled to set, and one of the easiest to craft, at least as regards its monetary component. However, the Budget Law for 2004 provides for co-funding by the state if a region decides to adopt a measure called Income of Last Resort (*Reddito di ultima istanza*). Although the details of such measure are still unclear, it is remarkable that the central government eschews social policy intervention in a matter, that of essential levels of provision, falling within its exclusive competence and leaves such intervention to regional voluntarism. It is tempting to guess that rich northern regions will introduce the measure, while the poorest southern regions will not. At the same time, in at least two instances, both related to policy interventions in favour of the family, the government has adopted a much more active (and confrontational) stance, trying to encroach upon the regions' constitutional rights in the social assistance field. The first episode has to do with the government unilaterally instituting, in Budget Law for 2002, a fund

---

would be instrumental towards the fertility objective, is absent" (interview V). "The proposal of a national OMC was in the White Paper because it is fashionable, but at present time it is a dead letter" (interview Z). "This is bunk. At the present time organisational preconditions are lacking and there are no initiatives" (interview A).

[36] The Budget Law for 2002 raised the amounts of the pension supplements and the social assistance old age pensions for beneficiaries over seventy years old (over sixty years old in the case of the invalidity pensions). As regards families, the Budget Law for 2002 raised the tax credit for dependent children, while the Budget Law for 2003 introduced the "no-tax area", an above-the-line tax deduction shielding a variable amount of earned income from the application of personal income tax. Neither of the latter measures seem to have had a considerable poverty reduction effect, due to the fact that the poor typically earn little if any income, so the tax credit instrument is utterly ineffective. From December 2003 to December 2004 mothers receive a one-off cash transfer worth 1,000 euros when they give birth to or adopt any child following their first one. The paucity of the transfer makes any pro-natalist or anti-poverty effect highly unlikely (see also Sacchi and Bastagli, 2005).

[37] Italy is one of the only two EU-15 Member States (the other is Greece) not to have a minimum income scheme.

earmarked for financing crèches, and those at the workplace in particular. The Constitutional Court has ruled against this[38]. The second episode relates to the earmarking of 10% of the 2003 Social Fund to reduce the cost of home loans for newly-wed couples, something that the state is probably not entitled to do under the new constitutional architecture. This triggered a harsh confrontation with the regions, resolved in favour of the latter before appeals to the Constitutional Court were lodged.

A third endogenous change has involved the organisation of the office responsible for social policies at the governmental level. A bill reforming state ministries, enacted by the centre-left government in 1999, provided for the establishment of a Ministry of Labour and Social Policies starting from the first government after the 2001 general elections[39]. This was done in order to take advantage of policy interdependencies in the employment and social policy areas. But the process of grafting the Department of Social Affairs onto the Ministry of Labour did not work out well. Because of wage and status differentials between the Presidency of the Council of Ministers and the Labour Ministry, when given the possibility to choose all but three officials (out of about one hundred) chose to remain in the Presidency of the Council of Ministers and did not follow their organisation's journey from a department of the Presidency to a department of the new Ministry of Labour and Social Policies. This almost completely deprived the new department of its former expertise. Moreover, only 80 new staff were hired, as opposed to 100 provided for by Law No.328 of 2000. Thus, from being prospectively staffed with 200 people, the new department was left rather understaffed, within a ministry employing more than 8,000 personnel in the labour departments. Moreover, a recent internal re-organisation cancelled the departments to establish a general secretariat, devoid of the power to allocate resources. This seems to have reinforced the structural weakness within the ministry, of those functions related to social policies as opposed to those related to employment policies, and at the same time to have reduced that capacity for co-ordinated action which was guaranteed by the departmental structure.

When jointly assessed, the endogenous dynamics taking shape between the first and the second Italian NAP/incl clearly obstructed the path towards a policy-making mode in the social assistance field more

---

[38] The Court ruled that the state cannot consider this matter under its exclusive competence, but also rejected the plaintiffs' (i.e. the regions') claim that this matter falls within the regions' exclusive competence, insofar as crèches perform educational functions, and education is a matter of shared competence. See footnote 27.

[39] The original reform provided that the Ministry should have competence over health policy as well, but the Berlusconi government changed it to maintain an autonomous Health Ministry.

attuned with that envisaged under the OMC. Processes of vertical and cross-sectoral integration have been upset by the constitutional reform and lack of political guidance on the part of the national government, while horizontal integration is now largely left to the will of the regions, a development in which the national government seems happy to acquiesce. Also the two most promising directions of the process of institutional capability building – the strengthening of its planning and the learning components – have suffered a hard blow from the loss of functions by central government and, in particular, from organisational changes and the lack of political backing for the fight against poverty and social exclusion. One of the initiatives we have mentioned as a sign of institutional capability strengthening, the creation of a territorially integrated system of information on social outlays, measures and needs, has never seen the light of day.

Italy's 2003 NAP/incl, and the way it was drafted, is a clear sign of the extent to which such endogenous dynamics of change have worked in the opposite direction as the adjustment towards the OMC processual objectives. Italy's NAP/incl for the period 2003-2005 was drafted in less than two months – between May and July 2003 – by a five-person staff comprised of the Director-General of the Directorate General for "Employment and Vocational Training", a senior officer and a junior officer from the same DG and two external consultants to the same DG. In no official document internal to the Ministry of Labour and Social Policies can there be found any formal assignment of the task of drafting the 2003 NAP/incl to a specific bureau. Apparently, the task of drafting the NAP /incl was assigned in May 2003 to the Director-General of a DG little connected with issues of poverty and social exclusion on the basis that the same officer had drawn up the first NAP/incl in 2001. This officer then involved her aides and staff, none of whom is directly concerned with stable administrative functions connected to poverty and social exclusion issues or social assistance. In addition to writing the NAP/incl, the same five people performed the task of involving the various offices within the Ministry and the regions, and of consulting the other governmental branches, the social partners and the NGOs. Some of the substantive aspects of Italy's NAP/incl 2003-2005 are particularly telling and useful for assessing the impact on Italian institutional capability of the Social Inclusion process.

The Plan is accompanied by a detailed and comprehensive statistical appendix, which was only completed in September 2003, two months after the NAP had been sent to Brussels. Presumably because of this, the NAP/incl is not informed by quantitative knowledge of social exclusion. However, it is the more inherently political aspect of the NAP that is utterly inadequate: no overall strategy for tackling and preventing poverty and social exclusion is presented, no targets are set and there is no indication of resources destined to listed policy measures[40]. In short: no commitments are made. With the exception of the scarcely useful "White Paper on Welfare", there were no political guidelines that the group of officials and consultants drafting the NAP/incl could follow, and no inputs on how to go about setting targets or identifying priorities for action came from the political level of the Ministry[41]. The lack of a strategy and political guidelines also influenced the way the NGOs and the social partners were involved in the making of the NAP: mere consultation took place, with the first meeting with the stakeholders convened only in July, so as to keep the drafting insulated while waiting for some political guidance which never came. All the stakeholders expressed their profound dissatisfaction with their involvement in the process of preparing the NAP/incl, as well as their disagreement with the substantive contents of the Plan[42]. But this did not trigger mobilisation on the part of NGOs and the social partners which, instead, put forward their negative comments to the plan, or – as was the case with the social partners – even refused to contribute to the NAP/incl, deemed impossible to improve[43]. This stance by the stakeholders is partly a consequence of their involvement in the preparation of the NAP/incl at a very late stage of the process, only few days before the document had to

---

[40] The only quantified targets in the NAP are the 2005 intermediate targets towards the Lisbon employment objectives. "This tells a lot about the imbalance between the two sectors (employment and social inclusion): once again, there is a vision of the fight against social exclusion running eminently through employment inclusion" (interview Z).

[41] "(The directions given by the White Paper are) so generic that it is extremely difficult to squeeze useful guidelines out of them, priorities for action, due to the lack of substance" (interview A). It is noteworthy, moreover, that the policy views set out in the White Paper concerning the role of the family within the welfare system run counter to much of mainstream contemporary social science. In the words of the European Anti-poverty Network "the Italian Plan sees the family as the main welfare provider and the most important tool for social inclusion, actually delegating to it almost the full range of those responsibilities that should be in the hands of society and public authorities, forgetting that many times the family alone cannot adequately respond or, put more simply, is just not there" (EAPN, 2003a: 10).

[42] See, for instance, the European Anti-poverty Network which reports that their Italian section feels that "the aim of 'mobilizing all relevant actors' has not been met even on a symbolic level" (EAPN, 2003a: 15). On the contents, see CILAP (2003), and its summary in English (EAPN, 2003b: 6).

[43] In a joint document issued on 22 July 2003 (a week after the draft NAP/incl was presented to them) Italy's three main trade unions state that "(our complete disagreement on the content of the draft NAP/incl) makes it impossible, for us, to put forward amendments to the presented document" (Letter of CGIL, CISL and UIL to the Welfare Minister and the Officer in charge of producing the NAP, available at www.uil.it/nap.htm).

be sent to Brussels. It can also be read, however, as a fatalistic attitude, showing resigned acceptance of the fact that a strategy to fight poverty and social exclusion is not on the government's agenda, except for issues related to the defence of the traditional family based on wedlock or when the attention of the media can be attracted to highly visible but scattered social policy interventions[44].

The absence of domestic commitment to the Social Inclusion process is illustrated by the way an inherently political document such as the NAP/incl is conceived by the political level of the Ministry: a mere "report to Brussels", rather than an action plan for the implementation of a strategy[45]. Since the preparation of the NAP/incl is regarded as an administrative task to be complied with in a token fashion, no effort is spent on creating a stable structure to draft it and monitor its implementation. Therefore, not only is there no dedicated office, but the task of drafting the NAP is not allocated to an existing office but rather to an identified officer whose stable functions do not include poverty and social exclusion issues[46]. What is relevant here is that the lack of a stable assignment of the task of preparing the NAP/incl hinders many achievements as regards the processual objectives that would otherwise be possible – and in particular reduces the likelihood of an impact of the social inclusion process on Italy's institutional capability in the field of social assistance.

---

[44] It is telling that the second European roundtable on poverty and social exclusion, held in Turin in October 2003 under the Italian Presidency of the EU, carried a subtitle: "The role of the family in promoting social inclusion".

[45] Much of our assessment of the Italian NAP/incl is shared by the second Joint Inclusion Report (CEC and Council of the European Union, 2004: 180-184). The lack of quantified targets, the scanty information on the allocation of financial resources, the inadequate involvement of the stakeholders and the social partners are all noted in the Report, which also utters words of caution as regards the overall territorial governance of the social assistance system given that "a strong co-ordination of policies and measures, as well as of monitoring and evaluation is still lacking to a degree" (CEC and Council of the European Union, 2004: 183). In addition, the Report also points to the NAP/incl's shortcomings as regards gender issues ("the principle of gender mainstreaming appears to have been implemented in the Italian NAP/incl only to a limited extent" [*ibid.*]) and immigrants ("social insertion of immigrants may also prove a bigger challenge that envisaged in the plan" [CEC and Council of the European Union, 2004: 184]). The issue of immigration, or better how immigration was dealt with in the NAP/incl, triggered a harsh confrontation in bilateral meetings between the Commission and Italian government officials in fall 2003.

[46] This might change in the future, as an projected internal reorganisation of the Ministry should explicitly allocate the function of preparing the NAP/incl to a Directorate General called "DG Family, Social Rights and Corporate Social Responsibility". This should be the same DG responsible for policy interventions to combat poverty and social exclusion.

For instance, if the collaborative relations initiated in the preparation of the NAP/incl between the group drafting it and the regions could develop and progress, institutional capability could be strengthened[47]. This requires the setting up of a stable and dedicated office, otherwise the links disperse and vanish as soon as the process of writing the NAP is concluded, as actually happened. Stable collaboration with the regions on co-ordination and monitoring of regional and local policies could clearly enhance all four components of Italy's institutional capability as regards social inclusion: the ability to identify policy options, local problems and interinstitutional strains could be improved, while agreements with regions and local actors could share decisions. By the same token, a parallel institutionalisation of relations with NGOs and social partners as regards social inclusion could broaden decision-making and improve legitimation of policy outputs. Moreover, the lack of a stable function of developing the action plan on social inclusion and monitoring its implementation increases the likelihood of the whole exercise occurring in an informational vacuum, disconnected from statistical evidence and knowledge. Monitoring of inclusion policies and social expenditure in Italy is scanty and extremely heterogeneous across regions, and an overall picture is virtually non-existent. The exigency of producing the NAP/incl could well be instrumental in monitoring social expenditure at all levels of government, something of the utmost importance for budgetary reasons and also because it is a precondition for setting essential levels of provision concerning social rights. Precisely for these reasons, however, surveys will be carried out in the near future with a view to establishing a permanent monitoring of social expenditure at the various levels of government, so this might be one of those endogenous dynamics of change that happen to facilitate adjustment towards the OMC processual objectives.

To sum up, the poor quality and the improvised way the 2003 NAP/incl was drafted testify to the detrimental influence of the changes occurring since 2001 on the process of institutional capability building. Causality can then be reversed, insofar as the necessity of preparing the

---

[47] Probably the most interesting aspects of Italy's NAP/incl 2003-2005 are to be found in Annexes I and II, where the state of affairs as regards the implementation of Law 328 of 2000 at subnational levels of government is detailed. This is the outcome of a collaboration between the officials writing the NAP and the representatives of the regions, who were involved in its preparation from the very beginning. In addition to contributing Annexes I and II (based on work carried out with ISFOL, a technical agency already mentioned in the section on the employment process), the regions also contributed to sections of the main text. Surprisingly enough, no mention is made of this collaboration in section five of the NAP/incl, which should have been dedicated – *inter alia* – to assessing "the process which was followed to monitor the 2001 NAP/incl and to develop the 2003 NAP/incl" (SPC, 2003).

NAP/incl is not being used as an instrument of institutional capability building and as a means for better governance of the chaotic social assistance sector in Italy. At the present time, we can only guess at the reasons why this has not happened so far, as we will do in the conclusions.

Conclusions

As we have seen, both as regards employment and social inclusion Italy's policy-making modes, at the time the OMC was applied to these fields, were quite dissonant with those envisaged under it. In both fields, moreover, there have been endogenous dynamics of change that seem to have inhibited the OMC's scope for inducing change towards the fourth process objective, that of institutional capability building. However, the two OMC processes have clearly had different impacts on Italy's policy-making, when assessed in terms of institutional capability. If our account is accurate, then the autonomous impact of the OMC has been relatively significant in the case of employment, and relatively insignificant in that of social inclusion. We have repeatedly pointed out evidence that can be taken as validating this claim: the different quality of National Action Plans in the two fields; the different strength, quality and degree of institutionalisation of supporting structures for planning and learning; the different degree of domestic institutionalisation of the employment as opposed to the social inclusion process, with the creation of a dedicated structure in one case and extemporaneous assignment of tasks in the other; and, finally, the different mode of participation in the process, with growing awareness and some acquired clout in promoting and "uploading" to the European level domestically relevant issues in the field of employment, as opposed to substantial lack of interest in that of social inclusion. More work is certainly needed to develop indicators for operationalising the concept of institutional capability and to assess the effects of the OMC on them. Nonetheless, we believe that the evidence we have collected so far is strong enough to highlight remarkable variance in the OMC's impact on Italy's policy-making modes and structures in the two fields. The next step is to explain this variance. Again, much more research is required on this front: at this stage we can only make a first attempt at singling out the explanatory factors, without trying to establish a hierarchy among them.

Retrospectively, it would seem that our *ex ante* conjectures, as outlined in the introduction, were indeed reasonable ones: differences in the external stimuli (OMC processes with different features) on the one hand and differences in the endogenous dynamics of change on the other to are evidently important factors in explaining the OMC's impact on national policy-making systems (apparently, variance in initial conditions was not available in this case). But two further clusters of plausible explanatory factors emerged from the analysis: differences in functional salience of the two policy areas, and differences in political conjunctures and agendas. As a way of organising future research in this field, let us consider each of these four clusters, while at the same time calling for comparative case study analyses that may introduce variance in the initial conditions.

As for differences in exogenous stimuli provided by different OMC processes, it seems that structural differences between the employment and the social inclusion process – outlined in table 1 below – were relevant factors in explaining why the first had some impact on Italy's institutional capability whereas the second had very little, if any. To enjoy a direct Treaty base makes the Luxembourg process a statutory OMC process, with specific guidelines to be implemented by each Member State and Council recommendations, none of which obtains in the social inclusion process. This has made a difference in the Italian case, forcing the national authorities to comply with more demanding statutory requirements in the employment field. Moreover, periodicity may well be an important factor, insofar as in the employment case Italy underwent a learning process (learning how to comply, how to draw up good NAPs, how to defend them at the European level, how to feed them back into the strategy itself, how to upload domestically relevant issues) that became tangible in its effects only after some rounds of the EES, so the more infrequent the periodicity of an OMC process, the less may be the scope for self-reinforcing changes to occur. This also points to the longer institutional life of the employment as opposed to the social inclusion process as an explanatory factor[48].

---

[48] Thus, the current difference in Italy's response to the requirements of the two OMC processes may simply be a matter of time (after all, institutionalisation takes time). Still, we believe that structural aspects make a difference, and therefore that the social inclusion process may develop in a way parallel, but not convergent to the one the employment process has done.

Table 1: Differences between the Employment
and the Social Inclusion Processes

	Employment Process	Social Inclusion Process
Treaty base	Specific provisions in the Employment Title (Article 128 TEC)	General provisions on co-operation between Member States in social policy (Article 137 TEC)
Periodicity	Annual	Biennial
Recommendations to Member States	Yes	No
Implementation of guidelines by the Member States	Yes	No (Member States pursue common objectives)

Note: This is an updated version of table 1 in Ferrera *et al.* (2002: 232).

The next cluster of explanatory factors relates to differences in endogenous dynamics of change, both their timing and nature. Although there have been processes of devolution of powers to the regions and the local authorities in both the employment and the social inclusion case, and in both cases such processes have worked in the opposite way as the objective of strengthening national institutional capability, their timing and nature have been very different. In the employment case, the constitutional reform of 2001 took place *after* the consolidation of the new system of employment policy management, and constitutionalised the already existing shared legislative competence between the state and the regions. The passage from *de facto* to *de jure* shared competence did not upset the existing system, which had moreover been cast following a precise organisational model imposed by the state. True, devolution of powers was concurrent with the launch of the EES and has somewhat disturbed institutional capability building at the national level, but the whole process has been rather smooth compared to what has happened in the social assistance field. In the latter, the European strategy for social inclusion started at the same time that a reform, similar in its guiding principles to what occurred in the employment field, was in its early stages of implementation. The model of social assistance governance envisaged by the reform – which configured a system of shared competences, with strong guidance and co-ordination powers of the state – was then completely disrupted by the 2001 constitutional reform. Proto-shared competence was transformed into exclusive competence of the regions and written into the Constitution. Therefore, the constitutional reform had a path-breaking character and happened *before* the consolidation of the system could take place, and institutionalisation of monitoring and supporting agencies at the national level – pushed by the OMC – could begin.

Moreover, endogenous organisational change was of a different nature in the two fields: while the ministerial branch dealing with employment policies remained the same, an organisational earthquake, striking the authority dealing with social assistance, intervened in the early stages of the social inclusion process, putting in jeopardy and even disrupting all that had been gained that far in terms of institutional capability.

The evidence we have exposed in the chapter, however, points to another important cluster of explanatory factors, related to differential functional salience of the two policy areas. For Italian policy-makers, the problem of unemployment is paramount, especially long-term unemployment, youth unemployment and unemployment in the south; poverty much less so. Moreover, it is a widely held view among policy-makers that raising employment levels and reducing unemployment would automatically raise many citizens above the poverty line *and* include them in social networks, thereby curing many problems on this front. It seems crystal clear, then, that the issues of unemployment and labour market reform were more salient than issues of social inclusion – or at least were perceived as such by policy-makers – and this entailed very different degrees of domestic organisational effort invested in the two strategies. This immediately leads to the fourth cluster of *explanantes*: political conjuncture and agenda. The Olive Tree coalition had a relatively clear agenda of labour market *cum* welfare state modernisation, encompassing both employment policies and social assistance reform. The Berlusconi government has so far had a clear agenda of labour market reform and flexibilisation, but has lost sight of a dedicated agenda for social inclusion issues. In the field of social assistance, the government has mainly focused on the defence of the traditional family model and – when the attention of the media could be attracted to them – on individual, flagship policy interventions such as raising benefits for the elderly or granting a one-off cash transfer for new-born babies. Social inclusion *per se*, moreover, has been framed almost uniquely in terms of work inclusion.

Given the lack of "hard", tangible positive and negative incentives to comply with the OMC, in a poorly institutionalised context where internalisation of norms is still incomplete, our analysis thus points to the ultimate importance of politics, and political commitment.

References

Baldini, M., Bosi, P. and Toso, S. (2000), "Targeting Welfare in Italy: Old Problems and Perspectives of Reform", *Materiali di discussione*, No.337, CAPP, Dipartimento di Economia Politica, Università degli Studi di Modena e Reggio Emilia.

Boeri, T. and Perotti, R. (2001), "Less Pensions, More Welfare", Paper presented at the conference on "The Frontiers of Economic Research in Italy", Rome, September 2001.

CEC (2001a), Communication from the Commission "Employment and Social Policies: A Framework for Investing in Quality", COM (2001) 313 final of 20 June 2001 (http://europa.eu.int/eur-lex/en/com/cnc/2001/com2001_0313en 01. pdf).

CEC (2001b), Communication from the Commission "Draft Joint Report on Social Inclusion", COM (2001) 565 final of 10 October 2001 (http://europa. eu.int/eur-lex/en/com/pdf/2001/com2001_0565en01.pdf).

CEC and Council of the European Union (2004b), Joint Report by the Commission and the Council on Social Inclusion, Document 7101/04, Brussels, 5 March 2004 (http://europa.eu.int/comm/employment_social/soc-prot/soc-incl/final_joint_inclusion_report_2003_en.pdf).

CILAP (2003), "Il Piano di azione nazionale contro la povertà e l'esclusione sociale", Commento del CILAP, EAPN Italia (http://www.eapn.org).

Council of the European Union (2002), Fight against Poverty and Social Exclusion: Common Objectives for the Second Round of National Action Plans – Endorsement, 14164/1/02 REV1, 25 November 2002.

Council of the European Union (2003), Council Decision 2003/8/EC of 22 July 2003 on Guidelines for the Employment Policies of the Member States, OJ L 197 of 5 August 2003, pp.0013-0021.

de la Porte, C., Pochet, P. and Room, G. (2001), "Social Benchmarking, Policy-making and New Governance in the EU", Journal of European Social Policy, Vol.11, No.4, pp.291-307.

de la Porte, C. and Pochet, P. (eds.) (2002), Building Social Europe through the Open Method of Co-ordination, P.I.E.-Peter Lang, Brussels.

EAPN (2003a), "National Action Plans on Inclusion 2003-2005. Where is the Political Energy? EAPN's response to the second round of Plans", EAPN Report, October 2003 (http://www.eapn.org).

EAPN (2003b), EAPN Network News, No.102, September-October 2003 (http:// www.eapn.org).

Esping-Andersen, G. (1999), Social Foundations of Postindustrial Economies, Oxford University Press, Oxford.

European Council (2002), Barcelona European Council, Presidency Conclusions, 15 and 16 March 2002.

Fargion, V. (2001), "Creeping Workfare Policies: The Case of Italy", in Gilbert, N. (ed.), Activating the Unemployed: A Comparative Appraisal of Work-oriented Policies, International Social Security Series, Vol.3, Rutgers, N.J. Transaction Publishers, pp.29-67.

Fargion, V. (2002), "Decoupling Passive and Active Labour Market Policies. The Italian Case in Comparative Perspective", Working Paper presented for the COST A13 "Unemployment Working Group meeting", Malta, 1-2 November 2002.

Ferrera, M., Matsaganis, M. and Sacchi, S. (2002), "Open Coordination against Poverty: The New EU 'Social Inclusion Process'", *Journal of European Social Policy*, Vol.12, No.3, pp.227-239.

Ferrera, M. and Gualmini, E. (2004), *Rescued by Europe? Social and Labour Market Reforms in Italy from Maastricht to Berlusconi*, Amsterdam University Press, Amsterdam.

Giubboni, S. (2003), "L'incerta europeizzazione. Diritto della sicurezza sociale e lotta all'esclusione in Italia", *Giornale di diritto del lavoro e di relazioni industriali*, No.99-100, pp.563-602.

Gori, C. (2003), "Applicare i livelli essenziali nel sociale", *Prospettive sociali e sanitarie*, No.15-17, pp.1-8.

Graziano, P. (forthcoming), "From a Guaranteed Labour Market to the 'Flexible Worker' Model? The Transformation of Italian Unemployment Policy in the '90s", in Clasen, J., Ferrera, M. and Rhodes, M. (eds.), *The Politics of Unemployment Insurance in Contemporary Europe*, Routledge, London.

Heclo, H. (1974), *Modern Social Politics: From Relief to Income Maintenance in Britain and Sweden*, Yale University Press, New Haven.

Hemerijck, A. and Visser, J. (2001), "Learning and Mimicking: How European Welfare States Reform", unpublished paper, University of Leiden and University of Amsterdam, June 2001.

Hodson, D. and Maher, I. (2001), "The Open Method of Coordination as a New Mode of Governance: The Case of Soft Economic Policy Coordination", *Journal of Common Market Studies*, Vol.39, No.4, pp.719-746.

Huntington, S. (1968), *Political Order in Changing Societies*, Yale University Press, New Haven.

Ministry of Labour and Social Affairs (2001), *Libro bianco sul mercato del lavoro in Italia. Proposte per una sociatà attiva e per un lavoro di qualità*, Ministero del Lavoro e delle Politiche Sociali, Rome, October 2001 (http://www.welfare.gov.it).

Ministry of Labour and Social Affairs (2003), *White Paper on Welfare State. Proposals for a Dynamic and Solidary Society*, Ministero del Lavoro e delle Politiche Sociali, Rome, February 2003 (http://www.welfare.gov.it).

Mosher, J. (2000), "Open Method of Coordination: Functional and Political Origins", *ECSA Review*, Vol.13, No.3, pp.6-7.

Radaelli, C. (2003), "The Open Method of Coordination: A New Governance Architecture for the European Union?", *SIEPS Report*, No.1, Swedish Institute for European Policy Studies, Stockholm, March 2003.

Sabel, C. F. and Zeitlin, J. (2003), "Active Welfare, Experimental Governance, Pragmatic Constitutionalism: The New Transformation of Europe", unpublished paper presented to the International Conference of the Hellenic Presidency of the European Union "The Modernisation of the European Social Model & EU Policies and Instruments", Ioannina, Greece, 21-22 May 2003.

Sacchi, S. and Bastagli, F. (2005), "Italy: Striving Uphill, but Stopping Halfway. The troubled Journey of the Experimental Minimum Insertion Income", in Ferrera, M. (ed.), *Welfare State Reform in Southern Europe: Fighting Poverty and Social Exclusion*, Routledge, London, (forthcoming).

Scott, J. and Trubek, D. M. (2001), "Mind the Gap: Law and New Approaches to Governance in the European Union", *European Law Journal*, Vol.8, No.1, pp.1-18.

Sestito, P. (2002), *Il mercato del lavoro in Italia*, Laterza, Bari.

SPC (2003), Common Outline for the 2003/2005 NAPs/Inclusion, Social Protection Committee (http://www.europa.eu.int/comm/employment_social/socprot/soc-incl/commonoutline2003final_en.pdf).

Strati, F. (2003), "Report on the Italian NAP Inclusion 2001", *First Report* (http://www.europa.eu.int/comm/employment_social/socprot/studies/studies_ en.htm).

Trubek, D. M. and Mosher, J. (2003), "New Governance, Employment Policy, and the European Social Policy", in Zeitlin, J. and Trubek, D. M. (eds.), *Governing Work and Welfare in a New Economy: European and American Experiments*, Oxford University Press, Oxford, pp.33-58.

CHAPTER 5

The OMC as Selective Amplifier for National Strategies of Reform

What the Netherlands Want to Learn from Europe

Jelle VISSER

Introduction: Europe's Underperformance and the Search for Reform

In the early 1990s, against the background of stagnating growth and employment, and rising unemployment, two main explanations were offered for Europe's underperformance[1]. The first explanation stressed the inability to handle economic shocks. Since the 1970s periods of job growth had been followed by periods of heavy job losses. After each recession, unemployment stabilised at a higher level and more jobless people entered the ranks of the long-term unemployed (Cameron, 2001; Layard *et al.*, 1991). In addition to the search for macroeconomic stabilisation, the "rigidities" of the labour market favouring the job and wage interests of "insiders" through employment protection became a target for research and reform (Bentolila and Bertola, 1990; Esping-Andersen and Regini, 2000; OECD, 1994; Nickell, 1997). With the realisation of the Monetary Union, following the decision of the Intergovernmental

[1] The author thanks Nynke Wiekenkamp and Paul de Beer, both at AIAS, for their assistance with the research and for constructive comments. Earlier versions of this chapter have been presented during the OMC workshop at the European University Institute in Florence in July 2003, the biennial conference of the Council of Europeanists in Chicago in March 2004 and the final conference of the COST A15 Action on Modernising Social Protection Systems in Nantes in May 2004. The author wishes to thank in particular David Cameron, Bernard Gazier and Noël Whiteside for inspiring comments. Finally, he thanks the Dutch Science Foundation (grant 450-02-170) for financial support and his colleagues in the Governance as Learning research program, in particular Jonathan Zeitlin, Anton Hemerijck and Marc van der Meer for stimulating criticisms. The responsibility for the views expressed in this chapter is solely his.

173

Conference of Maastricht (1991), labour market flexibility gained extra importance (Pissarides, 1997). The second explanation for Europe's unemployment predicament hinged on the inability of Europe's welfare states to handle the structural transformation of the economy. The result is a two-speed labour market, stratified between on the one hand older, mostly male workers and heads of family whose jobs in industry were made redundant, and on the other hand newly entering cohorts, among them many more women than in the past, who took up the new jobs in the service economy without the career prospects, employment security and social protection that had become associated with jobs in industry and in the public service (Esping-Andersen, 1999). Europe's various welfare states needed recalibration from protecting old rights to covering new risks, investing in skills and education, lowering the risks of dependency and encouraging labour market participation (Ferrera *et al.*, 2000).

Rather than attributing the problems of slow employment growth and job destruction to globalisation and technological change, both explanations underlined that Europe's problems were of its own making and that they could, or should, be addressed without abandoning the cause of free trade and product market liberalisation, both key to the European integration project. In this analysis, two discourses became intertwined: one about structural change and adaptation to the post-industrial labour market, another about modernising social protection systems in view of new social risks associated with the breakdown of families, single parenthood, a poor start in education, early school leaving, and lack of access to training. The main problem was formulated thus: how could Europe's social protection systems, presumably the best in the world, be maintained and modernised? To paraphrase Allan Larsson, the European Commission's Director-General Employment and Social Affairs until the Spring of 2000 and one of the architects of the European Employment Strategy (EES) in 1997: how could Europe's first-class social protection systems be transformed from safety nets, which defended acquired skills and social status, into springboards for new skills and new jobs (Larsson, 2000)? In short, how could social protection be restructured to become a productive factor?

This, it seems to me, is the *normative* and *cognitive* view underlying the EES in its infancy. The underlying analysis is anticipated in Delors' White Paper on "Growth, Competitiveness and Employment" (1993), which is rightly seen as the rallying call for a co-ordinated European policy (Goetschy, 1999). The normative message is that full employment is possible in a world of globalisation and rapid structural change and that it is the duty of Europe's leaders to raise participation and job levels and combat unemployment and dependency. The message gaining ground over a broad spectrum of European politics – from Nordic Social Democracy and New Labour, to Christian Democrats and mainstream Liberals – is that "good" social policy invests in people and makes them capable of surviving in tougher product and labour markets, thus saving the financial means and creating the solidarity needed for supporting those members of society who really need protection. The cognitive point is that a more employment-intensive growth path requires the modernisation of business and labour law and social protection systems, encouraging entrepreneurship and risk taking and removing the disincentives of moving from benefits into jobs. In the mid-1990s a co-ordinated European employment policy was emerging in order to get "full employment" back on the agenda and redirect politicians "away from managing unemployment towards managing employment growth" (CEC, 2002: 2). The demand side in the White Paper, in particular the proposal to stimulate growth by funding Trans-European Networks fell by the wayside when the European Council denied the needed finances. Yet, Delors' lasting result was that a multi-lateral surveillance procedure on employment became a permanent feature of European Council meetings. The first, in Essen (1994), addressed the need to promote employment, while calling for increasing flexibility in the organisation of work and extra measures for groups hard-hit by unemployment.

There were two arguments in favour of a *European* rather than *national* employment policy. Firstly, after the Maastricht IGC and the decision to prepare an Economic and Monetary Union, the European cause began to suffer from a legitimacy gap, showing in the Danish and French referendums and in an increasingly sceptical public opinion. This deficit could be closed, or so it was believed, through improved economic and social performance, with the help of better co-ordination among EU Member States. Secondly, with a centralised monetary policy and tighter rules for fiscal and budgetary policy, it was feared that Member States might export the problems caused by underperformance to each other and lack the will to reform. It did not follow, however, that Europe was the appropriate level for defining an employment policy, let alone executing such a policy. Surely, the Social Democratic "advocacy coalition" of Commission, Parliament and Member States that succeeded in inserting an Employment Title in the Amsterdam Treaty, was motivated by creating a stronger social profile for Europe. But the most active Member States in that coalition, like Sweden and the Netherlands, did not want to shift resources or power to Brussels (van Riel and van der Meer, 2002). Moreover, they needed the support from Member States like the UK and Germany where subsidiarity in this policy area is a major line of defence against European ambitions.

I. The European Employment Strategy, Lisbon and Social Inclusion

The employment chapter (Title VIII, TEC, articles 125-130) of the Amsterdam Treaty stipulates that Member States and the Community will work towards developing "a co-ordinated strategy for employment", in particular "for promoting a skilled, trained and adaptable workforce and labour markets responsive to economic change" (TEC 125). How this objective is being implemented through the European Employment Strategy (EES) is described elsewhere in this book (see chapter by Philippe Pochet in this volume and also Barbier's chapter on activation). Also in recent years the EU has expanded its competences in social policy, though under subsidiarity policies promoting social inclusion, like those promoting employment, remain the responsibility of Member States. Yet, Member States have signed up to a common objective, agenda and method. The so-called Lisbon process, adopted in March 2000 in order to make the EU "the most competitive and dynamic knowledge-based economy in the world, capable of economic growth with more and better jobs and greater social cohesion" (European Council, 2000: §5), considers "social cohesion" as one of the three pillars, together with employment and economic reform[2]. In seeking to promote convergence towards higher standards and performance, the Lisbon European Council adopted an Open Method of Co-ordination (OMC). Its key elements are the identification of common challenges, the agreement of common objectives and the exchange of "good practices" across Member States through comparison, benchmarking, peer review and monitoring. Beneath these common features there are important differences between the various OMC processes. The guidelines to Member States are a vital part of the EES. On their basis and following the deliberations over the Joint Employment Report the Council may issue critical recommendations to Member States upon a proposal by the Commission. Finally, since 2000, the EES operates with Community-wide targets. These elements are missing in the OMC on Social Inclusion.

This makes comparison of the two processes interesting, together with examining their interconnection. Are the two processes characterised by different patterns of compliance, participation and policy learning? Do they contribute to a common strategy, each strengthening the other, as intended by the Lisbon European Council, or are they working at cross-purposes, as is sometimes suggested by critics of the Lisbon

---

[2]   A year later, in June 2001, the Göteborg European Council agreed on a strategy for sustainable development and added the environment as the fourth pillar to the Lisbon strategy.

strategy[3]? The features of the OMC process – i.e. convergence through mutual learning, targets and scoreboards, peer reviews, the use of common indicators (in the case of social inclusion) or guidelines and recommendations (in the case of employment) – are interesting terrain for evaluating the mutual influence of European and national policies. Have OMC processes "narrowed the range of permissible policies", as is contended by Ashiagbor (2004) or have national policy choices merely been rephrased in a European language?

The methodological difficulties of answering such questions are notorious. They result from the fact that the OMC creates a recursive process in which it is hard to disentangle local, national and European influences. Moreover, it is an iterative process drawn out over many years. Political and economic conditions will not be constant and the influences coming "from Europe" will be hard to prove since we lack an observable counterfactual. Then, OMC processes have changed in their application, as was discussed in Philippe Pochet's chapter in this volume. Furthermore, national policies may be falsely dressed up as European and learning from Europe when it takes place tends to be denied or forgotten by politicians when it serves them. Then there is the question what we should evaluate. Allan Larsson (2000) once defined the EES simply as "management by objectives". In that case the evaluation should be about convergence or progress towards these objectives and not about the methods to reach them. Frank Vandenbroucke, who is cited in the introduction of this volume, defines OMC as "a mutual feedback process of planning, examination, comparison and adjustment of the policies of the EU Member States, all this on the basis of common objectives", admitting that different OMC processes operate differently ("a cookbook, not a recipe"). In this case evaluation is also about policies, programs and about policy learning. I take this as the basis for my own approach, distinguishing between various OMC processes, reform objectives and types of learning. Before turning to a discussion of the Dutch case, I shall first develop my argument about the rationale and types of international policy learning.

---

[3] In an open letter to Wim Kok, who headed a High-Level Group advising the European Council for the purpose of "identifying measures which together form a consistent strategy for (achieving) the Lisbon strategy", his former Cabinet colleague and current Minister of Economic Affairs Laurens-Jan Brinkhorst advises to drop the social inclusion process from the Lisbon process and concentrate on an "economy first" approach, since "one reason for the implementation gap is that the Lisbon process is burdened with side targets such as social inclusion" (*Financial Times*, 18 May 2004).

II. The OMC as an Opportunity to Learn Ahead of Failure

By committing the EU Member States to share information, compare themselves to one another and reassess current policies against relative performance, the OMC can be a valuable tool for promoting deliberative problem-solving and cross-national learning, precisely because it does not require a consensus on common policies and tolerates a certain openness, even vagueness, in its objectives and operation. It is probably for precisely these reasons that the OMC has so rapidly become a virtual template for Community policy-making in complex, domestically sensitive areas where diversity in interests and institutions among the Member States precludes harmonisation, but inaction is politically unacceptable and economically or socially harmful. Widespread uncertainty over "best practice" and over the division of responsibilities between the Union and its Member States, recommends a protracted phase of mutual learning and experimentation (Zeitlin, 2003; cf. also his introduction and conclusion in this volume).

Learning by mimicking others can be a useful strategy for rationally bounded actors in an uncertain environment (Hedström, 1998). Its current popularity in international politics reflects not only the ready availability of data and communication technologies, but also a decreasing autonomy of national (and local) state and non-state actors, and their increasing dependency on foreign (or central) resources and approval (Schludi, 2003). Organisational sociologists have shown that firms pervasively imitate their successful peers in order to minimise the chance of negative sanctions from various stakeholders (DiMaggio and Powell, 1983). Through borrowing solutions from others, policy-makers may avoid some of the costs of pure trial and error learning and save time in reaching solutions. They may thus extend the repertoire of potentially effective policies, i.e. solutions that they might not have discovered through examination of only their own experience or history.

In joint work with Anton Hemerijck, I have contended that knowledge and learning plays a significant role in the politics of reform of mature welfare states (Visser and Hemerijck, 1997; Hemerijck and Visser, 2001). Starting from the observation that major reforms in the Netherlands and elsewhere were motivated by structural decline and conditions or perceptions of crisis, we argue that most learning tends to be failure-induced. Often a "sense of urgency" and a perception that "things cannot go on as before" must be created as a condition for change. Under emergency conditions there tends to be a bigger propensity to reconsider existing assumptions and routines, and it will be easier to gain popular support for painful measures. This hypothesis has a basis in research on organisational behaviour and psychology as well as in neo-rational decision theory. Weaknesses are not analysed unless under conditions of crisis and repeated failure, and it takes major external shocks to change core beliefs, routines and existing distributions of resources and capabilities (Argyris and Schön, 1996; March, 1981; Siegenthaler, 1993; Simon, 1955).

"If it ain't broke, don't fix it". The corollary of failure-induced learning is that success breeds failure. According to Starbuck and Hedberg (2001: 338), repeated success in organisations tends to produce "introverted complacency". We speculate that a similar routinisation may be pervasive in politics. Often things have to go worse before they get better. The curse of success, and of the perception of success, is that it takes away the incentives for experimentation. At this point the OMC might be helpful in so far as policy-makers are invited to share information and compare performance with others, raising their awareness of future challenges and current weaknesses. It may thus contribute to "learning ahead of failure". Such pro-active learning involves precaution and the creation of buffers (slack); benchmarking towards the best; scanning the future (scenario learning); and systematic exposure to the experience and criticism of others.

In politics, as in organisations, the motivation and capability to invest in these learning strategies may be low, except under unusual circumstances when the choice is Reform or Decay. A strategy of precommitment based on international treaty obligations requiring countries to share and compare experiences and work towards "best practices" or commonly defined targets, may encourage politicians to invest more in proactive learning and make it more difficult to legitimise unsustainable policies such as lowering the retirement age or refusing public support for childcare available to young families. Raising participation and employment levels through the use of commonly defined targets is a precautionary strategy, a necessary buffer for the lean times when European populations have grown older. Benchmarking, exposure to the experience and criticism of others, mimicking best practice and mobilisation for future challenges are all ingredients of the OMC process. They create incentives and opportunities for pro-active learning, though they do not guarantee that such learning, or any learning, occurs.

Targets can raise ambitions and expose shortcomings, but they may also be unrealistic, biased, misleading, subject to statistical manipulation, contradict other goals and vulnerable to opportunistic selection in which all attention is given to the easiest attainable ones. Benchmarking may be a helpful tool to expose systematic shortcomings and blind spots in national policies, and it may help to identify attainable goals, policies and best practices, but can also be used for window dressing and beauty contests, creating a reason for contentment and self-congratulatory behaviour ("see how well we do") rather than discourage complacency. Openness to experiment and exposure of failure to others is rare in politics (as in academics) and the opportunities of "learning with others" may be unduly limited by presenting only "best" rather than "bad" practices. Moreover, best practice may be mimicked for trendy reasons, conformism or prestige, as happens often in business firms. Even a carefully designed process of best practice identification may result in inappropriate strategies if insufficient attention is paid to the institutional, political and cultural contexts in which such practices developed (Dollowitz and Marsh, 2000).

How the OMC actually works would seem to depend on two main conditions – how it is contextualised and how the balance between content and process, or ends and means, is managed. *Contextualised* mimicking allows "intensive consultation to set and modify standards" "targets that are wholly or partially negotiable", and "ample feedback on implementation" (Hemerijck and Visser, 2001: 25). *Decontextualised* mimicking is based on pre-defined excellence without much attention to local conditions or scope for local interpretation. On this aspect, there seems to be a major difference between the EES and the OECD Jobs Strategy, as I shall argue in the next section. Learning can be *adaptive* when there is full agreement about what the problem is and why it is important (the ends are given), and all attention can go to finding adequate solutions (the means to the ends). When the problem is not fully known, or when there is disagreement over its importance, learning must be *reflexive* as it involves a process of discovery of means and ends as part of the learning process. Learning by monitoring, as discussed by Sabel (1995) with regard to the institutional conditions propitious to economic development, is a case in point. In adaptive learning the key elements are consistency, competence, conditionality and outcome. Key to reflexive learning are multi-dimensionality, participation, openness and process[4]. Crossing the two dimensions yields the four-fold classification of figure 1.

Figure 1: Types of Learning and Mimicking

Mimicking Learning	De-contextualised	Contextualised
Adaptive	OECD Job Study	EES
Reflexive	?	OMC Social Inclusion

---

[4]   For this distinction I make use of joint work with Marc van der Meer, Ton Wilthagen and Paul van der Heijden (van der Meer *et al.*, 2003).

III. De-contextualised *vs.* Contextualised Mimicking: The OECD Jobs Strategy and the EES

The EES is in part modelled on and shares many features with the OECD Job Strategy (Noaksson and Jacobsson, 2003). In the early 1990s the OECD Secretariat gained a mandate to examine the labour market performance of its Member States, draw up a list of guidelines and communicate on a regular basis studies, policy surveys and recommendations to governments (OECD, 1994). The birth of the EES took place in the same period. In a comparison of the two strategies, Casey (2002) shows that there are many similarities in the diagnosis of the policy problem. Behind both campaigns lies an analysis that Europe's product and labour markets are rigid and too specialised in a small range of relatively secure goods, hampering growth and employment; unemployment is by a large measure structural; social security arrangements tend to discourage active search and create unemployment and poverty traps; and overprotective employment legislation works to the disadvantage of employment chances of women, the young, the old, the unskilled, and ethnic minorities. The EU has embraced the discourse of activating social policy, whereas the OECD is more reserved about the cost effectiveness of most active labour market policies (Calmfors *et al.*, 2001; Martin, 2000). The OECD, on the other had, has been more outspoken in criticising what it sees as "bad practices" in wage bargaining (generally, too much collectivism), an area where the EU, given its limited Treaty base in these matters and strong traditions of territorial and functional subsidiarity, has been more guarded in its criticism and more intent on seeking consensus from and promoting the social dialogue between trade unions and employers.

In its recommendations and as part of its effort to sell its flexibility prescription the OECD has held up the United States and, to a lesser degree, the United Kingdom as role models (Schmitt and Wadsworth, 2001). This element is missing in the EES, which tries to strike a more equal balance between flexibility and security, solidarity and competitiveness. The EES is, in the words of Casey (2002: 17), "more aware of the potentially negative outcomes that can result from following through some of its recommendations. Accordingly, it is more willing to counsel caution and suggest the need for compensatory actions. In contrast, the OECD is more willing to push one particular definition of excellence and blame failure on the lack of political will[5].

---

[5] According to one OECD analyst, the "key reason cited for slow and sporadic implementation of the OECD Jobs Strategy is the perception that undertaking reform involves conflict with policy objectives concerning equity and social cohesion" (Elmeskov, 1998). This view is not unique for the OECD; similar views exist regarding

Paradoxically, as an intergovernmental organisation specialising in diffusing "expert knowledge", the OECD can follow a more centralised approach than seems feasible in a political and semi-federal organisation like the EU. In OMC processes, Community and national politicians and officials, as well as non-governmental participants, prepare and examine their own descriptions and prescriptions, and the outcome is subject to constant reinterpretation and negotiation. In the OECD, aided by statistical and academic expertise within and outside the organisation, the "country desks" perform a seemingly academic, technocratic analysis, which can be finished almost entirely without the co-operation of Member States, though there are intense and frequent contacts with a limited selection of national officials, mostly in the Finance and Economic Ministries. This format allows stronger domination by one particular set of ideas on policy problems and solutions, and greater precision and sophistication in the use of econometrics. It may encourage "learning from others", though with a strong prescriptive bias and a narrow, economic and single-purpose definition of excellence. These prescriptions may be convincing for some, but only by abstracting from institutional detail and social context do they yield a practical "model for reform". It is therefore not surprising that the practical influence of the OECD's recommendations in matters of welfare reform appears to be rather limited (Armingeon and Beyeler, 2004).

The EES and other OMC processes, instead, are based on a model of mutual learning ("learning with others") and explicitly rely on co-operation between the Community and the Member States even in the provision of data on policies, outcomes and policy evaluation (the National Action Plans), with some support in the elaboration of common indicators. Arguably, the preparation of the National Action Plan (NAPs) and the Joint Report, drafted on the basis of the NAPs and finalised between Commission and Council, is the critical element of the Open Method in that it builds on all its components and includes a variety of government and non-government participants at different levels. In comparison to the OECD Job Strategy, the OMC model (as applied in the EES) appears to be more contextualised, not only by domestic institutions but also by political sensitivities (Hemerijck and Visser, 2001).

---

the Lisbon Strategy. For instance, Frits Bolkenstein, the leader of the Dutch Liberal Party until 1999 and European Commissioner for the Internal Market until 2004, prejudged the new High-Level Group on the Lisbon Strategy chaired by Wim Kok as superfluous since he sees no need "to analyse something we already know": that good plans are on the table but (some) Member States lack the will to act on their commitments.

It may be impossible to have it both ways. Policy analysis and advice is most useful when it is both valid and reliable (March and Olsen, 1995), i.e. when it correctly depicts what happened and why it happened, and when the description and analysis offered is recognised and shared by all involved. But there is often a tension between a *valid* account, with its emphasis on clean measurement and clear objectives, and a *reliable* analysis, with its emphasis on shared understanding and consensus in the face of political opposition. The OECD gives priority to what it believes is a valid analysis – within a view that is dominated by the academic and political standard bearers of economic liberalism. In the EES reliability would seem to win out over validity, almost by default, since the OMC procedure attaches great value to participation, both of state and non-state actors, at all levels. For some, participation is one of the defining characteristics of what is an "open" method of co-ordination (Telò, 2001; see also chapter by de la Porte and Pochet in this volume). This makes a stable and "single-peaked" policy preference unlikely. Consequently, in substantive terms, i.e. the problems to be solved or the ends to be reached, the European Employment Strategy, far more so than the OECD Jobs Strategy, means different things to different stakeholders and different things at different times. Does that mean that it is less effective? Or is it exactly this openness to contextualisation that allows the EES to serve as a selective amplifier of national reform strategies, within a certain range of permissible policies? I return to these questions in my analysis of the Dutch case. First, I want to distinguish between the EES and the Social Inclusion process, taking into account how they have evolved over time.

IV. Adaptive and Reflexive Learning: EES and Social Inclusion

Like the OECD Jobs Strategy, the EES started as a co-ordination strategy based on adaptive learning, with the ends and problems fairly well known, understood and accepted. With regard to the solutions there was more disagreement, with criticism of the exclusive attention to supply-side and activation measures, the support for increased flexibility in the organisation of work and the apparent neglect of the quality of jobs (Goetschy, 1999 and 2003). There were also disagreements over methods, for instance regarding the use and nature of quantitative targets, the number and precision of guidelines, the strictness of monitoring or the shift in attention from unemployment to employment indicators (Salais, 2004). Over time, the EES became more ambitious in its guidelines and targets, possibly at the price of its initial insistence on a "jobs first" approach. Doubts about the quality and sustainability of these jobs and concerns about equal opportunity and flexible employment contracts gained weight together with the economic recovery and the easing of the unemployment rate by the end of the 1990s.

In its evaluation of the first national action plans in 1998, the European Commission spoke of "a major political achievement" and "a shared commitment to a more transparent and politically-driven implementation of the commonly agreed employment policy objectives". The Commission was especially pleased with the new focus on active employment policies, intent on "reform in order to make work more attractive and jobs worth taking", also by "undertaking an in-depth review of tax and benefit systems to ensure that their impact is employment friendly and conducive to entrepreneurship, job creation, and active participation in working life". The Commission complained that "on several key aspects, such as the time horizons, resources, monitoring indicators and articulation between existing and planned measures, there is insufficient information" (CEC, 1998). Some of these problems were addressed in the second round.

In its initial years the main focus of the employment strategy was on a limited version of employability, putting pressure on Member States to move away from passive policies regarding the unemployed and abandon the "lump-of-labour" theory of employment. A broader version, stressing the importance of education and investment in human resources preparing people for volatile labour markets in which competence and skills must constantly be adapted, developed steadily but later. Quality of work and gender issues gained prominence in the course of time. How and why this happened is described elsewhere in this book (see chapter by Philippe Pochet in this volume and also Rubery's chapter on gender mainstreaming). What is to be stressed here is that none of this was uncontested, that differences in assigning importance to such issues differed among the Member States and within Member States between different political coalitions. Thus, it became possible that French working time policies, aimed at reducing labour force participation, hardly drew criticism in 2001 despite going against the spirit if not the declared commitments of the EES (Laulom, 2004) and that the UK government could simply ignore the job quality guidelines, stating in its 2002 NAP that the Commission and other EU Member States had their priorities wrong: "Our focus [...] is on getting people into work in the first place. [...] The basic prerequisite for quality in work is work itself – there is no quality for those without" (cited in Kilpatrick and Freedland, 2004). Italy came with two radically different versions of legal provisions allowing temporary employment before and after the government change in 2001, both times claiming the EES as its inspiration (Lo Faro, 2004). Not much of a narrowing of "the range of permissible policies" there.

It remains to be seen whether this will change as a consequence of the Kok Report. That report, commission by the 2003 Spring European Council and published in November 2003 under the title "Jobs, Jobs, Jobs" tried to instil a new sense of urgency in the EES. The report's message was: we know and agree about what we want, we even know what the best practices are, but we need more political will and better governance of reform delivery to make it work. In short, the EES is seen as a process or method of *adaptive* learning:

> More and better jobs can only be created through cooperation between all relevant actors. The success stories of a number of Member States shows that apart from a clear vision about the path to sustainable growth and social cohesion, strong political will and coordinated efforts of all actors are crucial for increasing adaptability, activating labour supply and equipping people for jobs (Kok *et al.*, 2003: 56).

The report mentions in particular the mobilisation of society to support reform (the content of which is given), a more effective manner of delivering reform and a more effective use of EU instruments, for instance by strengthening (rather than softening) the role of country-specific recommendations and by using the EU budget as a lever. This message was reiterated by the 2004 Spring European Council, which stated that "the critical issue now is the need for better implementation of commitments already made" and "the credibility of the (Lisbon) process requires stepping up the pace of reform at Member States" (European Council, 2004).

In its sixth year of implementation, the EES should probably be treated as a mature policy package. Hence, most problems in achieving the targets of the strategy are not due to the novelty or lack of understanding of the prescriptions, but rather caused by implementation failures based on the lack of commitment, co-ordination and political legitimacy (Lyberaki, 2004). The nascent European policy on social inclusion is in a different stage, with its status amidst European and national policies contested. Hence European social inclusion policy may require *reflexive* learning in order to find out what its ends and means are. It is for that reason that the struggle for high quality, policy-relevant, timely, and multi-dimensional indicators is so important (Atkinson *et al.*, 2002 and 2004) and why participation of various stake-holders in the OMC is crucial.

The division of labour between the EES and the Social Inclusion process was not clear at the outset, though recent changes in procedures and joint meetings of the Employment and Social Protection Committees are meant to create more synergy. The Joint Social Inclusion Report of 2003 stresses that the NAPs on employment and social inclusion should be read together to get a fuller picture of the measures being taken to combat social exclusion through participation in the labour market. The NAPs on employment provide the framework for the formulation of specific policies for the integration of disadvantaged groups in the labour market, as they cover the whole range of policy actions aimed at increasing employment levels towards the Lisbon targets, improving the functioning of labour markets and enhancing employability (CEC, 2003a: 44).

The special role for the NAP on social inclusion is seen in its focus on those individuals, groups and communities who are most distant from the labour market. Looking at the priorities, it is significant that activation holds first place in both the OMC processes on employment and social inclusion, though surely in its emphasis on housing, homelessness, poor health, disability, poor schooling, lack of (language) skills, and legal redress the OMC on social inclusion "goes beyond unemployment" (CEC, 2003a: 91).

V. From Miracle to Malaise

During the 1990s the Dutch economy performed above average, with higher GDP and employment growth than nearly all other European economies. By 2000, the unemployment rate (according to the international standards of Eurostat, ILO and OECD) had fallen below 3% – lower than in all OECD countries except Luxembourg (figure 2a). The employment rate, calculated as the proportion of all persons between 15 and 64 years of age with a job, rose by more than 1% point per year (figure 2b). Much of this growth came from the expansion of part-time jobs (Visser, 2002).

Figure 2a: Unemployment in the Netherlands and the EU 15

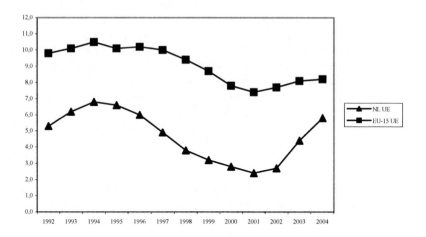

Figure 2b: Employment Rates in the Netherlands and the EU

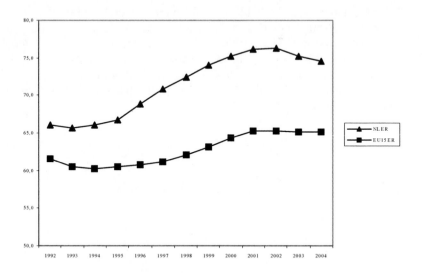

Source: CEC (2003b: Tables 87 and 93).

The strong growth and employment performance and the relatively small impact of the European recession of 1993-1994 had its basis in policy changes that had started a decade earlier: a combination of wage moderation, cost cutting in public finance and social security, and increased labour market participation, especially of women with the help of part-time employment (Visser and Hemerijck, 1997). Domestic growth benefited from a series of structural reforms, which had made Dutch product and labour markets more flexible. However, in the later 1990s the growth of labour productivity (among the highest per hour worked in the OECD) slowed down. Employment growth was consistently above levels elsewhere in Europe (with the exception of Ireland). Around 2000, with official unemployment below 3% and shortages of skilled workers and in the public sector, strong (wage) cost pressures undermining the competitiveness of Dutch industry re-emerged. A stronger rise in factor and labour productivity would have helped to achieve a more balanced growth path. Instead, together with pro-cyclical fiscal and budget policies, sanctioned under the Stability and Growth Pact, the Netherlands were set for a boom and bust pattern.

The economic situation changed dramatically in 2001 with a sharp drop in growth. This was a worldwide phenomenon, but just as the 1996-2000 boom was more exuberant in the Netherlands, so much bigger was the downturn. In 2003 the economy moved into recession. In 2002 the labour market held up well, thanks to government spending and continued strong consumer demand. But in 2003 employment levels fell for the first time since 1994 and unemployment began to rise fast, doubling from less than 3% in 2002 to 6.4% in the first quarter of 2004. In the same period, inflation fell from 4% in the aftermath of the introduction of the Euro in 2001 to 1.1% in first quarter of 2004 (De Nederlandsche Bank, 2003: 81).

**Table 1: Some Key Indicators: The Netherlands
Compared with the EU-15**

		1991-1995	1996	1997	1998	1999	2000	2001	2002	2003	2004
NL	Real GDP	2.1	3.0	3.8	4.3	4.0	3.5	1.2	0.2	-0.9	0.6
	Employment growth	1.3	2.3	3.2	2.6	2.6	2.2	1.8	0.9	-0.9	-0.6
	Employment rate	66.4	68.9	70.9	72.4	74.0	75.2	76.1	76.3	75.2	74.5
	Full-time empl. rate	53.2	54.8	56.3	57.7	58.7	59.5	59.8	59.6	58.6	57.9
	Unemployment rate	6.1	6.0	4.9	3.8	3.2	2.8	2.4	2.7	4.4	5.8
EU-15	Real GDP	1.5	1.6	2.5	2.9	2.8	3.6	1.7	1.1	0.8	1.3
	Employment growth	-0.4	0.7	1.0	1.7	2.0	2.2	1.4	0.5	0.0	0.4
	Employment rate	61.0	60.7	61.1	62.1	63.2	64.4	65.2	65.2	65.1	65.1
	Fulltime empl. rate	–	55.4	55.6	56.2	57.2	58.1	58.7	58.1	–	–
	Unemployment rate	9.5	10.2	10.0	9.4	8.7	7.8	7.4	7.7	8.1	8.2

Source: CEC (2003b).

The economic downturn and the increase in unemployment was a general phenomenon in the Euro area. However, compared to the massive job losses during past downturns, especially in 1993-1994, employment has not been as badly hit this time and the unemployment rate has increased less (see table 1). Some have attributed this to improved policies, as advocated by the EES[6]. Why, then, does this not apply to the Netherlands? Does this tell us something about the EES or about the particular application of the EES in the Netherlands? In a recent analysis, the Dutch Central Bank (De Nederlandsche Bank, 2004) singles out five factors explaining the sharp downturn after 2001: firstly, as a very internationalised economy the Netherlands are even more dependent on global economic trends than in the past; secondly, with the increased importance of price competitiveness, the rise in wages and inflation, and the appreciation of euro, caused more trouble; thirdly, the end of the home ownership boom with the recent change in tax treatment of home equity and the stock market crisis took away an important domestic

---

[6] There are indications that the "structural component" in unemployment has decreased somewhat, see the analysis in the annual report on the labour market of DG Employment (CEC, 2003c).

source of growth; fourthly, the 2001 tax reform, which gave an additional boost to an already overheating economy, came at the wrong time; and finally, budgetary policies of the government, with heavy spending and tax cuts between 1998 and 1992, and a sharp turn to austerity in 2003-2004, were strongly pro-cyclical. Interestingly, there is nothing even remotely relating to employment policy. Of the five points listed above, the Bank's governor selected (international) price competitiveness and wage moderation as the key issue for future policy. In his view future swings would be smaller if industry-wide bargaining were abandoned and wages would reflect more directly the differences among companies, skills and regions. The current government is above all obsessed with wage bargaining, a position which in the absence of agreement with the social partners leads to more rather than less government intervention, reversing the pattern of the past twenty years.

The economic downturn of 2001 preceded the dramatic political changes following the general elections of May 2002. Curiously, in the election campaign employment and economic issues played no role whatsoever and the incumbent government – a two-term coalition (1994-1998; 1998-2002) of Labour and two Liberal parties led by Wim Kok (Social Democracy) – was too divided to be able to claim the electoral rewards for the Dutch employment miracle. 11 September had changed the debate. In a general climate of discontent over failing public services and politicians who seemed too remote from people's daily concerns, the two key issues in the campaign were public security and immigration, thanks to a hugely effective campaign by Pim Fortuyn and his rightwing populist following. The elections took place within a week of the assassination of Fortuyn and produced a massive swing to the right. All three government parties lost, with the heaviest blow to the Social Democrats. The Christian Democratic party, which had lost the elections of 1994 and 1998, became again the largest party and its leader, Jan-Peter Balkenende, formed a cabinet with the main Liberal party and Fortuyn's party. That coalition fell apart in only a few months, leading to new general elections in January 2003. The Christian Democrats maintained their position as the country's largest party, though only by a slight margin. The social democrats came second, the two liberal parties lost and Fortuyn's party lost badly, losing nearly two-thirds of its 2002 electorate. After long but unsuccessful negotiations with the social democrats, Balkenende turned again to his right and formed his second cabinet with the two Liberal parties, both champions of economic liberalism and happy to be freed of the yoke of Social Democracy.

The Balkenende cabinets led a course towards austerity – though it is fair to say that the international economic downturn and the obligations of the Stability and Growth Pact would have forced any Dutch government in that direction. However, the parties making up the new coalition had promised huge savings in the various subsidised job programs for which successive Labour Ministers had successfully built up a large budget since 1994. Right from his start as Minister of Social Affairs and Employment in Kok's first cabinet, Ad Melkert, who became the Social Democratic leader in parliament during Kok's second term and Kok's designated successor, had started various programs of subsidised employment for the long-term unemployed. Ultimately the four programs of the so-called "Melkert jobs" offered 80,000 jobs in 2002, nearly all in local government. In addition, the first Kok cabinet which operated under the rallying call of "Jobs, Jobs, Jobs", a title he recycled for European use ten years later, phased in two tax relief programs lowering the social charges for firms employing unskilled workers with pay marginally above the statutory minimum wage and for employers hiring long-term unemployed workers. In total, the budget for active labour market programs tripled between 1994 and 2001, reaching nearly 6 billion euros, of which 3 billion euros on activation measures (including the Melkert jobs), 2 billion euros for the employment of disabled workers in special work shops and programs, and 1 billion euros for subsidies and fiscal compensation (Ministerie van Sociale Zaken en Werkgelegenheid, 2002: 53). In proportion to GDP, the Netherlands began to rival the Scandinavian countries in expenditure on active labour market policies, breaking away from its legacy of passive (income support) policies (Calmfors et al., 2001; Visser and Hemerijck, 1997).

Various critical evaluations, most prominently by an interdepartmental committee of top civil servants and experts (Ministerie van Sociale Zaken en Werkgelegenheid, 2001), criticised the high costs of these programs together with the low rate of outflow into regular jobs, the deadweight losses and the substitution effects of the tax relief programs (see for an overview Zijl et al., 2002: chapter 6). During the 2002 elections, the Christian Democrats promised to save 2 billion euros, the two liberal parties 1.5 billion euros on employment programs. In contrast to its predecessor, Balkenende opted for an exclusively supply-side approach, increasing the net benefits for people moving from benefits to jobs with extra tax breaks and tightening benefit eligibility, without the demand-stimulating elements of previous employment policies. The tax subsidies for employers hiring low-skilled and long-term unemployed workers have been ended and the Melkert job programs stopped or reduced.

Finally, there was a dramatic change in the social dialogue and partnership with trade unions and employers for which the Netherlands had received much international praise in previous years, starting with the celebrated Wassenaar agreement of 1982. In November 2002, the social partners and the first Balkenende cabinet were still able to reach a central agreement for 2003, including a softening of the turnaround in employment policy and a recommendation to settle pay increases within a limit of 2.5% cost increases, just under the expected rate of inflation. A year later, it proved much more difficult to negotiate another tripartite agreement. The trade unions were clearly disappointed that the 2003 elections had not produced a Centre-Left coalition and the largest union federation had markedly bad relations with the new administration. After a half-hearted mobilisation campaign against the government's plans, the social partners struck a deal, recommending a standstill in contractual wages in 2004 and, if need be, in 2005. This concession of an annual real wage decrease of -2% (at current inflation) came in exchange for a softening of the government's austerity measures in social security, sickness and disability insurance, health costs and a postponement of plans to phase out early retirement through punitive tax sanctions, subject to new negotiations in 2004. This compromise won a narrow yes vote in a unique referendum among the membership of the Dutch Confederation of Trade Unions (FNV). However, in May 2004 negotiations over the reduction of early retirement failed. The main trade union organised a "Them or Us" referendum leading to a massive rejection of the government's proposals and declared that it would seek to break the standstill on wages. The other unions joined in with a rejection of the 2003 Pact. The government retaliated by promising not to extend industry-wide collective agreements containing wage in-creases, expecting that this will strengthen the hands of employers to resist union wage claims. The government has also promised punitive sanctions in case unions and employers agree to soften the austerity measures regarding sickness and disability through collective agree-ments, as has been common practice in past decades. The unions see this as a frontal attack on their autonomy and are preparing an official complaint to the International Labour Organisation, marking a real low in Dutch social partnership. They also organised a massive protest rally against the government in October 2004, one of the largest the country has ever seen. Employers are divided, with the largest among them supporting the government's position and the small and medium-sized enterprises fearing industrial conflict.

VI. What Did the Netherlands (Want to) Learn from the EES?

Between the Amsterdam IGC in May and the Luxembourg Job Summit in November 1997, the Netherlands were actively involved in creating the EES. Top civil servants from the Department of Social Affairs and Employment were involved in its design. The Minister of

Social Affairs and Employment, Ad Melkert, used his influence in the meetings of the Council of Ministers and in the Party of European Socialists. He clearly wanted to give a higher social profile to Europe, countering the fears of "social dumping" in his own party and among critics to the party's left. In part this was a way to sell the Dutch success story and the policy approach on which it was based: financial conservatism; wage moderation; de-marginalisation of part-time work and negotiated flexibility through social dialogue.

By 1997 the Netherlands had become one of the fastest growing economies in Europe, rivalled only by Ireland. Various central agreements – on wage moderation and work sharing in 1982 and 1993; on Flexibility and Security in 1996 – had attracted international attention. The same became true for the extraordinary expansion of part-time work and its seemingly voluntary nature. All these elements had given the Netherlands the aura of an attractive exemplar in the European and global contest for reforms that might lead to growth and prosperity without destroying the underlying Social Model (Auer, 2000; Freeman, 1998; Schmid, 1997; Visser and Hemerijck, 1997). During the High-Level conference opening the Dutch Presidency of the European Union in January 1997, Melkert had coined the phrase of social policy as a productive factor (Hemerijck, 1998). At this time, the Netherlands radiated considerable enthusiasm towards the new European approach based on benchmarking and best practice learning. In an attempt to regain the initiative from the "friendly enemies" of Economic Affairs who had published a benchmarking study in order to argue their case that deregulation of product and labour markets would boost growth and innovation, Melkert's Ministry countered with a benchmarking study comparing Dutch social policy and labour market regulation with seven other European countries and the USA. That study flatly rejected the "working hypothesis" that a high level of social protection had been an obstacle to economic growth and innovation (SDU/Ministerie van Sociale Zaken en Werkgelegenheid, 1996). Four years later, the exercise was repeated, with the same conclusion, now using thirty-nine indicators in nine policy fields, including labour relations, employment, working conditions, social security, pensions, health, income distribution, collective services, and social cohesion. However, that study exercise also uncovered some notorious weaknesses in Dutch social policy: the low outflow from unemployment into regular jobs; the insufficiency of childcare services; the high poverty risk for lone parents; the high disability rate; and the low participation rates of older workers and ethnic minorities (SDU/Ministerie van Sociale Zaken en Werkgelegenheid, 2000).

Perhaps the EES needed the Netherlands, but the reverse was also true – especially with regard to the design and implementation of an effective activation policy. Even in the favourable overall context of the Dutch economy during the 1990s there were many bottlenecks, such as the prevention of sickness and disability, reintegration of partially handicapped workers, age discrimination, equal pay and training for part-time workers and women, the upgrading and productivity of low-skilled sectors, and the integration, training and employment of the immigrant labour force. The EES helped to consolidate and expand the Social Democratic version of the activation approach. Given the high level and extended duration of unemployment and disability benefits, and various add-ons to social assistance benefits, there were many unemployment and poverty traps built into the Dutch system. On this issue, the Netherlands were to receive many recommendations from the OECD as well as from the EU. For the OECD and for the Liberal opposition before 1994, the preferred policy option had been a lowering of the level and duration of benefits, a tightening of eligibility, a stricter application of sanctions, possibly completed by in-work tax breaks. For the Social Democrats that package was unacceptable; they were looking for in-work benefits, subsidies for low paid jobs and increased efforts at guiding and training the unemployed. In the two Kok cabinets the Social Democrats won the argument, helped by strong economic and job growth and much improved public finances. The Liberal parties secured their preference for tax reduction as well as various privatisation programs.

In 1992, after four years of experimenting, the Netherlands started a "comprehensive approach" to the activation of young people, in accordance with what later became guideline one of the EES. All jobless people under the age of 23 were offered a "fresh start" in the form of training or (subsidised) job placement within the first six months of unemployment. There was strong resistance from the Finance Ministry and within the Ministry of Social Affairs and Employment from the powerful Unit responsible for Social Security to extend this promise to the adult unemployed, as was called for in guideline two. The prevailing philosophy at Finance and of the opposition within the Ministry was that scarce resources should go to young people and to the worst-off among the long-term unemployed. The European pressure was clearly welcomed by those in favour of a more active as well as (in the short-run) more expensive approach. According to our interviews with politicians and officials, the external pressure through the EES was decisive for policy change (Zijl *et al.*, 2002). Implementation of guideline two required a huge extra expenditure in the order of 2 billion euros. During the introduction phase of the comprehensive approach, Dutch government officials organised meetings about the implementation of the new policy with colleagues from other Member States. In the process, Dutch officials learned that they tended to use instruments that were too strong. Instead of training, for instance, simpler (and less expensive) forms of support, like assistance in job search, might suffice for a return to employment (Zijl *et al.*, 2002).

The Netherlands had reservations about the prospect of introducing quantitative targets during the Luxembourg Job Summit, but three years later, when the European Council in Lisbon decided to introduce quantitative targets for employment, the Netherlands were one of only four Member States – with Denmark, Sweden and the UK – that had already reached the employment rate of 70%, the EU target set for 2010 (see figure 2b). The 60% employment rate target for women was also reached. The Barcelona Spring Council of 2002 called for drastic measures to increase the average exit age from the labour market from 60 to 65 years, to be reached by 2010. Most Member States, including the Netherlands, are still way off target and have only just begun to address the problem of early retirement. In the Netherlands, moreover, many workers, also of younger age, take the disability route out of employment. However, since the mid-1990s the employment rate of older workers is slowly increasing, from 28.9% of all those between the age of 55 and 64 having a job in 1994 to 42.3% ten years later. The realisation of the 50% target set in Lisbon for 2010 means that the increase of past years has to continue under much less favourable economic conditions. The Netherlands have set specific targets for women (65% in employment in 2010), for ethnic minorities (54% in 2005), for youth unemployment (not more than twice the general unemployment rate), and for the young entering the labour market, a lowering of 30% of those without qualifications compared to 1999. According to the Lisbon target 85% of the 22 year-olds should have at least a medium level education; the current rate in the Netherlands is 77% according to the NAP of 2003.

At this point we should note that meeting the targets depends on the definitions. In Eurostat Labour Force Surveys all people working one hour per week or more are counted as employed. The Dutch NAPs also present employment rates based on national definitions of employment, counting only jobs of twelve hours or more per week. In that case the 2002 employment participation rate in the Netherlands is 65%, for women 54%, for older workers 37%, and for ethnic minorities 50%. The official unemployment statistics, too, paint a picture that is too favourable, since a significant proportion of the labour force is absorbed in the disability insurance scheme or unavailable for work. Nor are unemployed workers above the age of 57 ½ years counted, since they need not apply for jobs in order to retain their insurance or benefit entitlements. This dispensation ruling was introduced in 1984 but was with-drawn in 2004, after several years of hesitation. According to Eurostat and ECHP data, the Netherlands had in 2001 the lowest long-term unemployment rate in the EU, only 0.7% of the potential labour force, after a significant drop since 1998 (CEC, 2003c; see also CEC, 2003d). The true rate is several percentage points higher. Approximately 9.5% of the potential labour force receives disability benefits: 7% of the potential labour force is regarded as being fully disabled and another 2.5% as partially disabled. Around 6% of the potential labour force is on social assistance, though not directly available for the labour market (Visser, 2003).

Under the EES guidelines, the Netherlands promised to be ready in four years to offer all people becoming unemployed assistance within the first year and start with offering activation measures to 20% (later changed to 25%) of the existing stock of long-term unemployed[7]. De-spite a sharp reduction in unemployment and a huge increase in the budget, the Netherlands did not keep their promise. In 2002, the "pre-ventive approach" is still not comprehensive for the adult unemployed (Zijl *et al.*, 2002). In 2003, reflecting the increased inflow in unem-ployment, the proportion of those entering the ranks of the long-term unemployed (after 12 months) without having been contacted with an offer of training, counselling, work or support has even increased (CEC, 2003e and CEC, 2004: 62). There may be several reasons for this: the unending restructuring of the public employment service, the insurance boards and municipal offices, the competence wars between them, perverse incentives, selection effects with the hardest to help remaining, wide-spread unemployment and poverty traps, and lower budgets at a time of rising unemployment. Together with a lack of clear definitions of the target groups and the lack of clear assessment criteria, these shortcomings were already highlighted in the report of a committee of top civil servants and experts in 2001, which all but concluded that active labour market policies were wasteful (Ministerie van Sociale Zaken en Werkgelegenheid, 2001). Remarkably, that report, although produced under the responsibility of the Ministry's top civil servants, made no mention of the EES. In our own evaluation study of five years EES we were also struck by the emphasis on input rather than output criteria for measuring policy performance.

The 2004 Joint Employment Report deplored the lack of comparable statistics and indicators in the Dutch National Action Plan on employ-ment. (The same criticism is applied to the NAP on social inclusion.)

---

[7]   Letter of the Minister of Social Affairs and Employment, Klaas de Vries, to Parlia-ment, session 1998-1999, 24 November 1998.

According to the Report, "notwithstanding budgetary constraints, there remains considerable scope for further redirecting of spending and greater efficiency through a better timing and focussing of measures". This point is also made by the Task Force on Employment: active policies should include more personalised services, better identification of real needs of job seekers and tailor-made solutions, rapid response schemes in case of plant closures, strengthened delivery systems, and, with a reference to social inclusion, they should address the needs of the most vulnerable, including disadvantaged young people and people with disabilities.

Repeatedly the EES had put pressure on the Netherlands to improve statistical monitoring, especially in connection with its activation policies. Twice, in 2000 and 2001, the Council issued a recommendation on this point. Why it did not in 2002 is unclear, perhaps it was part of the EES becoming "more diplomatic" (Goetschy, 2003). Other recommendations to the Netherlands included, in 2000, to remove tax and benefit disincentives to take up (low paid) jobs, and, in 2001 and 2002, to reduce disincentives in the benefit system leading to poverty traps and discouraging people receiving disability benefits from participating in the labour market. With the 2001 tax reform all rates of taxes on wages have been reduced and an in-work tax credit was introduced, the size of which was increased after 2002. The disability trap was again mentioned in 2003, together with a recommendation on lifelong learning and the gender pay gap. Disability has been the "open nerve" in Dutch politics for almost two decades (Visser and Hemerijck, 1997); the other two issues have hardly reached the national policy agenda, although the social partners, to whom these issues have been re-addressed, issued joint studies. In 2002, finally, the Council recommended that the Netherlands should invest in its partnership model with the social partners – a recommendation that fell on deaf ears.

The main policy failure, reflecting in poor and uncontrollable statistics, was related to the difficulty of getting all organisations involved in job placement, employee insurance and social assistance, both nationally and locally, working together. All recent NAPs announced major changes and promised improvement in the near future. The recommendations by the Council have probably added pressure, but the adoption of the "one counter approach" and a larger role for the municipalities was mainly inspired by studies and recommendations from the OECD.

In the Netherlands, the reform of the public employment service has been on the agenda ever since the first critical report on the absence of active and regional "manpower" policies, issued by the OECD in 1967! Various attempts to modernise the employment service and move away from a bureaucratic agency busy registering jobless people for the purpose of evaluating their claims on unemployment insurance (administrated by the social partners) or social assistance (the responsibility of local councils) failed. In 1991 a wholly new approach was tried: the employment service was decentralised and became the joint responsibility of the government and the social partners. Four years later this new tripartite organisation was accused of management chaos, lack of control over spending policies of its regional services and self-serving policies creating the appearance of success by helping only the easiest-to-place unemployed and abandoning the difficult cases. An official evaluation report, commissioned by parliament, declared the tripartite governance structure with "three commanders-in-chief" unworkable. The first Kok government seized the opportunity by taking away part of the funding, using the money for its expensive subsidised jobs programs. In 1996, the law was again changed and the social partners relegated to an advisory role. More or less the same happened in social insurance, following the 1993 Parliamentary Inquiry in the abuse of the disability insurance system (Visser and Hemerijck, 1997). After various experiments and intermediate solutions, a new structure of integrating the three public services dealing with employment and income became law in January 2002. The employment offices, the social insurance organisation, now both taken out of the hand of social partners, and the municipalities, responsible for social assistance, will be "chained" to each other through a system of "service level" contracts and financial transactions. The municipalities must negotiate service-level agreements with the public employment service, but are free to contract with private reintegration firms. They themselves are bound by performance targets negotiated with the central government.

The present Centre-Right coalition has made the outflow from (long-term) unemployment and inability the most pressing issue for the immediate future, with a stronger emphasis on sanctions. In the new "Work and Assistance" law of 2004, which replaces the National Assistance Act of 1996, there is a general presumption that those receiving social assistance should accept a job of at least 19 hours per week. This includes older unemployed workers, partially disabled workers and lone parents with young children. The criterion of "suitable jobs", i.e. a job of similar qualification and pay levels, has been deleted and welfare recipients can now be expected to accept any job offer made to them. The new Act empowers the municipalities to "own" their own assistance and integration budgets, which they can use according to choice (within some limits) and from which they are entitled to make savings. In theory, this power of the purse puts them in a controlling role regarding the employment office and private contractors for reintegration services. The government is optimistic that the new "chain" model will be fully operative in 2006. This optimism is not shared by the Council for Work and Income, the government's official advisory body with representatives from local government and social partners. In a recent advice, the Council warns that there are huge transaction costs, many organisational problems, too many interventions by the central government on details and too little central guidance by means of providing an adequate regulatory framework[8].

My overall conclusion from this brief account of European and Dutch employment policies is that the connection between the two is weak. There are phases in which the Netherlands actively used the "lessons for Europe" in order to change things at home, but this was always on the basis of existing *national* political priorities. The Social Democratic version of activation, translated in the preventive approach, is a case in point. It proved that Brussels can help to win an argument at home. Interesting in that example is that the pressure from Brussels is first created, with Melkert, his Ministry and his European party friends actively engaged in shaping a particular version of a co-ordinated European employment and activation policy. Here we have a classic case of what one might call, paraphrasing Max Weber, "eingeladene Gehorsamkeit", compliance with an international obligation you have asked for. It is a perfect illustration of how European integration works as a multi-level game.

This is not the only example. The Dutch contribution to the debate about reshaping and streamlining of the EES after the 2002 evaluation has gone in a direction of limiting ambitions, a narrower focus on activation, a jobs first approach, and more emphasis on delivery. Together with reducing administrative burdens, this has become the main plank of the Dutch Presidency of the EU in the second half of 2004[9]. The Ministry's preferred interpretation of job quality is sustainability in terms of pay and contract duration, which is important though by no means the only dimension. This squares with proposals to reduce domestic legislation and regulation in matters of work quality and working hours. If the EES can be reformed and its message be interpreted in this direction, difficult and unpopular changes in domestic law can be attributed, at least in part, as coming from Europe. Arguably, the strength of the EES is that it is a "strategy for all seasons". Thus, the EES has been used, in Italy, to defend two quite different versions of promoting part-time work and employment flexibility before and after the elections of

---

8   Advies Ketensamenwerking en -informatisering SUWI, advies van de Raad van Werk en Inkomen aan de Minister van Sociale Zaken en Werkgelegenheid, The Hague, 29 June 2004.

9   See, for instance, the program for the EU Presidency as presented on the website of the Ministry of Foreign Affairs and Social Affairs, calling for greater realism and more focus on reform delivery.

2001 (Lo Faro, 2004) and in the Netherlands for two versions of promoting participation and activating the long-term unemployed. In short, based on its political contextualisation, the EES can nicely serve as a selective amplifier of domestic policy choices.

In our interviews, conducted just before the general elections of May 2002, we found that the EES received broad political support, also from the Christian-Democratic opposition at the time (Zijl *et al.*, 2002). However, the Liberal members of parliament were clearly unenthusiastic. They feared that it would add pressure to increase European funds and tended to dismiss the EES as irrelevant and bureaucratic. The Finance and Economics Ministries, the fiefdoms of the two Liberal parties in both the Kok and Balkenende coalitions, favour their own European games based on the Cardiff process of structural reforms, the Broad Economic Policy Guidelines and Ecofin's guardianship of the Stability and Growth Pact. In their appraisal of employment policy, these Ministries share the OECD's rather than the EU's prescriptions, focussing on increased flexibility and supply-side measures. Regarding poverty and social inclusion, too, they favour a narrower focus, stressing the importance of activation through sanctions. Anti-poverty measures are seen as a stand-alone policy rather than as a general issue of social cohesion an inequality.

Nearly all respondents in our evaluation study believed that there is, or ought to be, a hierarchy in the guidelines (Zijl *et al.*, 2002). Employability issues are believed to be the most important ones, but given a rather narrow focus. Surely, the activation approach and the prevention of long-tem employment and partial disability had the strongest appeal for Dutch policy-makers. A separate pillar for Equal Opportunities was rejected as a nuisance by half of our respondents and the issue of pay differences received only a muted response. Part-time work, which is mainly women's work, has been de-marginalised through collective bargaining and legal interventions, but disadvantages in careers, training and pay are not really addressed (Visser *et al.*, 2004). The EES did help in defining more ambitious Dutch targets for women and ethnic minorities. In the case of women, the now defunct Unit for Emancipation in the Ministry of Social Affairs and Employment skilfully used the pressure from Europe in order to make the new target for female employment, 65% in 2010, into an official government position. The Commission has praise for the many special targets, but deplores that there appears to be little attention to the quality at work. The 2004 Joint Employment Report also notes that immigration is rejected as a measure to counterbalance ageing, and that immigration policies have become increasingly restrictive. In February the Netherlands, like other EU Member States, went back on their promises and decided to restrict the entry of citizens of the new EU Member States to the Dutch labour market for at least two more years.

Entrepreneurship, according to our respondents, was ill placed in the EES and received little attention, while the adaptability pillar is hardly developed, because the unions and employers resist government interference in what they see as their turf. This sentiment is particularly strong among employers, who insist that the NAP is a government document for which they do not want to share responsibility. The bad memories of the short-lived experience with the tripartite employment service do not inspire trust in the government. The unions complain that consultations in the preparation of the NAP have been perfunctory and that their influence was marginal, but probably their real problem is that they lack the ideas and resources to have a strong and creative pro-active influence. Employers, especially those organised in the main federation representing the larger and international firms, show considerable satisfaction, not only with their limited role but also with the recent turn of government policies[10].

VII. Poverty and Social Inclusion

On anti-poverty policies the Netherlands also preceded the European initiative. In the mid-1990s the Ministry of Social Affairs and Employment, under pressure from a coalition of churches, unions, NGOs and the larger cities, started to employ several instruments for tracking manifestations and causes of poverty and social exclusion. A prominent role was played by the so-called "Poverty Monitor" of the Social and Cultural Planning Office (SCP) in co-operation with the Central Bureau of Statistics (CBS)[11], and the annual series "Poverty in the Netherlands" published by a group of academic researchers[12]. In the second Kok cabinet (1998-2002) a special Ministry for "Large Cities and Integration" was created. Poverty is given a broad definition:

a complex phenomenon which commonly has interlinked dimensions (income, social participation, educational level, health, ability to cope, home and living environment), in which the future perspective is an important distinguishing characteristic, particularly in situations where there is little or no prospect of work or a change in living conditions. In this broad view poverty is similar to social exclusion[13].

---

[10] See also EIRO study (www.eiro.eurofound.ie/10/tfeature/nl10310102t).

[11] *Armoedemonitor 1997*, Sociaal en Cultureel Planbureau / Centraal Bureau voor de Statistiek, The Hague.

[12] The first of these reports was published in 1996 (Engbersen *et al.*, 1996).

[13] This definition appears in both NAPs on Social Inclusion, Ministerie van Sociale Zaken en Werkgelegenheid, The Hague, July 2001 and July 2003.

The sharp rise in unemployment during the 1980s had been accompanied by a rise in poverty. In reverse, it took a long time before the growth in employment translated into a fall in poverty. The number and share of households on the social minimum, the political definition of the poverty line in the Netherlands (operationalised as 105% of the lowest level of social benefits to which all residents are entitled, which in turn is linked to the statutory minimum wage) began to drop significantly after 1997, having remained constant during most of the 1990s. Currently, some 9% of all households are at or under the social minimum; one-third of these households during three years or longer (table 2). While (long-term) dependency on minimum income dropped slightly between 1997 and 2001, recent developments point to a rise.

**Table 2: Households in the Netherlands
on the Social Minimum**

	Households on social minimum x 1000	% of all households	Persistent on social minimum (>= 3 years) x 1000
1992	632	10.7%	236
1993	634	10.6%	247
1994	639	10.6%	250
1995	633	10.3%	254
1996	649	10.5%	243
1997	644	10.2%	244
1998	631	9.8%	243
1999	627	9.7%	235
2000	605	9.2%	228

Source: CBS (www.statline.nl). Social minimum is defined as 105% of the national minimum benefit entitlement, set at 50% of the statutory minimum wage in the case of a single person, yearly adjusted to the development in contractual wages.

Although the relationship with changes in employment and unemployment seems obvious, these changes are not the only cause of fluctuations in low income and poverty. Economic growth, leading to improved earnings and social security, may be the root cause behind both developments. The slump of the early 1980s not only caused considerable losses in employment, but also a fall in purchasing power of those in and out work. People on minimum wages and benefits experienced a further setback through the nominal lowering of the statutory minimum in 1984 and the suspension of the linking mechanism between contractual wages and the statutory minimum wage used for the calculation of the social minimum. This suspension was lifted in 1989 but again applied between 1992 and 1994. After 1994, the economic recovery translated into massive employment growth and a rise in the purchasing power of the employed population, from which recipients of (minimum) benefits also profited through the restoration of indexation of benefits to wages in 1995.

These figures seem to vindicate the strategy of combating poverty by a "jobs first" strategy. However, the relationship between employment growth and the development of poverty is more complicated than this simple reasoning suggests. The vast majority of poor people who find work do indeed rise above the poverty line if they remain in employment for a longer period. Dutch research, however, shows that almost half of those who find new work drop out of the labour market after a period of time (de Beer, 2001). As a consequence, employment offers a structural escape route from poverty for only half of all poor people who find paid employment. Though this is more than is achieved by any comparable measure, it is not comprehensive. The sustainability of jobs is an issue in its own right, not only in terms of productivity but also in terms of their contribution to the fight against poverty. Secondly, the effect of employment on poverty also depends on household composition. If the individuals who find work mainly come from households with a working partner, as was the case in the Netherlands during the "part-time job" boom of the 1980s and 1990s, then poor households with no earners hardly benefit. Indeed, until 1996 we find only a minor effect of job growth on the number of inactive households. However, in later years, at least until 2001 the number and share of households with no earners drop significantly, and so do the share and number of households below the poverty line. Finally, the impact of job growth on poverty will depend on the level at which these jobs are being paid. Many of the new jobs in the Netherlands were just above the statutory minimum wage and they were part-time.

According to the Joint Report on Social Inclusion of 2003 the Netherlands are one of the EU countries with the lowest poverty-risk rates (table 3). This is especially so in the case of older people, thanks to a multi-tiered old age pension system, based on a universal basic pension for all, indexed to wages, and a secondary earnings-related pension with wide-ranging coverage (van Riel *et al.*, 2003). The poverty-risk rate increases for the young and is strongly associated with unemployment and lone parenthood. The poverty-risk rate for lone parents is as high as 45%, which according the Joint Social Inclusion Report puts the Netherlands in 14th place in the EU-15 (only the UK does worse). The figures in table 3 also show a large effect of social transfers.

Table 3: Poverty-risk Rates in 2001,
The Netherlands and the EU

Age groups	All age groups	Children (< 15)	Adults (>= 16)		
			Total	*Men*	*Women*
After transfers	10 (15)	16 (19)	10 (15)	10 (13)	10 (16)
Before transfers	21 (24)	27 (31)	19 (22)	19 (20)	20 (24)
Status	Employed	Non-employed	Of whom		
			Unem-ployed	*Retired*	*Other*
	8 (7)	13 (22)	23 (38)	3 (17)	12 (25)
Household type	Households with children		Households without children		
	2 adults < 65	*Single parent*	*All*	*Single < 30*	*Single >= 65*
	4 (10)	45 (35)	7 (14)	49 (32)	3 (16)
Persistent poverty	All age groups	Children (< 15)	Adults (>= 16)		
			Total	*Men*	*Women*
	5 (9)	9 (12)	4 (9)	5 (8)	4 (9)

Source: based on *Statistical annex to the draft joint inclusion report* (CEC, 2003d);
figures for the EU are in brackets.

Combating poverty and social exclusion in the Netherlands is a joint effort of the national and local government. Voluntary organisations and church-related charities play an important role, especially in health and welfare. Their involvement of NGOs is mentioned as one of the four pillars of the Dutch anti-poverty strategy in the 2003 NAP. The first pillar is based on the promotion of social participation in the form of paid employment or when people are very remote from the labour market by means of social activities. Next comes the guarantee of income security for people who are unable to support themselves. This task is divided between the national and local governments. The third principle is based on promoting the accessibility of provisions in the areas of housing, education, care, ICT, public transport, legal assistance and integration, a task that is shared with local government and private organisations. Finally, in order to ensure the success of what is called "a comprehensive approach to poverty and social exclusion", the cabinet wants to encourage the partnership between the various public authorities and community organisations; to stimulate the involvement of (organisations of) vulnerable groups; and promote socially responsible business.

Compared to the first NAP, written under the second Kok cabinet, the second NAP, reflecting the priorities of the Balkenende cabinet, is more selective in its approach to poverty and exclusion. In the words of the Commission: "The Netherlands set a sharper demarcation of poverty and social exclusion issues and puts a stronger focus on the most vulnerable people" (CEC, 2003a: 38). These are identified as people with accumulated disadvantages, like lone mothers, immigrants and ethnic minorities, early school-leavers and young adults without qualifications, and people with chronic health problems. According to the Joint Report, this gives the report greater coherence, with planned policy measures and actions closely linked to achieving goals, but at the price of a "relatively narrow focus" (CEC, 2003a: 39). The Commission also notes that the Netherlands have taken a welcome turn towards decentralisation, giving the local councils responsibilities for budgets and implementations, with ample scope for outsourcing services to private contractors. But this raises doubt about adequate finances and effective strategies of monitoring, co-ordination and sharing information. Finally, the Commission strongly regrets that the Netherlands often use their own (non-Laeken) indicators, without making it easy to compare their own figures with the standardised measures based on the ECHP.

Although the encouragement of active input by and close co-operation with all stakeholders is mentioned as one of the strategic planks of Dutch anti-poverty policies, this is not reflected in the application of the OMC in the Netherlands. In preparing the NAP, both in 2001 and again in 2003 some fifty NGOs were twice given the opportunity to voice their opinion, during a "start-up" conference and just before the NAP is sent to Brussels. The main work is done and controlled by an interdepartmental working-party with participation from as many as eleven of the fourteen different Ministries and one representative of the Dutch Association of Local Government (VNG) who is there to check on the plan's feasibility in the local context. The co-ordination is in hands of the Ministry of Social Affairs and Employment, which devotes as much as one full-time equivalent position to co-ordinating the whole process (Idema, 2004: 194). The NGOs were given just two weeks to comment the draft version of the NAP and complained in both rounds about the lack of time, preparation and influence[14].

In 2001, NGOs also complained that consultations had been dominated by social insurance organisations at the expense of those from the welfare sector. Being organised at the local level, the latter felt unprepared. They have since organised together with the main churches and union organisations, human rights groups, anti-poverty leagues and

---

[14] There were two small evaluation studies, especially with regards to procedures and participation, conducted on behalf of the European Commission (see Nederland *et al.*, 2003a and 2003b).

groups defending the rights of immigrants in a loose Alliance for Social Justice (*Alliantie voor Sociale Rechtvaardigheid*). This coalition building is not the result of the OMC, however, but a response to the right turn in Dutch government policy in 2002 and since. The Alliance accuses the government of creating more poverty and social exclusion[15]. A general criticism is that the NAP, rather than being an occasion to develop a comprehensive and consistent policy, merely reports existing or intended government policies. Many NGOs criticised the lack of emphasis on the gender issue and on the cultural dimensions of poverty, and they were unhappy with what they see as an employment and financial bias in the indicators.

The NAP on social inclusion may be thought to replace the Social Account (*Social Nota*) which for many years was attached to the annual Budget but has since 2002 been discontinued for reasons of austerity. Yet its role in parliamentary proceeding is different and its contents are far more limited. Curiously, parliament appears to have no influence in what the Netherlands send to Europe or Europe wants from the Netherlands. (A similar finding is reported in Zijl *et al.* (2002) with regard to the European employment strategy and apparently there is no change since the electoral upheaval of 2002). The NAP is sent to the Lower House only after it has been sent to Brussels and it appears only months later as a small item in an inconspicuous meeting of the Social Affairs committee. The OMC on social inclusion (or the EES) never reaches the floor of the Lower or Upper House of Parliament. The draft Joint Social Inclusion Report remains a matter for closed-door discussions of European and national civil servants, with scarce attention from outside the Ministry of Social Affairs, NGOs or parliament. In his search through all parliamentary documents between January 2000 and March 2004, Idema (2004) did not find a single reference to the Joint Reports. Neither is the Joint Report explicitly dealt with in the National Action Plan. The assignment of peer review countries was only communicated (by Brussels) one week in advance and the government did not use the possibility to include other stake-holders in any discussion where "learning with others" might have taken place.

Timo Idema (2004: 196) concludes his study with the observation that the application of the OMC on social inclusion is characterised by a "lack of transparency" combined with a "lack of public debate". The role of NGOs is kept very limited in the sense that "there is no automatic feedback to input from society" and "reactions from the government to the input are not publicly available". His conclusion is that "the potential effects of OMC cannot be realised in the current method of

---

[15] Letter to the Cabinet and to Parliament of 16 September 2003.

working" (*ibid.*). I concur that the potentials of the OMC as a reflexive learning process are not appreciated or realised in the Netherlands (Raad voor Maatschappelijke Ontwikkeling, 2004).

Conclusions

Evaluating the lessons learnt by the Dutch participants in the OMC processes on employment and social inclusion, one might conceivably think of various influences: on the normative and cognitive views directing the definition of problems and solutions; on the level of ambitions, on the selection of policies; on the mobilisation of societal support in realising them; on the institutional setting, organisation and delivery of policies. My answer is that there was hardly any influence on the definition of the problems of (un)employment and poverty, or the way these problems should be tackled, but that "pressure from Europe" helped to reinforce existing national policy views, albeit in different directions depending on the political coalition that was in charge. The message from Brussels and the conception of the OMC process were flexible enough to allow selective learning, highly conditioned by what a particular country, a particular coalition or even a particular Minister wanted to hear and learn. I have also shown that Dutch policy-makers were not altogether without influence about what the message from Brussels should be.

I could find only little influence on policy programs or institutional aspects. Arguably, the biggest influence of the EES was that it helped the Dutch approach towards inactivity and long-term unemployment out of a blind alley and offered some new arguments and instruments for a preventive approach. There were some other lessons from abroad, for instance on how activation and job counselling might be organised or on cumulative risks-at-poverty might be analysed and tackled. Dutch government officials invited foreign colleagues to learn more about the preventive approach in 1999 and 2000. Other civil servants went to Sweden to learn about labour force participation of women and child care; some went to Britain for its "one-stop shop approach to social security, to Germany and France for the reintegration of occupationally handicapped, and to Denmark for the integration of ethnic minorities. In a similar way Germany perhaps has learned from the Dutch approach to part-time work and the Netherlands learned from the Belgian approach to funding career-breaks.

Arguably, the biggest impact of both OMC processes was on the level of ambitions – possibly a reflection of the Lisbon strategy of setting targets. In both OMC processes national ambitions have been raised and translated into a large number of special targets concerning employment, education and training, the reduction of poverty, access to resources, literacy, and integration. These targets may give a "sense of purpose" to policy-makers, but especially with regard to social inclusion many targets are hard to verify and perhaps also a form of window dressing.

In a recent opinion, the Netherlands Council for Social Development warns of a "practice of unfulfilled promises". Basing its verdict on the evaluation of the EES on Zijl *et al.* (2002) and of the OMC social inclusion on Idema (2004), the Council criticises the limitation of the OMC process to "policies without politics", In contrast, the Council would like to see more politics in the OMC as a way to strengthen its learning potentials, among others by improving feedback to input, evaluation and horizontal networking with NGOs across borders and generally making the processes more open for civil society. It would also help if the NAPs were made into the key document on employment and social policy, gaining central stage in Parliament.

The biggest limitation of the application of the OMC in the Netherlands is that the process has remained rather bureaucratic and isolated – from parliamentary influence, from NGOs, from the social partners and from public debate. The audience for learning remained very small, almost entirely limited to the Ministry of Social Affairs and a handful of local, national and European civil servants. Against the initial expectation that these European co-ordination strategies would narrow the range of permissible policies and put pressure on countries to improve policy performance through "naming and shaming" based on political and public debate, the public resonance of these processes has been extremely muted in parliament and in the press, at least in the Netherlands. Hence, the OMC is not fully used as a tool that could help to mobilise societal support for reform – a central theme in the Kok Report of 2003 and during the 2004 Spring European Council. In its Communication on the future of the EES, the Commission complains that involvement of parliaments is rare, not just in the Netherlands: "the NAPs are too often perceived as 'owned' by the ministerial departments and not fully or coherently integrated in the overarching national policy framework, partly as a result of a lack of parliamentary involvement" (CEC, 2003f: 18). This criticism is repeated in the Joint Employment Report of 2004.

With regard to NGOs and social partners, the government seems to have a more limited role in mind than what would seem appropriate for reflexive learning or even for only motivating and mobilising societal support for reform. When the government declares in the 2003 NAP on social inclusion that it wants partnerships of NGOs as the "fourth pillar of a comprehensive anti-poverty strategy", it has a limited version in mind. Rather than sharing the control over the direction of the reform process, it intends to share responsibility for policy delivery. This is part of its philosophy of promoting more self-reliance and self-help, with voluntary societal support and less state provision.

I can only speculate why the Netherlands have chosen such a reductionist approach to the OMC, after some initial enthusiasm. In many areas of employment and social inclusion, the Netherlands do or rather did better than many other EU countries, so its politicians may think that there is little to learn from other countries (except the US and the UK). Unfortunately, I have found little evidence that participation in the OMC helps to discourage the introverted complacency which tends to come with success. In this sense, one of my expectations on the benefits of OMC, benchmarking and best practice learning is falsified. A somewhat high-handed "we know best" attitude influences not only the approach to Europe – for instance, the decision to disregard commonly defined indicators – but is also found in relation to the social partners and the NGOs. They are invited to participate, of course, but only to help deliver a package of policies the direction of which is pre-defined in detailed coalition agreements. This reassertion of the "primacy of political direction" and the "authority of the state" over the messy entanglements of corporatism, in industrial relations no less than in the governance of labour markets, social security, pensions, health and social assistance, has become stronger after 2002. Rather than restoring the primacy of politics through electoral competition, parliamentary control, political debate or public involvement, it strengthened the authoritarian and elitist element in Dutch politics, in which the state likes not to learn from but to teach Europe and its citizens.

References

Argyris, C. and Schön, D. A. (1996), *Organizational Learning II: Theory, Method, and Practice*, Addison-Wesley, Reading, MA.

Armingeon, K. and Beyeler, M. (2004), *The OECD and European Welfare States*, Edward Elgar Publishing, Cheltenham.

Ashiagbor, D. (2004), "The European Employment Strategy and the Regulation of Part-time Work", in Sciarra, S., Davies, P. and Freedland, M. (eds.), *Employment Policy and the Regulation of Part-time Work in the European Union. A Comparative Analysis*, Cambridge University Press, Cambridge, pp.35-62.

Atkinson, A. B., Cantillon, B., Marlier, E. and Nolan, B. (2002), *Social Indicators: The EU and Social Inclusion*, Oxford University Press, Oxford.

Atkinson, A. B., Marlier, E. and Nolan, B. (2004), "Monitoring Social Inclusion in the EU", paper for the EU research network on Economic Change, Unequal Life-Chances and Quality of Life (CHANGEQUAL), Paris, May 2004.

Auer, P. (2000), *Employment Revival in Europe. Labour Market Success in Austria, Denmark, Ireland and the Netherlands*, ILO, Geneva.

Bentolila, S. and Bertola, G. (1990), "Firing Costs and Labour Demand: How Bad is Eurosclerosis?", *Review of Economic Studies*, Vol.57, No.3, pp.381-402.

Calmfors, L., Forslund, A. and Hemström, M. (2001), "Does Active Labour Market Policy Work? Lessons from the Swedish Experiences", Conference paper "Labour Market Institutions and Public Regulation", CESifo Conference Centre, Munich, 26-27 October 2001.

Cameron, D. (2001), "Unemployment, Job Creation, and Economic and Monetary Union", in Bermeo, N. (ed.), *Unemployment in the New Europe*, Cambridge University Press, Cambridge, pp.7-51.

Casey, B. (2002), "The OECD Jobs Strategy and the European Employment Strategy. Two Views of the Labour Market and of the Welfare State", Paper presented at the conference "Welfare and the Labour market in the EU" organised by CEPII together with FEDEA and DIW Berlin, 25-26 October 2002.

CEC (1998), Communication from the Commission "From Guidelines to Action. The National Action Plans for Employment", COM (1998) 316 final of 13 May 1998.

CEC (2002), Communication from the Commission "Taking Stock of Five Years of the European Employment Strategy", COM (2002) 416 final of 17 July 2002 (http://europa.eu.int/eur-lex/en/com/cnc/2002/com2002_0416en 01. pdf).

CEC (2003a), Communication from the Commission "Joint Report on Social Inclusion. Summarising the Results of the Examination of the National Action Plans for Social Inclusion (2003-2005)", COM (2003) 773 final of 12 December 2003 (http://europa.eu.int/eur-lex/en/com/cnc/2003/com2003_0773en01.pdf).

CEC (2003b), *European Economy 2003*, Office of Official Publications of the European Communities, Luxembourg

CEC (2003c), *Employment in Europe 2003. Recent Trends and Prospects*, Office for Official Publication of the European Communities, Luxembourg.

CEC (2003d), Statistical Annex to the Draft Joint Inclusion Report, SEC (2003) 1425 of 12 December 2003, Commission Staff Working Paper.

CEC (2003e), *National Action Plan for Employment 2003*, Commission of the European Communities, Brussels (http://europa.eu.int/comm/employment_ social/employment_strategy/nap_2003/nap_nl_en.pdf).

CEC (2003f), Communication from the Commission "The Future of the European Employment Strategy (EES). 'A Strategy for Full Employment and Better Jobs for All'", COM (2003) 6 final of 14 January 2003 (http://europa. eu.int/eur-lex/en/com/pdf/2003/com2003_0006en01.pdf).

CEC (2004), Communication from the Commission "Draft Joint Employment Report 2003/2004", COM (2004) 24 final of 27 January 2004 (http://europa. eu.int/eur-lex/en/com/rpt/2004/com2004_0024en02.pdf).

Davies, P. and Freedland, M. (2004), "The Role of EU Employment Law and Policy in the De-marginalisation of Part-time Work: A Study in the Interaction between EU Regulation and Member State Regulation", in Sciarra, S., Davies, P. and Freedland, M. (eds.), *Employment Policy and the Regulation of Part-time Work in the European Union. A Comparative Analysis*, Cambridge University Press, Cambridge, pp.63-82.

de Beer, P. (2001), *Werken in de post-industriële samenleving*, Sociaal en Cultureel Planbureau, Rijswijk.

de la Porte, C., Pochet, P. and Room, G. (2001), "Social Benchmarking, Policy, Policy-making and New Governance in the EU", *European Journal of Social Policy*, Vol.11, No.4, pp.291-307.

De Nederlandsche Bank (2003), *Annual Report 2003*, Amsterdam.

De Nederlandsche Bank (2004), "The Origins of Growth: The Dutch Economy in 1998-2006", *Quarterly Bulletin*, June 2004, pp.45-55.

DiMaggio, P. and Powell, W. W. (1983), "Institutional Isomorphism. The 'Iron Cage' Revisited", *American Sociological Review*, No.48, pp.147-160.

Dolowitz, D. P. and Marsh, D. (2000), "Learning from Abroad. The Role of Policy Transfer in Contemporary Policy-making", *Governance. An International Journal of Policy and Administration*, Vol.13, No.1, pp.5-24.

Elmeskov, J. (1998), "The Unemployment Problem in Europe: Lessons from Implementing the OECD Jobs Strategy", *EUI working papers*, RSC 98/24, European University Institute, Robert Schuman Centre, Florence.

Engbersen, G., Vrooman, J. and Snel, E. (1996), *Arm Nederland – het eerste jaarrapport armoede en sociale uitsluiting*, VUGA, The Hague.

Esping-Andersen, G. (1999), *Social Foundations of Post-industrial Economies*, Oxford University Press, Oxford.

Esping-Andersen, G. and Regini, M. (2000), *Why Deregulate Labour Markets?*, Oxford University Press, Oxford.

European Council (2000), Lisbon European Council, *Presidency Conclusions*, 23-24 March 2000.

European Council (2004), Brussels European Council, *Presidency Conclusions*, 25-26 March 2004.

Ferrera, M., Hemerijck, A. C. and Rhodes, M. (2000), "The Future of Social Europe: Recasting Work and Welfare in the New Economy", Report submitted to the Portuguese Presidency of the European Union, Celta, Lisbon.

Ferrera, M., Matsaganis, M. and Sacchi, S. (2002), "Open Coordination against Poverty: The New 'EU Social Inclusion Process'", *European Journal of Social Policy*, Vol.12, No.3, pp.227-239.

Freeman, R. B. (1998), "War of the Models: Which Labour Market Institutions for the 21st Century", *Labour Economics*, No.5, pp.1-24.

Goetschy, J. (1999), "The European Employment Strategy", *European Journal of Industrial Relations*, No.5, pp.117-137.

Goetschy, J. (2003), "The European Employment Strategy, Multi-level Governance and Policy Coordination: Past, Present and Future", in Zeitlin, J. and

Trubek, D. M. (eds.), *Governing Work and Welfare in a New Economy. European and American Experiences*, Oxford University Press, Oxford, pp.59-87.

Hedström, P. (1998), "Rational Imitation", in Hedström, P. and Swedberg, R. (eds.), *Social Mechanisms. An Analytical Approach to Social Theory*, Cambridge University Press, Cambridge, pp.306-327.

Hemerijck, A. C. (1998), "Social Policy and Economic Performance", Report of the High-level Conference organised by the Dutch Presidency, Ministerie van Sociale Zaken en Werkgelegenheid, The Hague, 23-25 January 1997.

Hemerijck, A. and Visser, J. (2001), "Learning and Mimicking: How European Welfare States Reform", unpublished paper, University of Leiden and University of Amsterdam, June 2001.

Idema, T. (2004), "European Coordination, Local Effects? Towards an Effective Implementation of the European Social Inclusion Strategy in the Netherlands", Appendix 5 in RMO advise No.28, SDU/The Netherlands Council for Social Development, The Hague.

Kilpatrick, C. and Freedland, M. (2004), "The United Kingdom: How Is EU Governance Transformative?", in Sciarra, S., Davies, P. and Freedland, M. (eds.), *Employment Policy and the Regulation of Part-time Work in the European Union. A Comparative Analysis*, Cambridge University Press, Cambridge, pp.299-357.

Kok, W. *et al.* (2003), "Jobs, Jobs, Jobs – Creating More Employment in Europe", Report of the Employment Task-force chaired by Wim Kok, Brussels, November 2003 (http://europa.eu.int/comm/employment_social/employment_strategy/pdf/etf_en.pdf).

Larsson, A. (2000), "Decent Work in the Information Society? Challenges to Work and Labour Relations in Europe", paper presented at conference on "The World of Labour in the 21st Century", University Pompeu Fabra, Barcelona, 19-20 October 2000.

Larsson, A. (2000), "The European Employment Strategy and EMU. You Must Invest to Save". The 1998 Meidner Lecture, *Economic and Industrial Democracy*, No.19, pp.391-415.

Laulom, S. (2004), "France: Part-time Work – No Longer an Employment Policy Tool", in Sciarra, S., Davies, P. and Freedland, M. (eds.), *Employment Policy and the Regulation of Part-time Work in the European Union. A Comparative Analysis*, Cambridge University Press, Cambridge, pp.85-120.

Layard, R., Nickel, S. and Jackman, R. (1991), *Unemployment: Macroeconomic Performance and the Labour Market*, Oxford University Press, Oxford.

Lo Faro, A. (2004), "Italy: Adaptable Employment and Private Autonomy in the Italian Reform of Part-time Work", in Sciarra, S., Davies, P. and Freedland, M. (eds.), *Employment Policy and the Regulation of Part-time Work in the European Union. A Comparative Analysis*, Cambridge University Press, Cambridge, pp.156-189.

Lyberaki, A. (2004), "Mobilisation and Governance: A View from Greece", in *Impulses for European Employment Policy – Impulses for Germany: the Re-*

port of the Employment Task Force, Report for the 2004 European Spring Council, IAB and BMWA, Nürnberg/Berlin.

March, J. (1981), "Footnotes to Organisational Change", *Administrative Science Quarterly*, Vol.26, No.2, pp.563-577.

March, J. G. and Olsen, J. P. (1995), *Democratic Governance*, The Free Press, New York.

Martin, J. P. (2000), "What Works Among Active Labour Market Policies: Evidence from OECD Countries' Experiences", *OECD Economic Studies*, No.30, pp.79-113.

Ministerie van Sociale Zaken en Werkgelegenheid (2001), *Aan de slag*, Report of interdepartmental working party on the future of the labour market, Ministerie van Sociale Zaken en Werkgelegenheid, The Hague.

Ministerie van Sociale Zaken en Werkgelegenheid (2002), *National Action Plan for Employment* (henceforth: NAP) of 2002, Ministerie van Sociale Zaken en Werkgelegenheid, The Hague.

Nederland, T., Stavenuiter, M. and Swinnen, H. (2003a), "Development and Implementation of the NAP 2001", An Evaluation of the National Action Plan the Netherlands for the Prevention of Poverty and Social Exclusion", Verwey-Jonker Instituut, Utrecht, July 2003.

Nederland, T., Stavenuiter, M. and Swinnen, H. (2003b), "NAP 2003 Development, Objectives and Contents", An Evaluation of the National Action Plan the Netherlands for the Prevention of Poverty and Social Exclusion, Verwey-Jonker Instituut, Utrecht, October 2003.

Nickell, S. J. (1997), "Unemployment and the Labour Market Rigidities: Europe *versus* North America", *Journal of Economic Perspectives*, Vol.11, No.3, pp.55-74.

Noaksson, N. and Jacobsson, K. (2003), "The Production of Ideas and Expert Knowledge in the OECD. The OECD Jobs Strategy in Contrast with the EU Employment Strategy", *SCORE rapport serie*, No.2003/7, Stockholm.

OECD (1994), *The OECD Jobs Study*. Part I, Organisation for Economic Co-operation and Development, Paris.

Pissarides, C. A. (1997), "The Need for Labour Market Flexibility in a European Economic and Monetary Union", *Swedish Economic Policy Papers*, Vol.4, No.2, pp.513-546.

Pochet, P. (2003), "Pensions: The European Debate", in Clark, G. L. and Whiteside, N. (eds.), *Pension Security in the 21st Century*, Oxford University Press, Oxford, pp.44-63.

Raad voor Maatschappelijke Ontwikkeling (2004), "Europa als sociale ruimte. Open coördinatie van beleid in de Europese Unie", *Advies*, No.28, The Hague, April 2004.

Sabel, C. F. (1995), "Learning by Monitoring: The Institutions of Economic Development", in Smelser, N. J. and Swedberg, R. (eds.), *The Handbook of Economic Sociology*, Princeton University Press, Princeton NJ, pp.137-165.

Salais, R. (2004), "La politique des indicateurs. Du taux de chômage au taux d'emploi dans la stratégie européenne pour l'emploi", in Zimmermann, B. (ed.), *Les sciences sociales à l'épreuve de l'action. Le savant, le politique et l'Europe*, Editions de la Maison des Sciences de l'Homme, Paris, pp.287-331.

Schludi, M. (2003), "Chances and Limitations of 'Benchmarking' in the Reform of Welfare State Structures – The Case of Pension Policy", *AIAS Working Paper*, No.03/10, Amsterdam Institute for Advanced Labour Studies, Amsterdam.

Schmid, G. (1997), "The Dutch Employment Miracle? A Comparison of Employment Systems in the Netherlands and Germany", *Discussion Paper FS*, No.1 97-202, Wissenschaftszentrum, Berlin.

Schmitt, J. and Wadsworth, J. (2001), "Is the OECD Jobs Strategy Behind US and British Employment and Unemployment Success in the 1990s", Paper prepared for conference on "Liberalization and Employment Performance in the OECD", CEPA, New School University, 18-19 May 2001.

SDU/Ministerie van Sociale Zaken en Werkgelegenheid (1996), *De Nederlandse verzorgingsstaat in economisch en sociaal perspectief*, SDU/Ministerie van Sociale Zaken en Werkgelegenheid, The Hague.

SDU/Ministerie van Sociale Zaken en Werkgelegenheid (2000), *De Nederlandse verzorgingsstaat. Sociaal beleid en economisch prestaties in internationaal perspectief*, SDU/Ministerie van Sociale Zaken en Werkgelegenheid, The Hague.

Siegenthaler, H. (1993), *Regelvertrauen, Prosperität und Krisen*, J.C. Mohr, Tübingen.

Simon, H. A. (1955), "A Behavioral Model of Rational Choice", *Quarterly Journal of Economics*, No.69, February 1955.

Starbuck, W. H. and Hedberg, B. (2001), "How Organizations Learn from Success and Failure", in Dierkes, M. *et al.* (eds.), *Handbook of Organizational Learning and Knowledge*, Oxford University Press, Oxford, pp.327-350.

Telò, M. (2001), "Governance and Government in the EU: OMC", in Rodrigues, M. J. (ed.), *The New Knowledge Economy in Europe*, Edward Elgar Publishing, Cheltenham, pp.242-271.

van der Meer, M., Visser, J., Wilthagen, T. and van der Heijden, P. F. (2003), *Weg van het Overleg? De Nederlandse overlegeconomie twintig jaar na Wassenaar*, Amsterdam University Press, Amsterdam.

van Riel, B. and van der Meer, M. (2002), "The Advocacy Coalition for European Employment Policy: The European Integration Process After EMU", in Hegemann, H. and Neumärker, B. (eds.), *Die Europäische Union aus politökonomischer Perspektive*, Metropolis Verlag, Marburg, pp.309-328.

van Riel, B., Hemerijck, A. and Visser, J. (2003), "Is There a Dutch Way to Pension Reform?", in Clark, G. L. and Whiteside, N. (eds.), *Pension Security in the 21ˢᵗ Century*, Oxford University Press, Oxford, pp.64-92.

Visser, J. (2000), "From Keynesianism to the Third Way. Labour Relations and Social Policy in Postwar Europe", *Economic & Industrial Democracy*, No.21, pp.421-456.

Visser, J. (2002), "The First Part-time Economy in the World. A Model to Be Followed?", *Journal of European Social Policy*, Vol.12, No.1, pp.23-42.

Visser, J. (2003), "Negotiated Flexibility, Working Time and Transitions in the Netherlands", in O'Reilly, J. (ed.), *Regulating Working-time Transitions in Europe*, Edward Elgar Publishing, Cheltenham, pp.123-169.

Visser, J. and Hemerijck, A. C. (1997), *"A Dutch Miracle". Job Growth, Welfare Reform, and Corporatism in the Netherlands*, Amsterdam University Press, Amsterdam.

Visser, J., Wilthagen, T., Beltzer, R. and Koot-van der Putte, E. (2004), "The Netherlands: From Atypicality to Typicality", in Sciarra, S., Davies, P. and Freedland, M. (eds.), *Employment Policy and the Regulation of Part-time Work in the European Union. A Comparative Analysis*, Cambridge University Press, Cambridge, pp.190-222.

Zeitlin, J. (2003), "Introduction: Governing Work and Welfare in a New Economy: European and American Experiments", in Zeitlin, J. and Trubek, D. M. (eds.), *Governing Work and Welfare in a New Economy: European and American Experiments*, Oxford University Press, Oxford, pp.1-32.

Zijl, M., van der Meer, M., van Seters, J., Visser, J. and Keuzenkamp, H. (2002), *Dutch Experiences with the European Employment Strategy*, Report for the Ministry of Social Affairs and Employment, SEO/AIAS, Amsterdam.

CHAPTER 6

The Leverage Effect

The Open Method of Co-ordination in France

Christine ERHEL, Lou MANDIN & Bruno PALIER

The Open Method of Co-ordination (OMC) was created in order to renew European policies, in fields where diversity was too high to impose the same policies on all, and in fields where national governments wanted to keep their hands on decisions. The OMC is supposed to work differently from the classical European method of integration. Instead of regulations or directives imposed from above to be uniformly implemented in all Member States, OMC is supposed to co-ordinate different national policies around the same kind of policy vision. Therefore, one should not ask the same question as when analysing the transposition of directives. The policy guidelines should not be read as directives that are more or less transposed and implemented in the different countries. One should not be looking for an impact of the OMC guidelines as there is an impact of a European directive on national law. Most of the research that took such a top down perspective and tried to assess the impact of OMC on national policies found very disappointing results. National social policies (in the fields of employment, pension, inclusion) remain oriented by national actors, trying to address national issues, maintaining national trajectories.

Nevertheless, enquiries on the interaction between French employment, social exclusion and pension policies on the one hand and European Employment Strategy (EES) and OMC on the other show that if OMC does not dictate the orientation of French policies, it provides domestic actors with European resources which might help them in their action at the national level (Barbier and Samba Sylla, 2001; Coron and Palier, 2002; Salais *et al.*, 2002). Therefore, the research question should be less to see whether the European guidelines have imposed or not new policies on the national level, but to look for the possible influence of the European process on a national dynamic, and to understand the reciprocal linkages between the European and the national levels in the developments of social policies.

There are two possible ways to observe a link between EU orientations and French social policies: logical and sociological. At the logical level, one can ask whether there are coincidences between European orientations and the content of French developments in social policy, both in terms of results and of contents of welfare reforms. The comparison between the French situation and the European orientation demonstrates a progressive and partial convergence. However, this coincidence does not prove that French trends are due to European orientations. Therefore, a second approach is necessary, which tries to trace the possible influence or usage of European tools at the national level. This would be the sociological tracing of European influence, through empirical enquiries, asking French actors whether what happens at the European level has been influential and moreover useful to them in their day-to-day actions. If French actors usually deny that they are merely implementing European prescriptions, they usually recognise that they sometimes used the tools and resources offered by the Open Method of Co-ordination to help them in their national actions (bargaining, legitimating, powering etc.). One can then distinguish among various ways the European resources are utilised in the French context, from which we can derive a broad picture of the "leverage effect" of the OMC on national developments.

From a methodological point of view, assessing these coincidences between French and European trends and grasping the leverage effect of OMC and EES in France appears challenging. Indeed, it relies on indicators and soft co-ordination procedures, and standard impact evaluation is unable to deal with this kind of policy. Therefore we must perform an evaluation in context, combining a series of tools, quantitative indicators, policy analysis, and actors' interviews.

In this chapter, we will combine:

– a macro-level analysis, identifying first the situation of France with regard to the existing guidelines and quantitative targets. Considering the content of European and national policies, is it possible to show certain coincidences between the national policies and the European orientations (section 1);

– a micro-level study of actors' perceptions and utilisation of OMC resources, based on interviews. We will analyse the policy-making process through interviews with the national actors in charge of employment, social and pension policies, in order to study whether there is an effect of the European orientations on the national policies and reciprocally, an effect of the national policies on the European orientations (section 2). Throughout our analysis, we will deal with both the EES and the two main OMC areas, namely pensions and social inclusion.

I. The French Situation in Relation to the European Guidelines

In this section, we will try to situate France in relation to the European guidelines. We have noticed some coincidences between the EU guidelines and French social policy orientations. In recent years, there has been a shift towards measures that do not fit with the traditional aim of French social policies: to contain costs by stopping the increase in social contribution rates, to develop active measures instead of passive transfers and to introduce fully-funded pension schemes. These reorientations of social policies follow the main ideas promoted at the EU level. These coincidences will be analysed through two sets of data. First, we will assess the French situation with regards to the European benchmarks set by the various OMCs, second, we will compare the content of recent reforms in French social policies with European policy orientations.

A. French Outcomes and European Benchmarks

Activity and employment levels represent a central reference in the European co-ordination processes, in the field of employment, as well as of social inclusion. We will consider here the most recent formulation of the Employment Guidelines, namely the three "overarching" objectives of the new EES, which are defined as follows: "full employment", "improving quality and productivity at work", and "strengthening social cohesion and inclusion". As decided at the Lisbon and Stockholm Summits, the achievement of the first objective should be measured through the employment rate[1]. The social inclusion OMC also relies on common objectives and indicators, which have been defined after the Stockholm European Council (SPC, 2001). According to European institutions and documents, a large part of the fight against poverty and social exclusion is related to the functioning of labour market: the objectives focus on employment participation and on the quality of employment, as well as on poverty indicators.

Facing these objectives, the question which arises is to identify the situation of every country and the main gaps between OMC indicators and national performances. The assessment of the French situation with regard to EES quantitative objectives is mixed[2]. It appears quite good

---

[1] Overall employment rate of 67% in 2005 and 70% in 2010; employment rate for women of 57% in 2005 and 60% in 2010; employment rate of 50% for older workers (55-64) in 2010.

[2] All the data in this paragraph come from the French Ministry of Labour (DARES, National Action Plan and evaluation report), except Eurostat and OECD data, which are specified in the text.

for all indicators except the employment rate[3] (see appendix, table 1). In the education and lifelong learning area, France fulfils the quantitative objectives. Indeed, in 1999, 92% of the youth leaving the education system have attained upper secondary education level (BEP, CAP). School drop outs (without any qualification) represent 7.8% of the youth leaving the education system. The average level of participation in lifelong learning was 29.1% in 1999-2000 (training rate), though it is characterised by many inequalities between jobs and/or qualification levels. Concerning childcare, the situation is also good in France. 57% of children under 3 benefit from childcare (and school provides free childcare from 3 to 6).

As for active programmes, the principle of preventative measures has been accepted and developed: the main programme in that respect is the *"Nouveau Départ"* (New Start), which takes the unemployed in charge after six months unemployment. In 2000, six months after their registration at the employment agencies, 91.2% of the unemployed youth and 93.3% of the unemployed adults have either gone out of unemployment, or benefited from the New Start. Besides, since July 2001, every unemployed person is entitled to individualised assistance through the *Projet d'Action Personnalisé pour un Nouveau Départ* (PAP-ND).

Nevertheless, taking the Lisbon and Stockholm employment rate targets, there are some gaps between the French situation and the European goals. France does not meet the global target (the employment rate stays at 60%), but stands close to the target for women: in 2000 the employment rate of women was 54.1%, which is not far from the objective. Besides the female employment rate follows an increasing trend (contrary to the global employment rate).

But the situation for older workers lags far behind: the employment rate is 46.4% for the 50-64 (Eurostat), but 34.2% for the 55-64 (OECD).

These figures already give an overview of some indicators of social exclusion, which are related to employment. More precisely, the main problems concerning the French situation are the following (CEC and Council of the European Union, 2004):

– the level of long-term unemployment and of very long-term unemployment (more than three years): the share of long-term unemployment has been declining since 1999, but has started to rise again in 2002, especially for older workers;

– the distribution of unemployment is unequal: the unemployment rate is higher among women than men, and substantial regional

---

[3] The figures come from the 2002 EES Evaluation report.

differences persist, with a coefficient of variation of 8.8% in 2001 according to the national figures;

- job insecurity is growing (temporary contracts, short-term employment contracts...), especially for young people (between 18 and 24).

According to Eurostat, the poverty risk rate (percentage of population whose income is less than 60% of the national median) was 15% in 2001, which corresponds to the European average. The number of RMI (minimum income) recipients has decreased between 1996 and 2000, but has begun to rise again since the second half of 2002. The groups most vulnerable to the risk of poverty and exclusion are: the unemployed, the working poor, children under 18, unskilled young people, large and single-parent families, women over 65. This situation is also close to the overall situation in Europe. Thus, from a quantitative point of view, the main difference between European objectives and French performances concerns mainly labour market performance, and especially employment rates.

In the 2002 evaluation report, the employment rate objective is criticised by the French reporters on the basis of three main arguments: first, the age group 15-64 includes young people, which means that an increase in the global employment rate could be achieved by an increase in young people's labour force participation, at the expense of their educational level; second, the legal retirement age is 60; third, the indicator should be calculated on a full-time equivalent basis (the inclusion of part-time jobs contradicts the quality of work objective). However, whatever the indicator, the relative performance regarding older workers' employment rates and situation on the labour market is bad in France (see appendix table 5). Concerning the 50-64 group, the situation is apparently better (employment rate close to the EU average; -0.5%). But this is the result of gender differentiated situations: women's employment rate is higher than the EU average (+3.9%), whereas men's employment rate is largely under the EU average (-5.1%) (Eurostat, see appendix). This reflects the higher participation rate of women in France for the baby boom generations, and the global figure, in comparison to EU average, is pushed up by a structural effect.

A flow approach confirms the negative diagnosis of older workers' situation on the labour market: the probability for unemployed people to move into inactivity is very high (and the probability for inactive or unemployed people to find a job is very low) (Bommier *et al*, 2003; de Larquier, 2001). This situation reinforces the difficulties encountered by the pensions system (and might partly explain the difficulties of reforming it). The 2002 French EES evaluation report concludes that employment policies have undergone important transformations since

1997, which are coherent with the European guidelines. Based on these coincidences and progressive convergences in outcomes, the report suggests that the EES has had an impact on the content and orientation of labour market policies, as well as on their institutional background. To prove this, the report emphasises the coincidences between the content of French policies and the European orientations.

B. The Content of the Reforms Compared with European Orientations

In this section, we will consider not only outcomes but also the content of recent reforms in order to assess further the verdict of convergence of France towards European orientation. To do so, we will look at the dynamics of labour market and social exclusion policies in France, as well as recent pension policies. If convergence is reassessed, it will mean that innovative or path shifting changes (Bonoli and Palier, 1998; Erhel and Palier, 2003; Erhel and Zajdela, 2004) have been introduced in France since the traditional ways of implementing employment and pension policies were often far from the European guidelines in the past (Palier, 2000). If innovative changes have been introduced, the hypothesis that this may be partly due to the OMC can be raised, although the identification of coincidences doesn't prove any causal link between the new policies and the OMC.

1. Employment and Social Exclusion: The Development of Active Measures

French labour market policy has experienced many reforms since 1997. In the following table, we provide a synthetic overview of these reforms and of their main function with regard to a standard distinction between labour demand and labour supply targeting. This table relies on a broad definition of employment policies, including tax and benefit systems, and pension systems characteristics. Among other things, the 2002 evaluation report advances the idea that such a global approach to employment also represents a major change in the French context.

The Main Policy Reforms in France 1997-2003

	Measure or Reform	Focus
1998	Aubry Laws (reduction of working time and social contribution cuts)	Labour demand
1998	Nouveau Départ TRACE	Labour supply
2001	Unemployment compensation: PARE (2001)	Labour supply
2001, 2003	PPE (negative income tax)	Labour supply
2003	Fillon reform	Pensions, labour supply
2003	Minimum income activation (RMA)	Labour supply

This overview does not provide any information about the nature of change: are these policy orientations and tools really new in the French context? This question implies a broader perspective on the dynamics of policies in the 1990s and beginning of 2000s.

The very recent reforms exhibit a trend towards labour supply orientation of employment and social policies (contrary to a former labour demand oriented LMP). In France, the diagnosis about "inactivity traps" and the incentive to work problem has emerged during the 1990s. The existence of incentive problems appears as a side effect of labour market policies, which have promoted part-time contracts, with monthly wages below the minimum wage level. The so-called employment reference norm has shifted from the level of the SMIC (i.e. the minimum wage) to the level of ½ SMIC since the end of the 1980s and beginning of the 1990s. This latter wage level is situated almost at the level of the minimum income, which generates work incentive problems, as well as a new working poor phenomenon. The minimum wage level is no longer a minimum income guarantee for workers.

In this context, a more global approach, involving social policies as well as labour market regulations and programmes, has been developed. First, some incentive problems related to the minimum income have been treated (for instance housing benefit reform).In addition, a negative income tax (*PPE – Prime pour l'Emploi*) has been created, and extended (in 2003). All these new programmes aim at enhancing the financial incentives to work. More recently (in 2003), the minimum income has been reformed in order to introduce a new welfare-to-work scheme (which is called the *Revenu Minimum d'Activité*, RMA). This new pro-gramme has two main characteristics which make it very close to other European welfare-to-work measures: first it involves a sorting process among minimum wage beneficiaries, so as to select those who are able to work; second, it provides a subsidy for employers who hire people who have been benefiting from the minimum income for at least two years.

All these reforms belong to a new consensus, which considers unem-ployment as the result of two factors: labour market "rigidities", and the influence of social policies, which discourage unemployed and inactive people from searching for a job (and accepting one), because of disin-centive problems. This interpretation has been diffused by OECD and EU Commission reports, and its controversial dimension seems to have weakened over time (see the French debates, where the Left parties have successively accepted labour costs as a cause of unemployment – at least for the less skilled – and the existence of "trap" problems). The EU, as well as the OECD, may have here played a role in the dynamics of ideas about employment policies (Serré and Palier, 2004).

Apart from the financial dimension of the incentive problem, preventative intervention on job supply has been developed: *Nouveau Départ* and PARE aim at providing early intervention for the unemployed, in order to avoid long-term unemployment. They also rely on individualisation and contractual relationships between the unemployed and the public employment service[4]. This trend is very much in line with the EES objectives. Its influence is recognised by the actors interviewed by Barbier and Samba Sylla (2001): preventative intervention on job supply is considered as the main innovation linked with OMC, and encompasses *Nouveau Départ* and PARE. Salais *et al.* show that OMC has also influenced the French national job placement agency (*ANPE – Agence Nationale pour l'Emploi*), which drew on the EES guideline on acting locally to decentralise and restructure its operations, and on the EES's emphasis on activation and prevention to expand its budget and staff (Salais *et al.*, 2002). There have therefore been a lot of innovative reforms within French employment and insertion policies. These innovative reforms may suggest that EES has met some national concerns (with certain adaptations).

However, the influence of the European guidelines remains limited in two major fields, which are partly related one to another: first, the labour market situation of older workers, second the lifelong learning perspective. In these two areas, the new policies or reforms which have been launched since 1997 seem far from innovative changes. In these cases, the weight of the past seem greater than the influence of new ideas.

2. Older Workers

The European influence doesn't seem to be very strong in this field, at least until the pension reform of 2003 (see below). Despite some attempts to reform existing policies, social partners, firms and workers resisted and stressed either the competitiveness constraints or the French social model. The second half of the 1990s was a good example of these inconsistencies. Indeed, an official objective of this period was to develop part-time early retirement (through the progressive early retirement programme, PRP). But this priority suffered from the creation of a new full-time scheme (ARPE), which appeared more attractive to workers and firms. Besides, the existence of functional equivalents to full-time early retirement within the unemployment benefit system also hindered the development of part-time early retirement: indeed, the ACA (*allocation de chômeur âgé*) provides constant (not decreasing)

---

[4] The same principle applies to TRACE, but it is targeted at a narrower population (young people with severe social difficulties).

unemployment benefit for people aged 57 ½ and over, who are also entitled to be exempted at the same time from any job search requirement (DRE). All these schemes, which are managed by the social partners, seem more attractive than part-time early retirement. Several studies have shown that such competition and crowding out effects have played a major role in the relative failure of part-time early retirement (DARES, 1998; Courtioux, 2002).

The complexity of the set of programmes targeted at older workers can be related to the existence of a social and political consensus around early retirement. From the firms' point of view, these schemes have represented a way to modernise work organisation and to renew their labour force. Unions see early retirement as a matter of social justice and social progress (compensating for difficult working conditions). And for governments, these programmes were a way to fight against unemployment. The existence of such a consensus, mixing economic efficiency and social justice considerations, has made any reform difficult until now. A recent synthesis by the Ministry of Labour (DARES, 2003) reveals that the share of older workers among active labour market policy inflows increased between 1994 and 2001, but that the number of early retirees and people benefiting from age related unemployment insurance (ACA and DRE) has not decreased. The recent debates around pensions reform, combined with the European guidelines, might have initiated a change in the representations of social partners and public opinion. Nevertheless, this is a field where institutions and policies are characterised by inertia and path dependence.

3. Further and Lifelong Training

In the field of further/vocational training, the influence of the EES is also limited, despite important organisational reforms (decentralisation), and reports on the subject (Gauron *et al.*, 2000). Further training suffers from two main problems: inequalities are very strong (the most skilled are the most likely to get training), and there is no real lifelong perspective. The Aubry laws allow negotiation on the possibility to obtain time off for training through individual "training accounts". But this measure had very little success (CGP, 2001). This lack of a lifelong perspective reinforces the age problem, as older workers are usually under-trained, because the firms (and the workers themselves) have usually preferred the development of early exit options since the 1980s.

On the whole, the period since 1997 has been characterised by important dynamics and reforms in employment and social insertion policies: incentives to work, job supply, individualisation are the keywords of innovative change. These orientations are consistent with the European guidelines. Nevertheless, it remains difficult to assess what really comes from the OMC at such a global policy level. Other influences might also have played an important role, especially OECD recommendations, the diffusion of evaluation techniques and "culture" in the field of labour market policy. Indeed, in the French context, micro evaluations, which put the stress on individual incentives, have been developed during the 1990s, and contrast with previous macro-evaluation on the basis of neo-Keynesian models. They might also have changed the perception of labour market programmes' impact. The same can be said about pension.

4. Pension Reform

In 2000, the EU Economic Policy Committee showed that public pension spending will consume between 3 and 5% more of GDP in 2050, and will threaten monetary stability if the national governments do not reform public pension systems (EPC, 2000). At the Lisbon Summit, the Economic Policy Committee (EPC) and the recently created Social Protection Committee (SPC), were charged with preparing reports to evaluate the state of pension reforms in the Member States and to make some recommendations. The joint report proposed eleven objectives (SPC and EPC, 2001). On the basis of this report, three main common goals have been defined. First, the Commission recommends respecting strict budgetary orientations and reducing the growth of public spending. This would lead to the development of a multi-pillar system and the introduction of private funded supplementary schemes. Second, the Council underlines the need to raise employment rates. The dependency ratio (number of people over 65/number of persons between 15 and 64) will double until 2050. The acceleration of demographic ageing should be partly contained by an improvement of the employment ratio (proportion of inactive people/proportion of active people). At the Lisbon summit, a quantitative objective was set: to attain a global employment rate of 70%, and of 60% for women in 2010. A few months later, at the Stockholm Summit, the Council fixed another specific objective for older workers: to reach an activity rate of 50% for workers between 55-65 by 2010. At the Barcelona Summit, the Member States also agreed to raise the effective age of retirement by encourage older workers to work five more years by 2010. The third objective is to adapt the pension systems to demographic, economic and societal changes, by taking account of the new forms of employment (flexibility, insecurity, periods of unemployment) and by guaranteeing intra- and intergenerational equity.

The first national reports were submitted in September 2002. The Joint Report, proposed in March 2003, evaluated the situation of older workers in Europe and insists on the importance of active ageing. According to its projection, the increase in public spending would be reduced by one third in 2050 if the employment objectives are attained (CEC and Council of the European Union, 2003). Even though these new orientations are not constraining because each Member State remains, according to the principle of subsidiarity, autonomous in its process of reform, it may here again have an impact on the representation of the problem and possible responses to it. Therefore, this would lead to a cognitive harmonisation of pension reforms, because each country is committed to respect the European objectives, even though there are different pathways of reforms (Mandin and Palier, 2004).

The situation in France appears quite deteriorated. Indeed, the 2003 Joint Report underlines that the baby-boom phenomenon in France will have soon some repercussions on the French PAYG pension system: the number of retirees will increase sooner than in other European countries, beginning in 2007, even though the financial consequences will not occur before 2010 (CEC and Council of the European Union, 2003: 145). According to the projection made in the French national report in September 2002, the public expenses will increase rapidly, from 12.6% of the GDP in 2000 to 16.3% in 2040. According to the European projection, the pension system will evolve from a surplus of 0.6% of the GDP in 2005 to a deficit of 1.8% of the GDP in 2020, and of 3.8% in 2040, what would lead to an increase in the contribution rate of 10% (CEC and Council of the European Union, 2003: 146). Furthermore, this situation is even more worrying, because of the widespread use of early retirement in France since the mid-1970s in order to face to the rising unemployment. Today, the activity rate of workers older than 55 is one of the lowest in Europe, at 31.9% in 2001, and the average age of effective retirement is around 58.1[5]. The financial weight of early retirement increases the pressure on the pension system.

Besides, the reforms in the 1990s have either failed, or remained limited. The Balladur reform, adopted in 1993, concerned only private sector employees. The main measure was to lengthen the period of contribution necessary to be entitled to a full pension (50% of the reference wage) from 37.5 years to 40 years. The Juppé plan proposed in 1995 to align civil servants with the new conditions but it was withdrawn after an important protest movement (Palier, 2000). Consequently, the nondecision of reform created some differences between private and public sector employees: the replacement rate in the public sector is still 75% of the reference wage. By contrast, the French Pension Steering Committee (*Conseil d'orientation des retraites*) showed in 2001 that, by 2040 the replacement rate in the private sector will diminish by 20% and

---

[5]   Eurostat, December 2002.

pass from 78% to 64% (Conseil d'orientation des retraites, 2002). Thus until 2003 France stood far from the European objectives, with structural financing problems and limited reforms.

The process of pension reform dates back to 2002. After the re-election of Jacques Chirac on 2002, the Prime Minister, Jean-Pierre Raffarin, set on pension reform his agenda. Between June and December 2002, the Ministers in charge of the reform, François Fillon (Social Affairs Minister) and Jean-Paul Delevoye (Civil Service Minister) elaborated a plan of reform, but also tried to avoid social contestation. The principal stake rapidly became the alignment of public sector employees with the private sector employees' regimes. In January 2003, all the trade unions called for a reform, showing their desire to act but also trying to impose their preferred condition: to maintain a high level of pension. Between January and April 2003, both ministers talked with the social partners, the political parties, and the experts. However, it was only on 18 April 2003, that the government presented its plan, which was very elaborate (a bill of 81 articles). The government announced that the contribution period in the public sector will be raised to 40 years as in the private sector, and that the period of contribution will be raised to 41 years for everybody in 2008 and almost 42 years in 2020. The government also introduced a system of *"surcote"*, a bonus for those, who decide to retire after the legal age of retirement, which is still in France of 60 years old, and *"décote"*, a sanction for those, who decide to retire before 60 and do not have the required period of contribution.

Even through there was a big protest movement and some important strikes in May, the Government obtained the agreement of the employers' organisations and of two trade unions, the CFDT and the CGC, to adopt the reform. The bill obtained the support of the strong government majority in Parliament and was adopted on 24 July 2003. Before Parliament, the government also showed more explicitly its desire to create an optional funded pension regime for private sector employees (*PERP – Plan d'épargne retraite populaire*), that was also accepted by the legislature.

Furthermore, the different pathways of early exit from work are being progressively closed. Consequently, the Fillon reform follows the main orientations of the EU: to ensure the financial sustainability of pension systems, by introducing some parametric measures (to lengthen the period of contribution) and by developing some supplementary private pensions plans in order to compensate for the diminution of the public pension. It also follows the orientation of the EU concerning the active ageing policy: to encourage people to work longer, through a system of bonuses and sanctions, to develop lifelong learning[6] in order to preserve their ability to work, and to close the early exit schemes. It also follows the orientation of the EU concerning the principle of equity and aligned the public and private sector pension regimes under the same conditions.

Thus the Fillon reform actually corresponds to an innovative change, and coincides with the European objectives. Whereas there are coincidences between the EU guidelines and the new French social policy measures, it is difficult to demonstrate a direct link of influence between the two levels. To do so, one has to go further than simply underlining the coincidences, and study the concrete policy-making process at the national level, to see whether and how European processes may have influenced national ones. It seems that EU processes appear more as a leverage effect that accompanies and/or accelerates the national policy reorientation than an independent variable that directly determines French social policy-making.

II. OMC and the Policy-making Process: The Leverage Effect

Contrary to the literature on "europeanisation", which analyses the impact of the European level on the national level as a top-down process (see Caporaso *et al.*, 2001; Featherstone and Radaelli, 2003), the politics of the reforms remain national. However, this does not mean that the effect of European integration is null. Europeanisation may not only be "adaptation of the members states to EU orientations", but may also occur through a "usage" of the European orientations by the national actors (Jacquot and Woll, 2003). The study of the policy-making process shows that that the national actors utilise the various European tools provided by the OMC as a resource in their domestic policy-making activities. These resources, the European instruments such as indicators, benchmarks, guidelines, models, and arguments – stem from the OMC, consequently from the EU, and can produce a "leverage effect", i.e. accelerate, legitimate or impede the developments of certain policy options. Thorough our study of the French social policy-making process, this is the main effect we could attribute to the OMC, since French actors usually deny any direct causal influence of OMC on national policy formation.

---

[6] An agreement has been signed on this topic by the social partners in autumn 2003.

A. There Is Little Direct Influence from EU Orientations on National French Policy-making

Two main reasons explain why it is difficult to identify a causal relationship between EU and French social policy-making: a temporal disjunction, and a denial by national actors of such influence.

First, there is a *temporal disjunction* between the EU orientation and the French reforms. In the three fields of employment, social inclusion and pensions policies, some innovative reforms occurred before the introduction of the European objectives.

1. Employment

Some French initiatives had been taken before the introduction of the EES, especially initiatives for reductions of or exemptions from "social charges" (social contribution paid by employers), in the early 1980s and extended in the 1990. This political desire to lower the social contributions was justified by the discursive claim that social contributions had a negative impact on low-paid labour and focused on specific groups: young people, low-paid and low-skilled workers. Between 1977 and 1982, successive "pacts for jobs" were proposed to encourage workers to recruit certain categories of workers in difficult situations (unskilled young people, long-term unemployed etc.). The "Emergency Plan for Youth Recruitment", proposed by the Minister for Social Affairs Philippe Séguin in 1986, sought to promote the recruitment of people under 25 thanks to exemptions from employers' social contributions. Then, the Back to Work Contract (*CRE – Contrat de retour à l'emploi*) was established in 1989 for the long-term unemployed, which offered a combination of exemption from social contributions and a flat-rate government subsidy (Coron and Palier, 2002). Other similar measures were proposed in the following years and increased in the 1990s (DARES, 1996).

2. Social Inclusion

In the same way, the problem of social exclusion was underlined in France before the introduction of the Social Inclusion OMC. The creation of the "insertion minimum income" (*RMI – Revenu minimum d'insertion*) was proposed at the end of the 1980s. During the electoral campaign of 1988, in his "Letter to All the French people" (*Lettre à tous les Français*), François Mitterrand proposed to create a minimum income, that was to become the *RMI*. He explained that the most important thing was to guarantee a means of living for all these people "who don't have anything" and "who cannot do anything". The proposal was accepted unanimously on 1st December 1988. A minimum income was guaranteed for "each person who, because of his or her age, a physical or a mental disease, the situation of the economy and of the labour market, is unable to work, and has the right to receive from the community the necessary means to live".

RMI is not only a minimum income: social and professional inclusion is seen as a "national imperative". This minimum insertion income is one of the elements of a global mechanism to fight poverty and suppress all the forms of exclusion especially in the fields of education, employment, training, health and housing. Therefore, RMI has also a re-insertion dimension, in the form of a contract between the recipient and 'society'. Recipients must commit themselves to take part in a re-insertion program, as stated in a contract, signed by the recipient and a social worker. Such a program can be either job-seeking, vocational training or activities designed to enhance the recipient's social autonomy. The bill was adopted with a great majority in the Parliament and become effective in 1989.

3. Pensions

Finally, in the field of pensions, the French policy-makers relied on numerous administrative reports, which have been made since the 1980s, and the specific problems of the pension system were well known[7]. The French policy-makers also relied on reports based on a comparison with the other European countries, and especially the recent works made by the Pension Steering Committee (Conseil d'orientation des retraites, 2001 and 2002). According to the interviewed actors, they did not learn that much from the OMC. The diagnosis and the solutions adopted abroad were well known. The problem of the reform was linked more to internal difficulties: the deep institutionalisation of the system, the weight of the trade unions as veto players, and the apparent incapac-

---

[7] L. Tabah (1986), *Vieillir solidaires*, Rapport du Commissariat général du Plan, La Documentation française, Paris; P. Schopflin (1987), *Evaluation et sauvegarde de l'assurance vieillesse*, Ministère des Affaires sociales; R. Teulade (1989), *Rapport de la Commission protection sociale*, La Documentation française, Paris; *L'avenir des retraites*, 1990, Rapport de l'INSEE; Livre blanc sur les retraites. *Garantir l'équité des retraites de demain*, 1991, Rapport du Commissariat général du Plan, Rapport de la mission Retraites, 1991, Mission Cottave; B. Bruhnes, Rapport sur les retraites, 1992, *Livre blanc sur les retraites. Garantir l'équité des retraites de demain*, La Documentation française, Paris, 1991; Rapport Charpin, *L'avenir de nos retraites*, rapport au Premier ministre, Paris, La Documentation française, 1999; suivi par le rapport de la Fondation Copernic, puis le rapport de Dominique Taddéi, "*Retraites choisies et progressives*" réalisé pour le *Conseil d'analyse économique* en septembre 1999; Rapport Teulade, *L'avenir des systèmes de retraite*, Conseil économique et social, Direction des journaux officiels, Paris, janvier 2000.

ity of the succeeding governments, since the failure of Alain Juppé in 1995, to get the reform adopted.

Furthermore, there is a *denial* by the French policy-makers: they affirm that the reforms are only national and that the EU orientations do not influence them. Since 1992 and the national referendum on the Maastricht Treaty in France, when the YES won with less than one percentage point, French high civil servants and politicians are accustomed to deny that Europe may impose or influence any policies at the national level. So, no one can really expect French actors to recognise explicitly an influence of Europe on national sovereignty. As mentionned in one of our interviews, "In France, there is a will to not show the importance of Europe: Brussels that regulate everything, this appears as a ghost"[8]. On the contrary, if domestic actors tend to see an interaction between France and Europe, it is often in the opposite direction, since they frequently claim that France was influential on the content of European policy orientations One should of course be as careful with these claims as one should be with the claim that Europe is directly influencing national policies.

4. Employment

In this way, one of the authors of the preparatory report for the French eleventh "National Plan" underlines a transmission of ideas from the national to the European level:

> I think it was more a matter of Paris influencing Brussels because our report, written in January 93, had been gestating throughout 1992. Obviously we had an alter ego who kept a very close eye on everything we were doing, and as far as Jérôme Vignon was largely responsible for drafting the relevant part. I believe he kept a very close eye on what was going on here and relayed it to the Community. In this instance, I think it was Paris influencing Brussels[9].

5. Social Inclusion

The same discourse appears in the field of social exclusion. In 1997, the dissolution of Parliament occurred during the discussion about a bill on social cohesion, presented by the Juppé government. Lionel Jospin promised to pass a new bill against social exclusion. The vote on this bill, announced for the autumn 1997, occurred in July 1998, the *Loi d'orientation relative à la lutte contre les exclusions*, which objective is to guarantee to everybody the access to existing social rights, especially

---

[8] Interview, Délégation aux affaires européennes et internationales (DAEI), 2 January 2004.

[9] Interview, Commissariat Général du Plan, 6 June 2001.

in the fields of health care, employment, housing and culture, and to prevent all the forms of exclusion. The objective of this law was to complete the RMI program and to make it more understandable. According to the interviewed actor in charge of the social exclusion NAPs, France was at the origin of the European orientations:

> France had the presidency of the EU after July. We created an informal group, it was our role to define the OMC concerning the social inclusion. For this policy field, it was inspired by the French initiatives, we based our work on the law of 1998. It was very important for Martine Aubry, the Minister of Employment and Social Affairs, to get this program accepted at the EU level. She intended to resign from her position in France in September, but she waited until the decision of the Social Affairs European Council, which was taken in Luxembourg in October. She only resigned the day after, the European orientations concerning social inclusion follow the French law of 1998[10].

6. Pensions

In the field of pensions, the situation is different. The policy-makers do not say that they influenced the European orientations, but that the OMC launched in the field of pensions, occurred too late in France, in order to be taken into account in the reform process. The national strategy reports on pension reform had to be presented to the Commission in September 2002, although the reform process was not yet underway in France. Consequently, the French policy-makers deny that they have used the OMC process:

> The national strategy report was a stylistic exercise. The French report respects the questions prepared by the Commission. We respected the number of pages (25-30 pages). However, it was difficult, as the last important reform occurred ten years ago. We were preparing the Fillon reform. During the elaboration of the Fillon reform, as for the elaboration of the national strategy report, we have juggled with the OMC. In September, the main objective was that we should not give the feeling that the reform was actually preconfected, although it still had to be discussed with the social partners. It was very important not to give the impression that the reform was imposed by Brussels. This was very present in the strategies of the successive governments[11].

Consequently, the French policy-makers chose not to transmit the content of the reform in their 2002 report, in order to preserve their own national policy-making process.

---

[10] Interview, Direction de la Sécurité Sociale, 13 January 2004.
[11] Interview, Direction de la Sécurité Sociale, 8 January 2004.

Looking at the policy-making processes at the French level, it is difficult then to argue that EU has imposed any of the recent trends observed in the first part of this chapter. However, this does not mean that there is no link between the EU and the national levels. The policymakers, even though they deny the influence, recognise that they made some use of the OMC. Consequently, European orientations do not appear as a causal influence on national actors but rather as a resource for the latter. This point converges with the political desire of the European Commission, which created the OMC as an opportunity to be taken up by the national actors. The interviews show that the French policymakers took these opportunities.

B. The Leverage Effect

Empirically, we will study the three different policy fields to see how this "leverage effect" occurred. We can distinguish four main processes that are triggered by the participation of French civil servants in the OMC, or by their usage of the OMC tools: rationalisation of policies; horizontal co-operation; vertical co-ordination; legitimisation.

1. Rationalisation of Policies through the Preparation of the NAPs

In the fields of employment and social exclusion, the drafting of the NAPs constitutes an important element, insofar as these plans bring together all the documents and measures launched and implemented. The NAPs are used by the national actors as a document of reference, which synthesise all the different measures, their implementation, their evaluation and their evolution. Consequently, the NAPs have provided an opportunity to highlight the contradictions of the various policies layered over time, and sometimes an opportunity to rationalise them.

As shown by Coron and Palier (2002), debates taking place in France around the compilation of the NAP/empl and, more broadly, the European employment guidelines provide an opportunity to view France's employment policies in the round, giving them a coherence which a growing succession of measures over the years has made invisible (or non-existent):

> The European Strategy and the guidelines are useful in that they provide an orientation. This lends overall coherence that didn't exist to such an extent before. In addition, what matters are obviously the four pillars. We get a general overview of the various facets, and we all move forward together. Everything is dealt with at the same time in the NAP [...] especially if there are elements of convergence. We're keen to co-ordinate our initial approach to an issue and to strike a coherent balance, which is perhaps a little more

awkward. But we have to tell ourselves: we must make headway not just on one of the pillars but on all four at once[12].

This element is also important in the field of social exclusion, although the process is a recent one. Even though, there is only the second generation of the NAPs in this policy field, the last report elaborated in July 2003, contains the program of social inclusion action for the next years 2003-2005. The NAPs have become the main documents of reference in France:

> In France, the NAP is the first support of the fight against the social exclusion. It's the document of reference, we follow the European rhythm. It has some national consequences. The national plan presented in Brussels represents our waybill[13].

The importance of the NAP has become a real theme at the French level. Policy-makers says that there is a gap concerning older people and long-term care:

> The NAP has become very important for our work at the national level. Indeed, it would be great if it could be extended to other themes, such as long term care. It would facilitate our action[14].

Consequently, the NAPs, especially in the field of employment and social exclusion became a way to rationalise the national policies and to develop some programs of action. Today, it is recognised as a resource by domestic actors, which facilitates their work at the national level.

2. Horizontal Co-operation

In France, on of the main problems is the dispersion of the ministries, and of the directions inside each ministry. The OMC involves an evolution of this method of work and a greater collaboration between the different services. As Coron and Palier (2002) show, preparation of the NAP not only fosters an overall harmonisation of policies; it also promotes co-ordination among the different employment policy-makers. One characteristic of the French method of compiling the NAPs seems to be active participation by various parts of the administration. Civil servants link the relative success of these measures with the fact that the procedure entails co-operation among the different ministries. A key role is played in this process by the SGCI (General Secretariat for Inter-Ministerial Co-operation on European Affairs). Once the guidelines have been received, this body apportions tasks and decides which departments will be project leaders, depending on what topics are

---

[12]   Interview, DGEFP, 6 June 2001.

[13]   Interview, Direction Générale de l'Action Sociale, 23 December 2003.

[14]   *Ibid.*

covered in the macroeconomic overview and the presentation of employment policies. A large majority of topics fall to the Ministry of Employment and Solidarity. Within that ministry, a specific service, the DGEFP, co-ordinates proceedings by holding a meeting of all assistant directors and heads of department; it also commissions a number of specific studies, while the Service in charge of statistics and studies (DARES) always retains primary responsibility in respect of statistical indicators. The final stage in the operation is to pull all the strands together, and this is done by the DGEFP. During this internal process within the Ministry of Employment, the inter-ministerial dimension is maintained by virtue of the SGCI.

> The NAP is a very demanding exercise; it requires inter-ministerial co-operation. It is carried out under the leadership of the Prime Minister, who steers it along with planning meetings at Matignon [the Prime Minister's office]. Therefore several ministries, especially those most directly affected, participate actively. First and foremost there's our own, obviously, but there's also the Ministry of Economics and Finance and the Ministry of Education. And this is important when we speak to other Member States in Brussels. We see that, when the Ministry of Employment is in sole command, they find it rather hard – so they tell us – to gather others around them and garner additional input. Here, the fact that a body exists, the SGCI, and that it is under the Prime Minister's direct leadership means that active participation takes place[15].

Therefore the NAP provides an opportunity for the various ministries to co-operate in putting forward employment policy objectives. It is a matter of jointly reviewing and co-ordinating provisions which have sometimes become fragmentary and even fossilised over time. According to all those we interviewed, the NAP makes it possible to identify the overriding logic behind employment policies and co-ordinate them.

The same appears to be true for helping to co-ordinate inclusion policies. According to an interviewed person in charge of the Social Inclusion OMC, this is one of the main problems:

> Many issues concern four or five directions, it is necessary to elaborate some inter-directional decisions. It is always necessary to work fast, with the colleagues of the DGAS, the DREES, the DARES, and the DGEFP. It is necessary to define very fast a common position with the other directions. It is very different from the traditional method of work. Most of the time, we work directly with the head of the Social Affairs Ministry[16].

This problem also appears concerning the work between the different ministries, especially the Employment and Social Affairs Ministry and

---

15 Interview, DGEFP, 5 June 2001.
16 Interview, Direction de la Sécurité Sociale, 13 January 2004.

the Economic and Financial Affairs ministries. This issue concerns more the field of pensions. Indeed, according to the actor in charge of the pension OMC: "We have the same problem at the EU and at the national levels. It is difficult to make the social and the economic spheres work together, and to arrive at a compromise between social and financial objectives"[17].

Consequently, writing the various NAPs necessitates developing collaboration between the directions and the ministries. Preparing the NAP is part of the interplay between institutions, and most notably the struggle between the Ministry of Employment and the Ministry of Finance. The Employment Ministry will for example try to prevent responsibility for writing certain passages being conferred on members of the Planning Directorate (in the Ministry of Economics and Finance). In 1998, it used the inclusion of the "fresh start" (*Nouveau Départ*) programme in the NAP as a justification for endowing it with a larger budget, contrary to the opinion of the Finance Ministry. The three-year commitment in the NAP was used as a bargaining chip in the budget debate that following autumn[18]. Experience gained over four years has enabled the Planning Directorate to manipulate such practices better, and, more generally, has caused France's various employment policy-makers to attribute growing importance to the preparation of the NAP.

In the same vein, we have already mentioned that ANPE referred to EES guidelines to obtain an expansion of its budget and staff (Salais *et al.*, 2002). Barbier and Samba Sylla show that the *Service du droit des femmes* was likewise strengthened as a result of the European gender mainstreaming and gender equality guidelines (Barbier and Samba Sylla, 2001).

3. Vertical Co-ordination

Aside from the co-ordination and conflicts triggered by the interministerial compilation of the NAPs, the Plans are in addition a vector of "vertical" co-ordination. Indeed, the Ministry of Employment strives to interest the lower tiers of the administration, the regional and local departments, in the compilation and then dissemination of the NAPs. The aim of so doing is to strengthen the local dimension of the work of the public employment services – another concern featuring in the NAPs. Thus the DGEFP disseminates the NAP to regional departments (of employment and vocational training), which then forward it to local departments. Moreover, use of the NAP enables a specific picture of employment policy to be presented to partners in public sector activities.

---

[17] Interview, Direction de la Sécurité Sociale, 8 January 2004.

[18] Interview, DGEFP, 6 June 2001.

And what we wanted to do this year was transmit it to Regional Directors, encouraging them to use it as back-up with their staff, their opposite numbers and their partners [...] Indeed, the Minister did so when she submitted it at the end of April[19].

One should also mention here the use of EES guidelines to trigger decentralisation and restructuring of the national job placement agencies (ANPE), as shown by Salais *et al.* (2002).

It would therefore seem that, at least within departments and among certain non-governmental partners in employment policy, the NAP is becoming an important tool for setting common goals and improving the actions undertaken.

The same kind of usage of OMC tools can be found for the Social Inclusion OMC. The OMC in the field of social inclusion will be used insofar as there is a move towards the decentralisation of the social exclusion programs at the level of the departments. DGAS participated to this work and use the indicators elaborated in the frame of the NAPs to define this new project: "We will use the program and the indicators elaborated in the NAPs in order to involve the departments. The NAP will become an operational document in France, it will oblige the departments to present their expenses and to justify them by their results"[20].

4. Legitimation of Actors and Orientations

OMC processes can increase the legitimacy of certain national actors when they use the tools or arguments provided by OMC within the national debate. The reference to European dynamics, to other countries sometimes help top reformulate national policies:

Today, there is a real dynamic at the EU level, and the importance given at the European level to the theme of poverty, makes it more important at the national level. The OMC and the NAPs are some elements which justify our action at the national level, it is the basis of our legitimacy. The theme of poverty has taken more importance, especially with the arrival of the new members. Today, half of all emergency social assistance goes to people from Eastern Europe. We do not want them to take advantage of free movement, so that we inherit the poverty of the rest of the Europe. The delocalisation of the poor may influence our national economy. The importance of OMC increases because there is a change in the national and the international environment. The new members are tempted by a movement of extremist liberalisation, and it is necessary to put the question of poverty on the table. Our wish is that these countries should fight against poverty and

---

[19] Interview, DGEFP, 6 June 2001.

[20] *Ibid.*

catch up with the high level of social protection, which is promoted in the rest of Europe.

The threatening arrival of poverty in France becomes an important stake that is taken into account both at the national and at the European level. In these conditions, the usage of the comparison is a way to prevent some undesirable events in France.

In the field of pensions, the question is different. The main objective is to preserve the social function of the French pension system: an adequate level of pensions, and to defend this point at the EU level so that the French pension system could be preserved:

> OMC permitted a materialisation of the social sphere at the European level, and its propositions especially in the frame of the Broad Economic Policy Guidelines. This principle was enacted at the Laeken Summit. At this time, it remains experimental, but we have insisted to work together with the economic actors, so that our point of view would be included in the Broad Economic Policy Guidelines. We know that the social actors have no weight and our possibility to influence the European orientations concerning the pension reform is to work with the economic actors, so that our voice could be heard[21].

In these different sectors, the OMC is used as an instrument, a re-source, to serve some national interests. We have seen the use by the Ministry of Employment or the Ministry of Social Affairs in their fights/bargain with the Ministry of Economics policy-making reference to EES or OMC as a support for their position, as another argument to promote policies aimed at individualising employment strategies, com-bating social exclusion, preserving a high level of pension... More and more, French policy-makers are using the EU tools and orientations, including them in their own policy-making process.

5. The Role of Social Partners

Other empirical studies, also based on interviews or seminars involv-ing the different social partners, have investigated more directly the implication of the French social partners in the OMCs (and especially the EES) (Raveaud, 2001; Barbier and Samba Sylla, 2001; Barbier, 2004 and Lefresne, 2004). They provide some interesting complements to our own enquiries. The participation of the social partners has been institutionalised in 1998 through the creation of the CDSEI (*Comité du dialogue social sur les questions européennes et internationales*, Na-tional Committee for Social Dialogue on European and International

---

[21] Interview, Direction de la Sécurité Sociale, 13 January 2004.

Questions). Since 2000, they are explicitly requested to play an active role and to write a contribution to the French NAP (Raveaud, 2001).

Empirical studies show the limits of their participation in the EES, from both a substantive and a procedural point of view[22]. Some reasons can be identified, like the differences among the positions of the various social partners, which lead to the impossibility to provide a synthetic overview of the "French social partners' position" (contrary to other countries). French social partners seem to use the European Employment Strategy according to their own objectives, which again indicates a leverage effect. Besides, they are very critical about the domination of the administration within the process, which is reinforced by the political situation since 2002. Indeed, this generates a kind of dilemma: on the one hand, not to participate actively means leaving the government free to limit the contribution of the social partners; on the other hand, active participation might be interpreted as support for the government's policy, which would limit their ability and credibility in raising criticisms. Thus there is a confusion between national and European agendas – a problem that has been reinforced by the change in the political majority. As for the administrative actors, it seems that the OMC process serves more a resource for social partners in the national context, than as a real way to intervene in European matters.

Nevertheless, this institutional process has led to some interesting results in the field of "quality of work". The debates around the definition of the concept and about the relevant indicators to measure it have involved a variety of actors, including the social partners, at the European as well as at the national level. According to Barbier's interviews (2004), the trade union representatives who have taken part in the process seem to be receptive to the concept of "quality of work", which opens a space for action. They stress the fact that it facilitates debates on the question of working conditions and "well-being at work", although they fear that the quality of work might hide a strategy of "dilution", when full employment is not attainable (Barbier, 2004: 109).

Conclusion

Despite the difficulties of establishing causality between European guidelines and national reforms, OMC is more than a virtual policy tool. It provides new resources for national actors, instead of imposing new policies from above. When national actors use these new instruments and resources, they meanwhile import and incorporate the general orientations on which the EES and OMC are based. One can of course

---

[22] This statement was already pointed out by Raveaud (2001), and is confirmed by the discussions in the IRES seminar (reported in Lefresne, 2004).

claim that the effect of EES and OMC on French policies is marginal, since the interests that have used OMC tools were already present in the national context, while political choices were already made without considering the European orientation. Yet, one could argue that this was also the case for the Maastricht Treaty and the Stability Pact: most of the new macro-economic orientation had already been adopted before 1992, the paradigmatic shift in economic policies having occurred during the 1980s in many European countries (Hall, 1986). However, the process of co-ordinating macro-economic policies associated with Maastricht and the Stability Pact has created a new institutional context which guarantees the continuity of the new policies at the European level. One could argue that the EES and OMC will have this kind of role, safe-guarding coherence and co-ordination of new social policies adapted and compatible with the new economic policy orientations. The fact that in 2003, both the Broad Economic Policy Guidelines and the Employment Guidelines (the so-called ten commandments) have been synchro-nised illustrates this.

OMC is developing new modes of co-ordination, based more on ideas than on legislation. If we do not consider reforms as either imme-diately dictated by the nature of the problems (a cybernetic view of government) or adequately adapted to objective interests of certain actors (public choice), but if we consider policy solution as constructed through social interaction, then, to understand how certain solutions prevail, the cognitive and normative aspects of the policy-making pro-cess have to be considered. The process of elaborating a reform is an intellectual one, in which European ideas may play a certain role. One should probably try to understand the kind of intellectual influence Europe may have on welfare state change if one wants to understand welfare state changes. However, this implies first a change in the con-ception of what a reform is, and second to use a particular approach, which focuses on the role of ideas. The European contribution to the transformation of welfare state will be more visible if we analyse re-forms less in terms of adjustments or adaptations to external shocks (such as globalisation or population ageing) and more in terms of public policies constructed through social interaction involving European insti-tutions more and more. The point here is not to deny the importance of "objective" problems, but rather to argue that identifying problems is not sufficient for understanding either the process or the outcome of reforms aimed at coping with them.

References

Barbier, J.-C. (2004), "La stratégie européenne pour l'emploi: genèse, coordination communautaire et diversité nationale", Rapport de recherche pour la DARES (ministère du Travail), Paris, January 2004.

Barbier, J.-C. and Samba Sylla, N. (2001), "Stratégie européenne de l'emploi: les représentations des acteurs en France", rapport pour la DARES et la Délégation à l'Emploi du ministère du Travail et de l'Emploi, Paris, December 2001.

Bommier, A., Magnac, T. and Roger, M. (2003), "Le marché du travail à l'approche de la retraite: évolution en France entre 1982 et 1999", Colloque Age et Emploi, DARES, 5 March 2003.

Bonoli, G. and Palier, B. (1998), "Changing the Politics of Social Programmes. Innovative Change in British and French Welfare Reforms", *Journal of European Social Policy*, Vol.8, No.4, November 1998, pp.317-330.

Caporaso, J., Cowles, M. G. and Risse, T. (2001), *Transforming Europe, Europeanization and Domestic Change*, Cornell University Press, Ithaca.

CEC and Council of the European Union (2003), Joint Report by the Commission and the Council on Adequate and Sustainable Pensions, Document 7165/03, Brussels, 10 March 2003.

CEC and Council of the European Union (2004), Joint Report by the Commission and the Council on Social Inclusion, Document 7101/04, Brussels, 5 March 2004 (http://europa.eu.int/comm/employment_social/soc-prot/soc-incl/final_joint_inclusion_report_2003_en.pdf).

CGP (2001), *Réduction du temps de travail: les enseignements de l'observation*, La Documentation française, Paris.

Conseil d'orientation des retraites (2001), *Age et travail, un axe de réflexion essentiel pour l'avenir des retraites*, La Documentation française, Paris.

Conseil d'orientation des retraites (2002), *Retraites: renouveler le contrat social entre les générations, orientations et débats*, La Documentation française, Paris.

Coron, G. and Palier, B. (2002), "Changes in the Means of Financing Social Expenditure in France since 1945", in de la Porte, C. and Pochet, P. (eds.), *Building Social Europe through the Open Method of Co-ordination*, P.I.E.-Peter Lang, Brussels, pp.97-136.

Courtioux, P. (2002), "Part-time Retirement *versus* Full-time Retirement: Labour Market Reform and Competition between Programmes in France", EALE Conference, Paris, 19-22 September 2002.

DARES (1996), *40 ans de politiques de l'emploi*, La Documentation française, Paris.

DARES (1998), "Les dispositifs publics de préretraite et l'allocation de remplacement pour l'emploi en 1996", *Premières informations et premières synthèses*, No.49.1, December 1998.

DARES (2003), "Les entrées en CES et en CEC en 2002", *Premières informations et premières synthèses*, No.50.1, December 2003.

de Larquier, G. (2001), "Dynamiques des marchés du travail, chômage et inégalités", in Bessy, C., Eymard-Duvernay, F., de Larquier, G. and Marchal, E. (dir.), *Des marchés du travail équitables? Approche comparative France/ Royaume-Uni*, P.I.E.-Peter Lang, Brussels, pp.21-50.

Dehousse, R. (2001), "Du bon usage de la méthode ouverte de coordination", Conference organised by the EU "Towards a New Architecture for Social Protection in Europe? A Broader perspective of Pension Policies", Leuven, 19-20 October 2001.

EPC (2000), Progress Report to the Ecofin Council on the Impact of Ageing Populations on Public Pension Systems, Economic Policy Committee, Brussels, 6 November 2000.

Erhel, C. and Palier, B. (2003), "Europe sociale et Europe de l'emploi: l'apport d'une perspective institutionnaliste à l'explication des trajectoires nationales", *Cahiers de la MSE*, No.2003-30.

Erhel, C. and Zajdela, H. (2004), "The Dynamics of Social and Labour Market Policies in France and UK: Towards Convergence?", *Journal of European Social Policy*, Vol.14, No.5, pp.125-142.

Featherstone, K. and Radaelli, C. (2003), *The Politics of Europeanization*, Oxford University Press, Oxford.

Gauron, A., Didier, M. and Piketty, T. (2000), "Formation tout au long de la vie", *Rapport du Conseil d'analyse économique*, No.22, La Documentation française, Paris.

Hall, P. A. (1986), *Governing the Economy: The Politics of State Intervention in Britain and France*, Oxford University Press, New York.

Jacquot, S. and Woll, C. (2003), "Usage of European Integration – Europeanisation from a Sociological Perspective", *European Integration online Papers (EioP)*, Vol.7, No.12 (http://eiop.or.at/eiop/texte/2003-012a.htm).

Lefresne, F. (2004), Intervention à l'atelier "Débats et enjeux nationaux: questions soulevées par les acteurs en France", conférence "Stratégie européenne pour l'emploi: débats et institutionnalisation", Observatoire social européen, Bruxelles, 30-31 août 2004.

Mandin, C. (2001), "L'Union européenne et la réforme des systèmes de retraites, de la nécessité d'une adaptation aux nouvelles normes socio-économiques à l'élaboration d'un compromis politique", mémoire de DEA, Institut d'études politiques, Paris.

Mandin, L. and Palier, B. (2004), "L'Europe et les politiques sociales: Vers une harmonisation cognitive des réponses nationales", in Lequesne, C. and Surel, Y. (eds.), *L'intégration européenne. Entre émergence institutionnelle et recomposition de l'Etat*, Presses de Sciences Po, Paris.

Palier, B. (2000), "'Defrosting' the French Welfare State", *West European Politics*, Vol.23, No.2, pp.113-136.

Raveaud, G. (2001), "La dimension européenne des politiques d'emploi françaises. Une analyse de la participation des partenaires sociaux à l'élaboration du PNAE 2001", Étude réalisée pour la Délégation Générale à l'Emploi et à la Formation Professionnelle du ministère de l'Emploi et de la Solidarité, November 2001.

Salais, R., Raveaud, G. and Mathieu, G. (2002), *L'évaluation de l'impact de la Stratégie Européenne pour l'Emploi – Thème 10: Elaboration des politiques*, DARES, Ministère de l'Emploi et de la Solidarité, Paris.

Serré, M. and Palier, B. (2004), "France: Moving Reluctantly in the OECD's Direction", in Armingeon, K. and Beyeler, M. (eds), *The OECD and European Welfare States*, Edward Elgar Publishing, Cheltenham, pp.101-112.

SPC (2001), Report on Indicators in the Field of Poverty and Social Exclusion, Social Protection Committee, Brussels, October 2001 (http://europa.eu.int/comm/employment_social/social_protection_commitee/laeken_list.pdf).

SPC and EPC (2001), Joint Report of the Social Policy Committee and the Economic Policy Committee on Objectives and Working Methods in the Area of Pensions: Applying the Open Method of Coordination, No.14098/01, Brussels, 23 November 2001.

Streeck, W. (1996), "Neo-voluntarism: A New European Social Policy Regime?", in Marks, G., Scharpf, P., Schmitter, P. and Streeck, W. (eds), *Governance in the European Union*, Sage Publications, London, pp.64-94.

Vandenbroucke, F. (2001), "Open Co-ordination on Pensions and the Future of Europe's Social Model", Closing speech at the Conference "Towards a New Architecture for Social Protection in Europe? A Broader Perspective of Pension Policies", Leuven, 19-20 October 2001.

Appendix: Statistical Annex

I. Some General Indicators for the French Labour Market and Employment Policies

Table 1: Unemployment Rate in France (1990-2000)

Year	Men	Women	Total
1990	7	12.1	9.2
1996	10.5	14.3	12.2
1997	10.9	14.2	12.4
1998	10.3	13.9	11.9
1999	10.3	13.7	11.8
2000	8.5	12	10.1

Source: OECD (2003).

Table 2: Employment and Activity Rates (1990-2000)

Year	Men	Women	Total
1990	69.7	50.3	59.9
2000	68.1	54.3	61.1
1990	75	57.2	66
2000	74.4	61.7	68

Source: OECD (2003).

Table 3: Share of Part-time Work in Total Employment by Gender in 1987 and 1999 (%)

	Men		Women	
	1987	1999	1987	1999
France	5.1	5.8	21.7	24.7

Source: OECD (2003).

Part-time employment refers to people usually working less than 30 hours a week.

Table 4: Proportion of Part-time Work in Total Employment and Share of Women in Part-time Work (%)

Year	Share PT	Share Women
1990	12.2	79.8
1997	14.9	78.8
1998	14.8	79.3
1999	14.7	79
2000	14.2	80.1

Source: OECD (2003).

II. Older Workers

Table 5a: Men and Women (% of Population in the Age Group)

	F	A	R-U	S	EU15
N 50-64	46.2	47.5	59.2	71.5	47.7
U 50-64	4.4	7.2	3	5.1	4.3
Inactive 50-64	49.4	45.3	37.8	23.5	48.1
N 25-49	*77.5*	*77.8*	*79.7*	*79.3*	*75.4*
U 25-49	*9.7*	*7.4*	*4.4*	*7.7*	*7.6*
Inactive 25-49	*12.8*	*14.8*	*15.8*	*13.1*	*17*

Source: Eurostat, *Labour Force Survey*, 1998.
N= Employment rate; U= Unemployment rate.

Table 5b: Men (% of Population in the Age Group)

	F	A	R-U	S	EU15
N 50-64	52.8	57.3	67.8	73.6	59.4
U 50-64	4.8	7.9	4.2	6.3	5
Inactive 50-64	42.5	34.8	28	20.1	35.6
N 25-49	*86.6*	*86.2*	*87.2*	*81.8*	*87.2*
U 25-49	*8.8*	*7.7*	*5.2*	*8.7*	*5.2*
Inactive 25-49	*4.6*	*6.1*	*7.6*	*9.5*	*7.6*

Source: Eurostat, *Labour Force Survey*, 1998.

Table 5c: Women (% of Population in the Age Group)

	F	A	R-U	S	EU15
N 50-64	39.8	37.7	50.8	69.3	36.3
U 50-64	4.1	6.6	1.7	3.9	3.6
Inactive 50-64	56	55.7	47.5	26.8	60.2
N 25-49	*68.6*	*69.1*	*72.1*	*76.7*	*64.4*
U 25-49	*10.6*	*7.2*	*3.6*	*6.6*	*8*
Inactive 25-49	*20.8*	*23.7*	*24.2*	*16.7*	*27.6*

Source: Eurostat, *Labour Force Survey*, 1998.

Table 6: Long Term Unemployment by Age Group
(% of Unemployed Population in Each Age Group)

	F	A	R-U	S
50-64	62.5	65.1	52.2	50.2
15-64	41.6	52.6	32.6	37.8

Source: Eurostat, *Labour Force Survey*, 1998.

III. Policies

Table 7: Employment Public Expenditure
(% GDP) – 1999 (France)

	France
1-Administration and PES	0.17
2-Training	0.28
Unemployment rate	0.25
Occupied adults	0.03
3-Youth	0.41
Unemployment rate	0.21
Training and apprenticeship	0.19
4-Recruitment subsidies	0.41
Employment subsidies (private sector)	0.21
Employment creation (public sector)	0.2
5-Disabled	0.09
6-Unemployment insurance	1.47
7-Early retirement programmes	0.29
TOTAL	3.12
Active measures (1-5)	1.36
Passives measures (6-7)	1.76

Source: OECD (2003).

CHAPTER 7

Surface Integration

The National Action Plans for Employment and Social Inclusion in Germany[1]

Milena BÜCHS & Dawid FRIEDRICH

Introduction

Discussions of the Open Method of Co-ordination (OMC) have been dominated by the supposed novelties of these new European governance mechanisms, such as increased participation and policy learning (see de la Porte and Pochet, 2002; Mosher and Trubek, 2003; Jacobsson, 2002 and 2005; Zeitlin, 2003). Less attention has been paid to the conditions which OMC processes encounter in their practical application within EU Member States. This chapter argues that a detailed examination of the OMC in action is essential for any research that aspires either to assess the extent to which it lives up to the expectations raised in the theoretical and political debate and/or to identify its policy impact. Without a stable political anchorage within Germany's social and employment policy-making structures, we argue, substantial and politically balanced effects of the OMC will be unlikely.

By analysing and comparing two examples of open co-ordination processes, namely the European Employment Strategy (EES) and the Open Method of Co-ordination for Social Inclusion (Social Inclusion process), we seek to fill this gap for the German case. By providing a detailed comparative overview of these two most elaborated OMCs, we will identify the extent to which the OMC is accepted by domestic actors and incorporated in both policy areas and seek to understand the reasons why this might or might not be the case. By incorporation we

---

[1] For helpful comments we wish to thank Philippe Pochet, Jonathan Zeitlin, David Trubek, Jochen Clasen, Sigrun Kahl, the participants of the workshop on the OMC at the European University Institute, Florence in July 2003, and one commentator who preferred to remain anonymous. We also thank Shona Hamilton for corrections of our Teutonic English on an earlier version of this chapter.

mean that the OMC must not remain an "alien" in the respective policy-making processes, dealt with by some civil servants in a "bureaucratic exercise" (Scharpf, 2001). Instead, public visibility, political commitment by policy-makers, active commitment of public actors (including parliaments) at all levels and participation of civil society actors would be needed to render it a domestic policy instrument that, in the end of the day, could live up to the expectations raised for it.

In Germany, the OMC faces a particularly complicated environment. Germany's policy-making process is characterised by two features: first of all, due to the country's federal structure, three levels of political responsibility have to be considered, namely the federal, the *Länder* and the local level. According to the Constitution (Articles 71ff.), competencies are divided among these levels, but many issues must be dealt with under the so-called "competing competencies", where in principle the *Länder* and/or the local level are in charge, but the federal level has to secure (almost) similar life conditions across the country and is, thus, also entitled to take legislative action. Both policy areas at stake belong to this category of shared competencies. In addition, a tradition of coalition governments and a proportional election system strengthen the need for a consensual policy approach. Thus, we face in our analysis a diverse institutional arena containing multiple actors at all levels, seeking to participate in the policy-making process. Each level of governance knows that it cannot succeed without the co-operation of the others within this "non-hierarchical multi-level system" (Mayntz, 1999: 101). The second aspect is the fact that the German "Rhine Model" is regarded as a co-ordinated "social market economy" with representatives of labour and industry playing an important role in the policy-making process, on the supervisory boards of companies as well as of banks and in the semi-autonomous administrative bodies of the social security system (Wood, 2001). Furthermore, the subsidiarity principle dominates the system of social provision. About two-thirds of all social services, such as nurseries or hospitals, are provided by six huge welfare associations which, accordingly, have also a significant voice in the social policy process. Against this institutional backdrop, characterised by its vertical and horizontal dispersion across a multitude of actors, we will analyse the preparation processes involved in the National Action Plans for employment (NAP/empl) and for social inclusion (NAP/incl) as the key national component of the OMC.

Here we will focus on the question how the NAP preparation processes are organised and what this means for their relevance to the policy-making process. First of all it is important to shed light on which actors are involved in the preparation process in which manner, what relevance is given to their contribution to the NAP, whether new working relationships have been developed through the preparation processes and what role they play in the policy-making process after their submission to the European Commission. Short considerations about the possible impact of both OMCs on policy processes and substantive policies follow.

In this chapter we will deal with these points firstly regarding the NAP/empl and then the NAP/incl. In the concluding section we compare these two processes, focussing on the role of actor constellations in these policy fields, the status of both policy areas for governmental politics in general and the shape of both OMCs at European level[2].

I. The NAP Employment Process

As pointed out in the introduction, the NAP preparation process and its role within the policy process more generally offer initial hints about whether the OMC can foster policy learning and lesson drawing across Member States. Accordingly, in this section we will describe the NAP preparation process, the role of various actors within it and our interviewees' views about it, before presenting some preliminary conclusions about the NAP's role in the German policy-making process.

Because of Germany's federal structure, it is necessary to consider the role of the various levels of government in this process: the federal and the *Länder* levels which share competencies for legislation and administration of labour market policies, and the local authorities which play an important role in their implementation. Further, we will examine the involvement of the social partners in the NAP process, as well as its role in the *Bundesrat* and the *Bundestag*.

Since the first NAP/empl was established in 1998 the preparation process has already changed in terms of the involvement of specific actors such as the *Länder* via the *Bundesrat*. The 2003 revision of the EES at EU level (see chapter by Pochet in this volume) will have further consequences for the preparation process in terms of timetables and co-

---

2   Methodological remark: the materials used in our examination were the NAPs, the evaluation report of the RWI/ISG, the joint employment reports, and German political documents such as guidelines of political programmes, draft laws and discussion scripts of *Bundestag* and *Bundesrat*. We also conducted thirty-seven intensive interviews and twelve shorter discussions with political actors from federal ministries, *Länder* ministries, representatives of the social partners, the central associations of the local authorities, the European Commission, welfare associations and experts. We want to thank all our interviewees very much for providing very helpful information. In order to guarantee anonymity, only our interview codes are used as references. Interviews about the Social Inclusion process are numbered A1ff., interviews about the EES are numbered B1ff.

ordination with actors responsible for implementing the Broad Economic Policy Guidelines (BEPG).

A. The Changing Responsibility for Co-ordinating the NAP Process

The NAP/empl preparation process is centrally co-ordinated by one federal ministry. The responsibility for this leading co-ordination role has changed several times since the introduction of the EES, for reasons also connected to changes of government in Germany. In the first NAP/empl round the Federal Ministry of Economics and Technology of the conservative-liberal Kohl-government was responsible for the overall co-ordination. After the Social Democrats and Bündnis 90/Die Grünen took over in autumn 1998, the responsibility for co-ordinating the NAP process was transferred to the Federal Ministry of Finance. This took place, because the unit for general affairs (*Grundsatzabteilung*), which was in charge of co-ordinating the NAP process, was transferred from the one ministry to the other. After the 2002 elections, which confirmed this coalition, a reshaping of some federal ministries occurred. The Federal Ministry of Economics and the former Federal Ministry of Labour and Social Affairs were merged into the new Federal Ministry of Economics and Labour (*Bundesministerium für Wirtschaft und Arbeit, BMWA*), whereas the former Federal Ministry of Health now became the new Federal Ministry of Health and Social Security. The unit for general affairs became part of the BMWA and several months later, in summer 2003, the responsibility for the overall co-ordination of the NAP process was also transferred to the BMWA.

The other participating federal ministries are requested to draft sections of the NAP that fall under their policy responsibilities, including collection and presentation of data (for more details, see Umbach, 2003: 61). If the task of compiling these data is transferred to sub-units within federal ministries, their contributions and draft texts are again reviewed firstly by the central co-ordinator in the respective ministry and, secondly, by the federal ministry in charge of the whole process. After the latter has compiled the whole NAP, it is circulated again to all actors involved, i.e. to the federal ministries, the peak organisations of the social partners (DGB and BDA)[3] and, via the respective federal ministry, to their colleagues at *Länder* level. The agreement on the final text of the NAP is reached by the cabinet. Only then is the NAP sent to the *Bundestag* and the *Bundesrat*, which (mainly) discuss it in their commit-

---

3   The DGB is the Federation of German Trade Unions (*Deutscher Gewerkschaftsbund*), the BDA the Association of German Employers (*Bundesvereinigung der Deutschen Arbeitgeberverbände*).

tees. Since 1999 this occurs before the NAP is submitted to the Commission.

B. Involvement of Actors at the Federal Level

1. The Federal Ministries

The ministry in charge of directing the whole NAP preparation process involves a range of other actors, some of which again involve further players. The ministry currently in charge, the Federal Ministry of Economics and Labour, involves other Federal Ministries, namely the Finance, Health and Social Security; Education and Research; Family Affairs, Senior Citizens, Women and Youth; Transport, Building and Housing; as well as the Federal Government Commissioner for Migration, Refugees and Integration[4], the Federal Government Commissioner for the Concerns of People with Disabilities[5] and the Federal Chancellery. Up to now two main meetings of all federal ministries involved have taken place annually to discuss the NAP preparation process. At the second of these meetings, a representative of the Conference of Ministers for Arts and Culture (*Kulturministerkonferenz, KMK*), an association of the *Länder* ministers of culture and education, also attended because of their competencies in this field. In 2003, it was planned to invite the central associations of local authorities to take part in this second meeting, due to their dissatisfaction regarding the level of their involvement. Separate meetings took place between federal ministries and the social partners to discuss the NAP procedures. In general, each of these federal ministries is responsible for those guidelines which fall under its responsibilities. However, as some guidelines concern several ministries, there are also inter-ministerial agreements on certain issues. These agreements are reached through the normal day-to-day inter-ministerial work, rather than through special working groups. Each individual federal ministry is requested to report on its activities concerning the relevant employment guidelines. Requests from the federal ministry in charge can be rather broad or rather detailed depending on the phase of the process.

2. Contacts with the European Level

Contacts between the German government and various actors at European level during the whole EES cycle are also important. There are bilateral contacts between the German government and the Commission, as well as multilateral contacts with the other Member States and

---

[4] Beauftragter der Bundesregierung für Migration, Flüchtlinge und Integration.

[5] Beauftragter der Bundesregierung für die Belange behinderter Menschen.

the Commission in the Employment Committee (EMCO) and the peer review processes, and with the labour ministers of other Member States in the European Council and the Council of Ministers. A regular meeting round with the German *Länder* and the Commission has been also established to discuss EES matters.

The general structure of the NAPs is agreed each year in the European Employment Committee, on the basis of a consensus among Member State representatives and the Commission. According to one interviewee, during the NAP preparation process no special co-ordination takes place between the federal level and the EU Commission (B25). Bilateral meetings between delegations from Germany and the Commission become crucial after the NAPs have been submitted (according to the new cycle mostly between February and March), and after the Commission has examined them and compiled the first draft of the joint employment report in which the challenges for individual Member States are outlined. This analysis also provides a basis for the proposed recommendations. Thus, after the draft joint employment report has been handed in to the Member States, bilateral meetings take place in which representatives of several DGs of the Commission (Employment, Industrial Relations and Social Affairs, Economics and Finance as well as DG Enterprise) and members of the German government, representatives of the *Länder* governments and the social partners participate. These meetings are said to be quite open in character and sensitive points are negotiated between the Commission and the government (Umbach, 2003: 34-37). Furthermore, the NAPs are reviewed by all other Member States and the Commission in EMCO. The German delegation in EMCO comprises three representatives of the BMWA and one representative of the *Länder*. The BMF indirectly feeds its opinion into these meetings via inter-ministerial co-ordinations which take place before the EMCO review (Umbach, 2003: 63).

Furthermore, direct contacts between Commission representatives and delegates from Germany take place at conferences or workshops on particular issues of the EES. This is especially the case in the peer review programme.

Germany also maintains bilateral contacts with other Member States regarding particular labour market policy issues. Such exchanges have, for example, been taking place with Italy on the entrepreneurship pillar, and with Denmark on job rotation (which then fed into the Job-AQTIV law, see below). Regular contacts on various issues take place with the UK and France (Umbach, 2003: 63f.)

3. The Federal Employment Agency (Bundesagentur für Arbeit)[6]

The Federal Ministry of Economics and Labour also involves the Federal Employment Agency (FEA), the semi-sovereign body responsible for labour market policy administration. The FEA is requested by the Federal Ministry in charge to report upon the measures that have been taken with regard to several guidelines, for example in active labour market policy, youth unemployment, disabled people, and gender mainstreaming. Within the FEA, several departments are again involved in writing reports on these activities. After the NAP/empl is submitted to the Commission and the Council, it is sent to the FEA which publishes the report on its intranet so that all agency employees can inform themselves or even comment on it (which has not so far occurred on a wide scale).

4. The Länder and the Local Authorities

The Federal Ministry of Economics and Labour involves its colleagues of the *Länder* labour ministries or departments. Other federal ministries also involve their *Länder* colleagues to some extent, but, according to one interviewee, the main exchange regarding the NAP/empl probably occurs between the BMWA and its *Länder* labour market policy colleagues (B23). For example, in each of the *Länder* equal rights offices exist which are involved in the NAP preparation process by the Federal Ministry for Family Affairs, Senior Citizens, Women and Youth (B4). The Federal Ministry of Education and Research involves the Conference of Ministers for Arts and Culture (*KMK*).

The *Länder* labour ministries are firstly asked to submit statistical material on their labour market situation and policies and secondly, to report on their activities in the relevant areas or to comment on passages written by other actors. Over the years it turned out that the *Länder* reports were too long to be completely integrated into the NAP. Hence the procedure has been changed and since 2002 the federal level drafts short reports on *Länder* activities to appear in an annex of the NAP which are then reviewed by the latter (B23).

The *Länder* are also involved in the policy-making process through the *Bundesrat* due to the constitutional obligation to involve them in matters where legislative competencies lie with the federal level. This applies also to EU matters (Article 23 GG). Therefore, the NAP/empl has been discussed from the beginning in the *Bundesrat*. However, the *Bundesrat* never took a decision on the NAP/empl and, particularly at

---

6   The new *Bundesagentur für Arbeit* is the former *Bundesanstalt für Arbeit* and has been given this new name in January 2004.

the beginning of the EES process, arguments about the degree of involvement of the *Länder* through the *Bundesrat* arose, as will be described below.

The federal ministry in charge also involves the central associations of the local authorities. The NAP/empl is sent to the four central associations of the local authorities[7] with a request for comment. However due to shortage of time, the central associations were not able to involve its local members or comment thoroughly on the report (B12, B20).

5. The Social Partners

The federal bodies of the social partners (DGB, BDA, BDI, DIHK, ZDH)[8] are involved by several federal ministries regarding particular policy areas belonging to the ministries' responsibilities. These social partner organisations are asked to report on their activities in the relevant areas, and to comment on texts already written by other actors. Regarding the former GL 13 on modernisation of work organisation[9] the social partners share the responsibility and decision for the whole text directed to that guideline. The federal bodies of the social partners also contact their affiliates on NAP/empl issues, although this mostly happens in the course of their normal activities rather than in order to work concretely on the NAP/empl (B3). This is also due to the fact that the federal bodies of the social partners in Germany have the main responsibility for European matters (B5, B3). At the *Länder* level, the social partners' involvement differs from federal state to federal state, depending on their organisation of labour market policy-making. In some of the *Länder*, e.g. in Mecklenburg-Western Pomerania, the social partners take part in decisions on the regional labour market policy programmes due to their special co-decision role in the committee of the structural funds (*Begleitausschuss*).

Other interest groups or NGOs have not been involved by the ministries or other bodies at federal and *Länder* level. One interviewee explained this by the fact that the process is already quite complicated and severe time shortages prevent involvement of further actors (B4).

---

[7] These four associations are: the Federal Association of Local Authorities (*Bundesvereinigung der kommunalen Spitzenverbände*), the German Congress of Municipalities (*Deutscher Städtetag*), German Congress of Rural Districts (*Deutscher Landkreistag*), German Association of Cities and Municipalities (*Deutscher Städte- und Gemeindebund*).

[8] DGB (Federation of German Trade Unions), BDA (Association of German Employers), BDI (Federal Association of German Industry), DIHK (German Chamber of Industry and Commerce), ZDH (Central Association of German Trade).

[9] GL 13 in 2001 respective GL 15 in 2000 and 16 in 1999.

6. The NAP/empl in the Bundestag

The NAP/empl has been submitted to the *Bundestag* each year. In the first year, 1998, this occurred after the NAP/empl was submitted to the EU Commission. However, this fact was not criticised in the *Bundestag*. In the following years the NAP/empl was submitted to the *Bundestag* before it was given to Brussels and after the decision of the cabinet. In the first discussion rounds, which usually took place sometime after the NAP/empl's submission, it was always "discussed" together with other topics and was only mentioned explicitly in the discussions in 1998 and 1999[10]. Consequently, the NAP/empl was transferred to the *Bundestag*'s committees. In the second discussion round, the NAP/empl was also dealt with alongside other topics. Only in 1999 and 2001 was the NAP/empl mentioned during the discussions and the *Bundestag* decided to "take notice" of the NAP/empl. This happened because in winter 1999 the NAP/empl became a topic together with a report of Chancellor Schröder about preparations for the Lisbon Summit and because it was discussed together with the Job-AQTIV Act in 2001. However, in all other years *Bundestag* committee chairs only announced to the plenum their decision to refrain from reporting about the NAP/empl[11]. This means that, all in all, the NAP/empl was not discussed as such in the *Bundestag* but rather dealt with in a similar but actually less important manner to several other reports on government activity. The same applies to the discussions within the committees where the NAP/empl was only discussed in a cursory manner (B24).

C. Assessment of the NAP/empl Process by the Actors Involved

In the following some general viewpoints on the preparation process, as well as the opinions of particular actors such as the social partners, the *Länder*, and the local authorities will be described. The NAP/empl is commonly perceived as a product of a variety of actors, ultimately directed by the federal government. Thus, disputes about formulations in the final text appeared when some actors were not satisfied with the presentation of their activities. However, those who mentioned such difficulties also clarified that they would not expect the NAP/empl to be

---

[10] Cf. for the first discussion rounds with decisions to transfer the NAP to the committees: BT-Plenarprotokoll 13/236, 8 May 1998: 21733, BT-Plenarprotokoll 14/77, 3 December 1999: 7089, BT-Plenarprotokoll 14/98 6 April 2000: 9117, BT-Plenarprotokoll 14/183, 6 July 2001: 18109, BT-Plenarprotokoll 14/239, 28 March 2002: 23932.

[11] Cf. for the second discussion rounds: BT-Plenarprotokoll 13/245, 25 June 1998: 22896; BT-Plenarprotokoll 14/98, 6 April 2000: 9116; BT-Plenarprotokoll 14/119, 15 September 2000: 11482; BT-Plenarprotokoll 14/1999, November 2001: 19530; BT-Plenarprotokoll 14/249, 5 July 2002: 25390.

a consensual product and they were aware that it was an activity report by the government to the European level. In addition, one of the interviewees commented that the NAP/empl would not deliver incentives to formulate new policy ideas because it is mainly a governmental product with many parties involved (B11). These are the reasons why the NAP/empl is not regarded as a strategic policy tool by all of the interviewees but merely as a report on activities related to the EES.

For most of the interviewed actors, the work on the NAP/empl was only a small part of their normal day-to-day activities. Most actors complained that they had far too little time to fulfil the requests before the deadline, and that the material demanded was far too encompassing. Many of them questioned the importance of the NAP/empl in the political process, some referring to the fact that they had additional responsibilities for submitting reports to the European level in other contexts and that all these reporting obligations tend to be an overload, consuming time which could be used for more important issues. Thus, all of the interviewees welcomed the recent procedural reforms of the EES aimed at reducing the number of guidelines, holding them more stable for three years and only having to submit follow-up NAPs in the years between a more thorough revision of the guidelines.

The social partners did not complain about their procedural involvement in the NAP preparation process, which they do not perceive as different from that in other similar issues. The political standpoints of unions and employers obviously differ regarding both the whole EES approach and particular areas covered by the guidelines. Both sides favoured certain components of the EES and also seek to use this process to strengthen their political demands in communicating with the government (B3, B5, B6, B11). Whereas in principle the trade unions welcome attempts to strengthen Europe's social dimension, active labour market policy, a gender equality approach and the demand to balance flexibility and security, they have greater reservations about some of the Employment Guidelines, which they perceive to be neo-liberal. The opposite is true for the employers' organisations, which are more sceptical about the EU's attempts to strengthen its social policy competencies, but welcome the principal direction of the EG and the recommendations about flexibilisation and activation policies. However, the government is very sensitive about policy presentation and the NAPs do not openly express the viewpoints of the social partners[12]. Also in this sense it becomes clear that the government regards the NAP as presenting its

---

[12] In the NAP 2003, however, a footnote on the pooling of unemployment assistance and social assistance is inserted, expressing the diverging positions of the unions and the employer organisations (NAP, 2003: 30, footnote 7).

own policy strategy and not as a document in which the pro and cons of policy approaches are discussed and different viewpoints of different actors integrated. At the same time, the NAP is regarded as a governmental product by the social partners themselves, thus limiting the status of this process because they cannot use it to influence policies directly.

Regarding the *Länder*, there is no homogeneous position towards the EES. At the beginning of the EES and during the first rounds of NAP/empl preparation, the *Länder* complained about not having been involved in an appropriate manner (cf. Müller, 2002; for the general position of the *Länder*, see Bauer and Knöll, 2003). In 1998 they complained that the NAP was only sent to the *Bundesrat* after it had been handed in to Brussels, thus, the procedure was changed afterwards.

Additionally, the *Länder* face very different labour market situations and, therefore, the EES creates different challenges for them. The labour market policy programmes of the *Länder* are financed to a significant degree by the European Social Fund (ESF)[13]. As the funding criteria of the ESF have been adapted to the EES, some *Länder*, especially some of the new eastern *Länder*, were quite keen to align their labour market programmes with the EES objectives (B8). However, certain other *Länder* – mainly those led by conservative governments – regard the whole EES quite critically, arguing this process would undermine the principle of subsidiarity and enable the European level to gain influence in areas belonging to their responsibility. The Social Democratic-led *Länder* governments however took a more positive standpoint towards the EES in recent years, which was also expressed in some of the interviews (B8, B10, B23). The *Bundesrat* in general is also used by the opposition-led *Länder* governments as a forum for criticising the policies of the federal government. Thus during the discussions on the NAP/empl, the main points of criticism by the Christian Democratic/ Liberal-led *Länder* governments were that labour market policy and, therefore, also the NAP/empl were not going far enough to establish the kind of neo-liberal approach prescribed by the EES. The opposition-led *Länder* governments also criticised the EES more generally, arguing that labour market policy is a reserved competency of the state and that the EES infringes the principle of subsidiarity, especially where issues of education are concerned (cf. BR-Drucksache 244/1/02: 7f.). Com-

---

[13] The labour market programmes of the new *Länder* belonging to the Objective-1 areas are financed by the ESF up to 75% (cf. the information on the ESF on the webpage of the Federal Ministry of Health and Social Security http://www.bmgs.bund.de/deu/ gra/themen/europa/esf/index_1427.cfm). In the new *Länder* ca. 30% of ESF resources are administered by the federal level and 70% directly by the *Länder*, in the old *Länder* the proportion amounts to ca. 50:50% (see http://www.bmgs.bund.de/deu/gra/ themen/europa/esf/index_1425.cfm, access 27 April 2003).

pared to the almost non-existent role of the NAP/empl in the *Bundestag* they give rise to slightly broader discussions in the *Bundesrat*. However, the NAP/empl is also not discussed as a complete document and its presentation is taken instead as an opportunity to criticise the whole labour market policy approach of the government. Nevertheless, procedural aspects connected to particularities of federalism in Germany were part of the discussions about the NAP/empl and the EES in the *Bundesrat*.

The local authorities, represented by their central association (*Kommunale Spitzenverbände*, cf. footnote 7), appear to face a dilemma regarding the NAP process. On the one hand, the central associations of the local authorities complained about not having been involved enough in the preparation process. The associations received the NAP/empl for comment before they were adopted by the Cabinet. But time at every stage was too short to work through the material thoroughly. According to an interviewee (B1) the federal level is now planning to involve the central associations of local authorities more intensely in the process, mainly through organising consultation rounds between the authorities and federal ministerial departments.

On the other hand, the central associations have few resources to get more deeply involved. For example, they lack resources to contact their members about the NAP. Also in general, the local administrative level takes a rather reserved position towards the EES and the OMC, fearing that the EU gains influence through these processes in areas where it does not have competencies. They are also opposed to the government taking further decisions which cannot be influenced by local authorities but which have to be carried out by them. However, this argument is far from specific to the OMC, but recurs in a variety of other domestic discussions about policy fields where local authorities have to implement decisions decided elsewhere but financed by them. Thus, this might be a general problem of externalising responsibilities and financial burdens from one level to another in federal systems.

D. Preliminary Conclusions about the Impact of the EES on Policies and Policy-making Processes in Germany

Despite severe methodological difficulties in assessing the possible impact of the EES on policy-making processes and policies in general (cf. for first studies on the impact dimension of the OMC in Germany and methodological difficulties of tracing such an impact, Büchs, 2003; Ostheim and Zolnhöfer, 2005; RWI/ISG, 2002; Thiel, 2003; Umbach, 2003 and Richardt, 2004[14]), some preliminary conclusions will be pre-

---

[14] N. Richardt (2004) found that EES demands for improving childcare facilities were influential in Germany in the sense that references to the EES have been made by the

sented in this section. Firstly, the status of the NAP/empl process has to be analysed because this provides initial hints about a possible impact on policy-making. Secondly, we will address the role of the employment guidelines and recommendations for policy-making in Germany as well as the potential for policy learning of different aspects of the EES.

According to almost all of our interviewees, the NAP/empl process does not enjoy a very important status within the overall policy-making process in Germany. It is mainly perceived as a rather bureaucratic process, obliging them to deliver information and reports to the government and, through the latter, to the EU. This process is not regarded as functioning as a policy planning tool. This is also indicated by the fact that the NAP/empl has not been discussed explicitly in the *Bundestag*, and only very cursorily in the *Bundesrat*, apart from the first two years, in which procedural aspects had to be clarified (see above). This is a clear sign that the NAP/empl is not seen as an instrument with which the government formulates new policy lines or programme proposals but as a pure reporting instrument which does not necessitate parliamentary discussion.

In this sense it can be claimed that the NAP process itself does not have the potential to influence policy planning, because it merely has the status of a governmental policy report. The process also does not provide substantial incentives for non-federal actors to discuss the government's policy approaches or to feed their political viewpoints into the policy-making process, because the NAP is rather conceptualised as representing the viewpoint of the government and the activities of other actors, not their political viewpoints.

Nevertheless, the NAP process – together with the processes connected to the implementation of the European Social Funds, see below – is the most important channel for disseminating information about the EES for the actors involved. Apart from that there is little publicity concerning the EES procedures, which is also due to the restricted status

---

government and by employer representatives to press for developing a coherent childcare strategy in Germany. This analysis shows that EES references can and are being used by political actors if these arguments fit with their interests and strategies (which are again influenced by the institutional framework of a specific political system). Richardt argues that the federal government has an interest in strengthening its position against the *Länder* and local authorities, who are responsible for childcare, and that employers are pressing for public funding of childcare in order to stave off demands for their own financial contributions in this sphere. This analysis shows that one has to analyse each particular aspect of the EES to develop a whole picture of whether and how the EES is used in the policy process. However, although actors made references to the EES in the case of childcare in Germany, provision of childcare still remains well below the EU targets (especially in the old *Länder*) and no national targets for improvement have been set.

of the NAP itself. Also according to an analysis by Umbach (2003), the NAP/empl and the EES more generally have a low public profile, and newspaper references have been steadily decreasing. Thus, it may be assumed that the NAP is not a document discussed by a broader public and is mainly relevant for those participating in its preparation.

All in all, the production of the NAPs has not created new working relationships between domestic policy actors because the requests for information and its delivery are transmitted through existing channels. The federal ministries also hold regular contacts with their *Länder* colleagues regarding policy issues in their area of responsibility. The individual federal ministries also contact the social partners regularly on policy issues which are "in the pipeline", so that the NAP process is sometimes only an additional step within contacts that are taking place anyway.

Thus, one has to look at other dimensions of the EES in order to draw conclusions on its possible impact on policy-making processes and policies. Here, one can distinguish between policy presentation, discourses and, instruments.

The requirement to produce the NAPs/empl and to submit them to Brussels entails in the first place a reorientation in the presentation of labour market policies according to the EES objectives and guidelines. Policies are now interpreted and presented according to the framework and the priorities of the EES, independently of whether they already existed previously, whether their development has been influenced by it, and whatever other internal reasons might have played a role in changing them. In the NAPs, policies and policy changes are mainly presented as responses to the requirements of the EES, not as outcomes of debates and struggles among domestic policy forces. Furthermore, to present national policies according to the requirements of the EES, new statistical data have to be produced. This is because in relation to several of the indicators agreed in the EMCO for monitoring, comparing and evaluating the development of labour market policies in the Member States, no data yet exist or are collected at either national or regional level (e.g. in federal systems). This can be regarded as an effect of the EES on the policy-making process, because the collection of data itself changes processes and communication between the bodies that request data and the bodies that collect the data. It also puts greater weight on the monitoring and the evaluation side of policy-making, which has been relatively underdeveloped in Germany compared to the political culture of other Member States, according to several interviewees (B34, B35).

Although there still exists a difference between the presentation of policies in the NAPs and the presentation of policy changes to the broader public – in which there is only very selective reference to EU influences – it is likely that EU-level policy concepts, priorities, and causal assumptions about the relationship between policies and their outcomes build a frame for domestic policy actors who are involved in European policy networks. In this sense it is also plausible to assume, as does Kerstin Jacobsson (2002 and 2005), that the EES has an impact on policy discourse and thus builds a cognitive frame of reference for domestic policy-making. In Germany, too, terms such as employability, activation, adaptability, and lifelong learning have entered labour market policy discourse and a general conceptual shift towards a work-welfare policy approach has taken place. In Germany this comes through most clearly through discussions of the so-called Hartz Acts and their frame, the government's Agenda 2010, as has been analysed by Brütt (2003).

Looking more concretely at the impact of the employment guidelines and EU recommendations[15] one can firstly conclude that especially the latter attracted some attention in the beginning, because it was very new in the German political culture that a body such as the EU would issue public policy recommendations to the country. The political elite was presumably afraid that these recommendations could cause some public embarrassment to the government and, thus, cause some political pressure. Several interviewees stated that it was just regarded as inconvenient to see some weak points of policy performance presented in such a way to the public. Despite this initial perception, other interviewees also remarked that over the years the actors have become used to the issuing of recommendations and that they are not taken as seriously as in the beginning. In order to estimate the potential effectiveness of the employment recommendations, one also has to consider that for them to be effective, broad publicity would be required. This, however, seems still to be lacking so that policy actors only make use of recommendations to put pressure on the government selectively and more through internal communications rather than through the wider media.

A further question is to what extent the employment guidelines and recommendations might have affected concrete policy instruments. Summarising the assessment of the interviewees on this issue provides some first indications about how the EES is perceived by policy-makers

---

[15] Since 2000 Germany has received five EU recommendations each year. These focus on strengthening the preventative approach to decrease long-term unemployment, removing disincentives to work for older people, reviewing the tax and the social security system (2000) and lowering taxes and social insurance contributions on labour (2001, 2002), especially at the lowest level of the wage scale (2002), strengthening the gender mainstreaming approach (2001), reducing the gender pay gap (2001, 2002), supporting the development of the service sector (2000), tackling skill gaps (2002) and making employment contracts and work organisation more flexible (2002).

or by actors who are intensely involved in the political process. Even if the interviewees' assessments of the influence of the EES on German labour market policy differed in detail, most of them were sceptical that the EES had introduced entirely new policies or ideas which had not previously been discussed. Some of the interviewees believed that active labour market policy has a long history in Germany and that, hence, there was no need to newly invent the general idea of an active and preventative approach (B6). Most of the interviewees thought that domestic factors had been more important for policy developments than the EES, for example, regarding the integration of older workers into the labour market which was supported by explicit references to the employment guidelines[16], while a limitation of the early retirement policy was also seen as domestically necessary in order to improve the financial sustainability of the pension insurance system. At the same time, a reduction of early retirement appears to be unpopular with the electorate, especially in areas with over 20% unemployment, so that a shift of policy approach needs external support, in this case, from the EU recommendations and guidelines.

An analysis of draft laws and related parliamentary discussions as well as other governmental publications about new policy programmes revealed that references to the EES were only made in a very few cases, mostly to point to European-wide performance comparisons or to give further reasons for introducing a particular policy initiative (cf. also Ostheim and Zolnhöfer, 2003 for this section)[17].

However, the EES guidelines and recommendations were regarded by many interviewees as stimulating discussions and reflections and, in some cases, as strengthening the position of actors advocating certain policy approaches. For example, the preventative approach to unemployment, which had already been included in the main labour market policy law in 1996, but which was strengthened in the Job-AQTIV law,

---

[16] BT-Drucksache 15/25: 34 and 40; BT-Drucksache 15/26: 21.

[17] References to the EES appeared, for example, in the drafts of the Job-AQTIV law, the Hartz laws, the second SBG III Änderungsgesetz, the 2002 guidelines of the JUMP programme and in the coalition agreement of 1998. However, in many other draft laws and government programmes referred to in the NAPs, no references to the EES can be found, e.g. in the draft laws on part-time work, on the implementation of equality between men and women (*Bundesgleichstellungsdurchsetzungsgesetz*), on pensions reform, and on fighting unemployment of severely disabled people. The value of these findings are naturally restricted from a methodological perspective because the both of the following scenarios are possible: a) policy actors may want to refer to the EES in order to legitimise unpopular reforms although it was not the driving force behind their development, or b) policy actors may wish to present ideas and proposals for reforms as elaborated by themselves although also some pressure of the European level played a role in their formulation.

and the introduction of the gender mainstreaming principle (which had, however, to be introduced according to binding EC law anyway) were perceived as having been intensified by the EES.

Thus, one could conclude on the one hand, that the EES did not have the power to introduce policies which were not supported previously or which would not be coherent with policy developments taking place anyway. As the formulation of the EES at European level is a process into which all Member States feed their viewpoints, it would anyway be unlikely that the Commission would propose policies that are not supported by the former to some degree. The same considerations hold true for the employment recommendations, on which the affected Member State government may have some input or, at least, corrective influence. On the other hand, the EES seems to provide a cognitive framework that strengthens the position of policy actors supporting this kind of strategy and, at the same time, limits the space for negotiation and discussion of policy alternatives. In Germany it appears that current labour market policies which are developing in a welfare-to-work direction – cutting unemployment benefits, putting greater pressure on the unemployed through stricter eligibility criteria such as intensifying demands to prove willingness to work and to accept jobs in farther away areas or in fields outside one's professional education and training – are supported by the EES, which may also have served as a catalyst speeding up their development[18]. At the same time, the position of policy actors advocating alternative strategies such as the trade unions and the left wing of the Green and Social Democratic Party lost considerable political attention and powers to influence policies. This is not to say that such a shift of power relationships has only occurred through the EES. Rather it is also due to other binding requirements of the EU related to what has been called "negative integration" (Scharpf, 2002) and to other domestic policy pressures such as the difficult financial situation of the state budget and the social security funds which are reinforced by high levels of unemployment.

A similar assessment applies to policy learning triggered by the EES: Exchanges with other Member States are not a new aspect of policy-making and contacts between Germany and other European (and non-European) countries on particular policy issues have a longer history than the EES. Clearly, the provision and the exchange of information for policy development have increased through the EES, in addition to that available through other international organisations such as the OECD

---

[18] Several authors already spoke of the possibly catalysing effects of the EES, e.g. de la Porte and Pochet (2002: 29) and Hemmann (2000: 37f.).

and German research institutes[19]. Hence, it has become easier for policy-makers in recent years acquire information on other countries' policies and "best practices". For example, an interviewee reported that other Member States' NAPs were used in the preparatory work of the Hartz Commission as a source for foreign good practice examples. However, it is no contradiction to observe, as our interviewees also did, that exchange and learning occurs mainly between countries that already have relatively similar approaches, or that governments search for information abroad which fits their own reform plans. In Germany, for example, there have been exchanges with Denmark on job rotation, a concept which was introduced in the Job-AQTIV law and there have also been intensified exchanges with the UK since the "third way/new centre alliance" of the late 1990s, which might partially explain the resemblance between some of German policy reforms in Germany and the UK's activation and welfare-to-work policies. In general, this means that the difficulties of policy transfer that are connected to questions of comparability of policies and policy contexts remain and that one cannot assume a greater willingness to learn from abroad due to the existence of the EES *per se*.

Furthermore it seems to be important also to look at the political content transported by "learning" potentially encouraged through the OMC. As Claus Offe already has critically pointed out, it is possible that the OMC might contribute to "unlearning"[20] (Offe, 2003: 463) the historical lessons of the "European social model". In our view, this judgement has a certain plausibility, since the EES has partially influenced policy discourses in Germany accompanying the strengthening of a welfare-to-work approach and since references to it have also been used to support unpopular labour market reforms while the position of opposing political actors has been considerably weakened[21].

---

[19] Such as the IAB (*Institut für Arbeitsmarkt- und Berufsforschung*), DIW (*Deutsches Institut für Wirtschaftsforschung*), Ifo (*Institut für Wirtschaftsforschung*).

[20] The argument in this context is that "learning" as policy change can also be interpreted as "unlearning" in the sense that previous arrangements are "demolished", e.g. if legislated minimum wages would replace collective agreements on wages between unions and employers. From this viewpoint "such 'unlearning' may in fact be the main purpose of the OMC, or its hidden agenda. The main purpose of this method of policy-making seems to be that of bringing home to Member States' political elites and constituencies the need for 'modernization' and 'recalibration' of their hitherto adopted arrangements of social security, industrial relations, and labour market policies. The negative message that 'nothing can stay as it is' does not imply, however, that what is going to replace present arrangements will be a consistent and consolidated Europeanized welfare state" (Offe, 2003: 463).

[21] A recent example for this usage of the EES is the presentation of the report of the Employment Task Force, chaired by Wim Kok (Kok *et al.*, 2003), on 8 December 2003 in Berlin. The German government supported the report and the Minister for

II. From "Europeans" to "Socials"? Cautious Movements of the German NAP/incl from a Merely European to a Domestic Policy Document

A. Institutional and Political Context

This section concentrates on the extent to which the rather new process of the Open Method of Co-ordination on social inclusion (Social Inclusion process) was successfully integrated into German social policy efforts. Special focus will be placed on the extent to which the NAP/incl has been accepted by the relevant actors and incorporated into existing policy structures as pre-conditions for the OMC to become a push-factor for future policy change.

As a reference point for the "incorporation" of the NAP/incl we chose the National Report on Poverty and Wealth[22] (NARB) from April 2001 as most visible example of a federal policy approach to poverty and social exclusion. The report is the first ever official confession by the German Federal Government that poverty and exclusion exist[23]. It is a comprehensive compendium of social data, orientated towards the life course concept, which, however, lacks concrete policy proposals and targets. Despite this, there is broad agreement among German social policy scholars that the NARB represents a first and important step towards a federal commitment to combat poverty and exclusion.

In comparison to the first NAP/incl we consequently seek to identify areas of progress and/or stagnation in the second NAP/incl 2003, particularly focussing on its relationship to the NARB and the perceptions and attitudes of the dominant actors. This analysis respects the fragmented institutional setting by differentiating three arenas. The first and most obvious is the federal arena, dominated by governmental actors who initiate and shape the whole process and have the final political responsibility. The second arena that reflects Germany's federal structure is essential because – as most interviewees stress – "bringing in the *Länder* and local authorities is a precondition for the success of the NAP/incl" (EAPN, 2002: 64), especially in the scattered social policy

---

Economy and Labour, Clement, used its arguments to underpin the urgency of the Hartz reforms (which were adopted by the two chambers in the second half of December).

[22] "Life courses in Germany. The first governmental poverty and wealth report" (Nationaler Armuts- und Reichtumsbericht – NARB) (Bundesregierung, 2001).

[23] Until recently, the prevalent attitude remained that of the previous Kohl – government, which claimed that social assistance effectively prevented the occurrence of poverty; hence, officially only "combated poverty" existed (cf. Neumann, 1999: 27; BT-Drs. 13/3339, 1995).

field[24]. Legislative competencies "are in principle with the *Länder* unless the constitution stipulates the competence for the federal level or declares shared competencies" (Müller 2002: 41), which is the case for social policy (see Article 74 Basic Law). The local authorities – as component parts of the *Länder* – are responsible for securing "a social balance in living conditions" (Hanesch, 2001: 1) by securing the "social infrastructure" (Bäcker *et al.*, 2000: 75) either through direct provisions or delegation to the six welfare associations[25] which, in fact, account for about two-thirds of social provision in Germany. Thirdly, due to the importance of the subsidiarity principle in Germany's social system, it is also crucial to consider the civil society arena. The high degree of "incorporation in the social protection system and the legal privilege" (Backhaus-Maul, 2000: 26) of the welfare associations provides them with an indispensable role in the horizontal dimension of Germany's social policies. In addition to the domestic arena we will look at the interaction of the actors in all these arenas with the European level, prominently with the European Commission.

B. The NAP/incl Process in Germany, More Than a Bureaucratic Exercise?

1. Formal Procedures

The formal procedure of the two NAP/incl processes is dominated by governmental actors who also have the political responsibility. The key actor is the responsible department – for the NAP 2001 it was the European Affairs Unit of the Labour and Social Affairs Ministry, for the NAP 2003 the NARB Unit of the new Ministry of Health and Social Security – which co-ordinates the process and finalises the NAP. The consultative body consists of the "usual suspects", i.e. sub-national representatives or their umbrella organisations, the welfare associations, social NGOs and experts; it discusses key concepts of the NAP and comments on the ministerial draft. Parliamentarians are invited to participate in this body. The final version is submitted to the cabinet which adopts it without much ado and passes it to the European Commission.

---

[24] See also the attempts of the European Anti-poverty Network (EAPN) to strengthen co-operation with Europcities (http://www.eapn.org/docs/reports/Athensreport_en. pdf).

[25] Diakonisches Werk; Caritas; Deutscher Paritätischer Wohlfahrtsverband; Arbeiterwohlfahrt; Deutsches Rotes Kreuz; Zentrale Wohlfahrtsstelle der Juden in Deutschland. Though privately organised, these associations become part of the functional administrative body through delegation of tasks by the state.

2. Participation and Interaction of Different Actors

a. The Federal Arena

The relationship of the NAP 2001 and the NARB, both in nature and in time of publication led observers to assume that the latter was already a result of the Social Inclusion process (cf. Degryse and Pochet, 2001). However, our data unanimously stress their mutual independence, a fact that is perhaps surprising but also revealing as regards the NAP/incl's (lack of) acceptance and incorporation.

Despite having been placed under the same roof, there was a clear institutional division between both processes, depending on their domestic or European nature. Whereas the NARB process was co-ordinated by a ministerial unit specialised in social assistance, the ministerial "European Affairs Unit" was placed in charge of the NAP 2001, despite its lack of specialised expertise. Co-ordination between these units, as well as with other ministries that were supposed to contribute to the NAP/incl "really crunched" (A4, A7, A10). Apparently, neither an internal nor an inter-ministerial project-group was set up, the progress and finalisation of the first NAP largely relied on the engagement and interest of the responsible department and its personnel which encountered considerable resistance from many colleagues of different units and ministries to writing their requested contributions. By 2003, this internal situation had improved, because the better institutionalised organisational structure of the NARB is now largely applied to the NAP/incl process, i.e. both documents are now co-ordinated by the same unit, the same inter-ministerial committee (IMA[26]) and even the same consultative body seeking to secure broad participation (A11, A18).

Parliamentary participation was scarce: only three parliamentarians participated in the consultative body of the NAP 2003 and the *Bundestag*'s Committee for Health and Social Affairs does not attach great political importance to the NAP/incl, considerably less than to the NARB. It was reported that the committee's debate on the NAP/incl lacked a European perspective and the principal divergent partisan views were merely exchanged.

Overall, the NAP/incl process in the federal arena remained largely dominated by civil servants who do not perceive it as relevant to their work but rather as a reporting mechanism to the EU. Only cautious signs suggest that some official actors understand the NAP/incl as a "national" plan and have started to reflect upon a closer relation to the NARB, e.g. strengthening the latter's analytic character as a *report* and the NAP's active character as a *plan for action* (A15).

---

[26] Interministerieller Ausschuss, the so-called "Ressortkreis".

b. The Sub-national Arena

Many observers believe that the litmus test for the Social Inclusion process within Germany's federal system is its ability to activate sub-national actors. This is because the fragmentation of the political system presents a serious challenge to successful implementation of a rather centralised top-down process like the Social Inclusion process, at least as it is perceived by most interviewed sub-national actors.

The *Länder*

In order to fully capture the *Länder*'s involvement in the NAP/incl-process, one needs to distinguish between the *Länder*'s activities at federal level via the *Bundesrat* and the individual Land domestically.

The *Länder* mainly participate in the national and increasingly also European policy-making process via the *Bundesrat*[27] (cf. Derlien, 2000). The EUZBLG does not address the OMC but this may have to change if and when the draft constitutional treaty is ratified. Until now, though, the *Länder* do not directly participate in EU-level decision-making on the OMC and, there is a dispute between the *Länder* and the federal government whether the latter has to respect the *Bundesrat*'s opinions (Müller, 2002: 41ff.)[28].

In the NAP process, the *Länder* are predominantly involved via the ASMK[29], the horizontal co-operative body for all sixteen *Länder* Social and Labour Ministries. The responsible unit of the federal ministry has an explicit interest in involving the ASMK in order to meet the requirements of the vertical character of poverty policies.

In 2001, the ASMK's EU working group, i.e. the EU experts of the *Länder*'s social ministries, prepared the *Bundesrat*'s opinion on the Social Inclusion process, co-ordinated the collection of the *Länder*'s best practice contributions to the first NAP and scrutinised the federal level's draft. As in the ministerial process at federal level, a shift from "Europeans" to "Socials" occurred within the ASMK. The co-ordinative responsability has now been transferred to the rather technocratic Conference of the Highest Social Authorities of the *Länder* (KOLS[30]).

---

[27] Germany's second parliamentary chamber, in which the *Länder* governments are represented.

[28] See *Bundesrat* Drucksache 352/01 (1 June 2001). The *Bundesrat* strongly expressed its objection to any attempts by the EU to intrude into domestic/sub-national competencies through the backdoor.

[29] Arbeits- und Sozialministerkonferenz (Conference of the Labour and Social Affairs Ministries).

[30] *Konferenz der Obersten Landessozialbehörden.*

Individual *Länder* hardly engage in the NAP/incl beyond the ASMK. Only a few participate directly in the federal consultative body and internal processes are almost non-existent. The spectrum of engagement ranges from fundamental resistance and blank rejection of the Social Inclusion process to the development of quite sustainable structures and attempts to use the NAP process within the Land's own policy-making. For instance the eastern Land of Sachsen-Anhalt initiated parallel to the NARB a *Länder* report that goes beyond the collection of data which "does not bring together the empirical findings" (Hanesch, 2001: 4) but seeks instead to formulate a coherent social policy strategy. The kinship to the NAP/incl is apparent and it is thus not surprising that Sachsen-Anhalt's attempts to further develop this report into a strategy is high-lighted in the 2003 NAP. A sustainable process was initiated by the Land's Ministry of Health and Social Affairs that even survived a governmental change from a Social Democratic to a conservative/liberal government.

Interviewees stated that political support, especially of the former Land government, for a coherent social policy strategy is a crucial feature that enabled the process to develop an independent dynamic. In addition to this, the administration seems to support this approach to policy-making and also to embrace the European dimension, despite principled reservations as regards the question of competencies. Active civil servants with close contact to the European level, especially the European Commission, facilitated this development, by which the Social Inclusion process lost its threatening character (A9, A11, A16).

Local Authorities

For the local authorities, the NAP process largely remained an "alien". Its involvement in this process seems to be confined to partici-pation of their umbrella organisations[31] in the consultative body and in commenting on the draft NAP without, however, informing its mem-bers. Principled reservations against further intrusion of another actor in what is perceived as their own realm of competencies remain dominant, as the following quotation demonstrates: "But also the consequence now to say: even if we had more time we would be more positive – well, I wouldn't say this. You know, I don't want at all that somebody else gives us instructions, it doesn't matter who it is" (B12). This attitude mirrors the "classic" conflict between local authorities and higher levels in Germany's federal structure, in which the former often feel their constitutionally guaranteed autonomy violated by decisions of the top

---

[31]   The three umbrella organisations co-ordinate their work and submit common opi-nions. These are: the "Deutscher Landkreistag", the "Deutscher Städtetag and the "Deutscher Städte- und Gemeindebund".

and forced to implement costly (social) policy measures despite suffering from severe tax deficits.

c. The Civil Society Arena

In contrast to the disinterest of most official actors, many actors in the civil society arena show a firm commitment to make political use of the NAP/incl. The limited dynamic of the NAP/incl process that we could identify largely depends on the engagement of welfare associations and other social NGOs. From the outset, the welfare associations and other social NGOs showed serious interest in the NAP/incl process. Their engagement commenced at federal level but in the meantime efforts have increased to initiate regional processes and to stimulate the local level.

A first stage of strategic reflection began in the aftermath of the March 2000 Lisbon European Council, in which the civil society actors sought to develop internal strategies in order to make the most out of this new policy instrument. The functioning co-operation between European NGO networks, such as the European Anti-poverty Network (EAPN), and domestic federal umbrella organisations, such as the National Poverty Conference (the German section of the EAPN), resulted in the establishment of NAP/incl working groups to prepare their contributions to the first NAP.

A second stage of improved co-ordination and consolidation began after the submission of the first NAP and resulted in the founding of a working group comprising most social umbrella organisations (A1, A11) together with some commonly organised workshops. These workshops were important for improving co-ordination among the civil society actors in order to overcome their fragmented approach to the NAP process, to provide better information to their *Länder*-level organisations and members in order to stimulate its vertical dimension, and to bring together not only civil society but also public actors, especially from the sub-national arena.

A third stage, according to several interviewees, now needs to begin after the 2003 NAP and will determine the Social Inclusion process's future in Germany: either structural improvements in the process will result in more substantive policy improvements or it will become increasingly difficult for activists to motivate colleagues/other actors to invest their time in it (A1, A10, A11, A13, A16).

After two NAPs/incl, and despite some improvements in 2003[32], a process of disillusionment can be observed among representatives of

---

[32] See www.eapn.org/inclusion/strategy_en.htm for a first and brief evaluation of the NAPs 2003.

social NGOs. The reality of the Social Inclusion process's implementation met neither their strategic expectations as regards increased involvement in policy-making procedures nor as regards substantive policy improvements in the wake of the current welfare reforms.

d. Interactions with the European Level

In relation to the NAP process, quite lively contacts exist between Commission representatives and actors from all three arenas analysed above.

Formal interactions between the Federal government and the European level take place primarily via participation in the Social Protection Committee (SPC) that *ex ante* defines the general structure of the NAPs consensually between all Member States and the Commission and that *ex post* is also responsible for the peer review. Moreover, there are bilateral consultations between the Commission and the Federal government during which the former gives its feedback on the NAP and explains its draft joint report on social inclusion[33]. During preparation of the NAP/incl there seems to be little (official) contact between the governmental actors and the Commission. This differs significantly as regards social NGOs. Their European awareness is sharpened not least through regular communication with the EAPN. This is mirrored in their conduct of several workshops over the last couple of years (see above) in which it was sought to bring together representatives of all levels of action, including the European level. In 2003 we could also see an increasing interest of the local level in the OMC social inclusion and in strengthening trans-European links[34].

C. Perceptions, Characteristics and Impact of the Social Inclusion Process in Germany

Faced with similar methodological difficulties to those as highlighted in the analysis of the EES above, but also recognising the relative youth of the Social Inclusion process, a direct impact on policy instruments seems unlikely and could, not in fact be found. This does not mean, however, that the Social Inclusion process has no significance at all but rather that a different, perhaps "softer" form of influence need to be

---

[33] This was highly conflictual in 2001 because of a proposed "league table", which presented Germany as a bad performer in social inclusion policies. This caused significant internal upheaval in the Federal government and even Chancellor Schröder learnt about this issue.

[34] See Turin, 14 and 15 October 2003 "Strengthening the Role of Local & Regional Government in the EU Strategy for Social Inclusion" (www.socialeurope.com) or Athens, 28 February-1 March 2003, EAPN – Eurocities Joint Conference on "The EU Strategy for Social Inclusion: Making It Work at the Local Level" (www.eapn.org).

identified. First and most importantly, the political support and commitment by policy-makers and the administration as well as participation of different civil actors should be taken as indicators to assess whether the NAP/incl remained an "alien" in the policy process or whether it has potential to become accepted as a national policy-making tool in its own right. We believe this to be a prerequisite for policy impact by placing the options available to domestic actors in a European frame of reference. Additionally, presentation of domestic policies in a European frame will arguably influence the policy discourse.

To a certain extent, incorporation of the NAP/incl into domestic policy-making processes seems to have taken place. The shift of responsibility for the NAP/incl process from "Europeans" to "Socials" at both federal and *Länder* level indicates that it succeeded in coming closer to the NARB and social policy experts. One could expect that the NAP/incl profits from the NARB's higher political leverage by its inclusion in the relevant process and will thus increase in quality and importance. The question is whether this incorporation is a mere bureaucratic improvement – to avoid double work – or whether it also signifies a qualitative development.

A sceptical and resistant attitude of the civil servants in the various participating federal ministries still remains prevalent. Our data gives no evidence that the new responsibility will ease these reservations; it remains, to be seen, however, whether the NARB unit will put more emphasis on the NAP 2005 by preparing it without the time constraints[35].

The sub-national level also remained largely unaffected in its attitudes by the procedural changes, considering the new responsibility of the rather technocratic KOLS instead of the EU working group of the ASMK. With only some exceptions, the interviews revealed a dominant concern that the Social Inclusion process might be a "Trojan horse" for increased European competencies to the detriment of the significant sub-national competencies for social policies in Germany. Moreover, scepticism remained unchanged whether the NAP/incl offers any surplus for the sub-national levels that would justify increased efforts. These strong resentments expressed in the interviews in spring 2003 are almost identical to the highly reserved *Bundesrat*'s opinion on the first NAP/incl from June 2001[36]. In a time of austerity the *Länder* are neither willing nor able to commit themselves to ambitious targets, especially

---

[35] As publicly indicated by the responsible ministry representative on the European Social Network's conference "Strengthening the Role of Local & Regional Government in the EU Strategy for Social Inclusion", Turin, 14 and 15 October 2003.

[36] See also Bavaria's position paper on the OMC http://www.bavaria.de/Europa/Offene Koordinierung.html (access 14 March 2003).

not, as several interviewees remarked, in policy documents such as the NAP/incl that will be scrutinised externally. In this regard, the *Länder*'s sceptical attitude does not necessarily mean a rejection of increased attempts to fight poverty and social exclusion, as the case of Sachsen-Anhalt shows, but rather signifies a "European extension" of the "usual" quarrels about competencies between the different levels of a federal system, complicated even in a time without financial crises[37], and, as many interviewees stressed, a mismatch between the German policy-making tradition and the "culture of evaluation" and "management by objectives" promoted by the Social Inclusion process.

A different picture presents itself as regards civil actors. Having been well-informed by their European umbrella organisations about the Social Inclusion OMC in 2000, most welfare associations and other social NGOs were committed to make use of this new process. The NAP/incl is perceived as a tool for their domestic lobbying efforts and the multi-dimensional conceptualisation of poverty and social exclusion is very much welcomed. The NAP/incl process provides social NGOs with additional arguments and political backing to strengthen their position in domestic debates. Additionally, they seek to push concrete aims with the NAP/incl. At federal level they try to avoid the report becoming "a graveyard for data" like the NARB. The incorporation of the NAP/incl into the NARB structures could be interpreted as a first success. Furthermore, increasing efforts are visible to stimulate regional processes since in the end of the day poverty policies have to be implemented locally.

In sum, the NAP/incl process seems to be marked by the following characteristics:

- A *public-private division* between formal compliance from public actors and active political aspirations for the NAP/incl by private actors. Whereas the former primarily seek to meet the requirements of the NAP in order to fulfil a "tiresome task", the latter combine political aspirations with this plan.

- An apparent *absence of policy-makers*. Only a few parliamentarians show interest in the NAP/incl and although the responsible committee did debate this issue, it was not a high priority. Moreover, the German administration needs explicit commitment from policy-makers in order to become more engaged. A lack of political backing was cited as a major obstacle for the NAP/incl to become a real success.

---

[37] Several sub-national interviewees blame the federal government for "making contracts at the cost of others" because the former has to implement the often costly social policy decisions.

- *Severe time constraints.* The time pressures of the process were almost unanimously stressed. As a result of this, a bottom-up debate within the civil society organisations was almost necessarily precluded and an elite-dominated process seems to be structurally favoured[38].

- The *horizontal dispersion of actors* in the social sphere resulted in a strong role for civil society actors. There attempts to stimulate the NAP process and to render it a policy tool considerably contributed to the (limited) dynamic of the process.

- Without question, the *federal structure* is a major aspect to be considered. The fragmented competencies in social policies make the co-ordination of a NAP a difficult task in Germany's "non hierarchical multi-level system" (Mayntz 1999: 101). The federalist argument, however, seems to be often used as a welcome excuse to hide policy area-specific and political reasons for inaction and reservations as regards the OMC.

- *Specific features of the policy area* represent a fundamental obstacle to successful implementation of the Social Inclusion process in Germany, namely the relatively low political salience of poverty and exclusion in national politics. In this respect, the NARB is an important, yet insufficient step towards a coherent poverty strategy in Germany, and the NAP/incl could be an important supporting instrument for proposing concrete measures. We thus encounter the interesting situation that the NAP/incl needs to be attached to the NARB in order to become integrated in domestic policy-making processes, but on the other hand the NARB is itself a rather weak policy tool that could profit from the NAP/incl The next couple of years will reveal whether both documents only play marginal roles or succeed in becoming more important.

Thus, the *process* of preparing the NAP/incl had to face several impediments. What does this mean, then, for the Social Inclusion process's (potential) impact? Unquestionably, as was stressed by several interviewees, the German discourse on social inclusion now takes place in a European frame, not least the term social inclusion itself stems from the European arena. The NAP/incl as a policy presentation document, together with accompanying aspects of the Social Inclusion process, most notably the definition of common indicators which requires increased statistical efforts (cf. Friedrich, 2002), arguably serves as a new frame of reference for national actors in this policy field. By strengthen-

---

[38] Similar results were found as regards the participation pattern in the Social Inclusion process at European level (Friedrich, 2002).

ing monitoring and evaluation processes and by forcing the government regularly to present the country's policy efforts, German administrative culture – which as several interviews underlined is not used to such transparency, evaluation and management by objectives – is also challenged. It is too early to judge, however, to what extent cognitive changes and learning processes strong enough to have policy impact have occurred. As remarked earlier, unlike employment policies, poverty and social exclusion policies in Germany have a relatively low political salience as well as a lower public visibility. Unsurprisingly, the current substantial reforms in German work-welfare relations are taking place with hardly any reference to issues of poverty and social exclusion, let alone the Social Inclusion process.

Conclusion

The foregoing analysis provides a preliminary overview of two different OMCs *in action* in Germany, namely the European Employment Strategy and the Social Inclusion process.

In our conclusion we pursue two aims: the results of the analysis of the preparation of the respective National Action Plans and their integration into the policy process will be assessed in a comparative perspective in order to identify the extent to which *policy-area specific factors* have influenced these processes in Germany and, furthermore, to discuss how far the identified differences and similarities are influenced by *domestic* and/or *OMC-specific*, i.e. *European factors*. Moreover, preliminary assessments are made of the impact of both OMCs. In doing so, we hope to contribute to a better understanding of the process and the potential effectiveness of policy co-ordination as a new instrument of European governance.

Obviously, the difference in maturity of the EES and the Social Inclusion process, the former having already been launched in 1997, the latter only in 2000, shaped the respective NAP processes. The procedures of the NAP/empl are already well-established in the sense that the actors deal with them routinely and have clear ideas of how much they can expect from the plan. The other side of the coin is that not as much attention is devoted to the whole process as in the beginning, e.g. less communication on this issue occurs and the handling of EU recommendations also appears to have become more relaxed. The decision to streamline the EES with the Broad Economic Policy Guidelines will change the process once again with tighter co-ordination required between the NAP/empl actors and those responsible for providing information about the implementation of the BEPG. This seems to be welcomed by most actors who argue that partial overlapping of co-ordination processes could be reduced this way.

The actors of the poverty and social inclusion policy area are, on the other hand, still not completely used to the NAP/incl process. Responsibilities have been substantially reshuffled since 2001 and there is no unanimous perception and expectation (yet) among the actors of what the Social Inclusion process and the NAP/incl can achieve nationally. One can expect in particular that civil society organisations will try to push the process further ahead.

It it thus not surprising that the NAP/incl process has a stronger bottom-up dynamic than the NAP/empl. Social NGOs significantly tried to establish a horizontal co-ordination and created new fora for discussion that are open also to governmental actors of all levels. This is less true for the EES, which mainly builds on the existing structures of social partnership in Germany. Sub-national actors do not tend to identify themselves with the NAPs. This is especially true for those *Länder* which are governed by parties opposing the federal government coalition. Our data also do not indicate that new relationships have been created or that inter-state relationships have been intensified through the OMC processes.

The acceptance of the OMC processes by domestic actors as national policy instruments is limited since the NAPs are regarded as mere reports to the European level rather than policy planning tools. A reason for this is that the NAP process occurs in an environment that does not provide incentives for political actors to use it as a strategic tool. In the public sphere there is no discussion on these processes. Thus, the government cannot be held accountable for substantive and procedural gaps between promises and outcomes in relation to the NAP. This is also reflected in an insufficient integration of both NAPs into the parliamentary process. Only the "weaker" actors, especially the social NGOs, try to use the NAPs more actively to make their case – but also without any publicity. The majority of actors perceive the task of producing the NAPs as an additional reporting obligation which is added to many others and therefore partially regard them as time-consuming and even superfluous.

Consequently, the incorporation of the NAP processes into domestic policy-making procedures is fairly limited. Neither the EES nor the Social Inclusion process seem to have *direct* influence on policy developments in Germany. In both areas, the European dimension plays very little if any role in wider public discussions and only those political actors who are directly involved in these processes or have regular contacts with the EU level seem to be aware of them. However, the awareness of European issues might be slightly higher in the EES than in the Social Inclusion process. Labour market policies have been discussed in a European context – at least at the elite level – for a long time, and the need to co-ordinate policies may be more accepted in this area than anti-poverty and social exclusion policies, which are also more decentralised than labour market policies in Germany. It also appears as if labour market policy and – where it is related – social policy discourse have increasingly but "silently" been framed by the welfare-to-work dimension of the EES in recent years, which might have sped up the pace of labour market policy changes in Germany, which now increasingly incorporates such neo-liberal elements. Policy actors seeking to discuss political alternatives have rather been discredited in the last years and lost their influence on policy discourses.

Our analysis suggests that the functioning of both OMCs and the respective NAP processes in Germany must still be characterised as "surface integration". Arguably, this can be explained by factors which are related on the one hand to the structure of the OMCs themselves and on the other hand to domestic conditions existing in each of these policy fields.

A. National Factors

The *federal structure* of Germany's political system affects both processes in a similar way. Inevitably, the NAP processes are rendered more complex than in more centralised systems. Considerable resistance of the sub-national level to both OMC processes exists, although it might even be stronger in the case of the Social Inclusion process because competencies for anti-poverty and social exclusion policies are more decentralised than labour market policies and because the subsidiarity argument is even more crucial in this field. However, resistance to the OMCs are not solely due to political reservations about Europeanisation of these policy fields but are also interwoven with "normal" struggles about competencies within a federal system, as well as to opportunities for partisan political advantage through coalition building in the *Bundesrat.* In an attitude that could be characterised as "watch out for the thin end of the wedge" this includes resistance to attempts by the European Commission to strengthen the regional and local dimension of the OMC.

Also the *actor constellation* contributes to the NAP processes' complexity. Germany is a co-ordinated social market economy which provides strong roles for the social partners, with a tradition of subsidiarity in social provision, i.e. welfare associations and social NGOs form essential components of the social system. The participation of those actors influences the NAP processes. As presented above, the NAP/incl benefits from the active commitment of civil society actors to make political use of the Social Inclusion OMC, for instance by trying to initiate regional processes. They welcome the existence of the Social

Inclusion process and broadly support the four Nice objectives which offer sufficient leeway to include their policy goals. Moreover, they hope that the multidimensionality of the concept of social exclusion will positively affect the German policy approach – at least in discussions this concept has found its way from Europe to Germany since the European poverty programmes of the 1990s. As regards the EES the social partners' relatively intense participation matches their usual degree of involvement in the policy-making process. The stance of the social partners towards the EES is however more ambiguous compared to that of the civil society actors in the Social Inclusion process. Whereas in principle the trade unions welcome the attempts to strengthen Europe's social dimension, they have greater reservations towards some of the Employment Guidelines, which they perceive as neo-liberal. The opposite is true for the employers' organisations, which are more sceptical towards the EU's attempts to increase social policy competencies, but welcome the main direction of the EG and the recommendations on flexibilisation and activation policies. Whether the more positive and collaborative attitude of the civil society actors in the Social Inclusion process will create further potential for influencing policy-making processes will be seen by the future development of both processes.

Some of our interviewees also expressed the opinion that the political culture of Germany does not really fit the new instruments used in the OMC processes such as benchmarking, management by objectives, monitoring etc. This might, particularly at the beginning, have caused further scepticism or reluctance of political actors to commit themselves to these kinds of policy tools of the EU.

Our analysis found some evidence for the importance of domestic *policy-area specific factors*. First of all, in the area of anti-poverty and social exclusion policies, the sub-national and particularly the local level have broader competencies than in labour market policies. Thus, the resistance to mainly federal government-driven processes appears to be stronger in the Social Inclusion process because competencies of the local and civil society arena are even more intensely defended. In addition, the labour market policy area seems to have clearer boundaries than the multidimensional policies required to combat poverty and social exclusion. The scope of the relevant actors is thus arguably more clearly specified in the former area, which renders implementation slightly easier than in social exclusion. Moreover, the political salience and visibility of employment policies is much higher than those concerning socially excluded people. Hence it might be easier to introduce a European dimension into employment policy discussions, whereas social exclusion issues still have to struggle for visibility in wider public discussions. However, labour market policies too are still regarded as a domestic prerogative, which makes it rather improbable that policy changes would be presented to the public as responses to "soft" demands of the EU.

B. European or OMC-specific Factors

A major difference between the EES and the Social Inclusion process is the former's clear *Treaty-base*, whereas the latter is only initiated by and based upon European Council conclusions. As we have seen, especially for the *Länder* this makes a fundamental difference because of their lack of a defined role in the process, despite their significant competencies in the field of poverty and social exclusion. This ambiguity causes significant resistance and suspicion as regards a possible transitional character of the OMC towards increased European social policy competencies.

Further, the *instruments* of the EES and the Social Inclusion process differ considerably: while the EES is based on a set of guidelines and a growing number of quantitative benchmarks or indicators, the Social Inclusion process has only four broad policy objectives, which leave broad scope for interpretation and (non-)implementation. The instrument of Council recommendations and joint European employment reports, which provide a systematic comparison of labour market performances of EU Member States, is also lacking in the Social Inclusion process. Together with the relative youth of the Social Inclusion process and its biennial cycle compared to the annual cycle of the EES, these features arguably diminish its potential influence on the policy-making process in comparison to the EES. Despite the lack of clear sanctions, the "naming and shaming" of the peer review process appears to matter, given its unpopularity among policy-makers in both fields. There is, however, a danger of creating even more resistance to these processes if EU assessments appear to misinterpret the domestic conditions and statistical data. In addition, the adaptation of the ESF criteria to the EES objectives increased the potential for the latter's direct influence on German labour market policies. Especially for the *Länder*, ESF funding provides an incentive to align policy measures with the EES. Conversely, the lack of an accompanying programme (e.g. via the Social Policy Agenda) or the structural funds is clearly a missed chance for the EU to render the Social Inclusion process more attractive, though this may now be changing with the development of the Community Action Programme in this field.

To summarise: we found it very useful to take two mutually linked sets of factors into account in analysing the role of the EES and the Social Inclusion OMC in the German policy process. On the one hand OMC-specific features, as defined at the European level, and on the other hand the various factors which shape the domestic use of each of these processes, such as the structure of the political system and the role of the public (which is relevant for actors' likely involvement), the political situation (which might provide "windows of opportunities" in fragile or exceptional situations, e.g. change of government after a lengthy period of time), the economic situation (which also determines the situation of the state budget and the social security system) and the policy-area specific factors as regards competencies of different levels, the financial system, leading policy principles, and policy legacies.

This analysis indicates that the differences between the EES and the Social Inclusion process depend firstly on the different shape of these instruments at EU level and secondly on the respective particularities of these policy fields regarding differing competencies of the local level and different actor constellations. In comparison to other EU Member States we presume that the usage of the OMCs is characterised by features of the German political system such as federalism, a public only weakly responsive to the European dimension of social issues, a contribution-based social security system and a political culture based on legal rulings rather than "soft instruments" such as management by objectives. In addition there is still no widely accepted and distinctive evaluation culture, which may additionally contribute to scepticism about EU monitoring mechanisms.

Our initial research question suggested that both the integration of the OMC in domestic policy processes and the extent of participation by various political actors are crucial for its effectiveness. In the light of our preliminary results, however, we argue that integration into the policy process and widespread participation are not values in themselves. Hence the question of the OMC's effectiveness needs to be reformulated. Understanding the OMC's effectiveness solely in procedural terms tends to be very affirmative as regards its content, while also underestimating asymmetries in participation. We believe that public visibility of the OMC's multi-level game is crucial for reasons of accountability and effectiveness, because it provides incentives for political actors openly to support or oppose OMC objectives, and forces them to justify themselves in case of failure. Furthermore, without being addressed in a public space the definition, interpretation, and practical implementation of the OMC's objectives remain elite-driven, opaque and illegitimate. In our view, future tasks for research on the OMC would be to discuss the role of the public sphere both in terms of effectiveness and political substance, as well as to review critically theories of decentralised deliberation in this regard.

References

Bäcker, G., Bispinck, R., Hofemann, K. and Naegele, G. (2000), *Sozialpolitik und soziale Lage in Deutschland. Band 1 Ökonomische Grundlagen, Einkommen, Arbeit und Arbeitsmarkt, Arbeit und Gesundheitsschutz*, Westdeutscher Verlag, Wiesbaden.

Backhaus-Maul, H. (2000), "Wohlfahrtsverbände als korporative Akteure. Über eine traditionsreiche sozialpolitische Institution und ihre Zukunftschancen", *Aus Politik und Zeitgeschichte*, B26-27, pp.22-30.

Bauer, M. W. and Knöll, R. (2003), "Die Methode der offenen Koordinierung: Zukunft europäischer Politikgestaltung oder schleichende Zentralisierung?", *Aus Politik und Zeitgeschichte*, B1-2, pp.33-38.

Bocklet, R. (without year), Positionspapier zur "offenen Koordinierung", Bayerisches Staatsministerium für Bundes- und Europaangelegenheiten (http://www.bavaria.de/Europa/OffeneKoordinierung.html).

BR-Drucksachen (various years), http://dip.bundestag.de/parfors/parfors.htm.

Brütt, C. (2003), "Von Hartz zur Agenda 2010. Die Realpolitik im, aktivierenden Sozialstaat", *Prokla 133*, Vol.33, No.4, pp.645-665.

BT-Drucksachen (various years), http://dip.bundestag.de/parfors/parfors.htm.

BT-Plenarprotokolle (various years), http://dip.bundestag.de/parfors/parfors.htm.

Büchs, M. (2003), "Methodological and Conceptual Issues in Researching the Open Method of Co-ordination", in Hantrais, L. (ed.), *Researching the European Social Model from a Comparative Perspective*, Cross-national Research Papers, Seventh Series: European Cross-national Research and Policy, No.1, November 2003, pp.31-41 (available under http://www.xnat.org.uk/).

Bundesrat (2001), "Nationaler Aktionsplan zur Bekämpfung von Armut und sozialer Ausgrenzung", Opinion of the Bundesrat, BR-Drucksache 352/01 (Beschluss) (1 June 2001).

Bundesregierung (2001a), *Lebenslagen in Deutschland: Der erste Armuts- und Reichtumsbericht der Bundesregierung*, Berlin.

Bundesregierung (2001b), *Nationaler Aktionsplan zur Bekämpfung von Armut und sozialer Ausgrenzung 2001-2003*, Berlin.

Degryse, C. and Pochet, P. (2001), *Social Developments in the European Union 2000*, European Trade Union Institute, Observatoire social européen and Saltsa, Brussels.

de la Porte, C. and Pochet, P. (2002), "Introduction", in de la Porte, C. and Pochet, P. (eds.), *Building Social Europe through the Open Method of Co-ordination*, P.I.E.-Peter Lang, Brussels, pp.11-26.

Derlien, H.-U. (2000), "Germany. Failing Successfully", in Kassim, H., Peters, G. P. and Wright, V. (eds.), *The National Co-ordination of EU Policy: The Domestic Level*, Oxford University Press, New York, pp.54-78.

EAPN (2002), *Making a Decisive Impact on Poverty and Social Exclusion?*, European Anti-poverty Network, Brussels.

Milena Büchs & Dawid Friedrich

Federal Republic of Germany (diverse years), National Action Plan for Employment (http://europa.eu.int/comm/employment_social/employment_strategy/national_en.htm, access 23 May 2003).

Friedrich, D. (2002), "The Open Method of Co-ordination: Bringing the Union Closer to the People? Participation in the Process of Defining Indicators for the OMC on Social Inclusion", Masters Dissertation in European Social Policy Analysis at the University of Bath.

Hanesch, W. (2001), "Poverty and Integration at the Local Level", *German Journal of Urban Studies*, Vol.40, No.1, n.a.

Hemmann, A. (2000), "Die nationalen Aktionspläne zur Beschäftigung und ihre arbeitsmarktpolitischen Schwerpunkte: Trends und erste Ergebnisse", *Arbeit und Sozialpolitik*, No.3-4, pp.36-41.

Jacobsson, K. (2002), "Soft Regulation and the Subtle Transformation of States: The Case of EU Employment Policy", *SCORE Working Paper*, No.2002/4, Stockholm Center for Organizational Research, Stockholm.

Jacobsson, K. (2005), "Between Deliberation and Discipline: Soft Governance in EU Employment Policy", in Mörth, U. (ed.), *Soft Law in Governance and Regulation: An Interdisciplinary Analysis*, Edward Elgar Publishing, Cheltenham (forthcoming).

Kok, W. *et al.* (2003), "Jobs, Jobs, Jobs – Creating More Employment in Europe", Report of the Employment Task Force chaired by Wim Kok, Brussels, November 2003 (http://europa.eu.int/comm/employment_social/employment_strategy/pdf/etf_en.pdf).

Mayntz, R. (1999), "Multi-level Governance: German Federalism and the European Union", *AICGS Research Report*, No.10, pp.101-114.

Mosher, J. S. and Trubek, D. M. (2003), "Alternative Approaches to Governance in the EU: EU Social Policy and the European Employment Strategy", *Journal of Common Market Studies*, Vol.41, No.1, pp.63-88.

Müller, M. (2002), "The Open Method of Co-ordination – A Coercive or Participatory Policy Tool of the European Union? Case Study of the Development of the Open Method of Co-ordination and the Interactions between the European Union and Germany Including the *Länder*", Masters Dissertation at the Free University of Brussels.

NAP (2003), National Action Plan for Employment Policy 2003 of the Federal Republic of Germany (http://europa.eu.int/comm/employment_social/employment_strategy/nap_2003/nap_de_en.pdf)

Neumann, U. (1999), "Verdeckte Armut in der Bundesrepublik Deutschland. Begriff und empirische Ergebnisse für die Jahre 1983 bis 1995", *Aus Politik und Zeitgeschichte*, B18/99, pp.27-32.

Offe, C. (2003), "The European Model of 'Social' Capitalism. Can it Survive European Integration?, *Journal of Political Philosophy*, Vol.11, No.4, pp.437-469.

Ostheim, T. and Zolnhöfer, R. (2005), "Europäisierung der Arbeitsmarkt- und Beschäftigungspolitik? Der Einfluss des Luxemburg-Prozesses auf die deutsche Arbeitsmarktpolitik", in Czada, R. and Lutz, S. (eds.), *Transformation und Perspektiven des Wohlfahrtsstaates*, Leske and Budrich, Opladen (forthcoming).

RWI/ISG (2002), *Wirkungsbewertung nationaler Politiken im Zusammenhang mit der Europäischen Beschäftigungsstrategie, Endbericht*, Rheinisch-Westfälisches Institut für Wirtschaftsforschung and Sozialforschung und Gesellschaftspolitik, Essen and Köln.

Richardt, N. (2004), "European Employment Strategy, Childcare, Welfare State Redesign – Germany and the United Kingdom Compared", Paper prepared for the Conference of Europeanists, Chicago, 11-13 March 2004.

Scharpf, F. W. (2001), "European Governance: Common Concerns vs. the Challenge of Diversity", *Jean Monnet Working Paper*, No.07/01, New York University of Law.

Scharpf, F. W. (2002), "The European Social Model: Coping with the Challenges of Diversity", *Journal of Common Market Studies*, Vol.40, No.4, pp.645-670.

Thiel, E. (2003), Govecor National Report for Germany, 3rd round, March 2003, Cologne.

Umbach, G. (2003), "Employment Policies in Germany and the United Kingdom – The Impact of Europeanisation", Research Project of the Anglo German Foundation, London and Cologne.

Wood, S. (2001), "Business, Government, and Patterns of Labor Market Policy in Britain and the Federal Republic of Germany", in Hall, P. A. and Soskice, D. (eds.), *Varieties of Capitalism. The Institutional Foundations of Comparative Advantage*, Oxford University Press, Oxford/New York, pp.247-274.

Zeitlin, J. (2003), "Introduction", in Zeitlin, J. and Trubek, D. M. (eds.), *Governing Work and Welfare in a New Economy: European and American Experiments*, Oxford University Press, Oxford/New York, pp.1-30.

CHAPTER 8

How Open is the United Kingdom
to the OMC Process on Social Inclusion?

Kenneth A. ARMSTRONG*

Introduction

In 1997, the "New" Labour government came to power in the United Kingdom (UK) promising a new relationship with the European Union (EU), pledging to tackle social exclusion, and committing itself to a process of constitutional reform, including the devolution of powers to Scotland, Wales and Northern Ireland. At the same time, the Amsterdam Treaty introduced into the European Community (EC) Treaty provisions for co-operation between the Member States to combat social exclusion: an objective later given meaning through the Lisbon European Council's commitment to make a "decisive impact on poverty". That commitment was given effect through the Nice European Council's decision to launch an Open Method of Co-ordination (OMC) in the area of social inclusion. The aim of this chapter is to consider the relationship between these parallel developments and, in particular, their implications for the development of the National Action Plan on Inclusion (NAP/incl) in the UK.

While debates about the emergence of the OMC within the governance architecture of the EU and about the relative significance of "hard" and "soft" law strategies have been important drivers of recent research, there is a danger that the focus on the tool of governance as the key explanatory variable comes at the expense of consideration of the domestic mechanisms of adaptation. Therefore, and adopting the methodological assumption of Jacobsson and Schmid (2002) – that there is a need for detailed case-studies of the adaptation mechanisms inside the Member State – this chapter seeks some answers to the question: "how open is the UK to the OMC process on inclusion?".

* This chapter draws on research funded through the award of a Leverhulme Trust Research Fellowship and the author gratefully acknowledges the support of the Trust.

This chapter also shares some of the same preoccupations as the now growing body of literature on the "Europeanisation" of domestic policy (see e.g. Featherstone and Radaelli, 2003) and on the implications of devolution for EU policy-making (see Bulmer *et al.*, 2002). Nonetheless, OMC poses a particular sort of conceptual challenge because of the absence of a transfer of substantive and binding rule-making competence to the EU and because the boundaries of governance between policy-making and policy-implementation are blurred. The issue for domestic actors is not one of how to seek influence on EU substantive rule-making, but rather one of adapting domestic policies and processes to the signals and steers emerging from the OMC process. The domestic dimension is both the object of adaptation pressures and the medium through which such pressures are mediated. It is, therefore, crucial to understand what happens at this level.

We begin by considering the significance of the discourse of "social inclusion" itself. Did the EU process introduce a new language into UK domestic policy? If not, did it create a new meaning or represent a shared meaning? Attention then turns to OMC as a governance technique and issues of the compatibility between the idea and practice of OMC with the UK's evolving governance architecture. The rest of the chapter focuses on institutional and actor adaptation to OMC with a focus on the preparation of the second generation of NAPs/incl submitted in July 2003 and covering the period 2003-2005. Emphasis is placed on the post-devolution dynamics of the UK and their impact on the NAP-building process. The chapter examines not only the activities of government institutions and actors but also the response of non-governmental organisations (NGOs) seeking to exploit the objective of "mobilising all relevant bodies" contained in the "Nice Objectives" that frame the social inclusion OMC.

I. The Idea of "Social Exclusion"

The discourse of "social exclusion" originally came to prominence in EU discussions in the late 1980s in preference to the language of "poverty" which had underpinned the earlier "Poverty Programmes" of the European Commission (for a discussion of which see Bauer, 2002). As Room suggests (1995), one reason for the change in language was the hostility of some national governments to talk about poverty. However, another reason lies with the adoption of the language by the research community to define a research agenda for the analysis and measurement of the multi-dimensional phenomenon of exclusion. Whatever the precise cause, the inclusion in the EC Treaty (Article 137 EC) of provisions to encourage co-operation between Member States "to combat social exclusion" together with the launch of the OMC process on social inclusion, consolidated the use of the language of social exclusion/inclusion in EU policy debates. The key question which we need to address here is how compatible this EU discourse is with the national discourse in the UK. We can analyse this in two ways: 1) visibility of the social exclusion/inclusion discourse and 2) the politics and political philosophy underpinning the discourse.

A. The Visibility of the Discourse of Social Exclusion

As Burchardt, Le Grand and Piachaud (2002) note in their introduction to a collection of essays entitled *Understanding Social Exclusion*, while the origins of the idea of social exclusion may lie in European policy discourses, the concept "is now part of the common currency of British social policy debates". One explanation for this lies with the increased visibility given to the discourse with the election of the Labour government in 1997 (for an extensive discussion of this see Levitas, 1998). In a lecture given to the Fabian Society in the summer of 1997 (the summer following Labour's election to government), Peter Mandelson (a key architect of the idea of "New" Labour and, in 2004, the UK's nominee for European Commissioner), described the need to tackle "the scourge and waste of social exclusion" as the key challenge facing New Labour in government. He announced the decision to establish by the end of 1997 a special unit in the Cabinet Office to be known as the Social Exclusion Unit (SEU) reporting directly to the Prime Minister and intended "to harness the full power of government to take on the greatest social crisis of our times" (Mandelson, 1997). The discourse of social exclusion soon spread. As a consequence of Peter Mandelson's announcement, and in the period prior to devolution of powers to the Scottish Parliament and Executive, the voluntary sector in Scotland mobilised to pressure Scottish Members of Parliament for a parallel Scottish strategy. After the establishment of the Social Exclusion Unit in December 1997, the Secretary of State for Scotland announced a consultation process on a Scottish Social Exclusion Strategy and the creation of a Social Exclusion Network (later becoming the Social *Inclusion* Strategy and the Scottish Social Inclusion Network). A heightened visibility of the language of social inclusion/exclusion is also evident in Wales and Northern Ireland.

The discourse of social exclusion is visible not only in UK political discourse but more broadly in academic and research discourses. At the same time as the SEU was being created, the UK Economic and Social Research Council (the main funding body for social science research) funded the establishment in October 1997 of the Centre for Analysis of Social Exclusion (CASE) within the London School of Economics. Research both within this Centre and in the wider academic community has utilised the concept of social exclusion to explore the multiple dimensions of exclusion (see Hills *et al.*, 2002) and the dynamic relationship between different aspects of exclusion. Moreover, the measurement of these dimensions of exclusion through the development of social indicators has been an important feature of UK social policy research and the work which Tony Atkinson of Oxford University and his collaborators have done on the development of social indicators has, of course, been of influence in shaping the common social indicators agreed at EU level [the Laeken indicators (see Atkinson *et al.*, 2002)].

It would be wrong, however, to say that the development of a discourse of social exclusion within UK has come at the expense of the language of "poverty". In political discourses we see the languages being used interchangeably: for example, while the Welsh Affairs Committee of the House of Commons chose to investigate *Social Exclusion in Wales*, in the same parliamentary session (1999-2000) the Scottish Affairs Committee studied *Poverty in Scotland*. We also find examples of the discourses being combined: for example, the unit within the Department of Work and Pensions (DWP) that is responsible for UK policy strategy (including preparation of the UK government's annual report to Parliament – *Opportunity for All* – as well as the NAP/incl) is known as the "Poverty and Social Exclusion Unit".

Thus, in its review of policy developments since the report of the Commission on Social Justice (established by the Labour Party in 1992 when in Opposition and often credited as laying the intellectual foundations for its strategy in Government), the left-leaning think tank the Institute for Public Policy Research (ippr) credits as one of the Labour government's "greatest achievements" that "poverty is no longer a dirty word" (ippr, 2004: 8). Perhaps the most visible aspect of the political discourse on poverty has been the particular commitment given by the Prime Minister to end child poverty within a generation. As Piachaud and Sutherland (2002) note, tackling child poverty has been given a heightened political attention under the Labour government. That attention also translated more specifically into policy debates about how to target and measure child poverty. As will be discussed in section 2 below, the UK government uses targets and indicators in Public Service Agreements (PSAs) concluded between HM Treasury and government departments as part of the budget planning process. The target of halving child poverty by 2010 is written into the PSA between the Treasury and DWP. The Chancellor of the Exchequer in 2003 announced a review of the child poverty indicator used to measure progress towards the 2010 target, and the consultation process surrounding this review added further visibility to the issue of child poverty. That said, while the language of poverty is used in respect of groups like children and pensioners and also in respect of access to certain resources or services (e.g. "fuel poverty"), it is perhaps less apparent in respect of the adult working age population. As the ippr report indicates (2004: 10), there is no explicit aspiration or target to tackle poverty associated with this group. As shall be discussed below, it is perhaps the case that when considering this group, the significance of the relative absence of an explicit discourse of poverty lies in the relative importance attached to tackling exclusion in the form of exclusion from the labour market.

In respect of the wider research community in the UK, the move towards analysis of social exclusion has served to generate a good deal of research on the processes, dynamics and multiple dimensions of exclusion (including but not limited to issue of income poverty). That this research agenda could have been accommodated within a broad poverty analysis is suggested by Hills: nonetheless, he concludes that "the emergence of the language of exclusion and inclusion into the UK policy debate since the late 1990s has, at least, not damaged more traditional concerns" (Hills, 2002: 242).

Whatever the causal connections, what is important for present purposes is that at the time of the launch of the OMC process on social inclusion, the UK policy and research communities were already familiar with the language of social exclusion/inclusion and in that sense there was no discursive barrier to UK adaptation to the EU process. More important however, is the need to analyse the meaning(s) to be attached to that discourse.

B. The Political Meaning of Social Inclusion

In her influential study of the discourses of social exclusion in UK domestic policy in the period preceding and immediately following the election of New Labour in the UK, Levitas attempts to recover the political meanings behind the discourse, highlighting three different interpretations (1998):

- RED: a redistributive discourse focussing on poverty as a key cause of social exclusion and the welfare state as a key mechanism for tackling poverty. Viewed as implying a concept of citizenship that emphasises egalitarianism and redistribution rather than minimal liberal commitments.

- MUD: a discourse that associates exclusion with an underclass, and which sees a moral connection between the behaviour of individuals and their situation of exclusion. Views problems as cultural rather than economic or structural.

- SID: this "social inclusion discourse" emphasises inclusion through paid work. Viewed as emphasising *economic* exclusion (exclusion from the labour market) rather than *social* exclusion.

While she finds evidence of all three discourses in New Labour policies, her anxiety is that there has been a gradual shift from RED to MUD and SID. In anticipating the question which Hills poses (2002) – "does the shift in language change the policy response?" – for Levitas the change does indeed alter the role of government from one of tackling inequality to the creation of opportunities (in particular the opportunity to participate in paid work). Levitas associates this meaning of social inclusion – the SID discourse – with EU discourses around social inclusion and she suggests that one reason why the discourse became so prevalent in UK political rhetoric was due to this EU influence (Levitas, 1998: 21). Viewed in this way, the heightened visibility of the discourse described above is not merely a shift in fashion, but points both to the influence of the EU and to a convergence of EU and UK policies around a shared meaning of social inclusion as inclusion through the labour market.

Certainly in terms of the meaning to be attached to the EU discourse on social inclusion, the OMC process adds some support to Levitas' claim that it is preoccupied with the issue of inclusion in the labour market. After all, the first of the Nice Objectives to be pursued through the OMC process is to "facilitate access to employment". The first of the six key priorities identified in the 2004 Joint Report on the 2003-2005 NAPs/incl is the promotion of investment in, and tailoring of, active labour market measures, while the fourth priority relates to the smooth transition from school to work (CEC and Council of the European Union, 2004: 5). In respect of the role of social protection systems, the second key priority identified in the Joint Report is that these systems must not only be adequate, they must provide effective work incentives. Thus, although recognising the big impact that social transfers make to the key "at-risk-of-poverty" measure, nonetheless, the political message delivered in the Report is that social protection systems are not a durable means of eluding poverty and that access to public services and integration into the labour market are necessary to promote "individual self-sufficiency" (CEC and Council of the European Union, 2004: 22-3). Not surprisingly then, and drawing on its first Joint Report (CEC, 2002), the Report identifies the development of an inclusive labour market and the promotion of employment as "a right and opportunity for all" as the first "core challenge" facing Member States (CEC and Council of the European Union, 2004: 32).

The "New Deal" policies of the Labour administration are very much oriented towards promoting a transition from welfare to work and preventing the risk of social exclusion through labour market inclusion. The *Opportunity for All* reports produced by the UK government continually reinforce the message that paid employment is the best protection against social exclusion. Whether or not the source of influence on UK policy is European, as Levitas appears to suggest, or perhaps a more American influence is open to debate (see Annesley, 2003; Wincott, 2003). But, while we can identify a consensus as to the centrality of inclusion in the labour market, it is difficult to determine whether there is a more fundamental convergence of political philosophy at work here.

John Gray, for example, has suggested that the discourse of social inclusion represents all that can be conserved from social democracy's values "because of the socially divisive consequences of the workings of late capitalism in the context of globalisation" (Gray: 2000, 19). For Gray, this means a turn from the egalitarian concerns that Levitas identifies as "RED", to a model of inclusion based on satisfying basic human needs in order to promote personal autonomy and individual well-being. Thus, in Levitas's critique of this model of inclusion (1998: 156): "Social inclusion now has nothing to do with distributional equality, but means lifting the poor over the boundary of a minimum standard [...]". The emphasis, then, is on government creating "opportunities" for individuals rather than with the more relational issue of inequality (see also Stewart, 2000). Viewed in this way we might then conclude that what we are really seeing is an end to a radical egalitarian politics and the beginning of a form of neutered social democracy that at best can hope to create opportunities (particularly to engage in paid work).

However as Clift notes, this interpretation may be to over-simplify both the nature of European social democracy and to ignore the different national interpretations of a European social democratic tradition (2004). As he argues, while other European social democrats may agree with the Lisbon Presidency conclusion that employment is the best safeguard against social exclusion, they do not necessarily agree that this alone suffices. Thus, Clift contends that "New Labour's conception of the (relatively low) minimum standards necessitated by the global economy is not shared by other social democrats" (Clift, 2004: 48). Clift's point is that beyond the consensus on the importance of labour market inclusion there are very different national interpretations of European social democracy.

The very openness of OMC and the vagueness of the Nice Objectives render different political visions of inclusion seemingly compatible with the EU strategy. These differences are reflected in the NAPs/incl and in the Joint Report itself. In respect of the latter we need to avoid too selective a reading of the Report: after all it does also highlight the clear correlation between expenditure on social protection and the at-risk-of-poverty rate and there is no condemnation of those states with strong universalistic ethics in their social protection systems. Indeed, the Joint Report is open to the criticism that it is so agnostic on the different national systems as to be virtually meaningless, tending simply to repeat back to states what those states have themselves reported in their NAPs/incl. All we can conclude then is that the strong emphasis placed in UK policy discourses on the creation of opportunities (especially work opportunities) is consistent with a core European consensus. But it is perhaps to go too far to conclude that labour market participation exhausts the meaning of social inclusion in European (EU and other Member States') discourses, and indeed, there may be some tension between competing value systems. Moreover, we also risk underplaying the extent to which issues of redistribution are still relevant to UK policies on poverty and low income. New Labour has also introduced a raft of tax credits designed to increase the incomes of working parents and has increased the value of the universal Child Benefit (see Piachaud and Sutherland, 2002). Even the New Deal designed to promote transition from welfare-to-work has been funded through the imposition of a "windfall tax" on privatised utility companies.

Where we do see a clearer alignment between the EU and the UK is in the conceptualisation of social exclusion as having an economic as well as a social cost, and therefore to tackle social exclusion is to contribute towards economic prosperity. In her analysis of the report of the Commission on Social Justice, Levitas notes its tendency to reiterate the interdependency of economic efficiency and social inclusion and in consequence the denial of a conflict of interest between capital and labour (1998: 33 and 114-115). The image of a virtuous "circle" of economic and social progress finds expression at EU-level in the Lisbon "triangle" of economic policy, employment policy and social policy co-ordination (see e.g. CEC, 2000). In this way, both the EU and UK approaches to social inclusion can be seen to downplay conflicts between economic and social progress.

II. The Idea of OMC as a Governance Technique

A different sort of consideration is how open is the UK to the very idea of OMC as a governance technique. New Labour has been the pioneer of new modes of governance, particularly the use of governance by objectives. The use of objectives, targets and indicators has been a hallmark of the Labour government's approach to domestic policy from poverty, health and education to transport and crime. It has also been a feature of techniques at the devolved level (e.g. the Scottish strategy on social inclusion contains numerous targets and milestones against which to measure progress). It is worth stating, however, that the creation of a "target culture" has, in more recent times, come under closer scrutiny both from within the Government and from the Opposition. The disquiet with targets is multi-faceted: from a concern of creating perverse incentives (e.g. in priorities in healthcare) to a sense that the technique is being over-used with the effect of increasing centralised control over service-provision. That is not to say that the UK has become resistant to targeting: rather that the role and function of targets has been questioned more openly and directly in political debates.

Nonetheless, it would seem that the very idea of OMC is very much in line with the governance approaches developed in the UK post-1997, and we might then hypothesise that the UK should have little difficulty accommodating OMC processes into its own decision-making processes (assuming a political willingness to do so). Nonetheless, this openness in principle encounters certain obstacles in practice. The UK Treasury has developed a budgetary planning process known as the Comprehensive Spending Review (CSR). The first CSR covered the period 1999-2002, the second that of 2003-2006, and the third announced in July 2004 covering the period up until 2008. To support the CSR, the Treasury agrees with spending departments so-called Public Service Agreements (PSAs) that incorporate objectives, targets and indicators. The areas of social inclusion and employment policy are covered by a PSA agreed between the Treasury and DWP. In this way, there is a close integration of economic, employment and social inclusion policies within the domestic arena in a way which is reminiscent of the aspiration for the streamlined and synchronised EU co-ordination processes.

However, the EU and UK cycles of planning are not themselves synchronised. The UK has already put in place its priorities and plans for the period up until 2008 according to the CSR announced in July 2004. The EU will be setting out its objectives for the three-year period 2006-2008 at the Spring Summit in 2006. Therefore, UK policy priorities (and the use of national targets and indicators) are set in advance of the EU policy-cycle. The national targets reported in Annex B of the second UK NAP/incl are those PSA targets already effective in April 2003 (i.e. those set in the 2000 CSR). In this way, while the UK can report on progress in respect of the Laeken indicators (agreed in 2001), it is not these indicators *per se* which drive the selection of national targets. Rather it is the Treasury-driven CSR process.

If there is a sense that the Lisbon process is having difficulty reaching into the national systems, then the evidence from the UK gives a good indication of why it might be that domestic systems encounter problems responding to OMC pressures. A system like the UK – which would appear to be in principle "open" to the idea of OMC – nonetheless, exhibits points of resistance to EU steering.

III. Adapting to OMC

In what remains of the chapter, attention turns to domestic adaptation to the OMC process on inclusion focussing specifically on the processes surrounding the preparation of the second generation UK NAP/incl.

A. Institutional Adaptation

In the following sections, we consider institutional adaptation at the level of central government, devolved government and parliamentary scrutiny of the OMC process. Section B below analyses the adaptation of social actors to the NAP-building process.

1. UK Government

It is noteworthy that despite the publicity surrounding the creation of the Social Exclusion Unit as a means of joining-up government, the task of preparing the UK NAP/incl fell not to the Unit but to the central government Department of Work and Pensions (DWP). Post-devolution, the geographical focus of the SEU was on England and its approach was project driven, producing substantive reports on specific social exclusion problems (like rough sleeping) rather than having a general policy delivery function like DWP. DWP is responsible for delivering on welfare and benefit reform (including New Deal programmes and Pension Credits). Either alone, or in conjunction with the Treasury, DWP is also accountable for meeting PSA targets relating to poverty and social exclusion. DWP produces the annual *Opportunity for All* report to the UK Parliament and, indeed, the first UK NAP/incl drew very much on that report. This was hardly surprising given that the New Labour government was not about to reinvent the wheel for the purposes of the first NAP/incl so soon after developing *Opportunity for All* as its domestic report to Parliament. DWP is also the author of the UK National Action Plan on Employment, emphasising the close connection institutionally between the employment and social inclusion co-ordination processes.

The NAP/incl was prepared within the Poverty and Social Exclusion Unit in DWP. Civil servants from within the Unit also sit on the Social Protection Committee ensuring a close interaction between the EU and domestic dimensions. A conscious decision was taken within the Unit that the second UK NAP/incl would do something different from the first and would not simply abridge the *Opportunity for All* report. The hope was to develop a shared understanding of the problems and strategies for tackling social exclusion by involving the devolved administrations, local and regional government as well as NGOs and grassroots organisations (discussed further below). While it was recognised that there was a traditional institutional resistance to this more participative style, that the production of the NAP/incl could be presented as an EU requirement (notwithstanding that there is no formal legal requirement to produce the NAP/incl) acted as a form of external driver on change: the "threat" of the EU could be turned into an "opportunity" to do something different and to break out of the traditional bureaucratic processes. Merely by virtue of its European provenance, the Nice Objective to "mobilise all relevant actors" has, in the UK context, been used to develop a more participatory NAP-building process. The NAP/incl has not only, then, provided opportunities for NGOs to mobilise (see below) it has also created opportunities for civil servants to do something different.

If this suggestion might be thought to be a rather generous interpretation of the facts there is some further evidence for the claim. In 2003, the European Commission produced its Communication on the "streamlining" of the social inclusion and "social protection" (i.e. pensions, healthcare, making work pay) co-ordination processes (CEC, 2003). The aim was to ensure a better fit with the timetable for the streamlined economic and employment co-ordination processes, but also to give greater visibility and political saliency to the social side of the Lisbon triangle by simplifying the different social OMC processes. The potential cost of rationalising the different social co-ordination processes lay with subsuming the social inclusion process – the most developed of the social co-ordination processes – into a broader "social protection" OMC. In particular, it was suggested that Member States produce a single national report on social protection to replace the NAPs/incl and the pensions strategy reports. It is understood that in its contribution to the debate within the Social Protection Committee, the UK defended the retention of the NAP/incl because of the visibility it gave to social inclusion issues within the UK and because any decision to replace it would undermine the work which had been done to develop a more participatory approach and to raise awareness about the EU process. It can be argued that the development of new ways of working within DWP and especially the creation of new relationships with NGOs and grassroots organisations around the NAP-building process, have resulted in a positive evaluation of the NAP element of the OMC process by UK civil servants in a way which led them to defend the retention of the NAP/incl.

In process terms, then, we can see an adaptation of the NAP-building process beginning to emerge with the second generation UK NAP/incl. As we will note below, this has been reinforced through the dialogue that has emerged with anti-poverty groups in the UK. To be sure, this new way of working may lack strong institutional foundations and may be conditioned by the personalities of the individuals involved. Nonetheless, there is perhaps a broader lesson to be learned from the UK experience.

The debate about streamlining the social OMC processes in order to give visibility and political clout to the EU's social dimension seems largely predicated on the desire for key political messages about the social dimension to emerge through the Spring Summit meetings. And indeed, the Kok Report on the Lisbon Strategy again reinforces the centrality of the Spring European Council as the driver of change (Kok *et al.*, 2004). This seems to over-emphasise domestic adaptation in response to "top-down" political signals, and under-appreciates the extent to which concrete achievements may lie in "bottom-up" shifts in domestic institutional cultures and routines.

2. Devolved Government in the UK

The election of the Labour government in 1997 not only brought with it a new attention towards tackling social exclusion, but also a commitment to a process of constitutional reform including the devolution of powers to Scotland, Wales and Northern Ireland. Devolution has a number of consequences for the development of a UK anti-poverty and exclusion strategy (whether inside or outside the context of the OMC process). Devolved government acquired policy responsibility for the delivery of anti-exclusion policies in a number of areas (including health, education, community regeneration), while central government retained responsibility for tax and welfare policies (and for the negotiation of EU policy matters). Overall fiscal policy is set at UK-level with the devolved governments funded through block-grants. Devolution was also asymmetric. In Scotland, as well as the creation of an Executive, a Parliament was created with primary law-making powers and a limited power to raise income taxes (as yet unused). In Wales, the Welsh Assembly Government is essentially an Executive body with a limited power to enact secondary legislation. In Northern Ireland an Assembly and Executive were established with powers similar to Scotland, but the institutions were suspended in October 2002 with direct rule from London reintroduced.

Not surprisingly, the devolved institutions – particularly in Scotland and Wales – have sought to use their newly acquired autonomy to develop their own inclusion strategies within the limits of their competences. In terms of reporting on progress, each devolved administration produces its own forms of reports, with the use of different targets and indicators. This emphasis, then, upon the autonomy and distinctiveness of the devolved strategies has limited the extent to which the devolved institutions have engaged in the NAP process. On the one hand, there is a desire to ensure that each jurisdiction has its appropriate representation in the UK NAP/incl. But, on the other hand, there is a clear sense that the "real" strategic work is at the devolved level. Accordingly, the first and second generation NAPs/incl have tended to be viewed by civil servants in the devolved administrations as "reports to Europe" which are at best distillations and at worst dilutions of the work being undertaken at the sub-state level and reported in other ways.

It would be misleading to see each of the devolved administrations in precisely the same way. This is particularly true of Northern Ireland where the devolved administration inherited a strategy – New Targeting Social Need (NTSN) – put in place in July 1998 (itself a revised version of a policy approach developed under the previous Conservative Government). The essence of the strategy is the skewing of existing spending programmes to the ends of tackling poverty and social exclusion: it is not a spending programme in its own right. Departments within the Executive produce action plans and reports on progress. However, NTSN, like its predecessor was subject to criticism as to the nature of its objectives – tackling poverty differentials between Nationalist and Unionist communities or meeting objective social need – and as to its effectiveness in "bending the spend". In agreeing to inherit NTSN, the devolved administration committed itself to an evaluation of the strategy. That evaluation found weaknesses: principally a lack of clarity in its strategic objectives; a focus on processes more than outcomes; and, a proliferation of departmental plans and targets. A consultation process was launched to consider the way forward. What is interesting about this consultation is its suggestion for a Northern Ireland Anti-poverty Strategy that not only has clearer objectives and targets but which would also be supported by a *regional* action plan in a format consistent with the EU social inclusion *national* action plan (including the use of indicators drawing on the Laeken indicators). In this way, the EU process and the idea of the NAP is being actively taken up as a model for the development of the Northern Ireland strategy.

It is clear, then, that whereas the Scottish and Welsh devolved administrations' launch of their new social inclusion strategies can be seen as rendering engagement with the NAP-building process seem less relevant, in Northern Ireland, the problems associated with NTSN created an opportunity to look to the EU process in order to seek a solution to these problems. It might also be suggested that the European origin of the model (rather than one drawing explicitly from either the Republic of Ireland or from mainland UK) might make it more politically acceptable.

The NAP/incl has created the opportunity to develop a truly national overview of what is going on in the UK post-devolution and therefore has, fortuitously, plugged a gap between the UK government's *Opportunity for All* report and the respective sub-state reports. But that is to view the NAP/incl only as a report and not a plan. It is not evident that the devolved administrations consider the NAP/incl as a vehicle for developing a UK-wide anti-poverty *strategy* (each level acting within its own powers), nor, has it been apparent that the devolved regions have sought to use the NAP/incl as a *resource* through which to gain insight into the experiences of others (including one another). This may well be a function of the novelty of devolution and of the NAP/incl itself. It will remain to be seen whether the NAP-process can indeed produce something that is more than an overview report.

Preparation of a "National" Action Plan, raised issues of how to co-ordinate the activities of central and devolved government. In anticipation of the need for post-devolution co-ordination of policy with central government, a number of structures were put in place to deal both with domestic and European policy-making (see Hogwood *et al.*, 2000). One such structure was the Joint Ministerial Committees (JMC) established to bring ministers from central and devolved government together. As well as meeting in plenary sessions, topic-specific configurations of the JMC were created. The JMC on Poverty – JMC(P) – first met in 2000, chaired by the Chancellor of the Exchequer, Gordon Brown (thereby ensuring a high level of Treasury and central government influence). However, no further meetings of the JMC committees were held after the autumn of 2002. The explanation for this is generally that bilateral meetings between central government and informal contacts have proved sufficient without the need for a formal committee to arrange meetings (see Trench, 2004). It, therefore, played no role in co-ordinating the UK NAP/incl. Instead, co-ordination fell to civil servants within DWP with contributions received from their colleagues in the devolved administrations.

3. Parliamentary Scrutiny

The role of national parliaments in scrutinising EU activities has assumed greater significance with the debate surrounding the negotiation of the Constitutional Treaty (for a discussion of this from the perspective of the UK see Cygan, 2003). And yet that debate has tended to revolve around the enduring centrality of the Community Method and issues of pre-*legislative* scrutiny (including subsidiarity monitoring) while finding difficulty engaging with OMC as an alternative mode of governance. To that extent, the debate is consistent with what is happening in the UK in respect of parliamentary scrutiny of OMC. While mechanisms have developed at both UK and devolved levels for parliamentary scrutiny of EU action, it is not evident that they have engaged to any significant extent with the OMC process on social inclusion.

When the Council of Ministers reached a political agreement on the Nice Objectives for the social inclusion OMC, the document received minimal scrutiny in the European Scrutiny Committee of the House of Commons and the document was cleared as not raising "specific questions" about the future direction of the European Social Policy Agenda[1]. It is noteworthy that when the SPC agreed revisions to the Nice Objectives in the Common Outline for the second generation of NAPs/incl, the UK entered a "scrutiny reserve" (the mechanism which constrains ministers from deciding on an issue in Council until the matter has cleared scrutiny through the European Scrutiny Committee). This mechanism usually only applies to legislative proposals under the EC Treaty or decisions under the Second and Third Pillars. The revised objectives were, however, cleared without any report by the Committee. As for the NAP/incl itself, it is not a "European" document and so would not be scrutinised by the Committee. However, the European Commission's Communication in advance of the 2004 Joint Report, was given minimal scrutiny by the Committee[2]. We can find similar limited scrutiny in respect of the Employment Strategy and revisions to the Employment Guidelines and Recommendations. Nor is there evidence that the House of Lords European Union Committee has been any more active in scrutiny of the OMC inclusion process, although it is noteworthy that in January 2004 a new "Social Policy and Consumer Affairs" sub-committee was established and it will be interesting to see whether this will engage more directly with the OMC process.

In Scotland, any potential scrutiny of the Scottish Executive's input into the second UK NAP/incl was affected by the end of the first parliamentary session in March 2003, and the ensuing hiatus during the election period. While the "legacy paper" of the Scottish Parliament's Social Justice Committee indicated that European issues should be taken up by its successor in the next Parliament, the result was that in reality there was no Parliamentary engagement with the second UK NAP/incl. We can contrast this with the year-long investigation into the European Employment Strategy and Corporate Social Responsibility undertaken by the Scottish Parliament's European Committee. In Northern Ireland, the Assembly was suspended in 2002 and direct rule re-imposed and so there was no opportunity for scrutiny. There is no evidence of debates on the issue within the Welsh Assembly.

---

[1] European Scrutiny Committee, Twenty-Ninth Report, Session 1999-2000.

[2] European Scrutiny Committee, Ninth Report, Session 2003-2004.

The suspicion that OMC is developing as a mode of governance acting outside the traditional scrutinising structures of representative democracy is, therefore, well illustrated in the UK. There is a sense that while structures and mechanisms for scrutinising "hard law" emanating from the EU have evolved, governance techniques which seek domestic policy influence by alternative means are slipping through the scrutiny net.

B. Mobilising Actors

The OMC inclusion process has a very specific commitment, in the Nice Objectives, to the mobilisation of all relevant bodies. To what extent, then, has mobilisation occurred in the UK? There was very little consultation on the first NAP/incl and it drew very much on the UK government's *Opportunity for All* report. Importantly, however, at least some NGOs picked up on perceived criticisms in the 2002 Joint Report's analysis of the first UK NAP/incl to seek better participation in the process of drawing-up the second NAP/incl. Therefore, it is not just the transnational NGO community that has used the Joint Reports as a resource: national NGOs have, at least to this extent, used the Joint Report to seek leverage.

In the following sections, the analysis concentrates on mobilisation around the second UK NAP/incl and is divided into consideration of: first, the role of sub-state umbrella groups representing the voluntary sector and second, the role of sub-state and national anti-poverty networks.

1. The Voluntary Sector

There are distinct "umbrella" bodies for the voluntary sectors in Scotland, England, Wales and Northern Ireland. To varying degrees they are involved in social inclusion and European policies. Yet, there has been limited involvement of voluntary sector organisations in either the first or second-generation NAP processes. One explanation is that the European dimension of these umbrella bodies is more concerned with issues of European funding than it is with the OMC process. Insofar as they are concerned with wider European governance issues, the drafting of the Constitutional Treaty has been more of a priority for the English umbrella group. Otherwise, they have been content to let more specific anti-poverty NGOs with a European dimension take the lead.

Another explanation relates to the development of distinctive sub-national social inclusion policies in the context of devolution. The social inclusion dimension of the work of these voluntary sector umbrella groups has been more towards involvement in the post-devolution new processes and structures than it has been on seeking to influence the

NAP/incl. And as one interviewee noted in respect of one of the devolved governments, insofar as the devolved administration was itself focused on developing its own social inclusion strategy, it was not looking to the voluntary sector for involvement in the NAP-building process. Another interviewee working in a different jurisdiction also suggested that the sub-state voluntary sector organisation had held-back from involvement in the second generation NAPs/incl because of the perception that it was simply a report to Europe (rather than a strategic document) with limited possibilities for consultation (the interviewee had actually attended a DWP-organised awareness-raising event on the first NAP/incl, but the experience had been evaluated negatively). Therefore, the priority was more to focus on engagement with the emerging sub-state strategy than with this EU process. That is not to say that there is no interest in the process: one interviewee – anticipating the potential linkage between OMC and the social inclusion strands of EU funding – indicated a desire to increase involvement in the OMC process. This suggests that were the connection, for example, between European funding and the OMC process to become more direct, then voluntary sector organisations would be more likely to mobilise around the OMC process.

2. Sub-state and National Anti-poverty Networks

We can contrast the picture in the previous section with that of the sub-state anti-poverty networks in Scotland, England, Wales and Northern Ireland. Before we consider the extent to which these networks have mobilised around the NAPs/incl we need to consider their capacity to do so. It should be recalled that the EU Action Programme which supports the OMC process (European Parliament and Council of the European Union, 2002: 1) does provide funding for capacity building but only for transnational networks (e.g. the European Anti-poverty Network – EAPN). While national level bodies may be able to source funding from this programme through involvement in specifically funded projects on particular issues, their core funding is largely dependent on domestic sources.

In the UK that has generally meant looking to the Community Fund[3] (distributing funds from the National Lottery) and to charities for support. It has also meant financial instability. For example, EAPN England – through its European expert Katherine Duffy – has been a vital source of information within the UK on European policies and strategies on social inclusion (including the OMC process). However, its Community

---

[3] From 1st June 2004, the Community Fund merged with the New Opportunities Fund to create The Big Lottery Fund.

Fund finance ended in 2001 and it subsequently continued as a voluntary board. Katherine Duffy has remained at the heart of the co-ordination of the sub-state networks but more on a voluntary and personal basis. In Wales, the Anti-poverty Network Cymru (APNC) only came into existence in 2002 as a result of work conducted by Oxfam and the UK Coalition Against Poverty (discussed further below). Upon its creation, the pre-existing EAPN Cymru (which had a small and diminishing membership) dissolved. However, since its creation, APNC has operated on a voluntary basis with no core funding and has found difficulty in accessing funding from the Welsh Assembly Government. In Northern Ireland, the Northern Ireland Anti-poverty Network (NIAPN) was established in 1991 but also suffered from funding difficulties. It secured new funding from the Community Fund from the spring of 2001. In Scotland, the Poverty Alliance received funding in 1998 from the Community Fund but by the beginning of 2002 that funding had ended. It did, however, receive funding from the Scottish Executive and from Communities Scotland (the community regeneration agency). In short, while devolution has given new impetus to the activities of sub-state networks, it has not necessarily produced a more stable funding basis for such networks, and there remains a strong reliance on the UK-wide funding provided by the National Lottery.

Devolution has, however, been a catalyst for the emergence of a new network in England. While in Scotland, Wales and Northern Ireland, the sub-state networks have a dual focus – sub-state and EU policies and strategies), this left England with an organisation – EAPN England – with a primarily European focus. In 2003, the England Anti-poverty Platform (EAPP) emerged to co-ordinate responses to poverty issues affecting England (and in this way to reflect the post-devolution emergence of distinctive sub-state networks). What the future relationship will be between EAPN England and EAPP is unknown.

Notwithstanding the very different capacities of the sub-state networks, we can point to a number of different ways in which, individually and collectively, they mobilised around the 2003-2005 NAP/incl. A number of NAP/incl awareness-raising events were held in each of the national territories together with seminars with a more substantive focus. Acting as the UK Liaison Group – the UK member of EAPN – collectively, EAPN England, EAPN Cymru (before its demise), NIAPN and the Scottish Poverty Alliance produced a submission to DWP in the spring of 2003 outlining what the networks wished to see in the NAP/incl. Given that DWP was producing the NAP/incl, it is not surprising that the sub-state networks, through UKLG, focused their attention at the central government department. But it is worth noting that there is no real sense that the sub-state networks saw the devolved administrations as opening up new opportunities for influencing the NAP/incl itself. In the same way that the devolved administrations might have felt that the NAP/incl was a distraction or dilution of their own new policy frameworks, the sub-state networks might have feared that communicating their desires through the devolved administrations would weaken their influence compared to the direct line of communication with DWP. That is not to suggest that sub-state networks were uninterested in developing working relationships with officials of the devolved administrations around the NAP-building process. Indeed in both Scotland and Northern Ireland, anti-poverty groups speak of having established generally good relationships with the relevant civil servants. Rather the point is that they tended to look to the direct channel of communication that was emerging with DWP as the primary source of influence (of particular relevance for NIAPN given the suspension of the Northern Ireland Executive and Assembly).

It is not just through the UK Liaison Group that sub-state networks have co-ordinated their NAP/incl mobilisation activities. The Poverty Alliance, NIAPN, APNC and (from 2003) EAPP form the four-nation umbrella group, the UK Coalition Against Poverty (UKCAP). UKCAP was formed in 1996, but reformed as a four-nation umbrella group with a focus on UK-wide decision-making. Together, UKCAP and EAPN England developed the idea of creating a Social Policy Task Force (SPTF) with the aim of influencing the process and content of the NAP/incl. The SPTF acted as a forum bringing together not just the sub-state networks but also a broader coalition of NGOs including OXFAM GB and ATD Fourth World (these bodies also made separate submissions to DWP on the second generation NAP/incl). Despite the loose nature of the Task Force and the limited resources of its component parts, by acting as a network, the SPTF was able to develop a strategy for influencing the NAP/incl, with some members being able to devote staff time to it (e.g. the Poverty Alliance initially provided the secretariat, but with UKCAP obtaining Community Funding in 2002 the SPTF secretariat moved to UKCAP).

The SPTF co-ordinated a number of seminars as a means of spreading awareness of the NAP/incl process to grassroots organisations. In a submission to DWP in spring 2003 (co-ordinated by EAPN England through Katherine Duffy), the SPTF set out submissions on the content and process of the NAP/incl; collated responses from grassroots organisations obtained at the awareness-raising seminars; and set out the vision and values that guided its approach. Certainly, the responses of participants in the SPTF seminars had a direct impact on the second UK NAP/incl in the sense that this aspect of the 2003 SPTF submission is reported directly as Annex E of the NAP/incl entitled "What People with Experience of Poverty Have Said". We can see, then, that anti-poverty groups did mobilise around the NAP-building process and sought to influence the content of the NAP/incl in a variety of ways. That the NAP/incl itself reports some of the outcomes of that work at least indicates a superficial responsiveness to this influence.

An interesting innovation that resulted from the development of a working relationship between DWP and the SPTF was the creation of a Participation Working Group. The aim of the group was to feed in views of those experiencing poverty into the NAP-building process. Notwithstanding that the second UK NAP/incl was developed over a slightly longer time-frame than the first, nonetheless, there was still a relatively short lead-time for the submission of the NAP/incl and it is questionable to what extent the Participation Working Group was able to do more than give voice to a limited number of participants (largely selected by the NGOs). But whatever the limitations, not only was the development of the Working Group an indication of the willingness of DWP officials to develop a dialogue outside the normal bureaucratic channels, what is more striking was the intention for this Group immediately to begin work on the third generation NAP/incl. Thus, in a Participation Working Group Plan agreed in April 2003, the aim of the Group was stated to be:

> to enable people in poverty to participate in the development of the UK NAP 2005 and beyond by establishing a real partnership between people living in poverty (women, men, children from all backgrounds) and government at all levels in order to improve anti-poverty policy and practice described in the NAP.

The Plan was included in the second UK NAP/incl in Annex F. In October 2004, the Working Group launched an on-line participation "tool-kit" (with support from Oxfam, DWP and UKCAP)[4]. The intention is to raise awareness and create a resource for a phased-participation in the 2006 NAP (the timetable for the NAPs/incl was revised from 2005 to 2006) beginning in Autumn 2004.

Despite the bewildering array of acronyms and over-lapping constellations of actors, what has emerged is an on-going participative process supported not only by sub-state anti-poverty networks and national NGOs but also by the DWP. That this dialogue exists at all is a remarkable achievement and can be contrasted with the history of the UK *Opportunity for All* report. Many NGOs reported having "no way in" to influence *Opportunity for All* and the emergence of a different process around the NAP/incl was seen by many interviewees as indicating a shift in the attitudes of key civil servants and as tentative evidence of the

---

4 The tool-kit entitled "Get Heard" can be accessed via the UKCAP website: http://www.ukcap.org.

emergence of new ways of working. Civil servants were even persuaded to give members of the SPTF a draft of the second NAP/incl for comments (albeit on a confidential basis). In short, the new process surrounding the second UK NAP/incl gave anti-poverty groups and networks access to central government civil servants in a way that simply had not been possible before within the domestic arena.

How then should we evaluate this mobilisation? What is striking is that while individually sub-state networks may have limited resources they have pooled their resources in developing strategies for influencing the NAP/incl. However, and despite the creation of the Participation Working Group, it is still a fairly small community of engaged individuals who are undertaking the mobilisation. The process surrounding the second UK NAP/incl was certainly different from the first and the level of awareness has risen, but this is far from being a process that is drawing in a broad range of actors.

Moreover, while the process may be different, substantively the policies and strategies indicated in the NAP/incl are not developed through the NAP-building process itself but are simply reported in it. The danger then is that process triumphs over substance. We need to be vigilant in assessing whether what has emerged is a new and more open process that is at best producing more process rather than real substantive deliberation. We, therefore, need to guard against heightening expectations of the leverage of the NAP-building process on domestic substantive policy.

In the context of devolution, the UK NAP/incl has provided an opportunity for sub-state networks to join together to seek to develop a UK-wide perspective on social exclusion. At the same time, the reality of devolution is that very different strategies are being developed at sub-state level and there is little reflection in the NAP/incl either upon the interaction of central and sub-state policies/strategies or upon what each of the devolved regions might seek to learn from one another. In other words, while the NAP/incl could potentially reconnect the different levels of government in the UK, it is not obvious that it actually succeeds in producing anything that could be seen as an overarching strategy. There may also be an unintended consequence of using the new channels of communication with DWP as the basis for sub-state NGOs to seek to develop a more UK-wide perspective on problems of social exclusion. The danger of using the NAP/incl as that vehicle is that unwittingly it may reinforce the role of central government because of DWP's role as both the institutional "owner" of the NAP/incl and as the mediator with EU institutions (particularly through the civil servants represented in the SPC).

Conclusions

This study has found examples of domestic adaptation to the OMC process on inclusion. They relate in particular to the mobilisation of anti-poverty networks and the willingness of central government civil servants to develop new working relationships with such networks. That DWP and NGOs have joined forces to develop a participation tool-kit for the next round of NAPs/incl is an indication of a desire to break out of traditional bureaucratic routines and at least gives the appearance of a commitment to the NAPs/incl. Attitudes towards the NAPs/incl from the devolved administrations are more ambivalent, although the idea that the EU process might serve as a model for recasting the Northern Ireland anti-poverty strategy suggests a stronger adaptation dynamic at work here.

The difficulty, however, is that it is hard to escape the conclusion that notwithstanding the elaboration of new processes, the UK NAP/incl remains primarily a report and not a plan. To be sure, it has filled a gap between the central and devolved government social exclusion and anti-poverty reports and acts as an overview of the UK as a whole. But that is not the same as developing a *strategy* for the UK as a whole. Devolution has compartmentalised central and devolved strategies.

In reflecting more generally on domestic adaptation to OMC, it is apparent that despite the affinity between the governance technique of OMC and techniques developed in the UK post-1997, the lack of synchronisation between the EU co-ordination processes and the domestic cycle of budget-planning and target-setting results in a reinforcement of the domestic arena as the key driver of social inclusion objectives, indicators and targets, which in turn undercuts the ability of the UK NAP/incl to do more than report on what has already been agreed.

The research reported here also highlights two different political visions of the future of OMC. The evidence of domestic adaptation – particularly at the level of central government – points to the importance of altering domestic mind-sets and routines in order to buttress commitments to political change. The alternative vision, however, is one that looks to EU institutions – in particular the European Council – to deliver high-level messages and to steer the Member States in the desired direction. It may not be a matter of choosing which vision to follow. But the evidence of the Lisbon Strategy to date has been that there remains a gap between the big statements of political intention and delivery within the Member States. More needs to be done to uncover the domestic mechanisms of adaptation in order to explain the success or failures of the commitments made at Lisbon.

References

Annesley, C. (2003), "Americanised and Europeanised: UK Social Policy Since 1997", *British Journal of Politics and International Relations*, Vol.5, No.2, pp.143-165.

Atkinson, A. B., Cantillon, B., Marlier, E. and Nolan, B. (2002), *Social Indicators – the EU and Social Inclusion*, Oxford University Press, Oxford.

Bauer, M. (2002), "Limitations to Agency Control in European Union Policy-making: The Commission and the Poverty Programmes", *Journal of Common Market Studies*, Vol.40, No.3, pp.381-400.

Bulmer, S., Burch, M., Carter, C., Hogwood, P. and Scott, A. (2002), *British Devolution and European Policy-making*, Palgrave Macmillan, Basingstoke.

Burchardt, T., Le Grand, J. and Piachaud, D. (2002), "Introduction", in Hills, J., Le Grand, J. and Piachaud, D. (eds.), *Understanding Social Exclusion*, Oxford University Press, Oxford, pp.1-12.

Clift, B. (2004), "New Labour's Second Term and European Social Democracy", in Ludlam, S. and Smith, M. J. (eds.), *Governing as New Labour: Policy and Politics under Blair*, Palgrave Macmillan, Basingstoke, pp.34-51.

Cygan, A. (2003), "Democracy and Accountability in the European Union – The View from the House of Commons", *Modern Law Review*, Vol.66, No.3, pp.384-401.

CEC (2000), Communication from the Commission "Social Policy Agenda", COM (2000) 379 final of 28 June 2000 (http://europa.eu.int/eur-lex/en/com/cnc/2000/com2000_0379en01.pdf).

CEC (2002), *Joint Report on Social Inclusion 2001*, Office for Official Publications of the European Communities, Luxembourg.

CEC (2003), Communication from the Commission "Joint Report on Social Inclusion Summarising the Results of the Examination of the National Action Plans for Social Inclusion (2003-2005)", COM (2003) 773 final of 12 December 2003 (http://europa.eu.int/eur-lex/en/com/cnc/2003/com2003_0773en 01.pdf).

CEC and Council of the European Union (2004), Joint Report by the Commission and the Council on Social Inclusion, Document 7101/04, Brussels, 5 March 2004 (http://europa.eu.int/comm/employment_social/soc-prot/soc-incl/final_joint_inclusion_report_2003_en.pdf).

European Parliament and Council of the European Union (2002), Decision No.50/2002/EC of the European Parliament and of the Council of 7 December 2001 Establishing a Programme of Community Action to Encourage Cooperation between Member States to Combat Social Exclusion, OJ L 10, 12 January 2002, pp.0001-0007.

Featherstone, K. and Radaelli, C. (2003), *The Politics of Europeanization*, Oxford University Press, Oxford.

Gray, J. (2000), "Inclusion: A Radical Critique", in Askonas, P. and Stewart, A. (eds.), *Social Inclusion: Possibilities and Tensions*, Palgrave Macmillan, Basingstoke, pp.19-36.

Hills, J. (2002), "Does a Focus on 'Social Exclusion' Change the Policy Response?", in Hills, J., Le Grand, J. and Piachaud, D. (eds.), *Understanding Social Exclusion*, Oxford University Press, Oxford, pp.226-243.

Hills, J., Le Grand, J. and Piachaud, D. (2002), *Understanding Social Exclusion*, Oxford University Press, Oxford.

Hogwood, P., Carter, C., Bulmer, S., Burch, M. and Scott, A. (2000), "Devolution and EU Policy Making: The Territorial Challenge", *Public Policy and Administration*, Vol.15, No.2, pp.81-95.

Ippr (2004), *The State of the Nation: An Audit of Injustice in the UK*, Institute of Public Policy Research, London.

Jacobsson, K. and Schmid, H. (2002), "Real Integration or Just Formal Adaptation? – On the Implementation of the National Action Plans for Employment", in de la Porte, C. and Pochet, P. (eds.), *Building Social Europe through the Open Method of Co-ordination*, P.I.E.-Peter Lang, Brussels, pp.71-97.

Kok, W. *et al.* (2004), "Facing the Challenge. The Lisbon Strategy for Growth and Employment", Report from the High Level Group chaired by Wim Kok, Office for Official Publications of the European Communities, Luxembourg, November 2004 (http://europa.eu.int/comm/lisbon_strategy/pdf/2004-1866-EN-complet.pdf).

Mandelson, P. (1997), "Labour's Next Steps: Tackling Social Exclusion", *Fabian Pamphlet*, No.581, Fabian Society, London.

Piachaud, D. and Sutherland, H. (2002), "Child Poverty" in Hills, J., Le Grand, J. and Piachaud, D. (eds.), *Understanding Social Exclusion*, Oxford University Press, Oxford, pp.141-154.

Room, G. (1995), "Poverty and Social Exclusion: The New European Agenda for Policy and Research", in Room, G. (ed.), *Beyond the Threshold: The Measurement and Analysis of Social Exclusion*, Polity Press, Bristol, pp.1-9.

Stewart, A. (2000), "Social Inclusion: A Radical Agenda?", in Askonas, P. and Stewart, A. (eds.), *Social Inclusion: Possibilities and Tensions*, Palgrave Macmillan, Basingstoke, pp.293-296.

Trench, A. (2004), "Devolution: The Withering-away of the Joint Ministerial Committee?", *Public Law*, Autumn 2004, pp.513-517.

Wincott, D. (2003), "The Idea of the European Social Model: Limits and Paradoxes of Europeanization", in Featherstone, K. and Radaelli, C. (eds.), *The Politics of Europeanization*, Oxford University Press, Oxford, pp.279-302.

Ireland: The Very Idea of an Open Method of Co-ordination

Rory O'DONNELL & Brian MOSS

Introduction[1]

Any attempt to identify and interpret the role of the Open Method of Co-ordination (OMC) in Ireland confronts a number of difficulties. These include the following:

- as a small country adjusting to deepening European integration, Ireland has for many years been feeling the pressure of competition and comparing its policy systems with other countries;
- Ireland's approach to wage and welfare policy since 1987 anticipated significant aspects of the European Employment Strategy (EES);
- since the deep crisis in the 1980s, Ireland has conducted economic and social governance by means of a flexible partnership process that involves a widening range of economic and social actors;
- through the 1990s Ireland's social partnership has been widened to include a range of new social actors;
- in 1997, Ireland formulated a National Anti-poverty Strategy (NAPS); and
- the OMC on employment and social inclusion arose after a period of dramatic change in economic and social policy and performance in Ireland.

In other words, since 1987 Ireland has been undertaking a kind of open method of co-ordination. As will be seen presently, this observation is not made in order to elevate Ireland nor to minimise the significance of the OMC.

---

[1] This paper is written in a personal capacity and does not represent the views of either the National Economic and Social Council or the National Probation and Welfare Service.

In section 1, we describe the Irish economic, social and political context in which the European employment and social inclusion strategies and OMC operated. In particular, note is made of a number of overarching policy frameworks and active labour market policies (ALMPs) that gave high priority to employment and social inclusion. This was reflected in Ireland's remarkable economic and employment performance in the 1990s and the early years of this decade.

Section 2 reviews the operation of the European Employment Strategy in Ireland. Drawing on our own interviews with various actors, the Joint Employment Reports and the formal impact evaluation, we identify a number of areas of policy that were significantly influenced by the European process. We also report stakeholders' views on the process and their proposals for how it could be improved. In section 3 we review the OMC on social inclusion, placing Ireland's contribution to the European process, its National Action Plans Against Poverty and Social Exclusion (NAP/incl), in the context of the evolving domestic anti-poverty strategy and the social partnership agreements. The community and voluntary pillar, speaking in the domestic policy process and through the European Anti-poverty Network (EAPN), have been critical of Ireland's approach and also suggest that the ambitious European goals and process should be more deeply reflected in, and connected, to the national partnership and budgetary processes.

While we accept the logic of various proposals for improving the OMC process, in section 4 we explore their meaning and implications further. We argue that if the OMC raises questions about Ireland's employment and social inclusion policies, and it does, then it also raises two other sets of questions, about both social partnership and Ireland's overall model of economy and society. In particular, it should force Irish actors to confront the fact that the country does not yet have systems of education, training, innovation, welfare and social services capable of supporting its aspiration to a high-participation, high-performance, economy linked to an inclusive society.

This chapter reflects work done on the OMC over several years. In 2002, Ireland's National Economic and Social Council (NESC) hosted the annual meeting of the economic and social councils of the EU Member States and the European Economic and Social Committee. The theme of that meeting was "The Open Method of Co-ordination and Social Concertation" (NESC, 2002a). Research for this chapter included interviews with the employers organisations, trade unions, voluntary and community organisations and government departments involved in Irish employment and social inclusion policy. In addition, in asking about the impact of these European processes on the Irish welfare system, we discovered the need for a systematic account of changes in the Irish welfare state since the mid-1980s. This prompted us to construct an inventory of changes in policy and work on the content and interpretation of that inventory is ongoing within the NESC secretariat. Our final discussion draws on ongoing policy analysis in the NESC on Ireland's welfare system, which explores ways in which it can be made more effective in addressing social problems and more closely aligned with Ireland's dynamic economy (Sweeney and O'Donnell, 2003).

I. Ireland: Economic, Social and Political Context

A. Introduction

In order to identify the impact of the EES and the OMC it is necessary to describe the Irish context in which they operated. Here we identify three policy frameworks that are closely related to the European employment and social inclusion strategies and note the content of Irish employment and social policy in the 1990s and the early years of the 21st century. Faced with a severe economic and employment crisis, and an attendant increase in poverty, the years after 1987 were ones of significant policy innovation on many fronts. The most important goal of these changes was undoubtedly employment creation and unemployment reduction.

B. Three Frameworks of Irish Policy: Social Partnership, EU Structural Funds and the National Anti-poverty Strategy

1. Social Partnership

Since 1987, Ireland's economic and social policy has been conducted within the context of social partnership. In 1990, the National Economic and Social Council (NESC) set out a framework which has informed its subsequent work, and which underlies the social partners' understanding of the process. It argued that there are three requirements for a consistent policy framework in a small, open, European democracy:

(1) macroeconomic: the economy must have a macroeconomic policy approach which guarantees low inflation and steady growth of aggregate demand;

(2) distributional: there must be an evolution of incomes which ensures continued improvement in competitiveness, and which handles distributional conflict in a way which does not disrupt the functioning of the economy (NESC, 1990);

(3) structural: there must be a set of complementary policies which facilitate and promote change in a range of supply-side factors.

Throughout the 1990s, the first of these requirements was met by sustained fiscal correction, adherence to the European Exchange Rate Mechanism and transition to EMU. The second was met by a negotiated determination of incomes. This negotiated approach also encompassed taxation, the public finances, monetary policy, the main areas of public provision and social welfare. In pursuit of the third requirement, NESC and others advocated a programme of structural reform in taxation, social welfare, housing, industrial policy, manpower policy and the management of public enterprises (NESC, 1996).

The content and process of social partnership has evolved significantly since 1987 (O'Donnell and O'Reardon, 1997 and 2000). All six programmes included agreement between employers, unions and government on the rate of wage increases in both the private and public sectors for a three-year period (with the exception of the 2003-2005 programme which sets wages for an 18-month period). The exchange of moderate wage increases for tax reductions has been an important feature of partnership, although the scope for this has been much reduced in recent years. Beyond pay and tax, the partnership programmes have contained agreement on an ever-increasing range of economic and social policies. One consistent theme has been the macroeconomic parameters of fiscal correction, the Maastricht criteria and transition to EMU. Another has been employment creation and the problem of long-term unemployment. While partnership began by addressing a critical central issue, looming insolvency and economic collapse, it has since focused more and more on a range of complex supply-side matters that influence either competitiveness or social inclusion (O'Donnell, 2001).

As partnership expanded to cover an ever wider set of issues, it also encompassed a set of actors beyond the traditional social partners. Representatives of the "community and voluntary sector" (organisations of the unemployed, women's groups, environmental organisations and others addressing social exclusion) were included in the national deliberative forums, such as the NESC and National Economic and Social Forum (NESF), and in negotiation and monitoring of the partnership programmes. Since 1996, the agreements included measures to promote partnership at enterprise level and modernise the public service.

2. EU Structural Funds and the Community Support Frameworks

A second important framework was that provided by the EU Structural Funds. In the context of the internal market programme and the Treaty of Maastricht, the Structural and Cohesion Funds were increased and reformed, in what are known as the Delors I and Delors II packages. As an Objective I region, Ireland was a major beneficiary of both these packages. During the decade from 1989 to 1999 Ireland's receipts from the Structural Funds averaged 2.6% of GNP per year (McAleese, 2000).

The process involved the Irish government and the European Commission jointly drafting a Community Support Framework (CSF), which was incorporated in a series of National Development Plans (NDP). The emphasis on programming, monitoring and evaluation in the reformed Structural Funds had a significant impact on the procedures of Irish public administration. In Ireland, a large share of the funds were spent on labour market programmes, education and training. This partly reflected the priorities of Irish policy and partly the fact the Ireland received a high proportion of funds under the European Social Fund (ESF). The CSF also included significant support for the partnership approach to local development. Overall, there is much evidence that the Structural Funds were not only a support for major investment at a time of national difficulty, but also a stimulus to policy innovation and experimentation (Adshead, 2002). In reviewing the OMC it is important not to lose sight of the fact that the traditional instruments of European integration, the internal market and cohesion policies, have quite profound effects, especially on countries seeking to address lagging economic and social development (O'Donnell, 2000).

3. The National Anti-poverty Strategy (NAPS)

Following a commitment given at the UN World Summit for Social Development in 1995, Ireland formulated a National Anti-poverty Strategy (NAPS). The strategy – adopted in 1997, some years ahead of the EU NAP/incl – prioritised five themes: unemployment, income adequacy, educational disadvantage, rural poverty and urban disadvantage. Single parents, single persons and households with three children or more, were identified as those most at risk of poverty. The overarching principles of the NAPS were: ensuring equal access and participation for all, guaranteeing the rights of minorities, reducing inequalities (especially in gender), developing partnership, actively involving the community and voluntary sector, encouraging self-reliance and appropriate consultation with service users.

The overall target adopted was reduction of the numbers experiencing "consistent poverty". "Consistent poverty" is defined as living on less than 50-60% of average household disposable income and experiencing enforced deprivation of at least one of a number of specific items. The fact that Ireland adopted an official target for poverty reduction was considered by many to be a major step forward in the development of an anti-poverty discourse (Nolan *et al.*, 2000).

The NAPS institutional structure borrowed that of social partnership, providing for access to well established channels of communication with central government. Nevertheless, in 2000, the government-sponsored Combat Poverty Agency (CPA) argued that while a shared analysis of poverty had emerged, key actors had been insufficiently involved and government departments had experienced difficulties with both operationalising the NAPS objectives and facilitating cross-cutting arrangements (CPA, 2000). The NAPS was reviewed in 2001 and a revised strategy published in 2002. We discuss this strategy and its revision in more detail in section 3.

C. The Content of Irish Employment and Social Inclusion Policies

1. Social Welfare and Taxation

It is commonly said that, unlike some other countries, Ireland's economic reform and recovery was not significantly based on modification of the welfare system. While there is some truth in this, an inventory of policy change, currently under construction by the NESC secretariat, reveals more extensive welfare reform than is commonly recognised. These should be considered in conjunction with tax reforms, which are widely recognised to have played a significant role in Ireland's economic and employment recovery.

Among the welfare and tax policy changes made after 1987 were:

– numerous tax reform measures, which, among other things, had the effect of reducing substantially the tax take out of low earnings;

– extension of social insurance coverage and entitlement to new groups, such as the self-employed, part-time workers, widows and people unable to enter the open labour market;

– steady increase in the real levels of welfare payments;

– introduction of a range of welfare supports to encourage labour market re-entry, such as the Back To Work Allowance, modified Family Income Supplement, retention of secondary benefits and increased Child Benefit;

– equal treatment of men and women in the welfare code;

– measures to reduce welfare fraud;

– introduction of a minimum wage.

It is clear that the content of Irish tax and welfare policy from 1987 onwards anticipated many aspects of the European employment and social inclusion strategies.

2. Active Labour Market Policies and Training

Active labour market policies (ALMPs) were a feature of Irish employment policy since the 1970s. With the dramatic increase in unemployment, especially long-term unemployment, in the 1980s, ALMPs became a central feature of Irish policy. This trend towards an activist approach to unemployment and employment was reinforced by the new acceptance that activist fiscal and monetary policy had almost no role in an economy as small and open as Ireland.

All manpower services were restructured and moved under the control of a single agency, FÁS, which subsequently became responsible for national training and employment schemes. Its services encompassed general training measures, specific training measures, direct employment programmes, employment subsidies and job search assistance.

Employment subsidies included the Employment Incentive Scheme (EIS), Employment Subsidy Scheme and Enterprise Allowance, introduced to encourage employers to offer unemployed individuals part-time work opportunities. The most important direct employment scheme was Community Employment (CE). Through the 1990s, several employment subsidy schemes were curtailed or abolished, while CE was expanded. This increase in the share of direct employment schemes, especially CE, and the associated fall in the share of training schemes, was strongly criticised by economists in their evaluation of the effectiveness of Ireland's ALMPs and this has figured strongly in Irish discussion of the EES and OMC (Denny *et al.*, 2000).

Reviewing ALMPs in 1997, O'Connell and McGinnity proposed the following classification of active labour market programmes:

Table 1: A Typology of Active Labour Market Programmes

	Market Orientation	
Labour Market Leverage	*Weak*	*Strong*
Supply	General Training	Specific Skills Training
Demand	Direct Employment Schemes	Employment Subsidies

Source: O'Connell and McGinnity, 1997.

They argued that ALMPs with strong labour market orientation – such as specific skills training and employment subsidies – appeared to significantly enhance the employment prospects, earnings potential and employment duration of programme participants. By contrast, ALMPs with weak orientation to the labour market – general training and direct employment schemes, such as CE – offered participants little advantage. Although we have some reservations about the categories and labels used by O'Connell and McGinnity to derive these inferences, they do provide important findings on the effect of various ALMPs. While the debate on the Community Employment scheme deserves a study of its own, we discuss it further in section 4, where we argue that it reveals important features of both the Irish social partnership system and the Irish social and economic model. An informative factual account of the CE programme can be found in Walker (2004).

3. Local and Community Development

In 1990, the Irish government established local partnership companies to develop and implement innovative approaches to long-term unemployment and local development. The local partnerships are made up of business, unions, community and voluntary groups and the local offices of public agencies. The extension of this approach was supported by the EU Structural Funds. In addition, the EU Leader Programme supported the creation of partnerships for local development of rural areas. New approaches to community development in disadvantaged areas were also adopted.

These new local partnership structures were initially unconnected to local government, which has long had a limited remit and autonomy in Ireland. Over time, government has sought to connect the new local and community development partnerships with the development and reform of elected local government (Sabel, 1996; Geddes, 1998; OECD, 2001; Turok, 2001; Hegarty and Honohan, 1998). Ireland's innovative approach to local social and economic development has attracted considerable international attention. Some observers consider that it has developed and delivered new services (NESF, 1994; Sabel, 1996), caused new services to be mainstreamed to the national level, led to more effective implementation of traditional top-down programmes, provided a "conduit for local involvement at all levels of policy" (OECD, 2001), demonstrated participatory and negotiated approaches (Geddes, 1998) and proved well placed to provide intensive supports and effective responses to the long-term unemployed (Goodbody Economic Consultants, 1999; NESF, 1999). Others are sceptical about the contribution of local partnerships to poverty and unemployment reduction (Hegarty and Honohan, 1998; Deloitte and Touche, 1998; Turok, 2001).

4. Other Policy Developments

Two other developments in social and welfare policy deserve mention. The first is child and family policy. There was a major change in the legislative framework protecting children. The welfare treatment of one-parent families was consolidated and improved. There were very large increases in Child Benefit, one of Ireland's few universal welfare payments. Although there has been acknowledgement of the inadequacy of childcare services, there has been no agreement on the best approach to provision and funding, an issue we discuss in section 4 below.

The second is legislative change on equality and the right to non-discrimination. The Employment Equality Act (1998) and the Equal Status Act (2000) prohibit discrimination on nine grounds: gender, marital status, family status, sexual orientation, religion, age, disability, race, and membership of the Traveller community. An equality infra-structure to underpin this legislation was created, comprising the Equality Authority and the Office of the Director of Equality Investigations. A National Disability Authority (NDA) was established to advise on policy and take a proactive role in developing standards.

D. Economic and Employment Performance

An important part of the context in which the EES and OMC must be evaluated is Ireland's economic and employment performance from 1987 to 2000. The period was one of unprecedented economic growth in Ireland, not only by comparison with the country's history, but also in global terms. This is illustrated by the following summary statistics. Between 1987 and 200, Ireland experienced:

- average real GNP growth of 6.1% per annum;
- average employment growth of 2.9% per annum;
- increase in Gross Average Industrial Earnings (GAIE) by 24.5%;
- increase in total employment rate from 51 to 67%;
- increase in labour force participation rates from 61 to 67%;
- reduction of debt/GNP ratio from 125 to 41.5%;
- unemployment reduced from 15.9 to 4.3%;
- long-term unemployment reduced from 8.9 to 1.6%;
- increase in earnings dispersion between top and bottom deciles.

Perhaps the most striking aspect of Ireland's economic performance has been the remarkable growth in employment and fall in unemployment. This is illustrated in figures 1 and 2 below.

Figure 1: Cumulative Employment Growth
(1987-2002)

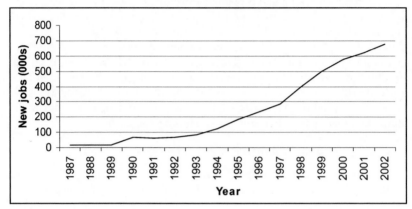

Source: ESRI databank, 2003.

Figure 2: Rates of Unemployment and
Long Term Unemployment

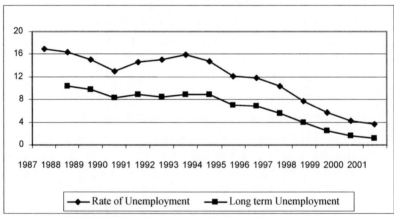

Source: ESRI databank, 2003.

The NESC has recently identified five key factors that drove Irish economic growth since 1987:

– domestic policy and institutional adaptation: the consistent combination of macroeconomic, distributional and structural policies, social partnership and evolving role of the state in industrial and development policy;

- competitiveness, reflected in strong export performance of foreign and indigenous firms;
- EU membership: the internal market, Structural Funds and transition to EMU;
- inward investment; and
- education and labour supply.

These combined to produce both intensive and extensive growth (NESC, 2003).

II. The OMC in Ireland: Employment

A. Introduction

We begin our examination of the OMC in Ireland with a summary of the Joint Employment Reports (JER) and the Recommendations to Ireland. We then report the main findings from our interviews with stakeholders and the earlier formal impact evaluation of the EES, distinguishing between comments on ALMPs and observations on the policy process.

B. The Joint Employment Reports and Recommendations to Ireland

The Joint Employment Reports (JER) and Recommendations to Ireland reflects the strengths and weaknesses of Irish policy and, we argue in section 4, some of the tensions within Ireland's distinctive model of economic and social development (CEC, 1996, 1999, 2000, 2001a and 2003).

Ireland's social partnership agreements were cited as a best practice, and attributed with a "decisive role in promoting strong economic growth and employment creation" (CEC, 1998: 15). Substantial progress in reducing the tax burden on low paid labour was acknowledged. In the area of ALMPs, note was made of a set of measures which aimed to integrate early school leavers into the labour market, offer advice and counselling to unemployed people and provide a "preventive package". We will see presently, that the Preventative Strategy was one of the most important pieces of policy learning in the Irish case. The CE programme was also discussed in the JERs.

Two weaknesses of Irish employment policy were consistently highlighted in the Joint Employment Reports, childcare and training. On both of these, the social partners remain disappointed with the European employment strategy and the OMC. But they see this as a direct reflection of the limited progress achieved on these issues in the *national* political and partnership process.

Gender and childcare issues were a persistent theme in the Joint Employment Reports. Frequent mention was made of the fact that employment rates for women have not reached 50%. The 1999 report pointed out significant developments in childcare planning and attention given to gender mainstreaming, through better statistical information and the creation of institutional frameworks. In offering recommendations to Member States for the first time in 1999, the Commission and Council noted that Ireland should adopt a comprehensive strategy to increase the participation of women in the labour force, further exploit the potential for job growth in the services sector and intensify policy efforts to expand and improve in-house training of employees. In 2001, childcare provision was judged to remain insufficient, and cited as a factor in exacerbating the gender pay gap and employment gap.

Ireland's poor performance on lifelong learning was frequently identified. The reports did acknowledge that Ireland was in the process of creating new arrangements for national certification, examining the need for new competences, curricula development, and new systems of credits. Nevertheless, the social partners seem to remain unhappy with the amount of progress made in addressing the skills deficit of Irish employees. This concern has become more urgent as intensified international competition increases redundancies in more traditional manufacturing sectors.

Many products of the wider social partnership process were acknowledged, including an agreement on teleworking, a new approach to health and safety and innovative approaches to enterprise-level partnership. Nevertheless, it was not uncommon for the JER to mention insufficient consultation of the social partners throughout the NEAP process. While social partnership was credited with contributing to Ireland's employment success, the 2002 report suggested that this could be further enhanced by strengthening the regional and local dimension. It was suggested that future development of both the local and regional element of labour market policies would determine the success or otherwise of Ireland's employment strategy. Recommendations to Ireland under the EES have also noted limited progress in advancing opportunities for people with disabilities and migrants and increasing the participation rates and working-life duration of older workers (CEC, 2002a). As in many countries, the report noted that the preparation and implementation of the NAP had given rise to increased inter-departmental and inter agency co-ordination.

C. The Content of Employment and Social Policy

1. Main Areas of Influence on National Policy

On the main impact of the EES and the OMC on the content of Irish employment policy, our research is in broad agreement with the earlier formal impact evaluation (O'Connell *et al.*, 2002) and ongoing work for the Govecor project (Lynch, 2004). Three main findings should be noted. First, Irish employment policy – shaped in the domestic political and partnership processes and in the European structural fund process, described above – has shown a high level of concurrence with the EU Employment Strategy and Guidelines. Second, the most significant impact of the EES and OMC on Irish employment policy was the Preventative Strategy (Guideline 1), which prompted significant modification of Ireland's active labour market approach. Third, in two other areas, gender and lifelong learning, the European process had a role in intensifying the national debate, but without much identifiable impact on the content of domestic policy or the quality of domestic outcomes.

2. Preventive Strategy

The authors of the formal impact evaluation considered that the Preventative Strategy "has had a profound effect on national labour market policy, it called for a major response and the allocation of related resources by the Irish employment and training system, and became for a time, the number one priority in Irish labour market policy" (Murphy, 2002: 109; O'Connell, 2002; Lynch, 2002). The Preventative Strategy was established in 1998 in response to Guideline 1 of the EES, which committed Ireland to assist the unemployed after a certain period by offering them a job or an employability support. The Department of Social and Family Affairs (DSCFA), which is responsible for welfare payments, refers persons to the national training agency FÁS as they reach a particular unemployment duration threshold. FÁS then interviews the persons, advises them on options and refers them to appropriate opportunities, including jobs, training or employment programmes. This process has been in place for young people since 1988 and for all persons aged 25-54 from July 2000. The current thresholds are six months for under 25s and nine months for older workers. In addition to the EAP process described above, FÁS initiated a pilot "full engagement" process in Kilkenny and Ballyfermot (Dublin) where all people who were on the unemployment register for over six months, and not just those crossing various duration thresholds, were referred to FÁS.

Research suggests that the referral process has achieved positive results for those involved, and that positive outcomes are by and large sustained beyond the short term. Overall, 64% of those referred leave unemployment within three months, and 93% do so within twelve months (FÁS, 2002; Corcoran, 2002; Barrett *et al.*, 2001; Indecon, 2002). Over half those referred left for "positive" reasons – to employment, or to attend a FÁS programme or education. Approximately one quarter left the unemployment register without informing the DSCFA or FÁS of their reason for doing so. One in ten left because they were no longer entitled to the welfare payments they had been receiving.

Overall, 34% of those referred to FÁS did not attend for interview. The timing and pattern of exit from unemployment differed significantly between those who did and those who did not attend for interview. More of those who did not attend for interview left the register in the period immediately after referral. Interviewees were more likely to have left the register for known positive reasons and a larger proportion of non-attendees left for unknown reasons. The latter are more likely to have left because they were no longer entitled to the welfare payment they had been receiving.

Some indication of the level of impact of the preventative strategy can be had from experience with the additional interventions undertaken in Kilkenny and Ballyfermot in 1999 and 2000 (FÁS, 2002; Corcoran, 2002). These pilots referred all people on the unemployment register for more than six months to FÁS. Despite the fact that this group would on average have been already unemployed for much longer than those involved in the general referral process, significant positive outcomes were achieved. Between 70 and 75% left the unemployment register. The results how that the overall impact of this incremental intervention was substantial, and this gives a strong indication, in turn, that the broader referral process had a strong impact on unemployment trends.

In considering the Preventative Strategy, mention should be made of the Local Employment Service (LES). This was conceived four years earlier in an NESF report on ending long-term unemployment (NESF, 1994). The aim of the LES was to prevent long-term unemployment and reintegrate long-term unemployed people in the labour market. A key aim was to increase the participation of the long-term unemployed on state or ESF-funded labour market programmes and thus their employment progression chances. The LES was to act as a gateway enabling a return to work via guidance, training, education and employment supports.

The LES was slowly implemented at local partnership area level after 1995 and integrated into the new National Employment Service under the direction of FÁS in 1999. In a review of the LES, the NESF found that limited progress had been made in combining counselling, guidance and placement advice (NESF, 2000). It concluded that the LES had not fulfilled its envisaged role. Consequently, the NESF welcomed its integration into the National Employment Service. However, it cautioned against doing away with the distinct ethos of the LES. A number of other studies also identified the absence of supportive co-ordination mechanisms and effective targeting as limiting the beneficial impacts of the LES (Forfás, 1997).

The NESF review is unusual in addressing the link between the EU-inspired Preventative Strategy, first mooted in the 1997 NEAP and introduced in the 1998 NEAP, and the partnership-generated LES. The review argued that the LES be given a "central role" within the preventative approach, even though LES providers themselves were divided over whether could safeguard the voluntary principle upon which the LES operated. Equally, the NESF was wary of the LES becoming or being perceived as a "hideaway" for the "not progression ready" or as a concerted attempt to counter welfare fraud. Therefore, so as to distinguish it from the National Employment Service component of the Preventative Strategy, the NESF recommended that the LES be focused primarily on certain groups: the registered long-term unemployed, dependent spouses of registered long-term unemployed, lone parents and those in receipt of Disability Allowance.

Following a review in 2002, FÁS launched the High Unemployment Area Programme, designed to identify and overcome the barriers facing unemployed people in accessing jobs, training, education and other progression options. A revamped High Supports Process, based on a co-ordinated multi-agency approach – combining training, welfare and education providers – has also been launched on a pilot basis.

"Full engagement" pilot projects similar to those reported above have been under way in Galway City and parts of Dublin since 2000 for all on the unemployment register for periods greater than six months. The NAP/incl 2003-2005 reported that between 75 and 87% of the referrals in each of the respective locations had left the unemployment register and that almost 90% of non-attendees had signed off during the programme. These results are higher than those recorded in the earlier pilots discussed above. In its annual report for 2002, FÁS indicated its intention to introduce "full engagement" to all areas on a phased basis during 2003, beginning with Dublin. The NAP/incl 2003-2005 identifies the Preventative Strategy as one "good practice" policy measure and institutional arrangement implemented during the first NAP/incl period.

3. Gender

The European process has influenced the Irish debate on gender, where the major issue has undoubtedly been childcare. The EES Gender Mainstreaming Guideline has been influential in keeping issues of gender equality in the labour market on the policy agenda. Murphy said "the impact has been gradual but significant, with a growing realisation of the benefits of such a policy and on how it should best be implemented" (Murphy, 2002: 109). Access to education and training was also highlighted as an obstacle to participation (Russell *et al.*, 2002). Nonetheless, Rubery (2002) identified a positive evolution of gender mainstreaming in Ireland since 1998, and particularly since 2000. This, she argued, owed more to adoption of the NDP than an outcome of the NEAP.

In noting the limited impact of the EES on Irish childcare policy and provision, it should be said that there has been significant deadlock on this issue in the Irish policy and partnership process. Partly in response to this, the government established a set of County Childcare Committees to explore ways of improving the provision of childcare, especially in disadvantaged areas. We consider this initiative more in our final discussion.

4. Training and Direct Employment Schemes

The formal impact evaluation on the EES echoed earlier criticism of Irish ALMPs by economists. Policies with weak labour market orientation, such as the Community Employment scheme, offered participants little progression to market employment. Secondly, it identified a tendency to wind down some of the more effective training programmes and to expand the major direct employment scheme, CE. These studies highlighted the need for better progression paths to eventual employment for the long-term unemployed (Denny *et al.*, 2000: xiii; Indecon, 2002).

Following a review of the CE in 1998, the Government has endeavoured to reduce the number of places available on the programme and promote training programmes instead, reflecting the much altered unemployment situation. However curtailment of CE proved highly contentious and brings to light interesting tensions in the Irish partnership and policy system, which we discuss in our final section.

Nevertheless, it has been argued that EES's lifelong learning guideline has had a "slow burning" effect on Irish labour market and employment policy (Murphy, 2002). Gradually, a coherent strategy to ensure both basic and on-going learning and skill development for young people, the unemployed and those at work is becoming a key element of national economic and social policy. But, as noted above, the social partners remain disappointed with progress on training.

An important training initiative was the establishment of Skillnets in 1999. Its task is to develop an enterprise-led approach to training, in which companies and their employees are directly involved in decision-making on the identification, design, delivery and evaluation of state-supported training systems. Since 1999, 55 sectoral and regional training networks have been created (Skillnets, 2004). The programme places special emphasis on the needs of small business and over 85% of the companies participating employ less than 50 people. The programme seems to demonstrate high levels of innovation in the content, scope and delivery of training. Within networks, enterprises are developing, piloting and disseminating new training programmes, materials and approaches to upskilling staff. Through the enterprise-led approach (a process that sees solutions to training needs being created by employers and employees), something of a new paradigm of in-company training and development in Ireland has emerged. The networks are increasingly aiming for certification and accreditation of work-based learning and training, by linked to the new National Qualifications Framework.

While Ireland's record on facilitating access to employment for people with disabilities is poor, two interesting developments should be noted. The first is the Workway Work Programme. In this initiative employers, unions and public agencies are using joint action and pilot projects to explore in great depth the complex barriers – legal, attitudinal, financial, educational and organisational – that prevent people with disabilities getting employment. They see this as an essential complement to wider legislative and policy change. They have created Workway Networks which designed specific strategies to encourage participation and buy-in of employers and people with disabilities, organised focus groups to explore barriers and designed employment guidelines. These ideas will be tested in pilot projects and a strategy to mainstream the new learning is to be developed. The second is the launch, in October 2004, of the National Disability Strategy, incorporating a new Disability Bill. While this is a major legal, political and expenditure initiative, it is too early to assess its effectiveness.

D. The Policy Process and Institutional Arrangements

1. The Experience to Date

Here we report the views of various stakeholders on the OMC processes and their suggestions on how those processes could be improved.

The most important finding on the policy process is that the EES and OMC have been secondary to both the national social partnership process and to the processes generated by European cohesion policy through the structural funds. This is confirmed in our interviews with the social partners and government departments, in the impact evaluation and in Lynch's work for the "Govecor" research programme (Lynch, 2003).

Second, all are agreed that the NEAP was seen primarily as a reporting rather than a planning document (Murphy, 2002: 114). In part, this reflected the tight timescale to which the process had to conform initially. Third, there is widespread agreement that the European-level peer review process has been of limited use to date. This would seem to derive, in large measure, from the nature of the Council of Ministers and the forms of interaction that are normal in and around it.

Fourth, the stakeholders are generally agreed that the NEAP accurately reported on progress achieved under each Guideline, even when they remain unhappy with the content of policy. Indeed, there has been considerable contention on the setting of national targets (on employment rates, participation rates, active measures and investment in human resource development). The government's response to the call for the setting of such targets is that the open nature of the Irish economy, and the likelihood of unexpected external economic shocks, would render many such targets meaningless. As we discuss in section 4, the setting of targets is a contentious and complex issue in the evolution of the Irish partnership process.

Fifth, the community and voluntary pillar were much less happy with the process of consultation and involvement on the employment action plan than on social inclusion. While they were formally consulted, they felt that there little was limited engagement with their observations by the lead department – despite their preparation of fairly detailed commentary at national level and contribution to the EAPN's reviews at EU level. A related observation on the process was that there was little link between the action plans on employment and social inclusion, despite a significant overlap in key issues.

A sixth observation, made by the social partners, but not always shared by government departments, was that the Commission's comments on the Irish reports and Irish policy were seen as accurate. For example, a number of partners felt that Commission observations on Ireland's training and childcare regimes were "spot on". But it should be said that, in making this observation, the partners referred more to the structural fund process than the OMCs on employment and social inclusion.

Seventh, as in other Member States, the NEAP process was seen to provide opportunities for increased cross-agency co-operation. This occurred particularly on the Activation Strategy and in the area of lifelong learning (Murphy, 2002). However, some argued that increased inter-departmental co-operation was mainly confined to data-gathering and information sharing, necessary to compile the annual reports, rather than in programme design and delivery.

Finally, in Murphy's view the role of the social partners in implementation of the NEAP was unclear. Neither the employer or the employee representatives consulted by her considered that they could implement planned actions on a unilateral basis. "The forum for joint action was seen to arise primarily within the context of the national partnership programme rather than the NEAP" (Murphy, 2002: 115). Nevertheless, as noted above, there are a number of important policy areas in which the social partners, sometimes acting in partnership with public agencies, have taken initiatives that address the goals of the EES.

Despite the many limitations identified by various stakeholders, almost all were in favour of European policies on employment and social inclusion and of continuing to participate in the process. The annual NEAP process provides a forum for reviewing Irish labour market and employment policy and for reporting on progress in its implementation. The updating of the action plan on an annual basis affords an opportunity to highlight areas where further action is required. The EU recommendations can ensure that areas that have not been adequately addressed in one report receive greater attention the following year (Murphy, 2002).

2. Views on How to Improve the Process

Across the EU, the most common proposal for improvement in the OMC would seem to be increased participation of the social partners and other stakeholders. The Irish case offers an interesting test of this proposal, because there has been a relatively high level of participation, given the extensive partnership approach to public governance.

The 2002 impact evaluation reported that the participants agreed that the guidelines would have a more significant role in national policy development if they focused on a limited number of key strategic issues at EU level, using a 2-3-year time horizon, and encouraged each Member State to identify its own priorities within this framework, rather than attempting to review and assess on an annual basis all areas of existing labour market and employment policy. This is, indeed, the direction in which the subsequent EU-level reform of the OMC on employment and social inclusion is moving.

The 2002 impact evaluation also included an interesting discussion of how the OMC process could be related to other consultation mechanisms. Two particular suggestions should be noted, one on streamlining the various policy and partnership processes, and the other on linking the NEAP process to the budgetary process. While these proposals are sometimes run together, there is good reason to distinguish them.

Murphy reported that "a very strong view was expressed that all the various reporting mechanisms currently in existence needed to be co-ordinated to minimise unnecessary duplication and to ensure that each added a particular value to the achievement of overall policy objectives" (Murphy 2002: 114). In that context, Murphy argued, the partners would be willing to participate more deeply in the planning, consultation and review process and it would be advisable to "formalise the institutional framework more". But, "if the NEAP remains largely a progress reporting mechanism the social partners would prefer to direct their resources to influencing the [national partnership] process" (Murphy, 2002: 116). Murphy argued that if the institutional framework was strengthened, the NEAP process would be an opportunity for the lead department to pull together all relevant labour market policies and actors, would provide a forum for sharing information, based on which the lead Department can draw together a co-ordinated strategy and related actions for addressing key labour market issues which will inform national policy-making (Murphy, 2002: 117).

The proposal to minimise duplication reflected a strong sense that the wide agenda of the national partnership agreements, combined with structural fund monitoring committees, was overloading the resources of the social partners and government departments. Accordingly, the subsequent social partnership agreement, "Sustaining Progress" (2003-2005) had a narrower agenda, spawned fewer working groups and created a simpler institutional structure for monitoring. While the partnership process has been simplified somewhat, the NEAP process still remains parallel to it.

The second proposal was that the NEAP process be linked to the budgetary process so that it could become more focused on policy development, supported by the necessary funding.

The emphasis in these suggestions is clearly on co-ordinated and coherence of two sorts: first, co-ordination of the many departments and actors in order to enhance the coherence of the overall strategy and, second, co-ordination of the NEAP process with two key domestic processes, the annual budget and tri-ennial social partnership process.

Overall, our assessment concurs with that in the impact evaluation that, while almost all of the Guidelines are reflected in Irish labour market and employment policy to some degree, the EU Guidelines were not the driving force behind the development of most policies. Many of these policies had already been identified at national level and formulated through national-level policy processes, including the national partnership programmes, the NDP and its Operational Programmes. Where these policies work, as they undoubtedly did in reducing unemployment, they confirm the wisdom of the EES. But, where these policies have less success – as in training, childcare and inclusion of people with disabilities in the workforce – they raise interesting questions about both the Irish policy process, including social partnership, and the impact of the OMC in stimulating policy learning. We address these questions in section 4.

III. The OMC in Ireland: Social Inclusion Policy

A. Placing NAP/incl in the Evolution of Domestic Policy and Partnership

A key to understanding the role of the OMC on social inclusion is to note how the National Action Plans Against Poverty and Social Exclusion (NAP/incl) occurred in the sequence of national partnership agreements and strategies. In particular, the timing and content of national agreements and policy strategies shaped the approach taken to the European social inclusion process. An account of this, combined with a brief report on the views of various actors, allows an initial assessment of how the European process has interacted with national processes and a discussion of how that interaction might evolve.

As noted in section 1, three-year partnership agreements were in place since 1987. The first National Anti-poverty Strategy (NAPS) was formulated in 1997. Its institutional structure, procedural arrangements and strategic method was very similar to that of national social partnership. It included a commitment to a review and revision in 2002. Ireland's first National Action Plans Against Poverty and Social Exclusion was submitted in June 2001. It set out the strategy to be adopted over the two-year period 2001 to 2003. Its preparation and content was somewhat compromised by the fact that a revision of the National Anti-poverty Strategy was about to be undertaken. A revised NAPS was published in 2002. Although its content was changed, and some significant new institutional arrangements were included, it adopted the some basic method: the setting of targets and commitments. In 2003, the social partners and government negotiated their sixth partnership programme, "Sustaining Progress", covering the period 2003 to 2005. It contained significant changes in institutional arrangements and method. Where previous programmes contained detailed commitments and created a large number of working groups, "Sustaining Progress" contained few if any spending commitments not already in the government's budget and National Development Plan. Instead it created a single Steering Group and ten "Special Initiatives" on which government would work with the social partners. As we discuss below, this has prompted the perception in the EAPN and among some in the community and voluntary sector that social partnership has turned its back on the anti-poverty agenda, as articulated in the first NAPS and the first NAP/incl.

Ireland's first NAP/incl reported positive developments in reducing consistent poverty, identified the challenges of income inequality homelessness and educational disadvantage. The plan also noted the formulation of a new National Drugs Strategy, a National Children's Strategy and a proposed study on the risk of social exclusion to non-national migrants (DSCFA, 2001).

Despite the pre-existing National Anti-poverty Strategy, impressive economic growth and a decline in both adult and child poverty since 1994, Ireland's first NAP/incl did not fare well in the 2001 Commission evaluation (CEC, 2001b). It was classified among those Member States deemed to have offered insightful analysis but no coherent strategy on poverty and social exclusion. Specifically, Ireland was deemed to face a growing disparity in incomes, compounded by a dearth of detailed data on poverty. Its NAP/incl was judged to have offered neither analysis of the problem, systematic identification of vulnerable groups nor mention of gender as a specific issue. Most importantly, the Irish NAP/incl was found to lack sufficient targets or evaluation of the on-going strategy. The involvement of stakeholders was gauged to be insufficient. Ireland was encouraged to enhance investment in service provision for those on low incomes, tackle rural and urban deprivation and implement a social care infrastructure. Further action was also required in raising overall educational achievement and literacy levels.

The EAPN review of Ireland's first NAP/incl, released after the first Commission report, noted that Ireland's anti-poverty networks were critical of the absence of any gender analysis, how plans were to be implemented or funded, the nature of specified targets and what they considered to be a lack of new initiatives (EAPN, 2002). The anti-poverty networks were less critical of the proposed monitoring mechanisms and follow-up procedures. The EAPN report reflected the community and voluntary sector's hope that the EU process could redress the problems it saw in the National Anti-poverty Strategy.

B. Revised National Anti-poverty Strategy

In response to criticism of its first NAP/incl, the Irish government argued that its commitment to the Nice goals should only be judged within the review of its own NAPS. That review was undertaken in late 2001 and published in February 2002 (Goodbody, Economic Consultants, 2001). The revised NAPS contained 36 targets, compared to 6 in the original strategy. It set a target to reduce consistent poverty to below 2%, but, once again, did not contain a target for reduction of relative income poverty. There was extended debate on whether to set a benchmark for welfare payments as a percentage of gross average equivalent earnings. The revised NAPS did not quite do that, but did set a target that by 2007 minimum welfare payments would be equivalent to 150 euros per week in 2002 terms. The revised NAPS also set targets of various kinds on children and young people, women, older people and travellers. It identified other vulnerable groups – people with disabilities, migrants and ethnic minorities – but did not set targets for them. It aimed to eliminate long term unemployment by 2007. Health, housing and accommodation were new themes in the strategy. Specific targets were set for public housing construction between 2002 and 2006.

The revised strategy placed greater emphasis on the provision of quality public services in combating poverty. It drew attention to the international interest in setting standards for public services and in systems by which standards could be monitored.

The revised NAPS included a number of significant institutional developments. It created a new Office of Social Inclusion, located within the Department of Social and Family Affairs. It functions are to monitor implementation of the NAPS, to prepare the NAP/incl, to enhance the poverty proofing process, to implement a data and research strategy and to develop a communications strategy. Another innovation was the creation of the Social Inclusion Consultative Group, involving the social partners and anti-poverty experts, to meet twice a year. In addition, provision was made for a new annual Social Inclusion Forum, to include groups not directly represented in the social partnership process.

The revised NAPS aimed to develop a more effective poverty proofing process, through enhanced proofing guidelines, and to integrate poverty proofing with equality proofing, gender proofing and rural proofing. It also committed to a two-yearly evaluation of the strategy, to coincide with the NAP/incl process.

Despite extensive involvement in the review, the community and voluntary sector in Ireland were critical of final outcome. While welcoming the setting of many more targets, they judged the revised strategy to be vague on concrete steps, policies and resources (EAPN Ireland, 2003a). In a related, but subtly different vein, the National Economic and Social Council observed that "Arguably, the more global are targets, the more articulated and detailed have to be the strategies for reaching them; otherwise little will be learned from attaining or missing them (NESC, 2003: 350). The NESC also underlined the importance of improved services, but drew attention to the scale of the challenge involved in setting standards and devising monitoring mechanisms.

The revision of the NAPS was soon followed by negotiation of a new national social partnership programme "Sustaining Progress". As usual, in the run up to the negotiations, the NESC prepared an extensive strategic overview of economic and social developments and challenges. It included a new analysis of the Irish economic boom and of the economic and social vulnerabilities that attend the particular pattern of economic development in Ireland. The negotiation and content of the programme was influenced by two factors that should be noted. The first was government reluctance to make any spending commitments not already included in the annual budget and the multi-annual National Development Plan. This reflected both the suddenly tight fiscal situation that followed the international economic slowdown and an apparent wish to reassert government authority in the partnership context. The second was fatigue, on all sides, with the massive agenda and large number of working groups that characterised the previous partnership programme. Consequently the programme created a central steering group and identified ten "Special Initiatives". Eight of these are on social problems:

- housing and accommodation;
- migration and interculturalism;
- long-term unemployed, vulnerable workers and those who have been made redundant;
- tackling education disadvantage – literacy, numeracy, and early school leaving;
- care – children, people with disabilities and older people;
- alcohol/drug misuse;
- including everyone in information society; and
- ending child poverty.

As a result of this change of approach the "Sustaining Progress" agreement was highly contentious within the community and voluntary sector. Some groups opted not to sign the programme and were subsequently excluded from the "pillar", through which relations with government are handled, and were not re-appointed to bodies such as the National Economic and Social Council. Others agreed to the programme and continue to work in all close collaboration with government and the other partners.

In a report prepared for DG Employment, as a background to the second Irish NAP/incl, Daly summarised well this perception that there was a decline in the quality of Irish programmes and strategies. She suggested that the "Sustaining Progress" agreement, and the prospects for the second NAP/incl, should be analysed by asking the extent to which each "advances the commitments made in the NAPS" (Daly, 2003: 10). In this regard, it was, she suggested, disappointing. First, in comparison to earlier agreements, and the trend towards a broadening of the issues and domains covered by partnership agreements, the 2003-2005 partnership agreement covers fewer issues, and could be said to be mainly a wage agreement.

Second, in relation to social issues, the agreement represents something of a paradigm shift in that, instead of making specific commitments to issues connected with social inclusion, it is planned that the social partners will work with government on a number of special initiatives. The idea is that a number of identified themes should be the subject of sustained focus of attention from all parties over the period of the agreement. Among other things, this orientation renders a new programme very different to its predecessor [...] which contained a large number of specific commitments in the social sphere. It also represents a different strategy to that of the revised NAPS which has very specific targets (*ibid.*).

Not only was there a retreat from specific commitments, time schedules and tasks, but Irish programmes and strategies had, Daly emphasised, continued to focus on "consistent poverty", rather than relative income poverty. In assessing the evolution of the Irish approach to poverty and social exclusion, Daly also cited a NESC review of the poverty proofing process (NESC, 2001). That review revealed numerous problems in poverty proofing and made a number of recommendations on how to improve the practice and extent of poverty proofing.

C. The Second National Action Plan for Social Inclusion

Criticism by the Commission seems to have determined the Department of Social and Family Affairs to put things right the second time (DSCFA, 2003). The 2003-2005 NAP/incl was evaluated in the Joint Report on Social Inclusion (CEC and Council of the European Union, 2004). This report noted continued income disparities – particularly among older people, large families and lone parents – and housing affordability and homelessness as outstanding issues. A greatly improved strategic approach, including a new data infrastructure, was welcomed. Significant institutional innovations included the establishment of an Office for Social Inclusion, a new Social Inclusion Forum and a Social Inclusion Consultative Group. As well as the wider engagement of civic society, initiatives for vulnerable groups, including support with personal health and finance issues, were identified as requiring further attention. A multi-layered challenge was identified for Ireland: to clarify monitoring arrangements; to continue to target migrants and educational disadvantage; and to ensure that sufficient resources were made available to underpin these commitments.

The EAPN acknowledged that the Irish NAP/incl for 2003-2005 was drawn up with very broad consultation run by the new Office of Social Inclusion and the Combat Poverty Agency. However, the anti-poverty groups were highly critical, particularly of government decisions in the wake of the National Action Plan. "Ireland has put more effort into anti-poverty plans than many other EU countries, but it is hard to see much real impact" (EAPN Ireland, 2003b). It pointed out that Ireland is now one of the richest countries in the EU, but has one of the worst levels of poverty. "This results from decades of low overall taxation, paid dispro-portionately by those on low incomes, and lack of spending on social protection and services". It was argued that the authors of the NAP had the impossible task of fulfilling the ambitious EU strategy, "without a mandate from Government to make the substantial policy changes or resource allocations needed to achieve this". "The plan relies heavily on the existing National Anti-poverty Strategy, revised in 2002, and the recent National Partnership Agreement "Sustaining Progress", which are both considered by anti-poverty groups to be too weak and vague to make serious impact on poverty. There is little to indicate how the com-mitments and targets in these documents will be timetabled, resourced and implemented" (EAPN, 2003: 5). Another criticism was that the NAP did not include a "rights-based approach" to poverty and social exclusion.

In the critical commentary on both the domestic strategies and Ire-land's contribution to the EU process, summarised above, we see four themes that have been central to the community and voluntary sector analysis and negotiating approach over the past decade: targets, proof-ing, spending commitments and the "rights-based approach". While their involvement in the partnership process has been hugely important, and very significant policy innovation has occurred, they have not, judged by their own commentary on Irish policy, persuaded the other partners and government to take action that would significantly reduce Ireland's social problems, beyond the reduction of unemployment. We argue in section 4 that the OMC not only challenges Irish government to look beyond overall employment and unemployment, but challenges all actors to recast the debate on social issues.

IV. Our Perspective

A. The OMC's Double Challenge to Ireland's Open Method of Co-ordination

In our review of the OMC on employment (in section 2) and the OMC on social inclusion (in section 3), we have reported criticisms of the process and suggestions that the ambitious European goals and processes be more closely connected to the domestic processes of social partnership and resource allocation. Here we explore in more depth the implications of the OMC for Irish policy and partnership and these proposed changes.

The account in sections 2 and 3 confirm that, despite the significant level of policy change and dynamic employment growth displayed by Ireland from 1987 to 2003, the OMCs in employment and social inclusion did ask important questions of the Irish system. In particular, they asked that Ireland look beyond *total employment* growth and *unemployment reduction*, in order to re-examine the effectiveness of its many activation measures, the adequacy of its training and lifelong learning, its achievement of flexible working arrangements, whether it was achieving equal opportunities in the labour market, and the effectiveness of its social inclusion and anti-poverty policies. But, in our view, these substantive questions, and Ireland's partial answer to them, raise additional questions for the country's social partnership system and about the overall model of economy and society that Ireland is developing. We state this argument briefly, before defending it in more detail.

Consider first the social partnership system. To address those substantive questions, Ireland has to ask why its policy process, highly influenced by partnership, expanded one employment creation scheme, Community Employment, that economic analysis suggests to be much less effective in achieving labour market progression than other, more market-oriented, training programmes. It has to ask why its partnership-inspired Local Employment Service, created in the mid-1990s, seems, on the face of it, to have been dramatically out performed by the EES-inspired Preventative Strategy. It has to ask why its generally effective partnership system has made so little progress on childcare and limited progress on training. It has to ask why a national partnership system that is virtually unique in including NGOs and community groups, has not made more progress in reducing poverty and social disadvantage, and in removing the enormous barriers that face people with disabilities. In short, it has to ask whether its social partnership system has retained the dynamic learning and problem solving capacity that marked it off, in the late 1980s and early 1990s, as one of the most important experiments in social concertation in Europe or, indeed, the world.

But when these questions are asked, they increasingly prompt Irish actors to ask even deeper questions about the country's economic and social trajectory. An open process of co-ordination and learning on labour market and social inclusion policy has already required that Irish partnership extend beyond high-level bargaining to multi-level problem solving (O'Donnell, 2001). This involves an element of "downward" movement: getting beyond high-level national bargaining, based on pre-conceived interests, to multi-level problem solving, based on disciplined monitoring and learning. We say "beyond" such bargaining, because it tends to lowest-common-denominator outcomes, and sometimes the lowest-common-denominator is deadlock, as on childcare. We call this a "downward" movement, because high-level actors in bargaining cannot devise solutions to many of the complex supply-side problems that influence both employment and social inclusion. While high-level bargaining can set a framework, only those close to these problems are able to do the experimentation and problem solving that is necessary. There are many examples of such multi-level problem solving in Irish social partnership, including the Skillnets approach to training and the Workway initiative on disability, mentioned above. Such a downward movement is a natural element of the OMC also, since OMC is based on the idea of suspending larger differences and dropping down to experimentation and comparison in order to identify what works. So the open method of co-ordination reflects and reinforces the challenge that Irish partnership has long faced and only partly met.

The second part of our argument is that the answers to the specific questions about Irish labour market and social policy, noted above, also reveal the need for an "upward" movement, a clearer look at where Ireland's economy and society is going. This is so, because some of the apparent weaknesses of Ireland's labour market and social policies – such the reliance on a direct employment scheme such as CE, poor progress on childcare and training, major barriers facing people with disabilities, and avoidance of the kind of radical intervention with the unemployed later achieved by the Preventative Strategy – should not just be criticised, but also understood. They arise from the limits of Ireland's employment miracle and the fact that it does not yet have a welfare, education, training and social services system capable of supporting its aspiration of a high-participation, high-skilled, high-performance economy based on an inclusive society. Indirectly, the OMC asks actors in the Irish system to evaluate *together* its policies for employability, taxes and benefits, equal opportunities and social inclusion measures. In short, the OMC in both employment and social inclusion prompts the Irish partners and government to look critically at the Irish "model" of economy, society and policy. This, in turn, suggests that new actors and institutions may need to become part of the conversation that is the OMC.

We explain this double argument in the remainder of the chapter. We look first at social partnership, its relation to the OMC and why the OMC prompts Irish actors to continue to review and improve their systems of consultation, co-ordination and implementation. This suggests that simply linking the European employment and social inclusion strategies to other policy processes, especially social partnership, might not be sufficient. It all depends on the nature and quality of the partnership and policy process. We then explain our rather surprising suggestion, that a review of labour market and social inclusion policies, which is what the OMC demands, prompts Irish actors to a deeper examination of Ireland's social and economic system.

B. OMC and National Social Partnership

We have suggested that a review of the OMC in Ireland prompts important and interesting questions for the Irish partnership-based policy process. The first of these is a general question that has been much discussed in the literature on the OMC: what is the relation of OMC to national social concertation? Others are more specific. Why did a partnership system highly focused on unemployment not devise a Preventative Strategy before 1998? Why did the partnership-based policy system apparently prefer to expand what economists see as a less effective programme, such as CE, and scale-down programmes that are considered in labour market analysis to be more effective ones? Why has an otherwise effective partnership system found it so hard to solve Ireland's childcare problem and to greatly improve training and lifelong learning? Indeed, a further question arises from both international research on OMC and Irish evaluations of the European employment and social inclusion strategies: would closer integration of the employment and social inclusion OMCs with national social partnership improve the visibility and effectiveness of the OMC? Our argument is that while each of these questions touches on significant aspect of Irish experience, they beg further questions of both the OMC and the Irish partners.

1. Relation of the OMC to National Social Concertation

In the emerging literature, we can identify three perspectives on the relation of national social pacts to the OMC. The first is that national pacts and the OMC have conflicting logics. This view derives from the idea that national social pacts are a form of "competitive corporatism" in which national actors seek to enhance *national* employment and economic prosperity in ways that damage other Member States. By contrast, the OMC is intended to achieve some convergence of national policies. Thus, the "competitive" element of national pacts conflicts with the "co-operative" or "co-ordinated" element of the OMC.

A second perspective is that the national social pacts and the OMC are more or less unconnected. Some argue that the OMC was initially based on, and still depends on, agreement on a dominant policy doctrine or orthodoxy, while the national pacts reflect divergent policy doctrines and approaches (Hodson and Maher, 2001). In addition, the process of negotiating a national pact – and indeed the content of it – can be seen as separate from the process of formulating a National Action Plan within the OMC.

A third perspective is that the process and content of national social pacts and the OMC are complementary. Each involves the engagement of a similar set of social actors – employers, unions and NGOs in the community and voluntary sector – in a process of policy dialogue with government. While the national pacts pursue a co-ordinated combination of macroeconomic policy, welfare reform and structural adjustment, the OMC has likewise extended beyond macroeconomic policy to encompass social protection and a range of structural adjustments. A stronger version of this third perspective would suggest that the national social pacts and OMC are, or can be, mutually reinforcing. If so, countries that adopted social concertation in the 1990s would find that the OMC continues and enhances that process. Conversely, participation in the OMC – especially the involvement of social actors in the formulation of National Action Plans – might increase the chance of successful social concertation where it does not exist.

In our view, Irish experience tends to support the third of these perspectives, at least the proposition that national social pacts and the OMC are complementary. As noted in the introductory section, Irish partnership and policy anticipated significant aspects of the European employment and social inclusion strategies and the OMC. But it is harder to defend the idea that the processes have yet become mutually reinforcing. Indeed, there is a real sense in which the three perspectives discussed in the literature, and summarised above, are insufficient to reveal the key issue concerning both OMC and national social pacts and the relationship between them: are they mechanisms of learning?

We have found a significant similarity between the OMC and Irish social partnership. This means that OMC has some of the strengths of Irish partnership. But also that it is likely to have its weaknesses (O'Donnell, 2001). Among these is the relatively centralised nature of partnership, which is a reflection of the centralised nature of the Irish public system. The result has tended to be an over-proliferation of national-level committees and working groups, many of which could do limited problem solving because they were too far from the problem that they were seeking to solve. In addition, partnership sometimes becomes a veto on change, especially in the public sector. The substantive social and economic tasks facing Ireland – in addressing social exclusion, improving social services, creating effective systems of childcare and training, investing in and regulating the utilities and networked sectors and improving physical planning and infrastructure – pose major organisational challenges (NESC, 2003). If partnership is not part of the solution to these, than it could be cast as part of the problem. This suggests that the substantive, participatory and procedural similarities between OMC and national social pacts are less relevant than the question of whether each is an effective mechanism for learning and problem solving. We need to evaluate the participatory routines of both OMC and national social concentration using our knowledge of learning (Rodrigues, 2001; Trubek and Mosher, 2003).

There is increasing international discussion of learning mechanisms promoting collective action towards best practice. Cohen and Sabel (2003) hypothesise that the OMC represents a key instrument for such a process in the EU. It preserves national diversity, yet reveals the defects of parochial solutions and provides best models to be emulated. It does this by widening participation in decision-making within and between governments. The wider organisational literature identifies a number of governance mechanisms that promote learning and innovation (Sabel, 1994; Easterby-Smith *et al.*, 2000). These include: mechanisms that destabilise existing understandings; bring together people with diverse viewpoints in settings that require sustained deliberation about problem-solving; facilitate erosion of boundaries between both policy domains and stakeholders; reconfigure policy networks; encourage decentralised experimentation; produce information on innovation; require sharing of good practice and experimental results; encourage actors to compare results with those of the best performers in any area and oblige actors collectively to redefine objectives and policies (Trubek and Mosher, 2003).

While significant elements of learning are evident in Irish policy and partnership over the period from 1987 to the present, there is evidence that problem-solving has sometimes been marginalised and replaced with a old-style bargaining and stand-offs. Some of this is evident in policy areas central to the OMCs on employment and social inclusion. Consequently, the open method of co-ordination challenges partnership to live up to its best deliberative standards, as we discuss further below.

2. Closer Integration of OMC and Social Partnership?

These arguments clearly have implications for the recommendation, found in many national studies of the OMC, for greater participation of the social partners and civil society in the Lisbon process. In the Irish case, this idea takes the form of the proposal that the OMC on employment and social inclusion be fused with the social partnership process. In addition, some argue that each process should be linked more closely with resource allocation in the budgetary process.

While closer alignment of the European employment and social inclusion strategies with existing partnership mechanisms is probably desirable in principle, its advantages are clearly dependent on the effectiveness of these domestic policy mechanisms. If these mechanisms were to be ineffective, over-centralised, characterised by bargaining more than problem solving, insufficiently outcome-orientated or captured, then aligning the OMC with them would be unlikely to invigorate either the national or the European process.

In this regard, two further conclusions and recommendations in the earlier formal impact evaluation are worthy of note. First, Murphy argued that within a modified EES process it would be possible to bring greater clarity to the role and responsibilities of the social partners in implementing specific aspects of the Plan. "The employer and employee representatives in particular can play a key role in helping to create climates that are supportive of initiatives to encourage greater in-company training and the adoption of more flexible work practices" (Murphy, 2002: 121). In our view, the most important way to clarify and extend the role of the social partners is to achieve a closer link between national-level partnership and the kind of local experimentation and action that is essential in training and other policy areas, such as the Skillnets and Workway initiatives.

Second, Murphy argued that if the NEAP process is to support the development and implementation of a more strategic and co-ordinated labour market policy approach, "authority to influence actions within all the relevant government departments and state agencies must be in-vested in the process. How this can best be done is not clear given the current system of departmental responsibility and lines of authority" (Murphy, 2002: 121). This observation resonates strongly with our view that Ireland's policy and partnership process faces significant chal-lenges. In its 2003 overview, the NESC observed that "the achievement of continuous improvement, supply-side infrastructures and services pose major organisational challenges to government, public agencies, business, trade unions and the community and voluntary sector" (NESC, 2003: 48).

We believe that there is a connection between the two challenges identified in Murphy's evaluation of the OMC: clarifying the role of the partners in OMC and reform of the public system. In our interviews on the OMC, one social partner observed that "people can be bought off with a few pet projects that avoid fundamental reform". This referred to the tendency to invent new iniatives, sometimes involving the social partners very actively, rather than change existing public programme and agencies. This certainly confirms the view that OMC asks important questions about Ireland's public system and that partnership needs to achieve more public sector reform. But our discussion suggests that there may be an important connection between what that partners called "pet projects" and "fundamental reform".

To some degree, we can distinguish between those policy areas and sectors which have displayed innovation and adopted an element of multi-level problem solving (housing management, homelessness, drug addiction, educational disadvantage, community development, aspects of training and others) from those which have been more resistant to reform and cling to high-level bargaining (for example, public transport and energy). The difference between them is sometimes indicated by the tendency to establish new programmes and entities rather than reform existing ones. But this is not an infallible guide. For example, in training and disability, the creation of new programmes and entities, involving new actors, is probably a necessary feature of a more effective problem solving approach. It is not just a reflection of a reluctance to reform the existing large scale public providers, although it is that in part. The real challenge seems to be to *combine* creation of new programmes and entities, that involve new actors in problem solving, with reform of large mainstream programmes and agencies. The first is necessary so that local actors find solutions to complex problems, and the second is necessary to monitor their progress and disseminate best practice across the system. Achieving this combination of local experimentation, creating new entities where necessary, and wider reform of the public system seems more important than seeking a closer link between national partnership negotiations and the annual budgetary process. While the latter is often seen as the key to strengthening both partnership and the open method of co-ordination, it may not be necessary and looks politically unlikely.

C. From Reviewing ALMPs to Examining Ireland's Social and Economic System

The second part of our argument is that that the review of labour market and social inclusion policies, required by the OMC, prompts Irish actors to a deeper examination of Ireland's social and economic system.

To see this, consider the two main criticisms of Ireland's active labour market policies, particularly of the CE. On the one hand, economists claim to reveal important limitations in Ireland's approach, especially in heavy reliance on a direct employment scheme like Community Employment. On the other hand, employers and trade unions are critical of the degree to which CE and other programmes directed at the long term unemployed and marginalised, absorbed the resources of Ireland's training agency, FÁS, thereby crowding out training for those in employment. There is force in both arguments, but neither can be given the last word.

The approach taken to employment and social inclusion policy in Ireland is more defensible, or at least understandable, than these criticisms allow. It is true that the CE and the Local Employment Service derived from an era in which managing high unemployment was a significant concern. It is true that the approaches taken sometimes reflected the ability of one or other social partner to defend schemes, institutions and practices in which they had a particular interest. But the approaches taken also reflected the reality of social exclusion, disadvantage and public service provision in Irish society.

The CE programme became a major source of employment, income and childcare for many lone parents with very limited educational attainment and for people with disabilities. While it began as a job creation programme, it became a source of provision of care and other local services that are chronically underprovided in the Irish welfare state. Some of the criticism of its failure to achieve progression to market employment gloss over the educational, training, childcare and social service deficits that both make CE attractive to its participants and essential to those who receive its services. If we turn to the second criticism reported above, we might say that Irish employers and unions are correct to want a better system of training for those in employment, but they could not have it because the extent of social disadvantage deflected FÁS from providing it. In the modern negotiated democracy, poverty and social exclusion do not "bite back" through rebellion of even party political mobilisation; they make themselves felt through the way they shape and sometimes dominate systems of public service provision, thereby preventing the mainstream population from acquiring what they want in training, health services, education and policing. While that effect is frustrating, it clearly has a democratic dimension and, furthermore, can prompt policy learning. This can be seen in a further intriguing twist to the story of CE and Irish training. It was partly because training of the unemployed and marginalised dominated the national training agency, FÁS, that employers, unions and government were prompted to create a somewhat parallel system of training, Skillnets. But they were thereby pushed in exactly the direction they needed to go. In an indirect way, they have the poor and the disadvantaged to thank for helping them in this critical piece of policy learning.

We can now see why looking beyond overall employment, to examine the effectiveness of Ireland's ALMPs and social policies prompts an examination of the wider economic and social reality. That reality is one in which a remarkable employment miracle and a dramatic reduction in the unemployment rate have coincided with a much more modest reduction in the benefit dependency rate and related social problems. Indeed, the continued high rates of benefit dependency are not explained by a large child cohort (as they would have been a few decades ago), nor by a large elderly population (as they might be in much of the EU), but by relatively high rates of non-participation in working age, especially among women with low levels of education. This, in turn, prompts wider questions about the nature and direction of Ireland's overall welfare state and its place within the Irish economic and social model.

Thus, many of the well-criticised weaknesses of Ireland's labour market policies actually arise from the limits of Ireland's employment miracle and the fact that it does not yet have a welfare, education and training system capable of supporting its aspiration of a high-participation, high-skilled, high-performance economy. The OMC in employment and social inclusion are prompting the Irish partners and government to look critically at the Irish "model" of economy, society and policy.

It seems that to adequately describe what the OMC means, and can mean, for Ireland, we require a more holistic understanding of Ireland's evolving social and economic system. What kind of welfare state is emerging from the changes created by social partnership and economic change? How should we characterise Ireland's open learning process, as shaped by social partnership and increasing engagement with the EU? In order to answer these questions, Ireland needs to describe to itself, and to the other Member States, the combination of substantive, procedural and institutional innovation undertaken by its partnership system since 1987. Ironically, a country that we described in our opening paragraph as undertaking a kind of OMC since 1987, has not yet fully applied to itself the OMC proposed by its European partners.

In order to address these wider questions about the nature and direction of Ireland's overall welfare state and its place within the Irish economic and social model, it seems necessary to widen the range of actors that participate in the OMC. In particular, it seems necessary to involve those agencies whose task is to analyse Ireland's long term economic and social development and to frame the evolution of the social partnership system. Among these are the National Economic and Social Council, the National Centre for Partnership and Performance (NCPP), the National Economic and Social Forum (NESF) and the industrial development body, Forfás.

In its last strategic overview, NESC argued that the major challenge is to explore how Ireland "networked developmental state", to use the term coined by O'Riain (2004), requires a "developmental welfare state" that is both more effective and more closely linked to the economy At the same time, it sketched the possibility a more decentralised public system, with a greater focus on outcomes, and a "new centre in public administration" that can monitor outcomes, benchmark progress and support continuous improvement (NESC, 2003).

The NESC is currently exploring in more depth its earlier sketch of a developmental welfare state. This involves a revised account of the evolution of the Irish welfare state and a redescription of the serious social deficits that remain despite Ireland's remarkable economic progress. This may allow a recasting of the social debate, in a way that balances a focus on income transfers with increased recognition of the role of services in providing protection against risks and of the important place that activist social policy initiatives in achieving reform. This can, in turn allow a reconceptualisation of the four themes that dominate the community and voluntary sector's criticism: targets, spending commitments, proofing and a "rights-based approach". Most important of all, it may allow a recasting of the social debate in a way that does not distinguish between the economic and the social and can, therefore, build consensus – across the social partners and government – on the need to urgently and radically address the social deficits.

References

Adshead, M. (2002), *Developing European Regions? Comparative Governance, Policy Networks and European Integration*, Ashgate Publishing Company, Aldershot.

Barrett, A., Whelan, C. and Sexton, J. J. (2001), "'Employability' and Its Relevance for the Management of the Live Register", *Policy Research Series*, No.40, The Economic Social Research Institute, Dublin.

CEC (1998), *Employment Policies in the EU and in the Member States – Joint Report 1997*, Office for Official Publications of the European Communities, Luxembourg.

CEC (1999), *Employment Policies in the EU and in the Member States – Joint Report 1998*, Office for Official Publications of the European Communities, Luxembourg.

CEC (2000), *Employment Policies in the EU and in the Member States – Joint Report 1999*, Office for Official Publications of the European Communities, Luxembourg.

CEC (2001a), *Employment Policies in the EU and in the Member States – Joint Report 2000*, Office for Official Publications of the European Communities, Luxembourg.

CEC (2001b), Communication from the Commission "Draft Joint Report on Social Inclusion", COM (2001) 565 final of 10 October 2001 (http://europa. eu.int/eur-lex/en/com/pdf/2001/com2001_0565en01.pdf).

CEC (2002a), *Employment Policies in the EU and in the Member States – Joint Report 2001*, Office for Official Publications of the European Communities, Luxembourg.

CEC (2002b), Communication from the Commission "Draft Joint Employment Report 2002", COM (2002) 621 final of 13 November 2002 (http://europa. eu.int/eur-lex/en/com/rpt/2002/com2002_0621en01.pdf).

CEC (2003), *Employment Policies in the EU and in the Member States – Joint Report 2002*, Office for Official Publications of the European Communities, Luxembourg.

CEC and Council of the European Union (2004), Joint Report by the Commission and the Council on Social Inclusion, Document 7101/04, Brussels, 5 March 2004 (http://europa.eu.int/comm/employment_social/soc-prot/soc-incl/final_joint_inclusion_report_2003_en.pdf).

Cohen, J. and Sabel, C. F. (2003), "Sovereignty and Solidarity: EU and US", in Zeitlin, J. and Trubek, D. M. (eds.), *Governing Work and Welfare in a New Economy – European and American Experiments*, Oxford University Press, Oxford, pp.345-375.

CPA (2000), *Planning for a More Inclusive Society – An Initial Assessment of the National Anti-poverty Strategy*, Combat Poverty Agency, Dublin.

Corcoran, T. (2002), "Retrospective Analysis of Referral under the Employment Action Plan", FÁS – Training and Employment Authority, Dublin.

Daly, M. (2003), First Background Report on Ireland available at http://europa.eu.int/comm/employment_social/soc-prot/studies/ireland_1st_report_final_en.pdf

Deloitte and Touche (1998), "Review of Community Employment Programme", *Final Report*, available at www.entemp.ie.

Denny, K., Harmon, C. and O'Connell, P. J. (2000), "Investing in People: The Labour Market Impact of Human Resource Interventions Funded under the 1994-1999 Community Support Framework in Ireland", *Policy Research Series*, No.38, The Economic and Social Research Institute, Dublin.

DSCFA (2001), *National Action Plan against Poverty and Social Exclusion*, Department of Social, Community and Family Affairs, Dublin.

DSCFA (2003), *National Action Plan against Poverty and Social Exclusion 2003-2005*, Department of Social, Community and Family Affairs, Dublin (http://portal.welfare.ie/index.xml).

EAPN (2002), "Making a Decisive Impact on Poverty and Social Exclusion?", A Progress Report on the European Strategy on Social Inclusion, European Anti-poverty Network, Brussels.

EAPN Ireland (2003a), "Submission on the National Action Plan against Poverty and Social Exclusion", European Anti-poverty Network, Ireland, Dublin.

EAPN Ireland (2003b), "First Evaluation of the 2003-2005 National Action Plan against Poverty and Social Exclusion", European Anti-poverty Network, Ireland, Dublin.

Easterby-Smith, M., Crossan, M. and Nicolini, D. (2000), "Organizational Learning: Debates Past, Present and Future", *Journal of Management Studies*, Vol.37, No.6, pp.783-796.

FÁS (2002), *The Irish Labour Market Review: 2002*, FÁS – Training and Employment Authority, Dublin.

Forfás (1997), *Initial Review of the Local Employment Service*, Forfás, Dublin.

Geddes, M. (1998), *Local Partnership: A Successful Strategy for Social Cohesion?*, European Foundation for the Improvement of Living and Working Conditions, Dublin.

Goodbody Economic Consultants (1999), *A Report on the Impact of the Local Urban and Rural Development Programme on Long Term Unemployment*, Goodbody Economic Consultants, Dublin.

Hegarty, D. and Honohan, P. (1998), "Mid-term Evaluation of CSF for Ireland", Paper prepared for European Conference on Evaluation Practices in the Field of Structural Policies in Seville, March 1998.

Hodson, D. and Maher, I. (2001), "The Open Method as a New Mode of Governance: The Case of Soft Economic Policy Co-ordination", *Journal of Common Market Studies*, Vol.39, No.4, pp.719-746.

Indecon (2002), *Review of Active Labour Market Programmes*, Department of Enterprise, Trade and Employment and Indecon International Economic Consultants, Dublin.

Lynch, B. (2002), National Report for Ireland (2nd Round) (www.govecor.org).

Lynch, B. (2003), National Report for Ireland (3rd Round) (www.govecor.org).

Lynch, B. (2004), National Report for Ireland (4th Round) (www.govecor.org).

McAleese, D. (2000), "Twenty-five Years 'A Growing'", in O'Donnell, R. (ed.), *Europe: The Irish Experience*, Institute of European Affairs, Dublin, pp.79-110.

Murphy, C. (2002), "Assessment of the Policy-making Process", in O'Connell, P. J. *et al.* (eds.), *Impact Evaluation of the European Employment Strategy in Ireland*, Department of Enterprise, Trade and Employment and ESRI, Dublin, pp.103-121.

NESC (1990), "Strategies for the Nineties: Economic Stability and Structural Change", *Report*, No.89, National Economic and Social Council, Dublin.

NESC (1996), "Strategy into the 21st Century", *Report*, No.99, National Economic Social Council, Dublin.

NESC (1999), "Opportunities, Challenges and Capacities for Choice", *Report*, No.104, National Economic and Social Council, Dublin.

NESC (2001), "Review of the Poverty Proofing Process", *Report*, No.106, National Economic and Social Council, Dublin.

NESC (2002a), The Open Method of Coordination and Social Concertation, paper presented at the annual meeting of the Chairpersons and Secretaries General of the Economic and Social Councils of the Member States of the European Union and the European Economic Goodbody Economic Consultants (2001), *Review of the National Anti-poverty Strategy: Framework Document*, Goodbody Economic Consultants, Dublin.

NESC (2002b), "An Investment in Quality: Services, Inclusion and Enterprise, Overview, Conclusions and Recommendations", *Report*, No.110, National Economic and Social Council, Dublin.

NESC (2003), "A Strategy for Quality: Services, Inclusion and Enterprise", *Report*, No.111, National Economic Social Council, Dublin.

NESF (1994), "Ending Long-Term Unemployment", *Forum Report*, No.4, National Economic Social Forum, Dublin.

NESF (1999), "Local Development Issues", *NESF Opinion*, No.7, National Economic and Social Forum, Dublin.

NESF (2000), "Enhancing the Effectiveness of the Local Employment Service", *Forum Report*, No.17, National Economic and Social Forum, Dublin.

NESF (2003), "NAPS Social Inclusion Forum: Report of Inaugural Meeting, January", National Economic and Social Forum, Dublin.

Nolan, B., O'Connell, P. J. and Whelan, C. T. (2000), *Bust to Boom? The Irish Experience of Growth and Inequality*, Institute of Public Administration, Dublin.

O'Connell, P. and McGinnity, F. (1997), *Working Schemes? Active Labour Market Policy in Ireland*, Aldershot, Ashgate.

O'Connell, P., Callan, T., Keeney, M., Russell, H., Gannon, B., Hughes, G. and Murphy, C. B. (2002), *Impact Evaluation of the European Employment Strategy in Ireland*, Department of Enterprise, Trade and Employment and ESRI, Dublin.

O'Connell, P. J. (2002), "Employability: Trends in Employment and Unemployment: The Impact of Activation Measures Unemployment Transitions", in O'Connell, P. J. *et. al.* (eds.), *Impact Evaluation of the European Employment Strategy in Ireland*, Department of Enterprise, Trade and Employment and ESRI, Dublin, pp.10-30.

O'Donnell, R. (2000), "The New Ireland in the New Europe", in O'Donnell, R. (ed.), *Europe: The Irish Experience*, Institute of European Affairs, Dublin, pp.

O'Donnell, R. (2001), "The Future of Social Partnership in Ireland", *Discussion paper*, National Competitiveness Council, May 2001 (www.forfas.ie/ncc/pdfs/discussion_social_may01.pdf).

O'Donnell, R. and O'Reardon, C. (1997), "Ireland's Experiment in Social Partnership 1987-1996", in Fajertag, G. and Pochet, P. (eds.), *Social Pacts in Europe*, European Trade Union Institute and Observatoire social européen, Brussels, pp.79-95.

O'Donnell, R. and O'Reardon, C. (2000), "Social Partnership in Ireland's Economic Transformation", in Fajertag, G. and Pochet, P. (eds.), *Social Pacts in Europe – New Dynamics*, European Trade Union Institute and Observatoire social européen, Brussels, pp.237-256.

O'Riain, S. (2004), *The Politics of High-tech Growth: Developmental Network States in the Global Economy*, Cambridge University Press, Cambridge.

OECD (2001), *Local Partnerships for Better Local Governance*, Organisation for Economic Co-operation and Development, Paris.

Rodrigues, M. J. (2001), "The Open Method of Co-ordination as a New Governance Tool", *Europa/Europe*, Special Issue, No.2-3, Fondazione Istituto Gramsci, Rome, pp.96-107.

Rubery, J. (2002), "Gender Mainstreaming and Gender Equality in the EU: The Impact of the EU Employment Strategy", *Industrial Relations Journal*, Vol.33, No.5, pp.500-522.

Russell, H., Smyth, E., Lyons, M. and O'Connell, P. J. (2002), *"Getting out of the House": Women Returning to Employment, Education and Training*, Liffey Press in association with the ESRI, Dublin.

Sabel, C. F. (1994), "Learning by Monitoring: The Institutions of Economic Development" in Rodwin, L. and Schon, D. (eds.), *Rethinking the Development Experience. Essays Provoked by the Work of Albert O. Hirschman*, The Brookings Institution, Washington D.C., pp.231-274.

Sabel, C. F. (1996), *Ireland: Local Development and Social Innovation*, Organisation for Economic Co-operation and Development, Paris.

Skillnets (2004), *Skillnets Network Profiles and Directory, 2002-2005*, Skillnets Ltd, Dublin.

Sweeney, J. and O'Donnell, R. (2003), "The Challenge of Linking Society and Economy in Ireland's Flexible Developmental State", paper presented at the Society for Advancement of Socio-Economics, Aix-en-Provence (France), June 2003.

Trubek, D. and Mosher, J. (2003), "New Governance, Employment Policy, and the European Social Model", in Zeitlin, J. and Trubek, D. (eds.), *Governing Work and Welfare in a New Economy: European and American Perspectives*, Oxford University Press, Oxford, pp.33-58.

Turok, I. (2001), "Innovation in Local Governance: the Irish Partnership Model", in OECD (ed.), *Local Partnerships for Better Local Governance*, Organisation for Economic Co-operation and Development, Paris, pp.135-173.

Walker, G. (2004), "Overview of the Community Employment Programme, 1984-2004", National Economic and Social Forum, Dublin, mimeo.

PART III

COMPARATIVE ASSESSMENTS

CHAPTER 10

Participation in the Open Method of Co-ordination

The Cases of Employment and Social Inclusion

Caroline DE LA PORTE & Philippe POCHET

Introduction[1]

The Open Method of Co-ordination (OMC) has generally been presented as a new form of governance, which differs from the traditional Community Method along various dimensions, including participation, our concern here[2]. Broad participation in the OMC is emphasised as a positive and desirable feature in the political rhetoric, as well as in the academic literature that has flourished since Lisbon (see the University of Wisconsin-Madison website http://eucenter.wisc.edu). In the document where the features of the OMC are defined as well as the Conclusions of the Lisbon European Council, there is an explicit reference to the need to include all concerned actors, from civil society to governmental actors, at different levels, from local to European, in a multi-level logic (Council of the European Union, 2000; European Council, 2000a: 10). This is confirmed by various academic and political agents supporting the OMC (Telò, 2002; Rodrigues, 2002). Participation is part of a broader governance agenda. Radaelli (2003: 45) underlines that participation "[…] is one dimension of the whole issue of accountability, democratisation and legitimacy of the new mode of governance".

In analysing the participation process, we consider decision-making in the OMC basically similar to the other processes at EU level. It is above all a process based on political bargaining, in which (relevant)

---

[1] We would like to thank David Natali and Jonathan Zeitlin for their very valuable comments.

[2] In this article we consider the European Employment Strategy as an OMC. Indeed, it is the benchmark for OMCs in other areas (European Council, 2000a).

actors seek to maximise their influence within the process on the basis of their politically-defined interests (de la Porte and Pochet, 2003). This does not mean that the political arena is devoid of contradictory interests within each Member State or within and between political parties or other organisations. Like other EU processes, there is room for manoeuvre for individual or collective political entrepreneurs to redefine the challenges and redesign the agenda. Concerning the political trade-off of the OMC we consider three dimensions that may but do not necessarily overlap. The first is a classic right/left divide; the second is a no less classic divide of more European integration *versus* more subsidiarity, and the third is a struggle between the economically and socially-oriented actors at both European (Ecofin and Social Affairs Councils) and national levels (Finance *versus* Social Affairs ministries) (see also Barbier, 2004).

To sum up, we consider the EES and the OMC as classic bargaining processes with some possibilities to develop a more deliberative dimension. These two dimensions are not (necessarily) conflicting or exclusive but could be also complementary.

In this chapter, we make a contextualised empirical analysis of participation/consultation practices in the OMC, rather than an analysis driven by a theoretical model derived from the academic literature. For more theoretically-driven analyses on participation in the OMC, see de la Porte and Nanz (2004) and Zeitlin (2002). Our main hypothesis is that (relevant) actors would variably be driven to become involved depending on three factors: a) their own political agenda, b) the specific policy area and c) how the OMC could be used (i.e. what added value) to influence the policy process compared to other channels.

For each area (employment and social inclusion), we first review the structural features of each process: we recall the mandate that launched each process, how it has developed and the link with European funding. We then briefly consider the recent changes to the processes, indicative of their political saliency. Secondly, we study the key actors. This analysis exposes how the policy processes are shaped. We begin to analyse first the institutional actors in their participatory dimension. Then we identify the key non-state actors in each process – social partners in the EES and NGOs in social inclusion – and analyse how they participate at European and at national level.

In the conclusion, we draw on our findings to plead for a more nuanced approach to participation in the OMC from a normative perspective – i.e the desirability of participation of the relevant actors needs to be contextualised.

I. European Employment Strategy (EES)

In the area of employment, social partners in the national context are the main relevant actors and are concerned above all with issues related to labour market (and employment) policy. However, the agenda of the EES sidesteps the main issues with which social partners are concerned: the EES is concerned mainly with increasing the EU employment rate, while social partners are mainly concerned with wage policies. In labour market and employment policy, social partners have well-rooted sources of legitimacy: they are integrated in the national decision-making process through bi- or tri-partite bargaining (Léonard, 2001). They thus would have a weak incentive to seek new sources of legitimacy from the European level, but would be likely to use it as another means of advancing the issues on their agenda if it would provide an element of added value. If it would prove to be qualitatively weak – i.e. they do not succeed in integrating their concerns on the agenda – then their incentive to participate would weaken. For the three factors of our hypothesis, the policy area is generally relevant, the agenda is intermediate, and the need for a source of legitimacy is weak. We would thus expect social partner participation to be weak to intermediate.

In this part, we first present the features of the EES and the major changes undertaken in 2003, that have increased its political status (see de la Porte and Pochet, 2004), which would thus be likely to increase the social partners' incentive to get involved. We also analyse the development of the link with the ESF, which is important in this context due to structurally incorporated features of participation in its partnership approach. Now there is an attempt to link the local and regional actors with the European EES perspective, partially through the ESF, that provides funding for the development of the Employment Strategy at the local level.

A. Structural Features of the Process and Recent Developments

1. EES and its Restructuration

The European Employment Strategy (EES) was launched in 1997. The steps involved in the process are defined in the Employment Chapter of the Amsterdam Treaty. Four policy "pillars" defined the strategy from 1997 to 2002 – employability, adaptability, entrepreneurship and equal opportunities. Throughout these five years, it developed both quantitatively and qualitatively, in particular due to the political initiatives of the European Commission and the rotating Presidency agendas (see de la Porte and Pochet, 2002). After the five-year evaluation of the strategy, significant changes were introduced. The first set of changes was introduced by the existing policy community around EMCO ensuring the continuity of the EES; the second set of changes was introduced by the *ad hoc* European Employment Task Force.

The EES was re-structured in a context where right-wing governments dominated the political landscape affecting employment priorities (Manow *et al.*, 2004). In this context, most governments wanted a stronger link between economic growth and the employment strategy. At the same time different governments wanted a stronger and clearer political message. Even Social Democratic governments, such as the Schroeder government in Germany, wanted to have a stronger reform message from EU[3].

Concerning the first set of changes, driven by the policy community dealing with the day-to-day policy-making process of the EES, three overarching objectives – to achieve full employment, to raise quality and productivity and work and to promote cohesion and inclusive labour markets (CEC, 2003a) – replaced the four "pillars". The guidelines were reduced in number from more than twenty to ten and were also rendered less complex, and linked more closely politically, and in terms of timing, to the Broad Economic Policy Guidelines (BEPG) that set out the economic policy of the Union. This has resulted in an increase in the political status of the EES, at least at the level of the European Council (Pochet, 2004a; introduction by Zeitlin in this volume).

Concerning the second set of changes, these were introduced by the ad-hoc Wim Kok Group, set up by the European Council in 2003 on the formal request of eight Member States. Led by Wim Kok, the former Dutch Prime Minister, another prominent member of the group was Maria Rodrigues, one of the key architects of the OMC and the Lisbon Strategy. Four members were academic experts, one representative from an employers' association, and one from industry (CEO of the Beneteau company). DG Employment of the European Commission provided the Secretariat of the Task Force, while the DG for Economic and Financial Affairs was granted an observer position. The group aimed to increase the political relevance of the EES in Member States and to strengthen its link with competitiveness.

The mandate of the Task Force was to focus on the reasons for Europe's low growth in employment and productivity. Its report, titled "Jobs, Jobs, Jobs: Creating More Employment in Europe" (Kok *et al.*, 2003), focussed essentially, but not exclusively, around the quantitative side of employment policy. The three main policy objectives put forward in the report were to increase adaptability of workers and enter-

---

[3]   It should be remembered that most of the *Länder*, on the basis of the principle of subsidiarity, were more concerned about Europe meddling with their affairs and showed some suspicion about the OMC (Büchs and Friedrich in this volume).

prises, to attract more people to the labour market and to invest more and more effectively in human capital. The fourth recommendation was for improved implementation through better governance. These object-tives have to a great extent superseded the objectives put forward by the policy community around EMCO, and structure the whole process: the peer review programme, and importantly, the recommenddations made to the individual countries. On its side, the Commission used the Kok Report to formulate sharper recommendations to the Member States (Tholoniat interview, June 2004).

In essence these changes and the streamlining process between the BEPG and the EES mean that the EES has become more coherent in terms of its policy message, in order to impact the national agenda of reform. Jelle Visser (2004: 7) summarises the underlying lessons of the Kok Report in two points.

> Firstly, for those governments intent on reforming labour markets and social protection system, but meeting opposition at home, the message from Europe cannot be strong enough. [...] Secondly, any process of "open coor-dination", exactly because of its openness and, hence, its ambiguity, needs a strong political engine for it to work as more than a free and non-committing process of deliberation over problem and solutions.

2. Links between the EES and the ESF

This section is devoted to underlining briefly the role of the Euro-pean Social Fund (ESF), in conjunction with the EES. This is an impor-tant point as on the one hand the ESF could influence the behaviour and the strategy of actors involved in the EES and on the other the ESF has a long tradition of broad partnership, which could be a reference point for the EES.

The objectives of the European Social Fund partially overlap with those of the EES. However, there is no direct reference to the EES in the Treaty provisions defining the ESF. Article 146 (in Title XI, Chapter 2) that provides the legal mandate for the ESF, indicates that its overall aim is to "improve employment opportunities for workers in the internal market and to contribute thereby to raising the standard of living" (the IGC did not change this article). At the level of secondary sources of legislation, the link is more direct in that the ESF regulation tasks every Member State to demonstrate that the ESF priorities are consistent with the NAP (Hartwig, 2004). EES documents consistently emphasise the linkage with the ESF in terms of financial support for the implementa-tion of the strategy. Even if the legal link remains weak, there has been some political will, essentially driven by the European Commission, to adapt the European Social Fund to the objectives of the EES. From 1999 onwards, the aims of the ESF became more explicitly oriented to support the EES. It also indicated that parallel to this the ESF shifted in character, from a training programme to a policy-oriented instrument, partly to do with the link with the EES. The Commission has recently presented its proposals for the next structural funds regulations (2006-2013) in July 2004. If the Commission proposal is accepted, then the link between the ESF and the EES should be enhanced.

The main financial commitment for the EES is for activation policies (60% – 34 billion euros). There is evidence of a shift towards preventive action in individual programmes of the ESF. Eight billion euros of the ESF is associated with the promotion of entrepreneurship, eleven billion for adaptability (in particular lifelong learning), and around four billion for equal opportunities (CEC, 2001a). In the preparation phase of the national documents for the EES and ESF, there is co-operation among actors in most countries, most often initiated by the actors involved in the ESF.

Concerning participation, the ESF structurally incorporates participation in its administration and implementation[4], in contrast to the EES, which is managed by the ministerial department in charge of national employment policy. Although this "principle of partnership" has been conceived as a major element of the Structural Funds system, the extent to which it is applied is determined by the particular political and administrative context of each individual Member State, and their tradition of dialogue between levels of government and with the other partners (Nauerz, 2004: 37). In general, national governments have been reluctant to support stronger involvement of a wider range of regional and local actors, while this has been pushed by the European Commission (Nauerz, 2004: 46; Bollen, 2001: 21). There are significant differences concerning the quality of participation in the different stages of the programme: preparations of the development plan, implementation and monitoring. Concerning development, there has been a progressive increase, but the key political choices are still predominantly made by the governmental authorities, due partly to their co-financing role (Bollen, 2001: 22-23; Nauerz, 2004: 35). In the implementation phase, there has generally been a wide range of participants, although these vary greatly in the different projects and countries (Bollen, 2001: 23). Monitoring committees have a wide-ranging set of participants (between 50 and 70),

---

[4] See for example the article 8 which states "In designating the most representative partnership at national, regional, local and other level, the Member State shall create a wide and effective association with all the relevant bodies [...]" (Council of the European Union, 1999: article 8). The ESF is managed by the Commission and a Committee presided over by a Member of the Commission and composed of representatives of governments, trade unions and employers organisations (article 147). At European level, these actors are different from those actors involved in the EES.

who include (local level) social partners and other non-governmental organisations. This broad participation has adversely affected the effectiveness of the committees (Bollen, 2001: 23-24). Evidence in the German case suggests that the monitoring committees fulfil their role merely as a formality (Nauerz, 2004: 35-36).

The European Commission itself has progressively obtained more direct decision-making power, specifically under a 40-million euro budget line for "innovative" projects, and pilots concerning labour markets, employment and vocational training (Nauerz, 2004: 38-39). Many of the projects aimed to establish a local action plan, on the basis of the objectives of the EES (Nauerz, 2004: 40). In order to complete the action carried out within the ESF context, the Commission has adopted in July 2004 a new programme entitled "Progress" which will cover five areas: employment, social protection and inclusion, working conditions, the fight against discrimination and diversity, and gender equality. The Commission proposes to allocate to it a budget of a little over 600 million euros in seven years.

To sum up, the EES has thus been politicised at European and national levels, while the linkages between the ESF and the EES are weak. But the ongoing reform of the structural funds should improve the coherence between EES and ESF action, which could be particularly beneficial to the new Member States.

B. Main Actors

Our analysis of participation in the EES proceeds in two stages. The first concerns the formal institutions with policy-making power – governmental and parliamentary institutions at both European and national levels. The second concerns the participation of the non state actors, mainly social partners, also at both European and national levels.

1. Formal Institutions

This section first presents the main actors involved at European and national levels, and then how the regional and local level involvement is developing.

a) European and National Levels

In the EES, the Employment and Social Affairs Council and European Commission are key decision-makers. As for the European Parliament (EP), up to now its role has been minor. According to the Employment Title of the Amsterdam Treaty, the EP has to be consulted on the EES, but in practice its role was marginalised during the first five years, due among other reasons to the lack of time to prepare positions or opinions that could be influential (European Parliament, 2003). The changed timetable of the EES should provide the EP the opportunity to be involved more closely by gaining additional time to prepare its opinion for the June European Council, where the EES is discussed (CEC, 2002a).

In essence, then, key decisions on the guidelines, and on where to include the quantitative benchmarks (and which ones) are made in the Employment Committee (EMCO) by a mixture of Commission and Member State expertise and interests. EMCO – made up of two delegates per Member State as well as two members from the Commission – is the intermediate body where the national and EU levels intersect[5]. Its composition and mandate are set out in article 130 of the Amsterdam Treaty. The secretariat of EMCO consists of a "support team" physically located at the Commission and *de facto* also providing expert advice to the Committee. EMCO has an advisory status in the co-ordination of employment and labour market policies among Member States. Its tasks include monitoring the employment situation and employment policies in the Member States and the Community; formulating opinions at the request of either the Council or the Commission or on its own initiative; and contributing to the preparation of the Council proceedings. According to article 130 "In fulfilling its mandate, the Committee shall consult management and labour".

While national parliamentary participation is not stipulated in the Treaty, it is important for legitimacy-conferring (as suggested in theories of democracy – see de la Porte and Nanz, 2004), as well as for bringing debate on policies under the EES into Member State arenas, at both the national and regional levels. The existing empirical evidence on parliamentary involvement in the EES suggests that it is unsatisfactory. For countries where parliament involvement is documented (United Kingdom, Ireland, Sweden, Belgium, the Netherlands)[6] participation is passive insofar as parliaments are informed. There is, crucially, no active debate on the issues of the EES NAP process that would aim for the parliament actually to feed into the process. A qualitative improvement in the participation of the parliament has been pushed by the Commission and also by the Kok Group (Kok *et al.*, 2003 and 2004). The European Parliament has suggested, to empower national parliaments, that the NAP should be presented as a bill for adoption in na-

---

[5] Jobelius (2003: 25) has characterised the EMCO as a kind of "deliberative institution" between the Commission and the Member States, driven dominantly by interest-driven bargaining. First hand sources of information confirm this interpretation, while others (Jacobsson and Vifell, 2005) suggest that open-ended deliberation also plays a role in defining the political objectives of the process.

[6] This is drawn from the 3rd and 4th round of national reports of the Govecor project (www.govecor.org).

tional parliaments. It also suggests that the EP should be more closely involved, through co-decision.

b) Regional and Local Levels

In the EES itself, the attention accorded to regional and local level actors increased considerably since Lisbon (Pochet, 2003). In line with its long-standing stance calling for broader involvement of relevant actors in the EES, the EP, too, supports broader participation by local actors in the EES (European Parliament, 2003).

Even if in many Member States, the local and regional authorities are responsible for areas linked to the EES, national governments have been reluctant to open the process to their subnational fellows. During the first years of the EES, regional and local stakeholders often knew little or nothing about the EES (for example on Denmark and Sweden, see Jacobsson and Schmid, 2002). Since 2000 in particular, actors at this level have been mobilised more (see conference of Committee of the Regions, 2002). There are some examples of local level actors using the EES as a vehicle to support their political agenda. The Flemish region in Belgium adopted a regional employment plan in line with the EES. In Italy, the action of regions in employment policies is uneven. Some began prior to the EES, some developed Regional Action Plans (RAPs) or analogous documents afterwards. Where the RAPs have been drawn up, their real political value – i.e. symbolic *versus* genuine political document – varies considerably from one region to another (Coordinamento delle regioni e province autonome per il lavoro e la formazione professionale, 2002) (see also chapter by Ferrera and Sacchi in this volume)[7]. A local government in Spain adopted the European guidelines to re-organise its local employment policy (López-Santana, 2004). In this volume Jacobsson shows how regional and local authorities are involved in Sweden. Büchs and Friedrich (in this volume) and Nauerz (2004) have analysed the extent of involvement of local level actors in Germany, with mixed results. The EES has thus been used instrumentally for local and regional level development, but the channels for local actors to actually influence the European level are thin.

The Commission has an ambiguous position with regard to regions and local governments.

At the beginning the Commission conceived its involvement mainly in terms of a top-down approach: the involvement of local actors was not seen as a process enabling new problems to come to the surface or highlighting areas where national plans are inappropriate, or indeed making it possible to use indicators more relevant to local circum-

---

[7]   Special thanks to Stefano Sacchi for this insight.

stances. The aim of their involvement was to increase the dissemination of the ideas and measures contained in the national plans. Local actors were expected to draw on the NAPs; Community, national and regional authorities were expected to keep local actors informed and ensure their involvement in the NAPs (CEC, 2001b: 9).

Based on this communication, the Commission has nevertheless taken initiatives to develop a more genuine involvement of local-level actors. Together with European-level representatives of regional and local actors like the Committee of the Regions, the Council of European Municipalities and Regions and Eurocities, the Commission has been pushing for the involvement of local and regional authorities in all stages of the process: formulation, implementation and dissemination. However, within the Employment Committee, the Member States have been resistant to such an increase in involvement, particularly concerning the formulation of the guidelines (Kristensen and Zeitlin, 2004: 288-9).

The regional and local actors have no legal Treaty-derived mandate to participate in the EES and the Commission has to take that into account. This could explain why the indicators working group (national delegates) of the Employment Committee has only proposed one indicator for the subnational level, which seeks to measure regional disparities. The European Court of Auditors has criticised the lack of data on local employment initiatives in the context of the EES (Groupe Bernard Brunhes Consultants and Economix, 2003). One initiative, contracted to an external consultant, seeks to foster the local dimension, including exchanging good practice (IDELE project) and an attempt to create specific regional indicators (Groupe Bernard Brunhes Consultants and Economix, 2003). In 2005 the Commission intend to develop a "European network of networks for local employment" (for an overview of the recent and future activities, see CEC, 2004b). The objective is to initiate a more bottom-up approach (on the bottom-up approach, see de la Porte *et al.*, 2001).

To sum up, there is a line of tension between a top-down approach through the employment guidelines and a more bottom-up approach, which seeks to guide the local and regional level actors in the view of these objectives, while also leaving them some degree of autonomy. There is more involvement of some of local and regional actors, but aside data from the Commission and national case studies, including those in this volume, there is no comparative information on the nature of their involvement.

2. Non-state Actors in the EES

This section first analyses the incentive structure for social partner participation, i.e which legal and political incentives have been put forward through the EES to enhance social partner participation. It secondly analyses European social partner participation and thirdly national social partner participation.

a) Incentive Structure for Social Partner Participation

A good deal of prominence has been given to participation and involvement of the social partners in the EES, at European and national levels. The social partners were attributed a Treaty-based mandate for participating in the Strategy, albeit rather vague. According to Article 130 EC, the Employment Committee, in fulfilling its mandate shall consult management and labour. Although not explicitly mentioned, this means the social partner organisations at European level. The main reference to national level social partner involvement in the Treaty is in article 126, paragraph 2, which states that "Member States, *having regard to national practices related to the responsibilities of management and labour*, shall regard promoting employment as a matter of common concern" (our emphasis in italics). Article 128.3, which asks the Member States to provide the Council and the Commission with an annual report, does not make any reference to the role of social partners in drafting the NAPs (Smismans, 2004).

As a complement to the legal incentives set out in the Treaty, the political incentives, pushed by the European Commission, have been prominent since Luxembourg. The Council conclusions state that "[...] the social partners at all levels will be involved in all stages of this approach and will have their contribution to make to the implementation of the "guidelines". Regular contact with the Council will properly pave the way for the six-monthly meeting of the social partners with a troika at the level of Heads of State or Government and the Commission before the European Council meeting (European Council, 1997). For the annual Spring Summit, instilled as an important part of the process since Lisbon, European level social partners formulate their position at a Tripartite Social Summit preceding the Summit itself (the IGC confirmed this formal meeting in the treaty, article 48).

The social partners have especially been encouraged to participate in issues related to work organisation, from decision-making to implementation. Like promotion of the partnership principle in the Structural Funds, the Commission is behind many incentives to encourage social partner participation. This is evident in various Commission communications on the subject. Concerning the performance of social partners, the Commission assesses that the social partners had difficulties using the incentives provided to them by the EES (CEC, 2002b: 15). The Commission has encouraged more genuine involvement and commitment of the social partners in different aspects of the EES. It calls for a reinforcement of the social partners' role throughout the whole OMC process, at a more political level, through contributions agreed to the broad policy guidelines that cover different aspects of the Lisbon agenda (CEC, 2002c: 15). The Commission also proposes that the social partners should prepare a position for each issue area of the Lisbon agenda (CEC, 2002b: 14). More specifically, the procedures for dialogue at technical and political level should be redefined in agreement with the Employment Committee and the Social Protection Committee, and the social partners should be fully involved in the preparation of these rules. This would increase the influence of the social partners in the actual decision-making process; so far, the proposals have not materialised.

To sum up, the participation falls short compared to the expectation of some strategic actors. For example, Allan Larsson, director general of DG Employment from 1995-2000, in charge of preparations under EES, has a severe judgment

[...] they should have played an independent role in their own systems. We designed a framework for the social partners to contribute significantly (instead of piecemeal contributions) to the strategy but they do not use it [...] I had hoped that the social partners could "reform themselves", take the guidelines and see what was for their competence, but the willingness lacked to get involved; the national stakes have remained dominant (interview done in December 2002 by Barbier and de la Porte published in Barbier, 2004).

b) European Level

At European level, the main social partners are the ETUC, UNICE and CEEP. The development of their position towards the EES will briefly be recounted here in the view of our hypotheses. The position of the EAPN, as a non-governmental actor that would like to get involved, will be examined as well.

The ETUC aims "to influence European legislation and policies by making direct representations to the various institutions (Commission, Parliament, Council), and by ensuring trade union participation in an extensive and multi-faceted consultation process with the European authorities, involving the Social Partners in areas such as employment, social affairs and macro-economic policy" (www.etuc.org). Along this line of reasoning, Ross (1995: 150) has argued that it "wanted more of everything in the social area" and also that it "[...] depended more on the Commission for support than on its national constituents". Similarly, Goetschy (1999: 119) has pointed to the fact that the "[...] long-term

ETUC strategy" was "to gain full integration in the inner circle of European institutions and recognition for its expertise and seriousness". Nevertheless, the main aim of ETUC was to create a layer of collective bargaining at European level and to foster negotiation with the employers. At the beginning they mainly saw the EES as a way to rebalance monetary integration (Jenson and Pochet, 2005) but they feared the soft law approach. As Trubek and Trubek show very clearly in their contribution to this book, ETUC shares the traditional vision of social Europe which also sees the necessity to counterbalance the inequality between the social partners as a way to increase legitimacy. On the contrary, defenders of the OMC insist on the participation of a broad range of actors with no specific priority for the labour movement.

In the EES the ETUC has on the one hand called for more participation in the process, but in practice, its participation has been moderate. This has not changed much since the increase in political status of the EES.

The development of the position of UNICE is quite different. There has been a shift away from a critical stance towards the EES, that was predominant from the Amsterdam Summit to the Lisbon Summit (see Pochet and Arcq, 1999; Arcq and Pochet, 2000) to a general support of the OMC from the 2000 onwards (this appears clearly in a position paper from Georges Jacobs, president of UNICE, to the Convention). The Lisbon agenda came closer to the priorities of the UNICE. They considered the EES as an integral part of a (high road) growth oriented reform agenda package (interview Thérèse de Liedekerke, June 2004). In particular, UNICE supported the quantified objectives (employment rates, quality of employment, lifelong learning, involvement of the social partners, attention to all four pillars in the guidelines and the definition of indicators). With regard to job creation, UNICE has been calling since Lisbon for fuller implementation of the "entrepreneurship" pillar, particularly the target of reducing taxation and other non-wage labour costs. On the other hand, it expressed concern with regard to the guidelines implying additional costs.

The European Centre of Enterprises with Public Participation and of Enterprises of General Economic Interest (CEEP), for its part, regrets that the guidelines do not lend greater weight to the local level. It argues for a stronger political commitment to the development of the local level (Pochet and Arcq, 2001).

In general, the participation of European level social partners, as well as their incentive to get involved, is patchy. Usually, the European level social partners prepared written position papers on the future of the EES after the EMCO had adopted its opinion. Evidence suggests that they could be more successful in lobbying their options through informal links with Members of the EMCO (King, 2003: 21-22).

The European level social partners have had difficulties to find common political aims in the EES. The recent joint programme of the European level social partners may reflect a slight increase in the will to undertake some activities together. This work programme represents a strategic feat by the trade unions: instead of relying on the Commission as their protector, they decided to explore a more autonomous path. For the employers, the approach is different: from a tactical point of view, they are attempting to deal with the trade unions as the weaker player (Branch and Greenwood, 2001, Arcq *et al.*, 2003). One of the three over-arching themes of the work programme is employment; the others are mobility and enlargement. In the area of employment, the key objective identified has been to report on social partner activity in the implementation of the guidelines. Aside that, there are also to be thematic focuses in areas that are addressed by the guidelines: lifelong learning, gender equality, ageing workforce, undeclared work (ETUC, UNICE/UEAPME and CEEP, 2004). Their joint social program can be considered the key document and strategy in relation to the EES. Their activities at plant or sectoral level often fit with the direction of the EES (flexi-security for example) but they depend on a completely different agenda. The actors involved in such negotiations are very far from the European jargon of the EES.

c) NGOs and European Anti-poverty Network (EAPN)

NGOs are not mentioned in the treaty and are for the most part not consulted on employment policies at national level. There are however few counter examples. The main one is Ireland, where the NGOs of the voluntary and community sector have since the outset been trying to use the EES to influence the policies and measures adopted within the national context. They have used both formal (written) and informal (meetings) channels to try and influence Irish employment policy, ultimately decided upon by the centralised governmental actors. However, they have had virtually no impact, which has adversely affected their desire to become more involved (author's participant observation in the Irish national EES process, July 2004). NGOs in Sweden have attempted to influence the employment policy there. There is also some evidence of voluntarily initiated involvement of NGOs in Spain and Portugal (Jacobsson and Vifell, 2005). But these rare attempts were an exception and the Danish account presented by Jacobsson in this volume illustrate much more the general situation "[...] during the revision of the EES, the Danish government outspokenly resisted a greater involvement of civil society actors in the EES, as proposed by the Commission. NGOs are perceived as an unpredictable factor in a stable and well-functioning social partnership".

Since 1998, EAPN[8] has prepared opinions and reports on how the EEG impacts poverty. It particularly puts forward the need not to side-line the issue of quality in employment (and the need to combat and avoid working poor) in the view of the concern with the quantitative increase of the employment rate that is central to the EES. (www.eapn. org). EAPN refers to the Lisbon definition of the OMC and the general call for the involvement of different actors in EU policies to legitimise its call for involvement (EAPN's response to the revised European Employment Guidelines, PR07-03). There is in particular a guideline in the new EES on poverty, which could legitimise EAPN's claim. Its re-peated expression of interest has been voluntarily initiated. Its involve-ment in the social inclusion strategy (2001) has given it an additional argument to express a wish to be involved in the EES. However, EAPN (like other civil society organisations and NGOs) have not been granted any formal role under the EES. The Commission and European Parlia-ment would be favourable to its further involvement, but Member State representatives in the Employment Committee are reluctant to grant any other actors aside social partners a formal role within the process (Zeitlin, 2003)[9]. Trade unions and employers are also reluctant to en-hance the participation of NGOs. NGOs are not consulted in the EES at national level, aside from a few exceptional cases (EAPN, 2003; Gove-cor, 2004). The nature of the policy area and (supposed) lack of legiti-mate representativeness of the EAPN as well as NGOs and civil society organisations, are used to prevent them from having an increased in-volvement in the EES.

3. National Level Social Partner Participation

The analysis undertaken here sheds some light on how the EES is used as a vehicle for mobilising the policy aims of social partners. The hypothesis is that the participation level of social partners in the EES would depend on three factors: one, the social partners' own political agenda; two, the specific policy area (e.g. work organisation or activa-

---

[8] EAPN is an independent coalition of non-governmental organisations (NGOs) and groups involved in the fight against poverty and social exclusion in the Member States of the European Union. It is made up of fifteen members representing the na-tional networks (voluntary organisations and grass-roots organisations in fight against poverty and social exclusion) and of three members representing the European Organisations.

[9] The 2003 EEG state that "relevant actors in the field of employment at national and regional level have important contributions to make" (Council of the European Union, 2003: 21).

tion) and three the EES as channel to influence the policy process, compared to other channels of influence within the national institutional setting. The European level would have to provide an element of added value.

Table 1 below draws on three European documents that analyse the participation of the social partners at national level. Though imperfect, they provide useful insights into the key issues regarding social partner participation in the EES. All misinterpretations of the data are our responsibility.

Table 1: Participation of Social Partners
in the NAPs of the Employment Strategy (2002 and 2003)

Country	Government Document/ Joint Document	Direct Contribution Social Partners in Writing NAP 2002/2003	Improved social partner participation 2003	Participation in implementation NAP
AT	GD	No	No	Yes
BE	GD	Yes	No	Yes
DK	GD	Yes	No	Yes
FIN	GD	Yes	No	Yes
FR	GD	Yes	Yes	Yes
DE	GD	No	Yes	Yes
GR	GD	No	Yes	Yes
IE	GD	Yes	No	Yes
IT	GD	No	No	Yes
LUX	JD	Yes	Yes	Yes
NL	GD	No	No	Yes
PT	GD	Yes	Yes	Yes
ES	GD	No	No	Yes
SE	GD	Yes	No	Yes
UK	GD	No	No	Yes

Sources: Where the data was drawn from and comments of the nature of the data:
(1) (3rd and 4th round) National Reports of the Govecor project (www.govecor.org) – for Austria, Belgium, France, Germany, Ireland, Italy, The Netherlands, Portugal, Spain, Sweden, the United Kingdom. In these reports, there were in some cases interviews with social partners. In other cases, the analyses were based on interviews and reports from the governmental perspective. The national reports of the Govecor project were the most uneven source of data, as the research focus was broader than social partner participation.
(2) a Survey by the European Foundation of Living and Working Conditions on the Participation of Social Partners in the NAPs (2002) of the Employment Strategy (www.eiro. eurofound.ie) – for all fifteen Member States. The survey was interested in the subjective evaluation of participation of the social partners; the survey by EIRO was the most uniform, in that it was based on a questionnaire sent out to all of the social partners.
(3) Joint Report on Social Partner Actions in Member States to Implement Employment Guidelines (ETUC, UNICE/UEAPME and CEEP, 2004). This report commented on social partner activity in the 2003 NAPs in all EU countries but France and Ireland. No reasons were given on their exclusion from the report. It is a self-evaluation of the

national social partners, but the report had a political finality, hence some bias in the way the data was presented. We compared sources and re-analysed conflicting data carefully.

It is difficult to draw general conclusions from the table. However, several observations (complemented or confirmed by qualitative data) are worth highlighting. First, there have progressively been more direct contributions and/or a qualitative improvement in the contributions: the crucial point here is a (slight) shift by the social partners to take the EES more seriously as a political vehicle. Nevertheless, this slight incremental improvement should not be over-stated, as major obstacles remain: the lack of time for adequate contributions, and also of financial resources. Second, the NAPs are essentially government documents. In countries where social partners do not have a tradition of negotiating with government, they manifest a reticence to use the NAP as a means to enhance tripartite negotiation. Especially in countries with a weak tradition of tripartite negotiation, the NAP is too often perceived as "owned" by ministerial departments. This issue can further be illustrated by the example of Eurexcter: a group of French public trade unions and employers that sought to exploit the EES as a means of action, and a forum for debate. The fact that the experience was not followed through was revealing of the difficulties of developing an independent social partner strategy (Eurexcter, 2002). Third, in *all* countries the social partners participate in the implementation of the policies under their remit in the NAP. This is logical as the NAP, at the very least, is a report that summarises all policies and measures undertaken throughout the year, including those involving the social partners.

Beyond these observations, several other points are worth emphasising. The first issue concerns the agenda mismatch. Wage negotiations, central to social partner activity, are not part of the EES guidelines, although the Wim Kok Group has managed to bring the issue on to the agenda in the country-specific recommendations (Casey, 2005). Employment policies on the other hand are mainly considered a government prerogative. That said, the political agenda of the social partners is broadening to debate issues related to employment policy as well (Léonard, 2004). Indeed, social partners have revealed interest in guidelines that are primarily addressed to governments: active and preventive measures for the unemployed and inactive, job creation and entrepreneurship, making work pay, transforming undeclared work into regular employment (ETUC, UNICE/UEAPME and CEEP, 2004). Concerning the EU policy agenda, the synchronisation of the EEG with the Broad Economic Policy Guidelines (BEPG) has not significantly changed social partner involvement. Only the social partners in Luxembourg delivered an opinion on the BEPG, while in Belgium social partner involvement was asked for in the preparation of the BEPG, as well as their evaluation. This was also confirmed in a recent research project organised by the Observatoire social européen in four countries (Belgium, France, Ireland and Sweden)[10]. Social partners did not mention the changed status of the EES or its closer linkage with economic policy as having changed their incentive to participate. This opposes our hypothesis, which links higher politicisation with participation. However, there is not (yet) much awareness of the implications of the changes.

From the literature (Foden, 1999) and the national contributions to this volume, it appears that trade unions prefer to influence the policy process in areas of their remit through means that pre-existed the EES, that are more rooted in the national institutional setting, and with which resources (either financial or power or a combination of both) would be associated.

The NAP/empl is conceived as a weak strategic document. To stimulate genuine social partner interest, the NAP would need to be beneficial, from both the trade union and employer organisations' perspective. According to Jacobsson (this volume) "Both trade union and employer representatives (in Sweden) have expressed that their willingness to continue to participate is a function of what they gain from it". In Germany, "the NAP is perceived as a governmental product by the social partners themselves, thus limiting the status of this process because it cannot be used by them to influence policies" (Büchs and Friedrich, in this volume). Concerning the Irish case, O'Donnell and Moss in this volume explain "While social partners would in principle, support a more in-depth consultation process, they were sceptical of the impact that such change would make, unless other more fundamental changes in the overall process is made. These include linking the NEAP to the partnership and budgetary process. If the NEAP remains largely a progress reporting mechanism, the social partners would prefer to direct their resources to influencing the national partnership process, where it is considered that significant influence on policy can be achieved". Visser in this volume makes a comparable argument for the Dutch case "The unions find it easier to influence government through pressure on the employers, as they proved in the last agreement of November 2003". In Italy, the involvement and position of trade unions regarding employment and labour market policy is reflected in the NAP, but has to do with endogenous political factors. Under the Berlusconi government, employment policy in Italy has been guided by the (controversial) Pact for Italy and the Biagi Law. It has brought about a split between trade unions: on the one hand, the CISL and UIL, which signed the Pact, and on the other, the CGIL which has refused to sign the Pact, in its critical

---

[10] For the results, see http://www.ose.be/SEE/mainEN.htm.

stance towards employment policy under the Berlusconi government. In Italy, the overall governmental stance towards social concertation and union involvement in employment and labour market policy does impact the nature of their involvement in the NAP[11].

The picture of social partner participation in the EES is shaky, despite the efforts made over time to improve their involvement. This is due not only to the financial resources and agenda mismatch, but also the lack of institutional rootedness of the EES within the national policy process. Furthermore, there is the issue of how the national political climate could influence the possibility for social partners to take part in the process. In Austria, Portugal and Italy, the shift towards the right has had a negative influence on the ability of social partners to participate.

II. Social Inclusion OMC

In the area of social inclusion, anti-poverty Non-Governmental Organisations (NGOs) are the main concerned actors. The fight against poverty which is the main objective of the OMC inclusion is in line with the concerns of these organisations, although the work-based focus of the OMC inclusion is not. Compared to social partners in the area of employment, NGOs in the domestic context have weaker legitimately recognised channels for putting forward their policy issues, although this has increased during the 1990s (Pochet, 2004a). Given their comparatively weak institutional means for setting issues on the national policy agenda, they would *a priori* be more likely to use the European level as a vehicle through which to put forward the policy issues on their agenda. For the three factors of our hypothesis, policy area is relevant, agenda generally coincides, and the NGOs would have a great incentive to use OMC as a source of legitimately voicing their concerns.

A. Structural Features of the Process

1. Treaty Provisions and OMC Inclusion

After the fighting between the Commission and some Member States around the legal base for initiatives in the domain of social exclusion in the 1990s, a treaty provision for the fight against poverty and social exclusion was introduced in the Amsterdam Treaty (1997). Even if it explicitly refers to "co-operation" that could be encouraged by the European level it is clear that the competency for this area is at national level (Armstrong, 2003). There is no equivalent to the "Employment Chapter" for the EES. In the Constitutional Treaty, there is now a provi-

---

[11] Special thanks to Stefano Sacchi for clarifying this point.

sion for the co-ordination process for social security with no reference to the need to involve NGOs or civil society organisations. Only the Commission and Council are mentioned as key actors (former article III-107, now III-307) (Barbier, 2003).

The mandate to tackle poverty and social exclusion through the OMC is a political one. When the OMC was coined, it was decided that it should be applied in a full-fledged manner for social inclusion, to eradicate poverty by 2010 (European Council, 2000a).

The decision to fight poverty and social exclusion at European level through OMC should be contextualised with the development of national level policies and activities. Poverty has become an issue or been raised in status in most Member States during the mid- and late-1990s. Albeit in different constellations, a wide range of public actors, NGOs, social partners and to a lesser extent persons experiencing poverty has characterised these different (national) instances of activity in the fight against poverty (Pochet, 2004a). In the political context of (mostly) left-wing governments during the Lisbon Summit, the OMC inclusion was agreed within a policy frame that had been developing within Member States (European Council, 2000a). "In this OMC, there is greater political commitment to wider participation, including social partner and civil society actors, from the national through local levels" (Peña Casas, 2004: 107-108). While the OMC inclusion is not yet included in the tri-annual economic policy co-ordination cycle, and is further away from the "high politics" of the European Union that the EEG, there is a political commitment to tie it closer to the this process from 2006 onwards.

The objectives of the strategy were approved in December 2000 (European Council, 2000b, see also Erhel *et al.* in this volume), organised around four objectives:

- ensuring the facilitation of participation in employment and access to resources, rights, goods and services for all;
- prevention of the risks of social exclusion;
- setting out actions for disadvantaged groups;
- mobilising all actors concerned in policy formulation and implementation.

The objectives of the OMC inclusion are akin to the four pillars of the EES from 1997 to 2002, and have become stable features of the social inclusion strategy. They have been developed mainly by the Member States and to a lesser extent by the Commission, through the SPC. The EAPN has also played a non-negligible role. The SPC calls for a higher profile for social inclusion in national contexts. For the second round of national plans, greater attention was accorded to gender mainstreaming, and the integration of vulnerable groups, particularly immigrants (SPC, 2003). This is in line with the aims of the European Anti-poverty Network (EAPN, 2003), that has emerged as the most active and influential European non-state player in the OMC inclusion.

In OMC inclusion, Member States submit national action plans for social inclusion (NAPs/incl) every two years, and have so far submitted the NAPs/incl twice, the first time in mid-2001 and the second in mid-2003. The first round of NAPs/incl was identified as an important starting point for the fight against poverty and social exclusion, but also too vague. In the second joint report, the Commission assessed most NAPs as qualitatively better than the first round substantively and also procedurally. In procedural terms, Member States had in most cases made progress in integrating the poverty policies with other policy processes, and had also made increased efforts to extend the process further to regional and local levels. Second, more efforts had been made to include civil society organisations in the NAP process. Although in agreement with the assessment of the Commission, the stance of the EAPN was slightly more critical, particularly concerning the quality of participation (EAPN, 2003).

2. Links with Funding: The Anti-poverty Programme and the Structural Funds

The activity of anti-poverty NGOs in the European context has been maturing over the past decade: "civil society organisations have *de facto* become better-organised and better-informed within the European sphere and the fight against poverty" (De Schutter, 2002: 206). However, the issue of which actors should be consulted, what that consultation should entail, have been identified through implementation. This can notably be reflected by the role of the EAPN in the OMC inclusion. In his analysis, Armstrong (2003) argues that the EAPN (and its national networks) is implicitly considered to be the most representative, although many important concerned actors are absent (particularly at the local level). He also provides examples of the exclusion of certain relevant actors.

In order to answer at least partially to these questions, the Commission adopted an anti-poverty programme (2000-2006) of 75 million euros with three objectives:

a) improve the understanding of social exclusion;
b) organise co-operation and reciprocal training in the context of national action plans;
c) develop the capacity of players to address social exclusion effectively.

Particularly the last objective has made it an important incentive structure for the mobilisation of non-governmental and civil society organisations within the OMC inclusion by providing fixed funding to a number of European networks. From the first set of networks funded, only the most efficient will receive funding in the second round. The aim of the Commission is to support structurally five or six European networks.

Many organisations have formed functional alliances to increase their chances of obtaining funding.

There is also a link, although weak, between the social inclusion OMC and the European Structural Funds, especially the Social Fund: the bulk of funding from the EQUAL programme ESF is directed towards the fight against poverty at regional level. However, similar to the loose link between the ESF and the EEG, this link has not been developed (EAPN, 2003).

B. Key Actors

In this section, we first analyse the formal institutions with policy-making power – governmental and parliamentary institutions at both European and national levels. We then analyse the participation of the non-state actors involved in the fight against poverty, at European level and national levels.

Formal Actors

At European level, the Social Protection Committee (SPC) was established in 2000 (officially endorsed in the Nice Treaty, article 144) with the mandate of working on social protection issues, where one of the four objectives was to work in the field of poverty and social exclusion[12]. Like EMCO, it has an "advisory status" and prepares reports and formulates opinions at the request of either the Council or the Commission or on its own initiative. Its mandate has in actual fact been guided by the European Councils, where one of its two key tasks has become social inclusion and the other pensions, both using the OMC. The SPC consists of two representatives per Member State and two representatives from the European Commission. Like EMCO, it has a support team that is located within the Commission. Similarly, the European Commission plays some role in the provision of expertise, and in monitoring, especially through its draft joint report on social inclusion, on which Member States through the Council have the final veto point.

---

[12] The other fields of its mandate are to make work pay, to make pension systems socially and financially sustainable, and to make health care systems accessible for all, of high quality and sustainable.

Also akin to the institutional structure in employment policy, an indicators sub-group has been established to work on the development of indicators and statistics to support the policy objectives of the OMC inclusion.

In this OMC, the role attributed to experts is greater, which can be reflected in the recently changed mandate of the SPC. The general structure of the Committee and membership remains the same. The proposed change on the one hand makes a broader reference to specific tasks (i.e. reporting). On the other, it leaves more leeway for working with other experts than those in the Commission, the Committee itself, or its indicators sub-group. Article 2.2 of the provision states that "the Committee may call on external experts where its agenda so requires" and article 4 states that it may establish working groups to work on specific issues.

Concerning social partners, article 144 states that the Committee should establish "appropriate" contacts with social partners, which is not a requirement in the same was as social partner consultation in the EES (CEC, 2003). The empirical evidence reveals that social partners have in most cases not played a role (EAPN, 2003). At national level, there is evidence of genuine social partner participation in the social inclusion strategy in Finland, and to a lesser extent in Belgium (interview ETUC, 14 January 2004). Social partners are in general not interested in getting involved in the OMC inclusion, as it is even further away from the mainstream of the social partner agenda than the EES. In general terms, it is not within the areas that are central to social partners. By contrast, there is no reference in article 144 about the need to involve or consult civil society organisations in any way.

The parliamentary involvement in OMC inclusion has not been well documents, but evidence suggests that it is virtually absent. The European Parliament calls for being closer involved and also calls for closer involvement of parliamentary bodies. It also emphasises the importance of involving civil society organisations further in OMC inclusion. It supports the Commission's initiatives for further integration of relevant stakeholders in the various OMC processes (European Parliament, 2003).

b) Non-governmental and Civil Society Organisations

* European Level

EAPN has been successful in gathering and centralising information on the objectives of the social inclusion OMC and on the participation of NGOs in the NAP process. It has also contributed to the development of the political objectives of the OMC inclusion through regular formal and informal contact with the SPC and written positions. Each round of the Action Plans for inclusion have been analysed by the national networks of the EAPN. To date, it has been the most active and influential non-governmental actor in the OMC inclusion process. EAPN has also contributed to the debate on indicators, and has been co-organising an annual roundtable on social inclusion with DG EMPL and the rotating EU presidency, as well as other EU-wide conferences financed by the Commission. While the involvement of the EAPN is a positive aspect, three issues must be kept in mind. First, while membership of the EAPN is quite broad-ranging, national networks of the EAPN are variably representative across Member States. Secondly, other European level non-governmental actors, that may include other relevant members, could (and have been) sidelined (Armstrong, 2003). Third, there is so far no representation at European level of the local authorities which are a key player in this field. Concerning this last point, some attempts to create stable networks have been made, such as one including EUROCITIES, the European Social Network, and the European Public Social Platform (see Armstrong, 2004) or another called RETIS.

* National Level

The issue of poverty and exclusion has been put (back) on the European agenda in a context where, over the past five years, renewed efforts have been made at national level, entailing a fresh openness to non-governmental actors. Of particular note are the establishment in France, in the wake of the law on exclusion, of a monitoring centre on poverty and social exclusion (1998) and the drafting of the first ever federal report on this topic in Germany (2001). Other countries too provide examples of the emergence of this issue on their political agendas since the second half of the 1990s (UNIOPSS, 2001): Belgium, with the elaboration of a general report on poverty (1994) which brought together all the stakeholders in this field; the Netherlands, with the holding of annual social affairs conferences around these issues; Ireland, by adopting a national anti-poverty strategy in 1997, reconfirmed in its latest Social Pact, complete with the involvement of social NGOs in negotiating Social Pacts.

Most of the information on this topic is from the EAPN, composed of sixteen national networks (UE15+Bulgaria). Based on analyses done by the networks themselves, the EAPN has made an overall assessment of the participation of NGOs in the NAP process. Overall, the EAPN assesses that its networks successfully engaged in dialogue with the concerned ministries. In fact, the EAPN believes that the "main value so far of the OMC in the field of inclusion has been moving the question of the institutional arrangements to centre stage". However, it also points to a general lack of financial resources, political commitment and legal pressure to actually develop "more open, democratic and integrated arrangements for developing effective anti-poverty strategies". Moreover, despite the inclusion of non-governmental actors in the core part of the NAP, the EAPN points out that in all but one country there was no consultation by government with NGOs for the selection of the "good practice" examples (EAPN, 2003).

Overall, compared to the EES, the OMC inclusion has led to a more voluntary and more genuine participatory dynamic among non-governmental organisations nationally. Furthermore, the extent of participation of NGOs and civil society improved considerably between the first and second rounds of the process.

Table 2 below is based on empirical data from each national EAPN network as well as the political document of the EAPN on the second round of NAP/incl.

The first column indicates whether the NAP process is a governmental dynamic, or rather, whether it is a joint effort by a variety of actors.

Then, the participation of two types of actors is analysed. The first actor is made up of anti-poverty NGOs, which vary considerably in composition (and representativity of organisations in the fight against poverty and social exclusion), sources and stability of financing, thematic areas of focus, and degree of centralisation across EU Member States[13]. The second actor is made up of people experiencing poverty. The representation of this group of people in one or several organisations is also variable across Member States. It is an explicit aim of the OMC/incl. to involve both these groups in the OMC social inclusion process.

The satisfaction of participatory conditions is not analysed here as there is not enough comparable information.

---

[13] In Ireland and Portugal, for example, the secretariat of the EAPN is a centralised structure and has a stable and continuous source of financing, and is very much oriented towards European level activities. In Italy and Spain, on the other hand, the EAPN is organised much more at a regional level with a corresponding regional focus of activities. In Germany, the principal members of the national EAPN network are big associations that are also service providers. In France, the members are a mix of big and small organisations. The Belgian EAPN network, on the other hand, is made up of three regional networks, two that have a stable source of financing and structure (Brussels and Flanders) and one that does not have a stable source of financing and structure (Wallonia) (telephone interview, EAPN representative, 13 January 2004).

Table 2: Participation of Anti-poverty NGOs
in the Social Inclusion OMC

Country	Governmental Document/Joint Document	Participation anti-poverty NGOs in dialogue with gov. on the social inclusion strategy (consultation)[1]	Participation of people experiencing poverty
AT	GD	Low	Low
BE	GD	Good	Medium
DK	GD	Good	Medium
FIN	JD	Good	Medium
FR	GD	Medium	Low
DE	GD	Good	Medium
GR	GD	Good	Medium
IE	GD	Good	Medium
IT	GD	Low	Low
LUX	GD	Good	Medium
NL	GD	Medium	Low
PT	GD	Low	Medium
ES	GD	Good	Low
SE	GD	Good	Medium
UK	GD	Good	Medium

(1) Good: indicates that there is genuine consultation by the government with non-governmental groups (EAPN network, other non-governmental groups, people experiencing poverty) during the drafting of the NAP/incl. In some cases, this means organising a specific meeting or a specific working group on the social inclusion.

Medium: indicates that there is only information by the government for the non-governmental groups.

Low: indicates that there is no *ex ante* consultation and weak information by the government for non-governmental groups.

Source: Second national round on National Action Plans for Social Inclusion; EAPN synthetic document on the participation of relevant anti-poverty NGOs in the second round of the NAPs inclusion; reports of the national networks of EAPN on the second round of the NAPs/incl (all documents downloadable from www.eapn.org). These results were completed by a telephone interview with a representative of the European Anti-poverty Network (EAPN). All erroneous interpretations of the results are ours.

Concerning the general thrust of the decision-making process on social inclusion, the only country where the OMC inclusion is a joint process is Finland, where the non-governmental organisations were involved in the actual negotiation of the political programme of the fight against poverty. In the other countries, the NAP is above all driven by the government.

The assessment by NGOs of their participation is positive overall (67% of the cases recording a good participation), and medium for people experiencing poverty (67% of the cases). For the participation of people experiencing poverty, the more mediocre (67% medium and 33% low) assessment could partially be attributed to the weak pre-existence of such practices in Member States. The EAPN has attributed the lesser extent of participation of this group in the NAP/incl to a problem of funding (EAPN, 2003).

There is a relatively high level of correspondence between the level of participation of NGOs and people experiencing poverty. In nine out of ten cases, where participation is good for NGOs, it is medium for people experiencing poverty. Conversely, a more mediocre (medium or low) level of participation of NGOs is associated with a low level of participation of people experiencing poverty.

Concerning NGO participation, the relatively good score could partially be attributed to existing consultation practices between governmental and non-governmental actors in national contexts. In the Netherlands, where consultation was characterised as medium, the government was conceived as seeking one solution to the different dimensions of poverty. In France, where consultation was also characterised as medium, the main problem was the involvement of the regional and local levels. The EAPN networks in both countries considered that their views were hardly taken into account (EAPN national reports France and the Netherlands). For the countries where the participation was low, this could be attributed to the strong right-wing orientation of the governments. In Austria, the participation of NGOs in the NAP/incl was reportedly worse in the second round compared to the first round (EAPN national reports Austria, Italy and Portugal).

In order to complement our analysis, we asked ATD-Quart Monde, an NGO that focuses on people experiencing poverty, to compare the extent to which the consultation practices in the NAP/inclusion correspond more generally to consultation practices in the national context. The information in the table, provided for seven countries, is the assessment of one of the most well-known NGOs, about its implication at national level comparing "normal" national anti-poverty policies and consultation in the NAP process.

Table 3: Participation of NGOs and People Experiencing Poverty in National Anti-poverty Policies (Existing Institutional Practices) Compared to their Participation in the NAPs/incl

Country	Participation in national anti-poverty policies		Participation in the NAP/incl	
	NGOs/ATD	People experiencing poverty	NGOs/ATD	People experiencing poverty
AT				
BE	Good	Good	Medium	Medium
FR	Good	Good	Medium	Low
LUX	Good	Low	Good	Low
IE	Good	Good	Good	Medium
ES	Medium	Low	Medium	Low
NL	Good	Good	Good	Medium
UK	Low	Low	Good	Medium

Good: indicates that there is genuine consultation by the government with non-governmental groups (non-governmental groups, people experiencing poverty) during the drafting of the NAP/incl. In some cases this means organising a specific meeting or a specific working group on the social inclusion.

Medium: indicates that there is only information by the government for the non-governmental groups.

Low: indicates that there is no *ex ante* consultation and weak information by the government for non-governmental groups.

According to this evaluation, in four countries out of seven (Belgium, France, Ireland, the Netherlands), the consultation practices are better in national anti-poverty policies than in the social inclusion process. In two countries (Luxembourg and Spain) consultation is the same in anti-poverty policy and the social inclusion process. In only one country (the United Kingdom), consultation was considered better in the NAP process for both NGOs and people experiencing poverty. According to Armstrong's study (2004) "The NAP has not only, then, provided opportunities for NGOs to mobilise; it has also created opportunities for civil servants to do something different". While not representative of all Member States, this comparison shows that the NAPs/incl need in most cases to be further integrated into national anti-poverty policies.

National chapters in this volume show contrasting situations. The worst case in term of participation seems to be the Italian one. In this country, the NAP/incl has been characterised as weak, and did not act as an incentive to enhance participation of social NGOs or civil society organisations in anti-poverty policies (see chapter by Ferrera and Sacchi in this volume). According to Jacobsson in this volume in Sweden, the administration was not open to a participatory approach, but the mere existence of the Social Inclusion process did instigate a broad informal network of NGOs to set out its own programme and action plan. The

380

group has continued to try and influence the NAP/incl process, including in the second round. In contrast to Sweden, she found that the government in Denmark genuinely seeks to enhance the involvement of NGOs. NGOs, civil society and other relevant actors have successfully been mobilised in the first, but especially the second round of the NAP/incl. This is also the case in Germany "From the outset, the welfare associations and other social NGOs showed serious interest in the NAP/incl process. Their engagement commenced at federal level but in the meantime efforts increase to initiate regional processes and to stimulate the local level". In this case, "the NAP/incl process provides the social NGOs with additional arguments and political backing to strengthen their position in domestic debates". Nevertheless, as indicated in the Irish case, the global impact on policies could be weak "while their involvement in the partnership process has been hugely important, and very significant policy innovation has occurred, they have, by their own admission, not persuaded the other partners and government to take action that would significantly reduce Ireland's social problems" (see chapter by O'Donnell and Moss in this volume).

Compared to EES, national participation is undoubtedly higher but the impact on policies and certainly on economic policies is still in most of the cases marginal. The same can be said at European level where the Social Inclusion process is very loosely connected with the BEPG.

Conclusion

The hypothesis guiding the analysis in this article is that the level of participation is to a great extent linked to the actors' own interests, political agenda, and that participation differs according to policy area. National circumstances also play an important role in the margin for manoeuvre left for participation. The two case studies confirm this hypothesis, while indicating important differences in the two areas.

In the European institutional landscape, an important actor is the Commission that has supported social partner involvement in the EES from the outset and also argued in favour of involving the social partners in the evaluation of the European Employment Strategy. It strongly supported the entry of new participants into the social exclusion OMC, notably through funding of networks. Other important and recently influential reports were those produced by Kok *et al.* (2003 and 2004), which support greater involvement of the social partners in all dimensions of the EES and the Lisbon strategy. The European Parliament, on the sidelines of the debate, has been calling for more involvement of relevant stakeholders, particularly parliaments, in the different OMC processes (European Parliament, 2003).

In essence, non-state actors do not participate in devising the over-arching political objectives of the OMC processes. They are however able to influence the process through formal written positions, combined with informal consultation with committee members. The dynamics of social partner participation in the Employment Strategy are different from the participation of non-governmental organisations in the OMC inclusion. This has to do *inter alia* with their institutionalisation at national level, their agenda, links with financing and their aims at European level.

At European level, in particular in the EES, the trade unions have for a long time privileged the creation of a new layer of industrial relations and the adoption of directives or collective agreements. Progressively, the European agenda has changed and the trade unions are reconsidering the importance of soft social law. The employers, after being reluctant toward the EES, now have a more positive position. The ETUC, UNICE and CEEP act essentially in the view of their strategic interests, as other political actors. In employment policy, national level social partners have a well-anchored institutional role in most Member States: they are consulted and/or informed formally or informally about labour market and employment policies. Bi- or tri-partite institutions structure ex-change amongst them and with public authorities. There are generally well-established formal and also informal channels through which the government and social partners collaborate. In certain areas, they have a co-regulatory role. The difficulty has been to link this autonomy with a position of dependence in the case of the European Employment Strat-egy. As the NAP/empl is generally not considered a strategic document, the incentive to increase the social partners' participation is weak. National social partner involvement in the EES has increased since 1997 for approximately half the EU Member States, but this is still weak compared to the incentives taken to encourage their participation. We have to remember too that the issues tackled under the EES only overlap partially with the main national bargaining agenda of the social partners. According to our perspective, this could change if the governments are taking the EES and his national side more seriously. It could also change if the traditional bi or tripartite institutions have their power and influ-ence reduced.

Concerning the potential interaction between the EES and ESF, it seems that the social partners involved in the ESF participatory bodies have little contact with those involved in the EES. However, there have been other initiatives, by the Commission, to involve other relevant actors at regional and local levels in the EES.

Financing is available from the Commission for local authorities to write up local action plans. Regional or local conditions will most probably guide the adaptation of the EES objectives to the context and priorities of the relevant level. The learning mechanism here is likely to be from the top-down.

In the area of social inclusion the actor dynamics and incentives for involvement are quite different. The anti-poverty associations are not as well anchored into the national contexts as the social partners, although, since the mid-1990s, there is evidence of a more permanent role in the institutional structures of the Member States (Pochet, 2004a). At European level, non-governmental organisations (in particular the EAPN), do not *a priori* have much say in political choices. As they are not in a bargaining position, they use resources instead: they push for their ideas to be included in the national and European agenda, on the basis of supporting analyses and data where available. They therefore have a more genuine motivation to take advantage of the window of opportunity offered by the Social Inclusion OMC.

At national level, the involvement of NGOs in the Social Inclusion process is better overall than that of social partners in the EES. The involvement of people experiencing poverty is not as successful, but is a less rooted practice nationally and more difficult to organise. In addition, the involvement of NGOs is directly supported by European financial resources. The agenda of the NGOs is likely to coincide with the anti-poverty objectives of the OMC inclusion. Some central NGOs, notably under the auspices of the EAPN, have acted strategically, mobilising their scarce resources to use the OMC to influence decision-makers at national and European levels. However, social exclusion is not a priority on most national agendas, and the financial resources for financing activities are scarce (EAPN, 2003).

This openness in the inclusion field should not be idealised. One of the two key factors Jacobsson found to explain the resistance of the Danish and Swedish government to OMC is that "the OMC poses challenges to the traditional institutional structures of policy-making, e.g. by engaging social NGOs in social and labour market policy".

It would nevertheless be mistaken to regard participation and deliberation as the converse of politicisation and bargaining. Politicisation can also strengthen the desire of certain actors to participate. Indeed, the more political the process, the higher the stakes. The EES and the OMC have launched a window of opportunity for participation by non-traditional actors. The discourse on new forms of governance keeps this window of opportunity open even during periods, such as the review of the Employment Strategy and the Kok Reports, when the negotiations are highly political.

References

Arcq, E. and Pochet, P. (2000), "UNICE and CEEP in 1999: Social Policy Perspectives", in Gabaglio, E. and Hoffmann, R. (eds.), *European Trade Union Yearbook 1999*, European Trade Union Institute, Brussels, pp.173-190.

Arcq, E., Dufresne, A. and Pochet, P. (2003), "The Employers: The Hidden Face of European Industrial Relations", *Transfer*, Vol.9, No.2, Summer 2003, pp.302-321.

Armstrong, K. A. (2004), "Combatting Social Exclusion through OMC: A UK Perspective", Paper presented to the Workshop "Nuove forme di decisione e nuove forme di regolazione: il metodo del coordinamento aperto nel processo di integrazione europea", Brescia, February 2004.

Armstrong, K. A. (2003), "Tackling Social Exclusion through OMC: Reshaping the Boundaries of European Governance", in Börzel, T. and Cichowski, R. (eds.), *The State of the European Union, Vol.6: Law, Politics, and Society*, Oxford University Press, Oxford, pp.170-194.

Barbier, C. (2003), "The European Convention: Establishment and Initial Results in the Field of Economic and Social Policy", in Degryse, C. and Pochet, P. (eds.), *Social Developments in the European Union 2002*, European Trade Union Institute, Observatoire social européen and Saltsa, Brussels, pp.19-59.

Barbier, J.-C. (2004), "La stratégie européenne pour l'emploi: genèse, coordination communautaire et diversité nationale", Rapport de recherche pour la DARES (ministère du Travail), Paris, January 2004.

Bollen, F. (2001), "EU Structural Funds and the Partnership Principle", in Bollen, F. (ed.), *Managing EU Structural Funds. Effective Capacity for Implementation as a Prerequisite*, European Institute of Public Administration, Maastricht, pp.21-24.

Branch, A. and Greenwood, J. (2001), "European Employers", in Compston, H. and Greenwood, J. (eds.), *Social Partnership in the European Union*, Palgrave, London, pp.41-70.

Casey, B. H. (2005), "Building Social Partnership? Strengths and Shortcomings of the European Employment Strategy", *Transfer*, Vol.11, No.1, Spring 2005 (forthcoming).

CEC (2001a), "European Governance: A White Paper", COM (2001) 428 final of 25 July 2001.

CEC (2001b), Communication from the Commission on the European Social Fund Support for the European Employment Strategy, COM (2001) 16 of 16 January 2001.

CEC (2001c), Communication from the Commission "Strengthening the Local Dimension of the European Employment Strategy", COM (2001) 629 final of 6 November 2001 (http://europa.eu.int/eur-lex/en/com/cnc/2001/com2001_0629en01.pdf).

CEC (2002a), Communication from the Commission on Streamlining the Annual Economic and Employment Policy Co-ordination Cycles, COM

(2002) 487 of 3 September 2002 (http://europa.eu.int/eur-lex/en/com/rpt/2002/com2002_0487en01.pdf).

CEC (2002b), Communication from the Commission "The European Social Dialogue, A Force for Innovation and Change" and Proposal for a Council Decision establishing a Tripartite Social Summit for Growth and Employment, COM (2002) 341 final of 26 June 2002 (http://europa.eu.int/eur-lex/en/com/pdf/2002/com2002_0341en01.pdf).

CEC (2002c), Communication from the Commission "Taking Stock of Five Years of the European Employment Strategy", COM (2002) 416 of 17 July 2002 (http://europa.eu.int/eur-lex/en/com/cnc/2002/com2002_0416en01.pdf).

CEC (2002d), Impact Evaluation of the European Employment Strategy, Technical Analysis Supporting COM (2002) 416 final of 17 July 2002 ("Taking Stock of Five Years of the EES"), October 2002 (http://europa.eu.int/comm/employment_social/publications/2002/cev102006_en.pdf).

CEC (2003), Communication from the Commission "The Future of the European Employment Strategy (EES) 'A Strategy for Full Employment and Better Jobs for All'", COM (2003) 6 final of 14 January 2003 (http://europa.eu.int/eur-lex/en/com/pdf/2003/com2003_0006en01.pdf).

CEC (2004a), Communication from the Commission "Draft Joint Employment Report 2003/2004", COM (2004) 24 final of 9 January 2004 (http://europa.eu.int/eur-lex/en/com/rpt/2004/com2004_0024en02.pdf).

CEC (2004b), Activity Report to EMCO Local Employment Development 2001-2004, 2 April 2004 (http://europa.eu.int/comm/employment_social/local_employment/publications/led_activity_report_en.pdf).

Coordinamento delle Regioni e Province autonome per il lavoro e la formazione professionale (2002), "Piano nazionale per l'occupazione, NAP 2002", Prima analisi delle politiche regionali per l'occupazione in funzione della costruzione del NAP 2002, Roma, 18 April 2002.

Council of the European Union (1999), Council Regulation (EC) No.1260/1999 of 21 June 1999 Laying Down General Provisions on the Structural Funds, OJ L 161, 26 June 1999, pp.1-42.

Council of the European Union (2000), "The On-going Experience of the Open Method of Coordination", *Presidency Note*, No.90088/00, Lisbon, 13 June 2000.

Council of the European Union (2003), Council Decision of 22 July 2003 on guidelines for the employment policies of the Member States, OJ L 197, 5 August 2003, pp.13-21.

de la Porte, C. and Nanz, P. (2004), "OMC – A Deliberative-Democratic Mode of Governance? The Cases of Employment and Pensions", *Journal of European Public Policy*, Vol.11, No.2, April 2004, pp.267-288.

de la Porte, C. and Pochet, P. (2002) (eds.), *Building Social Europe through the Open Method of Co-ordination*, P.I.E.-Peter Lang, Brussels.

de la Porte, C. and Pochet, P. (2003), "The OMC Intertwined with the Debates on Governance, Democracy and Social Europe: Research on the Open

Method of Co-ordination and European Integration", Report prepared for Frank Vandenbroucke, Belgian Minister for Social Affairs and Pensions, Observatoire social européen, Brussels, April 2003.

de la Porte, C. and Pochet, P. (2004), "The European Employment Strategy: Existing Research and Remaining Questions", *Journal of European Social Policy*, Vol.14, No.1, February 2004, pp.71-79.

de la Porte, C., Pochet, P. and Room, G. (2001), "Social Benchmarking, Policy-Making and the Instruments of New Governance", *Journal of European Social Policy*, Vol.11, No.4, November 2001, pp.291-307.

De Schutter, O. (2002), "Europe in Search of its Civil Society", *European Law Journal*, Vol.8, No.2, June 2002, pp.198-217.

EAPN (2003), Report "National Action Plans on Inclusion 2003-2005 – Where is the Political Energy? EAPN's response to the second round of plans", October 2003.

ETUC, UNICE/UEAPME and CEEP (2002), Work Programme of the European Social Partners 2003-2005, Brussels, 28 November 2002.

ETUC, UNICE/UEAPME and CEEP (2004), Report on Social Partner Actions in Member States to Implement Employment Guidelines, March 2004.

Eurexcter (2002), Contribution by National Social Partners to the Luxembourg Process, Association européenne de l'Excellence territoriale, Paris, November 2002 (http://europa.eu.int/comm/employment_social/news/2003/jan/coparso_en.pdf).

European Council (1997), Luxembourg European Council, *Presidency Conclusions*, 12-13 December 1997.

European Council (2000a), Lisbon European Council, *Presidency Conclusions*, 23-24 March 2000.

European Council (2000b), Nice European Council, *Presidency Conclusions*, 7 -9 December 2000.

European Parliament (2003), Report on analysis of the open coordination procedure in the field of employment and social affairs, and future prospects by the committee on employment and social affairs, Rapporteur Miet Smets A5-0143/2003 of 30 April 2003.

Foden, D. (1999), "The Role of Social Partners in the European Employment Strategy", *Transfer*, Vol.5, No.4, pp.522-541.

Goetschy, J. (1999), "The European Employment Strategy: Genesis and Development", *European Journal of Industrial Relations*, Vol.5, No.2, July 1999, pp.117-137.

Govecor (2004), "EU Governance by Self Co-ordination? Towards a Collective 'Gouvernement économique'", Final Report of the Govecor Project, August 2004 (http://www.govecor.org/intro/GOVECOR_Final_report.pdf).

Groupe Bernard Brunhes Consultants and Economix (2003), "Strengthening the local dimension of the European Employment Strategy: Feasibility Study on Indicators for Local and Regional Levels and for the Social Economy", Final Report on a Study conducted under the direction of Jacques Dahan and financed by the European Commission, DG Employment and Social Affairs, December 2003 (http://europa.eu.int/comm/employment_social/ local_employment/publications/ees_local_en.pdf).

Hartwig, I. (2004), "Towards a Communitarisation? Spill-overs between Structural Funds and the European Employment Strategy", Draft executive summary for final report of Govecor, February 2004.

Jacobsson, K. and Schmid, H. (2002), "Real Integration or Just Formal Adaptation? – On the Implementation of the National Action Plans for Employment", in de la Porte, C. and Pochet, P. (eds.), *Building Social Europe through the Open Method of Co-ordination*, P.I.E.-Peter Lang, Brussels, pp.69-95.

Jacobsson, K. and Vifell, Å. (2005), "New Governance Structures in Employment Policy-making? Taking Stock of the European Employment Strategy", in Linsenmann, I., Meyer, C. and Wessels, W. (eds.), *EU Economic Governance: A Balance Sheet of New Modes of Governance*, Palgrave Macmillan (forthcoming).

Jenson, J. and Pochet, P. (2005), "Employment and Social Policy Since Maastricht: Standing up to the European Monetary Union", in Fishman, R. and Messina, A. (eds.), *The Year of the Euro*, The University of Notre Dame Press, Notre Dame (forthcoming).

Jobelius, S. (2003), "Who Formulates the European Employment Guidelines? The OMC between Deliberation and Power Games", paper presented at the Annual ESPAnet conference "Changing European Societies – The Role for Social Policy", Copenhagen, 13-15 November 2003.

King, S.-J. (2003), "Legal and Institutional Dynamics of New Governance in the EU: Participation and Policy Learning in the Employment OMC", unpublished paper, European University Institute, Florence.

Kok, W. *et al.* (2003), "Jobs, Jobs, Jobs – Creating More Employment in Europe", Report of the Employment Task-force chaired by Wim Kok, Brussels, November 2003 (http://europa.eu.int/comm/employment_social/ employment_strategy/pdf/etf_en.pdf).

Kok, W. *et al.* (2004), "Facing the Challenge. The Lisbon Strategy for Growth and Employment", Report from the High Level Group chaired by Wim Kok, Office for Official Publications of the European Communities, Luxembourg, November 2004 (http://europa.eu.int/comm/lisbon_strategy/pdf/2004-1866-EN-complet.pdf).

Kristensen, P. H. and Zeitlin, J. (2004), *Local Players in Global Games – The Strategic Constitution of a Multinational Corporation*, Oxford University Press, New York.

Léonard, E. (2001), "Industrial Relations and the Regulation of Employment in Europe", *European Journal of Industrial Relations*, Vol.7, No.1, March 2001, pp.27-47.

Léonard, E. (2004), "Social Parts: The Employment Side", unpublished paper.

López-Santana, M. (2004), "How 'Soft' Pressure From Above Affects The Bottom: Europeanization, Employment Policy And Policy (Re)Formulation (The Spanish Case)", unpublished manuscript.

Manow, P., Schäfer, A. and Zorn, H. (2004), "European Social Policy and Europe's Party-Political Center of Gravity, 1957-2003", *MPIfG Discussion Paper*, No.04/6, Max Planck Institute for the Study of Societies, Cologne.

Marlier, E. and Berghman, J. (2004), "Open Coordination at EU Level in the Field of Social Protection and Social Inclusion: *Streamlining* without *Diluting*", in Girard, D. (ed.), *Solidarités collectives*, Famille et Solidarités (Tome I), L'Harmattan, Paris, pp.43-59.

Nauerz, M. (2004), "Does the European Employment Strategy Lead to a *Soft* Form of Europeanisation? An Analysis of the 'Local Dimension' in Germany", Thesis presented for the Degree of Master of European Studies, College of Europe, Bruges Campus.

Peña Casas, R. (2004), "Second Phase of the Open Method of Co-ordination on Social Inclusion", in Degryse, C. and Pochet, P. (eds.), *Social Developments in the European Union 2003*, European Trade Union Institute, Observatoire social européen and Saltsa, Brussels, pp.95-117.

Pochet, P. (2003), "OMC: A Way to Improve Democratic Europe or to Europeanise Social Rights", Paper prepared for the 8th EUSA Conference, Nashville, Tennessee, 27-30 March 2003.

Pochet, P. (2004a), "La MOC et la protection sociale: des développements ambigus", in Dehousse, R. (ed.), *L'Europe sans Bruxelles? Une analyse de la méthode ouverte de coordination*, L'Harmattan, Paris, pp.99-127.

Pochet, P. (2004b), "The New European Employment Strategy", in Degryse, C. and Pochet, P. (eds.), *Social Developments in the European Union 2003*, European Trade Union Institute, Observatoire social européen and Saltsa, Brussels, pp.77-94.

Pochet, P. and Arcq, E. (1999), "UNICE in 1998", in Gabaglio, E. and Hoffmann, R. (eds.), *European Trade Union Yearbook 1998*, European Trade Union Institute, Brussels, pp.179-195.

Pochet, P. and Arcq, E. (2001), "UNICE and CEEP in 2000", in Gabaglio, E. and Hoffmann, R. (eds.), *European Trade Union Yearbook 2000*, European Trade Union Institute, Brussels, pp.173-189.

Radaelli, C. (2003), "The Open Method of Coordination: A New Governance Architecture for the European Union?", *SIEPS Report*, No.1, Swedish Institute for European Policy Studies, Stockholm, March 2003.

Rodrigues, M. J. (2002) (ed.), *The New Knowledge Economy in Europe – A Strategy for International Competitiveness and Social Cohesion*, Edward Elgar Publishing, Cheltenham.

Ross, G. (1995), *Jacques Delors and European Integration*, Polity Press, Cambridge.

Smismans, S. (2004), "EU Employment Policy: Decentralisation or Central-isation through the Open Method of Co-ordination?", *EUI Working Paper LAW*, No.2004/1, European University Institute, Florence.

SPC (2003), Common Outline for the 2003/2005 NAPs/inclusion, Social Protection Committee (http://europa.eu.int/comm/employment_social/soc-prot/soc-incl/commonoutline2003final_en.pdf).

Telò, M. (2002), "Governance and Government in the European Union. The Open Method of Co-ordination", in Rodrigues, M. J. (ed.), *The New Knowledge Economy in Europe – A Strategy for International Competitiveness and Social Cohesion*, Edward Elgar Publishing, Cheltenham, pp.242-272.

UNIOPSS (2001), *Exclusion sociale et pauvreté en Europe*, La Documentation française, Paris.

Visser, J. (2004), "The EES as Selective Amplifier for National Strategies of Reform", document presented at COST A15 Final Conference, Nantes, 21-22 May 2004.

Zeitlin, J. (2002), "Opening the Open Method of Coordination", Presentation prepared for the Committee of the Regions Conference on "The Open Method of Coordination: Improving European Governance?", Brussels, 30 September-1 October 2002.

Zeitlin, J. (2003), "Social Europe and Experimental Governance: Towards a New Constitutional Compromise?" Revised draft of a paper presented to the International Conference of the Hellenic Presidency of the European Union, "The Modernisation of the European Social Model and EU Policies and Instruments", Ioannina, Greece, 21-22 May 2003.

CHAPTER 11

Gender Mainstreaming and the OMC

Is the Open Method Too Open for Gender Equality Policy?

Jill RUBERY

One of the distinctive features of the development of the European Employment Strategy (EES) has been the focus on gender equality issues; in 1997 the strengthening of equal opportunities between women and men was established as one of the four pillars of the Employment Strategy and in 1998 the commitment to gender mainstream all policies, under all four pillars, was added to the guidelines. Gender mainstreaming has been subsequently included in the social inclusion process. Council recommendations to Member States to improve performance under the EES have included recommendations with respect both to gender equality-specific policies and gender mainstreaming. Specific gender equality targets have been set, including a specific female employment rate target for 2005 and 2010 and related targets for the provision of childcare following the Barcelona summit. These developments – including the dual strategy of mainstreaming and gender-specific policies and the targets on employment and childcare – have been included in the new phase of the Employment Strategy, even though equal opportunities for women and men is no longer one pillar among four but one guideline among ten. The proposal by the European Commission for new targets to eliminate the gender gap in unemployment rates by 2010 and to halve the gender pay gap at the Member State level by the same date did not survive scrutiny by the Council but nevertheless the new guidelines include a commitment to substantial reductions by 2010 in the gender gaps in employment rates, unemployment rates and pay.

This chapter explores the conditions associated with the rise of this gender equality agenda, assesses its impact on both policy-making and outcomes at the Member State level, identifies the limitations of the current approach to gender equality and concludes by reviewing recent developments as potential indicators of the sustainability of the gender equality commitments[1].

I. The Rise of Equal Opportunities for Women and Men up the European Agenda

The development of the European Employment Strategy in the 1990s coincided and interacted with the development of a platform for action on gender equality at the UN world summit on women in Beijing in 1995. The EU played a major role in the negotiations over this platform for action and has recognised that it has an important responsibility in the implementation of that strategy; as a consequence it is impossible to separate out the increasing importance attached to equal opportunities at the EU level from the Beijing process itself. Nevertheless, by including the key commitment of the Beijing platform – to pursue gender equality objectives through gender mainstreaming in all policy areas – as an element of the European Employment Strategy, the EU has provided an example to other actors who have done very little to implement the agreed platform for action.

While the general political process in which the EU engaged around Beijing is a key factor in explaining the development of the gender equality perspective in the EES, the continued momentum behind the strategy must be explained by more proximate factors, associated with the European policy-making process. These proximate factors probably divide into three main types: first, and perhaps most important of all is the increasing awareness among officials and political actors responsible for the EES that the achievement of the employment targets at the heart

---

[1]   Much of the information in this paper has been collected as part of the author's role as co-ordinator of the European Commission's Expert Group on Gender and Employment (EGGE). This group acts as an advisory expert group to the Equal Opportunities Unit within DG Employment. It consists of an independent expert from each Member State who is responsible, *inter alia* for producing an evaluation of the National Action Plans on Employment (NAPs) from a gender perspective on an annual basis. Much of the information in this paper comes from the 2001 evaluation where the experts reviewed the evaluation of the NAPs – see Marage and Meudlers (2001) for Belgium, Emerek (2001) for Denmark, Maier (2001) for Germany, Moltó and Valiente (2001) for Spain, Silvera (2001) for France, Karamessini (2001) for Greece, Barry (2001) for Ireland, Villa (2001) for Italy, Plasman and Rusinek (2001) for Luxembourg, Plantenga (2001) for the Netherlands, Mairhuber (2001) for Austria, González (2001) for Portugal, Lehto (2001) for Finland, Gonäs (2001) for Sweden, Rubery (2001) for UK. The network is co-ordinated by Jill Rubery, together with colleagues at the European Work and Employment Research Centre, UMIST (Damian Grimshaw, Colette Fagan, Mark Smith and Hugo Figueiredo). The expert group is financed by the European Commission but the views expressed here are those of the author alone and do not necessarily represent the views of the European Commission nor of the other experts.

of the EES process are critically dependent on the behaviour of women. This awareness was by no means immediate but developed gradually. The 1993 so-called Delors White Paper that kick started the EES process made no mention of gender whatsoever and was heavily criticised by an expert group set up to consider the equal opportunities dimensions of the White Paper (Rubery and Maier, 1995), not only for ignoring the interests of women but for misdiagnosing and misunderstanding some of the fundamental changes taking place in the European labour market. For example, the White Paper presented the tendency for most new jobs to be taken by the inactive rather than the unemployed as a puzzle and not as a consequence of gendered nature of labour demand in a context of declining manufacturing and the rise of part-time and service sector jobs. The second set of factors are more political and personal. This increasing recognition of the gender dimension to the EES was not, as we have said, either immediate or automatic but depended on the understandings and initiatives taken by key officials and political actors. The attention paid to equal opportunities in the EES could well have been different if, for example, the director-general at DG Employment at the time, Allan Larsson, had not come from a Scandinavian country where high employment rates for women were a core element in labour market policy. Furthermore, the attention paid to gender equality in the EES is part of a process of defending but modernising the so-called European social model. Here there are clear differences in approach between for example DG Ecfin that takes a narrow economistic approach to employment and DG Employment where the EES is integrated with the development and modernisation of the European social model. The existence of these alternative perspectives on the European project is central to the understanding of how the attention paid to both employment and social issues rises and falls within the European agenda.

The importance of personalities and political processes is also evident within the series of European presidencies; the Austrian ministers for women and for labour in post during the 1998 Austrian presidency, both female, had their sights set on promoting equal opportunities further within the EES. To that end they organised an informal joint council of ministers for labour and gender equality, commissioned an extensive report (from the current author) and used this momentum to push for the successful inclusion of the commitment to gender mainstreaming in the EES guidelines at the December summit. The input from the presidencies has continued to be important in the development of the equal opportunities dimension to the EES. It was the Lisbon summit that established quantitative targets for both women and for childcare (made more specific at the Barcelona summit) and the presidencies of Finland, Belgium, France and Sweden have all continued to add to pressure to provide more and better information and indicators on gender equality. The third and related factor is the role of lobby groups and pressure groups that have created pressure at both the EU level and at the national level for the development of gender equality policies. The women's lobby is a well established pressure group at the EU level; at the nation-state level pressure groups and political parties have used the commitment to gender equality in the EES and perhaps more importantly within the structural funds to lobby for more attention at the national level. Thus the process has to some extent its own momentum as the inclusion of commitments at EU level opens up opportunities for national actors. However, as we will document below, while the question we are addressing at the moment is why equal opportunities has been given so much prominence at the EU level, an equally important question is why that prominence has not led to evidence of sustained commitments to equal opportunities and gender mainstreaming at the national level. One major factor, as we will discuss further below, is that national political processes explain not only the take up but also the dropping or the neglect of equal opportunities issues.

The development of the European Employment Strategy and indeed the social inclusion process through the Open Method of Co-ordination (OMC) necessarily requires that the commitment to gender equality at the EU level is mirrored at the Member State level. This is also to a large extent true of so-called hard law where the general approach to the implementation of law matters, not just the acceptability of the policy approach. The reliance on political will at the Member State level is both the strength and the weakness of the current phase of the equal opportunities agenda; it is a weakness because, as we shall illustrate, the Member States have very different commitments to, and concepts of gender equality. It is a strength in as much as the gender mainstreaming agenda can only really be effectively implemented at Member States level, as it requires the development of a policy-making approach or process and not the enactment of individually-specified policies. Moreover, the full development of gender mainstreaming involves a more holistic approach to policy-making where the implications and interactions between policies fields are considered in advance of design and implementation of policies; this approach is potentially "transformatory" (Rees, 1999; Council of Europe, 1998). As policy-making in all its various aspects still takes place primarily at the Member State level, it is implausible to imagine that a rethink of the interactions between social and economic policy could be effectively implemented through EU-level hard law. The European social model is in practice a collection of different models (Wickham, 2002) and each of these will need to find its own particular route to transformation, even if all aim to implement an equal opportunities perspective. There is, therefore, considerable complementarity between the OMC and the notion of gender mainstreaming;

nevertheless, one of the issues to be discussed is whether the soft law approach in this area has been too soft, not backed up by sufficiently specific targets, indicators or definitions of the desired outcome – a more gender equal society – for gender mainstreaming to really take root at the Member State level. However, before we come to dissect the weakness of the approach, we first of all have to review the achievements of the policy to date, bearing in mind that it is only ten years since the White Paper on employment was published that failed to identify any gender dimension to the employment problems faced by the European Union.

II. The Impact of the Gender Equality Perspective on Policy-making and Outcomes

The European Employment Strategy is much the most advanced process under the Open Method of Co-ordination. It is in fact now entering a second phase after a five-year period beginning 1997 that was evaluated under a joint impact assessment exercise between Member States and Commission. That assessment provided confirmation that, from both the Member States' and the Commission's perspective, the inclusion of the equal opportunities dimension had had significant outcomes (CEC, 2002). Seven Member States explicitly stated that equal opportunities policies had been "influenced by the EES, either through the setting up of institutions or through the spreading of practices (e.g. gender impact assessment)". Five Member States specifically mention gender mainstreaming and all Member States with the exception of France and Sweden refer to gender or equal opportunities issues in their summaries of the key policy changes associated with the EES (CEC, 2002: Annex to ch. 1). For Greece, equal opportunities policies became "more ambitious", while the impact of the EES on equal opportunities is "strong" in Spain and "notable" in Portugal. Finland reports that gender mainstreaming "became part of government policy, largely as a result of the EES".

These assessments are not fully in line with those carried out by the European Commission's Expert Group on Gender and Employment (EGGE) in their evaluations of the annual National Action Plans (NAPs) from a gender perspective (Rubery *et al.*, 2001). Nevertheless, there is agreement that the EES has put equal opportunities issues more on the map at both EU and the national level, although the extent of change at the national level varies according to the political priorities of the government in power. It is notable that the impact can be identified both in innovations in the policy-making process and in specific policy fields.

If we look at progress made in developing institutional arrangements for promoting gender mainstreaming it is clear that the EES has had a significant impact in stimulating institutional innovation. Box 1 highlights the main forms of institutional innovation that have been reported (see Rubery *et al.*, 2001). It should be noted that in 1997 most Member States had at best a weak and often a non-existent base for gender mainstreaming. In the first phase of the EES almost all Member States put in place some formal mechanism for gender mainstreaming of employment policy or government policy more generally. The role of the EU has been that of a catalyst, by putting gender mainstreaming on the agenda as an issue to be used within the internal political process by various interest groups and political parties. The reliance on local actors also means that the effectiveness of these mechanisms and the extent to which they are becoming deeply embedded in the policy-making process varies greatly (see section 3 below) and thus that the interpretation and meaning given to mainstreaming varies among EU states. The impact of the Beijing process can be seen in the development in some Member States of gender mainstreaming initiatives even before the introduction of the gender mainstreaming guideline into the EES in 1998-1999. Nevertheless, the gender mainstreaming guideline in 1999 not only represented a major step in the implementation of this Beijing commitment but also led to a more widespread development of institutional arrangements to implement gender mainstreaming in Member States. By 2001 only Spain and the Netherlands had failed to develop significant mechanisms for mainstreaming (Rubery, 2002).

The initiatives listed in box 1 refer mainly to central government policy. There are other direct and indirect impacts on gender mainstreaming from the EES, manifest in local or regional initiatives, often related to the gender mainstreaming dimension to the European structural funds that was introduced in parallel to the guideline in the EES. In some cases gender mainstreaming is more developed at the regional or local level. For example, the devolved governments of Scotland, Northern Ireland and Wales have made much stronger commitments to mainstreaming than the central United Kingdom government (for details see Rubery, 2000 and 2001).

Box 1: Examples of Gender Mainstreaming Initiatives and Institutional Developments

- Establishing a ministry with authority in gender mainstreaming (the Ministry for Women's Affairs in Luxembourg, Swedish Minister of Gender Equality);
- Setting up inter-ministerial committees (for example France, Belgium, Greece), inter-ministerial steering committees / work groups (the Netherlands, Germany, Austria), or committees at the office of the presidency (Portugal) with responsibilities for gender mainstreaming;
- Establishing departments, units or taskforces with specific competence in equal opportunities and/or evaluation and monitoring duties (UK, Denmark, Germany, Ireland, Sweden, Portugal) or providing an enhanced role for equal opportunities bodies (Spain);
- Appointing parity/equality advisors on key committees or in ministries (Austria, Italy, Finland, Belgium, France, Portugal) or committees or mechanisms established for gender analysis of the budget (Sweden, France);
- Passing new equal opportunities acts requiring mainstreaming (Denmark, Sweden) or drawing up national strategies or plans for equality (Portugal, Italy (planned), Greece, Belgium, Ireland (planned), France, Portugal);
- Introducing mainstreaming or gender assessment into individual ministries or public services (Finland, Sweden, Germany, Luxembourg (planned), Denmark, France, Ireland, Italy, Austria);
- Developing methodologies or guidelines for gender mainstreaming of government policies or employment policies (UK, Germany, Greece (planned), Ireland, Austria, Finland, Sweden);
- Making commitments to undertake gender assessment of all new pieces of legislation (Finland, Germany (planned)).

The interpretation of the significance of the initiatives reported in box 1 is complex. It may be that the impact of the EES has in some senses been greater in countries where a comparative evaluation would suggest that the actual measures are weaker or less strongly embedded in the policy-making process. That is because it is precisely those Member States without any significant tradition of gender mainstreaming where the EES may have done more to kick start a process, even if that process remains extremely fragile and underdeveloped. For example, in the Nordic countries commitments to include gender issues within public policy are well-established. Denmark has been mainstreaming its public employment service since 1981 when it first appointed equality consultants to regional labour market councils (Emerek, 2001) and in 1994 Sweden undertook to mainstream gender into all ministerial policy was also taken in 1994 (Gonäs, 2001). In part because gender mainstreaming is less novel in these countries, there is limited discussion of this approach within the Nordic National Action Plans. In contrast, the Southern countries of Greece and Italy together with Ireland have both weak traditions of equal opportunities policies and also relatively low female employment rates. It can thus be argued that the requirement to gender mainstream has had a significant impact on the approach to employment policy in all three countries. To some extent the reliance in all three countries, but particularly Greece and Ireland, on structural fund monies may have played a role in stimulating gender mainstreaming initiatives as the requirement to gender mainstream and to develop equal opportunities policies has also been strengthened within the structural funds. Indeed in Ireland the commitment to gender mainstreaming is much stronger in the National Employment Development Plan that relies on structural funds than in the employment NAP itself (Barry, 2001). However, while in 2001 Greece and Italy could be identified as two countries where a range of initiatives in gender mainstreaming were planned, by 2003 the situation has again changed, with Italy retreating on many of its former commitments. This illustrates not only the difficulty of comparing across countries but also in identifying what measures or developments constitute significant and sustainable changes. As we will see below, the changes in political complexion of governments in the EU has a major influence on the impact of the OMC on the development of an equal opportunities perspective. This was nowhere more true than in Austria where, having achieved the inclusion of the gender mainstreaming guideline during the Austrian presidency, the government of Austria changed and effectively dismantled many of the internal innovations in gender mainstreaming. France is another country where the election of a right wing government has placed questionmarks over the implementation of the significant programme of gender mainstreaming that it initiated in 2000 and 2001. In some countries, due to a range of factors including a strong commitment to gender equality that predated the EES, the process seems to be taking on a sustained life of its own. In Finland it is argued that gender mainstreaming has been accepted by policy-makers as a permanent part of the policy formation, implementation and evaluation process (Lehto, 2001) and Sweden has signalled the maturity of its policy by starting to evaluate the methodologies of mainstreaming that it has implemented (Gonäs, 2001). In Member States without such traditions of gender equality policies, it is too early to know which, if any, of the green shoots will eventually turn into mature policies. The large number of examples of Member States where initiatives have been reversed or ineffectively implemented provides scope for pessimism but there may still be a return to such developments, once the political or economic cycle swings again.

So far we have been discussing the development of gender mainstreaming from the perspective of the gender equality agenda. The other contribution that gender mainstreaming can make is to promote a more effective and holistic approach to employment policy, thereby improving the efficiency of policy-making in this area. Indeed the impact assessment of the EES used the interesting concept of "mainstreaming" employment "into other related areas such as social inclusion, education and training, fiscal policy and family policies" (CEC, 2002: 13). This positive assessment of the broadening of the scope of employment policy can be clearly related to the early decision to include equal opportunities and gender mainstreaming as part of the EES. This commitment necessarily leads on to a consideration of issues such as family policy (for example the childcare targets agreed at Barcelona) but also tax policies and social inclusion. This broader approach links the survival and the modernisation of the European social model much more closely to the EES and, furthermore, provides for more efficient and holistic approaches to policy-making, where the strategy is seen to require not just a change in the labour market but also in the institutional arrangements that underpin individuals' participation in that labour market. The development of a job quality dimension to the EES, particularly under the new guidelines, can also be in part attributed to the need to reconcile the search for gender equality with the changing nature of employment. If the focus had remained solely based around issues of access to employment, the problems of closing the gender gaps in quality of employment – as for instance indicated by the gender pay gap – could be expected to become increasingly apparent.

The second strand to gender mainstreaming is the inclusion of gender aspects in the design, implementation, monitoring and evaluation of specific measures included under all the EES guidelines. There is a general view that the EES has not been very successful in promoting a systematic approach to policy evaluation; it is therefore not that surprising that there is limited evidence of gender-based evaluation of mainstream policies. Perhaps more concerning is a rather general failure to set gender-specific or disaggregated targets within the first three pillars of the EES. There has been some more success in introducing gender aspects into the design or implementation of specific policies, particularly those related to active labour market policies, taxation and entrepreneurship. The record in other aspects of the EES has been even more limited, as we discuss in section 3 below.

Change in public policy is evident with respect to the access of women to active labour market policies. Such schemes were traditionally oriented towards displaced men, with eligibility restricted to being a benefit claimant (Rubery *et al.*, 1998 and 1999) or to redundancy from heavy industry or manufacturing. Many women who are without work but who want to work are not formally classified as unemployed for the purposes of claiming benefits, having been out of the labour market or working in non standard employment. Examples of countries which have opened up access to job seekers whether or not they are eligible for benefits since the beginning of the EU Employment Strategy in 1997 include Germany, France, Belgium and Austria, while other countries such as the Nordic countries do not face the same disparities in eligibility for programmes as women have similar employment patterns to men. Several countries have established targets or minimum quotas for women's share of these schemes – including France, Germany, Greece, Austria and Spain. For example, Greece introduced in 1999 a 60% quota (equal to the share of women in unemployment) in all active labour market programmes and schemes. Some schemes include more innovative gender equality approaches: for example in the traineeship scheme in Portugal the underrepresented sex is always to be encouraged and in Sweden some jobseekers are placed in "break projects" aimed at reducing gender segregation of the labour market. In Italy as part of the reform of the public employment service, personnel with equal opportunity competence were to be appointed in each local employment office. In contrast, the UK and Ireland have continued to restrict access to the main active labour market policies to those eligible for benefits, thereby excluding many female unemployed. The proportion of women on the New Deal programmes in the UK as a result is much lower than its share among the unemployed, using the ILO definition.

The second main area where there has been movement is that of tax where individualisation of taxation systems, aimed at removing disincentives to participation by women and other groups has been further developed or fully achieved in the Netherlands, Spain, Ireland, and Belgium. The Netherlands have a fully individualised system but within this have both retained a general tax benefit for everyone, including those who do not work, and has introduced a very small benefit for anyone who combines work and care (defined as looking after a child aged below twelve). This focus on taxation reform for promoting participation follows very much the line of the recommendations from the EU, although as we discuss below, in fact the impact of these policies on women's participation has possibly been exaggerated, except perhaps in Germany (Vermeulen *et al.*, 1994).

The majority of Member States have also established some specific programmes or set gender targets within existing programmes to support the development of female entrepreneurship but the impetus for this development may have come more from the structural funds that provide a good part of the support for business start-up programmes in many countries. In this context what is perhaps more surprising is how limited these developments are. Sometimes it is also difficult to know what has actually happened as programmes mentioned in one NAP disappear in the following NAP, with no information as to whether the measure has ended or has just been omitted.

While all the other areas of policy can be regarded as an almost gender-free zone (see section 3, point B), it is worth noting that, where efforts are made to expand or develop guidelines to point Member States at issues that have a gender perspective, there is some evidence that these developments may be followed up. Before 2001 there had been a relatively limited development of an equal opportunities dimension to lifelong learning initiatives, with many schemes still focused on those in full-time employment. In 2001 lifelong learning initiatives were stressed more and the guidelines revised to include a specification to pay attention to access for those in atypical jobs. There were some moves in 2001 to extend access in ways which may favour women. For example, in the Flanders region of Belgium training credits were introduced that allow for career breaks or reduced working time for training and learning leaves were introduced for part-timers; Spain expanded the range of organisations and workers eligible for state funded training; Italy's new law on parental leave gave a right to up to one year's unpaid leave for lifelong learning, Portugal required attention to gender balance in all its expanding training programmes and the UK began targeting part-timers in some training programmes.

In addition to the gender mainstreaming guideline in pillar 4, the equal opportunities pillar included guidelines that required Member States to enact specific policies to close gender gaps and to promote reconciliation of work and family life. In practice most of the attention was placed on the latter agenda – including improving childcare and leave arrangements. Policies to close the gender gaps were relatively underdeveloped, except for initiatives to address segregation, introduced largely in response to Council recommendations. Table 1 provides a summary of the positive and negative developments within EES within the equal opportunities pillar under the four main headings of segregation, pay, reconciliation and care provision (employment and unemployment being addressed primarily within pillar one). Here action has been greatest in the area of care provision, followed by leave entitlements, with relatively modest and not always productive steps taken to address issues of segregation and unequal pay.

Table 1: Positive and Negative Developments
under the Equal Opportunities Pillar

	Positive developments	Negative developments
Segregation	Initiatives include incentives or programmes aimed at diversifying the occupations or training programmes entered by the unemployed or by women returners; programmes designed to influence initial choices of education, training and career; schemes to increase women's representation in IT occupations; positive action programmes, particularly in public services; and some limited incentives for employers to diversify occupations (for example, rebates on social security in Spain if employers offer women permanent contracts in jobs in which they are underrepresented). Equality plans in Sweden and Finland should address segregation.	Most measures aimed at the unemployed, but male-dominated job sectors not fairing well at this level, so desegregation may not be productive. Limited measures aimed at addressing vertical segregation (e.g. almost no attention paid to the long hours culture). Women not seen as a potential source of easing skill shortages in IT and issues of skill shortages in women's job areas e.g. nursing not addressed. Equality plans in Sweden and Finland appear to be a promising idea for addressing segregation but implementation is low, an issue not addressed in the NAPs. Little attention is paid to reducing the costs of segregation through pay policies to provide for equal pay for work of equal value.
Pay	In Sweden and Denmark new laws introduced to give compulsory access to wage data by gender at enterprise level. Expanded interest in workplace equal pay reviews especially in the public sector. Some initiatives by trade unions with respect to job evaluation (e.g. Germany). New law in France requiring compulsory collective bargaining on occupational equality between women and men. National minimum wages introduced in Ireland and the UK with beneficial impacts on women.	Most countries have limited initiatives to new studies. Little attention paid by Member States to gender pay issues in NAPs; most of the momentum has come from the Commission (gender pay gap included in structural indicators for Broad Economic Policy Guidelines from 2002) and Belgian presidency adopted new indicators for monitoring progress, but little evidence of take up at national level or by social partners.

Reconciliation	Leave arrangements have generally been expanded, in length of time and to cover more needs (e.g. care of sick/elderly adults, sick children) and with more attention paid the involvement of fathers (including offer of longer family leaves if fathers participate).	In some case (e.g. Spain and Austria) the expansion of leave is feared to be reinforcing women's role as carers. Limited development of paid leave is inhibiting take up of leave by fathers.
Care provision	Almost universal improvements in childcare facilities, even for Member States with good provision already (for example moves to more flexible provision). Many of the initiatives in countries where childcare provision has been extremely limited.	More attention to the provision of places than to affordability issues; monitoring of achievement of stated targets not very evident; limited evidence of expansion of other forms of care provision.

III. Limitations of the EES/OMC

While the EES undoubtedly has served to put equal opportunities issues higher up the political agenda, the now rather lengthy experience with this process has served to reveal a number of shortcomings and limitations, some of which may not be susceptible to resolution, either because of a lack of political will or because of the presence of contradictory objectives. These problems can be classified under four headings. First, there is the problem of definition or lack of definition attached to the objectives of a more gender equal society. Second, there is the issue whether the pursuit of the EES as currently developed is compatible with the achievement of gender equality, or whether there are irresolvable conflicts in approach and objectives. Third, there is the extremely important issue of change and developments at the political level in Member States and that can be expected to be reflected at EU level and fourth there is the continuing problem of a lack of expertise among policy-makers, commentators and politicians concerning the development of a gender perspective on the European socio-economic system.

A. Towards a More Gender – Equal European Society – But What Does Such a Society Look Like?

One of the benefits of the OMC is held to be the possibility for Member States to combine their own traditions and approaches with the movement towards common EU wide objectives. On that basis it may therefore be regarded as hardly surprising that there are many definitions, implicit and explicit, within the Member States' National Action Plans as to what constitutes either equal opportunities or greater gender equality. Some Member States implicitly adopt the model of a dual earner dual carer society as the objective, while others – for example the Netherlands – see the one and a half earner model – that is where women combine wage and domestic work through part-time jobs as the objective. Still others – for example Spain – focus more on allowing women to continue with their care responsibilities with extended leaves, and the UK focuses on the sovereignty of choice, whereby the advantages of diversity in working time is stressed, without reference to the constraints that women may face in a context where their partners "choose" to work extended hours. The problem with this apparent free for all is not that there is one straight-jacketed model that has to be adopted immediately by all Member States but that the absence of any discussion of what gender equality actually means allows Member States extreme freedom in presenting their policies as promoting gender equality. Under these conditions the peer review process effectively breaks down as there is no clear set of criteria against which the policies can be assessed. In particular there is no agreement that a more gender equal society must involve change in men's and not just in women's behaviour; instead the focus is almost entirely on women, whether it is on promoting the male model for women to aspire to, or a different model – as in the one and a half earner model favoured in the Netherlands.

The "freedom" offered to Member States to set their own objectives within the OMC also has negative impacts on subsets of the EES. For example the guidelines up to 2003 required Member States to ensure that women are represented in active labour market policies according to their share of the unemployed but left it up to Member States to determine the definition of the unemployed. Thus states that restrict their definitions to those able to claim benefits on grounds of unemployment – thereby effectively ignoring all women returners who want to work but cannot find work – are deemed to fall within the policy guidelines. If gender mainstreaming and gender equality objectives are to have any serious impact on policy-making they must be used to challenge outdated and inappropriate ways of conceptualising the labour market. Unless this challenge is extended to the definitions and policies adopted by Member States under the guise of subsidiarity it will remain a policy tool without teeth.

B. Is the Goal of Equal Opportunity for Women and Men Compatible with or Potentially in Conflict with the European Employment Strategy, as Currently Formulated?

One of the characteristics of the EES, along with most other governmental or pan-governmental programmes is that there is no attempt to analyse the stated objectives for any implicit contradictions or tensions between the various elements. Equal opportunities is thus asserted as compatible with the other goals of the EES but, despite the principle of gender mainstreaming, there is no systematic analysis of the dangers to be avoided in order to enhance compatibility. From the analysis presented above, the changes that have come about associated with the dual development of the Employment Strategy and gender equality objectives are those where there is clear evidence of compatibility – in particular, where promotion of equal opportunities is treated as synonymous with improving the overall employment rate or increasing labour market flexibility. Where gender equality requires substantive change in the organisation of the labour market – with respect to pay, working time or other issues, where employers need to take action – there is very limited evidence of change. Indeed, one can argue that equal opportunities are being pursued as an input into the European Employment Strategy and not as an objective in their own right. This economic justification for equal opportunities has come to dominate over the human rights and social justice argument. This does not means that there are no benefits to women from this approach – in particular the new emphasis on childcare facilities will bring concrete improvements to the infrastructure – but it is important to be clear that these would not be being promoted if they were not seen as compatible with the employment objectives. Where further progress – for example on equal pay – requires action to change the behaviour of employers and indeed trade unions, the EES is in effect powerless, as there is no general consensus that the Strategy should "intervene" in areas deemed the prerogative of social partners and in particular of management. Trade unions appear to be either too weak or not interested in developing gender equality policies. The decision to leave change within the adaptability pillar up to social partners has meant in practice, in many areas and Member States, leaving change up to employer discretion. Issues such as working time, pay, job segregation (in contrast to, for example, educational choices and segregation) have attracted very limited attention. The EES is in fact primarily concerned with the social and legal infrastructure and the characteristics and behaviours of the labour supply; it has very little to say either about what currently happens or should happen within the skin of organisations or about distributional issues – such as the appropriate level of minimum wages. These are both critical areas for gender equality.

This limited approach to the role of government and pan-governmental policy-making leads also to a failure to analyse some of the contradictions within its own approach. The focus, for example, on promoting low taxes on low paid jobs is not framed within a more general policy approach designed to ensure the inclusion of all workers within social protection or the maintenance of adequate tax revenues to sustain the social services that facilitate women's entry to work. These are arguably much bigger issues for women than the rate of general taxation. Indeed, with the exception of Germany (which has maintained its income splitting tax system which does create strong financial incentives to non participation), research suggests that the impact of non-individualised taxation on female participation is at most weak (Vermeulen *et al.*, 1994). Much more important in creating disincentives are household-based means-tested benefit systems, but these issues have yet to be addressed in most countries. Instead there are moves in a number of cases towards employment conditional benefits as a means of promoting participation in low paid work. Belgium is planning an individualised approach (Marage and Meulders, 2001) but the UK and France have opted for household-based approach. These schemes have been recognised by the OECD (2003) as creating strong disincentives for female participation among couple households. It is therefore more than strange that the UK scheme was cited as a best-practice example of equal opportunities policy within the impact assessment of the EES (in contradiction to the analysis provided by the EC's Gender and Employment Expert Group and indeed by the Institute of Fiscal Studies; Rubery, 2000 and 2001; Rubery *et al.*, 2001; Brewer, 2003). There are therefore still contradictory forces at work in tax and benefit reform, at both the EU and the Member State level.

Within the guidelines on flexibility there are injunctions to combine flexibility with security, but there is no explicit analysis of the potential contradictions between flexibility to meet employer requirements and flexibility to facilitate reconciliation of work and family life. These two opposing types of flexibility are just presumed to be potentially compatible, and it is clear that if there were to be a conflict that the former would be prioritised over the latter. Where there are attempts to address the issue of gender equality within the flexibility strategy, these are rooted in particular developments at the national level. For example, in France under the socialist government, the implementation of the 35-hour week was much more sensitive to gender issues in its second than its first phase, reflecting the greater emphasis on gender mainstreaming within French public policy after 1999 (Silvera, 2000 and

2001). The second phase removed the fiscal incentives within the policy to create part-time jobs for in France the promotion of part-time work is regarded as undermining women's integration on an equal basis in the labour market. Instead the new law provided increased opportunities to move from part-time to full-time work.

The twin focus on job quality and full employment within the new guidelines could do something to focus attention on potential conflicts, but the main quantitative targets still apply to the full employment objective and there is little within the guidelines on job quality to point to the potential contradictions with gender equality if "modernisation" is pursued in particular directions. First analysis certainly suggests that the job quality theme has not been given a great deal of attention in the new round of National Action Plans and certainly not from a gender main-streaming perspective (Rubery *et al.*, 2004). The increased focus on social inclusion – both within the EES and as the social inclusion proc-ess develops maturity – should in principle alert policy-makers to some of the potential contradictions between elements of the EES and the related objectives of promoting social inclusion and gender equality. There is, however, a continuing danger that the approach to social inclusion will focus on the household level only, without reference to issues of individual entitlements and rights nor the fact that households are not stable entities, such that the socially excluded – lone parents, poor pensioners etc. – may at some stage have been part of an appar-ently "socially included" household. Again with the 2003 National Action Plans on Social Inclusion there is both a general failure to con-sider issues of individual rather than household risk and to promote gender equality as a goal in its own right, rather than as a means to reduce poverty within households and for children (Rubery *et al.*, 2004). In a context of increasing economic and family instability, more atten-tion needs to be paid to individual rights, an approach more consistent with the gender equality perspective than the primarily household-based approach to poverty and social inclusion.

C. Sustaining Commitment to Gender Equality in a Context of Political Cycles and Political Spin

The third and possibly most important problem in developing the equal opportunities agenda is its critical dependence on a political will to implement the agenda. The most obvious level at which that political will is critical is at the Member State level; it is here that there have been very obvious swings in commitment dependent upon the political persuasion and objectives of the government in power and their percep-tions of the possibility and desirability of making changes. The com-mitment to the equal opportunities agenda at the Commission level has remained somewhat more steadfast but the perception of the Commission of what is possible within the EES is also dependent upon the political will of the Member States as manifest in the Council. It is in fact worth noting that over recent years the presidencies of the Council have added to the momentum behind gender equality issues. Member States in charge of the presidency may have been rather keen to develop equal opportunities initiatives, to make their own mark on the EU equal opportunities agenda, and may also be susceptible to political lobbying at the Member State level to take some action in this field. The examples of Austria and France are instructive in this matter. Both Member States took significant steps during their presidencies to promote gender issues; in Austria the outcome was the inclusion of the gender mainstreaming guideline, in France the presidency called for and adopted proposals for better indicators on reconciliation of work and family life. These presidencies also coincided with the height of activity at the national level in promoting gender mainstreaming. The subsequent change in government in Austria brought these national developments to an effective halt (Rubery *et al.*, 2001) and the change in government in France in 2002 may yet also lead to some reversals of the gender mainstreaming process that was underway. The main role of the EU is in fact in placing equal opportunities and gender mainstreaming firmly on the policy agenda. This establishes equal opportunities as one of the list of options that internal political parties and leaders may decide to adopt for whatever reasons and ends. When the Member State is in the centre of European during a presidency, there is likely to be more attention paid, even at national level, to EU objectives.

Implementation of new approaches to policy-making take time and evaluations of the impact of recent commitments to gender mainstreaming is complicated not just because of volatile political conditions but also because many of the policies have not yet been implemented and are only in the planning phase. There is a further more general issue and that is the difficulty of acquiring anything other than positive perspectives on the progress made with respect to policy development and implementation. National Action Plans only tend to report positive developments and even evaluations of policies are only likely to be reported where these support rather than critique the government's chosen policy approach. This is not in any way surprising in that National Action Plans are overseen, and effectively the responsibility of active politicians who are only keen to present the positive side of the policies. These political dimensions are not however given sufficient consideration in the formulation of the Open Method of Co-ordination approach. There needs to be more independent assessment of the claims made in the National Action Plans, drawing on published work by acknowledged experts within the Member States who have subjected the policy approach to critical analysis. This function is provided by the European Commission's expert group on gender and employment, that consists of an equal opportunities and employment expert for each Member State, who are asked to write an evaluation of the NAP to assist the Commission in its own evaluation. This role of the expert group will be expanded under the next tender to include evaluations of the social inclusion NAPs. This utilisation of external expertise is rather more lacking in other areas. This approach is also of course more effective in Member States with strong traditions of policy-orientated social science research. In other cases there are relatively few independent sources of information on implementation or effects of the stated policies.

D. Limited Knowledge/Understanding on Part of Policy-makers at EU Member State Level

The fourth barrier we can identify to the full implementation of the equal opportunities agenda lies in the lack of both awareness of equal opportunities issues and developed expertise in implementation and analyses of this perspective among both policy-makers and political and economic analysts. Despite the gender mainstreaming requirement, equal opportunities remains compartmentalised and has not been mainstreaming into general analyses of the EES or the social inclusion process. Even in a book project such as this, there are remarkably few references to the gender dimension within the chapters not focused on gender issues. There is particular reluctance to address issues related to male behaviour and to continue to regard gender issues as only concerning women – and, therefore, apparently a minority interest. This approach leads to only partial and narrow perspectives on the changing nature of labour market and society. To what extent can the issues of skill shortage the role for migrant workers be considered without an understanding and analysis of women's labour market participation patterns and issues of gender segregation on the demand side of the labour market? And how can the prospects for re-employment for the unemployed in active labour market programmes be assessed without consideration of whether the problem is a shortage of jobs for unskilled workers or the creation of low skilled jobs designed for second income earners not dependent on their wage for their full living costs? Yet the discussion of active labour market policies on the one hand and skill shortage problems on the other remain a largely gender-free zone.

In addition to the lack of general interest and awareness, there are problems with respect to specific expertise in analysing developments with respect to equal opportunities or the use of indicators or benchmarks to assess progress. Two examples can be cited from the Joint Employment Reports that provide the official review of the NAPs and progress towards achieving stated objectives. In one case Greece was commended for achieving a closure of the gender employment gap, but without reference to the fact that this was only achieved through a fall in the male employment rate. Similarly changes in the segregation index were used to indicate progress in desegregating labour markets, without these changes being decomposed into affects related to structure and labour force change and into changes in the gender shares within occupational categories. Unless the EU raises its game in its analysis of the interrelations between equal opportunities objectives and labour market statistics, the result is likely to continue to include the use and misinterpretation of misleading indicators. Here one can contrast the relatively sophisticated analysis found in the Employment in Europe reports produced by the Commission with the more mechanistic and less satisfactory analysis in the Joint Employment Reports, where the focus is on the chosen indicators without analysis of the background factors necessary to interpret them. The decision from 2003 to produce only a very short joint employment report will not necessarily remedy but may reinforce these problems.

IV. Recent Developments and Future Prospects

So far we have primarily been discussing the development of gender mainstreaming and gender quality action under the first phase of the European Employment Strategy. We now need to confront the issue of whether the momentum that was identified during that phase is now spent, perhaps in line with other aspects of the EES (Goetschy, 2001), or whether there are grounds for optimism that the adoption of gender mainstreaming in the context of the Open Method of Co-ordination provides a basis for a continuing process within the policy-making agenda of both Member States and the European Union. Such an optimistic conclusion could be reached even if there was evidence of currently a retreat from new initiatives or full implementation of the current policy. Provided gender mainstreaming and gender equality remained clearly within the portfolio of policies promoted by the EU, the possibility or likelihood might be that this policy approach would be taken up again by agents in the Member States, when this suited their particular political interests. The likelihood of returning to gender mainstreaming would of course be enhanced the more that women's voices became stronger within the policy-making process, either as members of the policy-making elite or because the need to address women's concerns was recognised as an increasingly important matter for public policy. Moreover, as concerns about the ageing population in Europe increase, there may finally be a recognition that enhancing gender equality at work may actually promote rather than hinder fertility within the EU (Esping-Andersen, 2002).

A survey of recent developments in the EU provides several grounds for both pessimistic and for optimistic outcomes. On the optimistic side, the five-year impact assessment of the EES (CEC, 2002) provides clear confirmation of the importance of the equal opportunity and gender mainstreaming aspects of the strategy. To cynics that could be taken as an indication of the rather weak overall impact of the EES but it is notable that seven countries chose to include equal opportunities as one of the main strengths of the strategy. Furthermore the actions under a number of presidencies have added weight to the strategies being pursued within the EES, by calling for more action, more information and statistics in a number of areas with respect to gender equality. A report on gender gaps is currently being prepared by the Commission for the spring summit of 2004 and this is anticipated to be an annual report. If we turn to projected future developments there is a clear trend towards a streamlining and integration of a number of processes. First of all there is the synchronisation of the EES with the Broad Economic Policy Guidelines (BEPGs), requiring reports on both aspects of economic policy at the same time. This integration, as we outline further below, brings dangers, but it also brings the opportunity for the wider application of gender mainstreaming principles. This has already begun with the inclusion of the gender pay gap as one of the structural indicators under the BEPGs. There was initial opposition to the inclusion of this as a structural indicator but its eventual acceptance further reinforces the EU's commitment to gender equality (and not just high female employment rates). Another positive development is the consolidation of the social inclusion process with the second round of national action plans in the summer of 2003. The guidelines for these action plans, in line with those for employment, stress the need for a gender mainstreamed approach. Just as the promoters of the Employment Strategy have come to realise the centrality of women's employment issues for the overall objectives, a similar argument can be made for the social inclusion strategy – that unless gender issues are taken seriously there can be no effective development of a European social inclusion strategy. Women constitute a disproportionate share of the poor particularly among the older poor and women's' poverty has a particularly deleterious impact on the welfare of children. The possibilities for the development of a gender sensitive analysis may also be argued to be enhanced by the integration of the employment and social inclusion process by the specification of social inclusion as one of the overarching objectives of the new phases of the Employment Strategy. This brings us to the new phase of the EES and its new guidelines. Here again there can be grounds for optimism. The new strategy remains committed to the principles of gender mainstreaming, even if it only mentions this process under guideline six of the new strategy. Furthermore, it reiterates the targets set respectively at Lisbon and Barcelona with respect to women's employment and to childcare provisions and it adds the targets to achieve a substantial reduction in the gender gaps in employment, unemployment and the pay gap by 2010. The Commission's proposals to require a commitment to eliminating the gender gap in unemployment and halving, at the Member State level, the gender pay gap by 2010 were rejected by Council in favour of these weaker versions, but a commitment to a substantial reduction is significant, at least in principle. The three overarching objectives of full employment, improving job quality and productivity and promoting social inclusion also fit very well with the different needs of women in different parts of the European Union. In some Member States as a whole and some regions of other Member States the key concern is to generate more employment opportunities for women. In other Member States such as the UK there is significant progress in employment rates but much more limited progress on the job quality front. In regions such as the South of Italy one key concern is to promote social inclusion and here greater opportunities for women in the labour market could promote such developments.

Thus there is a lot in principle to be optimistic about. Yet pessimism is perhaps the more rational approach. The new EES no longer has equal opportunities as one of its four pillars; instead it is one guideline out of ten. The commitment to gender mainstreaming is not mentioned in the overall introduction but only under guideline 6. The changes to the structure of the EES do not call for a change in approach but by making the commitments to gender equality that much less visible, they also allow Member States to evade and ignore this aspect of the Strategy. What matters in the EES is Member States' perceptions of what is important. It is clear that the quantitative targets associated with the employability pillar led to much more concentration on the first pillar than on other pillars. Similarly downgrading equal opportunities to one guideline in ten allows Member States to interpret it as having lost political importance. First analysis of the new round of National Action Plans on employment has provided more support for the pessimistic than the optimistic interpretation (Rubery *et al.*, 2004). Similar problems have been found in the social inclusion strategy where there is very limited gender mainstreaming in practice of the policies included in the National Action Plans (Rubery *et al.*, 2004). Despite the integration of gender mainstreaming through the text, the policy-makers have yet to take this requirement seriously, even if progress has begun to be made in generating more gender disaggregated data. Further risks come with integration with the Broad Economic Policy Guidelines as here the risk is that the employment process will be seen as secondary to the overall economic strategy There is already evidence that this integration process is weakening commitments to elements that are seen as in conflict with the economic strategy; for example a requirement for policies to close the gender pay gap not to be in conflict with considerations fo productivity and labour market conditions was inserted into the new guidelines, following the line taken in documents of the BEPGs. As gender mainstreaming and equal opportunities is only beginning to be integrated into the BEPG, there is a danger that this momentum will be halted if the EES itself becomes a less important independent force within EU politics. Finally there is the general swing to the right within the Member States which is posing general problems for the more progressive aspects of the EES. Under these conditions perhaps the best the EU can do is hold the line, keep the requirements for gender mainstreaming and equal opportunities specified within the overall employment and social inclusion strategies and wait for the next swing of the political pendulum before a new push can be expected towards gender equality.

References

Barry, U. (2001), "Evaluation of the Irish National Action Plan 2001: A Gender Equality Perspective", European Expert Group on Gender and Employment Report to the Equal Opportunities Unit, DG Employment (http://www.umist.ac.uk/management/ewerc/egge/egge.htm).

Brewer, M. (2003), "The New Tax Credits", *Briefing Note*, No.35, Institute for Fiscal Studies, London, April 2003.

Council of Europe (1998), "Gender Mainstreaming: Conceptual Framework, Methodology and Presentation of Good Practices", Final Report of Activities of the Group of Specialists on Mainstreaming, EG-S-MS (98) 2, Strasbourg.

CEC (2002), Impact Evaluation of the European Employment Strategy, Technical Analysis Supporting COM (2002) 416 final of 17 July 2002 ("Taking Stock of Five Years of the EES"), October 2002 (http://europa.eu.int/comm/employment_social/publications/2002/cev102006_en.pdf).

Emerek, R. (2001), "Evaluation of the Danish National Action Plan 2001: A Gender Equality Perspective", European Expert Group on Gender and Employment Report to the Equal Opportunities Unit, DG Employment (http://www.umist.ac.uk/management/ewerc/egge/egge.htm).

Goetschy, J. (2001), "The European Employment Strategy from Amsterdam to Stockholm: Has it Reached its Cruising Speed?", *Industrial Relations Journal*, Vol.32, No.5, pp.401-418.

Gonäs, L. (2001), "Evaluation of the Swedish National Action Plan 2001: A Gender Equality Perspective", European Expert Group on Gender and Employment Report to the Equal Opportunities Unit, DG Employment (http://www.umist.ac.uk/management/ewerc/egge/egge.htm).

Gonzalez, M. P. (2001), "Evaluation of the Portuguese National Action Plan 2001: A Gender Equality Perspective", European Expert Group on Gender and Employment Report to the Equal Opportunities Unit, DG Employment (http://www.umist.ac.uk/management/ewerc/egge/egge.htm).

Karamessini, M. (2001), "Evaluation of the Greek National Action Plan 2001: A Gender Equality Perspective", European Expert Group on Gender and Employment Report to the Equal Opportunities Unit, DG Employment (http://www.umist.ac.uk/management/ewerc/egge/egge.htm).

Lehto, A.-M. (2001), "Evaluation of the Finnish National Action Plan 2001: A Gender Equality Perspective", European Expert Group on Gender and Employment Report to the Equal Opportunities Unit, DG Employment (http://www.umist.ac.uk/management/ewerc/egge/egge.htm).

Maier, F. (2001), "Evaluation of the German National Action Plan 2001: A Gender Equality Perspective European Expert Group on Gender and Employment Report to the Equal Opportunities Unit, DG Employment (http://www.umist.ac.uk/management/ewerc/egge/egge.htm).

Mairhuber, I. (2001), "Evaluation of the Austrian National Action Plan 2001: A Gender Equality Perspective", European Expert Group on Gender and Employment Report to the Equal Opportunities Unit, DG Employment (http://www.umist.ac.uk/management/ewerc/egge/egge.htm).

Marage, F. and Meulders, D. (2001), "Evaluation of the Belgian National Action Plan 2001: A Gender Equality Perspective", European Expert Group on Gender and Employment Report to the Equal Opportunities Unit, DG Employment (http://www.umist.ac.uk/management/ewerc/egge/egge.htm).

Moltó, M.-L. and Valiente, C. (2001), "Evaluation of the Spanish National Action Plan 2001: A Gender Equality Perspective", European Expert Group on Gender and Employment Report to the Equal Opportunities Unit, DG Employment (http://www.umist.ac.uk/management/ewerc/egge/egge.htm).

OECD (2003), *Employment Outlook*, Organisation for Economic Co-operation and Development, Paris.

Plantenga, J. (2001), "Evaluation of the Netherlands' National Action Plan 2001: A Gender Equality Perspective", European Expert Group on Gender and Employment Report to the Equal Opportunities Unit, DG Employment (http://www.umist.ac.uk/management/ewerc/egge/egge.htm).

Plasman, R. and Rusinek, M. (2001), "Evaluation of Luxembourg's National Action Plan 2001: A Gender Equality Perspective", European Expert Group on Gender and Employment Report to the Equal Opportunities Unit, DG Employment (http://www.umist.ac.uk/management/ewerc/egge/egge.htm).

Rees, T. (1999), *Mainstreaming Equality in the European Union*, Routledge, London.

Rubery, J. (2000), "Evaluation of the UK National Action Plan 2000: A Gender Equality Perspective", European Expert Group on Gender and Employment Report to the Equal Opportunities Unit, DG Employment (http://www.umist.ac.uk/management/ewerc/egge/egge.htm).

Rubery, J. (2001), "Evaluation of the UK National Action Plan 2001: A Gender Equality Perspective", European Expert Group on Gender and Employment Report to the Equal Opportunities Unit, DG Employment (http://www. umist.ac.uk/management/ewerc/egge/egge.htm).

Rubery, J. (2002), "Gender Mainstreaming and Gender Equality in the EU: The Impact of the EU Employment Strategy", *Industrial Relations Journal*, Vol.33, No.5, pp.500-522.

Rubery, J., Grimshaw, D. and Figueiredo, H. (2001), "Gender Equality and the European Employment Strategy: An Evaluation of the National Action Plans for Employment 2001", European Expert Group on Gender and Employment Report to the Equal Opportunities Unit, DG Employment (http://www.umist. ac.uk/management/ewerc/egge/egge.htm).

Rubery, J. and Maier, F. (1995), "Equal Opportunity for Women and Men and the Employment Policy of the EU – A Critical Review of the European Union's Approach", *Transfer*, Vol.1, No.4, October 1995, pp.520-532.

Rubery, J. Smith, M., Fagan, C. and Grimshaw, D. (1998), *Women and European Employment*, Routledge, London.

Rubery, J., Smith, M. and Fagan, C. (1999), *Women's Employment in Europe: Trends and Prospects*, Routledge, London.

Rubery, J., Smith, M., Figueiredo, H., Fagan, C. and Grimshaw, D. (2004), "Gender Mainstreaming and the European Employment Strategy and Social Inclusion Process", EU Expert Group on Gender and Employment, Report to the Equal Opportunities Unit in the European Union, DG Employment, February 2004 (http://www2.umist.ac.uk/management/ewerc/egge/egge_ publications/NapEmp_Inc2003.pdf)

Silvera, R. (2000), "Evaluation of the French National Action Plan 2000: A Gender Equality Perspective", European Expert Group on Gender and Employment Report to the Equal Opportunities Unit, DG Employment (http:// www.umist.ac.uk/management/ewerc/egge/egge.htm).

Silvera, R. (2001), "Evaluation of the French National Action Plan 2001: A Gender Equality Perspective", European Expert Group on Gender and Employment Report to the Equal Opportunities Unit, DG Employment (http:// www.umist.ac.uk/management/ewerc/egge/egge.htm).

Vermeulen, H., Dex, S., Callan, T., Dankmeyer, B., Gustafson, S., Schmaus, G. and Vlasblom, D. (1994), "Tax Systems and Married Women's Labour Force Participation: A Seven Country Comparison", *Working paper*, ESRC Research Centre on Micro-Social Change in Britain, University of Essex.

Villa, P. (2001), "Evaluation of the Italian National Action Plan 2001: A Gender Equality Perspective", European Expert Group on Gender and Employment Report to the Equal Opportunities Unit, DG Employment (http:// www.umist.ac.uk/management/ewerc/egge/egge.htm).

Wickham, J. (2002), "The End of the European Social Model – Before it Began?", Briefing paper for Infowork project, Employment Research Centre, Trinity College Dublin (http://www.tcd.ie/erc).

CHAPTER 12

The European Employment Strategy, a Channel for Activating Social Protection?

Jean-Claude BARBIER

I. Activation between Convergence and Diversity

An "activation" lens is especially promising for understanding the current restructuring of the so-called "welfare states" in the context of an increasing importance of the European Union (EU) level of government. Yet "activation" is all but a precise concept although it has indeed been extensively present in the political discourses of all EU Member States for nearly a decade, despite the continuing diversity of their labour markets and social protection systems.

On the one hand, the documentation of common tendencies in Europe is highly interesting. Accordingly, the longing to find convergence and sameness in a world of extreme diversity has proved very resilient in social research. Indeed, the European policy process itself provides strong incentives to focus primarily on what is common to all Member States, and to disregard what is not. Moreover a preference for universalism is strongly embedded in the most influential of scientific languages, i.e. mainstream economics. Yet apparently common features may easily be superficial and lead to misleading conclusions. The longing for uniformity may also be ascribed to the temptation to impose on other countries features that are documented in the researcher's own country. In this respect, the postulation of convergence[1] is certainly of

---

[1] A good example of "functional universalism" is provided by Gilbert (2002: 15), who, after commenting on the intrinsic variety of welfare systems and the traditionally used "clusters", eventually concludes that all systems are converging towards the same point where the UK and the USA have already arrived: "a basic shift has occurred in the institutional framework for social protection [...] most prominently in the United States and England, with the other advanced industrialized nations moving steadily in the same direction".

little use (Barbier, 2002a), especially when one fails to distinguish between convergence of rules and procedures, and convergence of substantive outcomes of change (Börzel and Risse, 2000).

On the other hand, there are many shortcomings of "culturalist" approaches that unilaterally privilege phenomena considered specific to a particular nation. Yet many aspects of institutions, playing key roles in social policy, are very much dependent on their initial historical stages, all being different across nations. Reducing diversity for the sake of achieving simple explanations is always possible, but at a considerable loss. The majority of research devoted to welfare states and social policy has documented diversity, along the clustering of countries proposed in Esping-Andersen's welfare regimes (Scharpf and Schmidt, 2000; Pierson, 2001). These typologies provide decisive tools and as Esping-Andersen suggested (1990: 2) lead to robust findings at a "big picture" level. Similarly, the traditional opposition between "Beveridgeism" and "Bismarckism" has certainly retained much of its robustness (Abrahamson, 1999). Both typologies might be relevant to understand "activation" as a common process of reform, adaptable to varying contents and resulting in diverse outcomes. What will interest us here is the fact that this process presently occurs in the context of the implementation of the European Employment Strategy (EES).

When it comes to analysing dynamics, clustering methods show important drawbacks (Barbier and Théret, 2003). Moreover, the threefold division of worlds of welfare capitalism does not apply evenly across all sectors of social protection: as we will show in the present paper, it is not possible to identify "three worlds of activation". At the present stage, features characterising the dynamics of activation seem to fit into two distinctive models, the "liberal" and the "universalistic" (Barbier, 2002b and 2003). Yet for the last decade in every country some sort of political discourse has promoted "active policies" ("an active society" as the OECD once phrased it, "an active welfare state" as the 2000 EU Lisbon summit put it). We first have to analyse what actual policies might be grouped under the activation banner, and to assess whether the fashionable policy slogan has remained rhetorical. Answering this question requires a rigorous separation between social science concepts and political discourse: an adequate analytical notion of "activation" will eventually turn out to be more encompassing than the most frequent use of the term.

Understanding the pertinence of "activation" in the context of the EES leads to a balancing exercise between diversity and similarity. Moreover, it leads to acknowledging that the interactive processes of influence between EU Member States cannot be captured as simple influences on one another, nor as a mechanical impact of the European level on the national. We will have to distinguish between different types of possible "convergence" or perhaps "hybridisation". So far, such exchange and interaction processes have not really prevented the resilience of national divergence. In these circumstances the European Strategy is confronted by the challenge of coordinating Member States' policies with very different activation rationales: so far as the procedure is concerned, the first five years of the EES have shown success. But what has happened in terms of substance? As with any EU-level policy, in the case of the EES, "outcomes" are a tricky notion: they might manifest themselves as the adoption of similar policies, whilst the question is left open as to the effects of these policies (in terms of employment, inequality etc.).

In this paper, we will pursue three goals. First, we will show that, despite being primarily a policy notion, "activation" can also be used for analysing a variety of policies, which might have very different influences on the welfare regime clients. Second, we stress that the trend to "activation" preceded the invention of the EES: it has existed for a much longer term, especially in certain countries and under different forms. Finally, because "activation" may be seen both from a processual and from a substantive perspective, we need to understand not only the interaction of national activation strategies and the OMC, but also the interaction of the OMC with types of such strategies in both these perspectives.

II. "Activation" as an EES Political Notion, "Activation" as a Concept

As part of the international political discourse, the term "activation" and associated words (active, activate) have inevitably borne multiple meanings (Serrano Pascual, 2002). Yet, the notion has also been increasingly used in social research (Gilbert and Van Voorhis, 2001; Esping Andersen *et al.*, 2001; Goul Andersen *et al.*, 2002; Schmid and Gazier, 2002; van Berkel and Möller, 2002) to characterise a type of programme which aims at transferring welfare recipients to the labour market ("welfare-to-work strategies"). However the on-going transformation in social and economic policies goes well beyond the introduction of welfare-to-work or a supposed return to the old spirit of the workhouse. The changes to social protection go well beyond the mere introduction of work-tests, and the punishment and/or incentivising of welfare recipients in America. Hence we need a more general and encompassing analytical notion to capture the essential features of contemporary "activation", while seeing their possible connection to the EES.

A. A Fuzzy International Political Notion with (Mainly) Scandinavian Roots

Politicians, policy-makers and administrators are used to ambiguous normative notions. Experts and officials working for international organisations constantly select new terms, which they use as universal categories, sufficiently ambiguous to apply to diverse situations. "Activation" has been one such category, along with many others, like "social exclusion" or the more recent "social inclusion'; it has featured high on the European Union's agenda, more visibly from the Essen Summit (1994) onwards, but the 1993 White Paper on Growth, Competitiveness and Employment also contained explicit recommendations for the activation of labour market policies[2].

Yet the introduction of the term into the international policy vocabulary occurred much earlier, and its dissemination has been gradual, while its content has also evolved. Very simply, three important stages can be identified. The first is related to the historical "Swedish model", as far back as the 1940s. The model was gradually implemented in the 1950s and 1960s and reached full gear in the 1970s – although with features which did not exactly fit the ideas of its inventors, G. Rehn and R. Meidner. With a prudent fiscal policy and selective expansionary instruments (to contain inflation – different in this respect to mainstream Keynesianism) the model combined a centrally bargained and solidaristic wage policy and active labour market policies. There, activation referred mainly to the necessity of tackling labour market adjustment problems through a variety of programmes fostering mobility, reallocation of the workforce, training etc. "Activation" in this sense was aimed at increasing the flexibility of the labour market in a safe and egalitarian environment for workers. The stress was on activation of the market and of policy, which was normatively preferred to the traditional provision of unemployment compensation (Milner and Wadensjö, 2001). A high level of public employment was also a distinctive feature of the model (including extensive temporary public employment). The model eventually was completely transformed, although it has actually retained its active labour market element, a Swedish tradition later extended to the other Nordic countries.

A second stage occurred in 1964 when the OECD adopted a recommendation to promote an active labour market policy[3], in a period where Keynesianism was still the mainstream economic policy reference. At

---

[2]   "Passive policies" were also sharply criticised in the 1993 EU White Paper.

[3]   "Recommandation du Conseil sur la politique de la main d'œuvre, instrument de la croissance économique". It is probably no pure coincidence that Gøsta Rehn was head of the Employment and Social Affairs secretariat at the OECD from 1962 to 1973.

that time, the OECD assessed the combination of policies implemented in Sweden positively. It is only after the neo-liberal turn, in a third stage during the 1980s, in the context of separation of macro-economic and social policies, that the notion of "active labour market policies" took on its present content, i.e. focussing on structural and supply-side labour market reforms. OECD reports have consolidated and emphasised this notion, while particularly criticising Member States with a high commitment to "passive policies" (chiefly unemployment compensation and early retirement programmes). This was particularly emphasised in the past ten years, after the publication of the 1994 OECD "Jobs Study". In the subsequent yearly Employment Outlook reports, OECD experts have kept praising labour market reforms which decreased eligibility and coverage of unemployment insurance or assistance. They particularly publicised the Danish introduction of an *"individual handlingsplan"* (action plan) in the early labour market reform[4], to "activate" the unemployed (Jørgensen *et al.*, 1998; Jørgensen, 2002; Barbier, 2004a). Actually the Danish example of activation (*aktivering*, as it was later known) was used extensively abroad to exemplify a virtuous type of reform, and a departure from presumed old style "passive" policies. This was for instance the case in the recent debate in France over the reform of unemployment insurance, but numerous examples appeared in other countries.

Hence, from 1994, a key OECD benchmark has been the activation of labour market policies, in the wider context of structural labour market reform and the connected idea of "welfare reform" (which was later translated into the now very current expression "tax-benefit reforms"). As we have shown, the OECD sharply criticised the policies of countries like France at the beginning of the 1990s. There was also a constant contrast of the supposedly high performances of the USA with the supposedly poor outcomes of the continental countries. From interviews with officials in France, in the Commission and in other EU Member States, we have come to the conclusion that the rivalry between the OECD and the European Commission was one important factor in the complex process of inventing the EES (Barbier and Samba Sylla, 2001).

At the European Council in Essen, in 1994, where a precursor of the EES was agreed, activation was mentioned in three of the five priorities adopted (Barbier, 1998). Hence, it was naturally introduced in the first version of the EES with its four pillars agreed at the Luxembourg summit of 1997, particularly in the first pillar (increasing employability).

---

[4] See for instance the report of the reform in the 1995 edition of *Employment Outlook* (p.125, French edition). The 1995 OECD report on the implementation of the Jobs Strategy also mentioned the introduction of individual plans in Denmark as a progress (p.32, French edition).

But gradually the notion that the tax and benefit systems had to be reformed in order to increase employment and incentives to take jobs, added in 1999, featured more and more prominently (Barbier, 2002c).

Now, activation is both a dimension of the EU economic recommendations (the Broad Economic Policy Guidelines – BEPGs) and of the EES Guidelines (Barbier, 2002c). It first applies to individuals in the working age population, whether they are active or inactive (for instance the disabled); it applies to women and lone parents, to the "socially excluded" persons, but also to early retirees and to pensioners. Here the common recommendation is for policies fostering the overall increase of employment rates, with specific targets for older people and women. But "activation" also applies to benefit programmes, to policies, to the whole array of instruments described as "tax and benefit" systems. In the current policy orthodoxy, not only individuals are to be "activated", but also whole systems of social protection (Barbier, 2002b; 2003 and 2004a), which are deemed too "passive" and inefficient, particularly adverse to job creation and to labour market flexibility. This set of economic assumptions and policy recommendations constitutes, in the area of labour markets, a kind of "universal policy mix" (Fitoussi, 2000).

As van Berkel and Möller have shown (2002: 51-56), these policies may be normatively justified in many ways. The mechanisms anticipated in such programmes and their normative justifications are in fact all but homogeneous, ranging from the traditional American conservative approach of "rights and responsibilities" aimed at fighting "welfare dependency" to the unconditional and universal access to Scandinavian activation programmes: we will come back to this. All in all, despite its fuzziness and ambiguity, taken out of its historical Swedish context and revisited, the international policy notion of activation is nevertheless interesting because of its capacity to encompass a wide range of reforms occurring across social protection systems in a number of countries.

B. An Encompassing Analytical Notion

The dynamics of activation should first briefly be set in the wider macro-economic context. It is true that "activation" took on a new aspect and scope once the "Fordist" regime compromises proved inefficient in the late 1970s and full employment policies were discarded. The new requirements for flexibility of work, as well as the change of paradigm in economic policy, have imposed new constraints upon national systems, now increasingly exposed to the impact of international monetary rules (Barbier and Nadel, 2000). The national actors (the state, social partners, "civil society") involved in the design and management of social protection systems have actively addressed this challenge: this has resulted in the diverse re-design of these systems within a common thrust towards more activation. The eventual compromises reached are certainly not exempt from contradictions of interest and power struggles, which can be very sharp and explode into wide-scale social protest, as was shown in recent years[5].

The notion of "activation" can be envisaged as the introduction of an increased and explicit linkage between "paid work" and social protection. Over the last decade, this dynamic has implied not only the redesign of pre-existing income support and, assistance programmes, but also the transformation of tax and social policies. This redesign, or sometimes even overhaul of the entire social protection systems has displayed common features, i.e. most prominently that of enhancing the various social functions of "paid work"[6] and labour force participation, which has even been seen increasingly compulsory in certain national cases. Precisely because there have been substantially different paths to activation, there is more to this transformation than a supposed "subordination" of "social policy to the needs of labour market flexibility and/or to the constraints of international competition" (Jessop, 1996: 176).

Areas of social protection potentially "activated" comprise (i) benefit programmes [unemployment insurance and various "assistance" schemes for working age groups (including disability and other family related benefits); (ii) pension systems and especially early retirement programmes[7]; (iii) employment (or labour market) programmes; but also, (iv) a policy area situated in between traditional social policy and tax policy. This policy area includes the extension of tax credits; programmes that partly allow people to keep their entitlements to benefits while being employed (supposed to incentivise them to take jobs[8]); various demand-side programmes for subsidising jobs, such as those introduced to decrease social contributions or to allocate wage subsidies to employers when they hire additional people.

From the individual's point of view, all these programmes are supposed to provide incentives (sometimes closely linked to compulsion and sanctions), but also, in some cases, a wide array of offers of services (for instance counselling, job search, training). At least in theory, they also indirectly or directly extend individual choice by increasing the number of job offers on the market (especially in the case of wage

---

[5] In 2001-2002, see for instance the mass refusal of the unemployment reform in Spain, the PARE controversy in France, the strikes in Italy.

[6] More precisely, in fact, "waged work" (*travail salarié*). A critical point here lies in the "wage-labour nexus" of the regulation school of economists (see, for instance, Boyer, 1986).

[7] In this case, the impact of the overall activation dynamics has only been emerging so far.

[8] "In-work benefit" was the British expression used before the extension of tax credits.

subsidies). From a system perspective, social protection is "activated" in the sense that the distribution of services and benefits mainly targets working age people in some sort of "work"[9] activities[10]. It is also activated in the sense that funding mechanisms and the allocation of resources are designed so as to foster increased job creation, even to the point that, with the 2000 Lisbon strategy of the European Union, a revised notion of "full employment" has returned to the political agenda. And indeed at EU level, "employment" or "work" now tends to be seen as a panacea for all sorts of social needs, certainly blurring the previous frontier existing between traditional social policy and social protection associated with the status of being employed.

C. Two Ideal Types of Activation and Maybe a Third?

The proposed notion can be confronted with the classical three welfare clusters. Seen as one form of restructuring in Pierson's terms (2001), activation can be differentiated according to them. So far, we have identified two really coherent ideal types of activation, the "universalistic" and the "liberal", which we will only briefly present here (for details, see Barbier, 2002b and 2003).

The liberal type chiefly enhances individuals' relationships to the labour market, which, aggregated, are assumed to yield social equity and efficiency. ALMPs as well as social policies thus take on a limited role, restricted to inciting individuals to seek work, providing quick information and simple matching services, as well as investing in short-term vocational training. Individuals in and out of the labour market are also the target of the wide-ranging implementation of "tax credits" and all sorts of "in-work" benefits. Similarly, activation manifests itself in the trend towards adopting measures inciting people to be as active as possible (accepting any job on the market as it is) across their life course and implementing pension reforms dispensing with any fixed age for retirement. Very generally, for an individual, having a conventional job on the market tends to be the normal way of accessing protection (pri-

---

[9] "Work" has to be seen here as a very broad notion, as was the case with the original US programmes of the 1970s (Rodgers, 1981; see also Greenberg and Rahmanou, 2003). In the typology they designed, van Berkel and Möller (2002) have rightly observed that "informal", "voluntary" and "community" work were not generally taken into consideration by public programmes.

[10] Despite its undeniably innovative character, the activation strategy, insofar as it links work and social protection, is certainly not completely new, because, from their start, social protection systems have been built upon relationships with employment statuses. Using the method of bilateral comparison, we have explored with colleagues this historical legacy in greater detail in the case of Germany, Austria, Italy, France, the UK, Slovenia, Norway and Denmark, for a special issue submitted to the journal "European Societies".

vate and social) from risks, and work systematically tends to replace assistance. Activation entails both re-commodification of the system (already highly commodified in comparative terms) and efforts to reduce social expenditure (for instance in the case of the disabled).

On the other hand, the universalistic type not only provides complex and extended services to all citizens, but simultaneously guarantees relatively high standards of living for the assisted, and, for the lower paid sections of the labour force, benefit levels amounting to a significant proportion of minimum wages. Hence the role of the market is not unilaterally prominent (although some re-commodification is implemented in a highly de-commodified system; Kvist, 2002). Not systematically submitted to work requirements, social policy retains its traditional role as a contribution to well-being. Activation applies to all citizens in a relatively egalitarian manner and the "negotiation" between the individual's and society's demands appears much more balanced. A fully active society seems to be able to yield employment opportunities tailored to a variety of needs and capacities. Activation applies to an already highly active population employed in a context of relatively good quality jobs. It entails recalibration of the previous income compensation mechanisms, in the overall context of cost containment, but the use of tax credits and subsidies plays a limited role.

No national case exactly fits these stylised types, but the countries of the liberal cluster are close to the liberal ideal-type and the Scandinavian countries are close to the universalistic. A third, coherent, "continental" ideal type has not yet clearly emerged, although the French could be a harbinger of a possible third type (Barbier, 2003).

III. Activation in EES Times (before and after 1998)

Activation as a policy rationale obviously pre-dates the existence of the EES. In the 1980s and 1990s, new approaches emerged, which certainly inspired its formulation, rather than the other way round. But since 1997, national and EES policy orientations have interacted, both in the area of assistance or unemployment programmes and in the reforming of the "tax and benefit systems".

A. The EES Has Inherited a Tradition of Programmes for the Unemployed and the Assisted

Over the past fifteen years a variety of new programmes, or reconfigurations of existing ones have been introduced. Because of the general use of the English language, the "Anglo-Saxon" reforms among them have not only featured prominently in comparative literature, but non-native speakers of English have been led to present and describe

continental programmes in English. Let's review some important milestones in this story.

1. Workfare, a Misnomer

Early analysis of the activation of assistance programmes made extensive reference to the term "workfare"[11], which proved misleading
(Barbier, 1996; 2002b). For instance, in the book they edited Lødemel
and Trickey (2000) included programmes which displayed heterogeneous characteristics, such as German social assistance and the French
"emplois-jeunes" and RMI (*revenu minimum d'insertion*). Indeed, they
defined "workfare" in very minimalist terms ("programmes and schemes
that require people to work in return for social assistance", page 6). The
notion of a "Schumpeterian workfare state" has also been used, following Jessop (1993 and 1996) in order to describe "workfare" under another avatar in Denmark[12] (Torfing, 1999). Peck (2001), on the contrary
has limited the analysis of "workfare states" to the Anglo-Saxon world.

As time and fads pass, the importance of substantive distinctions
among activation strategies has been taken into account by a growing
corpus of literature (Barbier, 1996; Kosonen, 1999; Geldof, 1999;
Abrahamson, 2001; Morel, 2000). The UK appears as the only European
country to have been greatly inspired by the USA, where the 1996
Clinton "welfare reform programmes" are currently being re-authorised
by Congress[13]. The British version of welfare-to-work has nevertheless
been implemented in the context of a very different welfare state.

Moreover, the most meaningful policy instrument pertaining to "activation" in the USA has not been "workfare" programmes. In the
context of a residual welfare state, it has instead been the EITC (Earned

---

[11] Although he did not exactly coin the term, Nixon gave it its classical meaning in
1969 in the context of US "welfare reform" (Peck, 1998: 138). Basically, the notion
of workfare has operated in the US as an "ideological totem" for conservative
thought on social assistance (Peck, 1998; Morel, 2000). This literature, of which
Charles Murray is a good example, has advocated the necessity of imposing work
obligations on individuals claiming "welfare", but this stance extended further to
other circles and became dominant before spilling over outside the USA.

[12] Torfing (1999: 17) explained that the Danish so-called "workfare" had five characteristics, which distinguished it from the UK and US programmes: all five actually
described a logic completely in opposition to the real workfare programmes in the
USA, notably the fact that the Danish programme was not about "punishment", but
rather about "empowerment", and that it was universal instead of stigmatising.

[13] One should further note that the outcomes of the reform in terms of *actual* activation
of individuals are not so clear-cut, as is shown for instance by the discussion going
on in the USA about "participation rates" (Greenberg and Rahmanou, 2003). The
main route to activation for individuals in the US programmes has remained ordinary
low-paid jobs.

Income Tax Credit, enacted in 1975), whose importance has kept increasing[14]. Here the USA appears more as a pace-setter, especially given the wide scale imitation of its policy in the UK, which, in a certain way remained an "activation laggard" till the end of the 1990s.

2. A Reformed Scandinavian Activation Rationale

As active policies of different brands existed on the continent, the designers of the EES did not have to turn to the USA for inspiration. But they certainly had to accommodate the indirect American influence that penetrated via British influence in the EU.

If, according to EES actors interviewed, the general economic policy framework bore Swedish and Scandinavian influence[15] (Barbier and Samba Sylla, 2001), the Scandinavian activation tradition of the 1960s had been altered, and Denmark, rather than Sweden (Hort, 2001), was the locus of inspiration for the reform of labour market policies in the early 1990s. Sweden was to follow only later, in the late 1990s. Active labour market policies born in Sweden had been imitated to various degrees by most European countries[16]. As successive OECD comparisons demonstrate, the Scandinavian countries constantly ranked among the highest spenders for such programmes in the years before the EES. Hence, the activation orientation is not new for them. Although much less generous and efficient, a similar trend has also existed in France since the beginning of the 1980s (Barbier and Théret, 2001). Presenting these programmes as an illustration of a recent and "Anglo-Saxon" inspired convergence for "promoting work" simply would not match facts.

---

[14] Whereas, in 2001, the number of participants of the TANF (Temporary Assistance for Needy Families) programme had dwindled to about two million households (caseloads are increasing now again), more than 19 million families and individuals claimed the federal EITC (a little under 20% of all American households). The federal tax credit now appears to lift more children out of poverty than any other programme in the USA. Some 4.8 million people, including 2.6 million children, are removed from poverty as a result of the federal EITC. The success of the federal EITC has led a number of states to enact *state* EITCs that supplement the federal credit. TANF accounts for less than 2% of the federal budget and is of relatively marginal importance when compared with European social budget standards. When not directed to ordinary jobs, workfare participants remain assisted (as opposed to accessing employee status), whereas the bulk of the poor are working EITC recipients (the "working poor").

[15] Among those interviewed: A. Larsson, former Swedish minister of finance, and director general of DG Employment and Social affairs; K. Löhnroth, the deputy director general of DG Employment.

[16] The most extensive temporary employment programme in France in the last twenty years, i.e. the "*contrats emploi solidarité* – CES" was directly inspired by the Swedish policies (Barbier and Théret, 2001).

In fact, Denmark was certainly the most innovative country in introducing, first for the young (from 1992) and then for all categories of working age people (even for the assisted[17]), the overall logic of "*aktivering*" within the context of a "capacious labour market" (Bredgaard, 2001)[18], a market deemed friendly for all. The Danish "*aktivering*" programmes fit with the tradition of an overall high level of labour market participation (especially for women). But they introduced a rupture in Danish policy, because they reduced the length of access to benefits and imposed work requirements in a country where a quasi-unconditional basic income existed. This did not amount to adopting a strict "supply side"-oriented OECD doctrine (Jørgensen, 2002).

3. "Insertion", the Republican Employer of Last Resort

The notion of "social exclusion" has passed from French into EU jargon. But this is not the case for "insertion" ("social integration") (Barbier and Théret, 2001), which appeared in the second half of the 1970s. At that time, various local initiatives from non-profit organisations helped create the base for what was to become "insertion" programmes of benefits and services and there had been no talk of "activation" in the country. New policies, which started from the introduction of schemes for the disabled in 1975 and were widely extended afterwards, were based on a rationale akin to the Scandinavian inspiration, but with a distinct Republican solidaristic flavour. They had their originality: "social integration" was not meant primarily or solely in terms of constraining people to take jobs on the market. In fact, due to the particularly low rate of job creation in France over that period, many programmes entailed the function of keeping people in welfare rather than transferring them over to work.

A particular aspect of these policies throughout the 1980s and 1990s was a constant and quantitatively important creation of temporary subsidised jobs in the public and the non-profit sectors (Barbier, 2001). Although the explicit justification of these programmes by successive governments (Left- or Right-wing alike) was precisely that they were intended to integrate people in society, and ultimately into the labour market, their eventual outcomes have remained controversial[19].

The programmes, in a way, manifested the duty of the state to act as an "employer of last resort" in times of supposed "market failure".

---

[17] At least in principle: see Jørgensen *et al.* (1998) and Larsen *et al.* (2002).

[18] Now more typically translated in English by the term "inclusive labour market", widely used in the EES and the EU Social Inclusion Process.

[19] Yet similar discussions have existed in other countries (Martin, 1998; Barbier, 2001; de Koning and Mosley, 2002).

Hence the ability of such programmes to really "activate" people in the sense of their eventual taking jobs on the conventional labour market, has remained limited. Although the French schemes – and particularly the RMI (*revenu minimum d'insertion*) activities – have certainly been less successful than their counterparts in Denmark or in Sweden, similarities exist between both. Yet even in the successful Scandinavian experience, there is talk about "open unemployment", with the clear implication that some unemployment remains "hidden" (Bredgaard, 2001; Abrahamson, 2001). Similar remarks have been made about programmes elsewhere, for instance in Italy, with the "Lavori socialmente utili" programme. However, in Italy, as well as in Spain, the implementation of comparable subsidised jobs in the public and non-profit sectors has remained limited, as well as the expenditures devoted to them.

This brings to the fore the observation that many so-called "activation" initiatives might remain at a rhetorical stage. Comparatively, continental countries, like Italy, Spain and Germany would be prone to this, because they have proved reluctant to adopt explicit activation strategies. A case in point has been Germany, where social partners and the state proved unable to engage into significant reforms for a long time: those following the report presented by the Hartz Kommission (in 2002) have, at the moment of writing just been initiated there. However, even in the cases of the Scandinavian countries and the UK, evaluation data about the actual outcomes of activation strategies have remained rather scarce so far.

4. The UK as Activation "Laggard"

When it came to power in 1997, the New Labour government embarked on a significant transformation of the welfare benefit rules and of the Employment Service, with the introduction of successive "New Deals", which first applied to the young unemployed and were subsequently extended to other groups. It is important to recall that the previous Conservative governments in Britain had constantly opposed the introduction of "workfare"[20]. Moreover, programmes similar to the continental labour market schemes had been gradually stopped in the mid-1980s by the Conservative governments, which privileged the conventional market, but at the same time allowed the growing transfer

---

[20] Only in 1996, just before Labour came to power, did John Major's government launch its short-lived "Project Work" for the long-term unemployed in ten pilot areas (Finn, 1998). Why the Thatcherites doggedly opposed such schemes is no mystery: they were acutely wary of the danger that the state, at the end of the day, would emerge as an "employer of last resort".

of unemployed working age people to disability schemes (Barbier, 2004a).

The new schemes, however different in scale and implementation, certainly display features similar to the American programmes, which were an inspiration for their creation (Deacon, 1999); they have appeared very much in line with the classical "punitive" dimension of the British legacy (King, 1995; Peck, 2001). However, as we have shown, the British welfare reform had a much broader scope than in the US, because, contrary to the latter, the British welfare state funds programmes with huge "caseloads" of recipients. Five years on, one of the principal potential target groups of "activation" in the UK, namely individuals receiving some sort of sickness or disabled benefit, has not shown clear signs of dwindling[21].

In the recent conversion of the UK to activating the welfare system, the market was given the central role. This policy has certainly been compatible with the EES and the British influence in drafting the employment guidelines has been important. The British reform was discussed in other countries, for instance in France, and the EES has certainly been a favourable factor for that. However, this does not mean that the recent French employment policy has been significantly influenced by the British one. Moreover, within the process of devising and discussing the guidelines and their associated indicators, France and Britain have often advocated divergent positions, as is for instance the case for the notion of "quality" of jobs (Barbier and Samba Sylla, 2001).

B. The Wider Scope: Activating the Systems

France and the UK have also differed in their strategies for reforming their "tax-benefit" systems. Both compatible with the general activation rationale recommended by the EES, these strategies contrast sharply and this contrast is obviously related to structural features of the welfare regime to which they belong. So far, no conclusive evaluation or research data are yet available to assess the precise outcomes of these reforms. Debates and controversies exist in France over the estimated outcome of the protracted reduction of indirect labour costs. Estimations vary about the number of jobs created, but also about the right timeframe to estimate them. In the UK, effects of the tax-benefit reforms on labour market participation have not yet been significantly assessed.

---

[21] Unlike the unemployed (claiming JSA – Job Seeker's allowance), the number of people on any of the sickness and disability *benefits* has continued to grow from 1997 to 2002 (from 2.792 to 3 million) (DWP, 2003). Whereas the number of unemployed claimants decreased by 600,000 in the same period, the number of disabled continued to increase slightly. The number of people on "key benefits" (excluding tax credits) comprise about 14% of the working age population.

The New Labour governments have embarked on a systematic extension of tax credits, imitating the US, but also Canadian programmes (notably the EITC and the Canadian Child Credit)[22]. From October 1999, the Labour administration has transformed and extended the existing Family Credit benefit. The new WFTC (Working Families Tax Credit) emerged as the most prominent "in-work" benefit in the UK system (presently catering for more than 1.2 million recipients, as the number of its recipients has grown sharply in recent years). The current "generalisation" of tax credits has not yet been completed, but it builds on the WFTC and other differential benefits[23]. A question is whether, via the on-going introduction of a "Working Tax Credit" for the low paid, the UK will eventually conform to the EITC model, thus extensively replacing traditional benefits for the poor out of the labour force, and transforming them into "US-style" working poor eligible for tax credits. The precise assessment of the extent of underemployment in the UK is obviously a crucial point here, as well as the potential capacity of the British economy to deliver an appropriate number of jobs (and, what is more, matching them with the slack labour force's skills and qualifications)[24]. This question also applies to the less "employable", particularly in certain areas affected by high unemployment and local labour market and economic development problems.

In France, policy has focused on labour demand instead of supply. The overall expenditure on "employment policies" has soared in the 1980s and 1990s, and its increase has only slowed slightly during the labour market boom from 1997 to 2001. During the same period, expenditure for subsidising employers" social contributions soared, because of (i) the implementation of "general" breaks on social contributions for low wages from 1993 on, and, (ii) the implementation of social contribution reductions associated with RWT (reduction of working time) subsidies in firms with more than 20 staff[25] from 1998. While the aggregate expenditure for "passive" and "active" programmes has remained

---

[22] Previously, over the 1990s, there had also been in Britain a continuous policy of decreasing National Insurance contributions, despite a recent increase announced in 2002 for the new budget.

[23] For instance, in March 2000, the Government announced that, from April 2001, all long-term unemployed were to be guaranteed a minimum income in their first year (£60 a week on top of wages up to yearly £15,000). Tax credits have also been introduced for disabled people.

[24] *Before* the introduction of the new credits, substantial evidence nevertheless had shown that there was a considerable gap between the politicians' rhetoric and the *actual* effects of welfare reforms on patterns of labour market participation and activity, at least with regard to lone parents (Bradshaw *et al.*, 2000).

[25] The full extension to all firms was delayed by the Socialist government and cancelled altogether by the new conservative government in 2002.

roughly unchanged, the amount spent on reductions of social contribu-tions has multiplied almost sixfold over seven years. Hence, one of the most important measures in the French "activation strategy", i.e. the reduction of employers' social contributions, funded by the state budget, has appeared structural and permanent, with the aim of decreasing labour costs for low wages, but also for medium wages (up to 1.8 SMIC – salaire minimum interprofessionnel de croissance, the minimum wage). Before the change of government, the principle of the reduction of social contributions was expected to be extended to about 11 million employees by 2005. Levels of reductions differ according to pro-grammes but are the highest at SMIC level (at around 30% of gross labour costs). It was estimated that the resulting decrease in labour costs was among the largest in Europe (DARES, 2002: 130). To our knowl-edge, this fundamental reform has not yet been documented extensively in comparative literature: activation, in the present sense, means an activation of the labour demand via funding mechanisms, not activation of the individuals, as is the case in the British strategy.

The complex structure of the French system (Barbier and Théret, 2001 and 2003) has been further complicated with the introduction of the PPE (*Prime pour l'emploi*), a "tax credit" for employees. PPE is not substitutive of other benefits. In 2001, one in four households was eligible for it. PPE is (until now) a relatively small tax credit with a very wide population of beneficiaries, a target group not strictly targeting poor households unlike the UK and US systems. One paradox is that, while bearing all appearances of a redistributive mechanism, it is fo-cused on lower median income earners and has had little chance so far either to act as a "work incentive" for the assisted or as a redistributive mechanism for the poorest. Given its present design[26], consequently, it is highly improbable that the PPE could effectively act as a significant "activating" mechanism for employees[27].

Despite their differences, both the UK and French strategies bear similarities: the reduction of social contributions is more adapted to the reform of the mainly contribution-based French system of funding, while the logic of incentives (make work pay) is more congruent with the tradition of the British welfare state, but both pertain to a liberal route to activation. The addition of a (so far) marginal tax credit in France, as well as other piecemeal incentives for the various minimum incomes, tend to complement the main trend of decreasing employers'

---

[26] Many reforms are being mooted presently in the wake of legislative and presidential elections (June 2002).

[27] The implicit philosophy that people "on welfare" are mainly moved by financial interests is also a moot point, as an extensive literature shows (see Esping-Andersen *et al.*, 2001).

social contributions in order to lower the cost of labour, especially for lower skilled people. Although less systematic than in the French case, activating mechanisms have also been introduced in Spain and in Italy. On the other hand, the universalistic model of activation has not shown significant resort to such mechanisms.

Pensions and early retirement schemes (early retirement pensions and disabled benefits for the ageing often play a similar role) are also an important area of social protection which will potentially be activated in the future. Repeated recommendations have figured in this respect in the EES guidelines. But important early retirement or disabled benefits programmes exist in many countries. So far, the Netherlands have been the most prominent example of an important number of people of working age in a very important programme for the disabled (the WAO – Wet op Arbeidsongeschiktheidsverzekering – caters for disabled people of whom 70% are older than 45) that successive governments seem to have tried to reform with limited success. Finally, another candidate for social protection activation has only started to emerge, but it is bound to be much higher on the agenda in the next few years, i.e. the on-going and anticipated efforts to increase labour force participation for older employees. The reform in Finland seems to be very much ahead of the general trend in Member States (Guillemard, 2002). The various EU-level policy recommendations will probably impact this trend, whose basic tenets nevertheless pertain to internal demographic factors.

All in all, our empirical review has confirmed that activation is a cross-cutting trend within welfare policies in Europe, with diverse national strategies. It is an adequate notion to group different programmes and policies often presented separately[28]. Only in the universalistic and the liberal models has the transformation displayed a coherent pattern, whereas in continental countries, activation policies are more diverse, piecemeal, drawing from each of the models. Activation was well under way when the EES started, which took it on board and which made this term one of its main general catchwords, at EU level, where the necessity to increase employment rates, is, in itself, an overarching activation objective. Numerous empirical interactions between the EES and national strategies have been mentioned. We now turn to a more systematic approach to these interactions.

---

[28] Esping-Andersen *et al.* (2001: 58) tend to present them in a piecemeal way, but they certainly point to the wide extension of the rationale, when they, for instance, explicitly classify the provision of day care for children within activation.

IV. Activation Policies and the EES: Processes, Substance and Models

Rather than looking for simple causal links between the EES and national policies it seems more interesting to try and unravel the complex cross-influences between countries and between the EU and national levels of government. Here a "cognitive" perspective seems promising. Yet, empirical analyses about the EES are still in their beginnings (Zeitlin and Trubek, 2003): we mostly draw here from our own on-going research[29]. Preliminary findings tend to show that the co-ordination procedure has been successful over the first five years, but it did not demonstrate any substantive convergence of policies. A complementary assumption is that national activation logics tend to interact differently with the EES. The EES actually is not the only "paradigm" or "framework of reference" for activation: also the Broad Economic Policy Guidelines (BEPG) are to be taken into account.

A. Two Common Assumptions

Especially in the domain of the EES, two simplistic and polar assumptions often impair realistic analysis of interactions between the EES and national policies.

The first one contends that the co-ordination is only superficial and symbolic (in Edelman's (1964) sense) because no sanctions are attached to following up recommendations. According to this assumption, there is little reason for the EES to have any influence, since there is no EU money attached to it (or very little), while the treaty of Amsterdam reaffirmed that competence in matters of employment policy is national. The second one, on the contrary, contends that the EES is a channel for substantive change. Actually there are two distinct versions of this assumption: according to the first, the employment strategy is a dangerous Trojan horse introduced in national policies to bend all of them towards the neo-liberal paradigm and degrade them; the proof lying in the substance of the guidelines and recommendations, which all fit very closely with the neo-liberal policy mix. According to the second, the EES is, on the contrary, introduced as a sort of protection of the social dimension of European integration, which, in its absence, would only be market and economy-based. Indeed both assumptions are myopic and impossible to vindicate from the current empirical material, which is limited so far. Both these assumptions are also inadequate, because they

---

[29] For a first approach to the transformation of French policies in the context of the EES, see Barbier and Samba Sylla (2001). This research has been extended through further interviews with European Commission officials and actors in various Member States (see Barbier, 2004b).

do not present a convincing empirical analysis of the actual processes of change, either in terms of the documentation of policies and programmes (a huge task indeed across the fifteen Member States and the ten future members), or in terms of conceptions and ideas.

1. Forget Programme Evaluation

The European Commission's communication on the assessment of the first five years of the EES (CEC, 2002) actually displayed an overall lack of evaluation findings of policy outcomes causally linked to the EES. This absence is all the more understandable since measurement problems are immense [the classical "programme evaluation" model is impossible to implement here]. Indeed, on top of the general limitations attached to traditional evaluation methods (Barbier and Simonin, 1997) in matters of European policy, the EES is certainly not a "programme". Should particular developments in "outcomes" be established as "fitting" with the explicit objectives and recommendations of the co-ordination, they would, at best, support "speculations" about possible links. But the reverse is also true. For instance, employment rates for older people may display increases or decreases: a particular decrease could, very hypothetically, offer evidence that, in the absence of EES recommendations, the employment rate would have sunk more rapidly. Documenting such causality is out of reach for the mainstream methods of programme evaluation. The "evaluation" reports handed by Member States to the Commission[30] vindicate the futility of efforts to objectify the EES as a causal mechanism in such a framework. We cannot for instance accuse the EES of being "symbolic", just on the basis of the fact that the Netherlands have failed to activate their disabled WAO recipients; or, similarly, on the basis of the fact that the employment rate of the 55+ in France has only slightly changed since the EES guidelines were first introduced. We have shown for the case of France, that recommendations have been stable and repetitive over the five first years of the EES (Barbier and Samba Sylla, 2001). Similar patterns are probable for the other Member States.

Observations should rather focus on the interplay of ideas and conceptions, but also on the possible changes in the policy processes.

---

[30] In the particular case of France (Barbier and Samba Sylla, 2001), we have shown that the National Action Plans for Employment (NAPs/empl) have contained very limited evaluation information, if evaluation is considered in terms of international practice standards. A preliminary survey of NAPs/empl tends to confirm this observation for various countries.

B. Cognitive Convergence, a Common Language

To the idea that the EES acts as a channel of the neo-liberal policy mix, contrary observations can be opposed. One is that there has been a continuous in-fighting, including in the recent stages (2002-2003) of the so-called "streamlining" of the co-ordination processes in different areas, between the differing conceptions embedded into the EES and the BEPG. Actually, the EES can be seen as fostering the adoption by all actors of a common language in employment policies, and especially in activation. But the overall compliance with the usage of the common language does not mean that conflicts between diverging conceptions have disappeared. The common language, moreover, also allows for "ritual compliance".

1. The "Neo-liberal" Turn: It Was Already Completed When the EES Started

Actually, factors explaining the conversion of Member States to activation are numerous and can be found at different levels: we have already mentioned the overall modification of the international regulatory regime. This has also entailed a general adoption by state elites of a "neo-liberal" economic framework, and the repudiation of Keynesianism. In this, key institutions have played an important role, among which the OECD. In terms of possible cognitive influence for adopting activation as a policy orientation, then, the OECD has historical precedence over the EES. The nearly simultaneous publication in 1993-1994 of the EU White Paper, the Essen priorities and the Jobs Study all referred to the activation imperative. It would be difficult to sort out each of their specific influence. However, a probably more important task is to go beyond the mere identification of the common economic policy framework as "neo-liberal".

Here two important aspects have so far received insufficient attention; the first is the actual differentiation of economic policies across Member States (especially with regard to their particular national mode of articulating social protection and their very gross conformity to mainstream orthodoxy). Throughout the five years of the EES, Scandinavian countries (Denmark and Sweden) and the UK have constantly featured as "good performers", despite the obvious contrast between their welfare systems[31]. The second aspect is the persistent differentiation that has existed, from their initial adoption, between the BEPGs, on

---

[31] Contrasts are in terms of the weight of social expenditure relative to GDP, of the generosity of benefits, and the universality of coverage. Numerous studies show that large differences appear in terms of inequality and poverty (see for instance Korpi, 2000).

one hand and the EES on the other. Important differences contrast the BEPGs policy discourse – which appears close, although not identical to standard OECD doctrine – from the EES policy discourse. Significant here is the latter's attention to the quality of jobs, to social exclusion, to discrimination between men and women, as well as to the role of social partners (Barbier, 2002c). These elements are often considered as features of a "Social Europe" model counterposed to the American brand of capitalism. One of the fields where the influence of the EES has seemed greatest is in the adoption of a policy discourse favourable to the equality of men and women.

Moreover, our present research tends to show that, in the various committees involved in the EES, rather stable associations tend to appear between certain Member States. While Belgium for instance has often sided with France, the Scandinavian countries' representatives often associate with their UK counterparts. This latter privileged association, at first glance, could appear contradictory in the light of their divergent welfare systems. Yet, many factors can explain such associations (for instance the influence of intergovernmentalism). However, the relatively high ranking of both the UK and the Scandinavian countries also has to be understood from the perspective of their domestic economic and welfare policies.

The continuous difference between the BEPGs and the EES (Barbier and Samba Sylla, 2001; Barbier, 2002c) has been rather well documented. Not only a war of words, it is also a persisting conflict between the DGs (Employment and Social Affairs, ECFIN) within the Commission, and it mirrors, in certain countries, internal conflicts between Finance and Employment ministers, which also emerge in the divergent opinions of the Employment and Economic Policy Committees. The BEPGs, even in their recent streamlined version (2003), still seem to have their own agenda for employment policy, structural reform of the labour market, more in line with traditional OECD doctrine. Although the BEPGs and the EES are strictly co-ordinated and deemed consistent and compatible with each other, the mere persistence of their different wording can be seen as a sign that various paths to activation compete. One dimension of this competition should be better documented, i.e., the role played by the notion of "quality of work" in the activation logics, but it is too early to identify clear findings. It is doubtful that the EES could be a simple channel for substantive impact on the quality of jobs in Member States; but at the same time, quality has also been a catchword for the forces in the Commission which push for more demanding social objectives.

Interviews with administrators in the Commission vindicate the fact that the proponents of the "social" dimension of the strategy are obliged to use the common economic language to formulate them: this is true of activation as well as more broadly. A recent example can be seen in one of the new priorities of the EES, which has been termed "quality and productivity". Conflicting views can be expressed in a common language. We have documented similar observations in France: whereas the EES has produced a certain homogenisation of the language used by actors competent in employment policies, this has not erased the divergence of their views and of their interests.

The impact of the common language also differs according to countries. For instance, in the UK, employment, social and financial policies all tend to be under the control of the Chancellor, so that the formulation of social policy at national level is already cast in a common economic language. By contrast, in countries like France, the impact of the EES on a cognitive level has also been to broaden the framework of reference in which employment and unemployment questions were previously formulated and envisage them more in economic terms. This cognitive adaptation has not, however, meant that the power of the Ministry of Finance was increased over employment and social policy: the contrary was true of the years 1998-2000 (Barbier and Samba Sylla, 2001).

2. Ritual Compliance and Domestic Usage

Because of the EES's nature as a procedure producing common guidelines and recommendations, it is no wonder that practices of "window dressing" and ritual compliance should be observed. Actually, in the initial stages of the EES, the nascent OMC only resulted in a common presentation of the existing programmes into a common framework agreed at Luxembourg (Barbier, 1998). Such a practice can be detected when the formulation and presentation of policies and programmes fits into the EES general normative framework, but at the same time, the former clearly differ in the way they are implemented. When one reviews the vast amount of documents, recommendations, national action plans and, notably the actual national evaluations presented to the Commission for the first impact assessment exercise in 2002, it is easy to show that Member States have tended to conform to the initial Luxembourg guidelines and EES pillars, in terms of activation. But, as we have shown (Barbier, 2002c) the essential basis for the EU co-ordination lies in national policies and these keep on diverging in substance, generosity, and expenditures.

Adaptation does not mean that guidelines have effectively been abided by, and the recommendations been heeded. Complying with EES guidelines might also be explained by internal motives. There often exist many ways of presenting national policies from a positive angle within the national action plans. Numerous examples may be taken as evidence: one is the opportunistic presentation of the *Prime pour l'emploi* in France and the PARE reform, which was actually promoted by the CFDT union and the MEDEF employers' confederation against strong opposition from the French government before being eventually approved; another is the complex and obscure presentation of figures in the Italian action plan for the main activation guidelines (ex-guidelines in the first pillar on employability). The successive versions of the Joint Employment Reports published by the Commission (which are political documents and not scientific analytical material) very clearly display numerous indicators. Many of them, among which the employment rates for the aged feature prominently, have shown that targets have not been met, in terms of activation or in other domains.

Ritual compliance nevertheless, can be accompanied by socialisation effects. Our interviews with members of the Employment Committee and administrators linked to the small elite of the EES show that the very process of its formulation and debate leads to interactions and learning from the part of officials in various countries.

C. The Brussels Arena and National Arenas: Power and Levers

Finally, the NAPs/empl are also political documents which can be used as power resources by actors in the various policy arenas. In the case of France, we have shown that key actors in the employment policy arena have been gradually obliged to cave in to the necessity of becoming direct or indirect participants in the "Brussels arena", where EES decisions are taken. This arena encompasses various institutions, such as for instance the Employment Committee created by the Amsterdam Treaty, but also of course the Economic Policy Committee (Barbier and Samba Sylla, 2001). Should they not participate in the Brussels arena, national actors would run a considerable risk of being also marginalised in the national arena where domestic decisions are taken, notably because the "Brussels insiders" are able to use the EES as a "lever", an additional resource to pursue their goals. We have presented numerous instances of this process in the French case: one was the Minister of Employment's victory over the Treasury about the funding of the Employment Service, another was the very significant increase in the relative position of the gender equality department of the Ministry of Social Affairs. However, participation in the EES Brussels arena has so far been limited to a tiny elite, and our observations in the French administration show that there has been very limited "spill-over" to other levels of administration and to regional or local authorities. This seems to be also true in other countries. For instance, the evaluation process, implemented under the direction of DG Employment and Social Affairs showed that social partners were very unevenly involved in the EES across Member States.

Conclusion

In Radaelli's sense (2000), the EES has clearly been a factor of "Europeanisation" and in many ways. This process is obvious with the adoption of a common language in the field of employment and social policy. Yet a common language practiced does not mean that conceptions have been homogenised or ideas of activation are converging.

So far, both the Scandinavian countries and the UK have fared rather well within the EES as good performers in matters of activation. Yet recommendations are made about the lack of vocational training in the UK and gender segregation of the Scandinavian labour markets. However, it should be recalled that Scandinavia and the UK share a common Beveridgean rationale. Their economic policies seem also to have been rather analogous in structural terms. Such structural similarity might explain their capacity to perform well within the EES procedure. However, in substantive terms, there has been no convergence of their systems, and the two models we have described have not been transformed into one, simply by the action of the EES, nor have they shown signs of hybridisation so far. As for the continental countries, the EES has not emerged as a determining cause for their conversion to some sort of activation strategy: internal factors here are probably more important than the EES influence, among them the traditional Bismarckian role of social contributions as an obstacle to activation. France, among the continental countries, has displayed a coherent activation strategy in this respect, although the effective results in terms of job creation remain very controversial. This may be linked to the fact that France's Bismarckianism is hybridised with a substantial dose of Beveridgeism, where the state has been able to impose reform in the last years (Barbier and Théret, 2003). It is too early to say whether, at the end of the day, the EES, in the medium term will be able to contribute to the formulation of a third "continental model" of activation but it is doubtful. The EES seems bound to remain a source for procedural rather than for substantive convergence.

Finally, it remains unclear whether substantive social policy aspects already present in EES guidelines might translate into effective changes across countries and transform their previous nation-specific policies (for instance altering the substantive nature of rights and obligations attached to nation-specific types of social citizenship). With regard to the relationship of these possible developments to the role of European-level regulation, if it is true, as Supiot (2003) observes, that the role of national legal frameworks of employment and social welfare is changing, while incorporating local and global norms into national models, it will be interesting to analyse how the implementation of the EES – a basically soft-law process, could interfere or spill-over with other types of regulations. But such effects cannot be documented at this early stage, in contrast to the direct effects of EU directives and regulations translated in national law.

References

Abrahamson, P. (1999), "The Welfare Modelling Business", *Social Policy and Administration*, Vol.3, No.4, pp.394-415.

Abrahamson, P. (2001), "L'activation des politiques sociales scandinaves: le cas du Danemark", in Daniel, C. and Palier, B. (eds.), *La protection sociale en Europe, le temps des réformes*, MIRE, La Documentation française, Paris, pp.123-140.

Barbier, J.-C. (1996), "Comparer workfare et insertion?", *Revue française des affaires sociales*, No.4, October-December 1996, pp.7-27.

Barbier, J.-C. (1998), "A la recherche de la politique européenne de l'emploi", in Barbier, J.-C. and Gautié, J. (dir.), *Les politiques de l'emploi en Europe et aux Etats-Unis*, Cahiers du CEE, Presses Universitaires de France, Paris, pp.357-380.

Barbier, J.-C. (2001), "Temporary Subsidized Employment in the Public and Non Profit Sector: A European Comparative Study", report for the Evaluation Committee, Noisy-Le-Grand, March 2001 (http://www.cee-recherche.fr).

Barbier, J.-C. (2002a), "Marché du travail et systèmes de protection sociale, pour une comparaison internationale approfondie", *Sociétés contemporaines*, No.45-46, pp.191-214.

Barbier, J.-C. (2002b), "Peut-on parler d'activation de la protection sociale en Europe?", *Revue française de sociologie*, No.43-2, April-June 2002, pp.307-332.

Barbier, J.-C. (2002c), "Une Europe sociale normative et procédurale: Le cas de la stratégie coordonnée pour l'emploi", *Sociétés contemporaines*, No.47, pp.11-35.

Barbier, J.-C. (2003), "Systems of Social Protection in Europe: Two Contrasted Paths to Activation and Maybe a Third", in Lind, J., Knudsen, H. and Jørgensen, H. (eds.), *Labour and Employment Regulation in Europe*, P.I.E.-Peter Lang, Brussels, pp.233-253.

Barbier, J.-C. (2004a), "Activation Policies: A Comparative Perspective", in Serrano Pascual, A. (ed.), *Are Activation Policies Converging in Europe? The European Employment Strategy for Young People*, European Trade Union Institute, Brussels, pp.47-84.

Barbier, J.-C. (2004b), "La stratégie européenne pour l'emploi: genèse, coordination communautaire et diversité nationale", Rapport de recherche pour la DARES (Ministère du Travail), Paris, January 2004.

Barbier, J.-C. and Nadel, H. (2000), *La flexibilité du travail et de l'emploi*, Domino, Flammarion, Paris.

Barbier, J.-C. and Samba Sylla, N. (2001), "Stratégie européenne de l'emploi: les représentations des acteurs en France", rapport pour la DARES et la Délégation à l'Emploi du ministère du Travail et de l'Emploi, Paris, December 2001.

Barbier, J.-C. and Simonin, B. (1997), "European Social Programmes: Can Evaluation of Implementation Increase the Appropriateness of Findings", *Evaluation*, Vol.3, No.4, pp.391-407.

Barbier, J.-C. and Théret, B. (2001), "Welfare to Work or Work to Welfare, the French Case?", in Gilbert, N. and Van Voorhis, R. (eds.), *Activating the Unemployed: A Comparative Appraisal of Work-oriented Policies*, Transaction Publishers, Rutgers, N.J., pp.135-183.

Barbier, J.-C. and Théret, B. (2003), "The French Social Protection System: Path Dependencies and Societal Coherence", in Gilbert, N. (ed.), *Changing Patterns of Social Protection*, Transaction Publishers, Rutgers, N.J., pp.119-167.

Börzel, T. and Risse, T. (2000), "When Europe Hits Home: Europeanization and Domestic Change", *European Integration online Papers (EIoP)*, Vol.4, No.15 (http://eiop.or.at/eiop/texte/2000-015a.htm).

Boyer, R. (1986), *La flexibilité du travail en Europe*, La Découverte, Paris.

Bradshaw, J., Terum, L. I. and Skevik, A. (2000), "Lone Parenthood in the 1990s: New Challenges, New Responses?", paper for the ISSA research conference, Helsinki, September 2000.

Bredgaard, T. (2001), "A Danish Jobtraining Miracle? Temporary Subsidised Employment in the Public and the Non-profit Sector", Preface by Henning Jørgensen and presentation by Jean-Claude Barbier, *CARMA Working Papers*, No.5, Centre for Labour Market Research, Aalborg University.

CEC (2002), Communication from the Commission "Taking Stock of Five Years of the European Employment Strategy", COM (2002) 416 of 17 July 2002 (http://europa.eu.int/eur-lex/en/com/cnc/2002/com2002_0416en01.pdf).

DARES (2002), "Bilan de la politique de l'emploi en 2000", *Dossier*, No.4/5, La Documentation française, Paris.

Deacon, A. (1999), "The Influence of European and American Ideas upon 'New Labour' Thinking on Welfare Reform", paper presented to Conference on "Global Trajectories: Ideas, Transitional Transfer and Models of Welfare Reform", Florence, 25-26 March 1999.

de Koning, J. and Mosley, H. (2002), "How Can Active Policies Be Made More Effective?", in Schmid, G. and Gazier, B. (eds.), *The Dynamics of Full Employment*, Edward Elgar Publishing, Cheltenham, pp.365-392.

DWP (2003), "Client Group Analysis, Quarterly Bulletin on the Population of Working Age on Key Benefits – November 2002", 17 April 2003, National Statistics, Department for Work and Pensions, Newcastle.

Edelman, M. (1964), *The Symbolic Uses of Politics*, University of Illinois Press, Chicago.

Esping-Andersen, G. (1990), *The Three Worlds of Welfare Capitalism*, Polity Press, Cambridge.

Esping-Andersen, G., Gallie, D., Hemerijck, A. and Myles, J. (2001), "A New Welfare Architecture for Europe?", Report submitted to the Belgian Presidency of the European Union, September 2001.

Finn, D. (1998), "Welfare to Work, Making It Work Locally", Report for the OECD Local Economic and Employment Development Programme (LEED), October 1998.

Fitoussi, J.-P. (2000), "L'avenir de l'Europe: l'ambition d'un autre contrat social", *Revue de l'OFCE*, No.75, October 2000, pp.165-182.

Geldof, D. (1999), "New Activation Policies: Promises and Risks", in Heikkilä, M. *et al.* (eds.), *Linking Welfare and Work*, European Foundation, Dublin, pp.13-26.

Gilbert, N. (2002), *Transformation of the Welfare State, The Silent Surrender of Public Responsibility*, Oxford University Press, Oxford.

Gilbert, N. and Van Voorhis, R. (2001), *Activating the Unemployed: A Comparative Appraisal of Work-oriented Policies*, Transaction Publishers, Rutgers, N.J.

Goul Andersen, J., Clasen, J., van Oorschot, W. and Halvorsen, K. (2002), *Europe's New State of Welfare, Unemployment, Employment Policies and Citizenship*, The Policy Press, Bristol.

Greenberg, M. and Rahmanou, H. (2003), "TANF Participation in 2001", CLASP internet paper, 18 March 2003 (www.clasp.org).

Guillemard, A.-M. (2002), "L'Europe continentale face à la retraite anticipée, barrières institutionnelles et innovations en matière de réforme", *Revue française de sociologie*, No.43-2, April-June 2002, pp.333-368.

Hort, S. (2001), "Sweden – Still a Civilised Version of Workfare?", in Gilbert, N. and Van Voorhis, R. (eds.), *Activating the Unemployed: A Comparative Appraisal of Work-oriented Policies*, Transaction Publishers, Rutgers, N.J., pp.243-266.

Jessop, B. (1993), "Towards a Schumpeterian Workfare State? Preliminary Remarks on Post-fordist Political Economy", *Studies in Political Economy*, No.40, pp.7-39.

Jessop, B. (1996), "Post-fordism and the State", in Greve, B. (ed.), *Comparative Welfare Systems, the Scandinavian Model in a Period of Change*, St. Martin's Press, New York, pp.165-183.

Jørgensen, H. (2002), *Consensus, Cooperation and Conflict, the Policy Making Process in Denmark*, Edward Elgar Publishing, Cheltenham.

Jørgensen, H., Larsen, F., Lassen, M. and Stamhus, J. (1998), "La politique active du marché du travail au Danemark: réforme et décentralisation", in Barbier, J.-C. and Gautié, J. (dir.), *Les politiques de l'emploi en Europe et aux Etats-Unis*, Presses Universitaires de France, Paris, pp.155-178.

King, D. (1995), *Actively Seeking Work, The Politics of Unemployment and Welfare Policy in the United States and Great Britain*, University of Chicago Press, Chicago.

Korpi, W. (2000), "Faces of Inequality: Gender, Class and Patterns of Inequalities in Different Types of Welfare States", *Social Politics*, Vol.7, No.2, Summer 2000, pp.127-191.

Kosonen, P. (1999), "Activation, incitations et workfare dans quatre pays nordiques", in *Comparer les systèmes de protection sociale en Europe du Nord et en France*, rencontres de Copenhague, Mire-Drees, Vol.4, Tome 1, Paris, pp.453-480.

Kvist, J. (2002), "Activating Welfare States. How Social Policies Can Promote Employment", in Clasen, J. (ed.), *What Future for Social Security? Debates and Reforms in National and Cross-national Perspectives*, Policy Press, Bristol, pp.197-210.

Larsen, F., Dalsgaard, L., Bredgaard, T. and Abildgaard, N. (2002), "Municipal Activation – Between Discipline and Integration", *CARMA Paper*, Centre for Labour Market Research, Aalborg University.

Lødemel, I. and Trickey, H. (2000), *An Offer You Can't Refuse, Workfare in International Perspective*, Policy Press, Bristol.

Martin, J.-P. (1998), "What Works Among Active Labour Market Policies: Evidence from OECD Countries' Experiences", *Labour Market and Social Policy Occasional Papers*, No.35, OECD, Paris.

Milner, H. and Wadensjö, E. (2001), *Gösta Rehn, the Swedish Model and Labour Market Policies*, Ashgate, Aldershot.

Morel, S. (2000), *Les logiques de la réciprocité, les transformations de la relation d'assistance aux États-Unis et en France*, Presses Universitaires de France, Paris.

Peck, J. (1998), "Workfare, a Geopolitical Etymology", *Environment and Planning, Society and Space*, Vol.16, pp.133-161.

Peck, J. (2001), *Workfare States*, Guilford Press, New York.

Pierson, P. (2001), *The New Politics of the Welfare State*, Oxford University Press, Oxford.

Radaelli, C. (2000), "Whither Europeanization? Concept Stretching and Substantive Change", *European Integration online Papers (EIoP)*, Vol.4, No.6 (http://eiop.or.at/eiop/texte/2000-008a.htm).

Rodgers, C. S. (1981), "Work Tests for Welfare Recipients, The Gap Between the Goal and the Reality", *Journal of Policy Analysis and Management*, Vol.1, No.1, pp.5-17.

Scharpf, F. W. and Schmidt, V. A. (2000), *Welfare and Work in the Open Economy, From Vulnerability to Competitiveness*, Vol.I, Oxford University Press, Oxford.

Schmid, G. and Gazier, B. (2002), *The Dynamics of Full Employment*, Edward Elgar Publishing, Cheltenham.

Serrano Pascual, A. (2002), "Are European Activation Policies Converging?", paper presented at the IREC Conference, Aalborg, 28 August 2002.

Supiot, A. (2003), "Governing Work and Welfare in a Global Economy", in Zeitlin, J. and Trubek, D. (eds.), *Governing Work and Welfare in a New Economy: European and American Experiments*, Oxford University Press, Oxford, pp.372-397.

Torfing, J. (1999), "Workfare with Welfare: Recent Reforms of the Danish Welfare State", *Journal of European Social Policy*, Vol.9, No.1, pp.5-28.

van Berkel, R. and Möller, I. H. (2002), *Active Social Policies in the EU, Inclusion through Participation?*, The Policy Press, Bristol.

Zeitlin, J. and Trubek, D. (2003), *Governing Work and Welfare in a New Economy: European and American Experiments*, Oxford University Press, Oxford.

The Open Method
of Co-ordination in Action

Theoretical Promise, Empirical Realities, Reform Strategy[1]

Jonathan ZEITLIN

Introduction

As we saw in the introduction, the Open Method of Co-ordination has aroused fierce controversies about its democratic legitimacy, practical effectiveness, and implications for European integration. Yet as we also saw, much of the debate surrounding the OMC has suffered from a serious empirical deficit, relying on a narrow range of often outdated evidence, and based mainly on official printed sources. Drawing on the previous chapters of this book, as well as on other recent research (both published and unpublished), this concluding essay seeks to redress the balance by reviewing the available evidence about the OMC in action, focussing particularly on the operations and impact of the European Employment and Social Inclusion Strategies at national and subnational levels. In order to establish appropriate criteria for the empirical assessment in the body of the chapter (Part II), the next section (Part I) briefly revisits the core claims for the theoretical promise of the OMC as a new mode or instrument of EU governance advanced by its proponents. Although the resulting assessment, as we shall see, is positive in many respects, it also highlights some significant practical limitations that inhibit the realisation of the OMC's theoretical promise. The final section (Part III) therefore considers how to overcome the shortcomings revealed by the empirical assessment, and proposes a reflexive strategy

---

[1] A preliminary version of this concluding chapter was presented at the conference organised by the Observatoire social européen on "The European Employment Strategy: Discussion and Institutionalisation", Brussels, 30-31 August 2004. I am grateful to the participants for helpful comments, including Robert Strauss and Luc Tholoniat of the European Commission's DG Employment.

for reforming the OMC by applying the method to its own procedures through benchmarking, peer review, monitoring, and iterative redesign.

I. Theoretical Promise of a New Mode of EU Governance

Among the theoretical claims for the OMC's potential as a new mode of EU governance enumerated in the introduction, two are arguably critical to any empirical assessment of its practical operations and impact[2]. First, the OMC has been hailed as a promising instrument for addressing common European concerns while respecting national diversity because it encourages convergence of objectives, performance, and broad policy approaches, but not of specific programmes, rules, or institutions. This is particularly important in the case of employment and social protection systems, where deep-rooted differences in national institutions and policy legacies largely preclude harmonisation at European level. Such capacity for reconciling common European action with legitimate national diversity has become more crucial than ever with the enlargement of the EU to include ten new Member States, which differ widely both from one another and from the original fifteen in their labour market institutions and social welfare regimes, as well as in their levels of economic development and rates of employment, unemployment, and income poverty (Hemerijck and Berghman, 2004; Galgóczi *et al.*, 2004).

Second, the OMC has been acclaimed as a promising mechanism for promoting experimental learning and deliberative problem-solving insofar as it systematically and continuously obliges Member States to pool information, compare themselves to one another, and reassess current policies against their relative performance. Diversity within Europe, on this view, should be regarded "not as an obstacle to integration but rather as an asset [...] a natural laboratory for policy experimentation", which enhances opportunities for cross-national learning through comparison of different approaches to similar or related problems (CEC, 2002a: 37; Cohen and Sabel, 2003: 368). Such capacity for mutual learning is likewise especially important in fields like employment, inclusion, and social protection, where EU Member States, whatever their differences have been struggling with similar challenges of reconfiguring inherited institutions and programmes to meet the demands of a

---

2 Empirical assessment of a third theoretical claim that the OMC can serve as a promising cognitive and normative tool for defining and building consensus around a distinctive European (or EU) social model based on shared values and policy paradigms as proposed by Vandenbroucke (2002) and Ferrera (2001), would require a fuller analysis of the historical evolution of EU social and employment policies than can be undertaken here. But see the discussion of the influence of OMC on national policy change in Part II below, as well as Pochet's chapter in this volume.

new economy, with its changing demographic trends, career patterns, household/family structures, and distributions of social risks. Some countries have coped more successfully with these challenges than others, but none can credibly claim to have discovered a comprehensive solution or model. Hence there is good reason to think that Europe might serve in a new way to enhance employment, inclusion, and social protection in a period of increasing uncertainty by creating a forum for discussing, evaluating, and generalising the results of different national adjustment strategies (Zeitlin, 2003; Sabel and Zeitlin, 2003).

This is not the place to respond to the various theoretical and political critiques of the OMC's legitimacy summarised in the introduction, a task which would require not only a broader analysis of EU governance, but also a reconceptualisation of key terms in the European debate such as subsidiarity, the "Community Method", and democracy itself[3]. But whether one believes that the OMC should be considered part of the solution to the EU's democratic deficit or instead part of the problem, participation and transparency are critical to any empirical assessment of its theoretical promise as a new mode of European governance. For not only the OMC's legitimacy, but also its effectiveness arguably depend on the participation of the widest possible range of actors and stakeholders at all levels, from the European through the national to the regional and local, in order to ensure the representation of diverse perspectives, tap the benefits of local knowledge and initiative, and hold public officials accountable for carrying out mutually agreed commitments. Transparency of deliberation and decision-making within the OMC is no less crucial, both as a procedural safeguard for European citizens and as a vital source of information on which both public and private actors at different levels can draw to drive the co-ordination process forward.

II. Empirical Realities: Impacts, Influences, Ambiguities

For many participants in the EU governance debate, the acid test of the OMC's value in enhancing the Union's problem-solving capabilities is whether it can deliver measurable performance improvements in relation to agreed objectives and metrics. Yet this type of question is exceptionally difficult to answer, as the five-year impact evaluation of the EES conducted in 2002 made abundantly clear. Between 1997 and 2001, as the Commission's technical evaluation showed, EU employment performance underwent a structural improvement, very much in line with the objectives of the EES. Unemployment across the EU fell

---

[3] For preliminary efforts in this direction, see Zeitlin (2005); Sabel and Zeitlin (2003), and Cohen and Sabel (2003), as well as the Trubeks' chapter in this volume.

by 3%, with sharper declines in its long-term and structural components. The employment rate likewise rose by 3%, with improvements concentrated among key groups targeted by the EES such as women, youth, older people, and the low skilled. Compared to previous economic upswings in the 1980s and 1990s, the job intensity of growth increased sharply, while the responsiveness of employment and labour-force participation to output also improved. Yet as the Commission itself acknowledged, "[...] the technical difficulties of a precise impact evaluation should not be under-estimated, considering the interaction between different policies, the simultaneous improvement of the economic situation and the relatively short period under review as compared to the long-term nature of certain structural reforms"(CEC, 2002b: 7-8; 2002c: ch. 2). The problem of evaluating the impact of the EES on EU employment performance is actually more complex still, because it involves a double relationship between national policies and employment outcomes on the one hand, and between the EES and national policies on the other, each of whose causal significance is open to question. Hence as Barbier's chapter rightly argues, classical models of programme evaluation cannot properly be applied to the EES – or to the OMC more generally – which is in any case a process rather than a programme (see also Barbier, 2004a: 22-31).

Following the example of previous chapters in this book and other recent case study research on the OMC in action, I adopt here instead what may be called a contextualised process-tracing approach to assessing the operations and impact of the European Employment and Social Inclusion Strategies. Consonant with the preceding discussion of the OMC's theoretical promise, the assessment focuses on four major issues: (A) substantive policy change (including broad shifts in policy thinking); (B) procedural shifts in governance and policy-making (including administrative reorganisation and institutional capacity building); (C) participation and transparency; and (D) mutual learning. By way of conclusion, the final section (E) evaluates the relative importance of different mechanisms whereby OMC processes may influence policy-making within EU Member States, emphasising their strategic utilisation by domestic actors.

A. Substantive Policy Change

Among the most widely attested findings of recent empirical work on the European Employment and Social Inclusion Strategies, including most of the chapters in this volume as well as official evaluation studies and reports, is that these OMC processes have raised the political salience and ambitions of employment and social inclusion policies at the national as well as the EU level. A second broadly supported finding is that these OMC processes have contributed to broad shifts in national policy orientation and thinking, involving the incorporation of EU concepts and categories into domestic debates. The most obvious examples of this cognitive influence of OMC on domestic policy orientations concern the shift of emphasis from reducing unemployment to raising employment rates as a core objective, from passive income support to activation services, and from a curative to a preventative approach to fighting unemployment. But many other key concepts associated with the EES and the Social Inclusion process have also entered or gained new prominence on the policy agendas of EU Member States, notably active ageing/avoiding early retirement, lifelong learning, gender mainstreaming, flexicurity (balancing flexibility with security), reconciling work and family life, an inclusive labour market, social exclusion as a multi-dimensional phenomenon beyond income poverty, and an integrated partnership approach to promoting employment, inclusion and local development[4].

Beyond these broad shifts in national policy thinking, there is also some evidence that these OMC processes have contributed to specific changes in individual Member States' policies. Such evidence is most abundant for the EES, which has been running considerably longer (seven rounds of NAPs and Joint Reports as against two for the Social Inclusion Process), and has been subjected to more extensive research and evaluation. In France, for example, the EES played a prominent part in the adoption of a preventative and individualised approach to the unemployed through programmes such as PAP-ND (*Projet d'Action Personnalisé pour un Nouveau Départ*) and PARE (*Plan d'Aide au Retour à l'Emploi*), the introduction of a modest negative income tax/in-work benefit for low earners (the *Prime pour l'Emploi*, or PPE), and the implementation of measures to close off pathways to early retirement and promote lifelong learning in the context of pension reform (itself the subject of a separate OMC process)[5]. In Germany, similarly, the Schröder government referred explicitly to the EES as part of the inspiration and justification for initiatives such as the "Immediate Programme for the Reduction of Youth Unemployment" (JUMP), the amendment of the Work Promotion Act to incorporate a more preventative and targeted approach, the Job-AQTIV (Active, Qualify, Train, Invest, and Place) Act, the development of gender mainstreaming, and the "Hartz Laws"

---

4   In addition to the chapters in this volume, on the EES see Jacobsson (2002); Jacobsson and Vifell (2005a); CEC (2002a: 9-15) and (2002b: ch. 1); on the Social Inclusion process, see Ferrera *et al.* (2002); CEC and Council of the European Union (2004b: esp. 36-42).

5   See, in addition to the chapters by Erhel *et al.* and Barbier in this volume, Barbier and Samba Sylla (2001); Salais *et al.* (2002) and Barbier (2004a).

on the reform of labour market regulation and unemployment insurance, as well as for its efforts to clamp down on early retirement and expand public childcare provision[6]. In both the Netherlands and Ireland, as the chapters by Visser and O'Donnell and Moss document, the EES's active and preventative approach had a significant impact on national labour market policy, shifting resources away from an exclusive emphasis on youth unemployment and training towards a broader effort embracing the adult unemployed in the former, and stimulating the introduction of a co-ordinated system of job referral, interview, guidance, and counseling for the young and long-term unemployed in the latter. In Sweden and Denmark, as Jacobsson's chapter shows, EU recommendations triggered the initiation of new policy measures aimed at combating gender segregation and improving the labour market integration of ethnic minorities.

Probably the greatest influence of the EES on national policy has come in the area of equal gender opportunities, cited specifically by nearly all Member States in their Five-Year Evaluation reports. Among the key substantive policy developments, as Rubery's chapter details, were improved access for women to active labour market and lifelong learning schemes, individualisation of tax systems, institutionalisation of gender mainstreaming and impact assessment practices, measures to reduce occupational segregation and the gender pay gap (embodied in private collective bargaining agreements in some countries such as France and Spain), and the adoption of childcare provision targets at both EU and national levels. The impact of the EES on gender equality policies has arguably been greatest, as she observes in relation to mainstreaming, "in those countries where a comparative evaluation would suggest that the actual measures are weaker or less strongly embedded in the policy-making process", because it did more there to kick start new initiatives. But the EES has also proved able to raise critical issues for even the best performing Member States, for example by highlighting the problem of occupational segregation in the Nordic countries despite their very high levels of female employment. The revised common objectives for the second round of the Social Inclusion process in 2003-2004 likewise underlined the need for a stronger gender mainstreaming approach, but as Rubery notes there appeared to be very

---

[6]   In addition to the chapter by Büchs & Friedrich in this volume, see Umbach (2004) and Richardt (2004). I have also benefited from reading an unpublished paper submitted to the *Journal of European Social Policy* entitled "Paving the Way for Employment? The Impact of the Luxembourg Process on German Labour Market Policies".

limited evidence of its practical influence on Member State policies as reported in the NAPs/incl[7].

Both in the case of broad cognitive shifts and of specific programmatic changes, however, identifying the precise causal impact of the EES and the Social Inclusion process on national policy-making raises difficult problems of interpretation. Thus changes in Member States' policy orientations, including enhanced attention to employment promotion and social inclusion, often preceded the launch of these OMC processes. Sweden, for example, had long been internationally renowned as a pioneer of active labour market policies, while Denmark reformed her unemployment benefit system, reinforced the "active line" in welfare policy, and began to develop an "inclusive labour market" approach to the disabled during the early 1990s[8]. The Dutch originated the concept of "flexicurity" through collective bargaining agreements and legislation in the mid-1990s, after they had already begun to take serious steps towards reducing the proportion of the workforce on disability schemes and reversing the trend towards early retirement[9]. France had developed the concept of social exclusion in the 1980s, which was then taken up and adapted by other European countries and the Commission during the 1990s, before appearing in rather different form alongside activation in the "New Deal" welfare reform programme of the British New Labour government elected in 1997[10]. A number of EU Member States had already launched high-profile national anti-poverty strategies during the late 1990s, including Ireland, Germany, Belgium, the Netherlands, and Portugal, as well as France and the UK. And as is well known, the 1993 Delors White Paper on "Growth, Employment, and Competitiveness" and the employment objectives agreed at the 1994 Essen European Council already anticipated important elements of both the substance and procedures of the EES.

Nor was the OMC the only external influence on the employment, inclusion, and social protection policies of EU Member States. The OECD and its 1994 Jobs Strategy also had a significant impact on policy orientations and programmes in a number of European countries, often through the channel of Finance rather than Employment and Social Affairs ministries, as the chapters by Barbier, Visser, and Erhel *et al.* illustrate. And the relationship between the EES and the OECD Jobs

---

[7] See also Rubery *et al.* (2004); CEC and Council of the European Union (2004b).

[8] On the Danish labour market and welfare reforms of the 1990s, see in addition to the chapters by Jacobsson & Barbier in this volume Madsen (1999).

[9] In addition to Visser's chapter in this volume, see Visser and Hemerijck (1997) and Hartog (1999).

[10] In addition to the chapters by Erhel *et al.* and Armstrong in this volume, see Atkinson and Davoudi (2000) and Mayes *et al.* (2001).

Strategy has itself become closer and less competitive in recent years, as the former has placed greater emphasis on concepts such as "active ageing" and "making work pay", while the latter has relaxed its critique of employment protection legislation and acknowledged the need to balance flexibility with security[11].

In important respects, moreover, these OMC processes cannot be considered truly external to national policy-making, since Member States actively supported their initiation and continuously participate in the definition of objectives, guidelines, and indicators, into which they often seek to "upload" (Börzel, 2002a) their own domestic priorities and preferences. Thus as recent historical research has shown, Sweden, the Netherlands, and other social democratic controlled Member States played a key part in launching the EES alongside the Party of European Socialists, the Commission's DG Employment (led by the former Swedish Social Democratic Finance Minister Allan Larsson), and the Luxembourg Presidency (led by the Christian Democratic Finance and Labour Minister Jean-Claude Juncker), with additional last-minute support from the newly elected Blair and Jospin governments of the UK and France. The conceptually heterogeneous four-pillar structure of the original EES (employability, entrepreneurship, adaptability, equal gender opportunities) clearly reflects its origins as a political compromise among Nordic social democrats, continental socialists and Christian Democrats, and British New Labourites. The incorporation of gender mainstreaming into the employment guidelines likewise resulted, as Rubery points out, from a successful EU-wide campaign orchestrated by the female Ministers for Women and Labour under the 1998 Austrian Presidency. More recently, the French and Belgian Presidencies fought hard to secure the integration of quality in work objectives and indicators into the EES to counterbalance what they saw as its one-sided quantitative emphasis, resulting in the revised goal of "more *and* better jobs" enunciated at Lisbon in March 2000 and retained in the new set of EU employment objectives and guidelines agreed in 2003. Even countries like Italy, which initially operated as passive "takers" of employment policy orientations defined by other Member States, have subsequently learned how to "upload" their own priorities such as regional disparities and undeclared work into the new employment guidelines, as Ferrera and Sacchi's chapter shows[12]. In the case of social inclusion, similarly, France, Portugal, the

---

[11] See, for example, the February 2004 presentation by John P. Martin, OECD Director of Employment, Labor, and Social Affairs to the EU Employment Committee (EMCO) (Martin, 2004).

[12] On the historical origins and evolution of the EES, see in addition to the chapters in this volume, Johansson (1999); Barbier and Samba Sylla (2001); Salais *et al.* (2002);

UK, and Belgium all played crucial roles in launching the new OMC process in 2000-2001, while the Dutch, Finnish, and Swedish Presidencies of the late 1990s also made important contributions to the emergence of a "concerted strategy for modernising social protection" at EU level, embodied in the ambitious European Social Agenda agreed at Nice in December 2000[13].

Not only have EU Member States actively participated in defining OMC goals and metrics, but they have also exercised considerable selectivity (both conscious and unconscious) in "downloading" (Börzel, 2002a) and inflecting European concepts and policy approaches in the fields of employment and social inclusion. Thus for example Barbier's chapter argues that EU Member States have interpreted their shared commitment to "activation" of labour market and social protection policies in sharply different ways, influenced but not fully determined by their pre-existing employment systems and welfare regimes, with the UK opting for a liberal model, Denmark and other Scandinavian countries a universalistic one, and some continental countries like France following a hybrid "insertion" approach, where the state serves as "republican employer of last resort". Other well-informed commentators like Lindsay and Mailand (2004) instead view the UK and Denmark, despite continuing differences in administrative arrangements, levels of expenditure, and benefit generosity, as converging towards a new hybrid activation model, based on a combination of some measure of compulsion, client-centred services, a human resource development approach, and a "real work" focus, delivered through local partnerships. But whichever interpretation may be closer to the truth, continuing variations in national interpretation and implementation of common policy concepts and approaches form an integral part of the OMC's logic.

As signaled in the introduction, interpretation of the OMC's substantive policy impact is further complicated by the strategic behaviour of national governments in communicating with domestic publics on the one hand and EU institutions on the other[14]. Thus governments often use references to OMC processes as a source of legitimation and blame-sharing in order to advance their own domestic agenda, sometimes irrespective of their real influence on policy decisions. Thus as the chapters by Visser and Büchs and Friedrich observe, the Schröder government in Germany has very deliberately sought to deploy the EES

van Riel and van der Meer (2002); Goetschy (2003); Trubek and Mosher (2003) and Barbier (2004a).

[13] On the historical evolution of EU social inclusion and social protection policies, see in addition to Pochet's chapter in this volume, Pochet (2002 and 2004); Ferrera *et al.* (2002) and Chassard (2001).

[14] For a subtle and insightful analysis of the Swedish case, see Vifell (2004).

and the 2003 report of the Employment Task Force chaired by former Dutch Prime Minister Wim Kok (for whose creation it pressed in the Council along with Britain, Spain, Portugal, and France) as levers for overcoming opposition to its unpopular Agenda 2010 package of labour market and social welfare reforms. And the Berlusconi government in Italy, as Ferrera and Sacchi's chapter notes, invoked a highly selective interpretation of the EES to support the controversial labour market reforms proposed in its 2001 White Paper and partially enacted by the 2003 Legge Biagi, even while sharply criticising the European strategy in its 2002 evaluation report for its limited relevance to Italian employment conditions[15].

Conversely, governments may also consciously play down the influence of OMC processes in communicating with domestic audiences, especially in Member States or policy areas where the legitimacy of EU intervention is weak. For example, as Jacobsson's chapter remarks, in neither Sweden nor Denmark did governments publicly explain the adoption of new measures to reduce gender segregation or improve labour market integration of immigrants as a response to EU recommendations, even though the linkage is clearly attested both in interviews and these countries' own NAPs (see also Vifell, 2004)[16].

Governments may likewise deliberately over- or understate the influence of OMC processes on domestic policy in reporting to the EU, depending on whether they want to burnish their credentials as "good Europeans" by demonstrating consummate compliance with guidelines and recommendations, or instead to present themselves as defenders of subsidiarity and the national interest against Brussels. Thus the French, German, and Danish national reports for the Five-Year Evaluation of the EES generally made stronger claims for its substantive impact on domestic policy than would be accepted by independent researchers (including the contributors to this volume), while the Italian national report, which followed a sharp political shift in government from centre-

---

[15] Other perhaps less blatantly instrumental appeals to the EES as a justification for domestic reforms include the Employment Conference organised by Frank Vandenbroucke as Belgian Federal Minister in September 2003. See Smets (2003); "Conclusions de la Conférence pour l'Emploi", http://www.vandebroucke.fgov.be/ zwerkgelegenheidsconferentie.htm, accessed 4 November 2003); and the references to the guidelines by the Spanish government in strengthening active labour market policies in López-Santana (2004).

[16] Even in private interviews, national officials may prefer, whether for reasons of *amour propre* or selective memory, to focus on the influence of their Member State on the direction of EU policy rather than vice versa. See for example the somewhat exaggerated claims of French officials quoted in the Erhel *et al.* chapter about national influence on the Delors White Paper and the EU Social Inclusion process, each of which arguably blended diverse elements from a much wider range of sources.

left to centre-right, downplayed the findings of its own preparatory studies concerning the strategy's positive influence on institutional capacity building[17].

Hence both on substantive and methodological grounds, the relationship between OMC processes and Member State policies should be analyzed as a two-way interaction rather than a one-way causal impact. The EES and the Social Inclusion process, as the chapters in this volume show, often operate as catalysts or "selective amplifiers" (Visser) for national reform strategies, increasing the salience and urgency of particular issues and policy approaches, which may already have been familiar domestically, at least in certain quarters. But there is also hard evidence of the OMC's ability to challenge and expand the terms of national policy debate, especially in fields like gender equality and social inclusion (see also Jacobsson and Vifell, 2005a). Yet given the ongoing variations in national interpretation and implementation of European concepts and policy approaches, OMC processes in employment and social inclusion should be viewed less as mechanisms for producing "cognitive harmonisation" (Palier, 2004) than for the creation of a common language and categorical framework to discuss and evaluate different solutions to similar problems.

B. Procedural Shifts in Governance and Policy-making

More profound and more easily traceable than the OMC's influence on substantive policy changes within EU Member States has been its contribution to shifts in governance and policy-making arrangements, including administrative reorganisation and institutional capacity building, though here too there are many other causal factors. Nearly all accounts of OMC processes in action at a national level report that they have stimulated improvements in horizontal or cross-sectoral integration across formally separate but practically interdependent policy fields: labour market policy, unemployment benefits, social assistance, pensions, taxation, education/training, and local development in the case of the EES; housing, health care, justice, sport/leisure, and transport as well as the above in the case of social inclusion. Production of NAPs typically requires collaboration among multiple ministries and government agencies: at a minimum the ministries of Labour and Finance in the case of employment, but usually also the ministries of Social Affairs, Education, and whatever unit is responsible for women's rights and/or gender equality (which were often created or strengthened, as Rubery's

---

[17] For a critical discussion of the French and other national evaluation reports, see Barbier (2004b: 22-31). For evidence of the positive influence of the EES on Italian institutional capacity building, see the chapter by Ferrera & Sacchi in this volume.

chapter shows, in response to the mainstreaming provisions of the EES). In many countries, especially those of southern Europe (Italy, Spain, Portugal, and Greece), the NAPs/empl have led to the creation of new inter-ministerial working groups or specialised co-ordination units, an arrangement which has also become normal for preparing the NAPs/incl in most Member States. In several cases, such as Denmark, the Netherlands, and Italy, the OMC has reinforced ongoing trends towards the merger of Labour/Employment and Social Affairs/Welfare ministries, though such developments have not always proved beneficial for their effective management, as Ferrera and Sacchi's chapter points out in relation to the Italian social inclusion process. Often too, the NAPs have served as a focus for general reviews and rationalisation of policy-making across ministries and agencies, as the chapters by Erhel *et al.* and O'Donnell and Moss report for France and Ireland respectively[18].

A second major effect of the OMC has been to stimulate improvements in national statistical and steering capacities. Thus participation in the EES and the Social Inclusion process has pushed Member States to upgrade their policy monitoring and evaluation capabilities, as well as to harmonise national and European statistics. In Italy, for example, Ferrera and Sacchi's chapter demonstrates how the EES spurred the enhancement of national data collection and assessment capacities, not only through the establishment of a new inter-departmental monitoring group, but also through reorganisation of the Directorate-General for Employment and Training, together with the development of new statistical tools and a computerised employment information system. In Spain, too, as López-Santana (2004) found, new data collection arrangements introduced to meet the demands of the EES exposed duplications of spending effort between the national government and the autonomous regions. But significant disparities between national and European statistics still persist in many countries even for OMC key indicators, as Visser's chapter on the Netherlands documents.

A third important influence of the EES and the Social Inclusion process has been to encourage the reinforcement of arrangements for vertical co-ordination among levels of governance. Such co-ordination has become both increasingly necessary and increasingly challenging as a result of the widespread decentralisation of the public employment services (to which the EES itself often contributed)[19] and the devolution

---

[18] On the NAPs as a stimulus to improved horizontal policy integration, see also CEC (2002c: 37-38); CEC and Council of the European Union (2004b: 113).

[19] In France, for example, the EES directly influenced the reorientation and restructuring of the French National Employment Agency (ANPE) from direct provision of centralised services to co-ordination of a mix of services provided by multiple bodies

of welfare and employment policies in federal or federalising polities such as Italy, Spain, Belgium, Austria, Germany, and the UK. Sometimes this vertical co-ordination occurs through well-established institutional channels such the National Institute for Employment (INEM) in Spain (López-Santana, 2004) or the *Länder* Conferences of Labour and Social Affairs Ministers (ASMK) and of the Highest Social Authorities (KOLS), as described in Büchs and Friedrich's chapter on Germany. In other cases, the NAP preparation process has led to the creation of new mechanisms for vertical co-ordination between federal and regional governments, whether through informal co-operation agreements as in Belgium, or formal co-ordination committees as in Austria (CEC, 2002c: 39; CEC and Council of the European Union 2004a: 113)[20]. In the UK, which has recently devolved a wide range of powers to new elected regional authorities in Scotland, Wales, and Northern Ireland, Armstrong's chapter suggests that "[...] [T]he NAP/incl has created the opportunity to develop a truly national overview of what is going on in the UK post-devolution" in a way that counteracts, to some degree, otherwise fragmentary governance tendencies.

The most contradictory case is that of Italy. There, as Ferrera and Sacchi's chapter shows, the EES led to a marked improvement in vertical as well as horizontal co-ordination capacities through the establishment of new inter-institutional co-ordination committees for employment at regional and provincial levels as well as common indicators for territorial monitoring of decentralised employment policies. A similar process of co-ordinated decentralisation appeared to have been set in motion for social assistance by the passage of a long-awaited framework law in 2000. But the emergent system of national social plans, data gathering, and guaranteed minimum standards which was supposed to guide the decentralisation process was almost immediately "disemboweled" by a constitutional reform in 2001 and the uncontrolled devolution of social welfare competences to the regions permitted by the incoming centre-right coalition (which includes the radical autonomist Lega Nord). Since then, the OMC has been proposed by the Berlusconi government itself as a possible template for vertical co-ordination of regional welfare

---

(internal and external, public and private) at a decentralised territorial level: see Salais *et al.* (2002).

[20] Co-ordination among the Belgian Federal, regional, and community authorities within the EES is also assured by a dedicated ESF-NAP Impact Assessment Cell (ENIAC) created in response to EU recommendations with support from the European Social Fund: see Plasschaert and Pochet (2004: 18).

policies and expenditure, but no concrete steps in this direction have actually been taken[21].

C. Participation and Transparency

Discussion of the impact of OMC processes on governance and policy-making arrangements leads naturally into the questions of participation and transparency. As the chapters in this book illustrate, the OMC and particularly the EES is widely regarded as a narrow, opaque, and technocratic process involving high domestic civil servants and EU officials in a closed policy network, rather than a broad, transparent process of public deliberation and decision-making, open to the participation of all those with a stake in the outcome.

Although OMC processes, objectives, guidelines, and recommendations are formally authorised by Member State governments in the European Council and the sectoral formations of the Council, most of the actual work is done by unelected committees of national civil servants and Commission officials (the Employment, Social Protection, and Economic Policy Committees), whose decisions are rarely overturned. The deliberations of these committees take place behind closed doors and remain far from transparent, though all three committees have now established public websites on which they post their formal opinions and reports[22]. The European Parliament has no direct decision-making or oversight role in OMC processes, although it does have the right to be consulted about the employment guidelines, which are the subject of regular committee hearings, reports, and parliamentary resolutions.

At a national level, too, NAP preparation has typically been dominated by bureaucratic insiders oriented towards relations with European institutions, though a clear tendency towards greater "domestication" of the process has become visible over time in many Member States, such as the shift in responsibility for the German NAP/incl from "Europeans" to "Socials" described in Büchs and Friedrich's chapter[23]. National parliaments are hardly involved in most countries even if they are formally consulted or informed (as for example in Germany, Denmark, the

---

[21] In addition to the chapter by Ferrera & Sacchi in this volume, see also Ministero del Welfare (2003) and Ferrara and Gualmini (2004: 165-8). For a similar proposal by Frank Vandenbroucke for open co-ordination of employment and social policy between the federal and regional governments in Belgium, see Plasschaert and Pochet (2004: 15).

[22] For a careful, well-informed, and balanced analysis of the operation of these committees, see Jacobsson and Vifell (2005b).

[23] For similar developments in the case of the EES, see the chapters by Jacobsson and Ferrera & Sacchi, as well as Vifell (2004) on Sweden, and Tholoniat (2001) and Barbier and Samba Sylla (2001) on France.

Netherlands, and the UK). In some countries, like Italy or France, key administrative bodies such as the public employment services or labour market boards have been effectively integrated into the NAPs, while in others like Sweden and Denmark they have not[24]. Often, too, as O'Donnell and Moss observe in their chapter, the NAPs are not well co-ordinated with other influential consultation and planning mechanisms, such as Ireland's social partnership programmes, Community Support Frameworks and National Development Plans for the use of EU structural funds, and National Anti-poverty Strategy. In most Member States, as recent research has shown, both media coverage and public awareness of OMC processes remain rather low, and have tended if anything to decline over time[25]. Behind each of these limitations lies the crucial fact that in almost every Member State, NAPs are presented domestically as backward-looking activity reports to the EU and government documents "owned" by the relevant ministries rather than as forward-looking action plans or strategic programming instruments subject to normal public scrutiny and debate[26].

1. Social Partners

What about participation in OMC processes by non-state and sub-national actors? Much of the debate on participation in the EES has focused on unions and employers' associations, whose co-operation is necessary for progress on issues subject to collective bargaining such as adaptability and modernisation of work organisation. The European social partner organisations (ETUC, UNICE/UEAPME and CEEP) are formally consulted about the employment guidelines, regularly comment on the evolution of the EES, and since 2003 participate in an annual tripartite social summit preceding the spring European Council. They also now report with assistance from the Dublin Foundation on actions by their national affiliates to advance the employment strategy, largely in response to ongoing pressure from the Commission and the Council. As mentioned in the introduction, the European social partners have developed their own independent multi-year work programme and are experimenting with non-binding framework agreements and guidelines on issues like teleworking and lifelong learning, whose implemen-

---

[24] Compare the chapters by Jacobsson and Ferrera & Sacchi, as well as Salais *et al.* (2002) on France.

[25] In addition to the chapters in this volume, see Meyer (2005). The major exception concerns critical recommendations from the EU to Member States about the (non)compliance of their fiscal and budgetary policies with the Broad Economic Policy Guidelines, which do receive extensive media coverage.

[26] For official endorsement of these criticisms, see CEC and Council of the European Union (2004a: 18).

tation by their national affiliates is monitored and followed-up along OMC lines.

At the national level, most Member States have sought to involve unions and employers' associations more fully in the preparation and implementation of their NAPs/empl, in response to the employment guidelines' growing emphasis on the role of the social partners, reinforced in some cases by country-specific recommendations from the Commission and the Council[27]. In most countries, the national social partner organisations now produce some kind of joint text, sometimes incorporated directly into the NAP, or more often attached as a separate appendix. The EES has not simply followed existing national patterns of social partnership (or lack thereof), but has also stimulated the creation of new bi- and tripartite consultative fora (e.g. France, Greece) or their reinvigoration after a period of decline (e.g. Sweden), with the UK as a conspicuous negative outlier. According to recent surveys, national unions and employers' organisations are generally satisfied with the NAP consultation arrangements, despite widespread criticisms of the excessively tight timetable and bureaucratic rigidity of the procedures (especially under the annual reporting schedule of the EES before 2003). Substantively, however, the social partners often complain about their lack of real influence over the NAPs' content, especially following the recent rightward changes of government in certain Member States, though there are also disagreements between unions and employers on this point, as Visser observes in the case of the Netherlands. More generally, fuller participation by the social partners in the implementation of the EES is inhibited by ongoing disagreements between unions and employers (and among unions themselves in some countries like France and Italy) about the objectives themselves. Thus employers typically embrace the tax-cutting and labour market flexibility guidelines, while unions are more enthusiastic about those aimed at lifelong learning and quality in work. Beyond these conflicting views, both unions and employers in many countries fear that more active involvement in the EES could compromise their autonomy and control of the bargaining agenda, even if they may be willing to integrate some of its objectives into collective agreements (e.g. on gender equality in France and Spain). And the social partners are also understandably reluctant to

---

[27] The number of guidelines specifically mentioning the role of the social partners increased from two in 1998 to six in 2002, including all those grouped under the adaptability pillar. A new "horizontal objective" was introduced in 2001 instructing the Member States to "develop a comprehensive partnership with the social partners for the implementation, monitoring and follow-up of the Employment Strategy". France, Greece, Portugal, and the UK all received country-specific recommendations in 1999-2003 to strengthen social partnership, especially in relation to modernisation of work organisation.

invest too much energy and resources in developing a National Action Plan that remains in their eyes fundamentally a government document[28].

2. *Civil Society and Social NGOs*

A second key category of non-state actors whose participation in OMC processes has been widely debated is "civil society", comprising in practice social NGOs and advocacy networks. The civil society group most active in both the European Social Inclusion and Employment Strategies is undoubtedly the European Anti-poverty Network (EAPN), which operates as a dynamic two-way pump between the European and national levels, drawing domestic information upwards from its national affiliates, mobilising pressure on EU institutions, diffusing European information downwards to its affiliates, and linking them horizontally. Financially supported by the EU under successive Community Action Programmes, EAPN has been granted a semi-official place in the Social Inclusion process. The network is consulted on key elements of the process such as the indicators, NAP common outlines, and objectives, while also regularly co-organising conferences and roundtables financed by the Commission. At the same time, however, EAPN also independently reviews and critically evaluates the NAPs and Joint Inclusion Reports, pushing for greater Member State commitment, a stronger social rights approach, and a more general "right to be heard" on the part of people experiencing poverty and organisations representing them. Other transnational NGO networks active in the Social Inclusion process include FEANTSA (the European Federation of National Organisations Working with the Homeless) and ATD Fourth World (an international organisation of people experiencing extreme poverty), both of which have also published evaluations of the NAPs/incl and JIRs based on submissions from their national affiliates, as well as the Platform of European Social NGOs to which all of these groups belong[29].

At the EU level, EAPN has also fought for a voice in the EES. The network produces regular independent reports on the NAPs/empl and

---

[28] On the participation of the social partners in the EES, see in addition to the chapters in this volume (especially that by de la Porte & Pochet); Foden (1999); Winterton and Foden (2001); Goetschy (2003) and CEC (2002c: 40-41), as well as ETUC, UNICE/UEAPME and CEEP (2004) and the national reports posted on EIROnline.

[29] For reports, position papers, information bulletins, and conferences on the European Social Inclusion process produced by these organisations, see the relevant sections of their websites: EAPN (http://www.eapn.org/code/en/publ.asp?section=x1x); FEANTSA (http://www.feantsa.org/code/en/theme.asp?ID=6); ATD Fourth World (http://www.atd-quartmonde.org/europe/del_ue_en.htm); Social Platform (http://www.socialplatform.org/code/EN/abou.asp?Page=107). For an assessment of their role in the Social Inclusion process, see in addition to the chapter by de la Porte & Pochet in this volume, Armstrong (2003).

the JERs and organises self-funded conferences on how to make the employment strategy work for social inclusion. EAPN is sharply critical of what it sees as a "jobs first" approach to the unemployed and an increasing turn towards sanctions in "making work pay", but supports the emphasis of the EES on opening up employment opportunities for all those who are genuinely able to work. On this basis, EAPN has vocally pressed for the right to be consulted alongside the social partners about the employment strategy at both EU and national level, complaining publicly for example about their exclusion from the preparatory hearings conducted by the Kok Employment Task Force[30].

At the national level, the Social Inclusion process has stimulated the development of new consultative bodies or structures to facilitate input from NGOs. In Finland, for example, both the 2001 and the 2003 NAP/incls were drafted by a joint committee of civil servants and NGOs. In the UK, as Armstrong's chapter reports, EU criticisms of the over-centralised character of the first NAP/incl resulted in the establishment of a new dialogue between the Department of Work and Pensions and a Social Policy Task Force of NGOs, which "gave anti-poverty groups and networks access to central government civil servants in a way that simply had not been possible before within the domestic arena", thereby not only providing opportunities for NGOs to mobilise but also for civil servants to "break out of the traditional bureaucratic processes" and "do something different". One striking consequence has been the creation of a joint Participation Working Group aimed at "enabl[ing] people in poverty to participate in the development of the UK NAP 2005 and beyond by establishing a real partnership [with] government at all levels in order to improve anti-poverty policy and practice [...]" In other Member States, such as Sweden, Germany, Denmark, and the Netherlands, new or existing national networks of social NGOs have been mobilised to co-ordinate their participation in the Social Inclusion process. NGO bodies have likewise been given a formal role in monitoring the implementation of the NAPs/incl in a number of countries like Denmark, Portugal, and Luxembourg[31].

As de la Porte and Pochet's chapter shows, the national affiliates of EAPN and ATD Fourth World in most Member States are moderately satisfied with the participation arrangements for the NAP/incls, with the partial exception of countries where centre-right governments less committed to the objectives of the process have recently come to power,

---

[30] See for example EAPN (2002a and 2002b); EAPN (2003a); EAPN (2004a and 2004b).

[31] See in addition to the chapters in this volume, CEC and Council of the European Union (2004b:113-28) and EAPN (2003b: 13-17).

such as Italy, Austria, Portugal, and the Netherlands. But both of these groups would like to see the NAPs/incl become more operational and politically committing documents[32]. NGOs, like other actors, are understandably reluctant to invest time and resources on participating in OMC processes if they do not yield substantive results, such as the positive influence on Danish national poverty reduction targets reported in Jacobsson's chapter. Thus Büchs and Friedrich's chapter finds some disillusionment with the second round of the social inclusion process setting in among German NGOs, though less for those more directly engaged in European policy networks.

At the national as at the European level, social NGOs have campaigned to participate in the EES, especially EAPN and organisations of the disabled. In some Member States, like Spain, Portugal, and Ireland, the NAP/empl process has been opened up to NGO consultation without much controversy. But in countries with highly institutionalised social partnership arrangements such as Belgium and Denmark, there has been strong resistance to any involvement by civil society groups. Perhaps the most interesting case is that of Sweden, where as Jacobsson's chapter describes, a network of social NGOs has consciously set out to "break the monopoly" of the social partners over the NAP/empl, and was invited to a separate dialogue on employment policy by the Ministry of Industry, Employment, and Communications for the first time in 2003[33].

3. Women's Organisations and Feminist Groups

Less visible in OMC processes than either the social partners or antipoverty NGOs have been women's organisations and gender equality networks. Insofar as feminist groups have played an active part in the European Employment and Social Inclusion Strategies, it seems to have been primarily behind the scenes, through linkages to "femocrats" in the Commission and the Expert Group on Gender and Employment (EGGE), recently extended to cover social inclusion[34]. At the national level, too, the most significant development has been the creation or strengthening of gender equality units within government, though as Rubery's chapter notes, "pressure groups and political parties have used

---

[32] See also EAPN (2003b) and ATD Fourth World (2003).

[33] In addition to the chapters in this volume, see Jacobsson and Vifell (2005a) and EAPN (2003a: 9-10).

[34] For the national and synthesis reports of EGGE (now EGGIE), see http://www2. umist.ac.uk/management/ewerc/egge/egge_publications/publications.html. The European Women's Lobby also publishes regular position papers on strengthening the gender equality dimension of OMC processes in employment, inclusion, and social protection, as well as of the Lisbon Strategy more generally: see http://www.women lobby.org/polselect.asp?SectionID=13&LangName=english.

the commitment to gender equality within the EES and perhaps more importantly within the structural funds to press for more attention". In the UK, as Richardt (2004) documents, women's organisations have not used the EES childcare targets as a mobilising tool, partly because of the top-down, closed character of the NAP/empl process there (in contrast to social inclusion) and partly because of these groups' established focus on using European law and the courts as primary tools for advancing gender equality.

4. Local and Regional Authorities

In most EU Member States, local and regional governments have extensive responsibilities and expertise in both employment and social inclusion policy. In some countries, as we have already seen, subnational authorities are formally consulted in OMC processes, especially in federal polities whose regions or states enjoy constitutional status. But such consultations have typically focused on the implementation and dissemination rather than the formulation, monitoring, and evaluation of the NAPs, especially in the case of the EES (CEC, 2002c: ch. 10). Local and regional authorities are often more deeply involved in the Social Inclusion process, as for example in Spain where the Social Services Commission of the Federation of Municipalities and Provinces (FEMPL) has been formally entrusted with responsibility for monitoring the implementation of the NAP/incl (López-Santana, 2004). In Germany, by contrast, as Büchs and Friedrich observe, the *Länder*, especially those controlled by the Christian Democrats, have remained suspicious of the NAPs for both inclusion and employment as a "Trojan horse" which might allow the EU (and through it the Federal Government) to encroach on their constitutionally reserved competences and saddle them with unfunded spending mandates.

From an early stage in the EES, local and regional authorities began to demand the right to participate more fully in the process, lobbying at a European level through horizontal networks like the EU's Committee of the Regions, the Council of European Municipalities and Regions (CEMR), and Eurocities. Between 1998 and 2001, the employment guidelines were progressively revised to call for the mobilisation of "all actors at regional and local levels" in the implementation of the EES; local and regional authorities in particular were encouraged to develop their own territorial employment strategies and to "promote partnerships between all actors concerned" in carrying them out. The Commission organised a year-long campaign and consultation process on "Acting Locally for Employment", and the European Parliament created a new budget line to support pilot projects that would "encourage co-operation, improve knowledge, develop exchanges of information, promote best practices, support innovative approaches and evaluate experience gained in implementing the National Action Plans for Employment at local and regional level" (CEC, 2000 and 2001a; Committee of the Regions, 2001: pp.20-24; CEMR, 2001; Eurocities, 2001). Among the innovative projects supported under this budget line are numerous Local and Regional Action Plans for Employment (LAPs and RAPs); the development of local and regional employment indicators; and the creation of a European network for identification, dissemination, and exchange of good practices in local and regional employment development (IDELE), capped by an annual Local Development Forum (Engender asbl, 2002; Groupe Bernard Brunhes Consultants and Economix, 2003; CEC, 2004a). In the Social Inclusion process, where the participation of local and regional authorities is less controversial, the Commission has likewise used the Community Action Programme to support horizontal networking through co-sponsorship of conferences and roundtables, as well as through the creation of new umbrella organisations such as the European Social Network (comprising directors of social service agencies) and the European Public Social Platform[35].

These EU initiatives have met with an active response from local and regional authorities in many Member States. In Sweden, as Jacobsson's chapter shows, associations of local authorities, county councils, and municipalities have sponsored a proliferation of LAPs, "intended to be tangible action plans, i.e. operational documents which should be followed up and results evaluated", and have pressed the central government for "more of a bottom up perspective" in the NAP/empl (see also Vifell, 2004). In Denmark, where the associations of local and county authorities already participate in the social partner consultation about the NAP/empl, they have also supported a number of municipalities in developing LAPs, and the new Ministry of Employment which has replaced the former Ministry of Labour is expected to integrate their work more fully into future NAPs. In Spain, the Autonomous Communities have embraced the OMC for their own purposes, especially in the case of social inclusion, where there are now thirteen regional plans. A number of other European regions have likewise adopted their own RAPs/empl, including not only relatively prosperous areas such as Lombardy, Tuscany, and Flanders, but also unemployment black spots

---

[35] See for example the EAPN-EUROCITIES conference on "The EU Strategy for Social Inclusion: Making It Work at the Local Level" EAPN-EUROCITIES (2003) and the 1st annual conference of the European Public Social Platform on "Strengthening the Role of Local and Regional Government in the EU Strategy for Social Inclusion", Turin, 14-15 October 2003 (http://www.socialeurope.com/english/e_ conferences.htm#Turin%20presentations). For the European Social Network (ESN), see also http://www.socialeurope.com/english/e_about.htm.

like Molise and Saxony-Anhalt. Often, too, local authorities have used EU support to integrate the EES into their employment policy-making. Thus for example a Spanish municipality reorganised its employment services around the four pillars of the first EES, while Offenbach am Main restructured its employment promotion, statistics, and European affairs departments into a single office. Perhaps the most imaginative such initiative was undertaken by the east German town of Döbeln, which used European funding to benchmark its local labour market situation against those of other areas experiencing similar structural problems of industrial decline[36].

5. Actors and Processes Compared

What accounts for the wide variations in participation patterns observable in these OMC processes? The much higher level of participation by non-state and subnational actors in the Social Inclusion Strategy than in the EES partly reflects underlying differences in the nature and objectives of the two processes. Thus "mobilising all the relevant bodies" figures as one of the four core objectives of the Social Inclusion process, but not of the EES, where the main emphasis has fallen instead on ensuring the involvement of the social partners because of their responsibility for many of the issues at stake in labour market reform, and Member States are more reluctant to open up their NAPs to input from social NGOs and local authorities, especially in unitary polities with historically centralised administrative structures.

But these variations in participation also reflect differences in the situation and strategies of the actors themselves. Thus the social partners, as we have seen, are profoundly ambivalent about deeper involvement in the EES, which they often regard as a threat to their bargaining autonomy, and feel less acute need than other actors for new channels of influence on public policy because of their privileged constitutional status in employment matters both at EU level and in many Member States (with the conspicuous exception of the UK). Social NGOs by contrast are hungry for new ways to make their voice heard by government, especially in countries where the national policy-making process offers them few such opportunities, as in the case of the UK's anti-poverty strategy. Women's organisations and feminist groups within the EU are accustomed to operating through parliamentary lobbying, court litigation, and linkages to sympathetic "femocrats" in EU and national administrations, which may have diminished their interest in pressing for participation rights in apparently soft, non-binding OMC processes.

---

[36] See in addition to the chapters in this volume López-Santana (2004) on Spain and Nauerz (2004) on Germany.

Local and regional authorities have a great deal at stake in the Employment and Social Inclusion Strategies, both of which bear directly on some of their core activities. They have pressed hardest for the right to participate in the preparation and implementation of the NAPs where their autonomy and prerogatives in national policy-making are newer or more contested (as for example in Sweden, Spain, and the UK), but have been most ambivalent or outright hostile to the OMC where the domestic division of competences is most constitutionally entrenched, giving rise to fears of disruption from Europe, as in Germany[37]. Finally, national Social Affairs ministries appear more interested than their Labour or Employment counterparts in mobilising external support for their policies from NGOs and civil society groups, while the Commission and the Parliament have long sought to cultivate allies at both European and subnational levels in their ongoing power struggles with Member State governments in the Council (see also Jacobsson and Vifell, 2005a).

Clearly, weaker and less constitutionally entrenched actors show greater interest in seizing opportunities for participation in both the EES and the Social Inclusion process. But the contrast between the creativity of the social NGOs on the one hand and the relative passivity of the trade unions on the other cannot be fully explained in such structural terms. Even among similarly situated actors, sharp differences in participatory behaviour within OMC processes can be observed, as for example among German regions and municipalities. More fundamentally, it is hard to believe that trade unions could not have found more proactive and imaginative uses for their privileged position in the EES, for example to demand increased joint influence over work reorganisation and other historic areas of managerial prerogative in the name of promoting adaptability, especially given their weakening organisational and political position in many Member States (see also Winterton and Foden 2001)[38].

---

[37] For a comparative analysis of the impact of Europeanisation on relations between national states and regions, see Börzel (2002b). Interestingly enough, the OMC appears to have reversed the pattern identified in her book, with the Spanish regions pursuing a strategy of co-operative federalism and the German *Länder* one closer to competitive regionalism.

[38] Among the rare examples of creative use of the EES by the social partners is the COPARSOC project, co-ordinated by the European Territorial Excellence Association (EUREXCTER), an action-research network sponsored by the European Centre of Enterprises with Public Participation (CEEP), with financial support from the European Commission. This project brought local and regional representatives of unions and employers from a dozen EU countries to France for a number of thematic workshops to share experiences, exchange good practices, and critically review the territorial dimension of the EES. It also involved a series of networked meetings between national union and employer representatives from nine EU Member States to evaluate jointly the operation of the EES through comparative discussion of each

For all non-state and subnational actors, however, the limited integration of OMC processes into domestic policy-making forms a crucial disincentive to greater participation. For even where they are allowed to participate in the preparation and implementation of the NAPs, as is often the case in social inclusion, civil society groups and subnational authorities will not continue to invest time, energy, and resources in the process unless it leads to forward policy commitments with real practical and financial consequences.

D. Mutual Learning

Perhaps the most critical claim for the novelty of the OMC concerns its capacity to promote mutual learning among EU Member States. As in the case of substantive policy change, the strongest impact of the European Employment and Social Inclusion Strategies in this area has come through a series of indirect or higher-order effects, which are not always recognised as "learning". Thus both OMC processes, as Ferrera and Sacchi suggest, have stimulated cross-national learning through heuristic, capacity-building, and maieutic effects (see in addition to the chapter by Ferrera and Sacchi in this volume, Ferrera *et al.*, 2002).

In heuristic terms, as we have already seen, the EES and the Social Inclusion process have been rather successful in identifying common European challenges and promising policy approaches, which have in turn contributed to broad shifts in national policy thinking. Both OMC processes have likewise enhanced mutual awareness of policies, practices, and problems in other Member States, even if such knowledge has largely been concentrated in EU committees and the higher echelons of national administrations. Beyond the formal framework of the OMC itself, moreover, EU Member States show increasing interest in learning from one another in preparing their own domestic policy reforms. Thus, for example, in early 2003 the French Minister of Social Affairs François Fillon led a study tour of parliamentarians and trade unionists to Spain, Germany, Sweden, and Finland to investigate the conditions

---

country's NAP. The project's methodology drew explicitly on the peer review and multilateral monitoring developed within the OMC, emphasising the importance of improving mutual understanding of cross-national differences in employment practices through reciprocal information about the institutional context and explanation of the local concerns motivating participants' questions. Based on the experience of the COPARSOC project, social partner representatives from a number of the participating countries expressed their support for establishing ongoing networks at both local and national levels for peer review, exchange of good practices, and multilateral monitoring of employment action plans: see Eurexcter (2002).

for successful pension reforms in Europe[39]. In Germany, as Büchs and Friedrich report in their chapter, not only did the Hartz Commission draw on other Member States' NAPs as a source for good practices in labour market reform, but government officials have also initiated bilateral exchanges with individual countries such as Denmark and the UK on specific issues such as job rotation, activation, and welfare-to-work policies. In the Netherlands, as Visser's chapter details, civil servants invited foreign colleagues to teach them how to implement the preventative approach to unemployment, while others traveled to Sweden, the UK, Germany, France, and Denmark to learn about subjects like child care and women's labour force participation, "one-stop shops" for social security, disability policies, and the integration of ethnic minorities, respectively[40].

In terms of capacity building, both the EES and the Social Inclusion process have given rise to the development of common European indicators and the creation of new data sources, such as the EU Statistics on Income and Living Conditions (EU-SILC). Despite continuing data limitations, moreover, they have also contributed to revisions and improvements in national social and employment statistics. In so doing, these OMC processes have stimulated cross-national debate and deliberation about the comparability, appropriateness, and significance of these indicators and the statistical data on which they are based, even if such discussions are largely confined to technical experts within the Employment and Social Protection Committees along with their academic interlocutors[41].

In maieutic or reflexive terms, the EES and the Social Inclusion process have pushed EU Member States to rethink established approaches and practices as a result of comparisons with other countries on the one hand and of the obligation to re-examine and re-evaluate their own policies and performance on the other. These OMC processes have undoubtedly "destabilize[d] existing understandings" (Trubek and Mosher,

---

[39] See in addition to the chapter by Erhel *et al.* in this volume, "Les retraites en Europe: bilan des voyages de François Fillon", 27 January 2003 (www.retraites.gouv.fr/rubrique32.html).

[40] Visser also suggests that Germany may have similarly learned from the Dutch approach to part-time work and the Netherlands from the Belgian approach to funding career breaks.

[41] On the social inclusion indicators, see Atkinson *et al.* (2002 and 2004). For a critical discussion of the employment indicators, see Salais (2004). Both the EMCO and SPC Indicators Groups regularly produce highly informative internal reports on their work. Those of the SPC are available on the Committee's website, http://europa.eu. int/comm/employment_social/social_protection_commitee/spc_indic_en.htm, whereas those of EMCO are regrettably unavailable to the general public at the present time.

2003: 46) and "pressured policy-makers to give a second thought to existing policy choices in the light of new ideas and the agreed common framework, and to accept being compared to better performers" (Jacobsson and Vifell, 2005a). In some cases, such reflexive learning has involved making new connections between hitherto separate policy issues, such as pensions and lifelong learning or women's employment and childcare provision. In others, it has entailed recognising that policies which seemed beneficial from one perspective can be harmful from another, such as early retirement as a palliative for unemployment created by industrial restructuring or high female employment in public social services as a source of occupational segregation and gender pay gaps.

At the same time, however, there are relatively few concrete cases at national level of direct or first-order policy learning from abroad about what works and what does not. Most of the examples of such direct learning cited in interviews and evaluation reports tend to focus on gender mainstreaming, the provision of personalised activation services, and the shift from a curative to a preventative approach to fighting unemployment[42]. Other examples of national policy learning tend to involve more problem recognition than adoption of foreign "best practice" solutions, as for example with lifelong learning, gender segregation, and labour market integration of immigrants and ethnic minorities. Even where national policy-makers refer explicitly to other countries' practices and the influence of OMC processes, they typically borrow selectively and adapt foreign programmes to the peculiarities of their own domestic social, institutional, and political contexts, as for instance in the case of French activation and tax-benefit policies or German labour market reforms.

The limited incidence of direct policy transfer, as Visser's chapter points outs, is a natural consequence of the OMC's "contextualised benchmarking" approach, which unlike the "decontextualised benchmarking" associated with the OECD Jobs Strategy, is more conducive to reflexive "learning with others" than to "adaptive mimicking" or what sociological institutionalists call "mimetic isomorphism", which can easily degenerate into uncritical trend following (see also Hemerijck and Visser, 2001 and 2003; DiMaggio and Powell, 1991). Such contextualised benchmarking as a mechanism for reflexive learning from others also fits well with the findings of comparative-historical research, which shows that foreign practices, whether in the economic or the political

---

42   Some Member States such as France and Belgium with high levels of long-term unemployment still have significant reservations about the latter shift. See Salais *et al.* (2002) and DULBEA (2002).

field, can rarely be successfully transferred from one social and institutional context to another without significant modification (Zeitlin, 2000 and 2003; Boyer *et al.*, 1998). The need for such contextualisation is explicitly recognised in OMC mutual learning programmes, which emphasise *in situ* explanation of "good practices" by host country experts on the one hand and creative adaptation to different local conditions by visiting participants on the other. Thus as a preliminary evaluation of the EES peer review programme reported:

> although Member States may not necessarily adopt the policies reviewed in an identical form, they are interested in adapting them to their own circumstances. In most cases, Member States have been inspired by their participation in the peer reviews to develop new initiatives or improve existing ones (CEC, 2001b: 3; ÖSB/INBAS, 2001).

More problematic, however, is the limited evidence of reflexive learning from the results of OMC processes at EU level. According to the Commission's own technical analysis of the impact evaluation reports, the EES did not do an especially good job during its first five years in identifying which types of active labour market policies or tax-benefit reforms were most effective under what circumstances, and revising the guidelines accordingly, despite all the political attention devoted to these issues, although the exercise itself generated a great deal of empirical material which could be used for that purpose (CEC 2002b: chs. 3-4; cf. also the chapters by Visser and O'Donnell and Moss in this volume). Nor does the new EES agreed in 2003 fully incorporate the empirical findings of the impact evaluation in this regard, even if they do respond to the widely expressed demands of Member State governments and other participating actors for fewer, simpler, and more outcome-oriented guidelines (CEC, 2003a; Council of the European Union, 2003).

Even more strikingly, the Member States do not seem to have made much tangible progress in drawing on cross-national learning at the level of local practice about how best to integrate labor market activation with social inclusion, balance flexibility with security, or extend the scope of lifelong learning to a wider section of the population (CEC, 2002b: chs. 5, 6, 8). As the Commission's technical analysis observes:

> a sufficient flow of information from the local and regional levels to the national level can enrich the basis upon which decisions are taken. Yet, there are *hardly any examples of a transfer of experiences from the bottom to the top* where nationally designed programmes have been modified according to the experiences or needs of the lower territorial levels [...] to date information has flowed only one-way – from the national to other levels (CEC, 2002b: 313, emphasis in original).

The potential for such "bottom up" and "horizontal" learning from local and regional experimentation is amply illustrated by reports of the European networking conferences and Commission-sponsored innovative local employment projects discussed in the previous section (see for example EAPN-Eurocities, 2003; CEC, 2004a). By stimulating the mobilisation of non-state and subnational actors, moreover, the EES, and still more the Social Inclusion process, appears to be creating the conditions for such "bottom up" learning in many EU Member States even where national governments do not formally acknowledge this in their NAPs or impact evaluation reports.

What accounts for these limitations on mutual learning within OMC processes? Part of the problem stems from the ambivalent commitment to this objective on the part of the key actors themselves. Thus the failure to capitalise at a European level on opportunities for reflexive learning from practical experience with the implementation of activation and prevention policies reflects the primary focus within the Commission and EMCO on ensuring national compliance with the action targets in the guidelines, rather than on reviewing the recommended measures in light of accumulated evidence about their effectiveness. The assumption has been, as Visser's chapter observes of the recent EU Employment Task Force report (Kok *et al.*, 2003), that "we know and agree about what we want, we even know what are the best practices, but we need more political will and better governance of reform delivery to make it work". And the failure to take full account of the empirical findings of the Five-Year Evaluation in the redesign of the EES likewise reflects the predominance of political bargaining over the new guidelines between the Commission and the Member States, even if the negotiations within EMCO also appear to have been subject to a certain deliberative discipline (Jobelius, 2003; Jacobsson and Vifell, 2005b; Vifell, 2004).

Other limitations on mutual learning, however, stem from more readily corrigible defects in OMC procedures and instruments. Thus, for example, there is broad agreement that the increasingly full agendas of EMCO and the SPC on the one hand and the very tight timetable for peer review of the NAPs on the other have crowded out opportunities for mutual learning among the participants. Although the EES peer review programme for the exchange of good practices is generally considered to have been more satisfactory, widespread criticisms have also been raised about its "show and tell" character, whereby Member States nominate "poster child" programmes, which are then selected through a "beauty contest" for presentation to a restricted audience of national officials and experts from those countries that choose to participate (see for example de la Porte and Pochet, 2003: 26; Jacobsson and Vifell, 2005b). These criticisms have been taken to heart by the members of EMCO and the SPC themselves, who have redesigned their peer review procedures and introduced new programmes to strengthen mutual learning, which will be examined in Part III below.

A second set of procedural limitations concern the indicators which are supposed to serve as crucial performance metrics within OMC processes. A major problem here is the persistent lack of comparable data for many key indicators, despite the development of new European survey instruments. This in turn necessitates continued reliance for many questions on national statistics, whose construction often reflects divergent policy choices and may produce misleading results when combined for comparative purposes, as for example in relation to definitions of unemployment (Salais, 2004) or the gender pay gap and segregation index (Rubery, in this volume). Some Member States like the Netherlands have also proved resistant to developing national equivalents for European indicators, preferring to rely on idiosyncratic domestic metrics in their NAPs (Visser, in this volume). A closely related issue regards the limited applicability of OMC employment and social indicators at local and regional levels due to the absence of corresponding data, though the Commission has been active in supporting the development of new territorially disaggregated metrics (see Groupe Bernard Brunhes Consultants and Economix, 2003 and the further discussion in Part III below).

Other problems with the indicators concern their definition and design, particularly in the case of the EES. Thus a number of the employment indicators, as Visser's chapter observes, focus on input rather than outcome measures, especially those dealing with activation and prevention. Other employment indicators are of questionable pertinence or lack clear causal significance, such as the ratio of educational spending to GDP or the new firm formation and survival rates. Even in the case of a key indicator like the employment rate, there are unresolved political disagreements among Member States about the appropriateness of different measures, such as the reliance on gross rather than full-time equivalent rates in the Lisbon targets, or the failure to adjust for varying proportions of young people in education (Salais, 2004). The situation is much better in the case of the Social Inclusion process, where the SPC has drawn up a clear and transparent set of methodological principles for the definition of OMC indicators, which should be balanced and multidimensional, outcome rather than means oriented, "responsive to policy interventions", and have a "clear and accepted normative interpretation", as well as being "robust and statistically validated, measurable in a sufficiently comparable way across Member States, and timely and susceptible to revision" (CEC and

Council of the European Union, 2004b: 129). But even there, the SPC has not yet managed to agree on common indicators for some contentious issues like decent housing and non-monetary indicators of poverty (SPC Indicators Group, 2001 and 2003).

Perhaps the most serious problem with OMC indicators from the perspective of mutual learning regards their use as "soft sanctions" to enforce Member State compliance with European targets rather than as diagnostic tools to highlight areas for improvement and self-corrective action by national and local actors[43]. This instrumental "naming and shaming" approach can provoke resistance from Member States to using European indicators in their NAPs, sometimes due to their genuine lack of policy pertinence, as in the case of Denmark's focus on social inclusion of the most vulnerable groups, for which there are no agreed indicators, but sometimes due to political preference for policy input rather than outcome-based measures, as in the Netherlands NAP/incl (CEC and Council of the European Union, 2004b: 129-30; Visser, in this volume). It can also lead to a counterproductive politicisation of the debate over the indicators themselves, as in the case of the employment rate discussed above.

A final set of procedural limitations on mutual learning within OMC processes concerns the barriers to participation and integration into domestic policy-making discussed in the previous section. Thus the paucity of "bottom-up" cross-national learning within the EES identified by the Five-Year Evaluation and the chapters in this volume is closely linked to the limited opportunities for participation by non-state and subnational actors in the process at all stages, from the definition of objectives, guidelines, and indicators, through the preparation, monitoring, and evaluation of the NAPs to the peer reviews and exchange of good practices. And the limited integration of both OMC processes into domestic policy-making, as we have likewise seen, inhibits the broad participation and public debate that is a necessary condition for experimental learning from local practice.

E. How Does It Work? Mechanisms of Domestic Influence

Among the most widely debated questions about the OMC concerns how it might work in influencing Member State policies in the absence of legally binding sanctions. A number of possible mechanisms of domestic influence have been proposed in the theoretical literature, including peer pressure; socialisation and discursive diffusion; mutual learning; and the strategic use of OMC processes as a "lever" or re-

---

[43] For this distinction between performance metrics as sanctioning mechanisms and diagnostic tools, see Sabel (2005) and Liebman and Sabel (2003).

source by domestic actors[44]. What light do the studies in this volume and other recent empirical research on the OMC shed on the relative importance and effectiveness of these mechanisms in practice?

There is certainly evidence that peer pressure and associated practices such as recommendations and rankings do have an influence on the behavior of Member State governments. National representatives in EU committee and Council meetings do feel pressure to reach common targets and carry out mutually agreed commitments (or at least to be seen to be doing so by the other participants). As one Swedish committee member quoted in the chapter by Jacobsson put it, "peer pressure feels", and conscientious compliance with the agreed procedures is also an important strategy for Member States (like Sweden) who want to influence the future evolution of OMC processes (cf. also Jacobsson and Vifell, 2005b; Vifell, 2004). Member State governments also want to avoid EU recommendations and low rankings on common indicators as a potential source of embarrassment in domestic politics, especially since these are sometimes taken up as points of criticism by opposition parties and interest groups (e.g. in relation to tax policy in Sweden). In many cases, national governments have been prepared to take some corrective action, such as increasing expenditure on activation and prevention services, stepping up consultation of the social partners in preparing the NAPs/empl, developing gender mainstreaming, and adopting measures to reduce gender segregation and improve the integration of immigrants and ethnic minorities in the labour market.

But as other commentators have observed in the context of economic policy co-ordination, the effectiveness of such peer pressure, and especially of public "naming, shaming, and blaming", depends on the perceived legitimacy of the recommendations, national sensitivity to criticism from the EU, and the domestic visibility of the process, including media coverage (see for example Hodson, 2004; Hodson and Maher, 2001). Where EU recommendations are perceived to be intellectually questionable, procedurally unfair, or politically illegitimate, Member State governments may be prepared to resist them publicly, and may even gain support by so doing (e.g. in the case of Swedish tax policy or the controversy over the Irish expansionary budget in 2001). Such criticism from Brussels will also bite less deeply where domestic public opinion is openly skeptical or hostile towards the EU (as in the UK) or where the recommendations themselves attract little media attention (as

---

[44] For discussions of these possible mechanisms of domestic influence, see in addition to the chapters in this volume (especially those by Trubek & Trubek on hard and soft law and Erhel *et al.* on the "leverage effect"); see also Jacobsson and Vifell (2005a and b); Jacobsson and Schmid (2003); Jacobsson (2005); Hodson (2004); Hodson and Maher (2001).

is increasingly true of the EES, though not of the Broad Economic Policy Guidelines and especially the Growth and Stability Pact)[45].

Precisely because such "naming, shaming, and blaming" by the EU can have significant domestic political repercussions for Member State governments, it may also generate perverse feedback effects on the evolution of OMC procedures. Thus after the shock produced by the first set of employment recommendations in 1999 (which were released by Commission without any prior consultation), Member State governments in a number of countries (notably Germany) have sought to tone down or pre-empt critical recommendations through bilateral negotiations between national officials and the Commission. More significantly, as discussed earlier fears of domestic political consequences have given rise to fierce struggles within EU committees over the adoption of OMC indicators which might cast particular Member States in an unfavourable light. Such domestic political concerns likewise lie behind the reluctance of Member State governments to agree quantitative targets for many OMC objectives and even in some cases to use common European indicators in their NAPs. In the Social Inclusion process, Member State representatives in the SPC have explicitly rejected any explicit performance ranking, and forced a modification of the first Joint Inclusion Report in 2001, which contained an implicit ranking of the various NAPs/incl. Member State governments have also remained so far unwilling to stiffen the procedures of the Social Inclusion process by adding formal guidelines and recommendations like those of the EES[46].

There is also evidence from the studies in this book and other recent empirical research of socialisation and discursive diffusion effects associated with the OMC. We have already underlined the influence of the EES and the Social Inclusion on national policy thinking, especially through the incorporation of European categories and concepts into domestic debate. Kerstin Jacobsson (2002 and 2005) in particular has analyzed in fine detail how the EES has contributed to the development of a common discursive frame of reference for national employment policies through participation of high civil servants in EU committees and the adoption of a common vocabulary, reporting format, and set of

---

[45] On changing patterns of media coverage of economic and employment policy coordination, see Meyer (2003 and 2005). Büchs and Friedrich's chapter reports that the influence of employment policy recommendations in Germany has tended to diminish over time as their novelty wore off.

[46] On such negotiations and conflicts between Member State and Commission representatives within EMCO and the SPC, see in addition to the chapters in this volume, Jacobsson and Vifell (2005b); Jobelius (2003); Barbier (2004a: esp. 83-85); Armstrong (2003). I have also drawn on my own interviews with Commission and Member State officials between 2002 and 2004.

performance metrics. Jacobsson and Åsa Vifell (Jacobsson and Vifell, 2005a and 2005b; Vifell, 2004) have likewise shown how participation in OMC processes can lead to a mutual socialisation of national officials and their internalisation of the discursive "rules of the game". Thus to operate persuasively in committees like EMCO and the SPC, Member State representatives cannot simply advance positions on the basis of naked national interest, but must instead offer reasoned arguments grounded in the common objectives, guidelines, targets, and indicators of the EES and Social Inclusion process. In this sense, the institutional setting and conceptual framework of these OMC processes serve as a deliberative discipline on interest-based bargaining, even where the participants may not be fully committed to their underlying principles[47]. But shared procedural norms and a common discursive frame of reference do not preclude sharp political disagreements and interpretive differences among the participants in these discussions, which is why it seems excessive to characterise their outcome as "cognitive harmonisation" (Palier, 2004). And such internalisation of European discursive categories and procedural norms is undoubtedly strongest within EU committees and among actors engaged in regular interactions with EU institutions, even if, as a number of chapters in this volume illustrate, there are also clear signs in many Member States of diffusion outwards and downwards to other groups within and beyond central government.

We have already examined in some depth the influence of mutual learning within the EES and the Social Inclusion process. Both OMC processes, we found, have contributed to indirect or higher-order shifts in national policy thinking through a combination of enhanced awareness of different approaches and performance standards elsewhere on the one hand, and reflexive self-assessment, including improvements in institutional capacity for information gathering and monitoring on the other. Conversely, we found relatively little direct or first-order learning and policy transfer at the national level, especially in terms of bottom-up learning from local experimentation, together with limited evidence of reflexive learning at the EU level itself. EU Member States remain vocally interested in the possibilities of mutual learning and exchange of good practices through the OMC, and are taking active steps to strengthen the mechanisms for this purpose within the EES and Social Inclusion process, as well as to extend them to new social policy fields such as health care, elder care, and social services. But so far, the mutual

---

[47] For the influence of deliberative settings and social norms of impartiality and reason-giving on public debates and decision-making, even where the participants themselves are not fully committed to such norms, see Elster (1998) and for an application of this argument to the Convention on the Future of Europe, see Magnette (2004) and Magnette and Nicolaïdis (2004).

learning potential of both OMC processes has remained underutilised at both European and national levels.

Probably the strongest and most effective mechanism of domestic influence identified by recent empirical research on the OMC is its strategic use by national and subnational actors as a resource for their own purposes: what Barbier and Erhel *et al.*'s chapters term the "leverage effect". Like other European policy commitments (most famously the Maastricht convergence criteria for EMU), national governments use the objectives, guidelines, targets, performance comparisons, and recommendations associated with OMC processes as a tool to advance their own domestic political agenda, promote desired reforms, and overcome entrenched veto positions. The OMC may thus serve as a "selective amplifier" (Visser), a source of external legitimation and blame-sharing device for unpopular or controversial measures that national governments would like to push through for their own reasons (see for example Büchs and Friedrich's chapter on Germany).

But this leverage effect of the OMC is by no means confined to national governments or their executives as unitary actors. As Erhel *et al.*, Visser, Jacobsson, and other contributors to this volume emphasise, OMC processes have also been widely used as a strategic resource in internecine struggles between different ministries and agencies within Member State governments themselves. Thus the EES and the Social Inclusion process have strengthened the hand of employment and social affairs ministries in negotiations over budgets and policy with finance and other ministries in fields such as activation and prevention services, training and lifelong learning, social assistance and support services for those most remote from the labour market, housing, transport, and so on. These OMC processes have also often been used to raise the profile and reinforce the position of specialised units and independent agencies within government, notably gender equality/mainstreaming units and public employment services. The "Brussels arena", as the chapters by Barbier and Erhel *et al.* observe, has thus become an increasingly crucial venue in domestic power struggles (even if Barbier claims that the strategic use of this arena is still largely confined to a small elite of insiders, at least in France).

Both the EES and the Social Inclusion process have also empowered non-state and subnational actors in different ways. Opposition parties and social partners have used EES guidelines, targets, and recommendations to challenge state policies, as for example over taxation in Sweden (Jacobsson) or childcare provision in Germany (Richardt, 2004). NGOs and civil society organisations, as we have seen, are among the most proactive users and beneficiaries of the Social Inclusion process, and have also gained influence through the EES in some countries. Local and regional authorities have likewise begun to use the EES and the Social Inclusion process as a vehicle for co-ordinating their own activities and engaging central administrations in new ways. Thus, for example, a representative of the Swedish Association of Municipalities and County Councils recently declared that the EES appeared as "the answer to a silent prayer" by his members who had been searching for ways to expand their participation in the country's historically centralised labor market and employment policies[48].

Member State governments, as Jacobsson's chapter observes, would clearly like to serve as gatekeepers between the European and domestic policy arenas. In Sweden, for example, as (Vifell, 2004) has shown, the national government very deliberately set out to "decouple" its active participation in shaping the EES at European level from any feedback effect on domestic policy-making. But even where Member States have rigorously sought to control the influence of OMC on domestic policy-making, evidence from the chapters in this book and other recent empirical studies suggests that they are decreasingly successful. Thus as we have already seen, despite the Swedish government's decoupling strategy, local and regional authorities have become increasingly active participants in the EES, with the assistance of innovative programmes and European networks supported by the Commission and the Parliament (cf. also Jacobsson and Vifell 2005a). In many Member States, as we also saw earlier, there has been a gradual "domestication" of OMC processes within national administrations, interest groups, and NGO networks, like the shift from "Europeans" to "Socials" described in Büchs and Friedrich's chapter on Germany[49].

Nor have these OMC processes simply reinforced existing power balances and institutional arrangements within EU Member States. As detailed above, both the EES and the Social Inclusion process have empowered weaker actors inside and outside government, rather than strengthening the executive and the authority of finance ministries within it, as much of the literature on "top-down" Europeanisation contends (see for example Featherstone, 2004; Featherstone and Radaelli, 2003; Börzel, 2002b; Cowles *et al.*, 2001). Careful empirical studies of the OMC in action, such as those presented in this volume,

---

[48] Statement made at a public conference on "The European Employment Strategy: Discussion and Institutionalisation", International Trade Union House, Brussels, 30-31 August 2004.

[49] In this sense, as Jacobsson and Vifell (2005a) also point out, the findings of empirical research on the OMC in action fit better with multi-level governance analyses of EU policy-making than with intergovernmentalist models of a two-level game controlled by the Member States. For the former, see Hooghe and Marks (2001); for the latter, Moravcsik (1998) and Pollack (1995 and 2003).

offer tangible evidence that it can stimulate the development of new channels of communication, participation, and negotiation between state and civil society, between national and subnational governments, and even between the social partners themselves. Among the unlikely examples are the collaboration between UK civil servants and anti-poverty NGOs in the Participation Working Group created for the NAP/incl, described in Armstrong's chapter, the emerging dialogue on employment policy between Swedish local authorities and central government, and the re-emergence of union-employer concertation around the Swedish NAP/empl, both discussed in Jacobsson's chapter. There is even evidence that participation in OMC processes can contribute not merely to advancing domestic actors' pre-existing interests and goals, but also to subtle shifts in their preferences and identities. Thus as Vifell (2004: 21) argues: "Local level actors in Sweden have increasingly come to define themselves as actors belonging to the European project and an augmentation of interest for the LAPs can also be noted at state level".

In relation to substantive policy change, procedural shifts in governance, and mutual learning, the strongest influence of the EES and the Social Inclusion Strategies on domestic policy-making in EU Member States has come through a series of indirect or higher-order effects, which are nonetheless consistent with the underlying theoretical principles of the OMC. These effects on national policy-making, as we have seen, are not only "pushed from above" through peer pressure, socialisation, and discursive diffusion, but also "pulled from below" through the strategic utilisation of OMC processes as a resource by domestic actors within and beyond government[50]. The confluence of these mechanisms of influence within the OMC, it should be noted, blurs standard conceptual distinctions between interest-based bargaining and adaptation to external pressure on the one hand and mutual learning and deliberative problem-solving on the other. Thus actors may be forced to learn by external pressures, which make it impossible to continue existing routines unchanged, while interests themselves must be interpreted and reinterpreted in order to serve as a basis for action. Hence "adaptation" may involve "learning", in the form of a redefinition of actors' goals in light of experience, while learning may also involve adaptation, in the sense of responding to external constraints and opportunities. More concretely, the fact that OMC processes pursue multiple objectives which are often considered to be mutually incompatible, such as "more and better jobs", "flexibility and security", or "socially adequate and financially sustainable pensions", may force Member State governments to find practical ways of reconciling them. It may likewise be through a

---

[50] For "push from above" and "pull from below" as complementary mechanisms of Europeanisation, see Börzel (2000).

combination of external pressure from EU institutions and internal mobilisation by domestic actors that issues such as gender pay gaps and occupational segregation acquire new political resonance, as has already begun to occur in the Nordic countries. In this sense, what Heclo (1974) terms "puzzling" and "powering" should not be counterposed to one another as alternative mechanisms of influence on domestic policy-making, but instead work hand-in-hand within OMC processes[51].

III. Opening the Open Method of Co-ordination: A Reflexive Reform Strategy

OMC processes in employment and social inclusion, as the preceding review shows, have produced genuine impacts and achievements at both EU and Member State levels. But neither have fully realised the OMC's theoretical promise in terms of reconciling common European action with national diversity while promoting experimental learning and deliberative problem-solving. These shortcomings, as I argued in the previous section, flow in large measure from procedural limitations: lack of transparency, barriers to broad participation, weak integration into domestic policy-making, and insufficient emphasis on mutual learning. Hence a potentially fruitful strategy for improving the operation of existing OMC processes would be to apply to their own procedures the key elements of the method itself: benchmarking, peer review, monitoring, evaluation, and iterative redesign. Ongoing initiatives and reform proposals within the EES and the Social Inclusion process already point in this direction, and provide evidence for the practical viability of such an approach. But this reflexive reform strategy is not self-actuating, and significant political obstacles would need to be overcome in order to make it work effectively, an issue to which I return below by way of conclusion.

A. Increasing Transparency

A first key step to improving existing OMC processes would be to increase transparency and make information about them more freely available. For lack of transparency and visibility, as we have seen, not

---

[51] This perspective has its roots in the pragmatist philosophy of Dewey, Peirce, Mead, and others, which underlies the literature on "learning by monitoring" and "directly-deliberative polyarchy" Sabel (1994 and 1997); Sabel and Cohen (1997); Cohen and Sabel (2003); Gerstenberg and Sabel (2002). This current of thought sees ends and means as reciprocally interdependent, with the former constantly being reassessed in the light of experience of their pursuit through particular courses of action, and re-jects sharp distinctions between instrumental, normative, and communicative action such as those assumed in different ways by rational-choice utilitarianism, sociological institutionalism, and Habermasian discourse ethics.

only tarnishes the OMC's democratic legitimacy, but also inhibits participation, integration into domestic policy-making, and mutual learning. One broad avenue of reform would be to open up the work of the EU committees responsible for running OMC processes to greater public scrutiny. Both EMCO and the SPC have recently created public websites on which they post their formal opinions and reports. But these committees should also make publicly available the full panoply of internal papers once they have been discussed, including agendas and minutes of meetings, following the best practice example set by the new European Food Safety Authority[52]. Another important dimension of transparency is that citizens are entitled to know the reasons for public decisions, and the deliberative quality of OMC processes (especially the EES and the BEPGs) would be by requiring more explicit explanations from the committees, the Commission, and the Council of the rationale for collective choices such as revisions of objectives and guidelines or country-specific recommendations. Both the legitimacy and the effectiveness of the EES and the Social Inclusion process would also be improved by greater visibility at national and subnational levels. According to Jacobsson and Vifell (2005a), opposition by a majority of Member State representatives in EMCO blocked proposals by the Commission for a joint campaign to disseminate knowledge about the EES nationally. But DG EMPL has since issued its own calls for tenders for projects to increase national awareness of the EES and the Social Inclusion process under the Employment Incentive Measures and Community Action Programmes respectively[53].

B. Ensuring Broad Participation

An obvious way to improve participation in the EES (and other OMC processes) would be to extend to them the Social Inclusion objective of mobilising all relevant bodies and stakeholders. Thus Member States should be expected to involve civil society organisations and local and regional authorities as well as the social partners in the preparation, monitoring, and evaluation, as well as the implementation and dissemination of their NAPs. To avoid any infringement of subsidiarity,

---

[52] For the EMCO and SPC websites, see http://europa.eu.int/comm/employment_social/ employment_strategy/emco_en.htm and http://europa.eu.int/comm/employment_ social/social_protection_commitee/index_en.htm, respectively. The Economic Policy Committee (EPC) also maintains a similar website, http://europa.eu.int/comm/ economy_finance/epc/epc_reports_en.htm. For the European Food Safety Authority, see http://www.efsa.eu.int/about_efsa/catindex_en.html.

[53] See VP 2004/15, "Awareness Raising for the European Employment Strategy", http://europa.eu.int/comm/employment_social/calls/2004/vp_2004_015/tender_en. htm, and VP 2004/05, "National Awareness Raising Actions on Social Inclusion", http://europa.eu.int/comm/employment_social/calls/2004/vp_2004_05/tender_en.htm.

they could be required to benchmark openness and participation within OMC processes according to national laws, traditions, and practices. During the first phase of the EES between 1997 and 2001, as we saw in the preceding section, Member States were pressed to step up involvement of the social partners and local and regional authorities through the addition of new guidelines and horizontal objectives, along with country-specific recommendations. Following the five-year impact evaluation and the European Parliament's resolution on the future of the EES (European Parliament, 2002), the Commission's proposals for the new Employment Guidelines in 2003 included a section on "promoting better governance, partnerships, and implementation" which called for "the mobilisation of all relevant actors":

- With due respect to different national traditions and practices [...] all main stakeholders, including civil society, should play their full part [in] the European Employment Strategy.
- Participation of regional and local actors in the development and implementation [of] the Guidelines should be supported notably through local partnerships, the dissemination of information and consultation (CEC, 2003b; see also CEC, 2002b).

But Member State representatives in EMCO insisted on watering down these proposals in the name of subsidiarity, deleting any explicit reference to civil society from the guidelines and acknowledging only that:

- Good governance and partnership are important issues for the implementation of the European Employment Strategy, while fully respecting national traditions and practices.
- In accordance with national traditions [...] relevant actors in the field of employment at national and regional level have important contributions to make (Council of the European Union, 2003).

Enhancing participation of non-state and subnational actors in OMC processes nonetheless remains a live and politically contested issue on the EU agenda. Thus the 2003 Kok Employment Task emphasised "mobilising for reforms" through "better governance" as one of its key messages, calling for consultation of social partners and civil society in the preparation of the NAPs/empl and the creation of "reform partnerships" involving local authorities alongside social partners and public agencies. The Task Force also recommended strengthening regional commitment to reforms in countries with devolved competences for employment policy by implementing "an open method of co-ordination between the national and regional levels of government. This would imply introducing open and transparent negotiation between national and regional government to agree regional objectives and reporting and monitoring mechanisms" (Kok *et al.*, 2003: 56-58). "Ensuring effective implementation of reforms through better governance" was included at the Commission's insistence as one of four common recommendations to all Member States in the 2004 Joint Employment Package (CEC, 2004b), and the EMCO Indicators Sub-Group is developing indicators for benchmarking governance in the NAPs/empl (EMCO Indicators Group, 2004)[54]. Regarding the OMC more generally, the Commission has proposed that the emphasis on openness and the involvement of a wide range of actors (including NGOs and subnational authorities as well as social partners) in the social inclusion process "could usefully be applied to the entire range of the future social protection process" under the new streamlined arrangements to be introduced in 2006, and this participatory approach is fully incorporated into its proposals for a new OMC process for health and elder care (CEC, 2003c and 2004a).

C. Mainstreaming OMC Processes into Domestic Policy-making

As with ensuring broad participation, Member States could be re-quired to mainstream OMC processes by benchmarking and reviewing their integration into domestic policy-making, according to national laws, traditions, and practices, with full respect for subsidiarity. Here again, the Social Inclusion process offers a partial model, which could be extended to the EES and the OMC more generally. Thus the Com-mission's proposals for "Taking the European Social Inclusion Strategy Forward" (CEC, 2002d) urged Member States in the second round of NAPs/incl to show how these were integrated into and add value to existing policy-making processes (including national budgetary and fiscal decision-making, as well as the use of EU structural funds), by providing a mechanism for reviewing and where necessary adjusting the latter. Member State representatives in the SPC responded by reaffirm-ing the principle of subsidiarity in the revised common objectives for the Social Inclusion Process: "Combatting social exclusion is first and foremost the responsibility of Member States and their national, regional and local authorities, in co-operation with the full range of the bodies concerned, in particular the social partners and NGOs" (CEC, 2002e). But the revised common outline for the NAPs/incl nonetheless enjoins Member States "to link [...] the NAPs/inclusion process more clearly with existing policy-making processes (including as appropriate the use of budgetary resources) and ensur[e] that a concern with poverty and social exclusion is mainstreamed into all policy areas, including the use of Structural Funds" (SPC, 2003). The 2003 Joint Inclusion Report

---

54 EAPN also continues to press actively for recognition of social NGOs' right to par-ticipate in the EES at both European and national levels (see EAPN, 2004a and 2004b).

observed that in many countries "significant progress has been made in strengthening institutional arrangements to mainstream a concern with poverty and social inclusion", but also complained that "in spite of the progress that has been made in several Member States to link their NAPs more strongly with national policy-making processes there is still little clear evidence of the NAPs directly impacting on national budgetary processes and thus on the overall allocation of resources" (CEC and Council of the European Union, 2004b: 112-13).

Following the Five-Year review of the Employment Strategy, the European Parliament (2002) emphasised "the need to better integrate the EES with national, regional and local labour market policy in the Member States and with the ESF policies". The Commission endorsed this judgement in its communication on the future of the employment strategy (CEC, 2003a), and its proposal for the new guidelines enjoined Member States to "ensure thei[r] effective implementation [...] including at the regional and local level", as well as to "ensure that adequate financial resources are allocated" for this purpose "while complying with the need for sound public finances in line with the Broad Economic Policy Guidelines" (CEC, 2003b). Member State representatives in EMCO responded by adding a blunt statement that "Responsibility for implementation of the Employment Strategy lies with the Member States", conceding only that they should "ensure transparency and cost-effectiveness in the allocation of financial resources to the implementation of the Employment Guidelines [...]" (Council of the European Union, 2003)[55]. But as in the case of participation, the question of ensuring better integration of the EES into national policy-making remains firmly on the EU agenda. Thus, for example, this issue was emphasised in the recommendations of the Kok Report (Kok *et al.*, 2003) and should figure in the proposed governance indicators for monitoring the EES.

Many proposals for improving the legitimacy and effectiveness of the EES and the OMC more generally have focused on enhancing the role of national parliaments in the process (European Parliament, 2002; 2003a and 2003b; CEC, 2003a; Jacobsson and Schmid, 2003)[56]. But

---

[55] But Member State representatives did accept the Commission's proposal that they should "fully exploit the potential contribution of the European Structural Funds, in particular the European Social Fund, to support the delivery of policies and to strengthen the institutional capacity in the field of employment" (Council of the European Union, 2003).

[56] The Commission proposed that "With due respect to different national traditions and practices, close involvement of relevant parliamentary bodies in the implementation of the [employment] guidelines should be ensured" (CEC, 2003b). But Member State representatives in EMCO conceded only that "relevant parliamentary bodies [...]

greater parliamentary involvement *per se* can hardly be regarded as a panacea for the OMC, since there is already a substantial democratic deficit in this respect at the national level, where legislatures have long experienced grave difficulties in exercising detailed control over policy-making and administration in complex fields like employment and social protection. National parliaments (and the European Parliament itself) could valuably participate in framing and debating OMC objectives and procedures, monitoring progress toward agreed goals, and revising the process in light of the results achieved. But this would involve a transformation of the conventional conception of parliaments' role in democratic polities as authoritative principals delegating detailed implementation of legislation to administrative agents, whose behaviour they seek to control through a combination of *ex ante* incentives and *ex post* sanctions. Effective participation by parliaments in OMC processes (as in the working of experimentalist democracies more generally) would require them to develop new roles in passing framework legislation embodying commitments to broad goals (such as OMC objectives); establishing administrative infrastructures to stimulate decentralised experimentation about how best to achieve these goals, monitor the efforts of local units to improve their performance against them, pool the resulting information, and set provisional standards in light of what they have learned; and reviewing the results and revising the framework objectives and administrative procedures accordingly[57]. The ability of parliaments to play such a new role in framing, reviewing, and revising OMC objectives and procedures (in collaboration with the Council and the European Parliament as EU legislators) thus depends on the reinforcement of mutual learning mechanisms at all levels, to which we now turn.

D. Reinforcing Mutual Learning

Increasing transparency, ensuring broad participation, and mainstreaming OMC processes into domestic policy-making would greatly enhance their contribution to mutual learning among EU Member States. But there are also a series of procedural reforms, many of them already initiated by EU institutions, which could significantly reinforce the mutual learning dimension of the EES and the Social Inclusion process. A first set of reforms concerns the procedures for mutual surveillance and peer review of NAPs at the EU level, which as we saw earlier, have been widely criticised for their cursory nature and limited

---

have important contributions to make", along with other actors (Council of the European Union, 2003).

[57] For this view of the transformed roles of the legislature and administration in experimentalist democracies, see Sabel (2005).

scope for substantive policy debate. In response to pervasive dissatisfaction among Member State representatives themselves, as well as to prepare for the challenge of enlargement, EMCO has revised its mutual surveillance procedures (the so-called "Cambridge Review") by breaking the NAP examinations into four smaller working groups, with a rapporteur to summarise the debates for the *ad hoc* Working Group charged with administering the review, whose report is then discussed by the full committee. "In order to promote mutual learning and to strengthen [...] peer pressure", the NAP review "should have an even stronger focus on the recommendations and a more in-depth exchange of views on the policy responses to the recommendations" (EMCO *Ad Hoc* Working Group, 2004). Informal reports of the SPC's operations suggest that this committee has adopted similar practices of breaking up into smaller working groups to facilitate genuine policy discussion in the face of enlargement from 15 to 25 Member States[58]. In social inclusion specifically, the SPC has also established a network of non-governmental experts to provide an independent critical perspective on Member States' NAPs/incl[59].

A second set of reforms concerns the procedures for peer review and exchange of good practices. The EES Peer Review Programme, as we also saw earlier, is in many respects an intelligently designed resource for mutual learning through contextualised benchmarking. But it has suffered from fragmentary coverage (as the choice of practices for examination is dependent on proposals from potential hosts), limited participation (confined to those Member States who wish to attend), and exclusion of non-state and subnational actors. Here again, EMCO has responded to internal dissatisfaction with these limitations by launching an expanded Mutual Learning Programme on Employment Policies, comprising a combination of EU-level thematic review seminars and national-level follow-up activities to be co-funded by the Commission and the Member States. The thematic review seminars will focus for six months at a time on a broad theme of general interest such as active ageing or adaptability, with discussions organised "on the basis of presentations from three to four Member States which perform particularly well in the area, or where major achievements recently have taken place". These seminars will be "open for a broader group of stakeholders", from both the national and the European levels, including independent policy experts. The existing peer review meetings on more

---

[58] Comments by Belgian members of the SPC to the first workshop on "La Méthode Ouverte de Co-ordination (MOC) en matière de pensions et de l'intégration européenne", Office National des Pensions, Brussels, 14 July 2004.

[59] For the reports of this network on the first round of NAPs/incl, see http://europa. eu.int/comm/employment_social/soc-prot/studies/studies_en.htm.

specific good practices will continue "with the participation of one Member State official and one independent policy expert from each of the participating countries", but they will be linked to the thematic seminars and may be opened up to representatives of the social partners. The joint national follow-up activities "would focus on furthering the dissemination of the results from the other activities under the Mutual Learning Programme and pursuing discussion on the theme or a more specific policy practice with the social partners and other national stakeholders", with special priority given to events with a transnational dimension or aimed at promoting closer co-operation among a group of Member States around mutual learning and the transferability of good practices (CEC, 2004c). For the Social Inclusion process, which has been running for a much shorter time, the SPC has just launched a Peer Review Programme modeled on that of the EES, whose first nine events in as many Member States will be completed by January 2005[60]. An unresolved issue for this programme is whether representatives of NGOs and local authorities will be permitted to participate in social inclusion peer review meetings, as EAPN for example has vocally demanded (EAPN 2003b: 19-20 and 2003c).

A final set of procedural reforms concerns the indicators used in OMC processes. Here again, as in other areas, the Social Inclusion process provides a partial model for the reform of the EES. Thus the employment indicators should be reviewed against the methodological principles outlined by the SPC Indicators Group (SPC Indicators Group, 2001 and 2003), notably that they should be outcome-oriented, responsive to policy interventions, subject to a clear and accepted normative interpretation, timely, and revisable. The Social Inclusion process likewise provides a good example of the participation of non-state actors in the formulation of non-state actors in the definition of OMC indicators, which should be extended to the EES as well[61]. OMC indicators as discussed earlier need to be sufficiently comparable and disaggregated to serve as diagnostic tools for self-corrective action by local actors, which has not been the case for either the EES or the Social Inclusion process, due to a lack of corresponding data at subnational level. But the Commission has recently sponsored the development of a workable set of regional and local employment indicators, which can be applied to existing national data, and a call for tenders has been issued for a similar project in the field of social inclusion. The Commission is also prepar-

---

[60] For details, see http://europa.eu.int/comm/employment_social/soc-prot/soc-incl/prp_en.htm.

[61] For a recent project co-ordinated by EAPN with support from the European Commission on "Poverty Indicators Starting from the Experience of People Living in Poverty", see Horemans (2003).

ing a "non-binding European methodological guide" to facilitate the use of such territorially disaggregated indicators by regional and local actors[62].

E. Overcoming Political Obstacles

Taken together, the procedural reforms discussed above would go a long way towards improving the operation of existing OMC processes and realising the method's theoretical promise. Despite the practical revisions to the EES and the Social Inclusion process initiated by the Commission and the EU committees, this reflexive reform strategy is not self-actuating, and significant political obstacles would have to be overcome to make it work effectively. The central problem here is resistance from Member State governments, as can be seen from the "battle of the clauses" over the governance section of the new Employment Guidelines, and the continuing reluctance of EU Social Affairs ministers to add guidelines or recommendations to the OMC processes in social inclusion and pensions. Even where national governments support the common objectives promoted by OMC processes, they often fear that these may lead to an erosion of their control over the content and timing of the domestic policy agenda. A noteworthy case in point is that of the 2003 French pension reforms, where as Erhel *et al.*'s chapter recounts the government played down its participation in the OMC pensions strategy review in order to avoid compromising its negotiations with the social partners by giving the impression that their outcome was already predetermined or imposed by Brussels.

Far from representing a "soft" option, Member State governments sometimes perceive the open-ended Europeanisation of a policy field entailed by the OMC as potentially more domestically intrusive than "hard" EU legislation itself. Thus as Caviedes (2004: 306) perceptively observes in relation to immigration policy:

> The present failure of the Council to adopt the Commission's proposal on a European immigration policy should not be read as a verdict on the innate unsuitability of the OMC in the immigration setting, but as a testament to the perceived discursive power of the OMC process. Being forced to compare and evaluate immigration policy in an open forum together with civil societal and international actors, whose views on immigration are often quite liberal, involves a risk of losing control over the agenda-setting process. This soft law learning process constitutes a greater threat to sovereignty in policy-making than an inchoate Community legislative competence in which the members still designate which areas are incorporated into Com-

---

[62] See Groupe Bernard Brunhes Consultants (2003); Open Call for Tender VT/2003/43, "Regional Indicators to Reflect Social Exclusion and Poverty", http://europa.eu.int/comm/employment_social/soc-prot/soc-incl/calls_en.htm.

munity law. The OMC certainly has the potential to be utilized as a mechanism for policy co-ordination (and as such seems more likely to be applied in areas such as asylum policy or combating illegal immigration), but in an issue area such as labour market-based immigration, characterized by a multitude of divergent policy goals and mechanisms, the OMC constitutes a greater obligation than the Member States are currently prepared to accept.

But if Member State governments find the OMC hard to live with, they also appear unable to live without it. Increasing interdependence, strategic uncertainty, and ongoing pressures to "do something" about urgent policy issues at a European level continually push Member States to expand the scope of the OMC and/or to apply closely related approaches based on mutual surveillance, peer evaluation, and exchange of good practices to new issue-areas. Thus for example, despite fears of "opening a box that can then never be closed" again by allowing EU-level discussion of national health-care policies (Baeten, 2003: 169), Member States now seem ready to accept a full-fledged OMC process for health and elder care (CEC, 2004d), as well as to extend mutual learning and exchange of good practices to other domestically sensitive issues such as the provision of social services[63]. In other thorny areas such as the fight against terrorism and regulation of genetically modified crops, the Council and the Commission have likewise reached for OMC-style mechanisms such as guidelines, peer evaluation, recommendations, and exchange of best practices in order to co-ordinate national policies (Council of the European Union, 2002a; CEC, 2003c)[64].

A necessary condition for reflexive reform and effective implementation of OMC processes is deeper commitment on the part of EU Member States (cf. also Jacobsson and Schmid, 2003). One possible approach to deepening Member State commitment might be to soften the prescriptions associated with OMC processes in exchange for hardening their procedures. Thus especially in relation to the EES, detailed prescriptions about means (such as targets for specific prevention and activation measures) should be replaced by a stronger focus on strategic objectives and performance outcomes. EU institutions, notably the Commission, should also resist the temptation to instrumentalise OMC reports, indicators, and recommendations to impose stronger European constraints on Member State policies through "naming, shaming, and blaming" (as proposed, for example, by the November 2004 Kok Report

---

[63] This latter proposal was supported close to unanimously by national ministers at the Maastricht Informal Council on Employment and Social Affairs, 8-10 July 2004, according to remarks by Belgian officials at the first workshop on "La Méthode Ouverte de Co-ordination (MOC) en matière de pensions et de l'intégration européenne", Office National des Pensions, Brussels, 14 July 2004.

[64] I am grateful to Gráinne de Búrca for these references.

on the review of the Lisbon Strategy). Conversely, however, OMC guidelines, targets, and indicators should become more precise and explicit, but also more diagnostic and revisable. Such steps might make it easier for Member States to accept a hardening of procedural requirements within OMC processes for transparency, participation, monitoring, review of weaknesses, and self-corrective action.

At the same time, however, these efforts to reinforce Member States' commitment to OMC processes would need to be supplemented by ongoing pressures both from above and from below. Hence EU institutions, from the Commission and the Parliament to the Committee of the Regions and the Economic and Social Committee, should continue to press for procedural reforms to the EES and the Social Inclusion process, while also supporting participation and networking by non-state and subnational actors at both European and national levels. A final consideration, which remains speculative for the moment, is whether European and national courts might also have a part to play in enforcing transparency and participation as procedural requirements for OMC processes, especially if the Constitutional Treaty is eventually ratified[65].

References

Armstrong, K. (2003), "Tackling Social Exclusion through the OMC: Reshaping the Boundaries of European Governance", in Börzel, T. A. and Cichowski, R. A. (eds.), *The State of the European Union, Vol.6: Law, Politics, and Society*, Oxford University Press, Oxford, pp.170-194.

ATD Fourth World (2003), *National Action Plans for Social Inclusion 2003-2005 as Instruments in the Fight against Extreme Poverty*, Brussels, October 2003.

Atkinson, R. and Davoudi, S. (2000), "The Concept of Social Exclusion in the European Union: Context, Development and Possibilities", *Journal of Common Market Studies*, Vol.38, No.3, September 2003, pp.427-448.

Atkinson, T., Cantillon, B., Marlier, E. and Nolan, B. (eds.) (2002), *Social Indicators: The EU and Social Inclusion*, Oxford University Press, Oxford.

Atkinson, T., Marlier, E. and Nolan, B. (2004), "Indicators and Targets for Social Inclusion the European Union", *Journal of Common Market Studies*, Vol.42, No.1, March 2004, pp.47-75.

Baeten, R. (2003), "Health Care on the European Political Agenda", in Degryse, C. and Pochet, P. (eds.), *Social Developments in the European Union 2002*, European Trade Union Institute, Observatoire social européen and Saltsa, Brussels, pp.145-176.

---

[65] For the strengthened commitments to transparency and participation in the Constitutional Treaty, see Intergovernmental Conference (2004: Articles I-47 and I-50).

Barbier, J.-C. (2004a), "La stratégie européenne pour l'emploi: genèse, coordination communautaire et diversité nationale", Rapport de recherche pour la DARES (ministère du Travail), Paris, January 2004.

Barbier, J.-C. (2004b), "Research on 'Open Methods of Coordination' and National Social Policies: What Sociological Theories and Methods?", unpublished paper presented to the RC 19 International Conference, Paris, 2-4 September 2004.

Barbier, J.-C. and Samba Sylla, N. (2001), "Stratégie européenne de l'emploi: les représentations des acteurs en France", rapport pour la DARES et la Délégation à l'Emploi du ministère du Travail et de l'Emploi, Paris, December 2001.

Börzel, T. A. (2000), "Why There is No 'Southern Problem'. On Environmental Leaders and Laggards in the European Union", *Journal of European Public Policy*, Vol.7, No.1, pp.141-162.

Börzel, T. A. (2002a), "Member State Responses to Europeanization", *Journal of Common Market Studies*, Vol.40, No.2, June 2002, pp.193-214.

Börzel, T. A. (2002b), *States and Regions in the European Union: Institutional Adaptation in Germany and Spain*, Cambridge University Press, Cambridge.

Boyer, R., Charron, E., Jürgens, U. and Tolliday, S. (1998), *Between Imitation and Innovation: Transfer and Hybridization of Productive Models in the International Automobile Industry*, Oxford University Press, Oxford.

Caviedes, A. (2004), "The Open Method of Co-ordination in Immigration Policy: A Tool for Prying Open Fortress Europe?" *Journal of European Public Policy*, Vol.11, No.2, April 2004, pp.289-310.

CEC (2000), Communication from the Commission "Acting Locally for Employment: A Local Dimension for the European Employment Strategy", COM (2000) 196 final, 7 April 2000 (http://europa.eu.int/eur-lex/en/com/cnc/2000/com2000_0196en01.pdf).

CEC (2001a), Communication from the Commission "Strengthening the Local Dimension of the European Employment Strategy", COM (2001) 629 final of 6 November 2001 (http://europa.eu.int/eur-lex/en/com/cnc/2001/com2001_06 29en01.pdf).

CEC (2001b), *Employment Strategy: Peer Review Programme 2002-2003*, European Commission, Employment Committee, *ad hoc* Working Group/ 007/190901/EN.

CEC (2002a), Report of the High Level Group on Industrial Relations and Change in the European Union, Office for Official Publications of the European Communities, Luxembourg, January 2002 (http://europa.eu.int/comm/employment_social/soc-dial/rapport_en.pdf).

CEC (2002b), Impact Evaluation of the European Employment Strategy, Technical Analysis Supporting COM (2002) 416 final of 17 July 2002 ("Taking Stock of Five Years of the EES"), October 2002 (http://europa.eu.int/comm/employment_social/publications/2002/cev102006_en.pdf).

CEC (2002c), Communication from the Commission "Taking Stock of Five Years of the European Employment Strategy", COM (2002) 416 of 17 July 2002 (http://europa.eu.int/eur-lex/en/com/cnc/2002/com2002_0416en01.pdf).

CEC (2002d), Communication from the Commission on Streamlining the Annual Economic and Employment Policy Co-ordination Cycles, COM (2002) 487 final, 3 September 2002 (http://europa.eu.int/eur-lex/en/com/rpt/2002/com2002_0487en01.pdf).

CEC (2002e), Taking the European Social Inclusion Strategy Forward: An Introductory Discussion Paper Prepared by the Commission, SPC/2002/June/02.

CEC (2003a), Communication from the Commission "The Future of the European Employment Strategy (EES). 'A Strategy for Full Employment and Better Jobs for All'", COM (2003) 6 final of 14 January 2003 (http://europa.eu.int/eur-lex/en/com/pdf/2003/com2003_0006en01.pdf).

CEC (2003b), Proposal for a Council Decision on Guidelines for the Employment Policies of the Member States, COM (2003) 176 final, 8 April 2003 (http://europa.eu.int/eur-lex/en/com/pdf/2003/com2003_0176en01.pdf).

CEC (2003c), Commission Recommendation of 23 July 2003 on Guidelines for the Development of National Strategies and Best Practices to Ensure the Co-existence of Genetically Modified Crops with Conventional and Organic Farming, OJ L 189, 29 July 2003, pp.0036-0047.

CEC (2004a), Activity Report to EMCO Local Employment Development: 2001-2004 (EMCO/14/220404/EN), Brussels, 2 April 2004 (http://europa.eu.int/comm/employment_social/local_employment/publications/led_activity_report_en.pdf).

CEC (2004b), Communication from the Commission "Strengthening the Implementation of the European Employment Strategy", Proposal for a Council Decision on Guidelines for the Employment Policies of the Member States, Recommendation for a Council Recommendation on the Implementation of Member States' Employment Policies, COM (2004) 239 final, 7 April 2004 (http://europa.eu.int/eur-lex/en/com/pdf/2004/com2004_0239en01.pdf).

CEC (2004c), Note to EMCO *Ad Hoc* Group Meeting 26 March 2004 "Mutual Learning Programme on Employment Policies", EMCO/11/220404/EN, March 2004.

CEC (2004d), Communication from the Commission "Modernising Social Protection for the Development of High-Quality, Accessible and Sustainable Health Care and Long-Term Care: Support for the National Strategies Using the 'Open Method of Coordination'", COM (2004) 304 final, 20 April 2004 (http://europa.eu.int/comm/employment_social/soc-prot/healthcare/com_04_304_en.pdf).

CEC and Council of the European Union (2004a), Joint Employment Report 2003-2004, Document 7069/04, Brussels, 5 March 2004 (http://europa.eu.int/comm/employment_social/employment_strategy/report_2003/jer20034_en.pdf).

CEC and Council of the European Union (2004b), Joint Report by the Commission and the Council on Social Inclusion, Document 7101/04, Brussels, 5 March 2004 (http://europa.eu.int/comm/employment_social/soc-prot/soc-incl/final_joint_inclusion_report_2003_en.pdf).

CEMR (2001), *Governance and the Open Method of Coordination*, Council of European Municipalities and Regions, Brussels, 10 October 2001.

Chassard, Y. (2001), "European Integration and Social Protection: From the Spaak Report to the Open Method of Co-ordination", in Mayes, D. G., Berghman, J. and Salais, R. (eds.), *Social Exclusion and European Policy*, Edward Elgar Publishing, Cheltenham, pp.291-321.

Cohen, J. and Sabel, C. F. (2003), "Sovereignty and Solidarity: EU and US", in Zeitlin, J. and Trubek, D. M. (eds.), *Governing Work and Welfare in a New Economy: European and American Experiments*, Oxford University Press, Oxford, pp.345-375.

Committee of the Regions (2001), *The Local Dimension of the European Employment Strategy: The Impact of the Committee of the Regions*, Committee of the Regions, Brussels.

Council of the European Union (2002), Council Decision 2002/996/JHA of 28 November Establishing a Mechanism for Evaluating the Legal Systems and their Implementation at National Level in the Fight against Terrorism, OJ L 349, 24 December 2002, pp.0001-0003.

Council of the European Union (2003), Council Decision 2003/578/EC of 22 July 2003 on Guidelines for the Employment Policies of the Member States, OJ L 197, 5 August 2003, pp.0013-0021.

Cowles, M. G., Caporaso, J. and Risse, T. (2001), *Transforming Europe: Europeanization and Domestic Change*, Cornell University Press, Ithaca, NY.

de la Porte, C. and Pochet, P. (2003), "The OMC Intertwined with the Debates on Governance, Democracy and Social Europe: Research on the Open Method Of Co-ordination and European Integration", Report prepared for Frank Vandenbroucke, Belgian Minister for Social Affairs and Pensions, Observatoire social européen, Brussels, April 2003.

Dimaggio, P. J. and Powell, W. W. (1991), *The New Institutionalism in Organizational Analysis*, University of Chicago Press, Chicago.

DULBEA (2002), "L'évaluation d'impact de la stratégie européenne pour l'emploi en Belgique", Rapport Final, Ministère de l'Emploi et du Travail, Brussels, 31 January 2002.

EAPN (2002a), "Does the Employment Strategy Work for Social Inclusion?" *EAPN Working Document*, EAPN, Brussels, April 2002.

EAPN (2002b), "EAPN Submission on the Review of the European Employment Strategy", EAPN, Brussels, 15 June 2002.

EAPN (2003a), "EAPN Response to the Commission's Communication on the Future of the European Employment Strategy", EAPN, Brussels, 25 March 2003.

EAPN (2003b), "National Action Plans on Inclusion 2003-2005: Where is the Political Energy? EAPN's Response to the Second Round of Plans", *EAPN Report*, Brussels, October 2003.

EAPN (2003c), "Final Declaration of the 2003 EAPN General Assembly: Local Actions in the Fight against Poverty and Social Exclusion", EAPN, Brussels, 24 November 2003.

EAPN (2004a), "EAPN National Network's Evaluation of the National Action Plans for Employment: Synthesis Report", *EAPN Report*, Brussels, April 2004.

EAPN (2004b), "EAPN Position Paper Regarding the Joint Employment Report 2003-2004", EAPN, Brussels, 8 April 2004.

EAPN-EUROCITIES (2003), "The EU Strategy for Social Inclusion: Making it Work at the Local Level", Report of the conference organised by EAPN and EUROCITIES, Athens, 28 February-1 March 2003.

Elster, J. (1998), "Deliberation and Constitution Making", in Elster, J. (ed.), *Deliberative Democracy*, Cambridge University Press, Cambridge, pp.97-122.

EMCO *ad hoc* Working Group (2004), "Future Focus and Format of the Cambridge Review Examination of the National Action Plans for Employment", EMCO/10/220404.

EMCO Indicators Group (2004), "Indicators Group Report to EMCO on Progress Made in the Field of Indicators to Monitor the Employment Guidelines", EMCO/22/130704/EN.

Engender asbl (2002), "Review of the Implementation of the Guidelines on Local Development in the Employment NAPs from 1998 to 2001 Across the EU", *Synthesis Report*, Brussels, April 2002.

ETUC, UNICE/UEAPME and CEEP (2004), "2004 Report on Social Partner Actions in Member States to Implement Employment Guidelines", European Trade Union Confederation, Brussels, 5 March 2004.

Eurexcter (2002), Contribution by National Social Partners to the Luxembourg Process, Association européenne de l'Excellence territoriale, Paris, November 2002 (http://europa.eu.int/comm/employment_social/news/2003/jan/coparso_en.pdf).

EUROCITIES (2001), *Strengthening the Local Dimension of the Future European Employment Strategy: Eurocities Recommendations*, Eurocities, Brussels.

European Parliament (2002), European Parliament Resolution on the Communication from the Commission to the Council, the Economic and Social Committee and the Committee of Regions on "Taking Stock of Five Years of the European Strategy" COM (2002) 416-2002/2152(INI), P5_TA(2002) 0442, 25 September 2002.

European Parliament (2003a), Resolution A5-0143/2003 on Analysis of the Open Coordination Procedure in the Field of Employment and Social Affairs and Future Prospects, Rapporteur: Miet Smet, Committee on Employment and Social Affairs, 5 June 2003.

European Parliament (2003b), Resolution B5-0282/2003 on the Application of the Open Method of Coordination, 5 June 2003.

Featherstone, K. (2004), "The Political Dynamics of External Empowerment: the Emergence of the EMU and the Challenge to the European Social Model", unpublished paper presented to the Conference of Europeanists, Chicago, March 2004.

Featherstone, K. and Radaelli, C. (2003), *The Politics of Europeanization*, Oxford University Press, Oxford.

Ferrera, M. (2001), "The European Social Model between 'Hard' Constraints and 'Soft' Co-ordination", unpublished paper presented to the "Social Models and EMU: Convergence? Co-existence? The Role of Economic and Social Actors", Economic and Social Committee, Brussels, 19 November 2001.

Ferrera, M. and Gualmini, E. (2004), *Rescued by Europe? Social and Labour Market Reforms in Italy from Maastricht to Berlusconi*, Amsterdam University Press, Amsterdam.

Ferrera, M., Matsaganis, M. and Sacchi, S. (2002), "Open Coordination against Poverty: The New EU 'Social Inclusion Process'", *Journal of European Social Policy*, Vol.12, No.3, pp.226-239.

Foden, D. (1999), "The Role of Social Partners in the European Employment Strategy", *Transfer*, Vol.5, No.4, pp.522-541.

Galgóczi, B., Lafoucriere, C. and Magnusson, L. (2004), *The Enlargement of Social Europe: The Role of the Social Partners in the European Employment Strategy*, European Trade Union Institute, Brussels.

Gerstenberg, O. and Sabel, C. F. (2002), "Directly Deliberative Polyarchy: An Institutional Ideal for Europe?" in Joerges, C. and Dehousse, R. (eds.), *Good Governance in Europe's Integrated Market*, Oxford University Press, Oxford, pp.289-343.

Goetschy, J. (2003), "The European Employment Strategy, Multi-level Governance, and Policy Coordination: Past, Present and Future", in Zeitlin, J. and Trubek, D. M. (eds.), *Governing Work and Welfare in a New Economy: European and American Experiments*, Oxford University Press, Oxford, pp.59-87.

Groupe Bernard Brunhes Consultants and Economix (2003), "Strengthening the Local Dimension of the European Employment Strategy: Feasibility Study on Indicators for Local and Regional Levels and for the Social Economy", Final Report on a Study conducted under the direction of Jacques Dahan and financed by the European Commission, DG Employment and Social Affairs, December 2003 (http://europa.eu.int/comm/employment_social/local_employment/publications/ees_local_en.pdf).

Hartog, J. (1999), "So What's So Special About the Dutch Model?", *Employment and Training Paper*, No.54, International Labour Organisation, Geneva.

Heclo, H. (1974), *Modern Social Politics in Britain and Sweden: From Relief to Income Maintenance*, Yale University Press, New Haven.

Hemerijck, A. and Berghman, J. (2004), "The European Social Patrimony: Deepening Social Europe through Legitimate Diversity", in Sakellaropoulos, T., Berghman, J., Hemerijck, A., Stergiou, A. and Stevens, Y. (eds.), *Connecting Welfare Diversity within the European Social Model*, Intersentia, Antwerp, pp.9-54.

Hemerijck, A. and Visser, J. (2001), "Learning and Mimicking: How European Welfare States Reform", unpublished paper, University of Leiden and University of Amsterdam, June 2001.

Hemerijck, A. and Visser, J. (2003), "Policy Learning in European Welfare States", unpublished paper, University of Leiden and University of Amsterdam, October 2003.

Hodson, D. (2004), "Macroeconomic Co-ordination in the Euro Area: The Scope and Limits of the Open Method", *Journal of European Public Policy*, Vol.11, No.2, April 2004, pp.231-248.

Hodson, D. and Maher, I. (2001), "The Open Method of Coordination as a New Mode of Governance: The Case of Soft Economic Policy Coordination", *Journal of Common Market Studies*, Vol.39, No.4, pp.719-746.

Hooghe, L. and Marks, G. (2001), *Multi-level Governance and European Integration*, Rowman and Littlefield, Lanham.

Horemans, L. (2003), "European Project on Poverty Indicators Starting from the Experience of People Living in Poverty", *Final Report*, Vlaams Forum Armoedebestrijding/Vlaams Netwerk van Verenigingen Waar Armen het Woord Nemen, September 2003.

Intergovernmental Conference (2004), "Treaty Establishing a Constitution for Europe", CIG 87/04, Brussels, 6 August 2004.

Jacobsson, K. (2002), "Soft Regulation and the Subtle Transformation of States: The Case of EU Employment Policy", *SCORE Working Paper*, No.2002/4, Stockholm Center for Organizational Research, Stockholm.

Jacobsson, K. (2005), "Between Deliberation and Discipline: Soft Governance in EU Employment Policy", in Mörth, U. (ed.), *Soft Law in Governance and Regulation: An Interdisciplinary Analysis*, Edward Elgar Publishing, Cheltenham (forthcoming).

Jacobsson, K. and Schmid, H. (2003), "The European Employment Strategy at the Crossroads: Contribution to the Evaluation", in Foden, D. and Magnusson, L. (eds.), *Five Years Experience of the Luxembourg Employment Strategy*, European Trade Union Institute, Brussels, pp.111-139.

Jacobsson, K. and Vifell, A. (2005a), "New Governance Structures in Employment Policy-making? Taking Stock of the European Employment Strategy", in Linsenmann, I., Meyer, C. and Wessels, W. (eds.), *Economic Governance in the EU*, Palgrave Macmillan, London (forthcoming).

Jacobsson, K. and Vifell, A. (2005b), "Towards Deliberative Supranationalism? Analysing the Role of Committees in Soft Co-ordination", in Linsenmann, I., Meyer, C. and Wessels, W. (eds.), *Economic Governance in the EU*, Palgrave Macmillan, London (forthcoming).

Jobelius, S. (2003), "Who Formulates the European Employment Guidelines? The OMC Between Deliberation and Power Games" presented to the Annual Conference of the ESPAnet "Changing European Societies – The Role for Social Policy", Copenhagen, 13-15 November 2003.

Johansson, K. M. (1999), "Tracing the Employment Title in the Amsterdam Treaty: Uncovering Transnational Coalitions", *Journal of European Public Policy*, Vol.6, No.1, pp.85-101.

Kok, W. *et al.* (2003), "Jobs, Jobs, Jobs – Creating More Employment in Europe", Report of the Employment Task-force chaired by Wim Kok, Brussels, November 2003 (http://europa.eu.int/comm/employment_social/ employment_strategy/pdf/etf_en.pdf).

Kok, W. *et al.* (2004), "Facing the Challenge. The Lisbon Strategy for Growth and Employment", Report from the High Level Group chaired by Wim Kok, Office for Official Publications of the European Communities, Luxembourg, November 2004 (http://europa.eu.int/comm/lisbon_strategy/pdf/2004-1866-EN-complet.pdf).

Liebman, J. S. and Sabel, C. F. (2003), "A Public Laboratory Dewey Barely Imagined: The Emerging Model of School Governance and Legal Reform", *New York University Review of Law and Social Change*, Vol.23, No.2, pp.183-304.

Lindsay, C. and Mailand, M. (2004), "Comparing Youth Activation Policies in Denmark and the United Kingdom", in Serrano Pascual, A. (eds.), *Are Activation Policies Converging in Europe? The European Employment Strategy for Young People*, European Trade Union Institute, Brussels, pp. 129-162.

López-Santana, M. (2004), "How 'Soft' Pressure from above Affects the Bottom: Europeanization, Employment Policy and Policy (Re)Formulation (The Spanish Case)", unpublished paper.

Madsen, P. K. (1999), "Denmark: Labour Market Recovery through Labour Market Policy", *Employment and Training Paper*, No.53, International Labour Organisation, Geneva.

Magnette, P. (2004), "Deliberation or Bargaining? Coping with Constitutional Conflicts in the Convention on the Future of Europe", in Eriksen, E. O., Fossum, J. E. and Menéndez, A. J. (eds.), *Developing a Constitution for Europe*, Routledge, London, pp.207-225.

Magnette, P. and Nicolaïdis, K. (2004), "The European Convention: Bargaining in the Shadow of Rhetoric", *West European Politics*, Vol.27, No.3, pp.381-404.

Martin, J. P. (2004), "Reflections on the OECD Jobs Strategy and the European Employment Strategy and Preliminary Lessons from the OECD's Older Worker Thematic Review" presented to the Meeting of the European Employment Committee, Brussels, 11-13 February 2004.

Mayes, D. G., Berghman, J. and Salais, R. (eds.) (2001), *Social Exclusion and European Policy*, Edward Elgar Publishing, Cheltenham.

Meyer, C. O. (2003), "The Soft Side of Hard Policy Coordination in EMU: Peer Review and Publicised Opinion in Germany and Ireland" presented to the Conference on Stability and Economic Governance, London, April 2003.

Meyer, C. O. (2005), "Towards a Grand Débat Européen? Exploring the Europeanization of Socio-Economic Discourses in Selected Member State", in Linsenmann, I., Meyer, C. O. and Wessels, W. (eds.), *EU Economic Governance: The Balance Sheet of Economic Policy Coordination*, Palgrave-Mcmillan, London (forthcoming).

Ministero del Welfare (2003), *Libro bianco sul welfare. Proposte per una societá dinamica e solidale*, Minestero del Lavoro e della Politiche Sociali, Rome, February 2003.

Moravcsik, A. (1998), *The Choice for Europe: Social Purpose and State Power from Messina to Maastricht*, Cornell University Press, Ithaca.

Nauerz, M. (2004), "Does the European Employment Strategy Lead to a Soft Form of Europeanisation? An Analysis of the 'Local Dimension' in Germany", College of Europe, Masters Thesis in European Political and Administrative Studies.

ÖSB/INBAS (2001), "Evaluation of Peer Review Programme on Active Labour Market Policy 2000-2001", Report prepared for the European Commission (DG EMPL), Brussels, October 2001.

Palier, B. (2004), "The Europeanisation of Welfare Reforms", unpublished paper presented to the Cost A15 Conference, Nantes, France, 20-22 May 2004.

Palier, B. (2004), "Social Protection Reforms in Europe: Strategies for a New Social Model", CPRN Social Architecture Papers, *Research Report* F|37 Family Network, Canadian Policy Research Networks, Ottawa, January 2004.

Plasschaert, S. and Pochet, P. (2004), "National Report for Belgium (4th Round 2003/2004), Govecor Project (http://www.govecor.org/data/20040213095204 _Belgian_ Report4.pdf).

Pochet, P. (2002), "La lutte contre la pauvreté et l'exclusion sociale et la méthode ouverte de coordination", *Revue belge de sécurité sociale*, No.1, March 2002, pp.159-177.

Pochet, P. (2004), "La MOC et la protection sociale: des développements ambigus", in Dehousse, R. (ed.), *L'Europe sans Bruxelles? Une analyse de la méthode ouverte de coordination*, L'Harmattan, Paris, pp.99-127.

Pollack, M. (1995), "Regional Actors in an Intergovernmental Play: The Making and Implementation of EC Structural Policy", in Mazey, S. and Rhodes, C. (eds.), *The State of the European Union*, Vol.3, Lynne Rienner Publishers, Boston, pp.361-390.

Pollack, M. (2003), *The Engines of Integration: Delegation, Agency, and Agenda Setting in the EU*, Oxford University Press, Oxford.

Richardt, N. (2004), "European Employment Strategy, Childcare, Welfare State Redesign: Germany and the United Kingdom Compared", unpublished paper presented to the Conference of Europeanists, Chicago, 11-13 March 2004.

Rubery, J., Smith, M., Figueiredi, H., Fagan, C. and Grimshaw, D. (2004), "Gender Mainstreaming and the European Employment Strategy and Social Inclusion Process: Report of EU Expert Group on Gender and Employment", European Work and Employment Research Center, Manchester School of Management, Manchester.

Sabel, C. F. (1994), "Learning by Monitoring: The Institutions of Economic Development", in Smelser, N. and Swedberg, R. (eds.), *Handbook of Economic Sociology*, Princeton University Press and Russell Sage Foundation, Princeton, pp.137-165.

Sabel, C. F. (1997), "Design, Deliberation, and Democracy: On the New Pragmatism of Firms and Public Institutions", in Ladeur, K. H. (ed.), *Liberal Institutions, Economic Constitutional Rights and the Role of Organizations*, Nomos Verlagsgesellschaft, Baden-Baden, pp.101-149.

Sabel, C. F. (2005), "Beyond Principle-Agent Governance: Experimentalist Organizations, Learning and Accountability", in Engelen, E. and Sie Dhian Ho, M. (eds.), *De Staat van de Democratie. Democratie Voorbij de Staat*, Amsterdam University Press, Amsterdam (forthcoming).

Sabel, C. F. and Cohen, J. (1997), "Directly-Deliberative Polyarchy", *European Law Journal*, Vol.3, No.4, December 1997, pp.313-342.

Sabel, C. F. and Zeitlin, J. (2003), "Active Welfare, Experimental Governance, Pragmatic Constitutionalism: The New Transformation of Europe", unpublished paper presented to the International Conference of the Hellenic Presidency of the European Union, "The Modernisation of the European Social Model & EU Policies and Instruments", Ioannina, Greece, 21-22 May 2003.

Salais, R. (2004), "La politique des indicateurs. Du taux de chômage au taux d'emploi dans la stratégie européenne pour l'emploi", in Zimmermann, B. (ed.), *Les sciences sociales à l'épreuve de l'action. Le savant, le politique et l'Europe*, Editions de la Maison des Sciences de l'Homme, Paris, pp.287-331.

Salais, R., Raveaud, G. and Mathieu, G. (2002), *L'évaluation de l'impact de la Stratégie Européenne pour l'Emploi – Thème 10: Elaboration des politiques*, DARES, Ministère de l'Emploi et de la Solidarité, Paris.

Smets, J. (2003), "Mobilisation Générale pour l'Emploi" presented to the "Conférence pour l'Emploi", Belgian Ministry for Employment and Pensions, Brussels, 18 September 2003.

SPC (2003), Opinion of the Social Protection Committee on the Commission's Communication "Strengthening the Social Dimension of the Lisbon Strategy: Streamlining Open Coordination in the Field of Social Protection", Brussels, 29 September 2003 (http://europa.eu.int/comm/employment_social/social_ protection_commitee/streamlining_en.pdf).

SPC Indicators Group (2001), Report on Indicators in the Field of Poverty and Social Exclusion, Social Protection Committee, Brussels, October 2001 (http://europa.eu.int/comm/employment_social/social_protection_commitee/l aeken_list.pdf).

SPC Indicators Group (2003), "Common Indicators Relating to National Strategies for Adequate and Sustainable Pensions", Second Progress Report of the

Indicators Sub-group to the Social Protection Committee, Social Protection Committee, Brussels (http://europa.eu.int/comm/employment_social/social_protection_commitee/2nd_prog_report_pensions_indicators_en.pdf).

Tholoniat, L. (2001), "L'Administration Française et la stratégie européenne pour l'emploi: jeux de legitimité et enjeux de gouvernance", unpublished manuscript.

Trubek, D. and Mosher, J. (2003), "New Governance, Employment Policy, and the European Social Model", in Zeitlin, J. and Trubek, D. M. (eds.), *Governing Work and Welfare in a New Economy: European and American Perspectives*, Oxford University Press, Oxford, pp.33-58.

Umbach, G. (2004), "Employment Policies in Germany and the United Kingdom: The Impact of Europeanisation", *Political Science Report*, The Anglo-German Foundation for the Study of Industrial Society.

van Riel, B. and van der Meer, M. (2002), "The Advocacy Coalition for European Employment Policy: The European Integration Process After EMU", in Hegemann, H. and Neumärker, B. (eds.), *Die Europäische Union aus politökonomischer Perspektive*, Metropolis Verlag, Marburg, pp.309-328.

Vandenbroucke, F. (2002), "Foreword: Sustainable Social Justice and 'Open Co-ordination' in Europe", in Esping-Andersen, G., Gallie, D., Hemerijck, A. and Myles, J. (eds.), *Why We Need a New Welfare State*, Oxford University Press, Oxford, pp.viii-xxiv.

Vifell, A. (2004), "Speaking with Forked Tongue – Swedish Employment Policy and European Guidelines: A Case of Europeanization through Soft Co-ordination" presented to the Conference of Europeanists, Chicago, 11-13 March 2004.

Visser, J. and Hemerijck, A. (1997), *'A Dutch Miracle': Job Growth, Welfare Reform and Corporatism in the Netherlands*, Amsterdam University Press, Amsterdam.

Winterton, J. and Foden, D. (2001), "The Role of Trade Unions in the European Employment Strategy", unpublished paper presented to the 6th European Industrial Relations Conference, Oslo, June 2001.

Zeitlin, J. (2000), "Introduction: Americanization and Its Limits: Reworking US Technology and Management in Post-War Europe and Japan", in Zeitlin, J. and Herrigel, G. (eds.), *Americanization and Its Limits: Reworking US Technology and Management in Post-war Europe and Japan*, Oxford University Press, Oxford, pp.1-50.

Zeitlin, J. (2003), "Introduction: Governing Work and Welfare in a New Economy: European and American Experiments", in Zeitlin, J. and Trubek, D. M. (eds.), *Governing Work and Welfare in a New Economy: European and American Experiments*, Oxford University Press, Oxford, pp.1-32.

Zeitlin, J. (2005), "Social Europe and Experimental Governance: Towards a New Constitutional Compromise?", in de Búrca, G. (ed.), *EU Law and the Welfare State*, Oxford University Press, Oxford (forthcoming).

Notes on the Contributors

Kenneth Armstrong

Kenneth Armstrong is Reader in European Union Law at Queen Mary, University of London. He has written widely on issues of European law and governance. His current research focuses on the Open Method of Co-ordination in the social inclusion sphere and more generally on the use of OMC in the context of the Lisbon Strategy.

Jean-Claude Barbier

A senior researcher (CNRS) at the Centre d'études de l'emploi (Noisy-le-Grand, France), Jean-Claude Barbier heads its "Employment and Social Protection" research unit. As a sociologist, he particularly specialises in comparative research. Social policies, employment policies and the broad social protection systems in a European context are his main fields. He also conducts empirical and theoretical research about the various EU level co-ordination mechanisms, especially the European Employment Strategy. In recent years, he published *Les politiques de l'emploi en Europe* (Flammarion, 1997); *Les politiques de l'emploi en Europe et aux Etats-Unis*, with J. Gautié (PUF, 1998); *La flexibilité du travail et de l'emploi*, with H. Nadel (Flammarion, 2000); *Le nouveau système français de protection sociale*, with B. Théret (La Découverte, 2004). He has contributed to many collective volumes, among which (also with B. Théret) "The French Social Protection System: Path Dependencies and Societal Coherence", in Gilbert, N. and Van Voorhis, R. (eds.), *Changing Patterns of Social Protection* (Transaction Publishers, 2003).

Milena Büchs

Milena Büchs is a PhD student at the Humboldt University, Berlin, Institute for Social Science. Her dissertation deals with the relationship of the EES and labour market policy development in Germany and the United Kingdom. During 2003, she spent almost one year of her dissertation research at the Marie Curie training site of the University of Stirling, Scotland. She teaches in the fields of European social policy, European "governance" and democratic theory.

Caroline de la Porte

Caroline de la Porte is currently writing her PhD thesis on the Open Method of Co-ordination at the European University Institute in Florence (Italy). Fields of research interest include new forms of European governance and social protection. Recent publications include, together with Patrizia Nanz, "OMC – A Deliberative-Democratic Mode of Governance? The Cases of Employment and Pensions", *Journal of European Public Policy* (Vol.11, No.2, May 2004) and together with Philippe Pochet, "The European Employment Strategy: Existing Research and Remaining Questions", *Journal of European Social Policy* (Vol.14, No.1, February 2004).

Christine Erhel

Christine Erhel is an Assistant Professor in Economics at the University Paris I Panthéon-Sorbonne, and a researcher at MATISSE (CNRS and Centre d'études de l'emploi). She has been working on labour market policies, especially in a comparative perspective, and she is actively involved in European networks focussing on LMP evaluation and reforms ("transitional labour markets", TRANSLAM network, and TLM.net since 2003). She has recently published about the French experience of working time reduction (*La RTT*, PUF), and about the dynamics of labour market and social policies in France and UK (*Journal of European Social Policy*, May 2004).

Maurizio Ferrera

Maurizio Ferrera is Professor of Comparative Social Policy at the University of Milan. He is also Deputy Director of the "Poleis" Center for Comparative Politics of Bocconi University (Milan) and Director of a Research Unit on European Governance (URGE) at the Fondazione Collegio Carlo Alberto of Moncalieri (Turin). He is a member of several academic bodies, including the Research Council of the European University Institute and the Executive Committee of the European Consortium for Political Research (ECPR). He has published extensively in the field of comparative public policy. His latest books in English are: *The Boundaries of Welfare. European Integration and the New Spatial Politics of Solidarity* (Oxford University Press, forthcoming, 2005) and *Rescued by Europe? Social and Labour Market Reforms in Italy from Maastricht to Berlusconi*, with E. Gualmini (Amsterdam University Press, 2004).

Dawid Friedrich

Dawid Friedrich received an MSc in "European Social Policy Analysis" from the University of Bath (UK) in 2002, and is currently a PhD candidate at the Graduate School of Social Sciences (GSSS), University of Bremen (Germany). He is a political scientist and particularly interested in international politics and European integration. His main research areas are questions of legitimation and participation in (new) governance arrangements, of democracy beyond the nation-state, and of developments of social policy in the "integrating" Europe. Accordingly, his PhD is on the (im-)possibility of democratising network governance in the EU. He is also a research affiliate at the Collaborative Research Center 597 "Transformations of the State" at Bremen University. Recently, he has written a review article on German political science and EU studies (together with Patrizia Nanz) for the *Journal of European Public Policy* (2005).

Kerstin Jacobsson

Kerstin Jacobsson is Associate Professor of Sociology. She is a Senior Lecturer at Södertörn University College and a Research Fellow at SCORE (Stockholm Center for Organizational Research) at Stockholm University and Stockholm School of Economics. Recent publications include *Learning to be Employable. New Agendas on Work, Responsibility and Learning in a Globalizing World*, co-edited with Christina Garsten (Palgrave Macmillan, 2004) and articles in *Journal of European Public Policy* and *Journal of European Social Policy*.

Lars Magnusson

Lars Magnusson is Professor of Economic History, Uppsala University, Sweden and Research Director at the National Institute for Working Life, Sweden. He is also the head of the SALTSA programme. He has written extensively on economic development, doctrinal history and the European labour market. He is the author of *An Economic History of Sweden* (2000), *Evolutionary Economics and Path Dependency* (1997), *From the Werner Plan to EMU* (2002), *Five Years Experience of the European Employment Strategy*, with David Foden (2003).

Lou Mandin

Lou Mandin, Young Researcher (Sciences Po Paris), contributed to the European research project "Welfare Reform and the Management of Social Change" between 2001 and 2004. Her main research field concerns active ageing in Europe, and the articulation between European orientations and national policies for older workers.

Brian Moss

Brian Moss is a social policy graduate of Trinity College, Dublin University, and University of Bath. He has worked as a Research Assistant at the Observatoire social européen and the Irish National Economic and Social Council and as a Researcher with the National Centre for Partnership and Performance. He is currently a Probation and Welfare Officer with the Irish Probation and Welfare Service (Dublin).

Rory O'Donnell

Dr Rory O'Donnell is Director of Ireland's National Economic and Social Council (NESC) and Chief Officer of the National Economic and Social Development Office (NESDO). In his work as Economist and later Director at NESC he has undertaken analysis for Ireland's social partnership programmes and has written extensively on partnership. He was formerly Jean Monnet Professor of Business at University College Dublin; where he edited *Europe – The Irish Experience* (Institute of European Affairs, 2000) and co-authored with Brigid Laffan and Michael Smith, *Europe's Experimental Union: Rethinking Integration* (Routledge, 2000).

Bruno Palier

Political scientist. Palier is CNRS researcher at the Centre d'études de la vie politique française (CEVIPOF), Paris (France). His research interests focus on welfare state reforms, from a French and a comparative perspective. He is currently working on specifying the characteristics of welfare changes in continental Europe, as opposed to both English-speaking and Nordic countries. Palier was a member of the Management Committee of Cost A15, "Reforming Welfare Systems in Europe" and was responsible for the Mire programme "Comparing Social Welfare Systems in Europe". He published *La réforme des systèmes de* santé (PUF, collection que sais-je?, 2004); *La réforme des retraites* (PUF, collection que sais-je?, 2003); *Gouverner la Sécurité sociale* (PUF, 2002). He co-edited a special issue of *Journal of European Social Policy* on "EU Accession, Europeanisation and Social policy", with Ana Guillen (Vol.14, No.3, 2004), and a special issue of *Global Social Policy* on "Globalisation/Europeanisation and Social Welfare", with Nick Manning (Vol.3, No.2, 2003). He co-edited *Globalization and European Welfare States: Challenges and Changes*, with Rob S. Sykes and P. Prior (Palgrave, 2001) and *La protection sociale en Europe, Le temps des réformes*, with Christine Daniel (La Documentation française, 2001).

Philippe Pochet

Director of the Observatoire social européen (Brussels) since 1992. He is the Digest Editor of the *Journal of European Social Policy*. Affiliate at the Centre of European Studies (Free University of Brussels) and also invited lecturer at the Catholic University of Louvain-La-Neuve, where he co-chairs the study group on Active Welfare State with Pascale Vielle. His main research fields are social impacts of the monetary union, the social dimension of the European Union and challenges of the globalisation process. He has recently edited *Wage Policy in the Eurozone* (P.I.E.-Peter Lang, 2002), and *Building Social Europe through the Open Method of Co-ordination*, with C. de la Porte (P.I.E.-Peter Lang, 2002). Recent publications include an article in the *Journal of European Social Policy*, with C. de la Porte (February 2004).

Jill Rubery

Jill Rubery is Professor of Comparative Employment Systems and Director of the European Work and Employment Research Centre at the Manchester Business School, University of Manchester. Her research focuses on the inter-disciplinary comparative analysis of employment systems, including the organisation of internal labour markets, wage structures and payment systems, working time arrangements and welfare systems. She is the co-ordinator of the European Commission's expert group on gender and employment that provides research and policy advice to the Equal Opportunities Unit of the European Commission. She as also worked as a consultant for the OECD, the International Labour Organisation and the UNECE. Recent publications include: *The Organization of Employment: an International Perspective* with Damian Grimshaw (Palgrave, 2002); *Managing Employment Change: the New Realities of Work*, with Huw Beynon, Damian Grimshaw, Kevin Ward (Oxford University Press, 2002); *Women's Employment in Europe: Trends and Prospects*, with Mark Smith, Colette Fagan (Routledge, 1999); *Equal Pay in Europe* (ed.) (ILO and Macmillan, 1998); plus articles on gender mainstreaming in the European employment strategy in the annual European review, December edition, *Industrial Relations Journal* 2002, 2003, 2004.

Stefano Sacchi

Stefano Sacchi is a PhD candidate in Political Science at the University of Pavia, and the research co-ordinator of the Research Unit on European Governance (URGE) of the Collegio Carlo Alberto Foundation of Turin. His main research interests are comparative political economy, comparative and European social policy. His most recent publication is "Italy: Striving Uphill, but Stopping Halfway. The Troubled Journey of the Experimental Minimum Insertion Income", with F. Bastagli, in M. Ferrera (ed.), *Welfare State Reform in Southern Europe* (Routledge, 2005). On the subject matter of this book, he co-authored the article "Open Co-ordination against Poverty: The New EU 'Social Inclusion Process'", *Journal of European Social Policy*, August 2002.

David M. Trubek

David M. Trubek is Voss-Bascom Professor of Law and Senior Fellow of the Center for World Affairs and the Global Economy (WAGE) at the University of Wisconsin-Madison. From 1998-2003 he was co-director of the UW's European Union Center. His research areas include the sociology of law, EU governance and social policy, and the role of law in economic development. He is co-editor with Jonathan Zeitlin of *Governing Work and Welfare in a New Economy: European and American Experiments* (Oxford University Press, 2003). Other recent publications include "EU Social Policy and the European Employment Strategy", *Journal of Common Market Studies*, with Jim Mosher (Vol.41, No.1, 2003); "Hard and Soft Law in the Construction of Social Europe: The Open Method of Co-ordination", with L. Trubek (*European Law Journal*, forthcoming, 2005); and "The Rule of Law in Development Assistance: Past, Present and Future", in M. Bauerle *et al.* (eds.), *Haben wir wirklich Recht?* (Nomos, 2004).

Louise G. Trubek

Professor Louise G. Trubek is a Clinical Professor at the University of Wisconsin Law School where she teaches Health Law and Alternatives Approaches to Regulation: Law and Policy. She directs the Health Law Project at the Law School that includes a health law externship program. Prof. Trubek writes extensively on health care law, public interest lawyering, and clinical legal education. Her current research fields are new approaches to governance in the Unites States and in the European Union, comparative health care law, and public interest lawyering around the world. Recent publications include "Health Care and Low-wage Work in the United States: Linking Local Action for

Expanded Coverage", in J. Zeitlin and D. M. Trubek (eds.), *Governing Work and Welfare in a New Economy: European and American Experiments* (Oxford, 2003), "Achieving Equality: Healthcare Governance in Transition", with Maya Das (*American Journal of Law and Medicine*, 2003), and "Crossing Boundaries: Legal Education and the New Public Interest Law" (*Wisconsin Law Review*, 2005, forthcoming).

Jelle Visser

Jelle Visser is Professor of Sociology at the University of Amsterdam, where he directs the Amsterdam Institute for Advanced Labour Studies (AIAS), an interdisciplinary centre for research and graduate teaching. He is the (co-)author of several books and articles on industrial relations, trade unions, organisational behaviour, labour markets, social policy and welfare states. Recent books include: *The Future of Collective Bargaining* (Oxford University Press, 2001), *Trade Unions in Western Europe since 1945*, with B. Ebbinghaus (Macmillan, 2000), and *'A Dutch Miracle'. Job Growth, Welfare Reform and Corporatism in the Netherlands*, with A. Hemerijk (Amsterdam University Press, 1997). In 2004 he edited the third *Industrial Relations in Europe* report published by the European Commission. In 2004-2005 he is visiting professor at the European University Institute, Florence.

Jonathan Zeitlin

Jonathan Zeitlin is Professor of Sociology, Public Affairs, and History at the University of Wisconsin-Madison, where he is also Director of the Center for World Affairs and the Global Economy (WAGE) and Founding Director of the European Union Center. His current research focuses on experimental governance, Europeanisation, and the reform of national welfare states and employment systems, with particular emphasis on the Open Method of Co-ordination. He edits the online Research Forum on the Open Method of Co-ordination, http://eucenter.wisc.edu/ OMC/index.htm, and has presented his policy research to numerous committee hearings and conferences organised by EU institutions. Among his recent publications are *Governing Work and Welfare in a New Economy: European and American Experiments*, co-edited with David Trubek (Oxford University Press, 2003) and *Local Players in Global Games: The Strategic Constitution of a Multinational Corporation*, co-authored with Peer Hull Kristensen (Oxford University Press, 2004).

"Work & Society"

The series "Work & Society" analyses the development of employment and social policies, as well as the strategies of the different social actors, both at national and European levels. It puts forward a multi-disciplinary approach – political, sociological, economic, legal and historical – in a bid for dialogue and complementarity.
The series is not confined to the social field *stricto sensu*, but also aims to illustrate the indirect social impacts of economic and monetary policies. It endeavours to clarify social developments, from a comparative and a historical perspective, thus portraying the process of convergence and divergence in the diverse national societal contexts. The manner in which European integration impacts on employment and social policies constitutes the backbone of the analyses.

Series Editor: Philippe POCHET, *Director of the Observatoire social européen (Brussels) and Digest Editor of the* Journal of European Social Policy.

Series Titles

No.49 – *The Open Method of Co-ordination in Action. The European Employment and Social Inclusion Strategies*, Jonathan ZEITLIN & Philippe POCHET (eds.), with Lars MAGNUSSON, SALTSA/Observatoire social européen, 2005, 511 p., ISBN 90-5201-280-6.

N° 48 – *Le « Moment Delors ». Les syndicats au cœur de l'Europe sociale* (provisional title), Claude DIDRY & Arnaud MIAS, forthcoming, ISBN 90-5201-274-1.

No.47 – *A European Social Citizenship? Preconditions for Future Policies from a Historical Perspective*, Lars MAGNUSSON & Bo STRÅTH (eds.), SALTSA, 2004, 361 p., ISBN 90-5201-269-5.

No.46 – *Restructuring Representation. The Merger Process and Trade Union Structural Development in Ten Countries*, Jeremy WADDINGTON (ed.), 2004, 414 p., ISBN 90-5201-253-9.

No.45 – *Labour and Employment Regulation in Europe*, Jens LIND, Herman KNUDSEN & Henning JØRGENSEN (eds.), SALTSA, 2004, 408 p., ISBN 90-5201-246-6.

N° 44 – *L'État social actif. Vers un changement de paradigme ?* (provisional title), Pascale VIELLE, Isabelle CASSIERS & Philippe POCHET (dir.), forthcoming, ISBN 90-5201-227-X.

No.43 – *Wage and Welfare. New Perspectives on Employment and Social Rights in Europe*, Bernadette CLASQUIN, Nathalie MONCEL, Mark HARVEY & Bernard FRIOT (eds.), 2004, 206 p., ISBN 90-5201-214-8.

No.42 – *Job Insecurity and Union Membership. European Unions in the Wake of Flexible Production*, M. SVERKE, J. HELLGREN, K. NÄSWELL, A. CHIRUMBOLO, H. DE WITTE & S. GOSLINGA (eds.), SALTSA, 2004, 202 p., ISBN 90-5201-202-4.

N° 41 – *L'aide au conditionnel. La contrepartie dans les mesures envers les personnes sans emploi en Europe et en Amérique du Nord*, Pascale DUFOUR, Gérard BOISMENU & Alain NOËL, 2003, en coéd. avec les PUM, 248 p., ISBN 90-5201-198-2

N° 40 – *Protection sociale et fédéralisme*, Bruno THÉRET, 2002, 495 p., ISBN 90-5201-107-9.

No.39 – *The Impact of EU Law on Health Care Systems*, Martin MCKEE, Elias MOSSIALOS & Rita BAETEN (eds.), 2002, 314 p., ISBN 90-5201-106-0.

No.38 – *EU Law and the Social Character of Health Care*, Elias MOSSIALOS & Martin MCKEE, 2002, 259 p., ISBN 90-5201-110-9.

No.37 – *Wage Policy in the Eurozone*, Philippe POCHET (ed.), Observatoire social européen, 2002, 286 p., ISBN 90-5201-101-X.

N° 36 – *Politique salariale dans la zone euro*, Philippe POCHET (dir.), Observatoire social européen, 2002, 308 p., ISBN 90-5201-100-1.

No.35 – *Regulating Health and Safety Management in the European Union. A Study of the Dynamics of Change*, David WALTERS (ed.), SALTSA, 2002, 346 p., ISBN 90-5201-998-3.

No.34 – *Building Social Europe through the Open Method of Co-ordination*, Caroline DE LA PORTE & Philippe POCHET (eds.), SALTSA/Observatoire social européen, 2002, 311 p., ISBN 90-5201-984-3.

N° 33 – *Des marchés du travail équitables ?*, Christian BESSY, François EYMARD-DUVERNAY, Guillemette DE LARQUIER & Emmanuelle MARCHAL (dir.), Centre d'Études de l'Emploi, 2001, 308 p., ISBN 90-5201-960-6.

No.32 – *Trade Unions in Europe: Meeting the Challenge*, Deborah FOSTER & Peter SCOTT (eds.), 2003, 200 p., ISBN 90-5201-959-2.

No.31 – *Health and Safety in Small Enterprises. European Strategies for Managing Improvement*, David WALTERS, SALTSA, 2001, 404 p., ISBN 90-5201-952-5.

No.30 – *Europe – One Labour Market?*, Lars MAGNUSSON & Jan OTTOSSON (eds.), SALTSA, 2002, 306 p., ISBN 90-5201-949-5.

No.29 – *From the Werner Plan to the EMU. In Search of a Political Economy for Europe*, Lars MAGNUSSON & Bo STRÅTH (eds.), SALTSA, 2001, 526 p., ISBN 90-5201-948-7.

N° 28 – *Discriminations et marché du travail. Liberté et égalité dans les rapports d'emploi*, Olivier DE SCHUTTER, 2001, 234 p., ISBN 90-5201-941-X.

Caroline DE LA PORTE & Philippe POCHET (eds.)
Building Social Europe
through the Open Method of Co-ordination

The Open Method of Co-ordination (OMC) is a multi-dimensional challenge for policy-makers, as well as social actors, researchers and other players. The aim of *Building Social Europe through the Open Method of Co-ordination* is to describe the role of the OMC as an instrument for the governance of Europe's social dimension from a multi-disciplinary perspective.

The underlying issues addressed concern its potential as an instrument of Europeanisation, as well as how the Member States influence EU policy formation. The complexities of national policy-making processes in the area of employment are scrutinised by researchers from different EU countries who seek to understand how, if at all, OMC employment is integrated into Member States' policies. Furthermore, the complex adaptational pressures of the EU on the reform of national public pension schemes (the Netherlands, Germany, Sweden and Italy) are analysed. The editors devote their efforts to understanding the national-European dynamics of OMC in the areas of employment, social exclusion and pensions.

The book is a first step towards a theoretical framework that explains the dynamics of OMC.

Caroline DE LA PORTE is a sociologist and a researcher at the Observatoire social européen and is particularly interested in the OMC, Social Europe, and the social dimension of enlargement.

Philippe POCHET is the director of the Observatoire social européen, Digest Editor of the Journal of European Social Policy, *affiliate at the Centre of European Studies (Université Libre de Bruxelles) and invited lecturer at the Université catholique de Louvain. He has published widely on the social dimension of the European Union.*

Brussels, P.I.E.-Peter Lang, 90-5201-984-3, 2002

39.00 SFR   26.60 €*   24.90 €**   16.00 £   29.95 US$
* includes VAT – only valid for Germany and Austria – ** does not include VAT
Our prices are subject to change without notice.